ACCOUNTING
CANADIAN EDITION

VOLUME 1
FINANCIAL ACCOUNTING

ACCOUNTING
CANADIAN EDITION

Carl S. Warren
University of Georgia, Athens

Philip E. Fess
University of Illinois, Champaign-Urbana

James M. Reeve
University of Tennessee, Knoxville

Sandra M. Felton
Brock University, St. Catharines, Ontario

H. Donald Brown
Brock University, St. Catharines, Ontario

VOLUME 1
FINANCIAL ACCOUNTING

 I(T)P Nelson

an International Thomson Publishing company

Toronto • Albany • Bonn • Boston • Cincinnati • Detroit • London • Madrid • Melbourne
Mexico City • New York • Pacific Grove • Paris • San Francisco • Singapore • Tokyo • Washington

I(T)P® **International Thomson Publishing**
The ITP logo is a trademark under licence.
www.thomson.com

Published in 1999 by
I(T)P® **Nelson**
A division of Thomson Canada Limited
1120 Birchmount Road
Scarborough, Ontario M1K 5G4
www.nelson.com

First published by South-Western Publishing Company, copyright 1996.

Canadian Cataloguing in Publication Data

Main entry under title:

Accounting

Canadian ed.
Includes index.
ISBN 0-17-616638-6 (v. 1)   ISBN 0-17-616748-X (v. 2)   ISBN 0-17-616639-4 (v. 3)

1. Accounting.   I. Warren, Carl S.

HF5635.A365 1998   657   C98-931794-3

Editorial Director:	Michael Young
Executive Editor:	Tim Sellers
Developmental Editor:	Anita Miecznikowski
Production Editor:	Valerie Adams
Copy Editor:	Anna Garnham
Production Coordinator:	Hedy Later
Marketing Manager:	David Tonen
Cover Image:	Dave Starrett
Cover and Interior Design:	Angela Cluer
Composition Analyst:	Marnie Benedict
Composition Manager:	Dolores Pritchard

Printed and bound in the U.S.A.

1 2 3 4   WCB   02 01 00 99

Contents

v

Preface

When we were first approached by ITP Nelson to consider adapting *Accounting* by Warren, Fess, and Reeve for the Canadian market, we were curious to know why it had been a best-seller in the American market for 18 editions. Upon examining the book, we found that it offered students a superlative learning system—complete with illustrations, real world examples, questions, exercises, problems, cases, and a full set of supplementary materials.

Warren, Fess, and Reeve have produced a truly student-friendly text. *Accounting* provides students with ample material to assist them in understanding accounting concepts, as well as preparing and using accounting information. Chapters are framed by clear sets of objectives, which are referenced throughout the text, and conclude with brief summaries of content related to these objectives. The writing is simple and the presentation well organized. The content is relevant and the context is real.

One of the chronic problems associated with teaching introductory accounting is the errors that are often found in the texts and solutions manuals. These errors confuse the students and aggravate the instructor. We found *Accounting* to be very free from errors and wanted to ensure that the Canadian edition upheld the same standards of accuracy. Consequently we have carefully reviewed the entire book for errors, and the Solutions Manual, which was prepared independently by Betty Wong and Richard Wright, was checked by both ourselves and a research assistant.

THE CANADIAN EDITION

The Canadian edition of *Accounting* is split into three volumes. Volumes 1 and 2 cover financial accounting and Volume 3 is on managerial accounting. The book has been published in three volumes thanks to feedback from the marketplace. The general consensus from reviewers and focus group participants alike was that such a split would make for maximum student benefit and flexibility. The book has been divided as follows:

- Volume 1 (Chapters 1–11) covers financial accounting topics up to and including current liabilities. This volume includes both inventories and payroll.
- Volume 2 (Chapters 12–16) covers the balance of the financial accounting material.
- Volume 3 (Chapters 17–26) covers all of the management accounting material.

Please note that each volume will contain some references to material in the companion volumes.

For those students who require two or three volumes for their courses, affordable shrink-wrapped packages of Volumes 1, 2, and/or 3 will be readily available from ITP Nelson.

This edition provides full integration of accounting concepts and practices within the Canadian context. Included is an introduction to the professional accounting organizations and the development of generally accepted accounting principles in Canada. The text contains numerous examples from the financial reports of Canadian companies and appropriate and up-to-date references to the *CICA Handbook,* including the most recent recommendations related to accounting for income taxes, financial instruments, and the statement of cash flows. We increased the conceptual content of the material, particularly in the early chapters, in order to provide students with a solid basis for preparing and understanding accounting information.

In addition, we compressed and rearranged the coverage of certain topics in the U.S. text. For example, we have included all of the essentials of accounting for corporations in one chapter (which we have completely rewritten from the Canadian perspective). Similarly, we have reorganized the material to group together long-term liabilities arising from various sources such as bonds, notes payable, leases, pensions, and income taxes. We have also revised and restructured the chapter on current liabilities to cover a broader range of items, and have moved some of the details of payroll calculation to an appendix at the end of the chapter.

In addition, we have aimed to improve the clarity of the writing by moving from the more traditional and cumbersome passive style to the active voice. Not only does this improve the readability for students and engage them more directly with the material, but we believe that it provides them with a model of good writing, as recommended by various handbooks on effective writing for accountants.

We believe that the scope and extent of problem, exercise, and case material in this book is unparallelled in any existing text. In keeping with the U.S. edition, we have included an extensive set of "A" and "B" problems at the end of each chapter. However, we have revised the "B" set of problems to increase variation and ensure that they are not an exact mirror of the "A" set. New to the Canadian edition is a selection of challenge problems in each chapter. We have also added several problems which specifically review accounting concepts as we proceed from topic to topic through the text.

Each chapter includes several cases, one or more of which is related to ethical issues in the preparation and use of accounting information. In addition, each chapter includes a case based on the Annual Report of Sears Canada Inc. (reproduced in Appendix C) to introduce the students to the use and analysis of financial statements.

We believe that the structure of the chapters, the writing style, the extensive collection of exercises, problems, and cases, and the balance of conceptual and procedural content set this book apart from other introductory accounting texts.

FEATURES

Perspective

Over the years we have used many different texts in our introductory accounting courses, from those labelled "preparer-oriented," to the "conceptual," to those described as presenting a "user perspective." We have concluded that a sound conceptual foundation is a necessary prerequisite to approaching both the preparation and use of financial reports. In addition, we think that preparation and use belong together (a preparer/user perspective). One of our goals in adapting this text was to ensure an appropriate balance among these three approaches (concepts, preparation, and use). To achieve this we increased and integrated the conceptual matter in the earlier chapters and eliminated the need for the traditional separate chapter on concepts part way through the book.

We believe that *Accounting, Canadian Edition,* can fulfill the needs of both those who wish to take either a more user-oriented, a more conceptual, or a more preparer-oriented approach. The focus can vary depending on the emphasis supplied by the instructor.

From the user's perspective, each chapter begins with an introductory section entitled "You and Accounting" which emphasizes how accounting information relates to so many areas of the student's everyday life. Each chapter also contains a case requiring the student to analyze some aspect of the financial statements of Sears Canada Inc., which appear in Appendix C. We chose Sears because it is a highly visible company with operations across Canada, and one that should be familiar to most students. The text also introduces the student to the various components of the annual report (such as the management report, historical summary, various notes to the financial statements, etc.). Although this material is included in the chapter on financial statement analysis, it could be included earlier in the course. We also introduce some of the more complex items which a user could encounter in the financial statements, such as capital leases, accrued/deferred pension costs, and future income tax assets and liabilities. We have covered these topics lightly, avoiding the excessive detail which might confuse an introductory accounting student. At the same time, we have ensured that our coverage reflects current practice in the area, and is not so overly simplistic as to be misleading.

The book can also be used effectively to emphasize a "preparer perspective." Each chapter contains clear examples of the accounting techniques presented along with journal entries, ledger account examples, and worksheets as appropriate. For example, reviewers have commented that Chapter 15 ("The Statement of Cash Flows") presents a very clear rationale and methodology for preparing the financial statement. With over 20 exercises per chapter, the book offers sufficient single-topic material to provide for mastery of principles and techniques prior to trying problems. A continuing problem built upon successive chapters ties together the basics introduced in the first section of the book. In later chapters, we have included comprehensive problems which review material covered earlier in the text. We were careful to reflect the latest professional accounting pronouncements in all areas and to present all topics in a way which is entirely compatible with a more in-depth study of the material so that, in the future, a student can make a smooth transition into intermediate accounting—without having to "unlearn" anything covered at the introductory level.

For either of the user or preparer approach, the integration of conceptual material provides the basis for understanding accounting. Accounting concepts are emphasized from the very beginning of the book and reinforced as each new topic is introduced. Aside from a comprehensive introduction of concepts in the first few chapters, each chapter contains principles, definitions, and concepts related to particular topics. Many chapters have two problems related to accounting concepts, which encourage the student to focus on the concepts which underlie the treatment of items discussed in that chapter, and many of the cases draw upon a conceptual understanding of what accounting is trying to do. Reviewers have commented that our presentation of present value concepts, effective interest rates, and statement of cash flow material was conceptually much clearer than material contained in other introductory texts.

Class Tested for Accuracy

As stated earlier, we know nothing is more upsetting to both students and instructors than to adopt a text with technical errors. We know the feeling first-hand having adopted error-filled books ourselves, in the past. That is why, in September of 1998, a group of seven instructors and over 500 students at our school used a pre-publication version of Volumes 1 and 2 of this text. The reason? We wanted to be sure the text you consider for adoption has been given a true "test drive"—and we knew the only way to do that was to put it through a rigorous class test. And believe us, we did! With over 500 students using the text, we were able to clean up any (and hopefully all) technical inaccuracies. And most importantly, the students enjoyed the text and performed well.

It's important to note this accuracy check was not limited to the text alone. The solutions manuals for Volumes 1 and 2 were also closely scrutinized at the same time, and corrections made to them as well. We are confident you will be very pleased with the accuracy of both our text and solutions manuals.

Format

Given the visual orientation of today's students, we have carefully integrated the use of colour and type style with the format of the book in order to attract and hold the students' attention.

"You and Accounting"

A short story at the beginning of each chapter relates the chapter's topic to the personal experience of the student. By capturing the student's attention at the beginning of the chapter, we hope to make the material more enjoyable to read and easier to grasp.

Chapter Objectives

A boxed and highlighted listing sets out the objectives to be covered at the beginning of each chapter. Throughout the text, we include the objectives as margin references for each section of text, and summarize them again at the end of the chapter in a "Key Points" recap, which includes brief explanatory notes.

"Using Accounting to Understand Business"

 Each chapter includes one or more informative examples, set apart in highlighted boxes, that clearly connect accounting to the business environment and show how students might use accounting information in their future business careers.

"Computer King"

 Introduced in Chapter 1 and continued throughout most of the text, the statements from this company help students tie together elements of the accounting cycle and more.

Glossary of Key Terms

Each chapter includes a glossary of definitions for terms introduced in the chapter. We have also combined these chapter glossaries into a comprehensive glossary included at the end of the text.

End-of-Chapter Material

We consistently conclude each chapter with the following pedagogy:

- Key Points
- Glossary of Key Terms
- Illustrative Problem
- Self-Examination Questions
- Discussion Questions
- Exercises (cross-referenced to topic and chapter objectives)
- Series A Problems (cross-referenced to topic and chapter objectives)
- Series B Problems (cross-referenced to topic and chapter objectives)
- Challenge Problems
- Cases
- Answers to the Self-Examination Questions

The assignment material encompasses a wide range of levels of difficulty: from straightforward exercises and questions to in-depth problems, conceptual analysis, comprehensive reviews, thought-provoking cases, and analysis of real-world financial data. The abundance and variety of this material is so extensive that it could provide the basis for numerous new assignments from year-to-year, providing for use of the text for an extended period.

Icons you will come across in the end-of-chapter material include:

 This continuing problem offers students the opportunity to practise what is being learned by following the accounting cycle step-by-step for a single company over Chapters 1–4. In addition, Chapters 4, 6, 11, and 14 include comprehensive problems, which integrate and summarize the concepts and principles covered over several chapters.

 "What's Wrong With This?"—We employ these unique exercises to challenge students to analyze and discover what is wrong with a financial statement, report, or management decision. Students will gain practical experience and critical thinking skills that will assist them in the business world.

 We use Ethics cases to stimulate discussion on ethical dilemmas in business.

 To help students develop essential communication skills, we have included communication exercises in the end-of-chapter material.

 "What Do You Think?"—These exercises require analyses beyond the material included in the text. Real companies are presented.

"Real World Examples"—We employ the annual report of Sears Canada Inc., as well as numerous other real world examples, to demonstrate how organizations use accounting and how it affects business in Canada and throughout the world. Integrated throughout the chapters and in the end-of-chapter cases and problems, these examples add concrete meaning to the concepts and principles.

End-of-Text Material

We have included the following appendices at the end of the text:

- **Appendix A: Accounting Concepts**
- **Appendix B: Interest Tables**
- **Appendix C: Annual Report for Sears Canada**
- **Appendix D: The Basics**—a review of basic accounting facts
- **Appendix E: Abbreviations and Acronyms Commonly Used in Business and Accounting**
- **Appendix F: Classification of Accounts**—a handy reference chart of account titles indicating classification, normal balance as debit or credit, and location in financial statements
- **Appendix G: A Classified Balance Sheet**

SUPPLEMENTS

For the Instructor

The following supplements are available for use with the Canadian edition of *Accounting*, Volumes 1, 2, and 3:

- **Solutions Manual**—adapted by the text authors and by Betty Wong of Athabasca University (Volume 1), Richard Wright of Fanshawe College (Volume 2), and Dave Kennedy of Lethbridge Community College (Volume 3). It provides complete written solutions for all exercises, questions, problems, and cases in the end-of-chapter assignment material.
- **Overhead Transparencies**—a complete set of acetates of the Solutions Manual (for adopters only).
- **Instructor's Manual**—adapted by Leo Gallant of St. Francis Xavier University. It provides lecture notes, overhead transparency masters, demonstration problems, group learning activities, and writing exercises.
- **PowerPoint Slides**—adapted by Dennis Wilson of Centennial College. These slides provide graphic presentations of accounting concepts.
- **Test Bank**—adapted by Irene Wiecek of the University of Toronto. It contains true/false questions, multiple-choice questions, and problems that test students' comprehension of the material presented in each chapter.
- **Computerized Test Bank**—adapted by Irene Wiecek of the University of Toronto. This electronic version of the Test Bank allows the instructor to produce customized, computer-generated examinations.

For the Student

The following student supplements are available for use with the Canadian edition of *Accounting*, Volumes 1, 2, and 3:

- **Study Guide** (Volumes 1, 2, and 3)—adapted by Kim Dyck of Red River Community College. These guides include chapter outlines, problems, and solutions to help the student understand the concepts presented in the text.

- **Working Papers** (Volumes 1, 2, and 3)—adapted by Michael Lee of Humber College. These include the forms needed for completing all problems in the end-of-chapter material.

In addition to the above supplementary materials, you can explore the world of accounting and conveniently access support for this text at

http://accounting.nelson.com

This resource site includes instructor supplements in a password-protected area, student activities, an accounting education page, a careers section, links to accounting software providers, accounting references and study resources, and a case/question of the month. We will be continually updating this site to keep the information current and to continue to meet your needs.

ACKNOWLEDGEMENTS

We would like to thank the following instructors who acted as consultants, reviewers, and/or participated in focus groups:

CONSULTANTS
- Kim Dyck, Red River Community College
- Robin Hemmingsen, Centennial College
- John Western, Kwantlen University College

FOCUS GROUP PARTICIPANTS
- Ted Carney, Humber College
- Sandy Caven, George Brown College
- Ron Francis, Seneca College
- John Glendenning, Centennial College
- Rob Harvey, Algonquin College
- Marie Madill-Payne, George Brown College
- Winston Marcellin, George Brown College
- Bonnie Martel, Niagara College
- Ann Paterson, Humber College
- Mike Perretta, Sheridan College
- John Varga, George Brown College

REVIEWERS
- Lewis Callahan, Lethbridge Community College
- Patricia Corkum, Acadia University
- Kim Dyck, Red River Community College
- Gordon Farrell, British Columbia Institute of Technology
- Mahlon Harvey, University of Winnipeg
- Rob Harvey, Algonquin College
- Bruce Hazelton, Sheridan College
- Dave Kennedy, Lethbridge Community College
- Guy Penney, College of the North Atlantic
- Ken Smith, College of the North Atlantic
- Ralph Sweet, Durham College
- Dennis Wilson, Centennial College
- Christopher Wright, University of Northern British Columbia
- Richard Wright, Fanshawe College
- Elizabeth Zaleschuk, Douglas College

We offer special thanks to our assistant, Miss Shari Leitch, who assisted us with searching the web for examples and statistics, and assisted with checking the detail of all answers for all of the discussion questions, exercises, problems, and cases. In addition, the enthusiasm, support, and expertise of the ITP Nelson College publishing staff have facilitated the completion of this project in a timely and professional manner.

Sandra M. Felton
H. Donald Brown

CARL S. WARREN

Dr. Carl S. Warren is the Arthur Andersen & Co. Alumni Professor of Accounting at the J.M. Tull School of Accounting at the University of Georgia, Athens. Professor Warren received his Ph.D. from Michigan State University in 1973. Dr. Warren's experience in listening to users of his texts sharpens his keen focus on helping students learn. When he is not teaching classes or writing textbooks, Dr. Warren enjoys golf, racquetball, and fishing.

PHILIP E. FESS

Dr. Philip E. Fess is the Arthur Andersen & Co. Alumni Professor of Accountancy Emeritus at the University of Illinois, Champaign-Urbana. He received his Ph.D. from the University of Illinois. Dr. Fess has been involved in writing textbooks for over twenty-five years, and his knowledge of how to make texts user-friendly is reflected on the pages of this edition. Dr. Fess plays golf and tennis, and he has represented the United States in international tennis competition.

JAMES M. REEVE

Dr. James M. Reeve is Professor of Accounting at the University of Tennessee, Knoxville. He received his Ph.D. from Oklahoma State University in 1980. Dr. Reeve is founder of the Cost Management Institute and a member of the Institute for Productivity Through Quality faculty at the University of Tennessee. In addition to his teaching experience, Dr. Reeve brings to this text a wealth of experience consulting on managerial accounting issues with numerous companies, including Procter and Gamble, AMOCO, Rockwell International, Harris Corporation, and Freddie Mac. Dr. Reeve's interests outside the classroom and the business world include golf, skiing, reading, and travel.

SANDRA M. FELTON

Dr. Sandra M. Felton is Associate Professor of Accounting in the Department of Accounting and Finance in the Faculty of Business at Brock University, St. Catharines, Ontario. She received her C.A. while employed with Clarkson Gordon in 1974, and her Ph.D. from the State University of New York at Buffalo in 1988. She is a Doctoral Fellow of the Institute of Chartered Accountants of Ontario. Dr. Felton has twenty-four years of experience teaching accounting and has published articles in the areas of financial accounting, accounting education, and accounting history.

H. DONALD BROWN

Donald Brown is an Adjunct Professor of Accounting and Academic Advisor for accounting and business students in the Department of Accounting and Finance at Brock University, St. Catharines, Ontario. He holds a Master of Divinity degree from the University of Emmanuel College, Saskatoon, and a Master of Science in Accounting degree from the University of Saskatchewan. He is a Chartered Accountant and Certified Management Accountant with experience in public accounting with national, regional, and local firms. He taught at the University of Lethbridge and the University of Saskatchewan before moving to Brock in 1985. With over twenty years of experience in teaching accounting, he has published and presented papers in the areas of accounting education, thinking skills, and problem solving.

A Brief Look at Accounting—Its Past, Present, and Future

Accounting is a profession similar to law and medicine. Such professions continually evolve and change as the needs of society change. In recent years, for example, the practice of medicine has changed significantly with the invention and use of lasers. Likewise, the practice of law has changed to reflect new specializations, such as environmental law.

The objective of this introduction is to make you aware of how accounting has changed over the years. This awareness will help you better understand the role and the importance of accounting in society and in your everyday life.

EARLY ACCOUNTING

Just as you may keep a record of the money you spend, people throughout history have maintained records of their business activities. Some of these records were clay tablets that indicated the payment of wages in Babylon around 3600 B.C. Record keeping also existed in ancient Egypt and in the Greek city-states. Some of the earliest English accounting records were compiled by William the Conqueror in the eleventh century. These early records included only some of the financial activities of an enterprise. A systematic recording of all activities of an enterprise developed later in response to the needs of the commercial republics of Italy.

DOUBLE-ENTRY SYSTEM

How did the early recording of financial activities evolve into a system of accounting? Luca Pacioli, a Franciscan monk, first wrote in the 1490s about the basic system of accounting, which is still used today. Pacioli was a mathematician who taught in various universities in Perugia, Naples, Pisa, and Florence. He was a close friend of Leonardo da Vinci, with whom he collaborated on a mathematics book. Pacioli wrote the text that included accounting and da Vinci drew the illustrations.

Pacioli wrote about the double-entry system of accounting in a work first published in Italy in 1494 in order to serve the financial needs of the Venetian merchants. Goethe, the German poet, novelist, and scientist, described the double-entry system as "one of the most beautiful inventions of the human spirit, and every good businessman should use it in his economic undertakings."[1]

What is so special about the double-entry system? It is unique because it documents financial activities in a way that creates an equilibrium within the accounting records. For example, assume that you borrow $1,000 from a bank. Within a double-entry system, you record the loan as $1,000 of cash received, and at the same time, you record an obligation for the eventual repayment of the $1,000. Each of the $1,000 amounts is balanced by the other. In a complex business environment, in which an enterprise may be involved in thousands of transactions daily, this balancing is a valuable control that ensures the accuracy of the recording process.

In spite of the enormous changes in business operations and their complexity since 1494, the basic elements of the double-entry system have remained virtually unchanged. This is a lasting tribute to the significance of Pacioli's invention and his contribution to society.

INDUSTRIAL REVOLUTION

In addition to the invention of the double-entry system, other major events significantly influenced the evolution of accounting. One such event was the Industrial Revolution. The Industrial Revolution occurred in England from the mid-eighteenth to the mid-nineteenth centuries. It changed the method of producing marketable goods from a handicraft method to a factory system.

The handicraft method of producing goods involved the coordinating of a network of independent artisans. For example, a textile business would coordinate separate weaving, spinning, and assembly artisans in order to finish completed garments. The final product price would include the sum of the individual artisan rates for work completed plus some profit to the manager for coordinating the activity. This form of business organization does not require sophisticated accounting records. The manager only needed a book of accounts to record transactions with the independent artisans and to record receipts for sales from customers.

Under the factory system, businesses took advantage of economies of scale by assembling machinery and labour in a centralized location under the control of a single manager. **Economies of scale** refers to the benefit obtained by spreading the cost of physical assets over a large quantity of production. The result was an increasing growth in productivity that only "size" could accomplish. For example, it was during this period that the early steel industry developed.

The factory system, however, introduced a new challenge for managers. No longer were the managers merely coordinators of independent artisans. Employees paid according to daily wage rates replaced the independent artisans. In turn,

---

[1] Johann Wolfgang von Goethe, *Samtliche Werke*, edited by Edward von der Hellen (Stuttgart and Berlin: J. G. Cotta, 1902– 07), Vol. XVII, p. 37.

single-manager businesses were replaced by large factories with several layers of management, where senior managers had responsibility over junior managers. As a result, a business enterprise now needed internal reporting measures to guide management in identifying the cost of their products and monitoring the results of operations. The fields of cost accounting and managerial accounting developed to meet these needs.

Even today, these disciplines continue to undergo major changes as accountants attempt to more accurately record, estimate, and report information for manufacturing operations.

CORPORATE ORGANIZATION

As you might expect, the Industrial Revolution created a demand for large amounts of money or capital to build factories and purchase machinery. The corporate form of business organization evolved to meet this need for capital. First established in England in 1845, it soon spread to other countries. In the United States, large amounts of capital were essential for the development of new industries, such as steel, transportation, mining, electric power, and communications. As in England, the corporation was the primary vehicle for raising the capital that was needed.

How does the corporate form of organization raise capital? If you answered "by issuing shares," you are correct. Corporate ownership is divided into shares of stock that can be readily transferred. The shareholders of a corporation normally do not exercise direct control over the operations of the corporation. The management runs day-to-day operations, and the shareholders only indirectly control the corporation through the election of a board of directors. The board of directors sets general policies and selects the officers who actively manage the corporation.

So how did the corporate form of organization affect accounting? The corporate form affected the evolution of accounting because the shareholders needed information about how well management was running the corporation. Since shareholders are not directly involved in day-to-day operations, they must rely on accounting reports in evaluating management's performance. These reports created additional demands upon accounting.

As corporations grew larger, the number of individuals and institutions relying on accounting reports increased. Potential shareholders and creditors needed information. Government agencies required information for purposes of taxation and regulation. Employees, union representatives, and customers requested information to judge the stability and profitability of corporations. Thus, largely due to the use of the corporate form of organization, accounting had to expand from serving the needs of a few owners to a public role of meeting the needs of a variety of interested parties.

PUBLIC ACCOUNTING

The corporate form of organization also created a need for an independent review or audit of reports prepared by the corporation's management. This audit was necessary to provide some assurance to users of the information that the reports were reliable. This audit function, called the **attest function,** was responsible for the development and growth of the public accounting profession. Unlike private accountants who work for a specific business entity, public accountants are self-employed. In this sense, they are independent of the businesses whose reports they audit. All provinces currently provide for the regulation and licensing of public accountants.

Although public accounting firms devote approximately 50% of their time to auditing, in recent years they have become increasingly involved in providing consulting services to assist clients in the planning and controlling of operations.

INCOME TAX

Income tax affects all of us. Since income taxes are based upon records of financial activities, the development of the income tax laws significantly affected the evolution of accounting, as you might expect.

The development of the federal income tax was made possible by legislation first enacted during World War I. The first federal income tax law was passed by the Canadian Parliament in 1917. Currently, individuals and all businesses organized as corporations are required to file income tax returns. To meet this requirement properly, filers must maintain adequate financial records. Because of the complexity of the tax laws and regulations, more and more organizations and individuals depend upon accountants. In addition to preparing tax returns, accountants advise clients on how to minimize their taxes.

GOVERNMENT INFLUENCE

Governments also have had a significant influence on the evolution of accounting. Current accounting systems must record and report financial data for a variety of governmental laws and regulations. You are probably aware of some examples of such laws and regulations at the local, provincial, and federal levels. For instance, the determination and collection of municipal property taxes, provincial sales taxes, and the Goods and Services Tax are based on accounting data. At the local level, public service commissions often approve utility rates. Such rate-making processes use and analyze accounting data. At the federal level, in addition to the income tax, the Canada Pension Plan and Employment Insurance laws require accounting record keeping and reporting by almost all businesses and many individuals.

ACCOUNTING'S FUTURE

As the preceding paragraphs emphasize, accounting touches all our lives in one way or another. Three areas of accounting that are undergoing intense study and review, and which will likely change significantly in the future, are international accounting, socioeconomic accounting, and managerial accounting.

International Accounting

As indicated earlier, accounting changes to meet the needs of society. As a result, accounting rules and regulations differ significantly among countries, each of which has unique cultural and societal needs. These differences create major accounting problems when a firm has foreign operations in more than one country. In such cases, the firm must adapt its accounting system to the rules and regulations of each country. This increases the costs of recording accounting data and preparing accounting reports. Also, there is potential for confusing the users of accounting reports. To overcome these problems, the accounting profession is seeking to develop uniform international accounting standards.

Socioeconomic Accounting

Accounting traditionally focuses on recording and reporting financial activities of businesses or other specific enterprises. Recently, there has been a suggestion that accounting should also record and report the impact of organizations on society. This area of accounting is called socioeconomic accounting.

Those proposing socioeconomic accounting have identified three main areas for study. The first area is recording and reporting the impact of various organizations on matters that affect the overall quality of life in society. The second area is recording and reporting the impact of government programs on achieving specific social objectives. The third area is recording and reporting the impact of corporate social performance. Corporate social performance refers to the corporation's responsibilities in such areas as water and air quality, conservation of natural resources, and equal employment practices.

The concept of socioeconomic accounting is relatively simple as a theory. However, additional study and research are needed before the socioeconomic costs and benefits of various activities can be recorded and reported. For example, the overall impact of a public utility's proposal to build a nuclear power plant is difficult to measure, record, and report.

Managerial Accounting

The role of managerial accounting is evolving as the information needs of managers change. One of the reasons for the change in information needs is **total quality management.** This new management concept is challenging many of the traditional methods of managing businesses.

Total quality management focuses on two major objectives. First, the business's primary objective is to earn customer loyalty by providing them with superior products and service. Second, the business should attempt to earn customer loyalty by continually improving employees, business processes, and products. This latter emphasis is called **continuous process improvement.**

Continuous process improvement extends traditional cost accounting and managerial accounting concepts beyond an emphasis of just the products that customers buy to everything that is done by the employees of the business. This philosophy envisions accountants providing information that will help managers and employees continually improve and re-engineer the business systems of which they are a part. As a result, cost accounting and managerial accounting systems are being revised to provide new and innovative types of information and reports.

DO YOU USE ACCOUNTING?

As this introduction suggests, we all use accounting to some degree. For some of us, accounting involves recording cheques in our chequebooks. For others, it may involve preparing our tax returns. As you begin your study of accounting, keep in mind the importance of accounting to your everyday life as well as its importance for your business career.

PART ONE

Basic Accounting Systems

1 Introduction to Accounting Concepts and Practice

YOU AND ACCOUNTING

Is accounting important to you? Do you use accounting information? The answer to both questions is yes. We all use accounting information in one form or another. For example, if you are thinking about buying a new car, you use accounting information to determine whether you can afford the monthly payments. Similarly, your decision to attend college or university implies that you considered the benefits (the ability to obtain a higher-paying or more desirable job). Most likely, you also considered the related costs of post-secondary education (the costs of tuition, textbooks, and so on).

Managers of businesses make decisions similar to this every day. For example, a manager of a chain of pizza restaurants must decide whether to acquire delivery cars. The manager will use accounting information about the pizza restaurants in determining whether to acquire the cars. Also, this information will be used in determining whether the business can obtain a loan to finance the purchase of the cars.

This chapter discusses the accounting framework by which businesses gather and report economic data to use in making decisions such as the ones described above.

Our primary objective in this text is to describe and illustrate basic accounting principles and concepts that will help you in your personal, as well as professional, lives. Accounting will be important to you, even though you may not be an accountant or a manager. If you are an engineer designing a product, for example, you should consider the costs of alternative manufacturing processes. If you are a lawyer, you will use accounting data in tax cases and in settling lawsuits.

In this text, we will focus primarily upon businesses organized for profit. However, the principles also apply to organizations that are not organized for profit, such as churches, charities, and governmental agencies.

After studying this chapter, you should be able to:

Objective 1
Define accounting as an information system.

Objective 2
Describe the profession of accounting and list its specialized fields.

Objective 3
Summarize the development of accounting principles and relate them to practice.

Objective 4
Summarize the three different forms of business organization.

Objective 5
List the characteristics of a business transaction.

Objective 6
State the accounting equation and define each element of the equation.

Objective 7
Explain the concepts of relevance and reliability, the entity and going concern concepts, the historical cost principle, and the monetary unit assumption.

Objective 8
Explain how business transactions can be stated in terms of the resulting changes in the three basic elements of the accounting equation.

Objective 9
Describe the financial statements of a sole proprietorship and explain how they interrelate.

Accounting as an Information System

Objective 1
Define accounting as an information system.

Accounting[1] may be defined as an information system that provides reports to various individuals or groups about economic activities of an organization or other entity. You might think of accounting as the "language of business," because it is the means by which most business information is communicated. For example, companies distribute accounting reports that summarize their financial performance to their owners, creditors, government regulators, and potential investors.

The process of using accounting to provide information to users is illustrated in Exhibit 1. First, accountants must identify user groups and their information needs. These needs determine which economic data and activities are recorded by the accounting system. Finally, accountants prepare reports that summarize this information for users.

Because individuals make decisions based upon the data in accounting reports, accounting has a major impact upon our economic and social system. For example, the management of **Canadian Airlines** may decide to lay off 50 pilots in Calgary based upon accounting projections and reports. Likewise, the federal government and provincial legislatures allocate monies to various programs, based at least partially upon accounting reports.

Profession of Accounting

SPECIALIZED ACCOUNTING FIELDS

Objective 2
Describe the profession of accounting and list its specialized fields.

All accounting is not the same. There are several specialized fields of accounting in practice. The two most common are financial accounting and managerial accounting. Within these two general areas there are further specializations,

---

[1] A glossary of terms appears at the end of each chapter. A complete glossary is included at the end of the text. The terms included in each glossary are printed in colour the first time they are defined in the text.

Exhibit 1

Accounting as a Process of Providing Information to Users

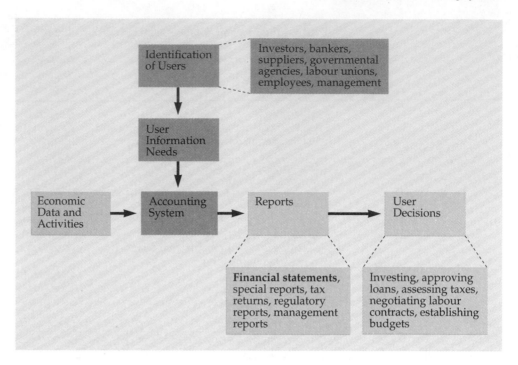

The scope of activities and duties of accountants varies widely and provides excellent training for top management positions.

including cost accounting, environmental accounting, tax accounting, systems, international accounting, not-for-profit accounting, and social accounting.

Financial accounting and managerial accounting are aimed at different groups of decision-makers. **Financial accounting** is primarily concerned with recording and reporting information about the economic activities of the enterprise for use by parties that are *external* to the firm itself. These are groups such as investors, creditors, government agencies, and the general public who do not have access to information that the firm may generate for its own internal use. Financial accountants follow generally accepted accounting principles (GAAP) in preparing reports for external users. These rules enable such users to compare the reports of different firms, since they ensure that all of the financial statements have been prepared on a common basis. The ability to compare financial reports is essential for an investor who is deciding between investing in one company or another.

Managerial accounting, on the other hand, involves the preparation of information for persons who work for the firm itself. These *internal* users, such as managers, department heads and top executives, need information to make decisions about the firm itself. Many different types of information, including projections and estimated data, are needed for running day-to-day operations and for making future plans. Unlike financial accountants, management accountants are not restricted to using generally accepted accounting principles. Instead, they gather and report any information that is useful to management. Thus, the nature and content of these reports can differ widely in form and content.

The demand for accounting services has increased with the increase in the number, size, and complexity of businesses. In addition, new laws and regulations have also created an increased demand for accounting.

You may wonder whether there are career opportunities in accounting. The answer is yes. Employment opportunities in the profession of accountancy are expected to continue to grow and expand. Between 1984 and 1994, employment grew by 51% in the field of financial auditing and accounting, compared to an economy-wide growth in employment of only 17% over the same period. Government projections indicate that employment trends in the accounting profession should remain favourable, as 93% of accountants are in full-time positions.[2] Earnings in this area are higher than average as a result of the education and experience of accounting professionals, and the higher levels of responsibilities of their work duties. If current growth rates continue, over 160,000 people will be employed in this field in Canada by the year 2000.

Accountants work in either (1) private accounting or (2) public accounting. Accountants employed by a business firm or not-for-profit organization are in private accounting. Accountants and their staff who provide services to clients on a fee basis are in public accounting.

Experience in private and public accounting provides excellent training for top management positions. For example, in its 1990 Special Bonus Issue on "The Corporate Elite," *Business Week* reported that 31% of the chief executives of the 1,000 largest public corporations followed a finance-accounting career path. Merchandising-marketing was the career path for 27%, and engineering-technical was the career path for 22% of the chief executives.

PRIVATE ACCOUNTING

Private accountants usually work for a single employer, which may be a business, the government, or some other not-for-profit organization. Private accountants are frequently called management accountants. Those employed by a manufacturing concern may be industrial or cost accountants. The chief accountant in a business is usually called the **controller.** The scope of duties of private accountants varies widely, and may include activities such as cost accounting, budgeting, internal auditing, and designing information systems.

Cost accounting analyzes the costs necessary to produce a product or render services. It is necessary to monitor these costs in order to help managers to control expenses. **Budgeting** involves the formulation of detailed plans that help managers to clearly set out the goals that they are trying to attain. Once established, these budgets can be used to measure how well management met their stated objectives. **Internal auditing** involves accountants who are employed by the firm to perform internal reviews of the company's accounting and operating procedures. Such reviews are undertaken in order to enhance the effectiveness and efficiency of the organization and to verify that employees are complying with the policies set out by upper management. Management accountants may also **design information systems** to collect and report data about the firm's economic activities to various interested groups.

PUBLIC ACCOUNTING

In public accounting, an accountant may practise as an individual or as a member of a public accounting firm. One of the primary functions of public accountants is to **audit** the financial reports prepared by business, government, and not-for-profit entities. In the role of auditor, the public accountant acts as an independent party who examines the accounting records of the enterprise to ensure that the financial reports prepared by management are reliable. An **audit report** must be attached to the financial reports published by companies whose shares are publicly traded, as well as by most government and many not-for-profit agencies. In the audit report the public accountant expresses his or her opinion as to whether the firm's financial statements are presented fairly and in accordance with **generally accepted accounting principles.** Investors, creditors, and other users of financial statements rely on the auditor's opinion for assurance that the statements are fair and not misleading.

---

[2] Minister of Supply and Services Canada, *Job Futures, Occupational Outlooks*, Ottawa, 1996.

Besides auditing, public accountants provide many other services to the public, such as the following. **Tax services** include both preparing of tax returns and advising clients on how to plan their business transactions so as to minimize taxes. **General accounting services** may entail helping small businesses to maintain their accounting records and to prepare their financial statements. **Management advisory services** includes assisting firms in designing new accounting and computing systems, as well as recommending other ways to improve their clients' business operations. In recent years, public practitioners have also become increasingly involved in **corporate and personal financial planning, business valuations,** and **risk assessment.** Public accountants may also serve as **trustees for firms that are insolvent** or engage in **forensic accounting and auditing.** The latter involves an in-depth analysis of accounting records to discover whether a fraud has occurred.

ACCOUNTING ORGANIZATIONS AND PROFESSIONAL CERTIFICATION

In Canada, education falls under provincial jurisdiction. At present, provincial laws recognize three accounting organizations as professional self-regulating bodies with authority to establish and enforce educational prerequisites, professional standards, and codes of conduct for their members.

To become a **Chartered Accountant (CA),** a student must complete 30 months of practical work experience in public accounting[3] and pass a national examination administered by the Canadian Institute of Chartered Accountants (CICA). Provincial CA Institutes set educational prerequisites that CA students must meet before attempting the national examinations. These generally include a university degree with completion of certain designated courses. After attaining their professional designation, approximately 50% of CAs leave public practice to work in business or government. The CICA supports research on current accounting and auditing topics, and issues accounting and auditing standards that are published in the *CICA Handbook.* The CICA also supports a monthly professional journal called *CA Magazine*.

The **Certified General Accountants Association of Canada (CGAAC)** administers a set of courses with national examinations for those pursuing the designation of **Certified General Accountant (CGA).** Students may obtain exemptions from some of these courses and examinations by completing specified community college or university courses. To become a CGA, a student must also complete a practical work experience requirement in industry, government, or a public accounting firm. Commencing with students enrolling in the CGA program in the fall of 1998, the educational requirements for the designation require all students to complete a university degree, meet specific course requirements, and pass a professional accreditation comprehensive examination. The CGAAC publishes the *CGA Magazine* and sponsors a Research Foundation that supports accounting research.

Those primarily interested in management accounting may seek accreditation as **Certified Management Accountants (CMAs).** To enter this program, a student must usually possess a university degree and must pass an entrance examination set by the **Society of Management Accountants of Canada (SMAC).** Requirements to obtain the CMA designation include successful completion of a two-year professional program, as well as a two-year experience requirement, usually in industry or government. The SMAC supports management accounting research, issues *Management Accounting Guidelines* and *Research Studies,* and publishes the *CMA Magazine*.

---

[3] Specific work experience with the provincial or federal government auditor general's office may also qualify to meet this requirement.

In 1997 there were approximately 60,000 CAs, 51,000 CGAs, and 27,000 CMAs registered in Canada. In addition to these three professional accounting designations, an individual interested in internal auditing may work towards becoming a **Certified Internal Auditor (CIA).** The **Institute of Internal Auditors (IIA)** is an international organization that administers this program and publishes its own professional journal, *The Internal Auditor.*

The **Canadian Academic Accounting Association (CAAA)** is an organization of accountants, including many academics, who are interested in promoting accounting education and research. The CAAA sponsors research projects and conferences and publishes an academic journal called *Contemporary Accounting Research.*

PROFESSIONAL ETHICS FOR ACCOUNTANTS

What are ethics? Ethics are moral principles that guide the conduct of individuals. In some cases, individuals may differ as to what is "right" or "wrong" in a given situation. For example, you may believe that it is unethical to copy another student's homework and hand it in as your own. Other students may feel that it is acceptable to copy homework, unless the instructor has told the class that it is prohibited. Likewise, business managers are often in situations where they may feel pressure to "bend the rules." For example, managers of automotive service departments are sometimes accused of recommending unnecessary repairs and overcharging customers for actual repairs in order to meet company goals and earn bonuses.

Regardless of differences among individuals, proper ethical conduct implies a behaviour that considers the impact of one's actions on society and others. In other words, proper ethical conduct implies that you not only consider what's in your best interests, but also what's in the best interests of others.

Ethical conduct is good business. A survey of top managers by the accounting firm of **Deloitte & Touche** reports that "an enterprise actually strengthens its competitive position by maintaining high ethical standards."[4] For example, an automobile manufacturer that fails to correct a safety defect to save costs may later lose sales from the loss of consumer confidence. Likewise, the management of a business that pollutes the environment may find itself the focus of lawsuits and customer boycotts.

Why is ethical conduct so important for accountants? As we indicated earlier, individuals, businesses, governmental agencies, and others rely on accounting reports in making decisions. Therefore, it is critical that such reports be prepared accurately and with minimal bias. In some cases, accountants may be pressured by supervisors to report activities or financial results that are more favourable than warranted by the facts. Accountants must resist such pressures. For example, a company's accountant might be pressured to delay recording a loss until after a bank has approved the company's loan. Providing misleading information would be unethical and, in this case, illegal.

In February of 1997 **KPMG,** an international public accounting firm, completed a survey of top executives of Canada's leading 1,000 companies on the topic of business ethics. Of the 251 responses received, over half were provided by Chief Executive Officers. Clearly, ethical management is of high interest for Canada's senior management. Sixty-six per cent of the respondents reported having a company code of ethics, practice, or conduct. Of the larger companies with over $1 billion in revenues, 90% published a code of ethics.

Respondents were asked to rate the level of importance of several ethical issues. Integrity of accounting books and records ranked as the overall top issue, with 71% of respondents rating it as "very important." KPMG concluded that:

---

[4] *Ethics in Business*, Deloitte & Touche (formerly Touche Ross), January 1988.

the top ranking of this issue reflects the fact that accurate books, accountable transactions, and consistent procedures are business fundamentals. When the integrity of these essential controls is compromised by carelessness or even well-intentioned "fudging," the door is left open to the risk of loss arising from incompetence, unethical conduct, and fraud.[5]

Although individuals and businesses may develop their own standards of moral and ethical conduct, accountants in both private and public practice have developed ethical standards to guide them. The provincial Institutes of Chartered Accountants, the provincial Societies of Management Accountants, and the Certified General Accountants of Canada have rules of professional conduct that provide standards of acceptable behaviour for their respective members.

These codes of professional conduct change as society changes. However, ethical conduct is more than simply conforming to written standards of professional behaviour. In a true sense, ethical conduct requires a personal commitment to honourable behaviour.[6]

Generally Accepted Accounting Principles

Objective 3
Summarize the development of accounting principles and relate them to practice.

What are generally accepted accounting principles (GAAP)? They are principles and concepts that are used by accountants in preparing financial reports. GAAP are necessary so that users of these reports can compare the financial condition and operating results across companies. If the management of a company could record and report transactions as they saw fit, then comparability between companies would be difficult, if not impossible.

Auditors use generally accepted accounting principles (GAAP) as a frame of reference in assessing the financial statements prepared by management. The audit report indicates whether the statements are presented fairly *and in accordance with GAAP.*

Because GAAP impact how and what companies report to external users, managers, auditors, investors, creditors, and others affected by these reports are interested in the establishment of these principles. Over time, GAAP have evolved in response to the demands of these various interest groups. In the future GAAP will continue to change and adapt to serve the various constituents of the financial reporting community (which includes investors, creditors, managers, auditors, and other users of financial information).

Accounting principles and concepts develop from many sources, including accounting research, accepted accounting practices, and the pronouncements of authoritative accounting bodies. In Canada, one of the most important sources for GAAP is the *CICA Handbook.* Both the Canada Business Corporations Act and provincial statutes have given the *CICA Handbook* legal authority by requiring that financial statements be prepared in accordance with the Accounting Recommendations that it contains. These Accounting Recommendations are issued and updated from time to time by the CICA's **Accounting Standards Board (AcSB).** The AcSB also publishes *Accounting Guidelines,* which do not have the same authority as its Recommendations but which provide guidance on handling specific accounting issues.

While the *CICA Handbook* contains recommendations about how to report many different types of transactions, it cannot deal with every possible accounting issue that might arise in recording the economic activities of an enterprise. Therefore,

---

[5] KPMG, *Business Ethics Survey Report,* Toronto, February 1997. Information found at KPMG's Web site: www.kpmg.ca.
[6] Ethics discussion cases are provided at the end of each chapter to focus attention on meaningful ethical situations that accountants often face in practice.

accountants and auditors must often use their professional judgment in interpreting and applying GAAP to specific situations that they encounter in practice. In areas where there is no official CICA pronouncement, accountants look to other sources to determine what is GAAP. These sources may include the pronouncements of other accounting organizations, accounting research, or common practice in the industry.

The body with the primary responsibility for developing accounting standards in the United States is the Financial Accounting Standards Board (FASB). The FASB issues *Statements of Financial Accounting Standards*, as well as *Interpretations* that explain and elaborate on existing standards. Other countries also have authoritative bodies that set their own accounting standards. The **International Accounting Standards Committee (IASC)** is a worldwide organization that attempts to harmonize the accounting practices of different countries. It suggests standards for universal adoption, but it has no legal authority to enforce its recommendations in any particular country.

GAAP includes both: (1) specific rules and practices for handling particular accounting transactions, and (2) broad principles and underlying concepts used in preparing financial statements. In this chapter and throughout this text, we emphasize accounting principles and concepts. It is through this emphasis on the "why" of accounting, as well as the "how," that you will gain an understanding of the full significance of accounting.

Accounting for All Types of Business Organizations

Objective 4
Summarize the three different forms of business organization.

Businesses may be organized in three different ways. A business with only one owner is a sole proprietorship. Many small retail businesses are owned and operated by a single individual. You have probably also encountered many professionals, such as lawyers, physicians, accountants, or architects, who run practices on their own. There are no special legal procedures required to set up a proprietorship. From a legal perspective, a sole proprietorship is not different from its owner. If the owner defaults on either personal or business loans, the creditors may lay claim to the owner's property, whether it is personal or used in the business.

Sometimes, two or more individuals will join together to form a partnership. Many professional practices and other businesses are operated as partnerships. Usually, the partners draw up a written agreement indicating how they will divide any income of the business. If a partner dies, the partnership ends and usually a new partnership must be drawn up for the business to continue. Like a sole proprietorship, a partnership has no legal status separate from its owners. Each partner can be held personally responsible for the debts of the business and creditors may seize business property in order to satisfy personal debts of individual partners.

A corporation is the only form of business organization that constitutes a legal entity separate from its owners. A firm may incorporate under provincial or federal law. The legal requirements for incorporation are complex and setting up this form of business will involve some legal expenses. A person participates in the ownership of a corporation by buying shares in the corporation. The shares of large, public corporations are traded in organized markets, such as the Toronto Stock Exchange. Since the firm can sell shares to a large number of investors, more individuals can participate in the ownership of a corporation than in a partnership. By appealing to a broader base of investors, the corporation should be able to raise money more easily than a sole proprietorship or partnership. Owners can buy and sell their shares or will their shares to their heirs without affecting the existence of the business. Because the corporation is a legal entity distinct from its owners, its property and obligations are also legally separate from those of its owners.

USING ACCOUNTING TO UNDERSTAND BUSINESS

In an editorial in *The Wall Street Journal*, Dennis R. Beresford, Chairman of the Financial Accounting Standards Board, discussed the role of generally accepted accounting principles. He asserted that the primary role of accounting principles should be to truthfully portray the economic consequences of events on the financial statements of a business enterprise. In doing so, Mr. Beresford asserted, ". . . the truth will set investors free." Mr. Beresford goes on to state that ". . . Truth in accounting means telling it like it is, without bias or intent to encourage any particular mode of behaviour by the user of the information."

Source: "In Accounting, Truth Above All," Letters to the Editor, *The Wall Street Journal*, March 21, 1994.

This means that the property of the business cannot be claimed to pay off the personal debts of any shareholder. Similarly, the shareholder cannot be held personally liable for the debts of the corporation.

The sole proprietorship is the most common form of business organization. However, since larger firms tend to be corporations, the corporate form of organization accounts for by far the largest share of dollars of business transactions in the economy. This is shown in Exhibit 2 below.

As indicated above, from a **legal** perspective, a corporation is very different from a sole proprietorship or partnership. However, from an **accounting** perspective, we generally treat all businesses the same way, no matter how they are legally organized. Generally accepted accounting principles apply to sole proprietorships and partnerships as well as to corporations.

Exhibit 2
Profit-Making Businesses

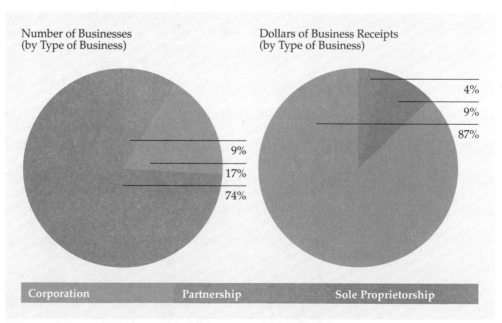

Number of Businesses (by Type of Business)

Dollars of Business Receipts (by Type of Business)

Corporation   Partnership   Sole Proprietorship

Source: *Understanding Canadian Business*, 2nd edition, Nickels, McHugh, McHugh and Berman, McGraw-Hill, 1997.

Business Transactions

Objective 5

List the characteristics of a business transaction.

Are all economic events affecting a business entity recorded in an accounting system? No. For example, a change in a business's credit rating by an agency such as **Dun and Bradstreet** is not recorded in the accounting records. Only business transactions are recorded in the accounting records.

A **business transaction** is an economic event or condition that directly changes the entity's financial position or directly affects its results of operations. For example, the payment of a monthly telephone bill of $68 affects the entity's financial position because the entity now has less cash on hand. Generally, we record only transactions or events that involve an exchange of economic consideration between the enterprise and another party. A sale is an example of such an exchange transaction. In this case, the firm provides goods or services to a customer in exchange for cash or for the customer's promise to make a payment in the future. The purchase of land for $50,000 is a transaction involving an exchange of property for cash. In contrast, the change in an entity's credit rating is not a transaction. It does not involve an exchange transaction and does not directly affect cash or any other element of the entity's financial position.

A business transaction may lead to an event or a condition that results in another transaction. For example, the purchase of $1,750 of merchandise on credit will be followed by the payment to the creditor. Each time a portion of the merchandise is sold, another transaction occurs. Each of these events must be recorded.

Assets, Liabilities, and Owner's Equity

Objective 6

State the accounting equation and define each element of the equation.

Assets are economic resources owned or controlled by an entity. Assets are the result of events or transactions that have already occurred and which are expected to bring future benefits to the firm. Examples of assets are cash, supplies, land, buildings, or equipment owned by the firm.

The rights or claims to the assets owned by a business entity are normally divided into two types: (1) the rights of creditors and (2) the rights of owners. The rights of creditors represent the debts or obligations due by the entity as a result of past transactions. These debts are called liabilities, and they will require the enterprise to pay out assets or render services to its creditors in the future. Examples of liabilities are loans owed to banks, wages owed to employees, and sales tax owed to the government.

The right of the owners to the assets of the business is called owner's equity.[7] The owners have the right to any assets of the entity that are left over after its creditors have been paid. Therefore, we can describe the owners' claims as a **residual interest**. The owners are entitled to the assets that remain after the firm has met all of its other obligations.

The relationship between assets, liabilities, and owner's equity may be written in the form of an equation, which states that the economic resources of the entity are equal to the total claims on those resources:

Assets = Liabilities + Owner's Equity

The preceding equation is known as the accounting equation. It is usual to place liabilities before owner's equity in the accounting equation because creditors

---

[7] The caption "owner's equity" refers to a single owner. If there is more than one owner, the correct heading would be "owners' equity" (the apostrophe after the "s" indicating that owners is plural).

have first rights to the assets. The claim of the owners is sometimes given greater emphasis by transposing liabilities to the other side of the equation, yielding:

Assets – Liabilities = Owner's Equity

To illustrate, if the assets owned by a business amount to $100,000 and the liabilities amount to $30,000, the owner's equity is equal to $70,000, as shown below:

Assets – Liabilities = Owner's Equity
$$\$100,000 - \$30,000 = \$70,000$$

Some Basic Accounting Concepts and Principles

Objective 7
Explain the concepts of relevancy and reliability, the entity and the going concern concepts, the historical cost principle, and the monetary unit assumption.

Before you can proceed to consider accounting for specific business transactions, you need to understand some of the basic principles that accountants follow in recording information and preparing financial reports. In this section we will define a few of the most important concepts and assumptions that underlie accounting practice. As we proceed through subsequent chapters, we will gradually introduce you to more of these general principles.

The **primary objective of financial statements** is to communicate information that is **useful** to investors, creditors, and other parties in making economic decisions.[8] The data should be **understandable** to those who have some knowledge of business and are willing to study it.[9] Accounting standard setters in both Canada and the United States have generally agreed that, in order to be useful to decision-makers, accounting information must possess two basic characteristics: it must be both relevant and reliable.

RELEVANCY CONCEPT

Accounting information is **relevant** *if it can influence the decisions of those who use it.* Accounting information can be relevant in two ways. It can have (1) **predictive value** and/or (2) **feedback value.**[10] Accounting information has predictive value if it helps the user to predict how the business will do in the future. For example, a bank might use a firm's financial statements to predict whether the firm would be able to repay a loan over the next two years. Accounting information has feedback value if it helps the user to assess how well the business has done in the past. For example, the owners of a company might use accounting information about the results of the firm's operations in order to determine whether management had been doing a good job or not. To be relevant, the information must be **timely.** That is, it must be made available early enough to influence the user's decision. A basic assumption underlying GAAP is that we should record information that is relevant to those who use the accounting reports.[11]

RELIABILITY CONCEPT

GAAP also requires that accounting information should be **reliable** or **objective.** This means that the information represents what it is supposed to represent and that it is **neutral** (free from bias) and verifiable. Data that are **verifiable** are not just based on personal opinion, but can be confirmed by independent observers.

---

[8] *CICA Handbook*, Section 1000, paragraph 15.
[9] *Ibid.*, paragraph 19.
[10] *Ibid.*, paragraph 20.
[11] *Ibid.*, paragraph 20.

Investors, creditors, and other parties who use financial reports need to know that this information is not just based on management's opinions, which could be overly optimistic or pessimistic. The information must be reliable so that an external auditor can verify its accuracy.[12]

ENTITY CONCEPT

The entity concept requires us to identify the individual economic units about which we need to collect and report data. The accounting entity could be an individual, a not-for-profit organization such as a church, a government agency, or a profitable enterprise such as a real estate agency. It could be an entire company or just one segment or branch of that company. For example, creditors who have made bank loans to **Eaton's** will want to see financial reports on how the business is doing overall. For this purpose, the entire company is the accounting entity. On the other hand, Eaton's owners will also need information on how well each store is performing, in order to decide whether certain unprofitable locations should be shut down. Reports prepared for each branch will treat the individual store as the accounting entity.

Once we have identified the entity for which information is needed, we can determine which economic data and activities to analyze, record, and summarize in reports. In accounting for any particular enterprise, we must keep track of its activities separate and distinct from the activities of any other entities and from the activities of its owners. For example, suppose that you are a lawyer running your own law practice. Every month you pay rent for both your law office and for the apartment in which you live. Financial reports for the law practice would show the office rent as an expense of the business, but would not include the rent on your personal residence. This is because the law practice is an accounting entity that is separate from you, the owner.

Be careful to differentiate the concept of an **accounting entity** from that of a **legal entity.** Every economic unit for which we keep records is an accounting entity, clearly separated from its owners. This applies to all forms of business, whether sole proprietorship, partnership, or corporation. Only a corporation is a legal entity separate from its owners, but all three are accounting entities separate from their owners.

GOING CONCERN CONCEPT

The going concern concept assumes that the entity will continue to operate indefinitely. This does not imply that the entity will last forever, but it does imply that the entity will continue its operations and not go out of business in the foreseeable future. This assumes that the business will be able to fulfil its objectives and will be able to pay off its debts when they come due.

HISTORICAL COST PRINCIPLE

The historical cost principle states that assets should be recorded and reported at the actual cost that was incurred to acquire them. The cost of the asset is the amount that the purchaser and the seller of the asset settle upon when the exchange takes place. If an asset is purchased for cash, we record the asset at the amount of cash paid at the date of acquisition. If an asset is purchased on account or in exchange for another asset, we still record the cost of the asset at the same amount as the purchaser would have paid if he or she had paid cash for the asset.

[12]*Ibid.*, paragraph 21.

The historical cost principle is linked to the accounting concept of reliability and the going concern assumption. Some have suggested that it would be more useful to report assets at their current market values; that is, at the amount that we would receive if we sold the assets today. One of the main reasons why we report assets at their historical cost is because this is more reliable. We can verify what an asset cost, but it is more difficult to determine what the asset could sell for today. This is a value on which opinions would differ. Also, the going concern concept assumes that the business will not have to sell off its assets immediately, but will be able to use its assets as it intended. If a business is going to use its plant and equipment in its operations and not sell them in the near future, the selling price of these assets may not be relevant.

The cost principle determines the amount entered into the accounting records for purchases of properties and services. For example, if a building is bought for $150,000, that amount should be entered into the buyer's accounting records. The seller may have been asking $170,000 for the building up to the time of the sale. The buyer may have initially offered $130,000 for the building. The building may have been assessed at $125,000 for property tax purposes. The buyer may have received an offer of $175,000 for the building the day after it was acquired. These latter amounts have no effect on the accounting records because they did not result in an exchange of the building from the seller to the buyer. *The exchange price, or cost, of $150,000 is the amount used in the accounting records for the building.*

Continuing the illustration, the $175,000 offer received by the buyer the day after the building was acquired indicates that it was a bargain purchase at $150,000. To use $175,000 in the accounting records, however, would record an illusory or unrealized profit. If, after buying the building, the buyer accepts the offer and sells the building for $175,000, a profit of $25,000 is then realized and recorded. The new owner would record $175,000 as the cost of the building.

In exchanges between buyer and seller, both try to get the best price. Only the final amount agreed on is objective enough for accounting purposes. If the amounts for which properties were recorded were constantly revised upward and downward based on offers, appraisals, and opinions, accounting reports would soon become unstable and unreliable.

The cost of an automobile is the amount agreed on between the buyer and the dealer.

MONETARY UNIT ASSUMPTION

Accountants measure and record business transactions in terms of money. For example, we record the cost of a building as the dollar amount required to purchase the asset. The monetary unit assumption presumes that money is the most relevant, understandable, and useful unit for recording accounting transactions. When we record transactions in dollars, we assume that the dollar is a reasonably stable measuring unit whose value does not change from period to period. This ignores the possibility of inflation (a decline in the purchasing power of the dollar). Because inflation has been fairly low in recent years in Canada, GAAP permits us to assume that the monetary unit is stable and to record accounting transactions in terms of dollars.

Transactions and the Accounting Equation

Objective 8
Explain how business transactions can be stated in terms of the resulting changes in the three basic elements of the accounting equation.

We can state all business transactions in terms of changes they cause in the three elements of the accounting equation. You will see how business transactions affect the accounting equation by studying some typical transactions. For example,

COMPUTER KING

assume that on November 1, 1999, Pat King begins a sole proprietorship to be known as Computer King. Using Pat's knowledge of microcomputers, the business will offer computer consulting services for a fee. We describe below each transaction or group of similar transactions during the first month of operations and show the effects of the transaction on the accounting equation.

Transaction a. Pat King deposits $15,000 in a bank account in the name of Computer King. The effect of this transaction is to increase the asset (cash), on the left side of the equation, by $15,000. To balance the equation, we increase the owner's equity on the right side of the equation by the same amount. We refer to the equity of the owner by using the owner's name and "Capital," such as "Pat King, Capital." The effect of this transaction on Computer King's accounting equation is:

$$
\left.\begin{array}{l}
\underline{\textit{Assets}} \\
\text{Cash} \\
\text{a. } 15,000
\end{array}\right\} = \left\{\begin{array}{l}
\underline{\textit{Owner's Equity}} \\
\text{Pat King, Capital} \\
15,000 \quad \text{Investment by} \\
\qquad\qquad \text{Pat King}
\end{array}\right.
$$

Note that the equation relates only to the business, Computer King. Pat King's personal assets, such as a home or personal bank account, and personal liabilities are excluded from the equation. The business is treated as a separate entity, with cash of $15,000 and owner's equity of $15,000.

Computer King offers computer consulting services for a fee. Each transaction will affect Computer King's accounting equation.

Transaction b. Computer King's next transaction is to buy land for $10,000 cash. The land is located near a shopping mall that contains three microcomputer stores. Pat King plans to rent office space and equipment for several months. If the business is a success, the company will build on the land.

The purchase of the land changes the makeup of the assets but does not change the total assets. We show the items in the equation prior to this transaction, the effect of the transaction, and the new amounts or *balances* of the items.

$$
\left.\begin{array}{lll}
\multicolumn{3}{c}{\underline{\textit{Assets}}} \\
\text{Cash} & + & \text{Land} \\
15,000 & & \\
\text{b.} \quad -10,000 & & +10,000 \\
\text{Bal.} \quad 5,000 & & 10,000
\end{array}\right\} = \left\{\begin{array}{l}
\underline{\textit{Owner's Equity}} \\
\text{Pat King, Capital} \\
15,000 \\
\\
\overline{15,000}
\end{array}\right.
$$

Transaction c. During the month, Computer King buys supplies for $1,350, agreeing to pay the supplier in the near future. This type of transaction is a purchase *on account.* The liability created is termed an account payable. Items such as supplies that will be used in the business in the future are called prepaid expenses, which are assets.

In practice, we normally record each purchase separately. However, to simplify this illustration, we have recorded all the purchases of supplies together. The effect is to increase assets and liabilities by $1,350.

$$
\left.\begin{array}{llllll}
\multicolumn{6}{c}{\underline{\textit{Assets}}} \\
& \text{Cash} & + & \text{Supplies} & + & \text{Land} \\
\text{Bal.} & 5,000 & & & & 10,000 \\
\text{c.} & & & +1,350 & & \\
\text{Bal.} & 5,000 & & 1,350 & & 10,000
\end{array}\right\} = \left\{\begin{array}{lcl}
\text{Liabilities} & + & \begin{array}{l}\textit{Owner's}\\ \textit{Equity}\end{array} \\
\text{Accounts} & & \text{Pat King,} \\
\text{Payable} & + & \text{Capital} \\
& & 15,000 \\
+1,350 & & \\
1,350 & & 15,000
\end{array}\right.
$$

Transaction d. Revenue is the amount charged to customers for goods or services sold to them. Special terms may be used for certain kinds of revenue, such as *sales* for the sale of merchandise. Revenue from providing services is called *fees earned*. For example, a physician would record fees earned for services to patients. Other examples of revenue terms include *rent earned* for the use of real estate or other property and *interest earned* on an investment in a Canada Savings Bond.

The amount of revenue earned during a period is measured by the amount of assets received from customers for the goods sold or services rendered to them. Earning revenue through business operations increases owner's equity. Thus, revenue increases assets and increases owner's equity.

During its first month of operations, Computer King earns fees of $7,500, receiving the amount in cash. These transactions increase cash and the owner's equity by $7,500.

	Assets					=		Liabilities	+	Owner's Equity
	Cash	+	Supplies	+	Land			Accounts Payable	+	Pat King, Capital
Bal.	5,000		1,350		10,000			1,350		15,000
d.	+7,500									+7,500 Revenue earned
Bal.	12,500		1,350		10,000			1,350		22,500

Instead of requiring the payment of cash at the time services are provided or goods are sold, a business may accept payment at a later date. Such revenues are called **fees on account** or **sales on account.** In such cases, the firm has an **account receivable,** which is a claim against the customer. An account receivable is an asset, and the revenue is earned as if cash had been received. When customers pay their accounts, there is an exchange of one asset for another. Cash increases and accounts receivable decreases.

Transaction e. The amount of assets or services used in the process of earning revenue is an **expense.** Expenses include supplies used, wages of employees, and other assets and services used in operating the business. As you might have guessed, the effect of expenses on owner's equity is the opposite of the effect of revenues. Expenses decrease owner's equity.

For Computer King, the expenses paid during the month were as follows: wages, $1,800; rent, $800; utilities, $450; and miscellaneous, $275. Miscellaneous expenses include small amounts paid for such items as postage due, coffee, and newspaper and magazine purchases. This group of transactions reduces cash and owner's equity, as shown.

	Assets					=		Liabilities	+	Owner's Equity
	Cash	+	Supplies	+	Land			Accounts Payable	+	Pat King, Capital
Bal.	12,500		1,350		10,000			1,350		22,500
e.	−3,325									−1,800 Wages expense
										− 800 Rent expense
										− 450 Utilities expense
										− 275 Misc. expense
Bal.	9,175		1,350		10,000			1,350		19,175

Transaction f. During the month, Computer King pays $950 to creditors on account, thereby reducing both assets and liabilities. The effect on the equation is as follows:

	Assets				=	Liabilities	+	Owner's Equity
	Cash	+ Supplies	+ Land			Accounts Payable	+	Pat King, Capital
Bal.	9,175	1,350	10,000			1,350		19,175
f.	−950					−950		
Bal.	8,225	1,350	10,000			400		19,175

You should note that paying an amount on account is different from paying an amount for an expense. The payment of an expense reduces owner's equity, as illustrated in transaction (e). Paying an amount on account reduces the amount owed on a liability.

Transaction g. During the month the business has used up some of its supplies, so that at the end of the month, the cost of the supplies on hand is $550. The remainder of the supplies ($1,350 − $550) was used in the operations of the business and is treated as an expense. This decreases supplies and owner's equity by $800.

	Assets				=	Liabilities	+	Owner's Equity
	Cash	+ Supplies	+ Land			Accounts Payable	+	Pat King, Capital
Bal.	8,225	1,350	10,000			400		19,175
g.		− 800						− 800 Supplies expense
Bal.	8,225	550	10,000			400		18,375

Transaction h. At the end of the month, Pat King withdraws $2,000 in cash from the business for personal use. This transaction is the exact opposite of an investment in the business by the owner. The cash payment is not a business expense but a withdrawal of a part of the owner's equity. Cash and owner's equity are decreased.

	Assets				=	Liabilities	+	Owner's Equity
	Cash	+ Supplies	+ Land			Accounts Payable	+	Pat King, Capital
Bal.	8,225	550	10,000			400		18,375
h.	−2,000							−2,000 Withdrawal
Bal.	6,225	550	10,000			400		16,375

You should be careful not to confuse withdrawals by the owner with expenses. Withdrawals do not represent assets consumed or services used in the process of earning revenues. The owner's equity decrease from the withdrawals is listed in the equation under Capital. This is because withdrawals are considered a distribution of capital to the owner.

Summary. We can now summarize the transactions of Computer King. The transactions are identified by letter, and the balance of each item is shown after each transaction.

	Assets					=	Liabilities	+	Owner's Equity	
	Cash	+	Supplies	+	Land	=	Accounts Payable	+	Pat King, Capital	
a.	+15,000					=			+15,000	Investment by Pat King
b.	−10,000				+10,000					
Bal.	5,000				10,000				15,000	
c.			+1,350				+1,350			
Bal.	5,000		1,350		10,000		1,350		15,000	
d.	+ 7,500								+ 7,500	Revenue earned
Bal.	12,500		1,350		10,000		1,350		22,500	
e.	− 3,325								− 1,800	Wages expense
									− 800	Rent expense
									− 450	Utilities expense
									− 275	Misc. expense
Bal.	9,175		1,350		10,000		1,350		19,175	
f.	− 950						− 950			
Bal.	8,225		1,350		10,000		400		19,175	
g.			− 800						− 800	Supplies expense
Bal.	8,225		550		10,000		400		18,375	
h.	− 2,000								− 2,000	Withdrawal
Bal.	6,225		550		10,000		400		16,375	

In reviewing the preceding illustration, you should note the following, which apply to all types of businesses:

1. The effect of every transaction is an increase and/or a decrease in one or more of the accounting equation elements.
2. The two sides of the accounting equation are always equal.
3. The owner's equity is increased by amounts invested by the owner and is decreased by withdrawals by the owner. In addition, the owner's equity is increased by revenues and is decreased by expenses. The effects of these four types of transactions on owner's equity are illustrated in Exhibit 3.

Financial Statements

Objective 9

Describe the financial statements of a sole proprietorship and explain how they interrelate.

After we have recorded and summarized the transactions, we can prepare reports for users. The accounting reports that provide this information are called **financial statements.** The principal financial statements of a sole proprietorship are the income statement, the statement of owner's equity, the balance sheet, and the statement of cash flows. The nature of the entity's data presented in each statement is as follows:

Exhibit 3

Effects of Transactions on Owner's Equity

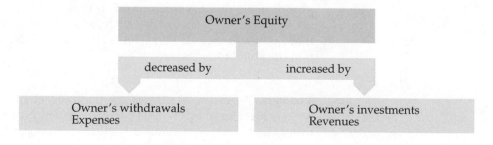

- **Income statement**—A summary of the revenue and expenses *for a specific period of time*, such as a month or a year. It indicates how well the entity has performed (as measured by net income or net loss) during the period.
- **Statement of owner's equity**—A summary of the changes in the owner's equity that have occurred *during a specific period of time*, such as a month or a year.
- **Balance sheet**—A list of the assets, liabilities, and owner's equity *as of a specific date*, usually at the close of the last day of a month or a year. It indicates the status of the entity's financial position at the end of the period.
- **Statement of cash flows**—A summary of the cash receipts and cash payments *for a specific period of time*, such as a month or a year.

Exhibit 4 illustrates the basic features of the four statements and their interrelationships. The data for the statements were taken from the summary of transactions of Computer King.

All financial statements should be identified by the name of the business, the title of the statement, and the *date* or *period of time.* The data presented in the income statement, the statement of owner's equity, and the statement of cash flows are for a period of time. The data presented in the balance sheet are for a specific date.

You should note the use of indentations, captions, dollar signs, and rulings in the financial statements. They aid the reader by emphasizing the sections of the statements. As well, the dollar signs indicate that the amounts represent currency in dollars (as distinct from the pound, yen, or mark).

INCOME STATEMENT

The excess of the revenue over the expenses incurred in earning the revenue is called **net income** or **net profit.** If the expenses of the business exceed the revenue, the excess is a **net loss.** It is impractical to determine the exact amount of expense for each revenue transaction. Therefore, the net income or the net loss is reported for a period of time, such as a month or a year, rather than for each revenue transaction.

We measure net income (or net loss) using a **matching** process involving two steps. First, we determine how much revenue has been earned during the period. We record revenue for providing a service when we earn the revenue, which is usually at the time the service is rendered to the customer. Second, we match against the revenue the expenses that were incurred in order to earn that revenue. Net income (or net loss) is the difference between the revenue earned in a period and the matched expenses that we record in the same period.

The effects of revenue earned and expenses incurred during the month for Computer King were shown in the equation as increases and decreases in owner's equity (capital). Net income for a period has the effect of increasing owner's equity (capital) for the period, whereas a net loss has the effect of decreasing owner's equity (capital) for the period.

The income statement in Exhibit 4 reports the revenue, expenses, and net income of $3,375 for Computer King. The order in which the expenses are listed in the income statement varies among businesses. One method is to list them in order of size, beginning with the larger items. Miscellaneous expense is usually shown as the last item, regardless of the amount.

STATEMENT OF OWNER'S EQUITY

We report the changes in the owner's equity of a sole proprietorship for a period in the statement of owner's equity. This statement links the balance sheet and the income statement.

Three types of transactions affected owner's equity for Computer King during November: (1) the original investment of $15,000, (2) the revenue and expenses that resulted in net income of $3,050 for the month, and (3) a withdrawal of $2,000 by the owner. Exhibit 4 summarizes this information for Computer King.

Exhibit 4
Financial Statements

Computer King
Income Statement
For the Month Ended November 30, 1999

Revenue earned		$7 5 0 0 00
Operating expenses:		
Wages expense	$1 8 0 0 00	
Rent expense	8 0 0 00	
Supplies expense	8 0 0 00	
Utilities expense	4 5 0 00	
Miscellaneous expense	2 7 5 00	
Total operating expenses		4 1 2 5 00
Net income		$3 3 7 5 00

Computer King
Statement of Owner's Equity
For the Month Ended November 30, 1999

Pat King, capital, November 1, 1999		$ 0
Investment on November 1, 1999	$15 0 0 0 00	
Net income for November	3 3 7 5 00	
	$18 3 7 5 00	
Less withdrawals	2 0 0 0 00	
Increase in owner's equity		16 3 7 5 00
Pat King, capital, November 30, 1999		$16 3 7 5 00

Computer King
Balance Sheet
November 30, 1999

Assets		Liabilities	
Cash	$ 6 2 2 5 00	Accounts payable	$ 4 0 0 00
Supplies	5 5 0 00	**Owner's Equity**	
Land	10 0 0 0 00	Pat King, capital	16 3 7 5 00
		Total liabilities and	
Total assets	$16 7 7 5 00	owner's equity	$16 7 7 5 00

Computer King
Statement of Cash Flows
For the Month Ended November 30, 1999

Cash flows from operating activities:		
Cash received from customers	$ 7 5 0 0 00	
Deduct cash payments for expenses and		
payments to creditors	4 2 7 5 00	
Net cash flow from operating activities		$ 3 2 2 5 00
Cash flows from investing activities:		
Cash payments for acquisition of land		(10 0 0 0 00)
Cash flows from financing activities:		
Cash received as owner's investment	$15 0 0 0 00	
Deduct cash withdrawal by owner	2 0 0 0 00	
Net cash flow from financing activities		13 0 0 0 00
Net cash flow and Nov. 30, 1999 cash balance		$ 6 2 2 5 00

USING ACCOUNTING TO UNDERSTAND BUSINESS

Financial statements such as those illustrated in Exhibit 4 are used to evaluate the current financial position of a business and to predict its future operating results and cash flows. For example, bank loan officers use an entity's financial statements in deciding whether to grant a loan to the entity. Once the loan is granted, the borrower may be required to maintain a level of assets in excess of liabilities. The bank will use the entity's financial statements to monitor this condition.

BALANCE SHEET

The amounts of Computer King's assets, liabilities, and owner's equity at the end of November are taken from the last line of the summary of transactions presented earlier. With the addition of a heading, we can prepare the balance sheet as shown in Exhibit 4. This form of balance sheet, called the account form, resembles the basic format of the accounting equation, with assets on the left side and the liabilities and owner's equity sections on the right side. An alternative form of balance sheet, called the report form, presents the liabilities and owner's equity sections below the assets section. We illustrate this form of balance sheet in a later chapter.

The assets section of the balance sheet normally presents assets in the order that they will be converted into cash or used in operations. We list cash first, followed by receivables, supplies, prepaid insurance, and other assets. Then we report the assets of a more permanent nature such as land, buildings, and equipment.

In the liabilities section of the balance sheet in Exhibit 4, accounts payable is the only liability. When there are two or more categories of liabilities, we list and show the total amount of liabilities as illustrated below:

	Liabilities	
Accounts payable	$12,900	
Wages payable	2,570	
Total liabilities		$15,470

STATEMENT OF CASH FLOWS

The statement of cash flows in Exhibit 4 consists of three sections: (1) operating activities, (2) investing activities, and (3) financing activities, as briefly described below:

CASH FLOWS FROM OPERATING ACTIVITIES. This section reports a summary of cash receipts and cash payments from operations. The net cash flow from operating activities will normally differ from the amount of net income for the period. This difference occurs because revenues and expenses may not be recorded at the same time that cash is received from customers and cash is paid to creditors.

CASH FLOWS FROM INVESTING ACTIVITIES. This section reports the cash transactions relating to the acquisition and sale of relatively long-term or permanent-type assets.

CASH FLOWS FROM FINANCING ACTIVITIES. This section reports the cash transactions related to long-term borrowings, cash investments by the owner, and cash withdrawals by the owner.

Preparing the statement of cash flows requires an understanding of concepts that we have not discussed in this chapter. Therefore, we will illustrate the preparation of the statement of cash flows in a later chapter.

KEY POINTS

Objective 1. Define accounting as an information system.
The goal of accounting is to record, report, and interpret economic data for use by decision makers. Accounting is often called the language of business. Accounting can be viewed as an information system that provides essential information about the economic activities of an entity to various individuals or groups.

Accounting provides the framework for gathering economic data and reporting these data to various users. Examples of users of accounting information include investors, bankers, creditors, government agencies, employees, and managers of the entity.

Objective 2. Describe the profession of accounting and list its specialized fields.
Accountants are engaged in either (1) private accounting or (2) public accounting. Accountants in both private and public accounting must adhere to codes of professional ethics.

Specialized fields in accounting have evolved as a result of technological advances and economic growth. The most common accounting fields are financial accounting and managerial accounting. The three main professional accounting organizations in Canada are the Canadian Institute of Chartered Accountants (CICA), the Society of Management Accountants of Canada (SMAC), and the Certified General Accountants Association of Canada (CGAAC).

Objective 3. Summarize the development of accounting principles and relate them to practice.
Generally accepted accounting principles (GAAP) have evolved to form a basis for accounting practice. The CICA issues authoritative pronouncements on accounting principles in Canada and the Financial Accounting Standards Board (FASB) issues standards in the United States. GAAP includes both rules for handling specific transactions and broad principles underlying financial statements.

Objective 4. Summarize the three different forms of business organization.
A business with only one owner is a sole proprietorship. A partnership has two or more owners, but is not a legal entity separate from its owners. A corporation is a legal entity separate from its owners who hold shares in the company.

Objective 5. List the characteristics of a business transaction.
A business transaction is an economic event or a condition that must be recorded by an entity. Some business trans-

actions cause future events or conditions that must also be recorded as transactions.

Objective 6. State the accounting equation and define each element of the equation.
The properties owned by a business and the rights or claims to properties may be stated in the form of an equation, as follows:

Assets = Liabilities + Owner's Equity.

Objective 7. Explain the concepts of relevance and reliability, the entity and going concern concepts, the historical cost principle, and the monetary unit assumption.
Relevant information is timely and capable of influencing the user's decision through its predictive or feedback value. Reliable information represents what it is supposed to represent and is free from bias and verifiable. The entity concept requires us to identify the individual economic unit about which we are collecting data and to separate the accounts of the business from those of its owners. The going concern concept assumes the entity will continue to operate indefinitely. The historical cost principle reports assets at the cost incurred to acquire them. The monetary unit assumption presumes that accountants should record transactions in terms of money (dollars).

Objective 8. Explain how business transactions can be stated in terms of the resulting changes in the three basic elements of the accounting equation.
All transactions can be stated in terms of the change in one or more of the three elements of the accounting equation. That is, the effect of every transaction can be stated in terms of increases or decreases in one or more of these elements, while maintaining the equality between the two sides of the equation.

Objective 9. Describe the financial statements of a sole proprietorship and explain how they interrelate.
The principal financial statements of a sole proprietorship are the income statement, the statement of owner's equity, the balance sheet, and the statement of cash flows. The income statement reports a net income or net loss for the period, which also appears on the statement of owner's equity. The ending owner's capital reported on the statement of owner's equity is also reported on the balance sheet. The ending cash balance is reported on the balance sheet and the statement of cash flows.

GLOSSARY OF KEY TERMS

Account form. The form of balance sheet with the assets section presented on the left-hand side and the liabilities and owner's equity sections presented on the right-hand side. *Objective 9*

Account payable. A liability created by a purchase made on credit. *Objective 8*

Account receivable. A claim against a customer for services rendered or goods sold on credit. *Objective 8*

Accounting. The process of identifying, measuring, and communicating economic information to permit informed judgments and decisions by users of the information. *Objective 1*

Accounting equation. The expression of the relationship between assets, liabilities, and owner's equity; it is most commonly stated as Assets = Liabilities + Owner's Equity. *Objective 6*

Assets. Economic resources owned or controlled by an entity. *Objective 6*

Balance sheet. A financial statement listing the assets, liabilities, and owner's equity of a business entity as of a specific date. *Objective 9*

Business transaction. The occurrence of an economic event or a condition that must be recorded in the accounting records. *Objective 5*

Canadian Institute of Chartered Accountants (CICA). The professional self-regulating accounting body whose *CICA Handbook Recommendations* have legal status as authoritative pronouncements regarding generally accepted accounting principles in Canada. *Objectives 2, 3*

Corporation. A separate legal entity that is organized in accordance with provincial or federal statutes and in which ownership is divided into shares of stock. *Objective 4*

Entity concept. The concept that accounting applies to individual economic units and that each unit is separate from the persons who supply its assets. *Objective 7*

Expense. The amount of assets or services used in the process of earning revenue. *Objective 8*

Financial Accounting Standards Board (FASB). An authoritative body for the development of accounting principles in the United States. *Objective 3*

Generally accepted accounting principles (GAAP). Generally accepted guidelines for the preparation of financial statements. *Objectives 2, 3*

Going concern concept. The principle that assumes the entity will not go out of business in the foreseeable future. *Objective 7*

Historical cost principle. The principle that assets should be recorded at the actual cost incurred to acquire them. *Objective 7*

Income statement. A summary of the revenues and expenses of a business entity for a specific period of time. *Objective 9*

Liabilities. Obligations due by an entity. *Objective 6*

Matching. The concept that expenses incurred in generating revenue should be matched against the revenue in determining the net income or net loss for the period. *Objective 9*

Monetary unit assumption. The principle that states that accounting transactions should be measured and recorded in terms of money (dollars). *Objective 7*

Net income. The final figure in the income statement when revenues exceed expenses. *Objective 9*

Net loss. The final figure in the income statement when expenses exceed revenues. *Objective 9*

Owner's equity. The rights of the owner to the residual assets in a business left over after creditors have been paid. *Objective 6*

Partnership. An unincorporated business owned by two or more individuals. *Objective 4*

Prepaid expenses. Purchased commodities or services that have not been used up at the end of an accounting period. *Objective 8*

Private accounting. The profession whose members are accountants employed by a business firm or not-for-profit organization. *Objective 2*

Public accounting. The profession whose members render accounting services on a fee basis. *Objective 2*

Relevancy concept. Accounting information is relevant if it is timely and can influence the decisions of those who use it. *Objective 7*

Reliability concept. Accounting information is reliable (objective) if it represents what it is supposed to represent, is free from bias, and is verifiable. *Objective 7*

Report form. The form of balance sheet with the liabilities and owner's equity sections presented below the assets section. *Objective 9*

Revenue. The gross increase in owner's equity as a result of business and professional activities that earn income. *Objective 8*

Sole proprietorship. An unincorporated business owned by one individual. *Objective 4*

Statement of cash flows. A summary of the major cash receipts and cash payments for a period. *Objective 9*

Statement of owner's equity. A summary of the changes in the owner's equity of a business that have occurred during a specific period of time. *Objective 9*

ILLUSTRATIVE PROBLEM

On July 1 of the current year, the assets and liabilities of the law practice of Cecil Jameson were as follows: cash, $1,000; accounts receivable, $3,200; supplies, $850; land, $10,000; accounts payable, $1,530. Cecil Jameson, Lawyer, is a sole proprietorship owned and operated by Cecil Jameson. Currently, office space and office equipment are being rented, pending the construction of an office complex on land purchased last year. Business transactions during July are summarized as follows:

a. Received cash from clients for services, $3,928.
b. Paid creditors on account, $1,055.
c. Received cash from Cecil Jameson as an additional investment, $3,700.
d. Paid office rent for the month, $1,200.
e. Charged clients for legal services on account, $2,025.
f. Purchased office supplies on account, $245.
g. Received cash from clients on account, $3,000.
h. Received invoice for paralegal services for July (to be paid on August 10), $1,635.
i. Paid the following: wages expense, $850; answering service expense, $250; utilities expense, $325; and miscellaneous expense, $75.
j. Determined that the cost of office supplies on hand was $980; therefore, the cost of supplies used during the month was $115.
k. Jameson withdrew $1,000 in cash from the business for personal use.

Instructions

1. Determine the amount of owner's equity (Cecil Jameson's capital) as of July 1 of the current year.
2. State the assets, liabilities, and owner's equity as of July 1 in equation form similar to that shown in this chapter. In tabular form below the equation, indicate the increases and decreases resulting from each transaction and the new balances after each transaction. Explain the nature of each increase and decrease in owner's equity by an appropriate notation to the right of the amount.
3. Prepare an income statement for July, a statement of owner's equity for July, a balance sheet as of July 31, and a statement of cash flows for July.

Solution

1. **Assets – Liabilities = Owner's Equity (Cecil Jameson, capital)**
   $15,050 – $1,530 = Owner's Equity (Cecil Jameson, capital)
   $13,520 = Owner's Equity (Cecil Jameson, capital)

2.

	Assets				=	Liabilities	+	Owner's Equity	
	Cash	+ Accounts Receivable	+ Supplies	+ Land	=	Accounts Payable	+	Cecil Jameson, Capital	
Bal.	1,000	3,200	850	10,000		1,530		13,520	
a.	+3,928							+ 3,928	Fees earned
Bal.	4,928	3,200	850	10,000		1,530		17,448	
b.	−1,055					−1,055			
Bal.	3,873	3,200	850	10,000		475		17,448	
c.	+3,700							+ 3,700	Investment
Bal.	7,573	3,200	850	10,000		475		21,148	
d.	−1,200							− 1,200	Rent expense
Bal.	6,373	3,200	850	10,000		475		19,948	
e.		+2,025						+ 2,025	Fees earned
Bal.	6,373	5,225	850	10,000		475		21,973	
f.			+ 245			+ 245			
Bal.	6,373	5,225	1,095	10,000		720		21,973	
g.	+3,000	−3,000							
Bal.	9,373	2,225	1,095	10,000		720		21,973	
h.						+1,635		− 1,635	Paralegal exp.
Bal.	9,373	2,225	1,095	10,000		2,355		20,338	
i.	−1,500							− 850	Wages exp.
								− 250	Answ. svc. exp.
								− 325	Utilities exp.
								− 75	Misc. exp.
Bal.	7,873	2,225	1,095	10,000		2,355		18,838	
j.			− 115					− 115	Supplies exp.
Bal.	7,873	2,225	980	10,000		2,355		18,723	
k.	−1,000							− 1,000	Withdrawal
	6,873	2,225	980	10,000		2,355		17,723	

3.

Cecil Jameson, Lawyer
Income Statement
For the Month Ended July 31, 20—

Fees earned		$5,953.00
Operating expenses:		
Paralegal expense	$1,635.00	
Rent expense	1,200.00	
Wages expense	850.00	
Utilities expense	325.00	
Answering service expense	250.00	
Supplies expense	115.00	
Miscellaneous expense	75.00	
Total operating expenses		4,450.00
Net income		$1,503.00

Cecil Jameson, Lawyer
Statement of Owner's Equity
For the Month Ended July 31, 20—

Cecil Jameson, capital, July 1, 20—		$13,520.00
Additional investment by owner	$3,700.00	
Net income for the month	1,503.00	
	$5,203.00	
Less withdrawals	1,000.00	
Increase in owner's equity		4,203.00
Cecil Jameson, capital, July 31, 20—		$17,723.00

Cecil Jameson, Lawyer
Balance Sheet
July 31, 20—

Assets		Liabilities	
Cash	$ 6,873.00	Accounts payable	$ 2,355.00
Accounts receivable	2,225.00	**Owner's Equity**	
Supplies	980.00	Cecil Jameson, capital	17,723.00
Land	10,000.00	Total liabilities and	
Total assets	$20,078.00	owner's equity	$20,078.00

Cecil Jameson, Lawyer
Statement of Cash Flows
For the Month Ended July 31, 20—

Cash flows from operating activities:		
Cash received from customers and on account	$6,928.00	
Deduct cash payments for expenses and payments to creditors	3,755.00	
Net cash flow from operating activities		$3,173.00
Cash flows from financing activities:		
Cash received as owner's investment	$3,700.00	
Deduct cash withdrawal by owner	1,000.00	
Net cash flow from financing activities		2,700.00
Net cash inflow for the month of July		$5,873.00
Add cash balance July 1		1,000.00
Cash balance July 31		$6,873.00

SELF-EXAMINATION QUESTIONS (ANSWERS AT END OF CHAPTER)

1. A profit-making business that is a separate legal entity and in which ownership is divided into shares of stock is known as a:
   A. sole proprietorship
   B. single proprietorship
   C. partnership
   D. corporation

2. The properties owned by a business are called:
   A. assets
   B. liabilities
   C. the accounting equation
   D. owner's equity

3. A list of assets, liabilities, and owner's equity of a business entity as of a specific date is:
   A. a balance sheet
   B. an income statement
   C. a statement of owner's equity
   D. a statement of cash flows

4. If total assets increased $20,000 during a period of time and total liabilities increased $12,000 during the same period, the amount and direction (increase or decrease) of the period's change in owner's equity is:
   A. $32,000 increase
   B. $32,000 decrease
   C. $8,000 increase
   D. $8,000 decrease

5. If revenue was $45,000, expenses were $37,500, and the owner's withdrawals were $10,000, the amount of net income or net loss would be:
   A. $45,000 net income
   B. $7,500 net income
   C. $37,500 net loss
   D. $2,500 net loss

DISCUSSION QUESTIONS

1. Name some of the categories of individuals and institutions who use accounting information.
2. Distinguish between private accounting and public accounting.
3. Describe in general terms the requirements that an individual must meet for (a) the CMA and (b) the CA designation.
4. What are ethics?
5. Name the two most common specialized fields in accounting.
6. Identify each of the following abbreviations:
   a. CGA
   b. CMA
   c. CA
   d. GAAP
7. Identify what the abbreviation CICA stands for and describe how the CICA sets generally accepted accounting principles.
8. a. Name the three principal forms of profit-making business organizations.
   b. Which of these forms is identified with the greatest number of businesses?
   c. Which of these forms is the dominant form in terms of dollars of business activity?
9. Explain the difference between the terms "legal entity" and "accounting entity."
10. Define each of the following generally accepted accounting principles:
    a. historical cost principle
    b. going concern concept
    c. relevancy concept
    d. reliability concept
    e. monetary unit assumption
11. On February 8, Allen Delivery Service extended an offer of $90,000 for land that had been priced for sale at $100,000. On February 20, Allen Delivery Service accepted the seller's counteroffer of $95,000. Describe how Allen Delivery Service should record the land.
12. a. Land with an assessed value of $60,000 for property tax purposes is acquired by a business for $75,000. Ten years later, the plot of land has an assessed value of $110,000 and the business receives an offer of $150,000 for it. Should the monetary amount assigned to the land in the business records now be increased?
    b. Assuming that the land acquired in (a) was sold for $175,000, how would the various elements of the accounting equation be affected?
13. What are the two principal rights to the properties of a business?
14. Name the three elements of the accounting equation.
15. Describe the difference between an account receivable and an account payable.
16. A business had revenues of $112,000 and operating expenses of $120,000. Did the business (a) incur a net loss or (b) realize a net income?

17. A business had revenues of $202,500 and operating expenses of $170,000. Did the business (a) incur a net loss or (b) realize a net income?
18. Name the two types of transactions that increase the owner's equity of a sole proprietorship.
19. List a sole proprietorship's four major financial statements illustrated in this chapter, and briefly describe the nature of the information provided by each.
20. Indicate whether the data in each of the following financial statements (a) cover a period of time or (b) are for a specific date:
    1. balance sheet
    2. income statement
    3. statement of owner's equity
    4. statement of cash flows
21. What particular item of financial or operating data appears on (a) both the income statement and the statement of owner's equity and (b) both the balance sheet and the statement of owner's equity?
22. Name the three types of activities reported in the statement of cash flows.

EXERCISES

EXERCISE 1–1
Professional ethics
Objective 2

Ethics

A fertilizer manufacturing company wants to relocate to Collier County. A 13-year-old report from a fired researcher at the company says the company's product is releasing toxic by-products. The company has suppressed that report. A second report commissioned by the company shows there is no problem with the fertilizer.

⬛━━▶ Should the company's chief executive officer reveal the context of the unfavourable report in discussions with Collier County representatives? Discuss.

Source: "Business Leaders Ponder Ethical Questions," *Naples Daily News*, May 12, 1991, p. 1E.

EXERCISE 1–2
Accounting equation
Objective 6

Determine the missing amount for each of the following:

	Assets	=	Liabilities	+	Owner's Equity
a.	X	=	$10,500	+	$31,500
b.	$62,750	=	X	+	20,000
c.	57,000	=	18,000	+	X

EXERCISE 1–3
Accounting equation
Objectives 6, 9

Diana Morley is the sole owner and operator of Dyn-A-Mo, a motivational consulting business. As of the end of its accounting period, December 31, 1999, Dyn-A-Mo has assets of $125,000 and liabilities of $85,000. Using the accounting equation and considering each case independently, determine the following amounts:

a. Diana Morley, capital, as of December 31, 1999.
b. Diana Morley, capital, as of December 31, 2000, assuming that during 2000, assets increased by $34,000 and liabilities increased by $21,000.
c. Diana Morley, capital, as of December 31, 2000, assuming that during 2000, assets decreased by $5,000 and liabilities increased by $6,000.
d. Diana Morley, capital, as of December 31, 2000, assuming that during 2000, assets increased by $45,000 and liabilities decreased by $15,000.
e. Net income (or net loss) during 2000, assuming that as of December 31, 2000, assets were $180,000, liabilities were $105,000, and there were no additional investments or withdrawals.

EXERCISE 1–4
Accounting concepts
Objective 7

In many instances one accounting principle can be used to justify another accounting principle. Explain how each of the following accounting concepts can be used to justify the historical cost principle:

a. reliability concept
b. going concern assumption
c. monetary unit assumption

EXERCISE 1–5
Accounting concepts
Objective 7

Bag-One Sports Co. sells hunting and fishing equipment and provides guided hunting and fishing trips. Bag-One Sports Co. is owned and operated by Marc Trailer, a well-known sports enthusiast and hunter. Marc's wife, Robin, owns and operates Red Bird Boutique, a women's clothing store. Marc and Robin have established a trust fund to finance their children's college education. The trust fund is maintained by Royal Trust in the name of the children, Sparrow and Trout.

For each of the following transactions, identify which of the entities listed should record the transaction in its records.

Entities

B Bag-One Sports Co.
T Royal Trust
R Red Bird Boutique
X None of the above

1. Marc received a cash advance from customers for a guided hunting trip.
2. Robin deposited a $5,000 personal cheque in the trust fund at Royal Trust.
3. Robin purchased three dozen spring dresses from a Montreal designer for a special spring sale.
4. Marc paid a local doctor for a physical, which was required by the insurance policy carried by Bag-One Sports Co.
5. Marc paid for an advertisement in a hunters' magazine.
6. Robin purchased mutual fund shares as an investment for the children's trust.
7. Marc paid for dinner and a movie to celebrate their tenth wedding anniversary.
8. Robin donated several dresses from inventory for a local charity auction for the benefit of a women's abuse shelter.
9. Marc paid a breeder's fee for an English springer spaniel to be used as a hunting guide dog.
10. Marc paid his dues to the Rotary Club.

EXERCISE 1–6
Asset, liability, owner's equity items
Objective 8

Indicate whether each of the following is identified with (1) an asset, (2) a liability, or (3) owner's equity:

a. revenue earned
b. supplies
c. wages expense
d. land
e. accounts payable
f. cash

EXERCISE 1–7
Effect of transactions on accounting equation
Objective 8

Describe how the following business transactions affect the three elements of the accounting equation.

a. Invested cash in business.
b. Received cash for services performed.
c. Purchased supplies for cash.
d. Paid for utilities used in the business.
e. Purchased supplies on account.

EXERCISE 1–8
Effect of transactions on accounting equation
Objective 8

a. A vacant lot acquired for $50,000, on which there is a balance owed of $35,000, is sold for $65,000 in cash. What is the effect of the sale on the total amount of the seller's (1) assets, (2) liabilities, and (3) owner's equity?
b. After receiving the $65,000 cash in (a), the seller pays the $35,000 owed. What is the effect of the payment on the total amount of the seller's (1) assets, (2) liabilities, and (3) owner's equity?

EXERCISE 1–9
Effect of transactions on owner's equity
Objective 8

Indicate whether each of the following types of transactions will (a) increase owner's equity or (b) decrease owner's equity:

1. owner's investments
2. revenues
3. expenses
4. owner's withdrawals

EXERCISE 1–10
Transactions
Objective 8

The following selected transactions were completed by Pronto Delivery Service during July:

e 1. Paid advertising expense, $625.
c 2. Received cash from owner as additional investment, $25,000.
D 3. Paid creditors on account, $250.
✗ *A* 4. Received cash from cash customers, $6,250.
c 5. Billed customers for delivery services on account, $2,900.
E 6. Paid rent for July, $2,500.
A 7. Purchased supplies for cash, $750.
✗ 8. Received cash from customers on account, $900.
é 9. Determined that the cost of supplies on hand was $180; therefore, $570 of supplies had been used during the month.
E 10. Paid cash to owner for personal use, $1,000.

Indicate the effect of each transaction on the accounting equation by listing the numbers identifying the transactions, (1) through (10), in a vertical column, and inserting to the right of each number the appropriate letter from the following list:

a. Increase in an asset, decrease in another asset.
b. Increase in an asset, increase in a liability.
c. Increase in an asset, increase in owner's equity.
d. Decrease in an asset, decrease in a liability.
e. Decrease in an asset, decrease in owner's equity.

EXERCISE 1–11
Nature of transactions
Objective 8

Kim Wong operates her own catering service. Summary financial data for March are presented in equation form as follows. Each line designated by a number indicates the effect of a transaction on the equation. Each increase and decrease in owner's equity, except transaction (5), affects net income.

	Cash	+ Supplies +	Land	= Liabilities +	Owner's Equity
Bal.	5,500	750	19,000	3,750	21,500
1.	+9,000				+ 9,000
2.	−4,000		+ 4,000		
3.	−3,250				− 3,250
4.		+600		+ 600	
5.	−1,950				− 1,950
6.	−2,300			−2,300	
7.		−800			− 800
Bal.	3,000	550	23,000	2,050	24,500

a. Describe each transaction.
b. What is the amount of net decrease in cash during the month?
c. What is the amount of net increase in owner's equity during the month?
✗ d. What is the amount of the net income for the month?
✗ e. How much of the net income for the month was retained in the business?

EXERCISE 1–12
Net income and owner's withdrawals
Objective 9

The income statement of a sole proprietorship for the month of February indicates a net income of $15,000. During the same period, the owner withdrew $25,000 in cash from the business for personal use.
➤ Would it be correct to say that the business incurred a net loss of $10,000 during the month? Discuss.

EXERCISE 1–13
Net income and owner's equity for four businesses
Objective 9

Four different sole proprietorships, A, B, C, and D, show the same balance sheet data at the beginning and end of a year. These data, exclusive of the amount of owner's equity, are summarized as follows:

	Total Assets	Total Liabilities
Beginning of the year	$425,000	$180,000
End of the year	570,000	225,000

On the basis of the above data and the following additional information for the year, determine the net income (or loss) of each company for the year. (Suggestion: First determine the amount of increase or decrease in owner's equity during the year.)

Company A: The owner had made no additional investments in the business and had made no withdrawals from the business.

Company B: The owner had made no additional investments in the business but had withdrawn $30,000.

Company C: The owner had made an additional investment of $110,000 but had made no withdrawals.

Company D: The owner had made an additional investment of $110,000 and had withdrawn $30,000.

EXERCISE 1–14
Balance sheet items
Objective 9

From the following list of selected items taken from the records of Magic Appliance Service as of a specific date, identify those that would appear on the balance sheet:

1. Utilities Expense
2. Fees Earned
3. Supplies
4. Wages Expense
5. Accounts Payable
6. Cash
7. Supplies Expense
8. Land
9. Susan Copperfield, Capital
10. Wages Payable

EXERCISE 1–15
Income statement items
Objective 9

Based on the data presented in Exercise 1–14, identify those items that would appear on the income statement.

EXERCISE 1–16
Statement of owner's equity
Objective 9

Financial information related to Kelvinator Company, a sole proprietorship, for the month ended June 30, 2000, is as follows:

Net income for June	$11,750
Kelvin Baer's withdrawals during June	8,000
Kelvin Baer, capital, June 1, 2000	79,950

Prepare a statement of owner's equity for the month ended June 30, 2000.

EXERCISE 1–17
Income statement
Objective 9

Leasing Services was organized on April 1. A summary of the revenue and expense transactions for April are as follows:

Fees earned	$15,400
Wages expense	7,700
Miscellaneous expense	250
Rent expense	2,500
Supplies expense	1,250

Prepare an income statement for the month ended April 30.

EXERCISE 1–18
Missing amounts from balance sheet and income statement data
Objective 9

One item is omitted in each of the following summaries of balance sheet and income statement data for four different sole proprietorships, I, II, III, and IV.

	I	II	III	IV
Beginning of the year:				
Assets	$370,000	$95,000	$90,000	(d)
Liabilities	260,000	45,000	76,000	$32,750
End of the year:				
Assets	355,000	125,000	94,000	99,000
Liabilities	165,000	35,000	87,000	42,000
During the year:				
Additional investment in				
the business	(a)	22,000	5,000	25,000
Withdrawals from the				
business	30,000	8,000	(c)	15,000
Revenue	97,750	(b)	88,100	99,000
Expenses	72,750	52,000	89,600	78,000

Determine the amounts of the missing items, identifying them by letter. (Suggestion: First determine the amount of increase or decrease in owner's equity during the year.)

EXERCISE 1–19
Balance sheets, net income
Objective 9

Financial information related to the sole proprietorship of Kate Interiors for March and April of the current year is as follows:

	March 31, 20—	April 30, 20—
Accounts payable	$ 5,720	$ 6,900
Accounts receivable	9,300	10,400
Kate Lynch, capital	?	?
Cash	10,150	12,050
Supplies	975	550

a. Prepare balance sheets for Kate Interiors as of March 31 and as of April 30 of the current year.
b. Determine the amount of net income for April, assuming that the owner made no additional investments or withdrawals during the month.
c. Determine the amount of net income for April, assuming that the owner made no additional investments but withdrew $2,000 during the month.

EXERCISE 1–20
Financial statements
Objective 9

Each of the following items is shown in the financial statements of **Exxon Corporation**. Identify the financial statement (balance sheet or income statement) in which each item would appear.

a. Operating expenses
b. Crude oil inventory
c. Income taxes payable
d. Sales
e. Investments
f. Marketable securities
g. Exploration expenses
h. Notes and loans payable

i. Cash equivalents
j. Long-term debt
k. Selling expenses
l. Notes receivable
m. Equipment
n. Accounts payable
o. Prepaid taxes

EXERCISE 1–21
Statement of cash flows
Objective 9

Indicate whether each of the following activities would be reported on the statement of cash flows as (a) an operating activity, (b) an investing activity, or (c) a financing activity:

1. Cash received as owner's investment
2. Cash paid for land
3. Cash received from fees earned
4. Cash paid for expenses

EXERCISE 1–22
Financial statements
Objective 9

Pastel Realty, organized March 1, 2000 as a sole proprietorship, is owned and operated by Erin Jones. Identify the errors in the following financial statements for Pastel Realty, prepared after its second month of operations.

Pastel Realty
Income Statement
April 30, 2000

Sales commissions		$16,100.00
Operating expenses:		
Office salaries expense	$3,150.00	
Rent expense	2,800.00	
Automobile expense	750.00	
Miscellaneous expense	550.00	
Supplies expense	225.00	
Total operating expenses		7,475.00
Net income		$ 8,650.00

Erin Jones
Statement of Owner's Equity
April 30, 2000

Erin Jones, capital, April 1, 2000	$ 8,450.00
Less withdrawals during April	2,000.00
	$ 6,450.00
Additional investment during April	2,500.00
	$ 8,950.00
Net income for the month	8,650.00
Erin Jones, capital, April 30, 2000	$17,600.00

Balance Sheet
For the Month Ended April 30, 2000

Assets	
Cash	$ 8,350.00
Accounts payable	1,300.00
Total assets	$ 9,650.00
Liabilities	
Accounts receivable	$ 9,200.00
Supplies	1,325.00
Owner's Equity	
Erin Jones, capital	17,600.00
Total liabilities and owner's equity	$28,125.00

PROBLEMS SERIES A

PROBLEM 1–1A
Transactions
Objective 8

On June 1 of the current year, Maria Mitra established a business to manage rental property. She completed the following transactions during June:

a. Opened a business bank account with a deposit of $28,000.
b. Purchased supplies (stationery, stamps, pencils, etc.) on account, $1,950.
c. Received cash from fees earned, $5,500.
d. Paid rent on office and equipment for the month, $3,000.
e. Paid creditors on account, $975.
f. Billed customers for fees earned, $2,250.
g. Paid automobile expenses (including rental charges) for month, $980, and miscellaneous expenses, $775.
h. Paid office salaries, $1,500.
i. Determined that the cost of supplies on hand was $925; therefore, the cost of supplies used was $1,025.
j. Withdrew cash for personal use, $1,000.

Instructions

1. Indicate the effect of each transaction and the balances after each transaction, using the following tabular headings:

Assets	=	Liabilities	+	Owner's Equity
Cash + Accounts Receivable + Supplies	=	Accounts Payable + Maria Mitra, Capital		

Explain the nature of each increase and decrease in owner's equity by an appropriate notation at the right of the amount.

2. ▬▬▶ Briefly explain why the owner's investment and revenues increased owner's equity, while withdrawals and expenses decreased owner's equity.

PROBLEM 1–2A
Financial statements
Objective 9

Following are the amounts of the assets and liabilities of Tursan Travel Agency, a sole proprietorship, at December 31, 1999, the end of the current year, and its revenue and expenses for the year ended on that date. The items are listed in alphabetical order. The capital of Joel

Tursan, owner, was $14,500 on January 1, 1999, the beginning of the current year. During the current year, Joel withdrew $25,000.

Accounts payable	$ 1,200
Cash	26,490
Miscellaneous expense	1,750
Rent expense	34,000
Revenue earned	114,530
Supplies	865
Supplies expense	2,125
Utilities expense	4,500
Wages expense	35,500

Instructions

1. Prepare an income statement for the current year ended December 31, 1999.
2. Prepare a statement of owner's equity for the current year ended December 31, 1999.
3. Prepare a balance sheet as of December 31, 1999.

PROBLEM 1–3A
Financial statements
Objective 9

Peggy Arnold established Arnold Services on May 1 of the current year. Arnold Services offers financial planning advice to its clients. The effect of each transaction and the balances after each transaction for May are as follows:

	Assets						=	Liabilities	+	Owner's Equity	
			Accounts					Accounts		Peggy Arnold,	
	Cash	+	Receivable	+	Supplies		=	Payable	+	Capital	
a.	+15,000									+15,000	Investment
b.					+725			+725			
Bal.	15,000				725			725		15,000	
c.	− 225							−225			
Bal.	14,775				725			500		15,000	
d.	+ 6,750									+ 6,750	Fees earned
Bal.	21,525				725			500		21,750	
e.	− 2,800									− 2,800	Rent expense
Bal.	18,725				725			500		18,950	
f.	− 1,600									− 1,250	Auto expense
										− 350	Misc. expense
Bal.	17,125				725			500		17,350	
g.	− 1,900									− 1,900	Salaries expense
Bal.	15,225				725			500		15,450	
h.					−450					− 450	Supplies expense
Bal.	15,225				275			500		15,000	
i.			+4,350							+ 4,350	Fees earned
Bal.	15,225		4,350		275			500		19,350	
j.	− 2,000									− 2,000	Withdrawal
Bal.	13,225		4,350		275			500		17,350	

Instructions

1. Prepare an income statement for the month ended May 31.
2. Prepare a statement of owner's equity for the month ended May 31.
3. Prepare a balance sheet as of May 31.

PROBLEM 1–4A
Transactions; financial statements
Objectives 8, 9

On September 1 of the current year, Jill Ivey established a real estate agency as a sole proprietorship under the name Ivey Realty. Ivey completed the following transactions during the month of September:

a. Opened a business bank account with a deposit of $7,500.
b. Purchased supplies (stationery, stamps, pencils, etc.) on account, $900.

c. Paid creditor on account, $500.
d. Earned sales commissions, receiving cash, $15,200.
e. Paid rent on office and equipment for the month, $2,000.
f. Withdrew cash for personal use, $3,000.
g. Paid automobile expenses (including rental charge) for month, $1,900, and miscellaneous expenses, $350.
h. Paid office salaries, $4,150.
i. Determined that the cost of supplies on hand was $350; therefore, the cost of supplies used was $550.

Instructions

1. Indicate the effect of each transaction and the balances after each transaction, using the following tabular headings:

Assets	=	Liabilities	+ Owner's Equity
Cash + Supplies	=	Accounts Payable + Jill Ivey, Capital	

Explain the nature of each increase and decrease in owner's equity by an appropriate notation to the right of the amount.
2. Prepare an income statement for September, a statement of owner's equity for September, and a balance sheet as of September 30.

PROBLEM 1–5A
Transactions; financial statements
Objectives 8, 9

Stansell Dry Cleaners is a sole proprietorship owned and operated by Joan Stansell. Currently, a building and equipment are being rented, pending expansion to new facilities. The actual work of dry cleaning is done by another company at wholesale rates. The assets and the liabilities of the business on July 1 of the current year are as follows: Cash, $8,250; Accounts Receivable, $12,100; Supplies, $1,200; Land, $25,000; Accounts Payable, $6,800. Business transactions during July are summarized as follows:

a. Received cash from cash customers for dry cleaning sales, $9,750.
b. Paid rent for the month, $2,000.
c. Purchased supplies on account, $750.
d. Paid creditors on account, $6,800.
e. Charged customers for dry cleaning sales on account, $5,920.
f. Received monthly invoice for dry cleaning expense for July (to be paid on August 10), $4,700.
g. Paid the following: wages expense, $2,400; truck expense, $1,580; utilities expense, $960; miscellaneous expense, $630.
h. Received cash from customers on account, $8,100.
i. Determined the cost of supplies used during the month was $1,050.

Instructions

1. Determine the amount of Joan Stansell's capital as of July 1 of the current year.
2. State the assets, liabilities, and owner's equity as of July 1 in equation form similar to that shown in this chapter. In tabular form below the equation, indicate increases and decreases resulting from each transaction and the new balances after each transaction. Explain the nature of each increase and decrease in owner's equity by an appropriate notation to the right of the amount.
3. Prepare an income statement for July, a statement of owner's equity for July, and a balance sheet as of July 31.

PROBLEM 1–6A
Financial statements
Objective 9

Kervar Services is an architectural firm operated as a sole proprietorship. Following are the amounts of the assets and liabilities of Kervar Services at December 31, the end of the current year, and its revenue and expenses for the year ended on that date. The capital of Thomas Kervar, owner, was $120,450 at January 1, the beginning of the current year, and the owner withdrew $50,000 during the current year.

Cash	$ 27,200
Accounts receivable	41,000
Supplies	2,750
Land	80,000
Accounts payable	13,100
Wages payable	1,500
Fees earned	129,250
Wages expense	29,700
Rent expense	12,000
Utilities expense	8,100
Supplies expense	4,800
Taxes expense	4,500
Advertising expense	3,000
Miscellaneous expense	1,250

Instructions

1. Prepare an income statement for the current year ended December 31.
2. Prepare a statement of owner's equity for the current year ended December 31.
3. Prepare a balance sheet as of December 31 of the current year.

PROBLEM 1–7A
Accounting concepts
Objective 7

Explain which generally accepted accounting concept(s) have been violated in each of the following situations:

a. Patel Enterprises published its first set of financial statements after it had been in operation for two years. The owner explained that he wanted to give the business time to "get on its feet" before publishing any financial information about the firm.
b. Cory Dykstra, owner of Dykstra Landscaping, signed a lease to rent a building for her business. She uses the first floor for her office and lives in an apartment on the second floor. She pays rent on the building by issuing a cheque on the company's account and recording it as "Office Rent Expense."
c. Ariano Company decided to build its own storage containers in order to save money. Ariano spent $10,000 building the containers. The assets were recorded at $12,000, since this was what it would have cost to purchase them from an outside supplier.

PROBLEMS SERIES B

PROBLEM 1–1B
Transactions
Objective 8

Jane Myers established an insurance agency as a sole proprietorship on March 1 of the current year and completed the following transactions during March:

a. Opened a business bank account with a deposit of $15,000.
b. Purchased supplies on account, $850.
c. Paid creditors on account, $625.
d. Received cash from fees earned, $4,250.
e. Paid rent on office and equipment for the month, $1,500.
f. Paid automobile expenses for the month, $780, and miscellaneous expenses, $250.
g. Paid office salaries, $1,800.
h. Determined that the cost of supplies on hand was $275.
i. Billed insurance companies for sales commissions earned, $3,350.
j. Withdrew cash for personal use, $2,000.

Instructions

1. Indicate the effect of each transaction and the balances after each transaction, using the following tabular headings:

Assets		=	*Liabilities*	+	*Owner's Equity*
Cash + Accounts Receivable + Supplies		=	Accounts Payable + Jane Myers, Capital		

Explain the nature of each increase and decrease in owner's equity by an appropriate notation to the right of the amount.

2. ▬▬► Briefly explain why the owner's investment and revenues increased owner's equity, while withdrawals and expenses decreased owner's equity.

PROBLEM 1–2B
Financial statements
Objective 9

Following are the amounts of the assets and liabilities of VIP Travel Service, a sole proprietorship, at April 30, 2000, the end of the current year, and its revenue and expenses for the year ended on that date. The capital of J. F. Pierce, owner, was $15,000 at May 1, 1999, the beginning of the current year, and the owner withdrew $20,000 during the current year.

Cash	$24,725
Supplies	1,675
Accounts payable	6,100
Fees earned	97,775
Wages expense	34,900
Rent expense	19,900
Utilities expense	9,500
Supplies expense	3,550
Taxes expense	2,800
Miscellaneous expense	1,825

Instructions

1. Prepare an income statement for the current year ended April 30, 2000.
2. Prepare a statement of owner's equity for the current year ended April 30, 2000.
3. Prepare a balance sheet as of April 30, 2000.

PROBLEM 1–3B
Financial statements
Objective 7

Ed Seaquist established Ed's Computer Services on August 1 of the current year. The effect of each transaction and the balances after each transaction for August are as follows:

	Assets				=	Liabilities	+	Owner's Equity	
	Cash	+	Accounts Receivable	+ Supplies	=	Accounts Payable	+	Ed Seaquist, Capital	
a.	+12,500							+12,500	Investment
b.				+550		+550			
Bal.	12,500			550		550		12,500	
c.	+ 5,000							+ 5,000	Fees earned
Bal.	17,500			550		550		17,500	
d.	– 1,500							– 1,500	Rent expense
Bal.	16,000			550		550		16,000	
e.	– 250					–250			
Bal.	15,750			550		300		16,000	
f.			+2,750					+ 2,750	Fees earned
Bal.	15,750		2,750	550		300		18,750	
g.	– 1,155							– 780	Auto expense
								– 375	Misc. expense
Bal.	14,595		2,750	550		300		17,595	
h.	– 2,500							– 2,500	Salaries expense
Bal.	12,095		2,750	550		300		15,095	
i.				–125				– 125	Supplies expense
Bal.	12,095		2,750	425		300		14,970	
j.	– 1,200							– 1,200	Withdrawal
Bal.	10,895		2,750	425		300		13,770	

Instructions

1. Prepare an income statement for the month ended August 31.
2. Prepare a statement of owner's equity for the month ended August 31.
3. Prepare a balance sheet as of August 31.

PROBLEM 1–4B
Transactions; financial statements
Objectives 8, 9

On May 1 of the current year, Lee McLaughlin established a sole proprietorship under the name McLaughlin Consulting Services and completed the following transactions during the month of May:

a. Opened a business bank account with a deposit of $10,000.
b. Purchased supplies (stationery, stamps, pencils, etc.) on account, $825.
c. Paid creditor on account, $500.
d. Earned consulting fees, receiving cash, $13,500.
e. Paid rent on office and equipment for the month, $4,600.
f. Paid a travel agency from the business account $2,000 for a personal vacation.
g. Paid automobile expenses (including rental charge) for the month, $900, and miscellaneous expenses, $550.
h. Paid office salaries, $3,950.
i. Determined that the cost of supplies used during May was $425.

Instructions

1. Indicate the effect of each transaction and the balances after each transaction, using the following tabular headings:

Assets	=	*Liabilities*	+	*Owner's Equity*
Cash + Supplies	=	Accounts Payable + Lee McLaughlin, Capital		

Explain the nature of each increase and decrease in owner's equity by an appropriate notation to the right of the amount.
2. Prepare an income statement for May, a statement of owner's equity for May, and a balance sheet as of May 31.

PROBLEM 1–5B
Transactions; financial statements
Objectives 8, 9

Print and Copy is a sole proprietorship owned and operated by Jill Smith. Currently, a building and equipment are being rented, pending expansion to new facilities. The actual work of large printing jobs is done by another company at wholesale rates. The assets and the liabilities of the business on November 1 of the current year are as follows: Cash, $5,400; Accounts Receivable, $8,750; Supplies, $1,560; Land, $15,000; Accounts Payable, $5,880. Business transactions during November are summarized as follows:

a. Paid rent for the month, $2,450.
b. Charged customers for services on account, $7,150.
c. Paid creditors on account, $1,680.
d. Purchased supplies on account, $840.
e. Received cash from cash customers for services, $4,600.
f. Received cash from customers on account, $4,750.
g. Received monthly invoice for printing expense for November (to be paid on December 10), $3,400.
h. Paid the following: wages expense, $1,800; truck expense, $725; utilities expense, $510; miscellaneous expense, $190.
i. Determined the cost of supplies on hand at the end of November was $1,500.

Instructions

1. Determine the amount of Jill Smith's capital as of November 1 of the current year.
2. State the assets, liabilities, and owner's equity as of November 1 in equation form similar to that shown in this chapter. In tabular form below the equation, indicate increases and decreases resulting from each transaction and the new balances after each transaction. Explain the nature of each increase and decrease in owner's equity by an appropriate notation to the right of the amount.
3. Prepare an income statement for November, a statement of owner's equity for November, and a balance sheet as of November 30.

PROBLEM 1–6B
Financial statements
Objective 9

Following are the amounts of the assets and liabilities of Yamada Consultants at March 31, 2000, the end of the current year, and its revenue and expenses for the year ended on that date. The items are listed in alphabetical order. The capital of Mort Yamada, owner, was $157,890 on April 1, 1999, the beginning of the current year. During the current year, the owner withdrew $60,000.

Accounts payable	$ 78,000
Accounts receivable	69,750
Advertising expense	30,000
Cash	64,515
Fees earned	727,500
Land	150,000
Miscellaneous expense	8,125
Rent expense	155,000
Supplies	6,250
Supplies expense	19,750
Taxes expense	33,500
Utilities expense	65,750
Wages expense	312,000
Wages payable	11,250

Instructions

1. Prepare an income statement for the current year ended March 31, 2000.
2. Prepare a statement of owner's equity for the current year ended March 31, 2000.
3. Prepare a balance sheet as of March 31, 2000.

PROBLEM 1–7B
Accounting concepts
Objective 7

Explain what is wrong with each of the following statements:

a. The entity concept states that each business is a legal entity that must be accounted for separately from its owners.
b. The practice of only accounting for economic events when there has been an exchange transaction is justified by the relevancy concept.
c. To be reliable, accounting information must be timely and free from bias.
d. The going concern assumption is unrealistic, since no business is going to last forever.

CONTINUING PROBLEM

Julian Felipe enjoys listening to all types of music and owns countless CDs, tapes, and records. Over the years, Julian has gained a local reputation for his knowledge of music from classical to rap and the ability to put together sets of recordings that appeal to all ages.

During the last several months, Julian served as a guest disc jockey on a local radio station. In addition, he has entertained at several friends' parties as the host deejay.

On November 1, 1999, Julian established a sole proprietorship known as Music A La Mode. Using his extensive collection of CDs, tapes, and records, Julian will serve as a disc jockey on a fee basis for weddings, parties, and other events. During November, Julian entered into the following transactions:

Nov. 1. Deposited $1,000 in a chequing account in the name of Music A La Mode.
      2. Received $500 from a local radio station to serve as the guest disc jockey for November.
      2. Agreed to share office space with a local real estate agency, Picasso Realty. Music A La Mode will pay ¼ of the rent. In addition, Music A La Mode agreed to pay $110 a month toward the salary of the receptionist and to pay ¼ of the utilities. Paid $250 for the rent of the office.
      3. Purchased supplies (blank cassette tapes, poster board, extension cords, etc.) from Ideal Office Supply Co. for $150. Agreed to pay $100 within 10 days and the remainder by December 3, 1999.
      5. Paid $75 to a local radio station to advertise the services of Music A La Mode twice daily for two weeks.
      8. Paid $300 to a local electronics store for rent on two CD players, two cassette players, and eight speakers.
    12. Paid $100 (music expense) to The Music Store for the use of its current demo CDs and tapes to make cassette tapes of various music sets.

Nov. 13. Paid Ideal Office Supply Co. $100 on account.
   16. Received $40 from a dentist for providing two music sets for the dentist to play for her patients.
   22. Served as disc jockey for a wedding party. The father of the bride agreed to pay $350 the 1st of December.
   25. Received $150 from a friend for serving as the disc jockey for a cancer charity ball hosted by the local hospital.
   29. Paid $120 (music expense) to Crescendo Music for the use of its library of demo CDs, tapes, and records.
   30. Received $300 for serving as disc jockey for a local club's monthly dance.
   30. Paid Picasso Realty $110 for Music A La Mode's share of the receptionist's salary for November.
   30. Paid Picasso Realty $100 for Music A La Mode's share of the utilities for November.
   30. Determined that the cost of supplies on hand is $70. Therefore, the cost of supplies used during the month was $80.
   30. Paid for miscellaneous expenses, $65.
   30. Withdrew $75 of cash from Music A La Mode for personal use.

Instructions

1. Indicate the effect of each transaction and the balances after each transaction, using the following tabular headings:

Assets	=	*Liabilities*	+	*Owner's Equity*
Cash + Accounts Receivable + Supplies	=	Accounts Payable + Julian Felipe, Capital		

   Explain the nature of each increase and decrease in owner's equity by an appropriate notation to the right of the amount.
2. Prepare an income statement for Music A La Mode for the month ended November 30, 1999.
3. Prepare a statement of owner's equity for Music A La Mode for the month ended November 30, 1999.
4. Prepare a balance sheet for Music A La Mode as of November 30, 1999.

CASES

CASE 1–1
Kelley Enterprises
Financial statements

Joan Kelley, president of Kelley Enterprises, applied for a $100,000 loan from the Toronto Dominion Bank. The bank requested financial statements from Kelley Enterprises as a basis for granting the loan. Joan Kelley has told her accountant to provide the bank with a balance sheet. Joan Kelley has decided to omit the other financial statements because there was a net loss during the past year.

➤ Discuss whether Joan Kelley is behaving in an ethical manner by omitting some of the financial statements.

CASE 1-2
Towering Enterprises
The internal auditor

Christine Markham is an internal auditor with Towering Enterprises. Recently Christine met with her superior Geoff Barkwell, Vice President of Finance, to discuss the upcoming visit of the external auditors. Geoff tells Christine that she is to keep some key financial information from the external auditors during their examination of the company's records. Christine is uncomfortable with Geoff's request, and discusses her reservations with him. Geoff argues that Christine's loyalties should be to her employer, Towering Enterprises.

➤ Comment on Geoff's point about where Christine's loyalties should lie. Suggest some ideas which could be implemented to increase Christine's independence within Towering Enterprises.

CASE 1–3
Bacall Partners
Net income

On January 3, 1997, Dr. Avery Bacall formed a partnership with two other doctors to establish a 24-hour emergency walk-in clinic. The following conversation occurred the following August between Dr. Bacall and a former medical school classmate, Dr. June Ivy, at a Canadian Medical Association convention in Halifax.

Dr. Ivy: Avery, good to see you again. Why didn't you call when you were in Ottawa? We could have had dinner together.

Dr. Bacall: Actually, I never made it to Ottawa this year. My wife and kids went up to our Muskoka condo twice, but I got stuck in Toronto for the rest of the year. I opened a new emergency clinic with two partners last January and I haven't had any time for myself since.

Dr. Ivy: I heard about it. I've thought about doing something like that. Are you making any money? I mean, is it worth your time?

Dr. Bacall: You wouldn't believe it. We started by opening a bank account of $50,000, and our July bank statement has a balance of $325,000. Not bad for seven months—all pure profit.

Dr. Ivy: Maybe I'll try it in Ottawa. Let's have breakfast together tomorrow and you can fill me in on the details.

Comment on Dr. Bacall's statement that the difference between the opening bank balance ($50,000) and the July statement balance ($325,000) is pure profit.

CASE 1–4
Sears Canada Inc.
Financial analysis

 The relationship between liabilities and owner's (shareholders') equity is often used in analyzing a corporation's ability to withstand adverse business conditions. It is also used to indicate the margin of safety for creditors. The ratio is computed as follows:

$$\text{Ratio of liabilities to shareholders' equity} = \frac{\text{Total liabilities}}{\text{Total shareholders' equity}}$$

The lower the ratio, the better the corporation can withstand poor business conditions and still meet its commitments to creditors. Moreover, the lower the ratio, the greater is the protection to the creditors. For example, a ratio of 1:1 indicates that the liabilities and shareholders' equity are equal and that the protection to the creditors is 100%. If the ratio decreases to 0.5:1, the protection to the creditors is 200%; that is, the corporation may suffer a loss equal to 200% of liabilities before the amount of the assets drops below the amount of the liabilities.

1. Determine the ratio of liabilities to shareholders' equity for Sears Canada Inc. at the end of current and preceding years.
2. What conclusions regarding the margin of protection to the creditors can be drawn from your analysis?

CASE 1–5
Village Tennis Services
Transactions and financial statements

Tega Hearst, a college student, has been seeking ways to earn extra spending money. As an active sports enthusiast, Tega plays tennis regularly at the Village Tennis Club, where her family has a membership. The president of the club recently approached Tega with the proposal that she manage the club's tennis courts on weekends. Tega's primary duty would be to supervise the operation of the club's four indoor and six outdoor courts, including court reservations.

In return for her services, the club would pay Tega $75 per weekend, plus Tega could keep whatever she earned from lessons and the fees from the use of the ball machine. The club and Tega agreed to a one-month trial, after which both would consider an arrangement for the remaining two years of Tega's college career. On this basis, Tega organized Village Tennis Services. During September, Tega managed the tennis courts and entered into the following transactions:

a. Opened a business account by depositing $500.
b. Paid $150 for tennis supplies (practice tennis balls, etc.).
c. Paid $75 for the rental of videotape equipment to be used in offering lessons during September.
d. Arranged for the rental of two ball machines during September for $100. Paid $60 in advance, with the remaining $40 due October 1.
e. Received $850 for lessons given during September.
f. Received $150 in fees from the use of the ball machines during September.
g. Paid $350 for salaries of part-time employees who answered the telephone and took reservations while Tega was giving lessons.
h. Paid $75 for miscellaneous expenses.
i. Received $300 from the club for managing the tennis courts during September.

j. Determined that the cost of supplies on hand at the end of the month totalled $80; therefore, the cost of supplies used was $70.

k. Withdrew $600 for personal use on September 30.

   As a friend and accounting student, you have been asked by Tega to aid her in assessing the venture.

1. Indicate the effect of each transaction and the balances after each transaction, using the following tabular headings:

Assets	=	Liabilities	+	Owner's Equity
Cash + Supplies	=	Accounts Payable +		Tega Hearst, Capital

Explain the nature of each increase and decrease in owner's equity by an appropriate notation to the right of the amount.

2. Prepare an income statement for September.

3. Prepare a statement of owner's equity for September.

4. Prepare a balance sheet as of September 30.

5. a. Assume that Tega Hearst could earn $6 per hour working 20 hours each of the four weekends as a waitress. Evaluate which of the two alternatives, working as a waitress or operating Village Tennis Services, would provide Tega with the most income per month.

   b. ◄█████► Discuss any other factors that you believe Tega should consider before discussing a long-term arrangement with Village Tennis Club.

ANSWERS TO SELF-EXAMINATION QUESTIONS

1. **D** A corporation, organized in accordance with provincial or federal statutes, is a separate legal entity in which ownership is divided into shares of stock (answer D). A sole proprietorship, sometimes called a single proprietorship (answers A and B), is an unincorporated business owned by one individual. A partnership (answer C) is an unincorporated business owned by two or more individuals.

2. **A** The properties owned by a business are called assets (answer A). The debts of the business are called liabilities (answer B), and the equity of the owners is called owner's equity (answer D). The relationship between assets, liabilities, and owner's equity is expressed as the accounting equation (answer C).

3. **A** The balance sheet is a listing of the assets, liabilities, and owner's equity of a business at a specific date (answer A). The income statement (answer B) is a summary of the revenue and expenses of a business for a specific period of time. The statement of owner's equity (answer C) summarizes the changes in owner's equity for a sole proprietorship or partnership during a specific period of time. The statement of cash flows (answer D) summarizes the cash receipts and cash payments for a specific period of time.

4. **C** The accounting equation is:

   Assets = Liabilities + Owner's Equity

   Therefore, if assets increased by $20,000 and liabilities increased by $12,000, owner's equity must have increased by $8,000 (answer C), as indicated in the following computation:

Assets	=	Liabilities + Owner's Equity
$20,000	=	$12,000 + Owner's Equity
$20,000 − $12,000	=	Owner's Equity
$8,000	=	Owner's Equity

5. **B** Net income is the excess of revenue over expenses, or $7,500 (answer B). If expenses exceed revenue, the difference is a net loss. Withdrawals by the owner are the opposite of the owner's investing in the business and do not affect the amount of net income or net loss.

2 Analyzing Transactions

YOU AND ACCOUNTING

Assume that a pizza restaurant has hired you to deliver pizzas and that you will be using your own car. You will be paid $8.00 per hour plus $0.20 per kilometre plus tips. What is the best way for you to determine how many kilometres you have driven each day in delivering pizzas?

One method would be to record the odometer reading before work and then at quitting time. The difference would be the kilometres driven. For example, if the odometer read 56,743 at the start of work and 56,889 at the end of work, you have driven 146 kilometres. However, this method is subject to error if you copy down the wrong reading or make a mathematical error. Is there a better method that would be more efficient and less subject to error? If your car has a trip odometer, you could set the trip odometer to zero when you begin work and simply read it at the end of work for the kilometres driven.

In running a business, managers need to have similar information readily available. Such information is useful for analyzing the effects of transactions on the business and for making decisions. For example, the manager of your neighbourhood dry cleaners needs to know how much cash is available, how much has been spent, and what services have been provided customers.

In Chapter 1 we analyzed and recorded this kind of information by using the accounting equation, Assets = Liabilities + Owner's Equity. Since such a format is not practical for most businesses, we will study more practical methods of recording transactions in Chapter 2. We will conclude this chapter by discussing how accounting errors may occur and how the accounting process can detect them.

After studying this chapter, you should be able to:

Objective 1
Explain why accounts are used to record and summarize the effects of transactions on financial statements.

Objective 2
Explain the characteristics of an account.

Objective 3
List the rules of debit and credit and the normal balances of accounts.

Objective 4
Analyze and summarize the financial statement effects of transactions.

Objective 5
Prepare a trial balance and explain how it can be used to discover errors.

Objective 6
Discover errors in recording transactions and correct them, and define the concept of materiality.

Usefulness of an Account

Objective 1
Explain why accounts are used to record and summarize the effects of transactions on financial statements.

Before making a major cash purchase, such as buying a CD player, you need to know the balance of your bank account. Likewise, managers need timely, useful information in order to make good decisions about their businesses. An accounting system must be designed to provide this information.

How are accounting systems designed to provide information? We illustrated a very simple design in Chapter 1, where we recorded and summarized transactions in the accounting equation format. However, this format is awkward and cumbersome for recording thousands of daily transactions. Thus, accounting systems are designed to show the increases and decreases in each financial statement item in a separate record. This record is called an account. For example, since cash appears on the balance sheet, we keep a separate record of the increases and decreases in cash. Likewise, we keep a separate record of the increases and decreases for supplies, land, accounts payable, and the other balance sheet items. A business maintains similar records for income statement items, such as revenue earned, wages expense, and rent expense.

We call a group of accounts for a business entity a ledger. A list of the accounts in the ledger is called a chart of accounts. The accounts are normally listed in the order in which they appear in the financial statements. The ledger usually lists the balance sheet accounts first, in the order of assets, liabilities, and owner's equity. It then lists the income statement accounts in the order of revenues and expenses. We discuss each of these major account classifications below.

Assets are economic resources owned or controlled by an entity. Assets may be either physical items (tangible) or rights (intangible) that have value. Examples of tangible assets include cash, supplies, buildings, equipment, and land. An example of an intangible asset is patent rights.

Liabilities are debts owed to outsiders (creditors). We often identify liabilities on the balance sheet by titles that include the word *payable*. Examples of liabilities include accounts payable, notes payable, and wages payable. Revenue received in advance, such as magazine subscriptions received by a publisher or tuition received by a university, is also classified as a liability. We call revenue received in advance *unearned* revenue.

Owner's equity is the owner's residual right to the net assets of the business. For a sole proprietorship, the owner's equity on the balance sheet is represented by the balance of the owner's *capital* account. A withdrawals account represents the amount of withdrawals made by the owner of a sole proprietorship.

USING ACCOUNTING TO UNDERSTAND BUSINESS

A review of the chart of accounts can provide a quick overview of a business's operations. For example, some revenue and expense accounts taken from the chart of accounts of a car dealership include the following:

- Revenue Accounts:
  - New Car Sales
  - Used Car Sales
  - Extended Warranty Sales
  - Financing Commissions
  - Parts Sales - Retail
  - Parts Sales - Wholesale
  - Service Sales

- Expense Accounts:
  - Cost of Sales - New Cars
  - Cost of Sales - Used Cars
  - Cost of Parts Supplies
  - Sales Commissions
  - Advertising
  - Vehicle Sales Administration
  - Parts Department Administration
  - Service Department Administration
  - Service Labour

These accounts tell us that the car dealership sells new and used cars, sells vehicle parts, and operates a service department. In addition, the accounts reflect some of the decision-making needs of management. For example, comparing the revenues from the service department with its related expenses assists management in determining whether this part of its operations is profitable. A loss from operating the service department might lead management to attempt to cut its costs in this area or to increase the rates it charges customers for car repairs.

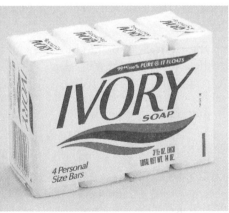

Procter & Gamble's account numbers have over 30 digits to reflect its different operations and regions. This can be typical for very large businesses.

Revenues are increases in owner's equity as a result of rendering services or selling products to customers. Examples of revenues include fees earned, fares earned, commissions revenue, and rent revenue.

Assets used up or services consumed in the process of generating revenues are **expenses.** Examples of typical expenses include wages expense, rent expense, utilities expense, supplies expense, and miscellaneous expense.

Accounts are numbered for use as references. Although accounts may be in numeric order, as are the pages of this book, a flexible system of indexing is desirable. Such a system has the advantage of allowing new accounts to be added in their proper order without affecting other account numbers.

In designing the chart of accounts for a company, you must analyze the company's expected operations and volume of business. In addition, you must also consider the extent to which reports are needed for taxes, managerial decisions, and credit purposes. For example, the type and number of accounts for a small retailer would be different from those needed by a lawyer or a real estate agency. For a large enterprise with many departments or operations, it is common for each account number to have four or more digits. For example, **Procter & Gamble's** account numbers have over 30 digits to reflect different operations and regions.

Exhibit 1 is Computer King's chart of accounts that we will be using in this chapter. We will be introducing additional accounts in later chapters. In Exhibit 1, each account number has two digits. The first digit indicates the major classification of the ledger in which the account is located. Accounts beginning with 1 represent assets; 2, liabilities; 3, owner's equity; 4, revenue; and 5, expenses. The second digit indicates the location of the account within its class.

Exhibit 1

Chart of Accounts for Computer King

Balance Sheet Accounts	Income Statement Accounts
1. Assets	**4. Revenue**
11 Cash	41 Revenue Earned
12 Accounts Receivable	**5. Expenses**
14 Supplies	51 Wages Expense
15 Prepaid Insurance	52 Rent Expense
17 Land	54 Utilities Expense
18 Office Equipment	55 Supplies Expense
2. Liabilities	59 Miscellaneous Expense
21 Accounts Payable	
23 Unearned Rent	
3. Owner's Equity	
31 Pat King, Capital	
32 Pat King, Withdrawals	

Characteristics of an Account

Objective 2

Explain the characteristics of an account.

The simplest form of an account has three parts. First, each account has a title, which is the name of the item recorded in the account. Second, each account has a space for recording increases in the amount of the item. Third, each account has a space for recording decreases in the amount of the item. The account form presented below is called a T account because it is similar to the letter T.

Title	
Left side	Right side
debit	*credit*

We call the left side of the account the debit side, and the right side the credit side.[1] Amounts entered on the left side of an account, regardless of the account title, are called debits to the account. When you enter debits in an account, the account is said to be **debited** (or charged). Amounts entered on the right side of an account are called credits, and the account is said to be **credited.** Sometimes, we abbreviate debits and credits as *Dr.* and *Cr.*

In the cash account shown at the top of the next page, we list transactions involving receipts of cash vertically on the debit side of the account. We list the transactions involving cash payments in similar fashion on the credit side of the account. If at any time we need the total of the cash receipts, we add the entries on the debit side of the account and insert the total ($10,950) below the last debit.[2] Similarly, we insert the total of the cash payments, $6,850 in the example, on the credit side. Subtracting the smaller sum from the larger, $10,950 − $6,850, identifies the amount of cash on hand, $4,100. This amount is the balance of the account. To identify this as a **debit balance,** we insert it in the account, after the total of the debit column. If the business were to prepare a balance sheet at this time, it would report cash of $4,100.

---

[1] The terms *debit* and *credit* are derived from the Latin *debere* and *credere*.

[2] This amount, called a memorandum balance, should be written in small figures or identified in some other way to avoid mistaking the amount for an additional debit.

	Cash		
	3,750	850	
Debit	4,300	1,400	Credit
Side of	2,900	700	Side of
Account	4,100 10,950	2,900	Account
		1,000	
		6,850	

Analyzing and Summarizing Transactions in Accounts

Objective 3
List the rules of debit and credit and the normal balances of accounts.

In this section we use the Computer King transactions from Chapter 1 to illustrate how to analyze and summarize transactions in accounts.

The effects of a transaction on a business and its accounts are initially recorded in a journal in the form of a **journal entry.** We call the journal the book of original entry because this is the first place in which we record a business transaction. A general journal contains a listing of journal entries in chronological order, leaving a line between each entry. The journal entry should indicate the date of the transaction and indicate the amount of the debits and credits made to each account, with a brief explanation immediately following the entry. Within a journal entry we list the title of each account to be debited, followed by the amount to be debited. After recording all of the debits first, we list the title of each account to be credited followed by the amount to be credited. We differentiate the credits from the debits by indenting the credits to the right (corresponding with the practice of recording credits on the right-hand side of a T account). The process of recording a transaction in a journal is called journalizing.

In the following section we first discuss those entries affecting only balance sheet accounts, transactions (a), (b), (c), and (f). We then discuss those transactions affecting income statement accounts, (d), (e), and (g). Lastly, we discuss the withdrawal of cash by the owner, transaction (h).

BALANCE SHEET ACCOUNTS

Balance sheet accounts consist of the assets, liabilities, and owner's equity accounts. Pat King's first transaction (a) was to deposit $15,000 in a bank account on November 1 in the name of Computer King. After the deposit, the balance sheet for the business is as follows:

Computer King
Balance Sheet
November 1, 1999

Assets		Owner's Equity	
Cash	$15,000	Pat King, Capital	$15,000

Every business transaction affects a business's financial statements and at least two accounts. The effect of the above transaction on the balance sheet is to increase cash and owner's equity. The business records this effect in the accounts as a $15,000 debit to Cash and a $15,000 credit to Pat King, Capital.

We initially record transaction (a) in the general journal as shown below.

Entry A.

Nov. 1	Cash	15,000	
	Pat King, Capital		15,000
	Owner invests $15,000 in the business.		

Next, we record the effects of this transaction in the accounts by transferring the amount and the date of the journal entry to Cash and Pat King, Capital, as follows:

Cash		Pat King, Capital	
Nov. 1 15,000		Nov. 1	15,000

We enter the amount of the asset, which is reported on the left side of the balance sheet, on the left (debit) side of Cash. We enter the owner's equity in the business, which is reported on the right side of the balance sheet, on the right (credit) side of Pat King, Capital. When the business acquires other assets, we enter the increases as debits to asset accounts. Likewise, we record other increases in owner's equity as credits to owner's equity accounts.

On November 5 (transaction b), Computer King bought land for $10,000, paying cash. This transaction increases one asset account and decreases another. This represents a $10,000 increase (debit) to Land and a $10,000 decrease (credit) to Cash. The journal entry for this transaction is:

Entry B.

Nov. 5	Land	10,000	
	Cash		10,000
	Buy land for $10,000 cash.		

We enter this entry in the accounts of Computer King as follows:

Cash		Land		Pat King, Capital	
Nov. 1 15,000	Nov. 5 10,000	Nov. 5 10,000			Nov. 1 15,000

On November 10 (transaction c), Computer King purchased supplies on account for $1,350. This transaction increases an asset account and increases a liability account. This represents a $1,350 increase (debit) to Supplies and a $1,350 increase (credit) to Accounts Payable. We show the journal entry for this transaction below. To simplify the illustration, we will show the effect of entry (c) and the remaining journal entries for Computer King later.

Entry C.

Nov. 10	Supplies	1,350	
	Accounts Payable		1,350
	Purchase $1,350 supplies on account.		

On November 30 (transaction f), Computer King paid creditors on account, $950. This transaction decreases a liability account and decreases an asset account. This decreases (debits) Accounts Payable by $950 and decreases (credits) Cash by $950. The journal entry for this transaction is:

Entry F.

Nov. 30	Accounts Payable	950	
	Cash		950
	Paid $950 on accounts payable.		

In the preceding examples, you should observe that we record increases on the left side of asset accounts and decreases on the the right side. However, we record increases on the right side of liability and owner's equity accounts and decreases to these accounts on the left side. The left side of all accounts, whether asset, liability, or owner's equity, is the debit side, and the right side is the credit side. Thus, a debit may be either an increase or a decrease, depending on the account affected. A credit may likewise be either an increase or a decrease, depending on the account. The general rules of debit and credit for balance sheet accounts are therefore as follows:

	Debit		Credit	
Asset accounts	Increase	(+)	Decrease	(−)
Liability accounts	Decrease	(−)	Increase	(+)
Owner's equity (capital) accounts	Decrease	(−)	Increase	(+)

Alternatively, we may state the rules of debit and credit in relationship to the accounting equation, as shown below.

Balance Sheet Accounts

ASSETS Asset Accounts		LIABILITIES Liability Accounts	
Debit for increases	Credit for decreases	Debit for decreases	Credit for increases

		OWNER'S EQUITY Owner's Equity Accounts	
		Debit for decreases	Credit for increases

INCOME STATEMENT ACCOUNTS

The analysis of business transactions affecting the income statement focuses on how each transaction affects owner's equity. Transactions that increase revenue will increase owner's equity. Just as we record increases in owner's equity as credits, we record increases in revenue accounts as credits. Transactions that increase expense will decrease owner's equity. Just as we record decreases in owner's equity as debits, we record increases in expense accounts as debits.

Computer King's transactions (d), (e), and (g) illustrate the analysis of transactions and the rules of debit and credit for revenue and expense accounts. On November 18 (transaction d), Computer King received fees of $7,500 from customers for services. This transaction increases an asset account and increases a revenue account. We increase (debit) Cash by $7,500, and increase (credit) Revenue Earned by $7,500. The journal entry for this transaction is:

Entry D.

Nov. 18	Cash	7,500	
	Revenue Earned		7,500
	Perform services for $7,500 cash.		

Throughout the month, Computer King incurred the following expenses: wages, $1,800; rent, $800; utilities, $450; and miscellaneous, $275. To simplify the illustration, we journalize the payment of these expenses on November 30 (transaction e), as shown below. This transaction increases various expense accounts and decreases an asset account.

Entry E.

Nov. 30	Wages Expense	1,800	
	Rent Expense	800	
	Utilities Expense	450	
	Miscellaneous Expense	275	
	Cash		3,325
	Paid $3,325 cash for various expenses.		

Regardless of the number of accounts, the sum of the debits is always equal to the sum of the credits in a journal entry. This equality of debit and credit for each transaction is inherent in the accounting equation: Assets = Liabilities + Owner's Equity. It is also because of this equality that we call the system double-entry accounting.

On November 30, Computer King recorded the amount of supplies used in the operations during the month (transaction g). This transaction increases an expense account and decreases an asset account. The journal entry for transaction (g) is shown below.

Entry G.

Nov. 30	Supplies Expense	800	
	Supplies		800
	Used $800 in supplies in November.		

The general rules of debit and credit for analyzing transactions affecting income statement accounts are stated below.

	Debit	Credit
Revenue accounts	Decrease (−)	Increase (+)
Expense accounts	Increase (+)	Decrease (−)

Alternatively, we may summarize the rules of debit and credit for income statement accounts in relationship to the owner's equity in the accounting equation:

Income Statement Accounts			
Debit for *decreases in owner's equity*		*Credit for* *increases in owner's equity*	
Expense Accounts		Revenue Accounts	
Debit for increases	Credit for decreases	Debit for decreases	Credit for increases

WITHDRAWALS BY THE OWNER

The owner of a sole proprietorship may withdraw cash from the business for personal use. This practice is common if the owner devotes full time to the business. In this case, the business may be the owner's main source of income. Such withdrawals decrease owner's equity. As decreases in owner's equity are debits, we record increases in withdrawals as debits. We debit withdrawals to an account with the owner's name followed by *Withdrawals, Drawings,* or *Personal.*

In transaction (h), Pat King withdrew $2,000 in cash from Computer King for personal use. This transaction increases the drawings account and decreases the cash account:

Entry H.

Nov. 30	Pat King, Withdrawals	2,000	
	Cash		2,000
	Owner withdrew $2,000 cash.		

ILLUSTRATION OF A GENERAL JOURNAL AND A LEDGER ACCOUNT

Exhibit 2 shows Computer King's general journal after the accountant has recorded transactions (a) through (h) described above for the month of November, 1999.

Exhibit 2
General Journal
Computer King

	Date	Description	Post. Ref.	Debit	Credit	
1	1999 Nov. 1	Cash	11	15 0 0 0 00		1
2		Pat King, Capital	31		15 0 0 0 00	2
3		Owner invests $15,000 in business.				3
4						4
5	5	Land	17	10 0 0 0 00		5
6		Cash	11		10 0 0 0 00	6
7		Buy land for $10,000 cash.				7
8						8
9	10	Supplies	14	1 3 5 0 00		9
10		Accounts Payable	21		1 3 5 0 00	10
11		Purchase $1,350 supplies on account.				11
12						12
13	18	Cash	11	7 5 0 0 00		13
14		Revenue Earned	41		7 5 0 0 00	14
15		Perform services for $7,500 cash.				15
16						16
17	30	Wages Expense	51	1 8 0 0 00		17
18		Rent Expense	52	8 0 0 00		18
19		Utilities Expense	54	4 5 0 00		19
20		Miscellaneous Expense	59	2 7 5 00		20
21		Cash	11		3 3 2 5 00	21
22		Paid $3,325 cash for various expenses.				22
23						23
24	30	Accounts Payable	21	9 5 0 00		24
25		Cash	11		9 5 0 00	25
26		Paid $950 on account payable.				26
27						27
28	30	Supplies Expense	55	8 0 0 00		28
29		Supplies	14		8 0 0 00	29
30		Used $800 of supplies in November.				30
31						31
32	30	Pat King, Withdrawals	32	2 0 0 0 00		32
33		Cash	11		2 0 0 0 00	33
34		Owner withdrew $2,000 cash.				34
35						35

JOURNAL PAGE 1

Exhibit 3 illustrates the posting of the first two transactions from the general journal to the ledger accounts. You will note that the T account form is not used in this exhibit. Although the T account clearly separates debit entries and credit entries, it is inefficient for summarizing a large quantity of transactions. In practice, a business will usually use a standard form similar to that shown in Exhibit 3. However, in subsequent chapters we still occasionally employ the T account format as a convenient way to visualize the impact of a transaction on the accounts.

The debits and credits for each journal entry are posted to the accounts in the order that they occur in the journal. In posting to the standard account, we enter ① the date and ② the amount of the entry. For future reference, we cross-reference the entry by inserting ③ the journal page in the Posting Reference column of the account and ④ the account number in the Posting Reference column of the journal.

After we post each entry to a general ledger account, we calculate the balance in the account and enter this in the Balance column of the account as a debit or a

Exhibit 3
Posting from the General Journal to the General Ledger

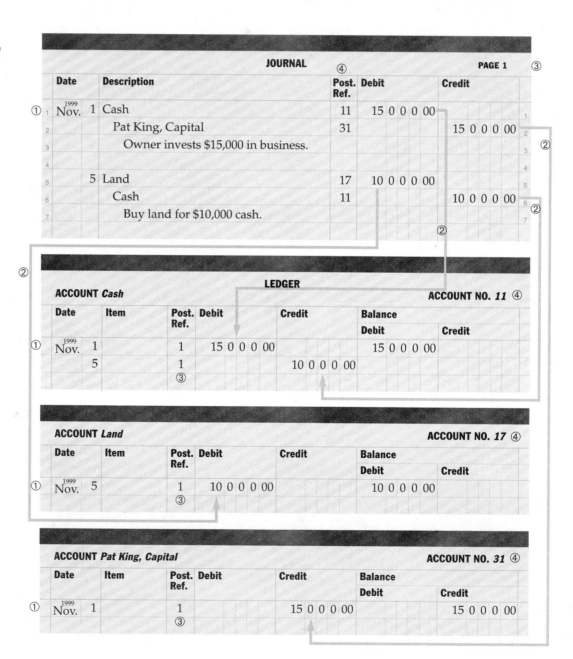

credit, as appropriate. For example, after we post the November 1 debit of $15,000 to the Cash account, we record $15,000 as a debit in the Balance column to show that this is the total amount in the account. After the November 5 credit of $10,000 is posted to Cash, we recalculate the amount remaining in the account and record the new amount in the Balance column as a $5,000 debit (the previous debit balance of $15,000 less the $10,000 credit).

NORMAL BALANCES OF ACCOUNTS

The sum of the increases recorded in an account is usually equal to or greater than the sum of the decreases recorded in the account. For this reason, the normal balances of all accounts are positive rather than negative. For example, the total debits (increases) in an asset account will ordinarily be greater than the total credits (decreases). Thus, asset accounts normally have debit balances.

We summarize the rules of debit and credit and the normal balances of the various types of accounts below:

	Increase *(Normal Balance)*	*Decrease*
Balance sheet accounts:		
Asset	**Debit**	Credit
Liability	**Credit**	Debit
Owner's Equity:		
Capital	**Credit**	Debit
Withdrawals	**Debit**	Credit
Income statement accounts:		
Revenue	**Credit**	Debit
Expense	**Debit**	Credit

When an account that normally has a debit balance actually has a credit balance, or vice versa, an error may have occurred or an unusual situation may exist. For example, a credit balance in the office equipment account could result only from an error. On the other hand, a debit balance in an accounts payable account could result from an overpayment.

Illustration of Analyzing and Summarizing Transactions

Objective 4

Analyze and summarize the financial statement effects of transactions.

How does a transaction occur in a business? A manager or other authorized employee normally initiates a transaction and generates a business document. For example, a purchase order is a business document used in purchasing supplies.[3] A billing statement or invoice is a business document used for billing customers for services or goods provided. We use business documents to analyze and record the effects of transactions on the financial statements. As we discussed in the preceding section, first we record the transaction in a journal. Periodically, we transfer the journal entries to the accounts in the ledger. We call this process of transferring the debits and credits from the journal entries to the accounts posting. We illustrate the flow of a transaction from its authorization to its posting in the accounts in the following diagram.

---

[3] In computerized accounting systems, some transactions are automatically authorized when certain events occur. For example, the salaries of managers may be paid automatically at the end of each pay period.

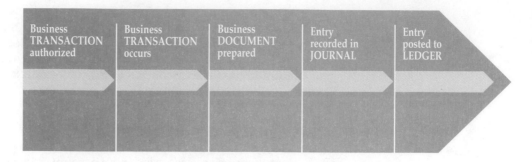

The ability to analyze the effects of transactions on financial statements is an essential skill for a successful career in business. As we illustrated earlier in the chapter, the double-entry accounting system is a very powerful tool in this analysis. We can summarize this system for analyzing transactions as follows:

1. Determine which accounts are affected by the transaction (for example, Cash and Accounts Payable).
2. Determine what type of accounts these are (asset, liability, owner's equity, revenue, or expense account).
3. For each account affected by the transaction, determine whether the account increases or decreases.
4. Determine whether each increase or decrease should be recorded as a debit or a credit using the rules listed on the previous page.

In practice, businesses use a variety of formats for recording journal entries. A business may use one all-purpose journal, sometimes called a general journal, or it may use several journals. In the latter case, each journal is used to record different types of transactions, such as cash receipts or cash payments. The journals may be part of either a manual accounting system or a computerized accounting system.[4]

To further illustrate recording transactions in the general journal and posting in a manual accounting system, we will use the December transactions of Computer King. The first transaction in December occurred on December 1.

Dec. 1. Computer King paid a premium of $2,400 for a comprehensive insurance policy covering liability, theft, and fire. The policy covers a two-year period.

ANALYSIS: Advance payments of expenses such as insurance are prepaid expenses, which are assets. For Computer King, the asset acquired for the cash payment is insurance protection for 24 months. The asset Prepaid Insurance increases and is debited for $2,400. The asset Cash decreases and is credited for $2,400.

27						27
28	Dec. 1	Prepaid Insurance	15	2 4 0 0 00		28
29		Cash	11		2 4 0 0 00	29
30		Paid premium on two-year policy.				30

We analyze the remaining December transactions for Computer King in the following paragraphs and post these transactions to the ledger in Exhibit 4, shown later. To simplify and reduce repetition, we state some of the December transactions

---

[4] The use of special journals and computerized accounting systems are discussed in later chapters, after the basics of accounting systems have been presented.

in summary form. For example, although a business would normally record cash received for services on a daily basis, in this example we record only summary totals at the middle and end of the month. Likewise, we journalize all revenues earned on account during December only at the middle and end of the month. In practice, each revenue transaction earned is recorded separately.

Dec. 1. Computer King paid rent for December, $800. The company from which Computer King is renting its store space now requires the payment of rent on the 1st of each month, rather than at the end of the month.

ANALYSIS: Like the advance payment of the insurance premium in the preceding transaction, the advance payment of rent is an asset. However, the asset Prepaid Insurance will not completely expire for 24 months, while the asset Prepaid Rent will expire in one month. When an asset that is purchased will be used up in a short period of time, such as a month, we usually debit an expense account initially. This avoids having to transfer the balance from an asset account (Prepaid Rent) to an expense account (Rent Expense) at the end of the month. Thus, when the rent for December is prepaid at the beginning of the month, we debit Rent Expense for $800 and credit Cash for $800.

30						30
31	Dec.	1	Rent Expense	52	8 0 0 00		31
32			Cash	11		8 0 0 00	32
33			Paid $800 for rent.				33

Dec. 1. Computer King received an offer from a local retailer to rent the land purchased on November 5. The retailer plans to use the land as a parking lot for its employees and customers. Computer King agreed to rent the land for three months, payable in advance. Computer King received $360 for three months' rent beginning December 1.

ANALYSIS: By agreeing to rent the land and accepting the $360, Computer King has incurred an obligation (liability) to the retailer. This obligation is to make the land available for use for three months and not to interfere with its use. The liability created by receiving the revenue in advance is called **unearned revenue.** We record the $360 received as an increase in an asset by debiting Cash. The firm records the increase in the liability account by crediting Unearned Rent for $360. As time passes, the unearned rent liability will decrease and will become revenue.

	JOURNAL				PAGE 2	
Date	Description	Post. Ref.	Debit	Credit		
1	1999 Dec. 1	Cash	11	3 6 0 00		1
2		Unearned Rent	23		3 6 0 00	2
		Received advance payment				
		for three months' rent.				

Dec. 4. Purchased office equipment on account from Executive Supply Co. for $1,800.

ANALYSIS: We debit Office Equipment for $1,800 to increase the asset. We credit Accounts Payable for $1,800 to increase the liability.

Dec.	4	Office Equipment	18	1 8 0 0 00	
		Accounts Payable	21		1 8 0 0 00
		Purchased $1,800 of office equipment			
		on account.			

Dec. 6. Paid $180 for a newspaper advertisement.

ANALYSIS: An expense increases and is debited for $180. Expense items that are expected to be minor in amount are normally included as part of the miscellaneous expense. Thus, we debit Miscellaneous Expense for $180. We credit Cash for $180 to decrease the asset.

Dec.	6	Miscellaneous Expense	59	1 8 0 00	
		Cash	11		1 8 0 00
		Paid $180 for miscellaneous expense.			

Dec. 11. Paid creditors $400.

ANALYSIS: We debit Accounts Payable for $400 to decrease the liability. We credit Cash for $400 to decrease the asset.

Dec.	11	Accounts Payable	21	4 0 0 00	
		Cash	11		4 0 0 00
		Paid $400 on accounts payable.			

Dec. 13. Paid receptionist and part-time assistant $950 for two weeks' wages.

ANALYSIS: This transaction is similar to the December 6 transaction, where we increased an expense account and decreased Cash. Thus, we debit Wages Expense for $950 and credit Cash for $950.

Dec.	13	Wages Expense	51	9 5 0 00	
		Cash	11		9 5 0 00
		Paid $950 for wages.			

Dec. 16. Received $3,100 from revenue earned for the first half of December.

ANALYSIS: We debit Cash to increase it by $3,100. We credit the revenue account Revenue Earned to increase it by $3,100.

		Dec. 16	Cash	11	3 1 0 0 00		
16			Revenue Earned	41		3 1 0 0 00	16
17			Received $3,100 cash for revenue				17
18			earned.				18

Dec. 16. Revenue earned on account totalled $1,750 for the first half of December.

ANALYSIS: When a business agrees that payment for services provided or goods sold can be accepted at another date, the firm has an **account receivable,** which is a claim against the customer. The account receivable is an asset, and the business has earned the revenue even though it has received no cash. Thus, we increase Accounts Receivable with a debit for $1,750. We increase the revenue account Revenue Earned with a credit for $1,750.

18							18
19		Dec. 16	Accounts Receivable	12	1 7 5 0 00		19
20			Revenue Earned	41		1 7 5 0 00	20
21			Earned $1,750 revenue on account.				21

Dec. 20. Paid $900 to Executive Supply Co. on the $1,800 debt owed from the December 4 transaction.

ANALYSIS: Similar to transaction of December 11.

20							20
21		Dec. 20	Accounts Payable	21	9 0 0 00		21
22			Cash	11		9 0 0 00	22
23			Paid $900 on accounts payable.				23

Dec. 21. Received $650 from customers in payment of their accounts.

ANALYSIS: When customers pay amounts owed for services they have previously received, one asset increases and another asset decreases. Thus, we debit Cash for $650, and credit Accounts Receivable for $650.

24							24
25		Dec. 21	Cash	11	6 5 0 00		25
26			Accounts Receivable	12		6 5 0 00	26
27			Collected $650 on accounts receivable.				27

Dec. 23. Paid $1,450 for supplies.

ANALYSIS: We debit Supplies $1,450 to increase the asset and credit Cash $1,450.

	Dec. 23	Supplies	14	1 4 5 0 00		
		Cash	11		1 4 5 0 00	
		Paid $1,450 for supplies.				

Dec. 27. Paid receptionist and part-time assistant $1,200 for two weeks' wages.

ANALYSIS: Similar to transaction of December 13.

	Dec. 27	Wages Expense	51	1 2 0 0 00		
		Cash	11		1 2 0 0 00	
		Paid $1,200 for wages.				

Dec. 31. Paid $310 telephone bill for the month.

ANALYSIS: Similar to transaction of December 6. We debit Utilities Expense for $310, and credit Cash for $310.

		JOURNAL			PAGE 3	
Date		Description	Post. Ref.	Debit	Credit	
1	Dec.[1999] 31	Utilities Expense	54	3 1 0 00		1
2		Cash	11		3 1 0 00	2
3		Paid telephone bill of $310.				3

Dec. 31. Paid $225 electric bill for the month.

ANALYSIS: Similar to the preceding transaction.

	Dec. 31	Utilities Expense	54	2 2 5 00		
		Cash	11		2 2 5 00	
		Paid electric bill of $225.				

Dec. 31. Received $2,870 from revenue earned for the second half of December.

ANALYSIS: Similar to transaction of December 16.

	Dec. 31	Cash	11	2 8 7 0 00		
		Revenue Earned	41		2 8 7 0 00	
		Received $2,870 for revenue earned.				

Dec. 31. Revenue earned on account totalled $1,120 for the second half of December.

ANALYSIS: Similar to transaction of December 16.

		Date	Description	Post. Ref.	Debit	Credit	
9							9
10		Dec. 31	Accounts Receivable	12	1 1 2 0 00		10
11			Revenue Earned	41		1 1 2 0 00	11
12			Earned $1,120 revenue on account.				12

Dec. 31. Pat King withdrew $2,000 for personal use.

ANALYSIS: The transaction resulted in an increase in the amount of withdrawals, which we record by a $2,000 debit to Pat King, Withdrawals. We decrease Cash by recording a $2,000 credit to Cash.

		Date	Description	Post. Ref.	Debit	Credit	
12							12
13		Dec. 31	Pat King, Withdrawals	32	2 0 0 0 00		13
14			Cash	11		2 0 0 0 00	14
15			Owner withdrew $2,000 cash.				15

   Exhibit 3, which we presented earlier in the chapter, illustrated page 1 of Computer King's general journal, showing the company's journal entries for November, 1999. Exhibit 4 below shows the portion of the general journal summarizing the entries for December, 1999. The wavy line on page 1 of the journal indicates that Exhibit 4 is only displaying the section of the page beginning with the December entries (since the first part of the page containing the November entries was already shown previously in Exhibit 3). Exhibit 4 also shows each of the general ledger accounts with the transactions posted through to the end of December.

Exhibit 4
Journal and Ledger—
Computer King

		Date	Description	Post. Ref.	Debit	Credit	
			JOURNAL			**PAGE 1**	
1		1999 Dec. 1	Prepaid Insurance	15	2 4 0 0 00		1
2			Cash	11		2 4 0 0 00	2
3			Paid premium on two-year policy.				3
4							4
5		1	Rent Expense	52	8 0 0 00		5
6			Cash	11		8 0 0 00	6
7			Paid $800 for rent.				7
8							8
9		1	Cash	11	3 6 0 00		9
10			Unearned Rent	23		3 6 0 00	10
11			Received advance payment for				11
12			three months' rent.				12
13							13

Exhibit 4 (continued)

	JOURNAL				PAGE 2
Date	**Description**	**Post. Ref.**	**Debit**	**Credit**	
1999 Dec. 4	Office Equipment	18	1 8 0 0 00		1
	Accounts Payable	21		1 8 0 0 00	2
	Purchased $1,800 of office equipment				3
	on account.				4
					5
6	Miscellaneous Expense	59	1 8 0 00		6
	Cash	11		1 8 0 00	7
	Paid $180 for miscellaneous expense.				8
					9
11	Accounts Payable	21	4 0 0 00		10
	Cash	11		4 0 0 00	11
	Paid $400 on accounts payable.				12
					13
13	Wages Expense	51	9 5 0 00		14
	Cash	11		9 5 0 00	15
	Paid $950 for wages.				16
					17
16	Cash	11	3 1 0 0 00		18
	Revenue Earned	41		3 1 0 0 00	19
	Received $3,100 for revenue earned.				20
					21
16	Accounts Receivable	12	1 7 5 0 00		22
	Revenue Earned	41		1 7 5 0 00	23
	Earned $1,750 revenue on account.				24
					25
20	Accounts Payable	21	9 0 0 00		26
	Cash	11		9 0 0 00	27
	Paid $900 on accounts payable.				28
					29
21	Cash	11	6 5 0 00		30
	Accounts Receivable	12		6 5 0 00	31
	Collected $650 on accounts receivable.				32
					33
23	Supplies	14	1 4 5 0 00		34
	Cash	11		1 4 5 0 00	35
	Paid $1,450 for supplies.				36
					37
27	Wages Expense	51	1 2 0 0 00		38
	Cash	11		1 2 0 0 00	39
	Paid $1,200 for wages.				40
					41
31	Utilities Expense	54	3 1 0 00		42
	Cash	11		3 1 0 00	43
	Paid telephone bill of $310.				44
					45

Exhibit 4 (continued)

JOURNAL   PAGE 3

	Date	Description	Post. Ref.	Debit	Credit	
1	1999 Dec. 31	Utilities Expense	54	2 2 5 00		1
2		Cash	11		2 2 5 00	2
3		Paid electric bill of $225.				3
4						4
5	31	Cash	11	2 8 7 0 00		5
6		Revenue Earned	41		2 8 7 0 00	6
7		Received $2,870 for revenue earned.				7
8						8
9	31	Accounts Receivable	12	1 1 2 0 00		9
10		Revenue Earned	41		1 1 2 0 00	10
11		Earned $1,120 revenue on account.				11
12						12
13	31	Pat King, Withdrawals	32	2 0 0 0 00		13
14		Cash	11		2 0 0 0 00	14
15		Owner withdrew $2,000.				15
16						16

LEDGER

ACCOUNT *Cash*   **ACCOUNT NO.** *11*

Date	Item	Post. Ref.	Debit	Credit	Balance Debit	Balance Credit
1999 Nov. 1		1	15 0 0 0 00		15 0 0 0 00	
5		1		10 0 0 0 00	5 0 0 0 00	
18		1	7 5 0 0 00		12 5 0 0 00	
30		1		3 3 2 5 00	9 1 7 5 00	
30		1		9 5 0 00	8 2 2 5 00	
30		1		2 0 0 0 00	6 2 2 5 00	
Dec. 1		1		2 4 0 0 00	3 8 2 5 00	
1		1		8 0 0 00	3 0 2 5 00	
1		2	3 6 0 00		3 3 8 5 00	
6		2		1 8 0 00	3 2 0 5 00	
11		2		4 0 0 00	2 8 0 5 00	
13		2		9 5 0 00	1 8 5 5 00	
16		2	3 1 0 0 00		4 9 5 5 00	
20		2		9 0 0 00	4 0 5 5 00	
21		2	6 5 0 00		4 7 0 5 00	
23		2		1 4 5 0 00	3 2 5 5 00	
27		2		1 2 0 0 00	2 0 5 5 00	
31		3		3 1 0 00	1 7 4 5 00	
31		3		2 2 5 00	1 5 2 0 00	
31		3	2 8 7 0 00		4 3 9 0 00	
31		3		2 0 0 0 00	2 3 9 0 00	

Exhibit 4 (continued)

ACCOUNT *Accounts Receivable*   **ACCOUNT NO.** *12*

Date		Item	Post. Ref.	Debit	Credit	Balance Debit	Balance Credit
1999 Dec.	16		2	1 7 5 0 00		1 7 5 0 00	
	21		2		6 5 0 00	1 1 0 0 00	
	31		3	1 1 2 0 00		2 2 2 0 00	

ACCOUNT *Supplies*   **ACCOUNT NO.** *14*

Date		Item	Post. Ref.	Debit	Credit	Balance Debit	Balance Credit
1999 Nov.	10		1	1 3 5 0 00		1 3 5 0 00	
	30		1		8 0 0 00	5 5 0 00	
Dec.	23		2	1 4 5 0 00		2 0 0 0 00	

ACCOUNT *Prepaid Insurance*   **ACCOUNT NO.** *15*

Date		Item	Post. Ref.	Debit	Credit	Balance Debit	Balance Credit
1999 Dec.	1		1	2 4 0 0 00		2 4 0 0 00	

ACCOUNT *Land*   **ACCOUNT NO.** *17*

Date		Item	Post. Ref.	Debit	Credit	Balance Debit	Balance Credit
1999 Nov.	5		1	10 0 0 0 00		10 0 0 0 00	

ACCOUNT *Office Equipment*   **ACCOUNT NO.** *18*

Date		Item	Post. Ref.	Debit	Credit	Balance Debit	Balance Credit
1999 Dec.	4		2	1 8 0 0 00		1 8 0 0 00	

ACCOUNT *Accounts Payable*   **ACCOUNT NO.** *21*

Date		Item	Post. Ref.	Debit	Credit	Balance Debit	Balance Credit
1999 Nov.	10		1		1 3 5 0 00		1 3 5 0 00
	30		1	9 5 0 00			4 0 0 00
Dec.	4		2		1 8 0 0 00		2 2 0 0 00
	11		2	4 0 0 00			1 8 0 0 00
	20		2	9 0 0 00			9 0 0 00

Exhibit 4 (continued)

ACCOUNT *Unearned Rent*   **ACCOUNT NO.** *23*

Date	Item	Post. Ref.	Debit	Credit	Balance Debit	Balance Credit
1999 Dec. 1		2		3 6 0 00		3 6 0 00

ACCOUNT *Pat King, Capital*   **ACCOUNT NO.** *31*

Date	Item	Post. Ref.	Debit	Credit	Balance Debit	Balance Credit
1999 Nov. 1		1		15 0 0 0 00		15 0 0 0 00

ACCOUNT *Pat King, Withdrawals*   **ACCOUNT NO.** *32*

Date	Item	Post. Ref.	Debit	Credit	Balance Debit	Balance Credit
1999 Nov. 30		1	2 0 0 0 00		2 0 0 0 00	
Dec. 31		3	2 0 0 0 00		4 0 0 0 00	

ACCOUNT *Revenue Earned*   **ACCOUNT NO.** *41*

Date	Item	Post. Ref.	Debit	Credit	Balance Debit	Balance Credit
1999 Nov. 18		1		7 5 0 0 00		7 5 0 0 00
Dec. 16		2		3 1 0 0 00		10 6 0 0 00
16		2		1 7 5 0 00		12 3 5 0 00
31		3		2 8 7 0 00		15 2 2 0 00
31		3		1 1 2 0 00		16 3 4 0 00

ACCOUNT *Wages Expense*   **ACCOUNT NO.** *51*

Date	Item	Post. Ref.	Debit	Credit	Balance Debit	Balance Credit
1999 Nov. 30		1	1 8 0 0 00		1 8 0 0 00	
Dec. 13		2	9 5 0 00		2 7 5 0 00	
27		2	1 2 0 0 00		3 9 5 0 00	

ACCOUNT *Rent Expense*   **ACCOUNT NO.** *52*

Date	Item	Post. Ref.	Debit	Credit	Balance Debit	Balance Credit
1999 Nov. 30		1	8 0 0 00		8 0 0 00	
Dec. 1		1	8 0 0 00		1 6 0 0 00	

Exhibit 4 (concluded)

ACCOUNT *Utilities Expense*   **ACCOUNT NO. 54**

Date		Item	Post. Ref.	Debit	Credit	Balance Debit	Credit
1999 Nov.	30		1	4 5 0 00		4 5 0 00	
Dec.	31		3	3 1 0 00		7 6 0 00	
	31		3	2 2 5 00		9 8 5 00	

ACCOUNT *Supplies Expense*   **ACCOUNT NO. 55**

Date		Item	Post. Ref.	Debit	Credit	Balance Debit	Credit
1999 Nov.	30		1	8 0 0 00		8 0 0 00	

ACCOUNT *Miscellaneous Expense*   **ACCOUNT NO. 59**

Date		Item	Post. Ref.	Debit	Credit	Balance Debit	Credit
1999 Nov.	30		1	2 7 5 00		2 7 5 00	
Dec.	6		2	1 8 0 00		4 5 5 00	

Trial Balance

Objective 5
Prepare a trial balance and explain how it can be used to discover errors.

How can you be sure that you have not made an error in posting the debits and credits to the ledger? One way is to determine the equality of the debits and credits in the ledger. This equality should be proven at the end of each accounting period, if not more often. Such a proof, called a trial balance, may be in the form of a computer printout or in the form shown in Exhibit 5.[5]

The first step in preparing the trial balance is to determine the balance of each account in the ledger. When the standard account form is used, the balance of each account appears in the balance column on the same line as the last posting to the account.

The trial balance does not provide complete proof of the accuracy of the ledger. It indicates only that the debits and the credits are equal. This proof is of value, however, because errors often affect the equality of debits and credits. If the two totals of a trial balance are not equal, an error has occurred. In the remainder of this chapter, we will discuss procedures for discovering and correcting errors.

Discovery and Correction of Errors

Objective 6
Discover errors in recording transactions and correct them, and define the concept of materiality.

Errors will sometimes occur in journalizing and posting transactions. In the following paragraphs, we describe and illustrate how to discover and correct errors.

[5] A trial balance is not a formal statement, but is used by the accountant to verify the accuracy of the accounting records. Thus, financial statement captions, subtotals, and dollar signs are normally omitted from a trial balance.

Exhibit 5
Trial Balance

Computer King Trial Balance December 31, 1999		
Cash	2 3 9 0 00	
Accounts Receivable	2 2 2 0 00	
Supplies	2 0 0 0 00	
Prepaid Insurance	2 4 0 0 00	
Land	10 0 0 0 00	
Office Equipment	1 8 0 0 00	
Accounts Payable		9 0 0 00
Unearned Rent		3 6 0 00
Pat King, Capital		15 0 0 0 00
Pat King, Withdrawals	4 0 0 0 00	
Revenue Earned		16 3 4 0 00
Wages Expense	3 9 5 0 00	
Rent Expense	1 6 0 0 00	
Utilities Expense	9 8 5 00	
Supplies Expense	8 0 0 00	
Miscellaneous Expense	4 5 5 00	
	32 6 0 0 00	32 6 0 0 00

In some cases, however, an error might not be significant enough to affect the decisions of management or others. A generally accepted accounting principle known as the materiality concept states that financial reports need only disclose information that is significant enough to impact a user's decision. Immaterial items are those whose omission would not influence or change a decision.[6] As it is not worth spending much time in accounting for such items, a business may deal with them in the easiest possible way. For example, an error of a few dollars in recording an asset as an expense for a business with millions of dollars in assets would be considered immaterial, and a correction would not be necessary. In the remaining paragraphs, we assume that errors discovered are material and should be corrected.

DISCOVERY OF ERRORS

As mentioned previously, the trial balance is one of the primary ways for discovering errors in the ledger. However, it indicates only whether the debits and credits are equal. If the two totals of the trial balance are not equal, it is probably due to one or more of the following types of errors:

1. Error in preparing the trial balance, such as:
   a. One of the columns of the trial balance was incorrectly added.
   b. The amount of an account balance was incorrectly recorded on the trial balance.
   c. A debit balance was recorded on the trial balance as a credit, or vice versa, or a balance was omitted entirely.
2. Error in determining the account balances, such as:
   a. A balance was incorrectly computed.
   b. A balance was entered in the wrong balance column.

---

[6] *CICA Handbook*, Section 1000, paragraph 17.

3. Error in recording a transaction in the ledger, such as:
    a. An erroneous amount was posted to the account.
    b. A debit entry was posted as a credit, or vice versa.
    c. A debit or a credit posting was omitted.

Among the types of errors that will not cause an inequality in the trial balance totals are the following:

1. Failure to record a transaction or to post a transaction.
2. Recording the same erroneous amount for both the debit and the credit parts of a transaction.
3. Recording the same transaction more than once.
4. Posting a part of a transaction correctly as a debit or credit but to the wrong account.

It is obvious that we must be careful in recording transactions in the journal and in posting to the accounts. The need for accuracy in determining account balances and reporting them on the trial balance is equally obvious.

You may discover errors in the accounts in various ways: (1) by audit procedures, (2) by chance, or (3) by looking at the trial balance. If the two trial balance totals are not equal, you must determine the amount of the difference between the totals before searching for the error.

The amount of the difference between the two totals of a trial balance sometimes gives a clue as to the nature of the error or where it occurred. For example, a difference of 10, 100, or 1,000 between two totals is often the result of an error in addition. A difference between totals can also be due to omitting a debit or a credit posting. If the difference is divisible evenly by 2, the error may be due to the posting of a debit as a credit, or vice versa. For example, if the debit total is $20,640 and the credit total is $20,236, the difference of $404 may indicate that a credit posting of $404 was omitted or that a credit of $202 was incorrectly posted as a debit.

Two other common types of errors are transpositions and slides. A transposition is the erroneous rearrangement of digits, such as writing $542 as $452 or $524. In a slide, the entire number is erroneously moved one or more spaces to the right or the left, such as writing $542.00 as $54.20 or $5,420.00. If an error of either type has occurred and there are no other errors, the difference between the two trial balance totals can be evenly divided by 9.

If an error is not revealed by the trial balance, you must retrace the steps in the accounting process, beginning with the last step and working back to the entries in the journal. Usually, you will discover errors causing the trial balance totals to be unequal before all of the steps are retraced. While there are no standard rules for searching for errors, we usually follow the steps presented below:

1. Prove the accuracy of the trial balance totals by re-adding the columns.
2. Compare the listings in the trial balance with the balances shown in the ledger. Make certain that no accounts have been omitted.
3. Recompute the balance of each account in the ledger.
4. Trace the postings in the ledger back to the journal. Place a small check mark beside each item in the ledger and also in the journal. If the error is not found, examine each account to see if there is an entry without a check mark. Do the same with the entries in the journal.
5. Prove the equality of the debits and the credits in the journal.

CORRECTION OF ERRORS

When you discover errors in journalizing and posting transactions, you may employ various procedures to correct them according to the nature of the error and when you discover it. We will discuss these procedures in the following paragraphs.

You may find an error in an account title or amount in the journal before you have posted the entry. In this case, you correct the error by drawing a line through it, and inserting the correct title or amount directly above. If there is any chance of questions arising later, the person responsible may initial the correction.

An entry in the journal may be prepared correctly but posted incorrectly to the account. In this case, you correct the error by drawing a line through it and posting the item correctly. As indicated above, if there is any chance of questions arising later, the person responsible may initial the correction.

An incorrect account title may appear in a journal entry and you may not discover the error until after posting is completed. In this case, it is best to journalize and post a correcting entry. To illustrate, assume that on May 5 a purchase of office equipment was incorrectly journalized and posted as a $12,500 debit to Supplies. The credit was correctly journalized and posted as a $12,500 credit to Accounts Payable. Before making a correcting entry, determine (1) the debit(s) and credit(s) of the entry in which the error occurred and (2) the debit(s) and credit(s) that should have been recorded. T accounts may be helpful in making this analysis, as in the following example:

Entry in which error occurred:

Supplies	Accounts Payable
12,500	12,500

Entry that should have been recorded:

Office Equipment	Accounts Payable
12,500	12,500

Comparing the two sets of T accounts shows that the incorrect debit of $12,500 to Supplies may be corrected by debiting Office Equipment for $12,500 and crediting Supplies for $12,500. Journalize and post the following correcting entry:

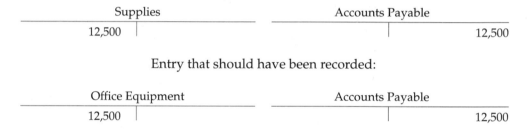

JOURNAL PAGE 30

	Date	Description	Post. Ref.	Debit	Credit	
1	2000 May 5	Office Equipment	18	12 5 0 0 00		1
2		Supplies	14		12 5 0 0 00	2
3		To correct erroneous debit to				3
4		Supplies on May 5. See invoice				4
5		from Bell Office Equipment Co. *CW*				5
6						6

The procedures for correcting errors are summarized in Exhibit 6.

Exhibit 6
Procedures for Correcting Errors

Error	Correction Procedure
Journal entry incorrect but not posted.	Draw line through the error and insert correct title or amount.
Journal entry correct but posted incorrectly.	Draw line through the error and post correctly.
Journal entry incorrect and posted.	Journalize and post a correcting entry.

KEY POINTS

Objective 1. Explain why accounts are used to record and summarize the effects of transactions on financial statements.

The record used for the purpose of recording individual transactions is an account. A group of accounts is called a ledger.

The system of accounts that make up a ledger is called a chart of accounts. We number and list the accounts in the order in which they appear in the balance sheet and the income statement.

Objective 2. Explain the characteristics of an account.

The simplest form of an account, a T account, has three parts. First, each account has a title, which is the name of the item recorded in the account. Second, each account has a left side, called the debit side. Third, each account has a right side, called the credit side. Amounts entered on the left side of an account, regardless of the account title, are called debits to the account. Amounts entered on the right side of an account are called credits. Periodically, we sum the debits and the credits in an account to determine the balance of the account.

Objective 3. List the rules of debit and credit and the normal balances of accounts.

General rules of debit and credit govern recording increases or decreases in asset, liability, owner's equity, revenue, expense, and withdrawals accounts. We record each transaction so that the sum of the debits is always equal to the sum of the credits. Initially, we enter transactions in a record called a journal. We transfer the data in the journal entry to the ledger accounts by a process known as posting.

The sum of the increases recorded in an account is usually equal to or greater than the sum of the decreases recorded in the account. For this reason, the normal balance of an account is indicated by the side of the account (debit or credit) that receives the increases.

The following table summarizes the rules of debit and credit and normal account balances:

	Increase (Normal Balance)	Decrease
Balance sheet accounts:		
Asset	**Debit**	Credit
Liability	**Credit**	Debit
Owner's Equity:		
Capital	**Credit**	Debit
Withdrawals	**Debit**	Credit
Income statement accounts:		
Revenue	**Credit**	Debit
Expense	**Debit**	Credit

Objective 4. Analyze and summarize the financial statement effects of transactions.

We employ a two-column journal with a debit column and a credit column for recording initial transactions in an accounting system. In practice, the T account is usually replaced with the standard account form. Periodically, we post journal entries to the accounts.

Objective 5. Prepare a trial balance and explain how it can be used to discover errors.

We prepare a trial balance by listing the accounts from the ledger and their balances. If the two totals of the trial balance are not equal, an error has occurred.

Objective 6. Discover errors in recording transactions and correct them and define the concept of materiality.

Errors may be discovered (1) by audit procedures, (2) by chance, or (3) by looking at the trial balance. Exhibit 4 summarizes the procedure for correcting errors.

GLOSSARY OF KEY TERMS

Account. The form used to record additions and deductions for each individual asset, liability, owner's equity, revenue, and expense. *Objective 1*

Balance of the account. The amount of difference between the debits and the credits that have been entered into an account. *Objective 2*

Book of original entry. The journal in which we first record a business transaction. *Objective 3*

Chart of accounts. The system of accounts that makes up the ledger for a business. *Objective 1*

Credit. (1) The right side of an account; (2) the amount entered on the right side of an account; (3) to enter an amount on the right side of an account. *Objective 2*

Debit. (1) The left side of an account; (2) the amount entered on the left side of an account; (3) to enter an amount on the left side of an account. *Objective 2*

Double-entry accounting. A system for recording transactions, based on recording increases and decreases in accounts so that debits always equal credits. *Objective 3*

Journal. The initial record in which we record the effects of a transaction on accounts. *Objective 3*

Journalizing. The process of recording a transaction in a journal. *Objective 3*

Ledger. The group of accounts used by a business. *Objective 1*

Materiality concept. Financial reports need only disclose information that is significant enough to affect a user's decision. *Objective 6*

Posting. The process of transferring debits and credits from a journal to the accounts. *Objective 4*

Slide. The erroneous movement of all digits in a number, one or more spaces to the right or the left, such as writing $542 as $5,420. *Objective 6*

T account. A form of account resembling the letter T. *Objective 2*

Transposition. The erroneous arrangement of digits in a number, such as writing $542 as $524. *Objective 6*

Trial balance. A summary listing of the titles and balances of the accounts in the ledger. *Objective 5*

Withdrawals. The amount of withdrawals made by the owner of a sole proprietorship. *Objective 1*

ILLUSTRATIVE PROBLEM

J. F. Outz, M.D., has been practising as a plastic surgeon for three years. During April, Outz completed the following transactions in her practice.

April 1. Paid office rent for April, $800.
    3. Purchased equipment on account, $2,100.
    5. Received cash on account, $3,150, from the government for services reimbursed under the provincial health insurance plan.
    8. Purchased supplies on account, $245.
    9. One of the items of equipment purchased on April 3 was defective. It was returned with the permission of the supplier, who agreed to reduce the account for the amount charged for the item, $325.
   12. Paid cash to creditors on account, $1,250.
   17. Paid cash for renewal of a six-month property insurance policy, $370.
   20. Discovered that the balance of the cash account and of the accounts payable account as of April 1 were overstated by $200. A payment of that amount to a creditor in March had not been recorded. Journalize the $200 payment as of April 20.
   24. Paid cash for laboratory analysis, $545.
   27. Paid cash from business bank account for personal and family expenses, $1,250.
   30. Recorded the cash received in payment of services (on a cash basis) to patients during April, $1,720. These payments were for cosmetic surgery not covered by the provincial health insurance plan.
   30. Paid salaries of receptionist and nurses, $1,725.
   30. Paid various utility expenses, $360.
   30. Recorded fees billed to the provincial health insurance plan for services to patients performed in April, $5,145.
   30. Paid miscellaneous expenses, $132.

Outz's account titles, numbers, and balances as of April 1 (all normal balances) are listed as follows: Cash, 11, $4,123; Accounts Receivable, 12, $6,725; Supplies, 13, $290; Prepaid Insurance, 14, $465; Equipment, 18, $19,745; Accounts Payable, 22, $765; J. F. Outz, Capital, 31, $30,583; J. F. Outz, Withdrawals, 32; Professional Fees, 41; Salary Expense, 51; Rent Expense, 53; Laboratory Expense, 55; Utilities Expense, 56; Miscellaneous Expense, 59.

Instructions

1. Open a ledger of standard four-column accounts for Dr. Outz as of April 1 of the current year. Enter the balances in the appropriate balance columns and place a check mark (✓) in the posting reference column. (You should verify the equality of the debit and credit balances in the ledger before proceeding with the next instruction.)
2. Journalize each transaction in a two-column journal.
3. Post the journal to the ledger, extending the month-end balances to the appropriate balance columns after each posting.
4. Prepare a trial balance as of April 30.

Solution

2. and 3.

<table>
<tr><th colspan="6">JOURNAL</th><th>PAGE 27</th></tr>
<tr><th>Date</th><th>Description</th><th>Post.
Ref.</th><th colspan="2">Debit</th><th colspan="2">Credit</th></tr>
<tr><td>1 April 1</td><td>Rent Expense</td><td>53</td><td colspan="2">8 0 0 00</td><td colspan="2"></td></tr>
<tr><td>2</td><td>Cash</td><td>11</td><td colspan="2"></td><td colspan="2">8 0 0 00</td></tr>
<tr><td>3</td><td>Paid office rent for April.</td><td></td><td colspan="2"></td><td colspan="2"></td></tr>
<tr><td>4</td><td></td><td></td><td colspan="2"></td><td colspan="2"></td></tr>
<tr><td>5   3</td><td>Equipment</td><td>18</td><td colspan="2">2 1 0 0 00</td><td colspan="2"></td></tr>
<tr><td>6</td><td>Accounts Payable</td><td>22</td><td colspan="2"></td><td colspan="2">2 1 0 0 00</td></tr>
<tr><td>7</td><td>Purchased equipment on account.</td><td></td><td colspan="2"></td><td colspan="2"></td></tr>
<tr><td>8</td><td></td><td></td><td colspan="2"></td><td colspan="2"></td></tr>
<tr><td>9   5</td><td>Cash</td><td>11</td><td colspan="2">3 1 5 0 00</td><td colspan="2"></td></tr>
<tr><td>10</td><td>Accounts Receivable</td><td>12</td><td colspan="2"></td><td colspan="2">3 1 5 0 00</td></tr>
<tr><td>11</td><td>Received cash on account.</td><td></td><td colspan="2"></td><td colspan="2"></td></tr>
<tr><td>12</td><td></td><td></td><td colspan="2"></td><td colspan="2"></td></tr>
<tr><td>13   8</td><td>Supplies</td><td>13</td><td colspan="2">2 4 5 00</td><td colspan="2"></td></tr>
<tr><td>14</td><td>Accounts Payable</td><td>22</td><td colspan="2"></td><td colspan="2">2 4 5 00</td></tr>
<tr><td>15</td><td>Purchased supplies on account.</td><td></td><td colspan="2"></td><td colspan="2"></td></tr>
<tr><td>16</td><td></td><td></td><td colspan="2"></td><td colspan="2"></td></tr>
<tr><td>17   9</td><td>Accounts Payable</td><td>22</td><td colspan="2">3 2 5 00</td><td colspan="2"></td></tr>
<tr><td>18</td><td>Equipment</td><td>18</td><td colspan="2"></td><td colspan="2">3 2 5 00</td></tr>
<tr><td>19</td><td>Returned defective equipment</td><td></td><td colspan="2"></td><td colspan="2"></td></tr>
<tr><td>20</td><td>for credit.</td><td></td><td colspan="2"></td><td colspan="2"></td></tr>
<tr><td>21</td><td></td><td></td><td colspan="2"></td><td colspan="2"></td></tr>
<tr><td>22   12</td><td>Accounts Payable</td><td>22</td><td colspan="2">1 2 5 0 00</td><td colspan="2"></td></tr>
<tr><td>23</td><td>Cash</td><td>11</td><td colspan="2"></td><td colspan="2">1 2 5 0 00</td></tr>
<tr><td>24</td><td>Paid $1,250 on accounts payable.</td><td></td><td colspan="2"></td><td colspan="2"></td></tr>
<tr><td>25</td><td></td><td></td><td colspan="2"></td><td colspan="2"></td></tr>
<tr><td>26   17</td><td>Prepaid Insurance</td><td>14</td><td colspan="2">3 7 0 00</td><td colspan="2"></td></tr>
<tr><td>27</td><td>Cash</td><td>11</td><td colspan="2"></td><td colspan="2">3 7 0 00</td></tr>
<tr><td>28</td><td>Paid premium for 6-month policy.</td><td></td><td colspan="2"></td><td colspan="2"></td></tr>
<tr><td>29</td><td></td><td></td><td colspan="2"></td><td colspan="2"></td></tr>
<tr><td>30   20</td><td>Accounts Payable</td><td>22</td><td colspan="2">2 0 0 00</td><td colspan="2"></td></tr>
<tr><td>31</td><td>Cash</td><td>11</td><td colspan="2"></td><td colspan="2">2 0 0 00</td></tr>
<tr><td>32</td><td>Record payment on accounts payable.</td><td></td><td colspan="2"></td><td colspan="2"></td></tr>
<tr><td>33</td><td></td><td></td><td colspan="2"></td><td colspan="2"></td></tr>
<tr><td>34   24</td><td>Laboratory Expense</td><td>55</td><td colspan="2">5 4 5 00</td><td colspan="2"></td></tr>
<tr><td>35</td><td>Cash</td><td>11</td><td colspan="2"></td><td colspan="2">5 4 5 00</td></tr>
<tr><td>36</td><td>Paid laboratory expenses.</td><td></td><td colspan="2"></td><td colspan="2"></td></tr>
<tr><td>37</td><td></td><td></td><td colspan="2"></td><td colspan="2"></td></tr>
<tr><td>38   27</td><td>J. F. Outz, Withdrawals</td><td>32</td><td colspan="2">1 2 5 0 00</td><td colspan="2"></td></tr>
<tr><td>39</td><td>Cash</td><td>11</td><td colspan="2"></td><td colspan="2">1 2 5 0 00</td></tr>
<tr><td>40</td><td>Owner withdrew $1,250.</td><td></td><td colspan="2"></td><td colspan="2"></td></tr>
<tr><td>41</td><td></td><td></td><td colspan="2"></td><td colspan="2"></td></tr>
<tr><td>42   30</td><td>Cash</td><td>11</td><td colspan="2">1 7 2 0 00</td><td colspan="2"></td></tr>
<tr><td>43</td><td>Professional Fees Revenue</td><td>41</td><td colspan="2"></td><td colspan="2">1 7 2 0 00</td></tr>
<tr><td>44</td><td>Performed services for cash.</td><td></td><td colspan="2"></td><td colspan="2"></td></tr>
<tr><td>45</td><td></td><td></td><td colspan="2"></td><td colspan="2"></td></tr>
</table>

	JOURNAL				PAGE 28
Date	**Description**	**Post. Ref.**	**Debit**	**Credit**	
¹ April³⁰ 30	Salary Expense	51	1 7 2 5 00		₁
²	Cash	11		1 7 2 5 00	₂
³	Paid salaries.				₃
⁴					₄
⁵	30 Utilities Expense	56	3 6 0 00		₅
⁶	Cash	11		3 6 0 00	₆
⁷	Paid utilities bill.				₇
⁸					₈
⁹	30 Accounts Receivable	12	5 1 4 5 00		₉
¹⁰	Professional Fees Revenue	41		5 1 4 5 00	₁₀
¹¹	Performed services on account.				₁₁
¹²					₁₂
¹³	30 Miscellaneous Expense	59	1 3 2 00		₁₃
¹⁴	Cash	11		1 3 2 00	₁₄
¹⁵	Paid miscellaneous expense.				₁₅
¹⁶					₁₆

1. and 3.

ACCOUNT *Cash*					ACCOUNT NO. *11*	
Date	**Item**	**Post. Ref.**	**Debit**	**Credit**	**Balance Debit**	**Credit**
April³⁰ 1	Balance	✓			4 1 2 3 00	
1		27		8 0 0 00	3 3 2 3 00	
5		27	3 1 5 0 00		6 4 7 3 00	
12		27		1 2 5 0 00	5 2 2 3 00	
17		27		3 7 0 00	4 8 5 3 00	
20		27		2 0 0 00	4 6 5 3 00	
24		27		5 4 5 00	4 1 0 8 00	
27		27		1 2 5 0 00	2 8 5 8 00	
30		27	1 7 2 0 00		4 5 7 8 00	
30		28		1 7 2 5 00	2 8 5 3 00	
30		28		3 6 0 00	2 4 9 3 00	
30		28		1 3 2 00	2 3 6 1 00	

ACCOUNT *Accounts Receivable*					ACCOUNT NO. *12*	
Date	**Item**	**Post. Ref.**	**Debit**	**Credit**	**Balance Debit**	**Credit**
April³⁰ 1	Balance	✓			6 7 2 5 00	
5		27		3 1 5 0 00	3 5 7 5 00	
30		28	5 1 4 5 00		8 7 2 0 00	

ACCOUNT *Supplies*   **ACCOUNT NO.** *13*

Date		Item	Post. Ref.	Debit	Credit	Balance Debit	Balance Credit
April 1		Balance	✓			2 9 0 00	
8			27	2 4 5 00		5 3 5 00	

ACCOUNT *Prepaid Insurance*   **ACCOUNT NO.** *14*

Date		Item	Post. Ref.	Debit	Credit	Balance Debit	Balance Credit
April 1		Balance	✓			4 6 5 00	
17			27	3 7 0 00		8 3 5 00	

ACCOUNT *Equipment*   **ACCOUNT NO.** *18*

Date		Item	Post. Ref.	Debit	Credit	Balance Debit	Balance Credit
April 1		Balance	✓			19 7 4 5 00	
3			27	2 1 0 0 00		21 8 4 5 00	
9			27		3 2 5 00	21 5 2 0 00	

ACCOUNT *Accounts Payable*   **ACCOUNT NO.** *22*

Date		Item	Post. Ref.	Debit	Credit	Balance Debit	Balance Credit
April 1		Balance	✓				7 6 5 00
3			27		2 1 0 0 00		2 8 6 5 00
8			27		2 4 5 00		3 1 1 0 00
9			27	3 2 5 00			2 7 8 5 00
12			27	1 2 5 0 00			1 5 3 5 00
20			27	2 0 0 00			1 3 3 5 00

ACCOUNT *J. F. Outz, Capital*   **ACCOUNT NO.** *31*

Date		Item	Post. Ref.	Debit	Credit	Balance Debit	Balance Credit
April 1		Balance	✓				30 5 8 3 00

ACCOUNT *J. F. Outz, Withdrawals*   **ACCOUNT NO.** *32*

Date		Item	Post. Ref.	Debit	Credit	Balance Debit	Balance Credit
April 27			27	1 2 5 0 00		1 2 5 0 00	

ACCOUNT *Professional Fees Revenue*   **ACCOUNT NO. 41**

Date	Item	Post. Ref.	Debit	Credit	Balance Debit	Balance Credit
April 30		27		1 7 2 0 00		1 7 2 0 00
30		28		5 1 4 5 00		6 8 6 5 00

ACCOUNT *Salary Expense*   **ACCOUNT NO. 51**

Date	Item	Post. Ref.	Debit	Credit	Balance Debit	Balance Credit
April 30		28	1 7 2 5 00		1 7 2 5 00	

ACCOUNT *Rent Expense*   **ACCOUNT NO. 53**

Date	Item	Post. Ref.	Debit	Credit	Balance Debit	Balance Credit
April 1		27	8 0 0 00		8 0 0 00	

ACCOUNT *Laboratory Expense*   **ACCOUNT NO. 55**

Date	Item	Post. Ref.	Debit	Credit	Balance Debit	Balance Credit
April 24		27	5 4 5 00		5 4 5 00	

ACCOUNT *Utilities Expense*   **ACCOUNT NO. 56**

Date	Item	Post. Ref.	Debit	Credit	Balance Debit	Balance Credit
April 30		28	3 6 0 00		3 6 0 00	

ACCOUNT *Miscellaneous Expense*   **ACCOUNT NO. 59**

Date	Item	Post. Ref.	Debit	Credit	Balance Debit	Balance Credit
April 30		28	1 3 2 00		1 3 2 00	

4.

J. F. Outz, M.D. Trial Balance April 30, 20—		
Cash	2 3 6 1 00	
Accounts Receivable	8 7 2 0 00	
Supplies	5 3 5 00	
Prepaid Insurance	8 3 5 00	
Equipment	21 5 2 0 00	
Accounts Payable		1 3 3 5 00
J. F. Outz, Capital		30 5 8 3 00
J. F. Outz, Withdrawals	1 2 5 0 00	
Professional Fees Revenue		6 8 6 5 00
Salary Expense	1 7 2 5 00	
Rent Expense	8 0 0 00	
Laboratory Expense	5 4 5 00	
Utilities Expense	3 6 0 00	
Miscellaneous Expense	1 3 2 00	
	38 7 8 3 00	38 7 8 3 00

SELF-EXAMINATION QUESTIONS (ANSWERS AT END OF CHAPTER)

1. A debit may signify:
   A. an increase in an asset account
   B. a decrease in an asset account
   C. an increase in a liability account
   D. an increase in the owner's capital account

2. The type of account with a normal credit balance is:
   A. an asset　　　　C. a revenue
   B. withdrawals　　D. an expense

3. A debit balance in which of the following accounts would indicate a likely error?
   A. Accounts Receivable　C. Revenue Earned
   B. Cash　　　　　　　　D. Miscellaneous Expense

4. The receipt of cash from customers in payment of their accounts would be recorded by a:
   A. debit to Cash; credit to Accounts Receivable
   B. debit to Accounts Receivable; credit to Cash
   C. debit to Cash; credit to Accounts Payable
   D. debit to Accounts Payable; credit to Cash

5. The form listing the titles and balances of the accounts in the ledger on a given date is the:
   A. income statement　　C. statement of owner's equity
   B. balance sheet　　　　D. trial balance

DISCUSSION QUESTIONS

1. What is an account?
2. Differentiate between an account and a ledger.
3. What is the name of the listing of accounts in the ledger?
4. Describe in general terms the sequence of accounts in the ledger.
5. Do the terms *debit* and *credit* signify increase or decrease, or may they signify either? Explain.
6. What is the name of the record in which a transaction is initially entered?

7. Define posting.
8. Explain why the rules of debit and credit are the same for liability accounts and owner's equity accounts.
9. What is the effect (increase or decrease) of debits to expense accounts (a) in terms of owner's equity and (b) in terms of expense?
10. What is the effect (increase or decrease) of credits to revenue accounts (a) in terms of owner's equity and (b) in terms of revenue?
11. Liebrandt Company adheres to a policy of depositing all cash receipts in a bank account and making all payments by cheque. The cash account as of June 30 has a credit balance of $575, and there is no undeposited cash on hand. (a) Assuming that there were no errors in journalizing or posting, what is the explanation of this unusual balance? (b) Is the $575 credit balance in the cash account an asset, a liability, owner's equity, a revenue, or an expense?
12. Rearrange the following in proper sequence: (a) entry is posted to ledger, (b) business transaction occurs, (c) entry is recorded in journal, (d) business document is prepared, (e) business transaction is authorized.
13. Describe the three procedures required to post the credit portion of the following journal entry (Revenue Earned is account no. 41):

	JOURNAL				PAGE 32
Date	**Description**	**Post. Ref.**	**Debit**	**Credit**	
1	June 11	Accounts Receivable	12	8 7 5 00		1
2		Revenue Earned			8 7 5 00	2
3						3

14. When you examine an entry that has been recorded in the journal, what indicates that the entry has been posted to the accounts?
15. Justice Company performed services in June for a specific customer, and the fee was $6,200. Payment was received the following July. (a) Was the revenue earned in June or July? (b) What accounts should be debited and credited in (1) June and (2) July?
16. a.   Describe the form known as a trial balance.
    b.   What proof is provided by a trial balance?
17. If the two totals of a trial balance are equal, does it mean that there are no errors in the accounting records? Explain.
18. Assume that a trial balance is prepared with an account balance of $36,750 listed as $3,675 and an account balance of $4,500 listed as $5,400. Identify the transposition and the slide.
19. When a purchase of supplies of $690 for cash was recorded, both the debit and the credit were journalized and posted as $960. (a) Would this error cause the trial balance to be out of balance? (b) Would the answer be the same if the $690 entry had been journalized correctly, but the credit to Cash had been posted as $960?
20. How is a correction made when an error in an account title or amount in the journal is discovered before the entry is posted?
21. In journalizing and posting the entry to record the purchase of supplies on account, the bookkeeper credited accounts receivable account in error. What is the preferred procedure to correct the error?
22. Banks rely heavily upon customers' deposits as a source of funds. Demand deposits normally pay interest to the customer, who is entitled to withdraw at any time without prior notice to the bank. Chequing accounts are the most common form of demand deposits for banks. Assume that The Exquisite Company has a chequing account at the Bank of Montreal. What type of account (asset, liability, owner's equity, revenue, expense, drawing) does the account balance of $8,500 represent from the viewpoint of (a) The Exquisite Company and (b) the Bank of Montreal?

EXERCISES

EXERCISE 2–1
Chart of accounts
Objective 1

Maurice Interiors is owned and operated by Maurice Katz, an interior decorator. In the ledger of Maurice Interiors, the first digit of the account number indicates its major account classification (1—assets, 2—liabilities, 3—owner's equity, 4—revenues, 5—expenses). The second digit of the account number indicates the specific account within each of the preceding major account classifications.

Match each of the following account numbers with its most likely account in the list below.

Account Numbers: 11, 12, 13, 21, 31, 32, 41, 51, 52, 53

Accounts:

Accounts Payable	Maurice Katz, Capital
Accounts Receivable	Maurice Katz, Withdrawals
Cash	Miscellaneous Expense
Revenue Earned	Supplies Expense
Land	Wages Expense

EXERCISE 2–2
Chart of accounts
Objective 1

The Charm Shop is a newly organized business that teaches young people how to behave in a socially acceptable way. The list of accounts to be opened in the general ledger is as follows:

Accounts Payable	Miscellaneous Expense
Accounts Receivable	Prepaid Insurance
Anni Vogel, Capital	Rent Expense
Anni Vogel, Withdrawals	Supplies
Cash	Supplies Expense
Equipment	Unearned Rent
Revenue Earned	Wages Expense

List the accounts in the order in which they should appear in the ledger of The Charm Shop and assign account numbers. Each account number is to have two digits: the first digit is to indicate the major classification (*1* for assets, etc.), and the second digit is to identify the specific account within each major classification (*11* for Cash, etc.).

EXERCISE 2–3
Identifying transactions
Objectives 2, 3

Pioneer Co. is a travel agency. Pioneer recorded nine transactions during April, its first month of operations, as indicated in the following T accounts:

Cash			Supplies		Accounts Payable	
(1) 20,000	(2) 2,500		(2) 2,500	(9) 1,450	(6) 6,000	(3) 12,000
(7) 9,500	(3) 3,000					
	(4) 2,725					
	(6) 6,000					
	(8) 2,500					

Accounts Receivable		Equipment		John Cabot, Capital	
(5) 12,500	(7) 9,500	(3) 15,000			(1) 20,000

John Cabot, Withdrawals		Service Revenue		Operating Expenses	
(8) 2,500			(5) 12,500	(4) 2,725	
				(9) 1,450	

Indicate for each debit and each credit: (a) whether an asset, liability, owner's equity, drawing, revenue, or expense account was affected and (b) whether the account was increased (+) or decreased (–). Present your answers in the following form [transaction (1) is given as an example]:

| | Account Debited | | Account Credited | |
Transaction	Type	Effect	Type	Effect
(1)	asset	+	owner's equity	+

EXERCISE 2–4
Journal entries
Objectives 3, 4

Based upon the T accounts in Exercise 2–3, prepare the nine journal entries from which the postings were made.

EXERCISE 2–5
Trial balance
Objective 5

Based upon the data presented in Exercise 2–3, prepare a trial balance, listing the accounts in their proper order.

EXERCISE 2–6
Normal entries for accounts
Objective 3

During the month, City Labs Co. has a substantial number of transactions affecting each of the following accounts. State for each account whether it is likely to have (a) debit entries only, (b) credit entries only, or (c) both debit and credit entries.

1. Revenue Earned
2. Cash
3. Miscellaneous Expense
4. Accounts Payable

5. Beth Wilson, Withdrawals
6. Accounts Receivable
7. Supplies Expense

EXERCISE 2–7
Normal balances of accounts
Objective 3

Identify each of the following accounts of Guillermo Services Co. as asset, liability, owner's equity, revenue, or expense, and state in each case whether the normal balance is a debit or a credit.

a. Accounts Payable
b. Equipment
c. Salary Expense
d. E. F. Guillermo, Withdrawals
e. Cash

f. Accounts Receivable
g. Revenue Earned
h. E. F. Guillermo, Capital
i. Supplies
j. Rent Expense

EXERCISE 2–8
Rules of debit and credit
Objective 3

The following table summarizes the rules of debit and credit. For each of the items (a) through (l), indicate whether the proper answer is a debit or a credit.

	Increase	Decrease	Normal Balance
Balance sheet accounts:			
Asset	Debit	Credit	(a)
Liability	(b)	(c)	(d)
Owner's Equity:			
Capital	Credit	(e)	(f)
Withdrawals	(g)	(h)	Debit
Income statement accounts:			
Revenue	Credit	(i)	(j)
Expense	(k)	Credit	(l)

EXERCISE 2–9
Capital account balance
Objective 2

As of January, 1, Karen Kahan, Capital had a credit balance of $12,000. During the year, withdrawals totalled $10,000 and the business incurred a net loss of $5,000.

a. Calculate the balance of Karen Kahan, Capital as of the end of the year.
b. ▬► Assuming that there have been no recording errors, will the balance sheet prepared at December 31 balance? Explain.

EXERCISE 2–10
Cash account balance
Objective 2

During the month, a business received $597,500 in cash and paid out $525,000 in cash.

a. ▬► Do the data indicate that the business earned $72,500 during the month? Explain.
b. If the balance of the cash account was $41,300 at the beginning of the month, what was the cash balance at the end of the month?

EXERCISE 2–11
Account balances
Objective 2

a. On March 1, the cash account balance was $8,750. During March, cash receipts totalled $16,500 and the March 31 balance was $11,150. Determine the cash payments made during March.
b. On March 1, the accounts receivable account balance was $23,900. During March, $21,000 was received from customers on account. If the March 31 balance was $27,500, determine the fees billed to customers on account during March.
c. During March, $40,500 was paid to creditors on account and purchases on account were $57,700. If the March 31 balance of Accounts Payable was $45,000, determine the account balance on March 1.

EXERCISE 2–12
Transactions
Objectives 3, 4

The Wildlife Co. has the following accounts in its ledger: Cash; Accounts Receivable; Supplies; Office Equipment; Accounts Payable; Jay Wren, Capital; Jay Wren, Withdrawals; Revenue Earned; Rent Expense; Advertising Expense; Utilities Expense; Miscellaneous Expense.

Journalize the following selected transactions in a two-column journal:

May 1. Paid rent for the month, $2,500.
      2. Paid advertising expense, $500.
      4. Paid cash for supplies, $770.
      5. Purchased office equipment on account, $7,200.
      8. Received cash from customers on account, $3,600.
     12. Paid creditor on account, $2,150.
     15. Withdrew cash for personal use, $1,000.
     25. Paid cash for repairs to office equipment, $120.
     30. Paid telephone bill for the month, $195.
     31. Fees earned and billed to customers for the month, $11,150.
     31. Paid electricity bill for the month, $430.

EXERCISE 2–13
Journalizing and posting
Objectives 3, 4

On April 2, 1999, Magnetic Co. purchased $3,150 of supplies on account. In Magnetic Co.'s chart of accounts, the supplies account is No. 15 and the accounts payable account is No. 21.

a. Journalize the April 2, 1999 transaction on page 10 of Magnetic Co.'s two-column journal. Include an explanation of the entry.
b. Prepare a four-column account for Supplies. Enter a debit balance of $2,200 as of April 2, 1999. Place a check mark (✓) in the posting reference column.
c. Prepare a four-column account for Accounts Payable. Enter a credit balance of $11,734 as of April 2, 1999. Place a check mark (✓) in the posting reference column.
d. Post the April 2, 1999 transaction to the accounts.

EXERCISE 2–14
Transactions and T accounts
Objectives 2, 3, 4

The following selected transactions were completed during February of the current year:

1. Billed customers for fees earned, $3,210.
2. Purchased supplies on account, $520.
3. Received cash from customers on account, $2,100.
4. Paid creditors on account, $400.

a. Journalize the foregoing transactions in a two-column journal, using the appropriate number to identify the transactions.
b. Post the entries prepared in (a) to the following T accounts: Cash, Supplies, Accounts Receivable, Accounts Payable, Revenue Earned. To the left of each amount posted in the accounts, place the appropriate number to identify the transactions.

EXERCISE 2–15
Trial balance
Objective 5

The accounts in the ledger of Asbury Park Co. as of March 31 of the current year are listed in alphabetical order as follows. All accounts have normal balances. The balance of the cash account has been intentionally omitted.

Accounts Payable	$ 13,710	Notes Payable	$ 27,000
Accounts Receivable	10,500	Prepaid Insurance	3,150
Cash	?	Rent Expense	48,000
Bob Dillon, Capital	110,290	Supplies	4,100
Bob Dillon, Withdrawals	18,000	Supplies Expense	5,900
Revenue Earned	315,000	Unearned Rent	4,000
Insurance Expense	5,000	Utilities Expense	41,500
Land	125,000	Wages Expense	190,000
Miscellaneous Expense	9,900		

Prepare a trial balance, listing the accounts in their proper order and inserting the missing figure for cash.

EXERCISE 2–16
Effect of errors on trial balance
Objective 5

Indicate which of the following errors, each considered individually, would cause the trial balance totals to be unequal:

a. A payment of $950 to a creditor was posted as a debit of $950 to Accounts Payable and a debit of $590 to Cash.

b. Payment of a cash withdrawal of $2,000 was journalized and posted as a debit of $200 to Salary Expense and a credit of $200 to Cash.

c. A payment of $5,000 for equipment purchased was posted as a debit of $5,000 to Equipment and a credit of $50,000 to Cash.

d. A receipt of $500 from an account receivable was journalized and posted as a debit of $500 to Cash and a credit of $500 to Revenue Earned.

e. A fee of $2,500 earned and due from a client was not debited to Accounts Receivable or credited to a revenue account, because the cash had not been received.

EXERCISE 2–17
Errors in trial balance
Objective 5

The following preliminary trial balance of O.K. Resales, a sports ticket agency, does not balance:

O.K. Resales
Trial Balance
December 31, 20—

Cash	83,000	
Accounts Receivable	26,200	
Prepaid Insurance		3,300
Equipment	4,500	
Accounts Payable		10,050
Unearned Rent		1,480
Earl Grey, Capital	68,550	
Earl Grey, Withdrawals	10,000	
Service Revenue		64,940
Wages Expense		33,400
Advertising Expense	5,200	
Miscellaneous Expense		1,380
	197,450	114,550

When you review the ledger and other records, you discover the following: (1) the debits and credits in the cash account total $83,000 and $65,300, respectively; (2) a billing of $1,100 to a customer on account was not posted to the accounts receivable account; (3) a payment of $2,100 made to a creditor on account was not posted to the accounts payable account; (4) the balance of the unearned rent account is $1,840; (5) the correct balance of the equipment account is $45,000; and (6) each account has a normal balance. Prepare a corrected trial balance.

EXERCISE 2–18
Effect of errors on trial balance
Objective 5

The following errors occurred in posting from a general journal:

1. A credit of $250 to Cash was posted as $520.
2. A debit of $1,200 to Supplies was posted twice.
3. A credit of $500 to Accounts Payable was posted as a debit.
4. A debit of $1,000 to Cash was posted to Wages Expense.
5. An entry debiting Accounts Receivable and crediting Revenue Earned for $4,500 was not posted.
6. A debit of $1,575 to Wages Expense was posted as $1,755.
7. A credit of $1,130 to Accounts Receivable was not posted.

Considering each case individually (i.e., assuming that no other errors had occurred), indicate: (a) by "yes" or "no" whether the trial balance would be out of balance; (b) if the answer to (a) is "yes," the amount by which the trial balance totals would differ; and (c) whether the debit or credit column of the trial balance would have the larger total. Answers should be presented in the following form [error (1) is given as an example]:

Error	(a) Out of Balance	(b) Difference	(c) Larger Total
1.	yes	$270	credit

EXERCISE 2–19
Errors in trial balance
Objective 5

How many errors can you find in the following trial balance? All accounts have normal balances.

J. Kelly, Interior Decorator
Trial Balance
For the Month Ending July 31, 20—

Cash	3,010	
Accounts Receivable		16,400
Prepaid Insurance	2,400	
Equipment	41,200	
Accounts Payable	1,850	
Salaries Payable		750
J. Kelly, Capital		34,600
J. Kelly, Withdrawals		5,000
Service Revenue	67,900	
Salary Expense	28,400	
Advertising Expense	7,200	
Miscellaneous Expense	1,490	
	153,450	153,450

EXERCISE 2–20
Entries to correct errors
Objective 6

Errors in journalizing and posting transactions are described as follows:

a. A withdrawal of $2,000 by J. Madden, owner of the business, was recorded as a debit to Miscellaneous Expense and a credit to Cash.
b. Rent of $1,800 paid for the current month was recorded as a debit to Accounts Payable and a credit to cash.

Journalize the entries to correct the errors.

EXERCISE 2–21
Entries to correct errors
Objective 6

Errors in journalizing and posting transactions are described as follows:

a. A $750 purchase of supplies on account was recorded as a debit to Cash and a credit to Accounts Payable.
b. Cash of $1,350 received on account was recorded as a debit to Accounts Payable and a credit to Cash.

Journalize the entries to correct the errors.

PROBLEMS SERIES A

PROBLEM 2–1A
Entries into T accounts and trial balance
Objectives 2, 3, 5

David Colletti, an architect, opened an office on August 1 of the current year. During the month, he completed the following transactions connected with his professional practice:

a. Transferred cash from a personal bank account to an account to be used for the business, $20,000.
b. Paid August rent for office and workroom, $2,500.
c. Purchased used automobile for $11,500, paying $2,500 cash and giving a non-interest-bearing note for the remainder.
d. Purchased office and drafting room equipment on account, $6,000.
e. Paid cash for supplies, $900.
f. Paid cash for insurance policies, $1,050.
g. Received cash from client for plans delivered, $3,100.
h. Paid cash for miscellaneous services, $75.
i. Paid cash to creditors on account, $3,000.
j. Paid installment due on note payable, $400.
k. Received invoice for blueprint service, due in September, $310.
l. Recorded revenue earned on plans delivered, payment to be received in September, $4,150.
m. Paid salary of assistant, $1,250.
n. Paid gas, oil, and repairs on automobile for August, $115.

Instructions

1. Record the foregoing transactions directly in the following T accounts, without journalizing: Cash; Accounts Receivable; Supplies; Prepaid Insurance; Automobiles; Equipment; Notes Payable; Accounts Payable; David Colletti, Capital; Professional Revenue Earned; Rent Expense; Salary Expense; Automobile Expense; Blueprint Expense; Miscellaneous Expense. To the left of the amount entered in the accounts, place the appropriate letter to identify the transaction.
2. Determine the balances of the T accounts having two or more debits or credits. A memorandum balance should be inserted in accounts having both debits and credits, in the manner illustrated in the chapter. For accounts with entries on one side only (such as Professional Revenue Earned), there is no need to insert the memorandum balance in the item column. For accounts containing only a single debit and a single credit (such as Notes Payable), the memorandum balance should be inserted in the appropriate item column. Accounts containing a single entry only (such as Prepaid Insurance) do not need a memorandum balance.
3. Prepare a trial balance for David Colletti, Architect, as of August 31 of the current year.

PROBLEM 2–2A
Journal entries and trial balance
Objectives 2, 3, 5

On July 1 of the current year, Diane Nehring established Oasis Realty, which completed the following transactions during July:

a. Diane Nehring transferred cash from her personal bank account to an account to be used for the business, $15,000.
b. Paid rent on office and equipment for the month, $3,500.
c. Purchased supplies on account, $1,500.
d. Paid creditor on account, $900.
e. Earned sales commissions, receiving cash, $19,750.
f. Paid automobile expenses (including rental charge) for month, $2,900, and miscellaneous expenses, $1,250.
g. Paid office salaries, $3,000.
h. Determined that the cost of supplies used was $1,125.
i. Withdrew cash for personal use, $1,000.

Instructions

1. Journalize entries for transactions (a) through (i), using the following account titles: Cash; Supplies; Accounts Payable; Diane Nehring, Capital; Diane Nehring, Withdrawals; Sales Commissions; Office Salaries Expense; Rent Expense; Automobile Expense; Supplies Expense; Miscellaneous Expense.

2. Prepare T accounts, using the account titles in (1). Post the journal entries to these accounts, placing the appropriate letter to the left of each amount to identify the transactions. Determine the account balances, after all posting is complete, for all accounts having two or more debits or credits. A memorandum balance should also be inserted in accounts having both debits and credits, in the manner illustrated in the chapter. For accounts with entries on one side only, there is no need to insert a memorandum balance in the item column. For accounts containing only a single debit and a single credit, the memorandum balance should be inserted in the appropriate item column.
3. Prepare a trial balance as of July 31, 20—.
4. Determine the following:
   a. Amount of total revenue recorded in the ledger.
   b. Amount of total expenses recorded in the ledger.
   c. Amount of net income for July.

PROBLEM 2–3A
Journal entries and trial balance
Objectives 3, 4, 5

On June 5 of the current year, Nezar Rghei established a sole proprietorship to be known as Progressive Designs. During the remainder of the month, Nezar completed the following transactions related to his interior decorating business:

June 5. Nezar transferred cash from a personal bank account to an account to be used for the business, $15,000.
        5. Paid rent for period of June 5 to end of month, $1,950.
        7. Purchased office equipment on account, $6,250.
        8. Purchased a used truck for $16,000, paying $9,500 cash and giving a note payable for the remainder.
      10. Purchased supplies for cash, $725.
      12. Received cash for job completed, $1,600.
      15. Paid wages of employees, $800.
      20. Paid premiums on property and casualty insurance, $725.
      22. Recorded jobs completed on account and sent invoices to customers, $1,950.
      24. Received an invoice for truck expenses, to be paid in July, $310.
      26. Received cash for job completed, $1,650. This job had not been recorded previously.
      28. Purchased supplies on account, $590.
      29. Paid utilities expense, $490.
      29. Paid miscellaneous expenses, $195.
      30. Received cash from customers on account, $1,200.
      30. Paid wages of employees, $1,200.
      30. Paid creditor a portion of the amount owed for equipment purchased on June 7, $1,500.
      30. Withdrew cash for personal use, $500.

Instructions

1. Journalize each transaction in a general journal, referring to the following chart of accounts in selecting the accounts to be debited and credited. (Do not insert the account numbers in the journal at this time.)

11 Cash	31 Nezar Rghei, Capital
12 Accounts Receivable	32 Nezar Rghei, Withdrawals
13 Supplies	41 Revenue Earned
14 Prepaid Insurance	51 Wages Expense
16 Equipment	53 Rent Expense
18 Truck	54 Utilities Expense
21 Notes Payable	55 Truck Expense
22 Accounts Payable	59 Miscellaneous Expense

2. Post the journal to a ledger of four-column accounts, inserting appropriate posting references as each item is posted. Extend the balances to the appropriate balance columns after each transaction is posted.
3. Prepare a trial balance for Progressive Designs as of June 30.

PROBLEM 2–4A
Journal entries and trial balance
Objectives 3, 4, 5

Reynalds Realty acts as an agent in buying, selling, renting, and managing real estate. The account balances at the end of March of the current year are as follows:

11	Cash	26,150	
12	Accounts Receivable	38,750	
13	Prepaid Insurance	1,100	
14	Office Supplies	715	
16	Land	0	
21	Accounts Payable		11,175
22	Notes Payable		0
31	K. Hamlet, Capital		39,840
32	K. Hamlet, Withdrawals	1,000	
41	Revenue Earned		124,500
51	Salary and Commission Expense	94,100	
52	Rent Expense	5,500	
53	Advertising Expense	3,900	
54	Automobile Expense	2,750	
59	Miscellaneous Expense	1,550	
		175,515	175,515

The following business transactions were completed by Reynalds Realty during April of the current year:

April 1. Paid rent on office for month, $2,500.
3. Purchased office supplies on account, $1,375.
5. Paid insurance premiums, $1,650.
7. Received cash from clients on account, $28,200.
15. Paid salaries and commissions for the first half of the month, $16,650.
15. Purchased land for a future building site for $45,000, paying $15,000 in cash and giving a note payable for the remainder.
15. Recorded revenue earned and billed to clients during first half of month, $20,100.
18. Paid creditors on account, $7,150.
20. Returned a portion of the office supplies purchased on April 3, receiving full credit for their cost, $275.
23. Received cash from clients on account, $16,700.
24. Paid advertising expense, $1,550.
27. Discovered an error in computing a commission; received cash from the salesperson for the overpayment, $350.
28. Paid automobile expense (including rental charges for an automobile), $715.
29. Paid miscellaneous expenses, $215.
30. Recorded revenue earned and billed to clients during second half of the month, $18,300.
30. Paid salaries and commissions for the second half of the month, $19,850.
30. Withdrew cash for personal use, $2,500.

Instructions

1. Record the April 1 balance of each account in the appropriate balance column of a four-column account, write *Balance* in the item section, and place a check mark (✓) in the posting reference column.
2. Journalize the transactions for April in a general journal.
3. Post to the ledger, extending the account balance to the appropriate balance column after each posting.
4. Prepare a trial balance of the ledger as of April 30.

PROBLEM 2–5A
Corrected trial balance
Objectives 5, 6

Anatole Carpet Installation, a sole proprietorship, has the following trial balance as of March 31 of the current year:

Cash	3,570	
Accounts Receivable	6,150	
Supplies	1,010	
Prepaid Insurance	250	
Equipment	15,500	
Notes Payable		5,000
Accounts Payable		4,620
Isham Anatole, Capital		15,300
Isham Anatole, Withdrawals	7,000	
Revenue Earned		49,980
Wages Expense	28,500	
Rent Expense	6,400	
Advertising Expense	320	
Miscellaneous Expense	945	
	69,645	74,900

The debit and credit totals are not equal as a result of the following errors:

a. The balance of cash was overstated by $750.
b. A cash receipt of $2,100 was posted as a debit to Cash of $1,200.
c. A debit of $1,000 for a withdrawal by the owner was posted as a credit to Isham Anatole, Capital.
d. The balance of $3,200 in Advertising Expense was entered as $320 in the trial balance.
e. A debit of $975 to Accounts Receivable was not posted.
f. A return of $125 of defective supplies was erroneously posted as a $215 credit to Supplies.
g. The balance of Notes Payable was understated by $5,000.
h. An insurance policy acquired at a cost of $150 was posted as a credit to Prepaid Insurance.
i. Gas, Electricity, and Water Expense, with a balance of $3,150, was omitted from the trial balance.
j. A debit of $710 in Accounts Payable was overlooked when determining the balance of the account.

Instructions

1. Prepare a corrected trial balance as of March 31 of the current year.
2. ▬▬➤ Does the fact that the trial balance in (1) is balanced mean that there are no errors in the accounts? Explain.

PROBLEMS SERIES B

PROBLEM 2–1B
Entries into T accounts and trial balance
Objectives 2, 3, 5

Simone Dion, a marketing consultant, opened an office on June 1 of the current year. During the month, she completed the following transactions connected with her professional practice:

a. Transferred cash from a personal bank account to an account to be used for her business, $25,000.
b. Purchased used automobile for $18,300, paying $5,300 cash and giving a non-interest-bearing note for the remainder.
c. Paid June rent for office, $2,200.
d. Paid cash for supplies, $225.
e. Purchased office equipment on account, $4,200.
f. Paid cash for insurance policies on automobile and equipment, $810.
g. Received cash from a client for plans delivered, $2,725.
h. Paid cash to creditors on account, $2,100.
i. Paid cash for miscellaneous expenses, $65.
j. Received invoice for office cleaning and maintenance, due in following month, $275.
k. Recorded fee earned on plans delivered, payment to be received in July, $3,500.
l. Paid salary of assistant, $1,500.
m. Paid cash for miscellaneous expenses, $68.

n. Paid installment due on note payable, $500.
o. Paid gas, oil, and repairs on automobile for June, $170.

Instructions

1. Record the foregoing transactions directly in the following T accounts, without journalizing: Cash; Accounts Receivable; Supplies; Prepaid Insurance; Automobiles; Equipment; Notes Payable; Accounts Payable; Simone Dion, Capital; Professional Revenue Earned; Rent Expense; Salary Expense; Automobile Expense; Maintenance Expense; Miscellaneous Expense. To the left of each amount entered in the accounts, place the appropriate letter to identify the transaction.
2. Determine the balances of the T accounts having two or more debits or credits. A memorandum balance should be inserted in accounts having both debits and credits, in the manner illustrated in the chapter. For accounts with entries on one side only (such as Professional Revenue Earned), there is no need to insert the memorandum balance in the item column. For accounts containing only a single debit and a single credit (such as Notes Payable), the memorandum balance should be inserted in the appropriate item column. Accounts containing a single entry only (such as Prepaid Insurance) do not need a memorandum balance.
3. Prepare a trial balance for Simone Dion, Consultant, as of June 30 of the current year.

PROBLEM 2–2B
Journal entries and trial balance
Objectives 2, 3, 5

On March 1 of the current year, Augie Ackman established Ace Financial Planning Services, which completed the following transactions during the month:

a. Augie Ackman transferred cash from his personal bank account to an account to be used for the business, $10,000.
b. Purchased supplies on account, $2,900.
c. Paid creditor on account, $1,000.
d. Paid rent on office and equipment for the month, $5,500.
e. Earned service revenue, receiving cash, $21,500.
f. Withdrew cash for personal use, $1,000.
g. Paid automobile expenses (including rental charge) for month, $1,900, and miscellaneous expenses, $1,050.
h. Paid office salaries, $4,000.
i. Determined that the cost of supplies used was $1,250.

Instructions

1. Journalize entries for transactions (a) through (i), using the following account titles: Cash; Supplies; Accounts Payable; Augie Ackman, Capital; Augie Ackman, Withdrawals; Sales Commissions; Rent Expense; Office Salaries Expense; Automobile Expense; Supplies Expense; Miscellaneous Expense.
2. Prepare T accounts, using the account titles in (1). Post the journal entries to these accounts, placing the appropriate letter to the left of each amount to identify the transactions. Determine the account balances, after all posting is complete, for all accounts having two or more debits or credits. A memorandum balance should be inserted in accounts having both debits and credits, in the manner illustrated in the chapter. For accounts with entries on one side only, there is no need to insert a memorandum balance in the item column. For accounts containing only a single debit and a single credit, the memorandum balance should be inserted in the appropriate item column.
3. Prepare a trial balance as of March 31, 20—.
4. Determine the following:
    a. Amount of total revenue recorded in the ledger.
    b. Amount of total expenses recorded in the ledger.
    c. Amount of net income for March.

PROBLEM 2–3B
Journal entries and trial balance
Objectives 3, 4, 5

On July 10 of the current year, Cecile Montoya, an architect, established a sole proprietorship. During the remainder of the month, Montoya completed the following transactions related to her business:

July 10. Cecile transferred cash from a personal bank account to an account to be used for the business, $20,000.

10. Paid rent for period of July 10 to end of month, $900.
11. Purchased a truck for $15,000, paying $7,000 cash and giving a note payable for the remainder.
12. Purchased equipment on account, $3,700.
14. Purchased supplies for cash, $885.
14. Paid premiums on property and casualty insurance, $750.
15. Received cash for job completed, $1,200.
16. Purchased supplies on account, $1,240.
17. Paid wages of employees, $600.
21. Paid creditor for equipment purchased on July 12, $3,700.
24. Recorded jobs completed on account and sent invoices to customers, $3,100.
26. Received an invoice for truck expenses, to be paid in August, $225.
26. Received cash for job completed, $1,050. This job had not been recorded previously.
27. Paid utilities expense, $1,205.
27. Paid miscellaneous expenses, $173.
28. Received cash from customers on account, $1,420.
31. Paid wages of employees, $1,350.
31. Withdrew cash for personal use, $1,500.

Instructions

1. Journalize each transaction in a two-column journal, referring to the following chart of accounts in selecting the accounts to be debited and credited. (Do not insert the account numbers in the journal at this time.)

11 Cash	31 Cecile Montoya, Capital
12 Accounts Receivable	32 Cecile Montoya, Withdrawals
13 Supplies	41 Revenue Earned
14 Prepaid Insurance	51 Wages Expense
16 Equipment	53 Rent Expense
18 Truck	54 Utilities Expense
21 Notes Payable	55 Truck Expense
22 Accounts Payable	59 Miscellaneous Expense

2. Post the journal to a ledger of four-column accounts, inserting appropriate posting references as each item is posted. Extend the balances to the appropriate balance columns after each transaction is posted.
3. Prepare a trial balance for Cecile Montoya, Architect, as of July 31.

PROBLEM 2–4B
Journal entries and trial balance
Objectives 3, 4, 5

Macbeth Realty acts as an agent in buying, selling, renting, and managing real estate. The account balances at the end of April of the current year are as follows:

11 Cash	29,500	
12 Accounts Receivable	38,600	
13 Prepaid Insurance	750	
14 Office Supplies	625	
16 Land	0	
21 Accounts Payable		13,250
22 Notes Payable		0
31 K. Lear, Capital		63,025
32 K. Lear, Withdrawals	10,000	
41 Fees Earned		157,750
51 Salary and Commission Expense	122,100	
52 Rent Expense	19,000	
53 Advertising Expense	8,900	
54 Automobile Expense	3,950	
59 Miscellaneous Expense	600	
	234,025	234,025

The following business transactions were completed by Macbeth Realty during May of the current year:

May 1: Paid rent on office for month, $2,500.
    2. Purchased office supplies on account, $925.
    3. Paid insurance premiums, $1,925.
    9. Received cash from clients on account, $19,500.
   15. Paid salaries and commissions for the first half of the month, $20,650.
   15. Purchased land for a future building site for $60,000, paying $10,000 in cash and giving a note payable for the remainder.
   15. Recorded revenue earned and billed to clients during first half of month, $30,900.
   18. Paid creditors on account, $7,650.
   20. Returned a portion of the office supplies purchased on May 2, receiving full credit for their cost, $150.
   29. Received cash from clients on account, $28,200.
   29. Paid advertising expense, $2,150.
   29. Discovered an error in computing a commission; received cash from the salesperson for the overpayment, $500.
   30. Paid automobile expense (including rental charges for an automobile), $850.
   30. Paid miscellaneous expenses, $215.
   31. Recorded revenue earned and billed to clients during the second half of the month, $15,300.
   31. Paid salaries and commissions for the second half of the month, $20,850.
   31. Withdrew cash for personal use, $5,000.

Instructions

1. Record the May 1 balance of each account in the appropriate balance column of a four-column account, write *Balance* in the item section, and place a check mark (✓) in the posting reference column.
2. Journalize the transactions for May in a two-column journal.
3. Post to the ledger, extending the account balance to the appropriate balance column after each posting.
4. Prepare a trial balance of the ledger as of May 31.

PROBLEM 2–5B
Corrected trial balance
Objectives 5, 6

Halpern Photography, a sole proprietorship, has the following trial balance as of December 31 of the current year:

Cash	5,225	
Accounts Receivable	9,350	
Supplies	1,277	
Prepaid Insurance	330	
Equipment	12,500	
Notes Payable		10,000
Accounts Payable		3,025
Jennifer Halpern, Capital		12,540
Jennifer Halpern, Withdrawals	6,700	
Revenue Earned		80,750
Wages Expense	48,150	
Rent Expense	750	
Advertising Expense	5,250	
Gas, Electricity, and Water Expense	3,150	
	92,682	106,315

The debit and credit totals are not equal as a result of the following errors:

a. The opening balance of cash was understated by $1,500.
b. A cash receipt of $1,200 was posted as a debit to Cash of $2,100.
c. A debit of $750 to Accounts Receivable was not posted.
d. A return of $252 of defective supplies was erroneously posted as a $225 credit to Supplies.
e. An insurance policy acquired at a cost of $310 was posted as a credit to Prepaid Insurance.
f. The balance of Notes Payable was overstated by $2,500.
g. A credit of $75 in Accounts Payable was overlooked when the balance of the account was determined.

h. A debit of $800 for a withdrawal by the owner was posted as a credit to Jennifer Halpern, Capital.
i. The balance of $7,500 in Rent Expense was entered as $750 in the trial balance.
j. Miscellaneous Expense, with a balance of $915, was omitted from the trial balance.

Instructions

1. Prepare a corrected trial balance as of December 31 of the current year.
2. ◖▬▶ Does the fact that the trial balance in (1) is balanced mean that there are no errors in the accounts? Explain.

CHALLENGE PROBLEMS

PROBLEM CP2–1

During your audit of Tremark (which has been in business for several years), you discover the following errors were made during the year ended December 31, 1999. Complete the following table to indicate the effect of each error (O = overstate, U = understate, NE = no effect) on 1999 total assets, total liabilities, and owner's equity at the end of 1999. Indicate the dollar amount of the effect in each case.

Error	Total Assets	Total Liabilities	Owner's Equity
a. Both sides of a journal entry to record $540 cash received for service revenue were recorded as $450.	U $90	NE	U $90
b. Recorded $3,000 payment for prepaid rent as a debit to salary expense.			
c. Both sides of a journal entry to record $6,000 of supplies purchased on account on Dec. 31 were recorded as $600.			
d. Recorded $600 payment of account payable by debiting accounts payable and crediting supplies expense.			
e. A $500 withdrawal by the owner was recorded as salary expense.			
f. Bookkeeper forgot to make a journal entry to record utilities expense payable of $350.			
g. $380 cash payment received for an accounts receivable was posted to both accounts as $830.			

PROBLEM CP2–2

You are given the following account balances for Trelevan Designs at the end of the current year:

Trelevan, Capital	30,000
Supplies Expense	1,600
Land	20,000
Accounts Payable	800
Wage Expense	9,550
Revenue Earned	32,680
Trelevan, Withdrawals	8,000
Supplies	5,200
Miscellaneous Expense	910
Equipment	3,600
Unearned Rent	720

Cash	2,900
Prepaid Rent	4,800
Rent Expense	3,200
Utilities Expense	1,970
Accounts Receivable	4,400

In addition, you discover the following errors are contained in the above accounts:

1. A credit of $250 to Cash was posted as $520.
2. A debit of $1,200 to Supplies was posted twice.
3. A credit of $500 to Accounts Payable was posted as a debit.
4. A debit of $1,000 to Cash was posted to Wages Expense.
5. A payment of $500 received from a customer on account was not journalized.

Instructions

Using the above information, prepare a corrected trial balance.

CONTINUING PROBLEM

The transactions completed by Music A La Mode during November 1999 were described at the end of Chapter 1. The following transactions were completed during December, the second month of the business's operations:

Dec. 1. Julian Felipe made an additional investment in Music A La Mode by depositing $2,000 in Music A La Mode's chequing account.

   1. Instead of continuing to share office space with a local real estate agency, Julian decided to rent office space near a local music store. Paid rent for December, $720.

   1. Paid a premium of $1,680 for a comprehensive insurance policy covering liability, theft, and fire. The policy covers a two-year period.

   2. Received $350 on account.

   3. On behalf of Music A La Mode, Julian signed a contract with a local radio station, CPRG, to provide guest spots for the next three months. The contract requires Music A La Mode to provide a guest disc jockey for 40 hours per month for a monthly fee of $500. Any additional hours beyond 40 will be billed to CPRG at $15 per hour. In accordance with the contract, Julian received $1,500 from CPRG as an advance payment for the first three months.

   3. Paid $50 on account.

   4. Paid a lawyer $75 for reviewing (on December 2) the contract with CPRG. (Record as Miscellaneous Expense.)

   5. Purchased office equipment on account from One-Stop Office Mart, $2,500.

   8. Paid for a newspaper advertisement, $100.

  11. Received $300 for serving as a disc jockey for a college fraternity party.

  13. Paid $250 to a local audio electronics store for rental of various equipment (speakers, CD players, etc.).

  14. Paid wages of $400 to receptionist and part-time assistant.

  16. Received $550 for serving as a disc jockey for a wedding reception.

  18. Purchased miscellaneous supplies on account, $375.

  21. Paid $120 to The Music Store for use of its current demo CDs and tapes in making cassettes of various music sets.

  22. Paid $50 to a local radio station to advertise the services of Music A La Mode twice daily for the remainder of December.

  23. Served as disc jockey for an annual holiday party for $780. Received $200, with the remainder due January 6, 2000.

  27. Paid electric bill, $280.

  28. Paid wages of $400 to receptionist and part-time assistant.

  29. Paid miscellaneous expenses, $88.

  30. Served as a disc jockey for a pre-New Year's Eve charity ball for $600. Received $300, with the remainder due on January 10, 2000.

  31. Received $1,000 for serving as a disc jockey for a New Year's Eve party.

  31. Withdrew $400 cash from Music A La Mode for personal use.

Music A La Mode's chart of accounts and the balance of accounts as of December 1, 1996 (all normal balances), are as follows:

11	Cash	$ 695
12	Accounts Receivable	350
14	Supplies	70
15	Prepaid Insurance	—
17	Office Equipment	—
21	Accounts Payable	50
23	Unearned Revenue	—
31	Julian Felipe, Capital	1,000
32	Julian Felipe, Withdrawals	75
41	Revenue Earned	1,340
50	Wages Expense	110
51	Office Rent Expense	250
52	Equipment Rent Expense	300
53	Utilities Expense	100
54	Music Expense	220
55	Advertising Expense	75
56	Supplies Expense	80
59	Miscellaneous Expense	65

Instructions

1. Enter the December 1, 1999 account balances in the appropriate balance column of a four-column account. Write *Balance* in the Item column, and place a check mark (✓) in the Posting Reference column. (Verify the equality of the debit and credit balances in the ledger before proceeding with the next instruction.)
2. Analyze and journalize each transaction in a two-column journal. Omit journal entry explanations.
3. Post the journal to the ledger, extending the account balance to the appropriate balance column after each posting.
4. Prepare a trial balance as of December 31, 1999.

CASES

CASE 2–1
Metro Services Co.
Errors in trial balance

At the end of the current month, Maurice Bouchard prepared a trial balance for Metro Services Co. The credit side of the trial balance exceeds the debit side by a significant amount.

Maurice has decided to add the difference to the balance of the miscellaneous expense account in order to complete the preparation of the current month's financial statements by a 5 o'clock deadline. Maurice will look for the difference next week when there is more time.

⬤▬▬▶ Discuss whether Maurice is behaving in an ethical manner.

CASE 2–2
Community College
Accounting for revenue

Community College requires students to pay tuition each term before classes begin. Students who have not paid their tuition are not allowed to enroll or to attend classes.

What journal entry do you think would be used by Community College to record the receipt of the students' tuition payments? Describe the nature of each account in the entry.

CASE 2–3
Prodata Company
Recording transactions

The following discussion took place between Jacob Mandy, the office manager of Prodata Company, and a new accountant, Harold Hartly.

Harold: I've been thinking about our method of recording entries. It seems that it's inefficient.

Jacob: In what way?

Harold: Well—correct me if I'm wrong—it seems like we have unnecessary steps in the process. We could very easily develop a trial balance by posting our transactions directly into the ledger and by-passing the journal altogether. In this way we could combine the recording and posting process into one step and save ourselves a lot of time. What do you think?

Jacob: We need to have a talk.

➤ What should Jacob say to Harold?

CASE 2–4
Beaverdam Construction Inc.
Debits and credits

The following is an excerpt from a conversation between Derrick Rawlins, the president and chief operating officer of Beaverdam Construction Inc., and his neighbour, Carrie Crymes.

Carrie: Derrick, I'm taking a course in night school, "Intro to Accounting." I was wondering—could you answer a couple of questions for me?

Derrick: Well, I will if I can.

Carrie: Okay, our instructor says that it's critical we understand the basic concepts of accounting, or we'll never get beyond the first test. My problem is with those rules of debit and credit . . . you know, assets increase with debits, decrease with credits, etc.

Derrick: Yes, pretty basic stuff. You just have to memorize the rules. It shouldn't be too difficult.

Carrie: Sure, I can memorize the rules, but my problem is I want to be sure I understand the basic concepts behind the rules.

For example, why can't assets be increased with credits and decreased with debits like revenue? As long as everyone did it that way, why not? It would seem easier if we had the same rules for all increases and decreases in accounts.

Also, why is the left side of an account called the debit side? Why couldn't it be called something simple . . . like the "LE" for Left Entry? The right side could be called just "RE" for Right Entry.

Finally, why are there just two sides to an entry? Why can't there be three or four sides to an entry?

➤ Help Derrick answer Carrie's questions.

CASE 2–5
Sears Canada Inc.
Financial analysis

 A single item appearing in a financial statement is often useful in interpreting the financial results of a business. However, comparing this item in a current statement with the same item in the prior statement often enhances the usefulness of the financial information. Such comparisons often take two forms: (1) the amount of the increase or decrease and (2) the percent of the increase or decrease for the current item when compared to the same item in the prior period. For example, the amount of the prior period's revenue and the amount of the change and the percent of change determined is indicated in the following table:

	Current Year	Prior Year	Increase (Decrease) Amount	Increase (Decrease) Percent
Revenues	$120,000	$100,000	$20,000	20%

a. For Sears Canada Inc., comparing the most recent year with the preceding year, determine the amount of change and the percent of change for
   1. revenues and
   2. cost of merchandise sold, operating, administrative, and selling expenses.

b. ➤ What conclusions can be drawn from this analysis of the revenues and the cost of merchandise sold, operating, administrative, and selling expenses?

CASE 2–6
Ace Caddy Service
Transactions and income statement

During June through August, Yu Li is planning to manage and operate Ace Caddy Service at Niagara Golf and Country Club. Yu will rent a small maintenance building from the country club for $150 per month and will offer caddy services, including cart rentals, to golfers. Yu has had no formal training in record keeping. During June, he kept notes of all receipts and expenses in a shoe box.

An examination of Yu's shoe box records for June revealed the following:

June 1. Withdrew $2,000 from personal bank account to be used to operate the caddy service.
      1. Paid rent to Niagara Golf and Country Club, $150.
      2. Paid for golf supplies (practice balls, etc.), $200.
      2. Paid miscellaneous expenses, $75.
      3. Arranged for the rental of 40 regular (pulling) golf carts and 10 gasoline-driven carts for $1,000 per month. Paid $750 in advance, with the remaining $250 due June 20.
      7. Purchased supplies, including gasoline, for the golf carts on account, $325. Niagara Golf and Country Club has agreed to allow Yu to store the gasoline in one of its fuel tanks at no cost.
      15. Received cash for services from June 1–15, $990.
      15. Accepted IOUs from customers on account for services from June 1–15, $210.
      15. Paid wages of part-time employees, $120.
      17. Paid cash to creditors on account, $180.
      20. Paid remaining rental on golf carts, $250.

      22. Purchased supplies, including gasoline, on account, $280.
      25. Received cash in payment of IOUs on account, $150.
June 28. Paid miscellaneous expenses, $60.
      30. Received cash for services from June 16–30, $1,475.
      30. For June 16–30, accepted IOUs from customers on account, $150.
      30. Paid electricity (utilities) expense, $55.
      30. Paid telephone (utilities) expense, $30.
      30. Paid wages of part-time employees, $110.
      30. Supplies on hand at the end of June, $180.

Yu has asked you several questions concerning his financial affairs to date, and he has asked you to assist with his record keeping and reporting of financial data.

a. To assist Yu with his record keeping, prepare a chart of accounts that would be appropriate for Ace Caddy Service.
b. Prepare an income statement for June in order to help Yu assess the profitability of Ace Caddy Service. For this purpose, the use of T accounts may be helpful in analyzing the effects of each June transaction.
c. Based on Yu's records of receipts and payments, calculate the amount of cash on hand on June 30. For this purpose, a T account for cash may be useful.
d. ◄■■■■► A count of the cash on hand on June 30 totalled $2,135. Briefly discuss the possible causes of the difference between the amount of cash computed in (c) and the actual amount of cash on hand.

ANSWERS TO SELF-EXAMINATION QUESTIONS

1. **A** A debit may signify an increase in an asset account (answer A) or a decrease in a liability or owner's capital account. A credit may signify a decrease in an asset account (answer B) or an increase in a liability or owner's capital account (answers C and D).

2. **C** Liability, capital, and revenue (answer C) accounts have normal credit balances. Asset (answer A), drawing (answer B), and expense (answer D) accounts have normal debit balances.

3. **C** Revenue Earned should normally have a credit balance. Hence, a debit balance in Revenue Earned (answer C) would indicate a likely error in the recording process. Accounts Receivable (answer A), Cash (answer B), and Miscellaneous Expense (answer D) would all normally have debit balances.

4. **A** The receipt of cash from customers on account increases the asset Cash and decreases the asset Accounts Receivable, as indicated by answer A. Answer B has the debit and credit reversed, and answers C and D involve transactions with creditors (accounts payable) and not customers (accounts receivable).

5. **D** The trial balance (answer D) is a listing of the balances and the titles of the accounts in the ledger on a given date, so that the equality of the debits and credits in the ledger can be verified. The income statement (answer A) is a summary of revenue and expenses for a period of time. The balance sheet (answer B) is a presentation of the assets, liabilities, and owner's equity on a given date. The statement of owner's equity (answer C) is a summary of the changes in owner's equity for a period of time.

3

Accrual Accounting and the Adjusting Process

YOU AND ACCOUNTING

Assume that you rented an apartment last month and signed a nine-month lease. When you signed the lease agreement, you were required to pay the final month's rent of $500. This amount is not returnable to you.

You are now applying for a student loan at a local bank. The loan application requires a listing of all your assets. Should you list the $500 deposit as an asset?

The answer to this question is "yes." The deposit is an asset to you until you receive the use of the apartment in the ninth month.

A business faces similar accounting problems at the end of a period. A business must determine what assets, liabilities, and owner's equity to report on its balance sheet. It must also determine what revenues and expenses to report on its income statement.

As we illustrated in previous chapters, we normally record transactions as they occur. Periodically, we prepare financial statements, summarizing the effects of the transactions on the financial position and the operations of the business.

At any one point in time, however, the accounting records may not reflect all transactions. For example, most businesses do not record the daily usage of supplies. Likewise, revenue may have been earned from providing services to customers, but the customers have not been billed when the accounting period ends. Thus, at the end of the period, we need to update the revenue and the receivable accounts.

In this chapter, we describe and illustrate this updating process. We will focus on accounts that normally require updating and the journal entries that update these accounts. We will also briefly discuss how some accountants use work sheets to aid them at the end of an accounting period.

After studying this chapter, you should be able to:

Objective 1
Explain how the revenue recognition and matching principles relate to the accrual basis of accounting.

Objective 2
Explain why adjustments are necessary and list the characteristics of adjusting entries.

Objective 3
Journalize entries for accounts requiring adjustment.

Objective 4
Enter adjustments on a work sheet and prepare an adjusted trial balance.

The Accounting Period Concept

Objective 1
Explain how the revenue recognition and matching principles relate to the accrual basis of accounting.

Accounting information is a tool that helps us to measure how well a business is doing. However, this measurement is only an estimate. We can never determine the success of a business with 100% accuracy until the business has actually ceased operations. Only then can we know, with absolute certainty, the total cash receipts that the firm generated and the cash outlays that it required. The accounting report that we could then produce would be completely reliable. But would the information be of much use to anyone?

Investors and creditors do not need information about a business after it has ceased operations. They need financial reports which indicate how well a firm has done in the past, so that they can predict how well it will do in the future. This information should be timely enough that it can help them decide whether to invest in, or loan money to, the firm while it is still operating. In order to provide information that is relevant to financial statement users, accountants must prepare reports on a timely basis. Firms issue financial statements at least once a year, although many publish results more often (perhaps on a quarterly or monthly basis). Preparation of these periodic statements is based on the **accounting period concept.** Also known as the **periodicity assumption,** this generally accepted accounting principle states that in order to produce relevant information for the users of financial reports we can divide the economic activities of an entity into artificial time periods.

ACCRUAL vs CASH BASIS OF ACCOUNTING

Using the accounting period concept, we must determine in which period the revenues and expenses of the business should be reported. To determine the appropriate period, we will use either (1) the **cash basis of accounting** or (2) the **accrual basis of accounting.**

Under the cash basis of accounting, we define revenues as the cash received during the period (excluding investments by owners) and we define expenses as cash paid out during the period (excluding withdrawals by owners). For example, we would record fees as earned only when we receive cash from clients. Similarly, we would record wage expenses only when we actually paid employees. Under this model, net income (or net loss) is simply the difference between the cash receipts (revenues) and the cash payments (expenses) made during the period.

Individuals sometimes use the cash basis of accounting, as do some small service businesses such as a barber shop, which may have very few receivables or payables. This method may also be acceptable for many charitable institutions for which determining net income is not a reporting objective. However, for most accounting entities, the cash basis of accounting does not provide a proper measurement of the success of the business's operations during the period, nor of the business's financial position at the end of the period.

For example, suppose that you were hired on a three-month contract to work as a consultant for Raisa Enterprises for a fee of $3,000 per month. When you sign the contract, you agree that Raisa Enterprises can pay your bill for consulting in one lump-sum payment of $9,000 at the end of the three-month period. After working for a month, wouldn't you feel that you had "earned" $3,000, even though you had to wait another two months before receiving your payment? Even if the contract were terminated at the end of the first month, Raisa would still owe you a month's fee for the time that you had worked.

Suppose you wanted to keep track of how your consulting business is doing on a monthly basis. Using a cash model of accounting, you would show no earnings for each of the first two months that you worked, but then the last month you would report earnings of $9,000. Is this a realistic portrayal of what is really happening in your business? Or is it misleading to indicate that you did nothing for two months and that all of your consulting activities took place in the last month?

The accrual basis of accounting attempts to record events in the period in which they actually occur, regardless of when the cash flows associated with these transactions take place. Thus, in the above example, you would recognize that you had earned revenue of $3,000 during each month that you worked, even though you would not receive the cash until later. Similarly, from the perspective of the firm that hired you, the accrual basis of accounting would recognize that Raisa had incurred an equal expense each month, even though it did not make the cash payment until the last period.

By the end of the contract you will have recognized $9,000 in earnings whether you use the cash or the accrual method of accounting. Similarly, Raisa Enterprises will have recorded $9,000 in expenses by the end of the three-month period under either method. The total income earned over the life of a business is always equal to the cash receipts generated by the business less the cash payments made in the course of its operations. Thus, both the cash and accrual methods of accounting will report the same amount of income in total over the life of a business. However, the cash and accrual methods will usually differ in the **timing** of the recognition of that income. Since users of financial reports need timely information for making decisions, the issue of *when* we report transactions is very important. Since users do not want to wait until the business is over to get an accurate measurement of its success, they will want accounting reports prepared using the method that best reflects the activities of the firm during each time period. That method is the accrual basis of accounting. Therefore, generally accepted accounting principles require us to prepare financial statements using the accrual, rather than the cash, basis of accounting.

Accrual accounting is based on two basic principles: (1) the **revenue recognition principle,** which tells us in which period to record revenue; and (2) the **matching principle,** which tells us the period in which to record expenses.

THE REVENUE RECOGNITION PRINCIPLE

Under the accrual basis of accounting, the **revenue recognition principle** leads to reporting revenues in the period in which they are earned. The revenue recognition principle sets out two basic criteria that must be met in order to record revenue: (1) performance and (2) measurability.

The **performance criterion** requires that the business must have carried out some action that entitles it to receive benefits from an outside party. For example, the business may have earned revenue by rendering a service to a client or by providing goods to a customer.

An understanding of the difference between the accrual and cash basis of accounting can be extremely important for many types of businesses. For example, a bank loan officer requires an individual, who normally keeps records on a cash basis, to list assets, such as automobiles, homes, investments, etc., on an application for a loan or a line of credit. In addition, the application often asks for an estimate of the individual's liabilities, such as credit card amounts outstanding and balances of automobile loans. In a sense, a loan application converts an individual from a cash-basis accounting system to an estimated accrual basis. The loan officer will also request other information, such as the amount of life insurance policies in force, estimated wages and other sources of income, and major monthly expenses. In this way, the completed loan application provides the loan officer with information that can be used in assessing the individual's ability to repay a loan.

The **measurability criterion** requires that the business be able to determine the amount of income generated by its performance. In order to satisfy this criterion, we must be able to measure three things:

- the amount of revenue arising from the sale;
- the amount of all costs associated with the sale;
- the likelihood of collecting the proceeds from the sale.

The measurability criterion for revenue recognition arises from the concept of reliability discussed in Chapter 1. Since accounting information must be reliable and verifiable, we cannot record a transaction unless we are able to measure it with reasonable accuracy.

Provided that a business can determine the amount of income associated with a sale, the business will normally report revenue in the period in which it transfers goods or provides services to a customer. This period may or may not be the same as the period in which the customer pays cash.

THE MATCHING PRINCIPLE

Under the accrual basis, we must report expenses in the same period as we report the revenues to which they relate. This is called the **matching principle.** Notice that we match expenses to revenues; we do not match revenues to expenses. The order is important. First, we use the revenue recognition principle to establish what revenues the business has earned during the period. It is only after we know the revenue earned that we can determine the expenses that were incurred in generating this revenue. If we decide to delay recording some revenue until a later period (because our revenue recognition criteria are not yet met), we must also delay recording expenses associated with that revenue. Suppose that in December of 1997, we paid cash to buy equipment to use in a new business that is opening in January, 1998. Since the equipment will not be generating revenues until 1998, we should not record any expense for it in 1997.

Under the matching concept, we report expenses in the same period as we report the revenues to which they relate. This period may or may not be the same as the period in which we make the cash payment for the expenditure. For example, employees usually generate revenues in the period in which they provide services to customers. Therefore, we will record wage expense in the period in which the employees work, regardless of when we actually pay the wages.

For most businesses, the cash basis of accounting will not provide accurate financial statements for user needs. For this reason, we will emphasize the accrual basis in the remainder of this text. The accrual basis and its related principles of revenue recognition and matching require an analysis and updating of some accounts whenever we prepare financial statements. In the following paragraphs, we will describe and illustrate this process, called the adjusting process.

Nature of the Adjusting Process

Objective 2
Explain why adjustments are necessary and list the characteristics of adjusting entries.

At the end of an accounting period, we can report many of the balances of accounts in the ledger without change in the financial statements. For example, we normally report the balance of the cash account on the balance sheet as the cash on hand at the end of the accounting period.

Some accounts in the ledger, however, require updating. For example, the balances listed for prepaid expenses may be out of date because we do not record the use of these assets on a day-to-day basis. The balance of the supplies account usually represents the cost of supplies at the beginning of the period plus the cost of supplies acquired during the period. To record the daily use of supplies would require many entries with small amounts. In addition, the total amount of supplies is small relative to other assets, and managers usually do not require day-to-day information on the amount of supplies on hand.

Another example of a prepaid expense account that requires updating is Prepaid Insurance. The balance in Prepaid Insurance may show the beginning balance plus the cost of insurance policies acquired during the period. Journal entries are not made daily for the premiums as they expire. To make such entries would be costly and unnecessary.

The journal entries at the end of an accounting period to bring the accounts up to date and to properly match revenues and expenses are called adjusting entries. By their nature, *all adjusting entries affect at least one income statement account and one balance sheet account.* Thus, an adjusting entry will always involve a revenue or an expense account and an asset or a liability account.

Is there an easy way to know when you need to make an adjusting entry? Yes, two basic classifications of items require adjusting entries. The first class of items, deferrals, is created by transactions that require us to delay or defer the recognition of an expense or a revenue. Deferrals may be either deferred expenses or deferred revenues, as described below.

Deferred expenses are items that are initially assets but which become expenses over time or through the normal operations of the business. The supplies and prepaid insurance discussed in the preceding paragraphs are examples of deferred expenses. The supplies become an expense as they are used, and the prepaid insurance becomes an expense as time passes and the insurance expires. Deferred expenses are often called **prepaid expenses.**

Deferred revenues are items that are initially liabilities but which become revenues over time or through the normal operations of the business. Examples of deferred revenues include tuition received by a college or university at the beginning of the term and magazine subscriptions received in advance by a publisher.

The college or university earns the tuition revenue throughout the term as students attend class. The publisher earns the subscription revenue as it publishes and distributes the magazines. Deferred revenues are often called **unearned revenues.**

The second class of items that gives rise to adjusting entries is accruals. **Accruals** arise when an expense has been incurred or a revenue has been earned but we have not yet entered the transaction in the accounting records. Accruals may be either accrued expenses or accrued revenues, as described below.

Accrued expenses are expenses that have been incurred *but have not been recorded* in the accounts. Examples of accrued expenses include unrecorded wages owed to employees at the end of a period and unrecorded interest owed on loans. Accrued expenses are often called **accrued liabilities.**

Accrued revenues are revenues that have been earned *but have not been recorded* in the accounts. Examples of accrued revenues include unrecorded fees earned by a lawyer or unrecorded commissions earned by a real estate agent. Accrued revenues are often called **accrued assets.**

How do you tell the difference between deferrals and accruals? Deferrals normally arise when cash is received or paid in the current period but some of the related revenue or expense is to be recorded in a future period. Accruals normally arise when a revenue or expense is recorded in the current period but the related cash is received or paid in a future period. These differences are illustrated in Exhibit 1.

Exhibit 1
Deferrals and Accruals

	Current Period	Future Period
Deferral	Cash received or paid	Revenue or expense recorded
Accrual	Revenue or expense recorded	Cash received or paid

Recording Adjusting Entries

Objective 3
Journalize entries for accounts requiring adjustment.

The examples of adjusting entries in the following paragraphs are based on the ledger of Computer King as reported in the December 31, 1999 trial balance in Exhibit 2. An expanded chart of accounts for Computer King is shown in Exhibit 3. The additional accounts that will be used in this chapter are shown in colour. To simplify the examples, T accounts are used. The adjusting entries are shown in colour in the accounts to separate them from other transactions.

DEFERRED EXPENSES (PREPAID EXPENSES)

We introduced the concept of adjusting the accounting records in Chapters 1 and 2 in the illustration for Computer King. In that illustration, supplies were purchased on November 10 (transaction c). We recorded the supplies used during November on November 30 (transaction g). In practice, this matching of revenues and

Exhibit 2
Unadjusted Trial Balance for Computer King

Computer King
Trial Balance
December 31, 1999

Cash	2 3 9 0 00	
Accounts Receivable	2 2 2 0 00	
Supplies	2 0 0 0 00	
Prepaid Insurance	2 4 0 0 00	
Land	10 0 0 0 00	
Office Equipment	1 8 0 0 00	
Accounts Payable		9 0 0 00
Unearned Rent		3 6 0 00
Pat King, Capital		15 0 0 0 00
Pat King, Withdrawals	4 0 0 0 00	
Revenue Earned		16 3 4 0 00
Wages Expense	3 9 5 0 00	
Rent Expense	1 6 0 0 00	
Utilities Expense	9 8 5 00	
Supplies Expense	8 0 0 00	
Miscellaneous Expense	4 5 5 00	
	32 6 0 0 00	32 6 0 0 00

Exhibit 3
Expanded Chart of Accounts for Computer King

Balance Sheet Accounts	Income Statement Accounts
1. Assets	4. Revenue
11 Cash	41 Revenue Earned
12 Accounts Receivable	42 Rent Income
14 Supplies	5. Expenses
15 Prepaid Insurance	51 Wages Expense
17 Land	52 Rent Expense
18 Office Equipment	53 Amortization Expense
19 Accumulated Amortization	54 Utilities Expense
2. Liabilities	55 Supplies Expense
21 Accounts Payable	56 Insurance Expense
22 Wages Payable	59 Miscellaneous Expense
23 Unearned Rent	
3. Owner's Equity	
31 Pat King, Capital	
32 Pat King, Withdrawals	

expenses is part of the normal adjusting process that takes place only at the end of the accounting period, which is typically monthly and at least yearly.

The balance in Computer King's supplies account on December 31 is $2,000. Some of these supplies (computer diskettes, paper, envelopes, etc.) were used during December, and some are still on hand. If we know either amount, we can readily determine the other. It is normally easier to determine the cost of the supplies on hand at the end of the month than it is to keep a record of those used daily.

Assuming that the inventory of supplies on December 31 is $760, we must transfer $1,240 from the asset account to the expense account.

Supplies available (balance of account) $2,000
Supplies on hand (inventory)   760
Supplies used (amount of adjustment) $1,240

As we discussed in Chapter 2, we record increases in expense accounts as debits and decreases in asset accounts as credits. Hence, at the end of December, we debit the supplies expense account for $1,240 and credit the supplies account for $1,240 to record the supplies used during December. The adjusting journal entry and T accounts for Supplies and Supplies Expense are as follows:

Supplies Expense   1,240
    Supplies   1,240
        Record December supplies used.

Supplies				Supplies Expense		
Bal.	2,000	Dec. 31	1,240	Bal.	800	
760				Dec. 31	1,240	
					2,040	

After we have recorded and posted the adjustment, the supplies account has a debit balance of $760. This balance represents an asset that will become an expense in a future period.

The debit balance of $2,400 in Computer King's prepaid insurance account represents a December 1 prepayment of insurance for 24 months. At the end of December, we should increase (debit) the insurance expense account and decrease (credit) the prepaid insurance account by $100, the insurance for one month. The adjusting journal entry and the T accounts for Prepaid Insurance and Insurance Expense are as follows:

Insurance Expense   100
    Prepaid Insurance   100
        Record December insurance expense.

Prepaid Insurance				Insurance Expense		
Bal.	2,400	Dec. 31	100	Dec. 31	100	
2,300						

After we have recorded and posted the adjustment, the prepaid insurance account has a debit balance of $2,300. This balance represents an asset that will become an expense in future periods. The insurance expense account has a debit balance of $100, which is an expense of the current period.

What is the effect of omitting adjusting entries? If we had not recorded the preceding adjustments for supplies ($1,240) and insurance ($100), the financial statements prepared as of December 31 would be misstated. On the income statement, Supplies Expense and Insurance Expense would be understated by a total of $1,340 and net income would be overstated by $1,340. On the balance sheet, Supplies and Prepaid Insurance would be overstated by a total of $1,340. Since net income increases owner's equity, Pat King, Capital would also be overstated by $1,340 on the balance sheet. The effects of omitting these adjusting entries on the income statement and balance sheet are as follows:

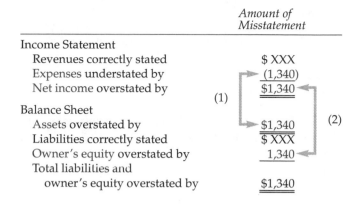

Arrows (1) and (2) indicate how omitting adjusting entries affects both the income statement and the balance sheet. Arrow (1) indicates the effects on the expenses and assets. Arrow (2) indicates the effect of the overstated net income on owner's equity. On the balance sheet, the assets and the total liabilities and owner's equity are misstated by the same amount.

Supplies and prepaid insurance are two examples of prepaid expenses that may require adjustment at the end of an accounting period. Other examples of prepaid expenses that may require adjustment are prepaid advertising and prepaid interest.

We will now discuss an alternative method for recording deferred expenses.

ALTERNATIVE METHOD OF RECORDING DEFERRED EXPENSES

As previously discussed, a deferred expense arises from a transaction in which the business has paid cash, but must delay recognition of some of the expense until a future period. In the previous examples, we debited an asset account when the cash was paid. Alternatively, we might have debited an *expense account* at the time of the cash payment. This practice is common with many small businesses, which keep simple records: when the cash expenditure is made, the bookkeeper debits an expense account.

To illustrate this alternative method of recording deferred expenses, we reconsider the insurance premium paid by Computer King in Chapter 2. The amounts related to this insurance are as follows:

Prepayment of insurance for 24 months, starting December 1	$2,400
Insurance premium expired in December	100
Unexpired insurance premium at the end of December	$2,300

On December 1, 1999 when the firm pays $2,400 for a two-year insurance premium, we could have debited the entire amount to insurance expense:

Insurance Expense	2,400	
Cash		2,400
Paid $2,400 for insurance.		

In this case, on December 31, 1999 we need an adjusting entry to set up the amount of the premium not yet expired by the end of the period. If we did not make the adjustment, insurance expense for 1999 would be overstated and the asset, prepaid insurance, would be understated at the end of 1999. The adjustment required in order to **match the expense** to the correct period is as follows:

Prepaid Insurance   2,300
    Insurance Expense   2,300
        To record prepaid insurance on December 31, 1999

Exhibits 4 and 5 compare the accounting entries made to insurance, depending on whether we record the original cash payment for the insurance premium as an *asset* or as an *expense*.

Either of the two methods of recording deferred expenses (prepaid expenses) is acceptable. As illustrated in Exhibits 4 and 5, both methods result in the same account balances after the adjusting entries have been recorded. Therefore, the amounts reported as expenses in the income statement and as assets on the balance sheet will not be affected by the accounting method used. To avoid confusion, a business should use the same accounting method for each kind of prepaid expense consistently from year to year.

Some businesses record all deferred expenses using one method. Other businesses use one method to record the prepayment of some expenses and the other method for other expenses.

Prepayments of expenses are sometimes made at the beginning of the period in which they will be *entirely consumed.* On December 1, for example, Computer King paid rent of $800 for the month. On December 1, the rent payment represents the asset prepaid rent. The prepaid rent expires daily, and at the end of December, the entire amount has become an expense (rent expense). In cases such as this, we record the initial payment as an expense rather than as an asset. In this case, no adjusting entry is needed at the end of the period.

DEFERRED REVENUE (UNEARNED REVENUE)

According to Computer King's trial balance on December 31, the balance in the unearned rent account is $360. This balance represents the receipt of three months' rent on December 1 for December, January, and February. At the end of December, we must debit (decrease) the unearned rent account by $120 and credit (increase) the rent income account by $120. The $120 represents the rental income for one month ($360 ÷ 3). We show the adjusting journal entry and T accounts on page 103.

Exhibit 4	**Exhibit 5**
Expenditure Recorded Initially as Asset	*Expenditure Recorded Initially as Expense*
Initial entry (to record initial payment):	Initial entry (to record initial payment):

Dec. 1   Prepaid Insurance   2,400
              Cash   2,400
	Dec. 1 Insurance Expense 2,400
	              Cash 2,400

Adjusting entry (to transfer amount **used** to proper expense account):	Adjusting entry (to transfer amount **unused** to the proper asset account):

Dec. 31   Insurance Expense   100
              Prepaid Insurance   100
	Dec. 31 Prepaid Insurance 2,300
	              Insurance Expense 2,300

Prepaid Insurance Dec. 1 2,400 | Dec. 31 Adjusting 100	Prepaid Insurance Dec. 31 Adjusting 2,300 |
Insurance Expense Dec. 31 Adjusting 100 | Dec. 31	Insurance Expense Dec. 1 2,400 | Dec. 31 Adjusting 2,300

```
Unearned Rent                    120
    Rent Income                           120
        Record rent earned in December.
```

	Unearned Rent				Rent Income		
Dec. 31	120	Bal.	360			Dec. 31	120
		240					

After we have recorded and posted the adjustment, the unearned rent account, which is a liability, has a credit balance of $240. This balance represents a deferral that will become revenue in a future period. The rent income account has a balance of $120, which is revenue of the current period.

ALTERNATIVE METHOD OF RECORDING DEFERRED REVENUES

As previously discussed, a deferred revenue arises from a transaction in which the business has received cash, but must delay recognition of some of the revenue until a future period. In the previous examples, we credited a liability account when the cash was received. Alternatively, we might have credited a *revenue account* at the time of the cash receipt. Again, this practice is common with many small businesses that keep simple records: when the cash is received, the bookkeeper credits a revenue account.

To illustrate this alternative method of recording deferred revenues, we reconsider the rent received in advance by Computer King in Chapter 2. The amounts related to this rent are as follows:

Rent revenue received in advance for three months, starting December 1	$360
Rent revenue earned in December	120
Unearned rent at the end of December	$240

On December 1, 1999 when the firm receives $360 for three months' rent, we could have credited the entire amount to rent income:

```
Cash                         360
    Rent Income                       360
        Received $360 for rent.
```

In this case, on December 31, 1999 we need an adjusting entry to set up the amount of the rent income not yet earned by the end of the period. If we did not make the adjustment, rent income for 1999 would be overstated and the liability, unearned rent, would be understated at the end of 1999. The adjustment required in order to **recognize the revenue** in the correct period is as follows:

```
Rent Income                      240
    Unearned Rent                         240
        To record unearned rent on December 31, 1999.
```

Exhibits 6 and 7 compare the accounting entries made to rent, depending on whether we record the original cash received for rent as a *liability* or as a *revenue*:

Exhibit 6	**Exhibit 7**
Cash Receipt Recorded Initially as Liability	*Cash Receipt Recorded Initially as Revenue*

Initial entry (to record initial receipt):

Dec. 1   Cash   360
                 Unearned Rent   360

Initial entries (to record initial receipt):

Dec. 1   Cash   360
                 Rent Income   360

Adjusting entry (to transfer amount **earned** to proper **revenue** account):

Dec. 31   Unearned Rent   120
                 Rent Income   120

Adjusting entry (to transfer amount **unearned** to proper **liability** account):

Dec. 31   Rent Income   240
                 Unearned Rent   240

Unearned Rent

Dec. 31 Adjusting   120 | Dec. 1   360

Unearned Rent

                               | Dec. 31 Adjusting   240

Rent Income

                               | Dec. 31 Adjusting   120

Rent Income

Dec. 31 Adjusting   240 | Dec. 1   360

As illustrated in Exhibits 6 and 7, both methods result in the same account balances after the adjusting entries have been recorded. Therefore, the amounts reported as revenues in the income statement and as liabilities on the balance sheet will not be affected by the method used. Either of the methods may be used for all revenues received in advance. Alternatively, a business may use the first method for advance receipts of some kinds of revenue and the second method for other kinds. To avoid confusion, a business should use the same method for each kind of unearned revenue consistently from year to year.

If we did not record the preceding adjustment of unearned rent and rent income, the financial statements prepared on December 31 would be misstated. On the income statement, Rent Income and the net income would be understated by $120. On the balance sheet, Unearned Rent would be overstated by $120, and Pat King, Capital would be understated by $120. We show the effects of omitting this adjusting entry below.

	Amount of Misstatement
Income Statement	
Revenues understated by	$ (120)
Expenses correctly stated	XXX
Net income understated by	$ (120)
Balance Sheet	
Assets correctly stated	$ XXX
Liabilities overstated by	$ 120
Owner's equity understated by	(120)
Total liabilities and	
owner's equity correctly stated	$ XXX

The only unearned revenue for Computer King was unearned rent. Other examples of unearned revenue that may require adjustment include tuition received in advance by a school, an annual retainer fee received by a lawyer, premiums received in advance by an insurance company, and amounts received in advance by an advertising firm for advertising services to be rendered in the future.

ACCRUED EXPENSES (ACCRUED LIABILITIES)

We normally pay for some types of services, such as insurance, before they are used. These prepayments are deferrals. We pay for other types of services *after* the service has been performed. For example, wages expense accumulates or *accrues* hour by hour and day by day, but payment may be made only weekly, biweekly, or monthly. The amount of such an accrued but unpaid item at the end of the accounting period is both an expense and a liability. For this reason, we call such accruals **accrued expenses** or **accrued liabilities.** In the case of wages expense, if the last day of a pay period is not the last day of the accounting period, we will record the accrued expense and the related liability in the accounts by an adjusting entry. This adjusting entry is necessary to properly match expenses to the period in which they were incurred.

At the end of December, accrued wages for Computer King were $575. This amount is an additional expense of December and is debited to the wages expense account. It is also a liability as of December 31 and is credited to Wages Payable. We show the adjusting journal entry and T accounts below.

Wages Expense	575	
Wages Payable		575
Record images payable on December 31, 1999.		

Wages Expense			Wages Payable	
Bal.	3,950		Dec. 31	575
Dec. 31	575			
	4,525			

After we have recorded and posted the adjustment, the debit balance of the wages expense account is $4,525, which is the wages expense for the two months, November and December. The credit balance of $575 in Wages Payable is the amount of the liability for wages owed as of December 31.

We summarize the accrual of the wages expense for Computer King in Exhibit 8. You should note that Computer King paid wages of $950 on December 10 and

Exhibit 8
Accrued Wages

1. Wages are paid on the second and fourth Fridays for the two-week periods ending on those Fridays. The payments were $950 on December 10 and $1,200 on December 24.

2. The wages accrued for Monday, December 27 through Friday, December 31 are $575.

3. Wages paid on Friday, January 7, total $1,275.

December 1999

S	M	T	W	T	F	S	
			1	2	3	4	
5	6	7	8	9	10	11	Wages expense (paid), $950
12	13	14	15	16	17	18	
19	20	21	22	23	24	25	Wages expense (paid), $1,200
26	27	28	29	30	31		

Wages expense (accrued), $575

January 2000

						1
2	3	4	5	6	7	8

Wages expense (paid), $1,275

$1,200 on December 24. These payments represent biweekly payroll payments made on alternate Fridays for the pay periods ending on those days. The wages of $575 earned from Monday, December 27 through December 31 are accrued at December 31. The wages paid on January 7, 2000 totalled $1,275, including the $575 accrued wages of December 31.

What would be the effect on the financial statements if we did not record the adjustment for wages ($575)? The income statement for the period and the balance sheet as of December 31 would be misstated. On the income statement, Wages Expense would be understated by $575, and the net income would be overstated by $575. On the balance sheet, Wages Payable would be understated by $575, and Pat King, Capital would be overstated by $575. We show these effects of omitting the adjusting entry below.

	Amount of Misstatement
Income Statement	
Revenues correctly stated	$ XXX
Expenses understated by	(575)
Net income overstated by	$ 575
Balance Sheet	
Assets correctly stated	$ XXX
Liabilities understated by	$ (575)
Owner's equity overstated by	575
Total liabilities and owner's equity correctly stated	$ XXX

Accrued wages is an example of an accrued expense that we record by an adjusting entry. Other accrued expenses include accrued interest on notes payable and accrued taxes.

ACCRUED REVENUES (ACCRUED ASSETS)

All assets belonging to a business at the end of an accounting period and all revenue earned during a period should be recorded in the ledger. During an accounting period, we record some revenues only when we receive cash. Thus, at the end of an accounting period, there may be items of revenue that have been earned *but have not been recorded.* In such cases, we should record the amount of the revenue by debiting an asset account and crediting a revenue account. Because of the dual nature of such accruals, we call them **accrued revenues** or **accrued assets.**

To illustrate, assume that Computer King signed an agreement with Dankner Co. on December 15. The agreement provides that Computer King will be on call to answer questions and render assistance to Dankner Co.'s employees concerning computer problems. The services provided will be billed to Dankner Co. on the fifteenth of each month at a rate of $20 per hour. As of December 31, Computer King had provided 25 hours of assistance to Dankner Co. Although the revenue of $500 (25 hours × $20) will be billed and collected in January, Computer King earned the revenue in December. We show the adjusting journal entry and T accounts to record the claim against the customer (an account receivable) and the revenue earned in December below. We debit accounts receivable for $500 and credit revenue earned for $500.

Accounts Receivable	500	
Revenue Earned		500
Record accrued revenue at December 31, 1999.		

Accounts Receivable		Revenue Earned	
Bal. 2,220		Bal. 16,340	
Dec. 31 500		Dec. 31 500	
2,720		16,840	

If we did not record the adjustment for the accrued asset ($500), the income statement for the period and the balance sheet as of December 31 would be misstated. On the income statement, Revenue Earned and the net income would be understated by $500. On the balance sheet, Accounts Receivable and Pat King, Capital would be understated by $500. We show these effects of omitting the adjusting entry below.

	Amount of Misstatement
Income Statement	
Revenues understated by	$ (500)
Expenses correctly stated	XXX
Net income understated by	$ (500)
Balance Sheet	
Assets understated by	$ (500)
Liabilities correctly stated	$ XXX
Owner's equity understated by	(500)
Total liabilities and	
owner's equity understated by	$ (500)

Accrued legal fees in a law firm are an example of an accrued revenue that we must record by an adjusting entry to recognize revenue in the period in which it is earned. Other accruals that require similar treatment include commissions earned but not billed, accrued interest on notes receivable, and accrued rent on property rented to others.

CAPITAL ASSETS

Tangible assets that are owned by a business, are permanent or have a long life, and are used in the business are called capital assets. In a sense, capital assets are a type of long-term deferred expense. However, because of their nature and long life, we discuss them separately from other deferred expenses, such as supplies and prepaid insurance.

Computer King's capital assets include office equipment that is used much like the supplies are used to generate revenue. Unlike supplies, however, there is no visible reduction in the quantity of the equipment. Instead, as time passes, the equipment loses its ability to provide useful services. This decrease in usefulness is called *amortization*.

All capital assets, except land, lose their usefulness. Any decrease in an asset used to generate revenue is an expense. However, it is difficult to objectively measure the decrease in usefulness of a capital asset. For this reason, amortization in accounting is the systematic allocation of a capital asset's cost to expense. This allocation occurs over the asset's estimated life during which we expect it to generate revenue. We will discuss methods of computing amortization in a later chapter.

The adjusting entry to record amortization is similar to the adjusting entry for supplies used, in which we debit an expense account and we credit an asset account. However, we do not credit the asset account Office Equipment because

Computer King's capital assets such as office equipment and furniture will decrease in usefulness, or depreciate, over time.

we need to report both the original cost of a capital asset and the amount of amortization recorded since its purchase. The account credited is an accumulated amortization account, which we report on the balance sheet as a deduction from the asset account. We call accumulated amortization accounts contra accounts or **contra asset accounts** because we report them as deductions from the related asset accounts.

Normal titles for capital asset accounts and their related contra asset accounts are as follows:

Capital Asset	Contra Asset
Land	None—Land is not amortized.
Buildings	Accumulated Amortization—Buildings
Equipment	Accumulated Amortization—Equipment

The ledger could have a separate account for each of a number of buildings. We may also subdivide Equipment according to function, such as Delivery Equipment, Store Equipment, and Office Equipment, with a related accumulated amortization account for each capital asset account.

We illustrate the adjusting entry to record amortization for December for Computer King in the following journal entry and T accounts. The estimated amount of amortization for the month is $50.

Amortization Expense	50	
Accumulated Amortization —Office Equipment		50
Record amortization expense for December, 1999.		

We subtract the $50 in the accumulated amortization account from the $1,800 cost in the related capital asset account. The difference between the two balances is the unexpired, unamortized, or unallocated cost. This amount ($1,750) is called the net book value of the asset. We present the net book value on the balance sheet in the following manner:

Office equipment	$1,800	
Less accumulated amortization	50	$1,750

You should note that the market value of a capital asset normally differs from its net book value. This is because amortization is a cost allocation method, not a valuation method. That is, amortization allocates the cost of a capital asset to expense over its estimated life. Amortization does not attempt to measure changes in market values, which may vary significantly from year to year.

If we did not record the previous adjustment for amortization ($50), the financial statements as of December 31 would be misstated. On the income statement, Amortization Expense would be understated by $50, and the net income would be overstated by $50. On the balance sheet, the net book value of the office equipment and Pat King, Capital would be overstated by $50. We show the effects of omitting the adjustment for amortization below.

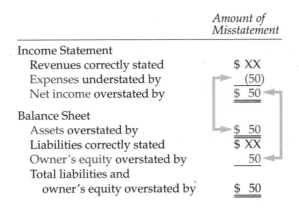

	Amount of Misstatement
Income Statement	
Revenues correctly stated	$ XX
Expenses understated by	(50)
Net income overstated by	$ 50
Balance Sheet	
Assets overstated by	$ 50
Liabilities correctly stated	$ XX
Owner's equity overstated by	50
Total liabilities and owner's equity overstated by	$ 50

Work Sheet

Objective 4
Enter adjustments on a work sheet and prepare an adjusted trial balance.

Before we can prepare adjusting entries such as those described above, we must assemble the relevant data. For example, we need to determine the cost of supplies on hand and the wages accrued at the end of the period. Accountants use **working papers** to summarize such data and analysis.

A working paper often used by accountants to summarize adjusting entries and assist in preparing the financial statements is the work sheet. We list the name of the business, the type of working paper (work sheet), and the period of time at the top of the work sheet, as shown in Exhibit 9. Such work sheets are normally not

Computer King
Work Sheet
For the Two Months Ended December 31, 1999

Account Title	Trial Balance Dr.	Trial Balance Cr.	Adjustments Dr.	Adjustments Cr.	Adjusted Trial Balance Dr.	Adjusted Trial Balance Cr.	Income Statement Dr.	Income Statement Cr.	Balance Sheet Dr.	Balance Sheet Cr.
Cash	2,390									
Accounts Receivable	2,220									
Supplies	2,000									
Prepaid Insurance	2,400									
Land	10,000									
Office Equipment	1,800									
Accounts Payable		900								
Unearned Rent		360								
Pat King, Capital		15,000								
Pat King, Withdrawals	4,000									
Revenue Earned		16,340								
Wages Expense	3,950									
Rent Expense	1,600									
Utilities Expense	985									
Supplies Expense	800									
Miscellaneous Expense	455									
	32,600	32,600								

Exhibit 9
Work Sheet with Trial Balance Entered

Accountants use the work sheet for assembling data and summarizing the effects of adjusting entries. It also aids in the preparation of financial statements.

prepared in computerized accounting systems, since computer programs automatically post to the accounts and prepare financial statements after the adjusting entries are entered into the program.

TRIAL BALANCE COLUMNS

We can prepare the trial balance discussed in Chapter 2 directly on the work sheet. The work sheet in Exhibit 9 shows the trial balance for Computer King at December 31, 1999.

ADJUSTMENTS COLUMNS

We enter the adjusting entries on the work sheet in the Adjustments columns, inserting both the debit and the credit amounts for the proper accounts for each adjustment. Cross-referencing the debit and credit of each adjustment by letters is useful in reviewing the work sheet. It also helps when we record the adjusting entries in the journal.

The order in which you enter the adjustments on the work sheet is not important. Most accountants enter the adjustments in the order in which the data are assembled. If the titles of some of the accounts to be adjusted do not appear in the trial balance, you should insert them in the Account Title column, below the trial balance totals, as needed. We have entered the adjustments for Computer King that were explained and illustrated earlier in the chapter on the work sheet in Exhibit 10.

Explanations for the entries in the Adjustments columns of the work sheet follow:

(a) **Supplies.** The supplies account has a debit balance of $2,000. The cost of the supplies on hand at the end of the period is $760. Therefore, the supplies expense for December is the difference between the two amounts, or $1,240. We enter the adjustment by writing (1) $1,240 in the Adjustments Debit column on the same line as Supplies Expense and (2) $1,240 in the Adjustments Credit column on the same line as Supplies.

(b) **Prepaid Insurance.** The prepaid insurance account has a debit balance of $2,400, which represents the prepayment of insurance for 24 months beginning December 1. Thus, the insurance expense for December is $100 ($2,400 ÷ 24). We enter the adjustment by writing (1) Insurance Expense in the Account Title column, (2) $100 in the Adjustments Debit column on the same line as Insurance Expense, and (3) $100 in the Adjustments Credit column on the same line as Prepaid Insurance.

(c) **Unearned Rent.** The unearned rent account has a credit balance of $360, which represents the receipt of three months' rent, beginning with December. Thus, the rent income for December is $120. We enter the adjustment by writing (1) $120 in the Adjustments Debit column on the same line as Unearned Rent, (2) Rent Income in the Account Title column, and (3) $120 in the Adjustments Credit column on the same line as Rent Income.

(d) **Wages.** Wages accrued but not paid at the end of December total $575. This amount is an increase in expenses and an increase in liabilities. We enter the adjustment by writing (1) $575 in the Adjustments Debit column on the same line as Wages Expense, (2) Wages Payable in the Account Title column, and (3) $575 in the Adjustments Credit column on the same line as Wages Payable.

(e) **Accrued Revenue.** Revenue accrued at the end of December but not recorded total $500. This amount is an increase in an asset and an increase in revenue. We enter the adjustment by writing (1) $500 in the Adjustments Debit column on the same line as Accounts Receivable and (2) $500 in the Adjustments Credit column on the same line as Revenue Earned.

Exhibit 10
*Work Sheet with Trial Balance
and Adjustments Entered*

	Computer King Work Sheet For the Two Months Ended December 31, 1999									
	Trial Balance		Adjustments		Adjusted Trial Balance		Income Statement		Balance Sheet	
Account Title	Dr.	Cr.	Dr.	Cr.	Dr.	Cr.	Dr.	Cr.	Dr.	Cr.
Cash	2,390									
Accounts Receivable	2,220		(e) 500							
Supplies	2,000			(a)1,240						
Prepaid Insurance	2,400			(b) 100						
Land	10,000									
Office Equipment	1,800									
Accounts Payable		900								
Unearned Rent		360	(c) 120							
Pat King, Capital		15,000								
Pat King, Withdrawals	4,000									
Revenue Earned		16,340		(e) 500						
Wages Expense	3,950		(d) 575							
Rent Expense	1,600									
Utilities Expense	985									
Supplies Expense	800		(a)1,240							
Miscellaneous Expense	455									
	32,600	32,600								
Insurance Expense			(b) 100							
Rent Income				(c) 120						
Wages Payable				(d) 575						
Amortization Expense			(f) 50							
Accumulated Amortization				(f) 50						
			2,585	2,585						

Add accounts, as needed to complete the adjustments.

(a) Supplies used, $1,240 ($2,000 – $760).
(b) Insurance expired, $100.
(c) Rent earned from amount received in advance, $120.
(d) Wages accrued but not paid, $575.
(e) Revenue earned but not received, $500.
(f) Amortization of office equipment, $50.

(f) **Amortization.** Amortization of the office equipment is $50 for December. We enter the adjustment by writing (1) Amortization Expense in the Account Title column, (2) $50 in the Adjustments Debit column on the same line as Amortization Expense, (3) Accumulated Amortization in the Account Title column, and (4) $50 in the Adjustments Credit column on the same line as Accumulated Amortization.

We total the Adjustments columns to verify the mathematical accuracy of the adjustment data. The total of the Debit column must equal the total of the Credit column.

ADJUSTED TRIAL BALANCE COLUMNS

We add or subtract the adjustment data to the data in the Trial Balance columns and extend the balance to the Adjusted Trial Balance columns, as shown on the work sheet in Exhibit 11. For example, we extend the cash account at its original amount of $2,390, since no adjustments affected Cash. Accounts Receivable has an initial balance of $2,220 and a debit adjustment (increase) of $500. The amount we extend is the debit balance of $2,720. We continue the same procedure until we have extended all account balances to the Adjusted Trial Balance columns. We then total the Debit and Credit columns to verify the equality of the Debit and Credit columns.

COMPLETING THE WORK SHEET

We will complete the work sheet, including the use of the Income Statement and Balance Sheet columns, in Chapter 4. Also, we will discuss the use of the work sheet in preparing financial statements and the journalizing and posting of the adjusting entries. Finally, we will illustrate how to prepare the accounting records for the next accounting period.

Computer King
Work Sheet
For the Two Months Ended December 31, 1999

Account Title	Trial Balance Dr.	Trial Balance Cr.	Adjustments Dr.	Adjustments Cr.	Adjusted Trial Balance Dr.	Adjusted Trial Balance Cr.	Income Statement Dr.	Income Statement Cr.	Balance Sheet Dr.	Balance Sheet Cr.
Cash	2,390				2,390					
Accounts Receivable	2,220		(e) 500		2,720					
Supplies	2,000			(a)1,240	760					
Prepaid Insurance	2,400			(b) 100	2,300					
Land	10,000				10,000					
Office Equipment	1,800				1,800					
Accounts Payable		900				900				
Unearned Rent		360	(c) 120			240				
Pat King, Capital		15,000				15,000				
Pat King, Withdrawals	4,000				4,000					
Revenue Earned		16,340		(e) 500		16,840				
Wages Expense	3,925		(d) 575		4,525					
Rent Expense	1,600				1,600					
Utilities Expense	985				985					
Supplies Expense	800		(a)1,240		2,040					
Miscellaneous Expense	455				455					
	32,600	32,600								
Insurance Expense			(b) 100		100					
Rent Income				(c) 120		120				
Wages Payable				(d) 575		575				
Amortization Expense			(f) 50		50					
Accumulated Amortization				(f) 50		50				
			2,585	2,585	33,725	33,725				

Exhibit 11
Work Sheet with Trial Balance, Adjustments, and Adjusted Trial Balance Entered

Determine the adjusted trial balance amounts by extending the trial balance amounts plus or minus the adjustments. For example, the Wages Expense debit of $4,525 is the trial balance amount of $3,925 plus the $575 adjustment debit.

KEY POINTS

Objective 1. Explain how the revenue recognition and matching principles relate to the accrual basis of accounting.

The accrual basis of accounting requires the use of an adjusting process at the end of the accounting period to recognize revenues in the correct periods and match expenses properly. We report revenues in the period in which they are earned, and match expenses with the revenues they generate.

Objective 2. Explain why adjustments are necessary and list the characteristics of adjusting entries.

At the end of an accounting period, some of the amounts listed on the trial balance are not necessarily current balances. For example, amounts listed for prepaid expenses are normally out of date because we do not record the use of these assets on a daily basis. A delay of the recognition of an expense already paid or a revenue already received is called a deferral.

Some revenues and expenses related to a period may not be recorded at the end of the period, since these items are normally recorded only when cash has been received or paid. We call a revenue or expense that has not been paid or recorded an accrual.

The entries required at the end of an accounting period to bring accounts up to date and to ensure the proper matching of revenues and expenses are called adjusting entries. Adjusting entries require a debit or a credit to a revenue or an expense account and an offsetting debit or credit to an asset or a liability account.

Adjusting entries affect amounts reported in the income statement and the balance sheet. Thus, if we do not record an adjusting entry, these financial statements will be incorrect (misstated).

Objective 3. Journalize entries for accounts requiring adjustment.

In this chapter we illustrated adjusting entries for deferred (prepaid) expenses, deferred (unearned) revenues, accrued expenses (accrued liabilities), accrued revenues (accrued assets), and amortization of capital assets.

Objective 4. Enter adjustments on a work sheet and prepare an adjusted trial balance.

In this chapter we illustrated a work sheet with a trial balance, adjustments, adjusted trial balance, income statement, and balance sheet columns. We entered adjustments on the work sheet in the Adjustments columns. The adjustments were added to or subtracted from the trial balance amounts, and the resulting amounts extended to the Adjusted Trial Balance columns. We then totalled the Debit and Credit columns to verify the equality of the Debit and Credit columns.

GLOSSARY OF KEY TERMS

Accounting period concept. In order to provide timely information relevant to users, accountants divide the economic activities of the entity into artificial time periods. *Objective 1*

Accrual basis. Recognizes revenues in the period earned and expenses in the period incurred in the process of generating revenues. *Objective 1*

Accruals. Expenses incurred or revenues earned that have not yet been recorded. *Objective 2*

Accrued expenses. Expenses incurred, but not yet recorded. Sometimes called accrued liabilities. *Objective 2*

Accrued revenues. Revenues earned, but not yet recorded. Sometimes called accrued assets. *Objective 2*

Accumulated amortization. Contra asset account used to accumulate the amortization recorded to date on capital assets. *Objective 3*

Adjusting entries. Entries required at the end of an accounting period to bring the ledger up to date and ensure that revenues and expenses are recorded in the correct period. *Objective 2*

Adjusting process. The process of updating the accounts at the end of the period. *Objective 1*

Amortization. Systematic allocation of the cost of a capital asset over its useful life in order to match the cost of the asset with the periods in which it provides service to the business. *Objective 3*

Capital asset. Long-lived asset owned by a business that provides benefits over more than one period and is used in business operations. *Objective 3*

Cash basis. Recognizes revenue when cash is received and expenses when cash is paid. *Objective 1*

Contra account. Account that is offset against (deducted from) another account in the financial statements. *Objective 1*

Deferral. Delay in recognizing a cash payment as an expense or a cash receipt as a revenue. *Objective 2*

Deferred expense. Cash expenditure recorded as an asset, which will be recognized as an expense in the future as it is used up over time or through the normal business operations. Sometimes called prepaid expense. *Objective 2*

Deferred revenue. Cash receipt recorded as a liability, which will be recognized as revenue in the future when it is earned. Sometimes called unearned revenue. *Objective 2*

Matching principle. Accountants should record expenses in the same period as the revenue that they helped to generate. *Objective 1*

Net book value of a capital asset. The difference between the cost of a capital asset and the accumulated amortization that has been recognized to date on the asset. *Objective 3*

Revenue recognition principle. Recognizes revenue in the period in which it is earned. Requires that both performance and measurability criteria can be met before revenue is recorded. *Objective 1*

Work sheet. A working paper used to summarize adjusting entries and assist in preparation of financial statements. *Objective 4*

ILLUSTRATIVE PROBLEM

Three years ago, T. Roderick organized Harbour Realty. At July 31, 1999, the end of the current year, the trial balance of Harbour Realty is as follows:

Cash	3,425	
Accounts Receivable	7,000	
Supplies	1,270	
Prepaid Insurance	620	
Office Equipment	51,650	
Accumulated Amortization		9,700
Accounts Payable		925
Unearned Revenue		1,250
T. Roderick, Capital		29,000
T. Roderick, Withdrawals	5,200	
Revenue Earned		59,125
Wages Expense	22,415	
Rent Expense	4,200	
Utilities Expense	2,715	
Miscellaneous Expense	1,505	
	100,000	100,000

The data needed to determine year-end adjustments are as follows:

a. Supplies on hand at July 31, 1999, $380.
b. Insurance premiums expired during the year, $315.
c. Amortization of equipment during the year, $4,950.
d. Wages accrued but not paid at July 31, 1999, $440.
e. Accrued revenue earned but not recorded at July 31, 1999, $1,000.
f. Unearned revenue on July 31, 1999, $750.

Instructions

1. Enter the July 31, 1999 trial balance on a work sheet.
2. Using the adjustment data, enter the necessary adjustments on the work sheet.
3. Extend the adjustment data on the work sheet to the Adjusted Trial Balance columns.

Solution

1., 2., and 3. (See page 115.)

SELF-EXAMINATION QUESTIONS (ANSWERS AT END OF CHAPTER)

1. Which of the following items represents a deferral?
    A. Prepaid insurance   C. Revenue earned
    B. Wages payable   D. Accumulated amortization

2. If the supplies account, before adjustment on May 31, indicated a balance of $2,250, and supplies on hand at May 31 totalled $950, the adjusting entry would be:
    A. debit Supplies, $950; credit Supplies Expense, $950
    B. debit Supplies, $1,300; credit Supplies Expense, $1,300
    C. debit Supplies Expense, $950; credit Supplies, $950
    D. debit Supplies Expense, $1,300; credit Supplies, $1,300

3. The balance in the unearned rent account for Jones Co. as of December 31 is $1,200. If Jones Co. failed to record the adjusting entry for $600 of rent earned during December,

the effect on the balance sheet and income statement for December is:
    A. assets understated $600; net income overstated $600
    B. liabilities understated $600; net income understated $600
    C. liabilities overstated $600; net income understated $600
    D. liabilities overstated $600; net income overstated $600

4. If the estimated amount of amortization on equipment for a period is $2,000, the adjusting entry to record amortization would be:
    A. debit Amortization Expense, $2,000; credit Equipment, $2,000
    B. debit Equipment, $2,000; credit Amortization Expense, $2,000

Harbour Realty
Work Sheet
For the Year Ended July 31, 1999

Account Title	Trial Balance Debit	Trial Balance Credit	Adjustments Debit	Adjustments Credit	Adjusted Trial Balance Debit	Adjusted Trial Balance Credit
1 Cash	3 4 2 5 00				3 4 2 5 00	
2 Accounts Receivable	7 0 0 0 00		(e)1 0 0 0 00		8 0 0 0 00	
3 Supplies	1 2 7 0 00			(a) 8 9 0 00	3 8 0 00	
4 Prepaid Insurance	6 2 0 00			(b) 3 1 5 00	3 0 5 00	
5 Office Equipment	51 6 5 0 00				51 6 5 0 00	
6 Accumulated Amortization		9 7 0 0 00		(c)4 9 5 0 00		14 6 5 0 00
7 Accounts Payable		9 2 5 00				9 2 5 00
8 Unearned Revenue		1 2 5 0 00	(f) 5 0 0 00			7 5 0 00
9 T. Roderick, Capital		29 0 0 0 00				29 0 0 0 00
10 T. Roderick, Withdrawals	5 2 0 0 00				5 2 0 0 00	
11 Revenue Earned		59 1 2 5 00		(e)1 0 0 0 00		60 6 2 5 00
12				(f) 5 0 0 00		
13 Wages Expense	22 4 1 5 00		(d) 4 4 0 00		22 8 5 5 00	
14 Rent Expense	4 2 0 0 00				4 2 0 0 00	
15 Utilities Expense	2 7 1 5 00				2 7 1 5 00	
16 Miscellaneous Expense	1 5 0 5 00				1 5 0 5 00	
17	100 0 0 0 00	100 0 0 0 00				
18 Supplies Expense			(a) 8 9 0 00		8 9 0 00	
19 Insurance Expense			(b) 3 1 5 00		3 1 5 00	
20 Amortization Expense			(c)4 9 5 0 00		4 9 5 0 00	
21 Wages Payable				(d) 4 4 0 00		4 4 0 00
22			8 0 9 5 00	8 0 9 5 00	106 3 9 0 00	106 3 9 0 00
23						

C. debit Amortization Expense, $2,000; credit Accumulated Amortization, $2,000

D. debit Accumulated Amortization, $2,000; credit Amortization Expense, $2,000

5. If the equipment account has a balance of $22,500 and its accumulated amortization account has a balance of $14,000, the net book value of the equipment is:

A. $36,500   C. $14,000
B. $22,500   D. $8,500

DISCUSSION QUESTIONS

1. How are revenues and expenses reported on the income statement under (a) the cash basis of accounting and (b) the accrual basis of accounting?
2. Fees for services provided are billed to a customer during 1999. The customer remits the amount owed in 2000. During which year would the revenues be reported on the income statement under (a) the cash basis? (b) the accrual basis?
3. Employees performed services in 1999 but the wages were not paid until 2000. During which year would the wages expense be reported on the income statement under (a) the cash basis? (b) the accrual basis?
4. Is the matching concept related to (a) the cash basis of accounting or (b) the accrual basis of accounting?
5. Is the balance listed for cash on the trial balance, before the accounts have been adjusted, the amount that should normally be reported on the balance sheet? Explain.

6. Is the balance listed for supplies on the trial balance, before the accounts have been adjusted, the amount that should normally be reported on the balance sheet? Explain.

7. Why are adjusting entries needed at the end of an accounting period?

8. What is the difference between *adjusting entries* and *correcting entries*?

9. Identify the five different categories of adjusting entries frequently required at the end of an accounting period.

10. If the effect of the credit portion of an adjusting entry is to increase the balance of a liability account, which of the following statements describes the effect of the debit portion of the entry?

    a. Increases the balance of a revenue account.
    b. Increases the balance of an expense account.
    c. Increases the balance of an asset account.

11. Does every adjusting entry have an effect on the determination of the amount of net income for a period? Explain.

12. What is the nature of the balance in the prepaid insurance account at the end of the accounting period (a) before adjustment? (b) after adjustment?

13. On May 1 of the current year, a business paid the May rent on the building that it occupies. (a) Do the rights acquired at May 1 represent an asset or an expense? (b) What is the justification for debiting Rent Expense at the time of payment?

14. What are capital assets?

15. What is amortization?

16. In accounting for amortization on equipment, what is the name of the account that would be referred to as a contra asset account?

17. (a) Explain the purpose of the two accounts: Amortization Expense and Accumulated Amortization. (b) What is the normal balance of each account? (c) Is it customary for the balances of the two accounts to be equal in amount? (d) In what financial statements, if any, will each account appear?

18. What term is applied to the difference between the balance of a capital asset account and its related accumulated amortization account?

19. What is a work sheet?

20. What purpose do the Adjusted Trial Balance columns serve in a work sheet?

EXERCISES

EXERCISE 3–1
Classifying accruals and deferrals
Objectives 2, 3

Classify the following items as (a) deferred expense (prepaid expense), (b) deferred revenue (unearned revenue), (c) accrued expense (accrued liability), or (d) accrued revenue (accrued asset).

1. Utilities owed but not yet paid.
2. Revenue received but not yet earned.
3. Salary owed but not yet paid.
4. A two-year premium paid on a fire insurance policy.
5. Revenue earned but not yet received.
6. Taxes owed but payable in the following period.
7. Supplies on hand.
8. Tuition collected in advance by a university.

EXERCISE 3–2
Classifying adjusting entries
Objectives 2, 3

The following accounts were taken from the unadjusted trial balance of Lapierre Ltd., a consulting firm. Indicate whether or not each account would normally require an adjusting entry. If the account normally requires an adjusting entry, use the following notation to indicate the type of adjustment:

AE—Accrued Expense
AR—Accrued Revenue
DE—Deferred Expense
DR—Deferred Revenue

To illustrate, the answers for the first two accounts are shown below:

Account	Answer
Marcel Lapierre, Withdrawals	Does not normally require adjustment.
Accounts Receivable................	Normally requires adjustment (AR).
Accumulated Amortization.....	
Cash	
Insurance Expense	
Interest Payable	
Interest Receivable	
Land	
Office Equipment	
Prepaid Rent	
Supplies Expense	
Unearned Revenue..................	
Wages Expense	

EXERCISE 3–3
Adjusting entry for supplies
Objective 3

The balance in the supplies account, before adjustment at the end of the year, is $1,725. Journalize the adjusting entry required if the amount of supplies on hand at the end of the year is $420.

EXERCISE 3–4
Determining supplies purchased
Objective 3

The supplies and supplies expense accounts at December 31, after adjusting entries have been posted at the end of the first year of operations, are shown in the following T accounts:

Supplies		Supplies Expense	
Bal.	375	Bal.	1,750

Determine the amount of supplies purchased during the year.

EXERCISE 3–5
Effect of omitting adjusting entry
Objective 3

At December 31, the end of the first *month* of the year, the usual adjusting entry transferring supplies used to an expense account is omitted. Which items will be incorrectly stated, because of the error, on (a) the income statement for December and (b) the balance sheet as of December 31? Also indicate whether the items in error will be overstated or understated.

EXERCISE 3–6
Adjusting entries for prepaid insurance
Objective 3

The balance in the prepaid insurance account, before adjustment at the end of the year, is $6,650. Journalize the adjusting entry required under each of the following *alternatives* for determining the amount of the adjustment: (a) the amount of insurance expired during the year is $1,900; (b) the amount of unexpired insurance applicable to future periods is $4,750.

EXERCISE 3–7
Adjusting entries for prepaid insurance
Objective 3

The prepaid insurance account had a balance of $3,750 at the beginning of the year. The account was debited for $1,150 for premiums on policies purchased during the year. Journalize the adjusting entry required at the end of the year for each of the following situations: (a) the amount of unexpired insurance applicable to future periods is $2,300; (b) the amount of insurance expired during the year is $2,150.

EXERCISE 3–8
Adjusting entries for unearned fees
Objective 3

The balance in the unearned fees account, before adjustment at the end of the year, is $9,000. Journalize the adjusting entry required if the amount of unearned fees at the end of the year is $2,500.

EXERCISE 3–9
Effect of omitting adjusting entry
Objective 3

At the end of January, the first *month* of the year, the usual adjusting entry transferring rent earned to a revenue account from the unearned rent account was omitted. Indicate which items will be incorrectly stated, because of the error, on (a) the income statement for January and (b) the balance sheet as of January 31. Also indicate whether the items in error will be overstated or understated.

EXERCISE 3–10
Adjusting entries for accrued salaries
Objective 3

Chan Realty Co. pays weekly salaries of $7,500 on Friday for a five-day week ending on that day. Journalize the necessary adjusting entry at the end of the accounting period, assuming that the period ends (a) on Tuesday, (b) on Wednesday.

EXERCISE 3–11
Determining wages paid
Objective 3

The wages payable and wages expense accounts at December 31, after adjusting entries have been posted at the end of the first year of operations, are shown in the following T accounts:

Wages Payable		Wages Expense	
Bal.	420	Bal.	21,800

Determine the amount of wages paid during the year.

EXERCISE 3–12
Effect of omitting adjusting entry
Objective 3

Accrued salaries of $3,000 owed to employees for December 30 and 31 are not taken into consideration in preparing the financial statements for the year ended December 31. Indicate which items will be erroneously stated, because of the error, on (a) the income statement for the year and (b) the balance sheet as of December 31. Also indicate whether the items in error will be overstated or understated.

EXERCISE 3–13
Effect of omitting adjusting entry
Objective 3

Assume that the error in Exercise 3–12 was not corrected and that the $3,000 of accrued salaries was included in the first salary payment in January. Indicate which items will be erroneously stated, because of failure to correct the initial error, on (a) the income statement for the month of January and (b) the balance sheet as of January 31.

EXERCISE 3–14
Adjusting entries for prepaid and accrued taxes
Objective 3

Edwards Financial Planning Co. was organized on April 1 of the current year. On April 2, Edwards prepaid $1,080 to the city for taxes (licence fees) for the *next* 12 months and debited the prepaid taxes account. Edwards is also required to pay in January an annual tax (on property) for the *previous* calendar year. The estimated amount of the property tax for the current year (April 1 to December 31) is $13,600. (a) Journalize the two adjusting entries required to bring the accounts affected by the two taxes up to date as of December 31, the end of the current year. (b) What is the amount of tax expense for the current year?

EXERCISE 3–15
Effects of errors on financial statements
Objective 3

The balance sheet for **J Mart Stores Ltd.** as of February 28, 1999, includes the following accrued expenses as liabilities:

Accrued expenses	$86,826,000
Accrued income taxes	38,582,000

The net income for J Mart Stores Ltd. for the year ended February 28, 1999, was $132,400,000. (a) If the accruals had not been recorded at February 28, 1999, by how much would net income have been misstated for the fiscal year ended February 28, 1999? (b) What is the percentage of the misstatement in (a) to the reported net income of $132,400,000?

EXERCISE 3–16
Effects of errors on financial statements
Objective 3

The accountant for Econoline Travel Services mistakenly omitted adjusting entries to set up (a) unearned revenue ($2,500) and (b) accrued wages ($850). Indicate the effect of each error, considered individually, on the income statement for the current year ended December 31. Also indicate the effect of each error on the December 31 balance sheet. Set up a table similar to the following, and record your answers by inserting the dollar amount in the appropriate spaces. Insert a zero if the error does not affect the item.

	Error (a)		Error (b)	
	Over-stated	Under-stated	Over-stated	Under-stated
1. Revenue for the year would be	$	$	$	$
2. Expenses for the year would be	$	$	$	$
3. Net income for the year would be	$	$	$	$
4. Assets at December 31 would be	$	$	$	$
5. Liabilities at December 31 would be	$	$	$	$
6. Owner's equity at December 31 would be	$	$	$	$

EXERCISE 3–17
Effects of errors on financial statements
Objective 3

If the net income for the current year had been $31,700 in Exercise 3–16, what would be the correct net income if the proper adjusting entries had been made?

EXERCISE 3–18
Adjusting entry for accrued fees
Objective 3

At the end of the current year, $1,150 of revenue have been earned but have not been billed to clients.

a. Journalize the adjusting entry to record the accrued revenue.
b. ➤ If the cash basis rather than the accrual basis had been used, would an adjusting entry have been necessary? Explain.

EXERCISE 3–19
Adjusting entries for unearned and accrued fees
Objective 3

The balance in the unearned revenue account, before adjustment at the end of the year, is $11,300. Of this revenue, $8,500 have been earned. In addition, $2,750 of revenue have been earned but have not been billed. Journalize the adjusting entries (a) to adjust the unearned revenue account and (b) to record the accrued revenue.

EXERCISE 3–20
Effect on financial statements of omitting adjusting entry
Objective 3

The adjusting entry for accrued revenue was omitted at December 31, the end of the current year. Indicate which items will be in error, because of the omission, on (a) the income statement for the current year and (b) the balance sheet as of December 31. Also indicate whether the items in error will be overstated or understated.

EXERCISE 3–21
Adjusting entry for amortization
Objective 3

The estimated amount of amortization on equipment for the current year is $4,100. Journalize the adjusting entry to record the amortization.

EXERCISE 3–22
Determining capital asset's net book value
Objective 3

The balance in the equipment account is $115,000, and the balance in the accumulated amortization—equipment account is $80,000.

a. What is the net book value of the equipment?
b. ➤ Does the balance in the accumulated amortization account mean that the equipment's loss of value is $80,000? Explain.

EXERCISE 3–23
Net book value of capital assets
Objective 3

Canadian Airlines Corporation reported Capital Assets (*Property, Plant, and Equipment*) of $1,533 million and *Accumulated Amortization* of $304 million at the end of June, 1996.

a. What was the net book value of the capital assets at June 30, 1996?
b. ➤ Would the net book value of Canadian Airlines Corporation's capital assets normally approximate their fair market values?

EXERCISE 3–24
Adjusting entries for amortization; effect of error
Objective 3

On December 31, a business estimates amortization on equipment used during the first year of operations to be $1,800. (a) Journalize the adjusting entry required as of December 31. (b) If the adjusting entry in (a) were omitted, which items would be erroneously stated on (1) the income statement for the year and (2) the balance sheet as of December 31?

EXERCISE 3–25
Entering adjustments data on work sheet
Objective 4

The unadjusted trial balance for Coral Services Co. has been prepared on the following work sheet for the year ended December 31, 1999.

Coral Services Co.
Work Sheet
For the Year Ended December 31, 1999

Account Title	Unadjusted Trial Balance Dr.	Unadjusted Trial Balance Cr.	Adjustments Dr.	Adjustments Cr.	Adjusted Trial Balance Dr.	Adjusted Trial Balance Cr.
Cash	6					
Accounts Receivable	18					
Supplies	4					
Prepaid Insurance	6					
Land	12					
Equipment	20					
Accumulated Amort.—Equip.		3				
Accounts Payable		13				
Wages Payable		0				
Jill Tolbert, Capital		40				
Jill Tolbert, Withdrawals	4					
Revenue Earned		34				
Wages Expense	12					
Rent Expense	4					
Insurance Expense	0					
Utilities Expense	2					
Amortization Expense	0					
Supplies Expense	0					
Miscellaneous Expense	2					
Totals	90	90				

The data for year-end adjustments are as follows:

a. Revenue earned but not yet billed, $5.
b. Supplies on hand, $1.
c. Insurance premiums expired, $4.
d. Amortization expense, $2.
e. Wages accrued but not paid, $1.

Set up the above work sheet on separate paper, enter the adjustments data, and extend the balances to the Adjusted Trial Balance columns.

EXERCISE 3–26
Work sheet
Objective 4

The accountant for All-Washed-Up Laundry prepared the following portion of a work sheet. Assume that all balances in the unadjusted trial balance are correct in amount. How many errors can you find in the accountant's work? What are they?

All-Washed-Up Laundry
Work Sheet
For the Year Ended August 31, 1999

Account Title	Trial Balance Dr.	Trial Balance Cr.	Adjustments Dr.	Adjustments Cr.	Adjusted Trial Balance Dr.	Adjusted Trial Balance Cr.
Cash	17,790				7,790	
Laundry Supplies	4,750		(a) 3,910		8,660	
Prepaid Insurance	2,825			(b) 1,500	1,325	
Laundry Equipment		85,600				85,600
Accumulated Amortization	55,700		(c) 5,720		61,420	
Accounts Payable		4,950				4,950
Jim Leland, Capital		30,900				30,900
Jim Leland, Withdrawals	8,000				8,000	
Laundry Revenue		76,900				76,900
Wages Expense	24,500		(d) 850		24,500	
Rent Expense	15,575				15,575	
Utilities Expense	8,500				5,800	
Miscellaneous Expense	910					
	138,550	198,350				
Laundry Supplies Expense			(a) 3,910		3,910	
Insurance Expense					1,500	
Amortization Expense			(c) 5,720		5,720	
Wages Payable			(d) 850			850
			15,240	7,220	144,200	199,200

EXERCISE 3–27
Adjusting entries for office supplies

The office supplies purchased during the year total $3,450, and the amount of office supplies on hand at the end of the year is $830.

a. Record the following transactions directly in T accounts for Office Supplies and Office Supplies Expense, using the system of initially recording supplies as an asset: (1) purchases for the period; (2) adjusting entry at the end of the period. Identify each entry by number.

b. Record the following transactions directly in T accounts for Office Supplies and Office Supplies Expense, using the system of initially recording supplies as an expense: (1) purchases for the period; (2) adjusting entry at the end of the period. Identify each entry by number.

EXERCISE 3–28
Adjusting entries for prepaid insurance

During the first year of operations, insurance premiums of $7,300 were paid. At the end of the year, unexpired premiums totalled $2,750. Journalize the adjusting entry at the end of the year, assuming that (a) prepaid expenses were initially recorded as assets and (b) prepaid expenses were initially recorded as expenses.

EXERCISE 3–29
Adjusting entries for advertising revenue

The advertising revenues received during the year total $160,000, and the unearned advertising revenue at the end of the year is $22,000.

a. Record the following transactions directly in T accounts for Unearned Advertising Revenue and Advertising Revenue, using the system of initially recording advertising revenue as a liability: (1) revenues received during the period; (2) adjusting entry at the end of the period. Identify each entry by number.

b. Record the following transactions directly in T accounts for Unearned Advertising Revenue and Advertising Revenue, using the system of initially recording advertising revenue as revenue: (1) revenues received during the period; (2) adjusting entry at the end of the period. Identify each entry by number.

EXERCISE 3–30
Year-end entries for deferred revenues

In their first year of operation, Snyder Publishing Co. received $530,000 from advertising contracts and $875,000 from magazine subscriptions, crediting the two amounts to Unearned Advertising Revenue and Circulation Revenue, respectively. At the end of the year, the unearned advertising revenue amounts to $175,000, and the unearned circulation revenue amounts to $240,000. Journalize the adjusting entries that should be made at the end of the year.

PROBLEMS SERIES A

PROBLEM 3–1A
Adjusting entries
Objective 3

On December 31, the end of the current year, the following data were accumulated to assist the accountant in preparing the adjusting entries for Wyckoff Realty:

a. The supplies account balance on December 31 is $2,450. The supplies on hand on December 31 are $490.
b. The unearned rent account balance on December 31 is $2,400, representing the receipt of an advance payment on December 1 of three months' rent from tenants.
c. Wages accrued but not paid at December 31 are $1,500.
d. Revenue accrued but unbilled at December 31 are $7,500.
e. Amortization on office equipment for the year is $850.

Instructions

1. Journalize the adjusting entries required at December 31.
2. ◖▬▬▶ Briefly explain the difference between adjusting entries and entries that would be made to correct errors.

PROBLEM 3–2A
Adjusting entries
Objective 3

Selected account balances before adjustment for Byte Computer Services at December 31, the end of the current year, are as follows:

	Debits	Credits
Accounts Receivable	$11,250	
Supplies	4,750	
Prepaid Rent	27,000	
Equipment	42,500	
Accumulated Amortization		$10,900
Wages Payable		—
Unearned Revenue		5,000
Revenue Earned		87,950
Wages Expense	29,400	
Rent Expense	—	
Amortization Expense	—	
Supplies Expense	—	

Data needed for year-end adjustments are as follows:

a. Unbilled revenue at December 31, $3,650.
b. Supplies on hand at December 31, $1,275.
c. Rent expired during year, $24,000.
d. Amortization of equipment during year, $2,750.
e. Unearned revenue at December 31, $1,250.
f. Wages accrued but not paid at December 31, $1,150.

Instructions

Journalize the six adjusting entries required at December 31, based upon the data presented.

PROBLEM 3–3A
Adjusting entries
Objective 3

Octavius Company specializes in the repair of music equipment and is owned and operated by Cecil Virgil. On June 30, 1999, the end of the current year, the accountant for Octavius Company prepared a trial balance and an adjusted trial balance. The two trial balances are as follows:

Octavius Company
Trial Balance
June 30, 1999

	Unadjusted		Adjusted	
Cash	11,825		11,825	
Accounts Receivable	29,500		29,500	
Supplies	6,950		2,635	
Prepaid Insurance	3,750		1,150	
Equipment	92,150		92,150	
Accumulated Amortization—Equipment		53,480		61,270
Automobiles	36,500		36,500	
Accumulated Amortization—Automobiles		18,250		22,900
Accounts Payable		8,310		9,730
Salaries Payable		—		2,400
Unearned Service Fees		5,000		1,225
C. Virgil, Capital		55,470		55,470
C. Virgil, Withdrawals	5,000		5,000	
Service Revenue Earned		244,600		248,375
Salary Expense	172,300		174,700	
Rent Expense	18,000		18,000	
Supplies Expense	—		4,315	
Amortization Expense—Equipment	—		7,790	
Amortization Expense—Automobiles	—		4,650	
Utilities Expense	4,700		6,120	
Taxes Expense	2,725		2,725	
Insurance Expense	—		2,600	
Miscellaneous Expense	1,710		1,710	
	385,110	385,110	401,370	401,370

Instructions

Journalize the seven entries that adjusted the accounts at June 30. None of the accounts was affected by more than one adjusting entry.

PROBLEM 3–4A
Adjusting entries
Objective 3

Blair Company, an electronics repair store, prepared the following trial balance at the end of its first year of operations:

Blair Company
Trial Balance
November 30, 20—

Cash	1,150	
Accounts Receivable	5,500	
Supplies	1,800	
Equipment	17,900	
Accounts Payable		750
Unearned Revenue		2,000
G. Orwell, Capital		10,000
G. Orwell, Withdrawals	1,500	
Revenue Earned		35,250
Wages Expense	8,500	
Rent Expense	8,000	
Utilities Expense	2,750	
Miscellaneous Expense	900	
	48,000	48,000

For preparing the adjusting entries, the following data were assembled:

a. Revenue earned but unbilled on November 30 were $1,550.
b. Supplies on hand on November 30 were $480.
c. Amortization of equipment was estimated to be $1,100 for the year.
d. The balance in unearned revenue represented the September 1 receipt in advance for services to be provided. Only $800 of the services was provided between September 1 and November 30.
e. Unpaid wages accrued on November 30 were $275.

Instructions
Journalize the adjusting entries necessary on November 30.

PROBLEM 3–5A
Work sheet and adjusting entries
Objectives 3, 4

Dickens Company is a small editorial services company owned and operated by E. Scrooge. Dickens Company's accounting clerk prepared the following trial balance on December 31, the end of the current year:

Dickens Company
Trial Balance
December 31, 20—

Cash	6,700	
Accounts Receivable	23,800	
Prepaid Insurance	3,400	
Supplies	1,950	
Land	50,000	
Building	141,500	
Accumulated Amortization—Building		91,700
Equipment	90,100	
Accumulated Amortization—Equipment		65,300
Accounts Payable		7,500
Unearned Rent		6,000
E. Scrooge, Capital		81,500
E. Scrooge, Withdrawals	10,000	
Revenue Earned		218,400
Salaries and Wages Expense	80,200	
Utilities Expense	28,200	
Advertising Expense	19,000	
Repairs Expense	11,500	
Miscellaneous Expense	4,050	
	470,400	470,400

The data needed to determine year-end adjustments are as follows:

a. Unexpired insurance at December 31, $800.
b. Supplies on hand at December 31, $450.
c. Amortization of building for the year, $1,620.
d. Amortization of equipment for the year, $5,500.
e. Rent unearned at December 31, $1,500.
f. Accrued salaries and wages at December 31, $2,000.
g. Revenue earned but unbilled on December 31, $2,750.

Instructions

1. Enter the trial balance on a 10-column work sheet.
2. Enter the data for the seven adjustments in the Adjustments columns of the work sheet. Add additional accounts as needed.
3. Complete the Adjusted Trial Balance columns in the work sheet.
4. On the basis of the adjustment data in the work sheet, journalize the adjusting entries.

PROBLEM 3–6A
Adjusting entries and errors
Objective 3

At the end of June, the first month of operations, the following selected data were taken from the financial statements of K. Martin, a lawyer:

Net income for June	$ 39,750
Total assets at June 30	189,700
Total liabilities at June 30	20,200
Total owner's equity at June 30	169,500

In preparing the financial statements, adjustments for the following data were over-looked:

a. Supplies used during June, $1,750.
b. Unbilled revenue earned at June 30, $2,900.
c. Amortization of equipment for June, $2,500.
d. Accrued wages at June 30, $1,500.

Instructions

1. Journalize the entries to record the omitted adjustments.
2. Determine the correct amount of net income for June and the total assets, liabilities, and owner's equity at June 30. In addition to indicating the corrected amounts, indicate the effect of each omitted adjustment by setting up and completing a columnar table similar to the following. Adjustment (a) is presented as an example.

	Net Income	Total Assets	Total Liabilities	Total Owner's Equity
Reported amounts	$39,750	$189,700	$20,200	$169,500
Corrections:				
Adjustment (a)	−1,750	−1,750	0	−1,750
Adjustment (b)	_____	_____	_____	_____
Adjustment (c)	_____	_____	_____	_____
Adjustment (d)	_____	_____	_____	_____
Corrected amounts	══════	══════	══════	══════

PROBLEMS SERIES B

PROBLEM 3–1B
Adjusting entries
Objective 3

On December 31, the end of the current year, the following data were accumulated to assist the accountant in preparing the adjusting entries for Michelle Marvan, Architect:

a. Revenue accrued but unbilled at December 31 are $5,250.
b. The supplies account balance on December 31 is $3,100. The supplies on hand at December 31 are $1,050.
c. Wages accrued but not paid at December 31 are $1,350.
d. The unearned rent account balance at December 31 is $4,500, representing the receipt of an advance payment on December 1 of three months' rent from tenants.
e. Amortization of office equipment for the year is $900.

Instructions

1. Journalize the adjusting entries required at December 31.
2. ⬤▬▬➤ Briefly explain the difference between adjusting entries and entries that would be made to correct errors.

PROBLEM 3–2B
Adjusting entries
Objective 3

Selected account balances before adjustment for Ace Engineering at December 31, the end of the current year, are as follows:

	Debits	Credits
Accounts Receivable	$ 9,250	
Supplies	2,700	
Prepaid Rent	21,000	
Equipment	50,500	
Accumulated Amortization		$16,900
Wages Payable		—
Unearned Fees		6,500
Revenue Earned		99,850
Wages Expense	40,750	
Rent Expense	—	
Amortization Expense	—	
Supplies Expense	—	

Data needed for year-end adjustments are as follows:

a. Supplies on hand at December 31, $825.
b. Amortization of equipment during year, $3,950.
c. Rent expired during year, $18,000.
d. Wages accrued but not paid at December 31, $1,525.
e. Unearned revenue at December 31, $2,250.
f. Unbilled revenue at December 31, $3,750.

Instructions
Journalize the six adjusting entries required at December 31, based upon the data presented.

PROBLEM 3–3B
Adjusting entries
Objective 3

Aneid Company specializes in the maintenance and repair of signs, such as billboards. On December 31, the end of the current year, the accountant for Aneid Company prepared a trial balance and an adjusted trial balance. The two trial balances are as follows:

Aneid Company
Trial Balance
December 31, 20—

	Unadjusted		Adjusted	
Cash	9,750		9,750	
Accounts Receivable	20,400		20,400	
Supplies	7,880		1,460	
Prepaid Insurance	2,700		700	
Land	47,500		47,500	
Buildings	107,480		107,480	
Accumulated Amortization—Buildings		79,600		85,100
Trucks	72,000		72,000	
Accumulated Amortization—Trucks		32,800		43,900
Accounts Payable		8,920		9,420
Salaries Payable		—		1,450
Unearned Service Revenue		7,500		920
V. Homer, Capital		93,890		93,890
V. Homer, Withdrawals	8,000		8,000	
Service Revenue Earned		152,680		159,260
Salary Expense	81,200		82,650	
Amortization Expense—Trucks	—		11,100	
Rent Expense	9,600		9,600	
Supplies Expense	—		6,420	
Utilities Expense	6,200		6,700	
Amortization Expense—Buildings	—		5,500	
Taxes Expense	1,720		1,720	
Insurance Expense	—		2,000	
Miscellaneous Expense	960		960	
	375,390	375,390	393,940	393,940

Instructions
Journalize the seven entries that adjusted the accounts at December 31. None of the accounts was affected by more than one adjusting entry.

PROBLEM 3–4B
Adjusting entries
Objective 3

Western Trout Co., an outfitter store for fishing treks, prepared the following trial balance at the end of its first year of operations:

Western Trout Co.
Trial Balance
June 30, 20—

Cash	1,150	
Accounts Receivable	3,500	
Supplies	1,300	
Equipment	9,900	
Accounts Payable		750
Unearned Revenue		2,000
Erich Remarque, Capital		10,500
Erich Remarque, Withdrawals	1,000	
Revenue Earned		36,750
Wages Expense	19,500	
Rent Expense	9,000	
Utilities Expense	3,750	
Miscellaneous Expense	900	
	50,000	50,000

For preparing the adjusting entries, the following data were assembled:

a. Supplies on hand on June 30 were $275.
b. Revenue earned but unbilled on June 30 were $1,025.
c. Amortization of equipment was estimated to be $750 for the year.
d. Unpaid wages accrued on June 30 were $510.
e. The balance in unearned revenue represented the May 1 receipt in advance for services to be provided. Only $1,200 of the services were provided between May 1 and June 30.

Instructions
Journalize the adjusting entries necessary on June 30.

PROBLEM 3–5B
Work sheet and adjusting entries
Objectives 3, 4

Phelps Service Co., which specializes in appliance repair services, is owned and operated by Silas Loftus. Phelps Service Co.'s accounting clerk prepared the following trial balance at December 31, the end of the current year:

Phelps Service Co.
Trial Balance
December 31, 20—

Cash	3,200	
Accounts Receivable	17,200	
Prepaid Insurance	3,900	
Supplies	2,450	
Land	50,000	
Building	141,500	
Accumulated Amortization—Building		95,700
Equipment	90,100	
Accumulated Amortization—Equipment		65,300
Accounts Payable		7,500
Unearned Rent		4,000
Silas Loftus, Capital		65,900
Silas Loftus, Withdrawals	5,000	
Revenue Earned		218,400
Salaries and Wages Expense	78,700	
Utilities Expense	28,200	
Advertising Expense	19,000	
Repairs Expense	13,500	
Miscellaneous Expense	4,050	
	456,800	456,800

The data needed to determine year-end adjustments are as follows:

a. Unexpired insurance at December 31, $825.
b. Supplies on hand at December 31, $700.
c. Amortization of building for the year, $1,500.
d. Amortization of equipment for the year, $5,500.
e. Rent unearned at December 31, $3,000.
f. Accrued salaries and wages at December 31, $1,250.
g. Revenue earned but unbilled on December 31, $1,950.

Instructions

1. Enter the trial balance on a 10-column work sheet.
2. Enter the data for the seven adjustments in the Adjustments columns of the work sheet. Add additional accounts as needed.
3. Complete the Adjusted Trial Balance columns in the work sheet.
4. On the basis of the adjustment data in the work sheet, journalize the adjusting entries.

PROBLEM 3–6B
Adjusting entries and errors
Objective 3

At the end of July, the first month of operations, the following selected data were taken from the financial statements of Nicole Lietch, an accountant:

Net income for July	$ 70,500
Total assets at July 31	177,250
Total liabilities at July 31	36,500
Total owner's equity at July 31	140,750

In preparing the financial statements, adjustments for the following data were overlooked:

a. Unbilled revenue earned at July 31, $6,500.
b. Supplies used during July, $3,100.
c. Amortization of equipment for July, $5,300.
d. Accrued wages at July 31, $2,250.

Instructions

1. Journalize the entries to record the omitted adjustments.
2. Determine the correct amount of net income for July and the total assets, liabilities, and owner's equity at July 31. In addition to indicating the corrected amounts, indicate the effect of each omitted adjustment by setting up and completing a columnar table similar to the following. Adjustment (a) is presented as an example.

	Net Income	Total Assets	Total Liabilities	Total Owner's Equity
Reported amounts	$70,500	$177,250	$36,500	$140,750
Corrections:				
Adjustment (a)	+6,500	+6,500	0	+6,500
Adjustment (b)	_____	_____	_____	_____
Adjustment (c)	_____	_____	_____	_____
Adjustment (d)	_____	_____	_____	_____
Corrected amounts	_____	_____	_____	_____

CHALLENGE PROBLEMS

PROBLEM CP3–1

Kenny Dewitt operates a sole proprietorship, Dewitt's Management Consultant Services, which has a December 31, 1999 fiscal year-end. Kenny's accountant has determined the 1999 net income for this sole proprietorship to be $50,000. Kenny is unsure if this amount is correct and requested you to review the accounting records. Your review disclosed the following transactions that were not adjusted in the preparation of the 1999 financial statements.

a. On October 1, 1998 Dewitt purchased for cash a three-year insurance policy costing $4,200. In recording this transaction, Dewitt debited an income statement account. The 1998 financial statements correctly reflected the effects of this transaction.

b. On December 15, 1999 the firm received $6,000 for management services to be rendered during the 2000 fiscal year. In recording this transaction, Dewitt debited cash and credited a correct liability account when this was received.

c. During 1999 Dewitt paid $2,200 cash for office supplies and debited an income statement account when recording the transaction. On December 31, 1998 the balance in the office supplies inventory account was $425. A physical count of office supplies on December 31, 1999 showed $615 still on hand.

d. On July 1, 1998 the firm received $3600 in cash for the rental of excess office space for a two-year period commencing on that date. The bookkeeper recorded the transaction by debiting cash and crediting an income statement account for $3,600. A review of the December 31, 1998 balance sheet revealed no adjusting journal entry relating to this transaction.

e. The firm pays office salaries on a monthly basis on the 15th of each month. Office salaries are $1,500 per month.

f. Dewitt completed management services for the law firm, P.E.I. Law, on December 29, 1999, but did not issue an invoice for $2,200 for these services until January 3, 2000.

g. The bookkeeper recorded $35,000 for Kenny's withdrawals for the 1999 fiscal year into the salaries and wages expense account. The $35,000 is still recorded in this account.

h. The December 1999 bank statement received on January 15, 2000 showed interest income earned during that December to be $150. No entry was made in 1999 to record this interest income.

Instructions

Complete the table below, indicating for each of the above transactions: (1) whether an adjusting journal entry needed to be made at the end of 1999, and (2) the effect of the adjusting journal entry, if any, on 1999 net income. Indicate whether income increased or decreased and by what amount.

ITEM	ENTRY REQUIRED		NET INCOME	
	Yes	*No*	*Amount of Increase*	*Amount of Decrease*
a.				
b.				
c.				
d.				
e.				
f.				
g.				
h.				

PROBLEM CP3–2

Keywest began operations on January 1, 1998, with a new line of merchandise. Although the business started out well, sales dropped drastically in 1999 after a new competitor entered the market. By the end of 1999, Keywest closed its doors. The following data pertain to Keywest's operations during 1998 and 1999:

a. Sales were $100,000 in 1998; $20,000 in 1999.

b. Keywest bought inventory supplies for $48,000 on account in 1998. During 1998, the firm paid $12,000 of this. Inventory supplies on hand at the end of 1998 totalled $18,000. Keywest had a huge going-out-of-business sale in 1999 and sold all of its remaining merchandise.

c. In January, 1998 Keywest paid $2,000 for a two-year insurance policy.

d. Other expenses paid in cash were $50,000 in 1998 and $30,000 in 1999.

e. There were no accounts payable at the end of 1999.

Instructions

1. Prepare income statements for 1998 and 1999 using the cash basis of accounting.
2. Prepare income statements for 1998 and 1999 using the accrual basis of accounting.
3. Prove that income over the life of the business is the same under either method.

PROBLEM CP3–3

Simp Lee Wrong Enterprises has prepared a cash basis report for its fiscal year ending September 30, 1999. The summarized statement is as follows:

Cash Receipts	$250,000
Cash Disbursements	125,000
Increase in Cash	125,000

Simp Lee Wrong's new accountant has informed the firm that generally accepted accounting principles require that it must prepare its income statement on the accrual basis. The bookkeeper has done some analysis work and summarized the relevant information as follows:

	1999	1998
Accounts Receivable	$80,000	$90,000
Accrued Revenues	1,250	2,100
Unearned Revenues	6,900	7,025
Accounts Payable	36,775	34,850
Prepaid Expenses	2,310	3,890
Accrued Expenses	4,640	2,935

Instructions

Compute the net income for 1999 on an accrual basis of accounting.

PROBLEM CP3–4

DJ Vue Company has prepared its financial statements for its fiscal year ending September 30, 1999. The summarized income statement is as follows:

Revenues	$300,000
Expenses	200,000
Net Income	100,000

In order to do some analysis, two CA wannabes, Bin Thar and Dun That, are asked to compute cash receipts and cash disbursements from operations. To aid them in their computation, Bin and Dun have compiled the following amounts from opening and closing balance sheets:

	1999	1998
Accounts Receivable	$80,000	$70,000
Accrued Revenues	2,500	2,100
Unearned Revenues	7,000	6,900
Accounts Payable	36,000	34,000
Prepaid Expenses	2,300	3,800
Accrued Expenses	1,600	2,800

Instructions

Assume the role of Ben or Dun and compute the cash receipts and disbursements for DJ Vue's 1999 fiscal year.

PROBLEM CP3–5

TriBall Company, a locally owned hardware store, sells most of its products on a cash basis, but extends short-term credit to a few of its customers. Invoices for sales on account are placed in a file and are not recorded until cash is received, at which time the sale is recorded in the same manner as a cash sale. The net income reported for the first three years of operations was $121,500, $150,000, and $202,000, respectively. The total amount of the uncollected sales invoices in the file at the end of each of the three years was $6,500, $12,500, and $9,100, respectively. In each case, the entire amount was collected during the first month of the succeeding year.

a. Determine the amount by which net income was overstated or understated for each of the three years.
b. Determine the items on the balance sheet that were overstated or understated, and the amount of overstatement or understatement, as of the end of each year.

CONTINUING PROBLEM

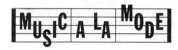

The trial balance that you prepared for Music A La Mode at the end of Chapter 2 should appear as follows:

Music A La Mode
Trial Balance
December 31, 1999

Cash	2,282	
Accounts Receivable	880	
Supplies	445	
Prepaid Insurance	1,680	
Office Equipment	2,500	
Accounts Payable		2,875
Unearned Revenue		1,500
Julian Felipe, Capital		3,000
Julian Felipe, Withdrawals	475	
Revenue Earned		4,570
Wages Expense	910	
Office Rent Expense	970	
Equipment Rent Expense	550	
Utilities Expense	380	
Music Expense	340	
Advertising Expense	225	
Supplies Expense	80	
Miscellaneous Expense	228	
	11,945	11,945

The data needed to determine adjustments for the two-month period ending December 31, 1999, are as follows:

a. During December, Music A La Mode provided guest disc jockeys for CPRG for a total of 70 hours. For information on the amount of the accrued revenue to be billed to CPRG, see the contract described in the December 3, 1999 transaction at the end of Chapter 2.
b. Supplies on hand at December 31, $320.
c. The balance of the prepaid insurance account relates to the December 1, 1999 transaction at the end of Chapter 2.
d. Amortization of the office equipment is $40.
e. The balance of the unearned revenue account relates to the contract between Music A La Mode and CPRG, described in the December 3 transaction at the end of Chapter 2.
f. Accrued wages as of December 31, 1999 were $80.

Instructions

1. Enter the unadjusted trial balance on a 10-column work sheet. Include the following additional accounts in the unadjusted trial balance:

    18   Accumulated Amortization—Office Equipment
    22   Wages Payable
    57   Insurance Expense
    58   Amortization Expense

2. Enter the data for the adjustments in the Adjustments columns of the work sheet.
3. Complete the Adjusted Trial Balance columns in the work sheet.

CASES

CASE 3–1
Sunrise Real Estate Co.
Cash basis versus accrual basis

 Addison Stein opened Sunrise Real Estate Co., a small sole proprietorship, on January 11 of the current year. Her nephew, a fourth-year accounting student, explained the accrual basis of reporting revenue and expenses, noted that it was the most widely used method, and suggested its use for Sunrise Real Estate Co. Addison decided that the accrual basis was too complicated and unnecessary for her business. She decided to use the cash basis for preparing financial statements, even though some receivables and payables existed at the end of the year.

➤ Discuss whether Addison Stein behaved in an appropriate manner by using the cash basis for preparing the financial statements for Sunrise Real Estate Co.

CASE 3–2
Baird & Associates
Financial disclosures

 John Baird is negotiating the sale of his law practice, Baird & Associates, to Lavoir Terry. As part of the negotiations, John has prepared a list of his clients, with an estimate of revenue expected to be earned from each. In some cases, the estimated revenue differs from the amounts earned from clients and that have been included in the preceding year's financial statements. In other cases, an amount has been listed as an expected revenue from a client for whom no services have been rendered in the past.

➤ Discuss whether John Baird is behaving in an ethical manner.

CASE 3–3
Ford Motor Co.
Accrued expense

  On December 30, 1998, you buy a Ford Explorer. It comes with a three-year, 60,000-kilometre warranty. On January 21, 1999, you return the Explorer to the dealership for some basic repairs covered under the warranty. The cost of the repairs to the dealership is $150. In what year, 1998 or 1999, should Ford Motor Co. recognize the cost of the warranty repairs as an expense? Give reasons for your answer.

CASE 3–4
Canadian Airlines
Accrued revenue

  The following is an excerpt from a conversation between Margaret Nelms and Dave Jerkins just before they boarded a flight to Banff on Canadian Airlines. They are going to Banff to attend their company's annual sales conference.

Margaret: Dave, aren't you taking an introductory accounting course at Mohawk College?

Dave: Yes, I decided it's about time I learned something about accounting. You know, our annual bonuses are based upon the sales figures that come from the Accounting Department.

Margaret: I guess I never really thought about it.

Dave: You should think about it! Last year, I placed a $100,000 order on December 21. But when I got my bonus, the $100,000 sale wasn't included. They said it hadn't been shipped until January 3, so it would have to count in next year's bonus.

Margaret: A real bummer!

Dave: Right! I was counting on that bonus including the $100,000 sale.

Margaret: Did you complain?

Dave: Yes, but it didn't do any good. Elmer, the head accountant, said something about not meeting the criteria for revenue recognition. I figure I'd take the accounting course and find out whether he's just jerking me around.

Margaret: I never really thought about it. When do you think Canadian Airlines will record its revenues from this flight?

Dave: Mmm . . . I guess it could record the revenue when it sells the ticket . . . or . . . when the boarding passes are taken at the door . . . or . . . when we get off the plane . . . or when our company pays for the tickets . . . or . . . I don't know. I'll ask my accounting instructor.

➤ Discuss when Canadian Airlines should recognize the revenue from ticket sales to properly match revenues and expenses.

CASE 3–5
Sears Canada Inc.
Financial analysis

 Analytical procedures can take many forms. One form would be comparing an item on the current statement with the same item on a prior statement. For example, the net income for the current year may be compared to the net income of the prior year. Also, an item in the current statement may be compared to other items in the same statement. For example, the amount of the net income for the current year can be compared with the amount of the revenues for the same year.

a. Determine for Sears Canada Inc.:
   1. The amount of the change and percent of change in net income for the current year.
   2. The percentage relationship between net income and net sales (net income divided by net sales) for the current and preceding years.
b. What conclusions can be drawn from the analysis performed in (a)?

CASE 3–6
Niki Television Repair
Adjustments and financial statements

Several years ago, your neighbour opened Niki Television Repair. He made a small initial investment and added money from his personal bank account as needed. He withdrew money for living expenses at irregular intervals. As the business grew, he hired an assistant. He is now considering adding more employees, purchasing additional service trucks, and purchasing the building he now rents. To secure funds for the expansion, he submitted a loan application to the bank and included the most recent financial statements (shown at right) prepared from accounts maintained by a part-time bookkeeper.

After reviewing the financial statements, the loan officer at the bank asked Mr. Niki if he used the accrual basis of accounting for revenues and expenses. He responded that he did and that is why he included an account for "Amounts Due from Customers." The loan officer then asked whether or not the accounts were adjusted prior to the preparation of the statements. Mr. Niki answered that they had not been adjusted.

a. Why do you think the loan officer suspected that the accounts had not been adjusted prior to the preparation of the statements?
b. Indicate possible accounts that might need to be adjusted before an accurate set of financial statements could be prepared.

Niki Television Repair
Income Statement
For the Year Ended December 31, 20—

Service revenue		$66,900
Less: Rent paid	$18,000	
Wages paid	16,500	
Supplies paid	7,000	
Utilities paid	3,100	
Insurance paid	3,000	
Miscellaneous payments	2,150	49,750
Net income		$17,150

Niki Television Repair
Balance Sheet
December 31, 20—

Assets	
Cash	$ 3,750
Amounts due from customers	2,100
Truck	25,000
Total assets	$30,850
Equities	
Owner's capital	$30,850

CASE 3–7
Neptune Software Co.
Recognizing revenue

Neptune Software Co. creates and produces computer software for various office applications. The majority of the software is designed to run on a networked system of personal computers.

Neptune Software licenses its software to its customers under an agreement that requires a fee payment within 30 days. Neptune has designed authorization codes into all its software. These authorization codes allow the user to run the software only if the proper code is entered. When a customer initially enters into the licensing agreement for software, Neptune provides the customer with a temporary authorization code that will expire in 30 days. Thus, if the customer has not paid within 30 days, Neptune can deny use of the software by not providing the customer a permanent authorization code. In some cases, Neptune will provide an additional temporary authorization code if the customer has made partial payment within 30 days and has agreed to a payment plan. A permanent authorization code is provided only when full payment has been received.

The controller for Neptune Software is uncertain as to when to recognize revenue associated with the licensing of the software; specifically, the following three times for recognizing revenue are being considered:

(1) Record the revenue when the software is delivered to the customer.
(2) Record the revenue as payments from customers are received.

(3) Record the revenue only when the permanent authorization code has been provided to the customer and full payment has been received.

➤ When would you suggest the controller of Neptune recognize revenue from the licensing agreements? Explain your answer.

ANSWERS TO SELF-EXAMINATION QUESTIONS

1. **A** A deferral is the delay in recording an expense already paid, such as prepaid insurance (answer A). Wages payable (answer B) is considered an accrued expense or accrued liability. Revenue earned (answer C) is a revenue item. Accumulated amortization (answer D) is a contra account to a capital asset.

2. **D** The balance in the supplies account, before adjustment, represents the amount of supplies available. From this amount ($2,250) is subtracted the amount of supplies on hand ($950) to determine the supplies used ($1,300). Since increases in expense accounts are recorded by debits and decreases in asset accounts are recorded by credits, answer D is the correct entry.

3. **C** The failure to record the adjusting entry debiting unearned rent, $600, and crediting rent income, $600, would have the effect of overstating liabilities by $600 and understating net income by $600 (answer C).

4. **C** Since increases in expense accounts (such as amortization expense) are recorded by debits and it is customary to record the decreases in usefulness of capital assets as credits to accumulated amortization accounts, answer C is the correct entry.

5. **D** The net book value of a capital asset is the difference between the balance in the asset account and the balance in the related accumulated amortization account, or $22,500 − $14,000, as indicated by answer D ($8,500).

4 Completing the Accounting Cycle

YOU AND ACCOUNTING

When you ride in a taxi, you get in, you tell the driver where you want to go, and the driver lowers the meter lever (flag) to start the meter running. At the end of the trip, the driver stops the meter. You then pay the driver for the amount indicated. As the next passenger is picked up, the driver lowers the lever, and the cycle starts all over again.

Businesses also go through a cycle of activities. At the beginning of the cycle, management plans where it wants the business to go and begins the necessary actions to achieve its operating goals. Throughout the cycle, which is normally one year, the accountant records the operating activities (transactions) of the business. At the end of the cycle, the accountant prepares financial statements, which summarize the operating activities for the year. The accountant then prepares the accounts for the recording of the operating activities in the next cycle.

We begin this chapter by completing our discussion of how to use the work sheet in preparing financial statements. We then describe and illustrate the journalizing and posting of adjusting entries and how we should go about preparing the accounting records for the next accounting period.

We will also discuss how to classify assets according to how quickly the entity can convert them to cash and how to classify liabilities by their due date. These classifications are important because a company must be able to pay its debts as they come due. If, for example, it has a large amount of assets invested in equipment that cannot be readily converted to cash, the company may have difficulty paying its debts on time.

After you have finished studying this chapter, you will have covered all the basic steps in the accounting process. We conclude the chapter by summarizing these steps.

135

Work Sheet

Objective 1
Prepare a work sheet.

In Chapter 3, we illustrated the use of a work sheet for assembling data and summarizing the effects of adjusting entries on the accounts. We prepared the December 31, 1999 trial balance for Computer King directly on the work sheet, as shown in Exhibit 1 on page 141A. We then entered the adjustments in the Adjustments Debit and Credit columns, and extended the Trial Balance amounts through these columns to the Adjusted Trial Balance columns, as shown in the first transparency overlay (Exhibit 2). In the following paragraphs, we describe how the extension of the Adjusted Trial Balance amounts to Income Statement and Balance Sheet columns can aid in the preparation of financial statements.

INCOME STATEMENT AND BALANCE SHEET COLUMNS

The Income Statement Debit and Credit columns are directly to the right of the Adjusted Trial Balance columns in the work sheet. The Balance Sheet Debit and Credit columns are directly to the right of the Income Statement columns.

We could expand the work sheet to include Statement of Owner's Equity columns. However, because of the few accounts affected (Capital and Withdrawals), we do not normally include separate columns for the statement of owner's equity in the work sheet. Instead, we extend the owner's equity accounts to the Balance Sheet columns.

COMPLETING THE WORK SHEET

We complete the work sheet by extending the Adjusted Trial Balance amounts to the Income Statement and Balance Sheet columns. We extend the amounts for assets, liabilities, owner's capital, and withdrawals to the Balance Sheet columns and the amounts for revenues and expenses to the Income Statement columns.

In the Computer King work sheet, the first account listed is Cash and the balance appearing in the Adjusted Trial Balance Debit column is $2,390. We extend this amount to the proper column. Cash is an asset. It is listed on the balance sheet and it has a debit balance. We extend the $2,390 to the Debit column of the Balance Sheet section. We extend the $2,720 balance of Accounts Receivable in similar fashion. We continue the same procedure until we have extended all account balances to the proper columns, as shown in the second transparency overlay (Exhibit 3). We extend the balances of the capital and withdrawals accounts to the Balance Sheet columns because this work sheet does not provide for separate Statement of Owner's Equity columns.

After we have extended all of the balances, we add each of the four statement columns, as shown in the third transparency overlay (Exhibit 4). The difference between the two Income Statement column totals is the amount of the net income or the net loss for the period. Likewise, the difference between the two Balance Sheet column totals is also the amount of the net income or net loss for the period.

If the Income Statement Credit column total (representing total revenue) is greater than the Income Statement Debit column total (representing total expenses), the difference is the net income. If the Income Statement Debit column total is greater than the Income Statement Credit column total, the difference is a net loss. For Computer King, we compute net income as follows:

Total of Credit column (revenues)	$16,960
Total of Debit column (expenses)	9,755
Net income (excess of revenues over expenses)	$ 7,205

As shown in Exhibit 4, we insert the amount of the net income, $7,205, in the Income Statement Debit column and the Balance Sheet Credit column. We also insert the term *Net income* in the Account Title column. If there had been a net loss instead of net income, we would have entered the amount in the Income Statement Credit column and the Balance Sheet Debit column, and inserted the term *Net loss* in the Account Title column. Inserting the net income or net loss into the statement columns on the work sheet shows the effect of transferring the net balance of the revenue and expense accounts to the owner's capital account. We discuss journalizing this transfer later in this chapter.

After we have entered the net income or net loss on the work sheet, we total each of the four statement columns. The totals of the two Income Statement columns must be equal. The totals of the two Balance Sheet columns must also be equal.

Financial Statements

Objective 2
Define the full disclosure and cost benefit principle, and prepare financial statements from a work sheet.

In deciding what information to report in financial statements, accountants should follow the generally accepted accounting principle known as the full disclosure principle. This principle requires that financial reports provide any information that is important enough to influence the decisions of an informed user. However, this does not mean that the statements must include every small detail about the firm's operations. Since excessively detailed data could overwhelm the reader, the accountant will often group similar items together and condense the information in order to keep the statements **understandable** to the user. The cost-benefit principle also requires that the statements only disclose information whose benefit to users is greater than the costs of presenting it.[1]

The work sheet is an aid in preparing the income statement, the statement of owner's equity, and the balance sheet, which are presented in Exhibit 5 on page 141B. In the following paragraphs, we discuss these financial statements for Computer King, prepared from the completed work sheet in Exhibit 4. The basic form of the statements is similar to those presented in Chapter 1.

INCOME STATEMENT

We normally prepare the income statement directly from the accounts listed in the work sheet. However, we may change the order of the expenses. One method used

---

[1] *CICA Handbook*, Section 1000, paragraph 16.

in preparing the income statement is to list the expenses in order of size, beginning with the larger items. Miscellaneous expense is usually shown as the last item, regardless of the amount. This is the method that we will follow in this text.

STATEMENT OF OWNER'S EQUITY

The first item normally presented on the statement of owner's equity is the balance of the proprietor's capital account at the beginning of the period. On the work sheet, however, the amount listed as capital does not always represent the account balance at the beginning of the period. The proprietor may have invested additional assets in the business during the period. Hence, for the beginning balance and any additional investments, you must refer to the capital account in the ledger. We then use the amount of net income (or net loss) and the amount of the withdrawals to determine the ending capital account balance. We obtain the net income (or net loss) and the withdrawals amounts from the Balance Sheet columns of the work sheet.

Exhibit 5 shows the basic form of the statement of owner's equity. For Computer King, the amount of withdrawals by the owner was less than the net income. If the owner's withdrawals had exceeded the net income, we would have reversed the order of the net income and the withdrawals and deducted the difference between the two items from the beginning capital account balance. Other factors, such as additional investments or a net loss, also require some change in the form, as shown in the following example:

Allan Johnson, capital, January 1, 20—	$39,000	
Additional investment during the year	6,000	
Total		$45,000
Net loss for the year	$ 5,600	
Withdrawals	9,500	
Decrease in owner's equity		15,100
Allan Johnson, capital, December 31, 20—		$29,900

BALANCE SHEET

We prepare the balance sheet directly from the accounts listed in the work sheet. The Computer King balance sheet in Exhibit 5 includes the addition of subtitles for current assets, capital assets, and current liabilities. A more complex example is included in Appendix G. We describe such a balance sheet as a *classified* balance sheet. In the following paragraphs, we describe some of the sections and subsections that may be used in a balance sheet. We will introduce additional sections in later chapters.

Assets

We divide assets for presentation on the balance sheet into two classes: (1) current assets and (2) long-term assets.

CURRENT ASSETS. Current assets are those that we expect to be converted to cash or to sell or use up usually within one year or less, through the normal operations of the business. In addition to cash, current assets usually owned by a business are short-term notes receivable, accounts receivable, supplies, and other prepaid expenses. Short-term notes receivable and accounts receivable are current assets because they will usually be converted to cash within one year or less.

Notes receivable are written claims against debtors who promise to pay the amount of the note, and possibly interest at an agreed rate, to a specified person or bearer at a specified date. Accounts receivable are also claims against debtors but are less formal than notes and do not provide for interest or a specified payment date. Accounts receivable normally arise from providing services or selling merchandise on account.

LONG-TERM ASSETS. Long-term assets include any assets not classified as current. Normally, the business is not planning to sell these assets within the next year. This classification includes capital assets, which are expected to generate benefits for the firm over more than one time period. Capital assets include equipment, machinery, buildings, and land. With the exception of land, the benefits associated with these assets are used up over several time periods. We amortize their cost over their useful life, as discussed in Chapter 3. We usually report the acquisition cost, accumulated amortization, and net book value of each major type of capital asset in the balance sheet. Long-term assets can include other types of economic resources besides capital assets, such as long-term notes receivable and long-term investments. We will discuss these in a later chapter.

Liabilities

Liabilities are debts of the business owed to outsiders (creditors). We divide liabilities into: (1) current liabilities and (2) long-term liabilities.

CURRENT LIABILITIES. Current liabilities are liabilities that will fall due within a short time (usually one year or less) and that are expected to be paid out of current assets. Two common liabilities in this group are short-term notes payable and accounts payable. These liabilities are like their receivable counterparts, except that the debtor-creditor relationship is reversed. Other typical current liability accounts are Wages Payable, Interest Payable, Taxes Payable, and Unearned Revenue.

LONG-TERM LIABILITIES. Long-term liabilities are liabilities that will not fall due for a long time (usually more than one year) If Computer King had long-term liabilities, we would report them below the current liabilities. As long-term liabilities come due and are to be paid within one year, we reclassify them as current liabilities. If we are sure that they are to be renewed rather than paid, we would continue to classify them as long-term. When a capital asset is pledged as security for a liability, we usually call the obligation a *mortgage note payable* or a *mortgage payable*.

Owner's Equity

We present the owner's right to the assets of the business on the balance sheet below the liabilities section. We add the owner's equity to the total liabilities and this total must be equal to the total assets.

Journalizing and Posting Adjusting Entries

Objective 3
Journalize and post the adjusting entries

At the end of the accounting period, we use the adjustment data appearing in the work sheet to record the adjusting entries in the journal. After we have posted all the adjusting entries, the ledger should agree with the data reported on the financial statements. The adjusting entries are dated as of the last day of the period, even though they may be recorded at a later date. We may support each entry by an explanation, or just include a caption above the first adjusting entry.

The adjusting entries for Computer King are as follows. The accounts to which they have been posted appear in the ledger in Exhibit 7 (pages 143–147).

	Date	Description	Post. Ref.	Debit	Credit	
		JOURNAL			**PAGE 4**	
1		Adjusting Entries				1
2	1999 Dec. 31	Supplies Expense	55	1 2 4 0 00		2
3		Supplies	14		1 2 4 0 00	3
4		Record December supplies used.				4
5						5
6	31	Insurance Expense	56	1 0 0 00		6
7		Prepaid Insurance	15		1 0 0 00	7
8		Record December insurance expense.				8
9						9
10	31	Unearned Rent	23	1 2 0 00		10
11		Rent Income	42		1 2 0 00	11
12		Record rent earned in December.				12
13						13
14	31	Wages Expense	51	5 7 5 00		14
15		Wages Payable	22		5 7 5 00	15
16		Record wages payable at				16
17		December 31, 1999.				17
18						18
19	31	Accounts Receivable	12	5 0 0 00		19
20		Revenue Earned	41		5 0 0 00	20
21		Record accrued revenue at				21
22		December 31, 1999.				22
23						23
24	31	Amortization Expense	53	5 0 00		24
25		Accumulated Amortization—				25
26		Office Equipment	19		5 0 00	26
27						27

Nature of the Closing Process

Objective 4

Journalize and post the closing entries and prepare a post-closing trial balance.

At the end of an accounting period, we report the revenue and expense account balances in the income statement. We deduct expenses from revenues to determine the net income or net loss for the period. Since revenues and expenses are reported for each period, the balances of these accounts should be zero at the beginning of the next period. The zero balances allow us to record the next period's revenues and expenses separately from the preceding period. Because the balances of revenue and expense accounts are not carried forward, they are sometimes called tempo-rary accounts or nominal accounts. The balances of the accounts reported in the balance sheet are carried forward from year to year. Because of their permanent nature, balance sheet accounts are sometimes called real accounts.

How do we convert the end-of-period balances of the temporary accounts to zero? To begin, the revenue and expense account balances are transferred to an account called Income Summary. The balance of Income Summary is then transferred to the owner's capital account.

At the end of an accounting period, we report the balance of the owner's withdrawals account on the statement of owner's equity. We deduct the owner's withdrawals from the net income or add them to the net loss for the period to determine the net increase or decrease in owner's equity. Since withdrawals are reported for each period, the balance of the owner's withdrawals account should be zero at the beginning of the next period. Thus, the owner's withdrawals account is also a temporary account. We transfer its balance to the owner's capital account at the end of the period.

JOURNALIZING AND POSTING CLOSING ENTRIES

We transfer revenue, expense, and withdrawals account balances to the owner's capital account by a series of entries called closing entries. This transfer process is called the **closing process**. For a sole proprietorship, we make the following four closing entries at the end of the period.

1. Debit each revenue account for the amount of its balance and credit Income Summary for the total revenue.
2. Credit each expense account for the amount of its balance and debit Income Summary for the total expense.
3. If the balance in Income Summary is a credit (net income), debit Income Summary for the amount of the balance and credit owner's capital for this amount. If the balance in Income Summary is a debit (net loss), credit Income Summary and debit owner's capital for this amount.
4. Credit the withdrawals account for the amount of its balance and debit the capital account for the same amount.

We obtain the account titles and balances needed in preparing the closing entries from either the (1) work sheet, (2) income statement and statement of owner's equity, or (3) ledger. If we used a work sheet, the data for the first two entries appear in the Income Statement columns. The amount for the third entry is the net income

COMPUTER KING

		JOURNAL			PAGE 5	
	Date	Description	Post. Ref.	Debit	Credit	
1		Closing Entries				1
2	1999 Dec. 31	Revenue Earned	41	16 8 4 0 00		2
3		Rent Income	42	1 2 0 00		3
4		Income Summary	33		16 9 6 0 00	4
5						5
6	31	Income Summary	33	9 7 5 5 00		6
7		Wages Expense	51		4 5 2 5 00	7
8		Rent Expense	52		1 6 0 0 00	8
9		Amortization Expense	53		5 0 00	9
10		Utilities Expense	54		9 8 5 00	10
11		Supplies Expense	55		2 0 4 0 00	11
12		Insurance Expense	56		1 0 0 00	12
13		Miscellaneous Expense	59		4 5 5 00	13
14						14
15	31	Income Summary	33	7 2 0 5 00		15
16		Pat King, Capital	31		7 2 0 5 00	16
17						17
18	31	Pat King, Capital	31	4 0 0 0 00		18
19		Pat King, Withdrawals	32		4 0 0 0 00	19
20						20

Exhibit 1

Work Sheet with Trial Balance Entered

Computer King
Work Sheet
For the Two Months Ended December 31, 1999

Account Title	Trial Balance Dr.	Trial Balance Cr.	Adjustments Dr.	Adjustments Cr.	Adjusted Trial Balance Dr.	Adjusted Trial Balance Cr.	Income Statement Dr.	Income Statement Cr.	Balance Sheet Dr.	Balance Sheet Cr.
Cash	2,390									
Accounts Receivable	2,220									
Supplies	2,000									
Prepaid Insurance	2,400									
Land	10,000									
Office Equipment	1,800									
Accounts Payable		900								
Unearned Rent		360								
Pat King, Capital		15,000								
Pat King, Withdrawals	4,000									
Revenue Earned		16,340								
Wages Expense	3,950									
Rent Expense	1,600									
Utilities Expense	985									
Supplies Expense	800									
Miscellaneous Expense	455									
	32,600	32,600								

> We use the work sheet for assembling data and summarizing the effects of adjusting entries. It also aids in the preparation of financial statements.

Exhibit 5

*Financial Statements
Prepared from Work Sheet*

**Computer King
Income Statement
For the Two Months Ended December 31, 1999**

Revenue earned	$16 8 4 0 00	
Rent income	1 2 0 00	
Total revenues		$16 9 6 0 00
Expenses:		
Wages expense	$ 4 5 2 5 00	
Supplies expense	2 0 4 0 00	
Rent expense	1 6 0 0 00	
Utilities expense	9 8 5 00	
Insurance expense	1 0 0 00	
Amortization expense	5 0 00	
Miscellaneous expense	4 5 5 00	
Total expenses		9 7 5 5 00
Net income		$ 7 2 0 5 00

**Computer King
Statement of Owner's Equity
For the Two Months Ended December 31, 1999**

Pat King, capital, November 1, 1999		$ 0
Investment on November 1, 1999	$15 0 0 0 00	
Net income for November and December	7 2 0 5 00	
	$22 2 0 5 00	
Less withdrawals	4 0 0 0 00	
Increase in owner's equity		18 2 0 5 00
Pat King, capital, December 31, 1999		$18 2 0 5 00

**Computer King
Balance Sheet
December 31, 1999**

Assets				Liabilities		
Current assets:				Current liabilities:		
Cash	$ 2 3 9 0 00			Accounts payable	$ 9 0 0 00	
Accounts receivable	2 7 2 0 00			Wages payable	5 7 5 00	
Supplies	7 6 0 00			Unearned rent	2 4 0 00	
Prepaid insurance	2 3 0 0 00			Total liabilities		$ 1 7 1 5 00
Total current assets		$ 8 1 7 0 00				
Long-term assets:						
Land	10 0 0 0 00					
Office equipment				**Owner's Equity**		
(less accum. amort.)	1 7 5 0 00			Pat King, Capital		18 2 0 5 00
Total capital assets		11 7 5 0 00		Total liabilities and		
Total assets		$19 9 2 0 00		owner's equity		$19 9 2 0 00

or net loss appearing at the bottom of the work sheet. The withdrawals account balance appears in the Balance Sheet Debit column of the work sheet.

The closing entries for Computer King are shown on page 141.

Exhibit 6 shows a flowchart of the closing process for Computer King. The balances in the accounts are those shown in the Trial Balance columns of the work sheet in Exhibit 1.

After we have posted the closing entries to the ledger, the balance in the capital account should agree with the amount reported on the statement of owner's equity and the balance sheet. In addition, the revenue, expense, and withdrawals accounts should have zero balances.

You should note that we use the Income Summary account only at the end of the period. At the beginning of the closing process, Income Summary has no balance. During the closing process, we will debit and credit Income Summary for various amounts. At the end of the closing process, Income Summary will again have no balance. Because Income Summary has the effect of clearing the revenue and expense accounts of their balances, it is sometimes called a **clearing account**. Other titles used for this account include Revenue and Expense Summary, Profit and Loss Summary and Income and Expense Summary.[1]

Exhibit 6

Flowchart of Closing Process for Computer King

1. Transfers revenues to Income Summary.
2. Transfers expenses to Income Summary.
3. Transfers net income to Pat King, Capital.
4. Transfers Pat King, Withdrawals to Pat King, Capital.

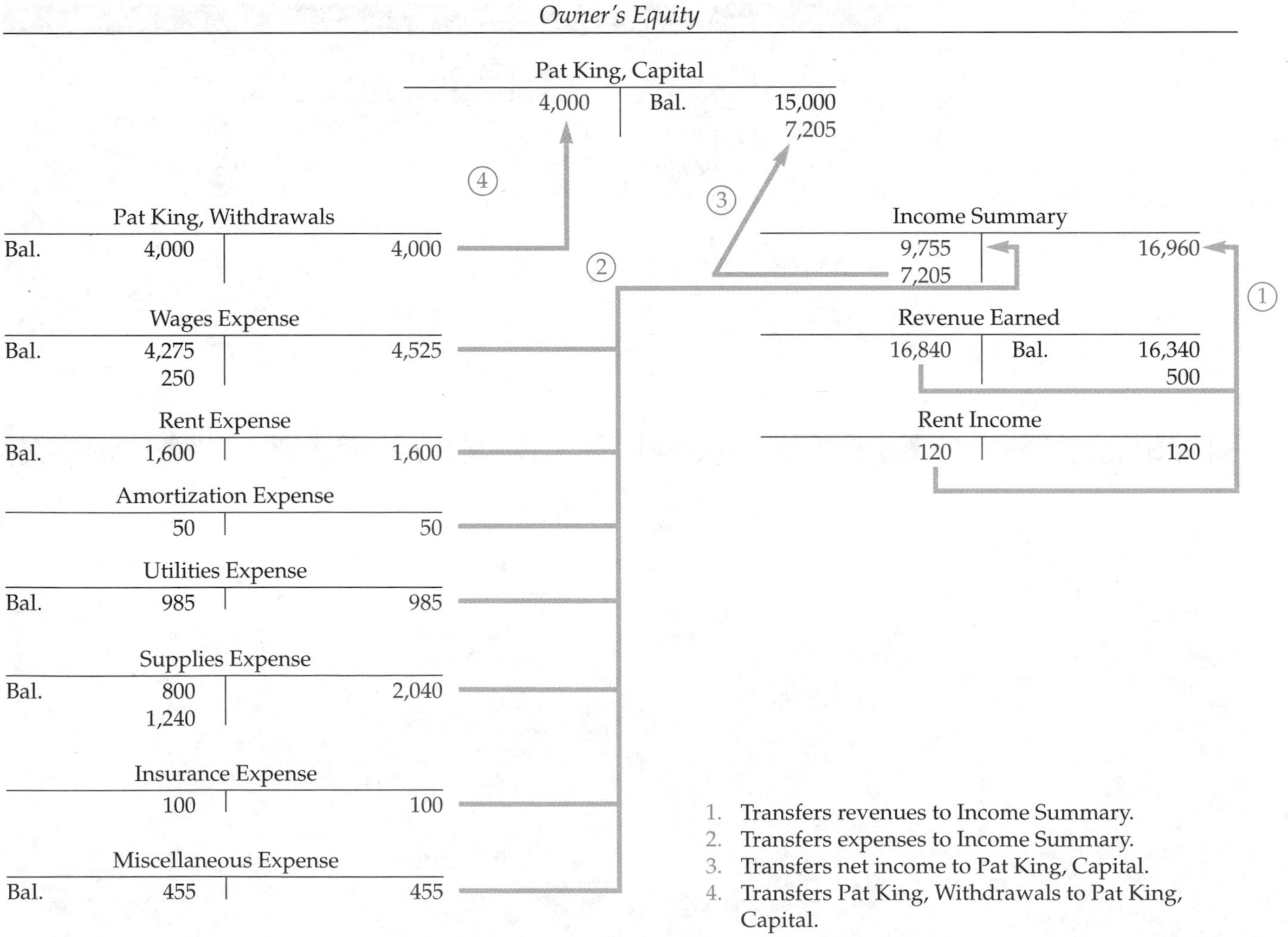

[1] It is possible to close the temporary revenue and expense accounts without using a clearing account such as Income Summary. In this case, we credit the balances of the revenue accounts and debit the balances of the expense accounts directly to the owner's capital account.

Exhibit 7 shows the ledger of Computer King after posting the adjusting and closing entries.

Exhibit 7
Ledger for Computer King

ACCOUNT *Cash*   **ACCOUNT NO.** *11*

Date		Item	Post. Ref.	Debit	Credit	Balance Debit	Balance Credit
1999 Nov.	1		1	15 0 0 0 00		15 0 0 0 00	
	5		1		10 0 0 0 00	5 0 0 0 00	
	16		1		9 5 0 00	4 0 5 0 00	
	18		1	7 5 0 0 00		11 5 5 0 00	
	30		1		3 6 5 0 00	7 9 0 0 00	
	30		1		2 0 0 0 00	5 9 0 0 00	
Dec.	1		2		2 4 0 0 00	3 5 0 0 00	
	1		2		8 0 0 00	2 7 0 0 00	
	1		2	3 6 0 00		3 0 6 0 00	
	6		2		1 8 0 00	2 8 8 0 00	
	11		2		4 0 0 00	2 4 8 0 00	
	13		2		9 5 0 00	1 5 3 0 00	
	16		2	3 1 0 0 00		4 6 3 0 00	
	20		2		9 0 0 00	3 7 3 0 00	
	21		2	6 5 0 00		4 3 8 0 00	
	23		2		1 4 5 0 00	2 9 3 0 00	
	27		2		1 2 0 0 00	1 7 3 0 00	
	31		3		3 1 0 00	1 4 2 0 00	
	31		3		2 2 5 00	1 1 9 5 00	
	31		3	2 8 7 0 00		4 0 6 5 00	
	31		3		2 0 0 0 00	2 0 6 5 00	

ACCOUNT *Accounts Receivable*   **ACCOUNT NO.** *12*

Date		Item	Post. Ref.	Debit	Credit	Balance Debit	Balance Credit
1999 Dec.	16		2	1 7 5 0 00		1 7 5 0 00	
	21		2		6 5 0 00	1 1 0 0 00	
	31		3	1 1 2 0 00		2 2 2 0 00	
	31	Adjusting	4	5 0 0 00		2 7 2 0 00	

ACCOUNT *Supplies*   **ACCOUNT NO.** *14*

Date		Item	Post. Ref.	Debit	Credit	Balance Debit	Balance Credit
1999 Nov.	10		1	1 3 5 0 00		1 3 5 0 00	
	30		1		8 0 0 00	5 5 0 00	
Dec.	23		2	1 4 5 0 00		2 0 0 0 00	
	31	Adjusting	4		1 2 4 0 00	7 6 0 00	

Exhibit 7 (continued)
Ledger for Computer King

ACCOUNT *Prepaid Insurance*   **ACCOUNT NO. 15**

Date		Item	Post. Ref.	Debit	Credit	Balance Debit	Balance Credit
1999 Dec.	1		2	2 4 0 0 00		2 4 0 0 00	
	31	Adjusting	4		1 0 0 00	2 3 0 0 00	

ACCOUNT *Land*   **ACCOUNT NO. 17**

Date		Item	Post. Ref.	Debit	Credit	Balance Debit	Balance Credit
1999 Nov.	5		1	10 0 0 0 00		10 0 0 0 00	

ACCOUNT *Office Equipment*   **ACCOUNT NO. 18**

Date		Item	Post. Ref.	Debit	Credit	Balance Debit	Balance Credit
1999 Dec.	4		2	1 8 0 0 00		1 8 0 0 00	

ACCOUNT *Accumulated Amortization*   **ACCOUNT NO. 19**

Date		Item	Post. Ref.	Debit	Credit	Balance Debit	Balance Credit
1999 Dec.	31	Adjusting	4		5 0 00		5 0 00

ACCOUNT *Accounts Payable*   **ACCOUNT NO. 21**

Date		Item	Post. Ref.	Debit	Credit	Balance Debit	Balance Credit
1999 Nov.	10		1		1 3 5 0 00		1 3 5 0 00
	16		1	9 5 0 00			4 0 0 00
Dec.	4		2		1 8 0 0 00		2 2 0 0 00
	11		2	4 0 0 00			1 8 0 0 00
	20		2	9 0 0 00			9 0 0 00

ACCOUNT *Wages Payable*   **ACCOUNT NO. 22**

Date		Item	Post. Ref.	Debit	Credit	Balance Debit	Balance Credit
1999 Dec.	31	Adjusting	4		5 7 5 00		5 7 5 00

Exhibit 7 (continued)
Ledger for Computer King

ACCOUNT *Unearned Rent*   **ACCOUNT NO. 23**

Date		Item	Post. Ref.	Debit	Credit	Balance Debit	Balance Credit
1999 Dec.	1		2		3 6 0 00		3 6 0 00
	31	Adjusting	4	1 2 0 00			2 4 0 00

ACCOUNT *Pat King, Capital*   **ACCOUNT NO. 31**

Date		Item	Post. Ref.	Debit	Credit	Balance Debit	Balance Credit
1999 Nov.	1		1		15 0 0 0 00		15 0 0 0 00
Dec.	31	Closing	5		7 2 0 5 00		22 2 0 5 00
	31	Closing	5	4 0 0 0 00			18 2 0 5 00

ACCOUNT *Pat King, Withdrawals*   **ACCOUNT NO. 32**

Date		Item	Post. Ref.	Debit	Credit	Balance Debit	Balance Credit
1999 Nov.	30		1	2 0 0 0 00		2 0 0 0 00	
Dec.	31		3	2 0 0 0 00		4 0 0 0 00	
	31	Closing	5		4 0 0 0 00	—	—

ACCOUNT *Income Summary*   **ACCOUNT NO. 33**

Date		Item	Post. Ref.	Debit	Credit	Balance Debit	Balance Credit
1999 Dec.	31	Closing	5		16 9 6 0 00		16 9 6 0 00
	31	Closing	5	9 7 5 5 00			7 2 0 5 00
	31	Closing	5	7 2 0 5 00		—	—

ACCOUNT *Revenue Earned*   **ACCOUNT NO. 41**

Date		Item	Post. Ref.	Debit	Credit	Balance Debit	Balance Credit
1999 Nov.	18		1		7 5 0 0 00		7 5 0 0 00
Dec.	16		2		3 1 0 0 00		10 6 0 0 00
	16		2		1 7 5 0 00		12 3 5 0 00
	31		3		2 8 7 0 00		15 2 2 0 00
	31		3		1 1 2 0 00		16 3 4 0 00
	31	Adjusting	4		5 0 0 00		16 8 4 0 00
	31	Closing	5	16 8 4 0 00		—	—

Exhibit 7 (continued)
Ledger for Computer King

ACCOUNT *Rent Income* **ACCOUNT NO. 42**

Date		Item	Post. Ref.	Debit	Credit	Balance Debit	Balance Credit
1999 Dec.	31	Adjusting	4		1 2 0 00		1 2 0 00
	31	Closing	5	1 2 0 00		—	—

ACCOUNT *Wages Expense* **ACCOUNT NO. 51**

Date		Item	Post. Ref.	Debit	Credit	Balance Debit	Balance Credit
1999 Nov.	30		1	1 8 0 0 00		1 8 0 0 00	
Dec.	13		2	9 5 0 00		2 7 5 0 00	
	27		2	1 2 0 0 00		3 9 5 0 00	
	31	Adjusting	4	5 7 5 00		4 5 2 5 00	
	31	Closing	5		4 5 2 5 00	—	—

ACCOUNT *Rent Expense* **ACCOUNT NO. 52**

Date		Item	Post. Ref.	Debit	Credit	Balance Debit	Balance Credit
1999 Nov.	30		1	8 0 0 00		8 0 0 00	
Dec.	1		2	8 0 0 00		1 6 0 0 00	
	31	Closing	5		1 6 0 0 00	—	—

ACCOUNT *Amortization Expense* **ACCOUNT NO. 53**

Date		Item	Post. Ref.	Debit	Credit	Balance Debit	Balance Credit
1999 Dec.	31	Adjusting	4	5 0 00		5 0 00	
	31	Closing	5		5 0 00	—	—

ACCOUNT *Utilities Expense* **ACCOUNT NO. 54**

Date		Item	Post. Ref.	Debit	Credit	Balance Debit	Balance Credit
1999 Nov.	30		1	4 5 0 00		4 5 0 00	
Dec.	31		3	3 1 0 00		7 6 0 00	
	31		3	2 2 5 00		9 8 5 00	
	31	Closing	5		9 8 5 00	—	—

Exhibit 7 (continued)
Ledger for Computer King

ACCOUNT *Supplies Expense*   **ACCOUNT NO. 55**

Date		Item	Post. Ref.	Debit	Credit	Balance Debit	Balance Credit
1999 Nov.	30		1	8 0 0 00		8 0 0 00	
Dec.	31	Adjusting	4	1 2 4 0 00		2 0 4 0 00	
	31	Closing	5		2 0 4 0 00	—	—

ACCOUNT *Insurance Expense*   **ACCOUNT NO. 56**

Date		Item	Post. Ref.	Debit	Credit	Balance Debit	Balance Credit
1999 Dec.	31	Adjusting	4	1 0 0 00		1 0 0 00	
	31	Closing	5		1 0 0 00	—	—

ACCOUNT *Miscellaneous Expense*   **ACCOUNT NO. 59**

Date		Item	Post. Ref.	Debit	Credit	Balance Debit	Balance Credit
1999 Nov.	30		1	2 7 5 00		2 7 5 00	
Dec.	6		2	1 8 0 00		4 5 5 00	
	31	Closing	5		4 5 5 00	—	—

After posting the entry to close an account, we should insert a line to rule off both balance columns after the final entry. The next period's transactions for the revenue, expense, and drawing accounts will be posted directly below the closing entry.

POST-CLOSING TRIAL BALANCE

The last accounting procedure for a period is to prepare a trial balance after posting the closing entries. The purpose of the post-closing (after closing) trial balance is to make sure that the ledger is in balance at the beginning of the next period. The accounts and amounts should agree exactly with the accounts and amounts listed on the balance sheet at the end of the period. The post-closing trial balance for Computer King is shown in Exhibit 8.

Instead of preparing a formal post-closing trial balance, we could list the accounts directly from the ledger, using a printing calculator or a computer. The calculator tape or computer printout, in effect, becomes the post-closing trial balance. Without such a tape or printout, there are no efficient means of determining the cause of an inequality of trial balance totals.

Exhibit 8
Post-Closing Trial Balance

Computer King Post-Closing Trial Balance December 31, 1999		
Cash	2 3 9 0 00	
Accounts Receivable	2 7 2 0 00	
Supplies	7 6 0 00	
Prepaid Insurance	2 3 0 0 00	
Land	10 0 0 0 00	
Office Equipment	1 8 0 0 00	
Accumulated Amortization		5 0 00
Accounts Payable		9 0 0 00
Wages Payable		5 7 5 00
Unearned Rent		2 4 0 00
Pat King, Capital		18 2 0 5 00
	19 9 7 0 00	19 9 7 0 00

Fiscal Year

Objective 5

Explain what is meant by the fiscal year and the natural business year.

The maximum length of an accounting period is usually one year, which includes a complete cycle of business activities. Income, property taxes, and other financial reporting requirements are often based on yearly periods.

In the Computer King illustration, the length of the accounting period was for two months, November and December. Computer King began operations November 1, and chose the end of its fiscal reporting period to be December 31. The federal income tax law generally requires a sole proprietorship to use the calendar year as its fiscal year. Thus, Computer King must also close its accounts on December 31, 1999. In future years, the financial statements for Computer King will be prepared for 12 months ending on December 31 each year.

The annual accounting period adopted by a business is known as its fiscal year. Fiscal years begin with the first day of the month selected and end on the last day of the following twelfth month. The period most commonly used is the calendar year. Other periods are not unusual, especially for businesses organized as corporations. Often a corporation will adopt a fiscal year that ends when business activities have reached the lowest point in the corporation's annual operating cycle. Such a fiscal year is called the natural business year.

The 1995 edition of *Financial Reporting in Canada*, published by the Canadian Institute of Chartered Accountants, reported the following results of a survey of 300 industrial, transportation, and merchandising companies concerning the month of their fiscal year-end.

Percentage of Companies with Fiscal Years Ending in the Month of:

January	5%	July	2%
February	2	August	5
March	6	September	4
April	3	October	3
May	2	November	2
June	2	December	64

The financial history of a business may be shown by a series of balance sheets and income statements. If the life of a business is expressed by a line moving from left to right, the series of balance sheets and income statements may be graphed as follows:

Balance Sheet dated Dec. 31, 1997	Balance Sheet dated Dec. 31, 1998	Balance Sheet dated Dec. 31, 1999	Balance Sheet dated Dec. 31, 2000	
	Income Statement for Fiscal Year 1998	Income Statement for Fiscal Year 1999	Income Statement for Fiscal Year 2000	

Accounting Cycle

Objective 6

List the seven basic steps of the accounting cycle.

We have presented the primary accounting procedures of a fiscal period in Chapters 2, 3, and 4. We call this sequence of procedures the accounting cycle. It begins with the analysis and the journalizing of transactions and ends with the post-closing trial balance. The most important output of the accounting cycle is the financial statements.

An understanding of the steps of the accounting cycle is essential for further study of accounting. The following basic steps of the cycle are shown, by number, in the flowchart in Exhibit 9.

1. Transactions are analyzed and recorded in journal.
2. Transactions are posted to ledger.
3. Trial balance is prepared, adjustment data are assembled, and work sheet is completed.
4. Financial statements are prepared.
5. Adjusting entries are journalized and posted to ledger.
6. Closing entries are journalized and posted to ledger.
7. Post-closing trial balance is prepared.

USING ACCOUNTING TO UNDERSTAND BUSINESS

Companies whose business operations are highly seasonal often select their accounting period to coincide with the lowest point in their normal operations. At this point, they have more time to analyze the results of operations and to prepare financial statements. **Future Shop** is an example of a company whose fiscal year is other than the calendar year. Future Shop's fiscal year-end is March 31. This should not surprise you, since you would expect that Future Shop experiences a high volume of sales around the December holiday season, followed by relatively low sales in January, February, and March.

Because companies with fiscal years often have highly seasonal operations, investors and others should be careful in interpreting partial-year reports for such companies. That is, you should expect the results of operations for these companies to vary significantly throughout the fiscal year. For example, during its 1996 fiscal year, Future Shop reported the following net sales and operating revenues:

	Net Sales and Operating Revenue (in thousands of dollars)
First Quarter	$ 258,580
Second Quarter	314,284
Third Quarter	439,635
Fourth Quarter	291,329

Exhibit 9
Accounting Cycle

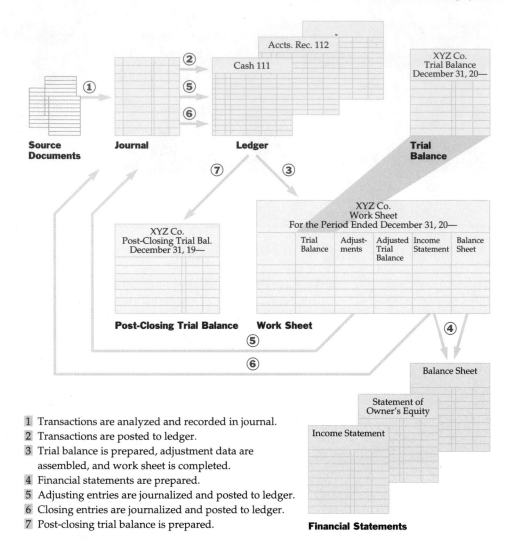

1. Transactions are analyzed and recorded in journal.
2. Transactions are posted to ledger.
3. Trial balance is prepared, adjustment data are assembled, and work sheet is completed.
4. Financial statements are prepared.
5. Adjusting entries are journalized and posted to ledger.
6. Closing entries are journalized and posted to ledger.
7. Post-closing trial balance is prepared.

Appendix: Reversing Entries

Some of the adjusting entries recorded at the end of an accounting period have an important effect on otherwise routine transactions that occur in the following period. A typical example is accrued wages owed to employees at the end of a period. If we have made an adjusting entry for accrued wages expense, the first payment of wages in the following period will include the accrual. In the absence of some special provision, we should debit Wages Payable for the amount owed for the earlier period, and debit Wages Expense for the portion of the payroll that represents expense for the later period. However, an *optional* entry—the reversing entry—may be used to simplify the analysis and recording of this first payroll entry in a period. As the term implies, a **reversing entry** is the exact reverse of the adjusting entry to which it relates. The amounts and accounts are the same as the adjusting entry; the debits and credits are reversed.

We will illustrate the use of reversing entries by using the data for Computer King's accrued wages, which were presented in Chapter 3. These data are summarized in Exhibit 10.

Exhibit 10
Accrued Wages

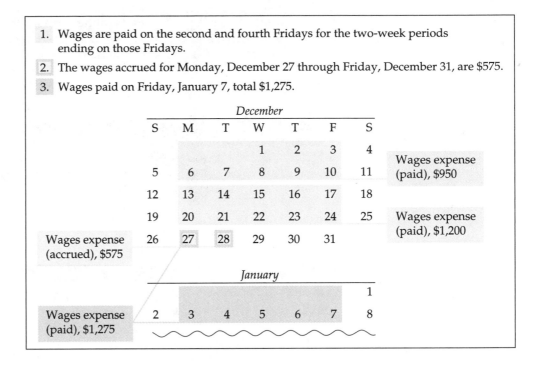

1. Wages are paid on the second and fourth Fridays for the two-week periods ending on those Fridays.
2. The wages accrued for Monday, December 27 through Friday, December 31, are $575.
3. Wages paid on Friday, January 7, total $1,275.

The adjusting entry for the accrued wages of December 27 through December 31 was as follows:

Dec. 31	Wages Expense	51	5 7 5 00	
	Wages Payable	22		5 7 5 00

After we post the adjusting entry, Wages Expense has a debit balance of $4,525 ($3,950 + $575), and Wages Payable has a credit balance of $575. After the closing process is completed, Wages Expense has a zero balance and is ready for entries in the next period. Wages Payable, on the other hand, has a balance of $575. Without the use of a reversing entry, we should record the $1,275 payroll on January 7 as a debit of $575 to Wages Payable, a debit of $700 to Wages Expense, and a credit of $1,275 to Cash. The employee who records this entry must refer to the prior period's adjusting entries to determine the amount of the debits to Wages Payable and Wages Expense.

Because the bookkeeper is not recording January payroll in the usual manner, there is a greater chance that an error may occur. We can reduce this chance of error by recording the following reversing entry as of the first day of the fiscal period:

Jan. 1999	1 Wages Payable	22	5 7 5 00	
	Wages Expense	51		5 7 5 00

The reversing entry transfers the $250 liability from Wages Payable to the credit side of Wages Expense. The nature of the $250 is unchanged—it is still a liability. When the payroll is paid on January 7, the bookkeeper can now make the usual entry debiting Wages Expense and crediting Cash for the entire amount of the payment, $1,275. After this entry is posted, Wages Expense has a debit balance of $1,025. This amount is the wages expense for the period January 1–7. We illustrate the sequence of entries, including adjusting, closing, and reversing entries in the following accounts:

ACCOUNT *Wages Payable*   **ACCOUNT NO.** *22*

Date		Item	Post. Ref.	Debit	Credit	Balance Debit	Balance Credit
1999 Dec.	31	Adjusting	4		5 7 5 00		5 7 5 00
2000 Jan.	1	Reversing	6	5 7 5 00		—	—

ACCOUNT *Wages Expense*   **ACCOUNT NO.** *51*

Date		Item	Post. Ref.	Debit	Credit	Balance Debit	Balance Credit
1999 Nov.	30		1	1 8 0 0 00		1 8 0 0 00	
Dec.	13		2	9 5 0 00		2 7 5 0 00	
	27		2	1 2 0 0 00		3 9 5 0 00	
	31	Adjusting	4	5 7 5 00		4 5 2 5 00	
	31	Closing	5		4 5 2 5 00	—	—
2000 Jan.	1	Reversing	6		5 7 5 00		5 7 5 00
	7		6	1 2 7 5 00		7 0 0 00	

In addition to accrued expenses (accrued liabilities), we can also journalize reversing entries for accrued revenues (accrued assets). For example, the following reversing entry could be recorded for Computer King's accrued revenue earned:

	Date		Item	Post. Ref.	Debit	Credit	
4	Jan.	1	Revenue Earned	41	5 0 0 00		4
5			Accounts Receivable	12		5 0 0 00	5

We can also use reversing entries for prepaid expenses that are initially recorded as expenses and unearned revenues that are initially recorded as revenues. However, you should note that there are three types of adjusting entries for which we never make reversing entries:

1. adjusting entries that record the amount of prepaid expense expired at the end of the period, where we initially recorded Prepaid Expense as an asset when the cash was paid;
2. adjusting entries to record the amount of unearned revenue earned by the end of the period, where we initially recorded a liability for Unearned Revenue when the cash was received;
3. adjusting entries to record amortization expense on capital assets.

As mentioned, the use of reversing entries is optional. However, with the increased use of computerized accounting systems, data entry personnel may be inputting routine accounting entries. In such an environment, reversing entries may be useful, since these individuals may not recognize the impact of adjusting entries on the related transactions in the following period.

KEY POINTS

Objective 1. Prepare a work sheet.

Prepare the work sheet by first entering a trial balance in the Trial Balance columns. Then enter the adjustments in the Adjustments Debit and Credit columns. Extend the Trial Balance accounts plus or minus the adjustments to the Adjusted Trial Balance columns. Complete the work sheet by extending the Adjusted Trial Balance amounts of assets, liabilities, owner's capital, and withdrawals to the Balance Sheet columns. Extend the Adjusted Trial Balance amounts of revenues and expenses to the Income Statement columns. Enter the net income (or net loss) for the period on the work sheet in the Income Statement Debit (or Credit) column and the Balance Sheet Credit (or Debit) column. Total each of the four statement columns.

Objective 2. Define the full disclosure and cost benefit principle, and prepare financial statements from a work sheet.

The full disclosure principle requires that financial reports provide any information that would be important enough to influence an informed user. Such disclosure is modified by the cost-benefit principle, which requires statements only to disclose information where the benefits to users exceed the cost of providing the information. This limits the amount of excessive detail included in financial statements.

You normally prepare the income statement directly from the accounts listed in the work sheet. On the income statement, the expenses are normally presented in the order of size, from largest to smallest.

Prepare the basic form of the statement of owner's equity by listing the beginning balance of owner's equity, adding investments in the business and net income during the period, and deducting the owner's withdrawals. The amount listed on the work sheet as the capital of a sole proprietor does not always represent the account balance at the beginning of the accounting period. The proprietor may have invested additional assets in the business during the period. Hence, for the beginning balance and any additional investments, refer to the capital account.

Various sections and subtitles are used in preparing a balance sheet. Show separately current assets and long-term assets. Current assets include cash and other assets that are normally expected to be converted to cash or sold or used up within one year or less. Long-term assets include capital assets such as property, plant, and equipment. The cost, accumulated amortization, and net book value of each major type of capital asset are normally reported on the balance sheet.

Report separately current liabilities and long-term liabilities. Current liabilities are those that will be due within a short time (usually one year or less) and that are expected to be paid out of current assets. Liabilities that will not be due for a long time (usually more than one year) are called long-term liabilities.

Present the owner's claim against the assets below the liabilities section and add it to the total liabilities. The total liabilities and total owner's equity must equal the total assets.

Objective 3. Journalize and post the adjusting entries.

At the end of the accounting period, record the adjusting entries appearing in the work sheet in the journal and post these to the ledger. This brings the ledger into agreement with the data reported on the financial statements.

Objective 4. Journalize and post the closing entries and prepare a post-closing trial balance.

The four entries required in closing the temporary accounts of a sole proprietorship are:

1. Debit each revenue account for the amount of its balance, and credit Income Summary for the total revenue.
2. Credit each expense account for the amount of its balance, and debit Income Summary for the total expense.
3. Debit Income Summary if it has a credit balance for the amount of its balance (net income), and credit the capital account for the same amount. (Debit and credit are reversed if there is a net loss.)
4. Credit the withdrawals account for the amount of its balance, and debit the capital account for the same amount.

After the closing entries have been posted to the ledger, the balance in the capital account should agree with the amount reported on the statement of owner's equity and balance sheet. In addition, the revenue, expense, and withdrawals accounts should have zero balances.

The last step of the accounting cycle is to prepare a post-closing trial balance. The purpose of the post-closing trial balance is to make sure that the ledger is in balance at the beginning of the next period.

Objective 5. Explain what is meant by the fiscal year and the natural business year.

The annual accounting period adopted by a business is known as its fiscal year. A business may adopt a fiscal year that ends when business activities have reached the lowest point in its annual operating cycle. Such a fiscal year is called the natural business year.

Objective 6. List the seven basic steps of the accounting cycle.

The basic steps of the accounting cycle are:

1. Analyze and record transactions in a journal.
2. Post transactions to the ledger.
3. Prepare the trial balance, assemble the adjusted data, and prepare the work sheet.
4. Prepare financial statements.
5. Journalize and post adjusting entries to ledger.
6. Journalize and post closing entries to ledger.
7. Prepare the post-closing trial balance.

GLOSSARY OF KEY TERMS

Accounting cycle. The sequence of basic accounting procedures during a fiscal period. *Objective 6*

Closing entries. Entries necessary to eliminate the balances of temporary accounts in preparation for the following accounting period. *Objective 4*

Cost-benefit principle. Financial statements should only disclose information whose benefit to users is greater than the costs of presenting it. *Objective 2*

Current assets. Cash or other assets that are expected to be converted to cash or sold or used up usually within a year or less, through the normal operations of a business. *Objective 2*

Current liabilities. Liabilities that will be due within a short time (usually one year or less) and that are expected to be paid out of current assets. *Objective 2*

Fiscal year. The annual accounting period adopted by a business. *Objective 5*

Full disclosure principle. Financial reports should provide any information that is important enough to influence the decisions of an informed user. *Objective 2*

Income summary. The account used in the closing process for transferring the revenue and expense account balances to the owner's capital account at the end of the period. *Objective 4*

Long-term assets. Assets that will not be sold or used up within one year. *Objective 2*

Long-term liabilities. Liabilities that are not due for a long time (usually more than one year). *Objective 2*

Natural business year. A year that ends when a business's activities have reached the lowest point in its annual operating cycle. *Objective 5*

Nominal accounts. Revenue or expense accounts that are periodically closed to the income summary account; temporary owner's equity accounts. *Objective 4*

Post-closing trial balance. A trial balance prepared after all of the temporary accounts have been closed. *Objective 4*

Real accounts. Balance sheet accounts. *Objective 4*

Temporary accounts. Revenue or expense accounts that are periodically closed to the income summary account; nominal accounts. *Objective 4*

ILLUSTRATIVE PROBLEM

Three years ago, T. Roderick organized Harbour Marina. At July 31, 1999, the end of the current fiscal year, the trial balance of Harbour Marina is as follows:

Harbour Marina Trial Balance July 31, 1999		
Cash	3 4 2 5 00	
Accounts Receivable	7 0 0 0 00	
Supplies	1 2 7 0 00	
Prepaid Insurance	6 2 0 00	
Office Equipment	51 6 5 0 00	
Accumulated Amortization		9 7 0 0 00
Accounts Payable		9 2 5 00
Unearned Fees		1 2 5 0 00
T. Roderick, Capital		29 0 0 0 00
T. Roderick, Withdrawals	5 2 0 0 00	
Revenue Earned		59 1 2 5 00
Wages Expense	22 4 1 5 00	
Rent Expense	4 2 0 0 00	
Utilities Expense	2 7 1 5 00	
Miscellaneous Expense	1 5 0 5 00	
	100 0 0 0 00	100 0 0 0 00

The following adjustment data have been entered on the 10-column work sheet.

a. Supplies on hand at July 31, 1999 are $380.
b. Insurance premiums expired during the year are $315.
c. Amortization of equipment during the year is $4,950.
d. Wages accrued but not paid at July 31, 1999 are $440.
e. Accrued revenue earned but not recorded at July 31, 1999 are $1,000.
f. Unearned revenue on July 31, 1999 are $750.

Instructions

1. Complete the 10-column work sheet.
2. Prepare an income statement, a statement of owner's equity (no additional investments were made during the year), and a balance sheet.
3. On the basis of the adjustment data in the work sheet, journalize the adjusting entries.
4. On the basis of the data in the work sheet, journalize the closing entries.

Solution

1.

Harbour Marina
Work Sheet
For the Year Ended July 31, 1999

Account Title	Trial Balance Dr.	Trial Balance Cr.	Adjustments Dr.	Adjustments Cr.	Adjusted Trial Balance Dr.	Adjusted Trial Balance Cr.	Income Statement Dr.	Income Statement Cr.	Balance Sheet Dr.	Balance Sheet Cr.
Cash	3,425				3,425				3,425	
Accounts Receivable	7,000		(e)1,000		8,000				8,000	
Supplies	1,270			(a) 890	380				380	
Prepaid Insurance	620			(b) 315	305				305	
Office Equipment	51,650				51,650				51,650	
Accumulated Amortization		9,700		(c)4,950		14,650				14,650
Accounts Payable		925				925				925
Unearned Fees		1,250	(f) 500			750				750
T. Roderick, Capital		29,000				29,000				29,000
T. Roderick, Withdrawals	5,200				5,200				5,200	
Revenue Earned		59,125		(e)1,000		60,625		60,625		
				(f) 500						
Wages Expense	22,415		(d) 440		22,855		22,855			
Rent Expense	4,200				4,200		4,200			
Utilities Expense	2,715				2,715		2,715			
Miscellaneous Expense	1,505				1,505		1,505			
	100,000	100,000								
Supplies Expense			(a) 890		890		890			
Insurance Expense			(b) 315		315		315			
Amortization Expense			(c)4,950		4,950		4,950			
Wages Payable				(d) 440		440				440
			8,095	8,095	106,390	106,390	37,430	60,625	68,960	45,765
Net income							23,195			23,195
							60,625	60,625	68,960	68,960

2.

Harbour Marina
Income Statement
For the Year Ended July 31, 1999

Revenue earned		$60 6 2 5 00
Operating expenses:		
Wages expense	$22 8 5 5 00	
Amortization expense	4 9 5 0 00	
Rent expense	4 2 0 0 00	
Utilities expense	2 7 1 5 00	
Supplies expense	8 9 0 00	
Insurance expense	3 1 5 00	
Miscellaneous expense	1 5 0 5 00	
Total operating expenses		37 4 3 0 00
Net income		$23 1 9 5 00

Harbour Marina
Statement of Owner's Equity
For the Year Ended July 31, 1999

T. Roderick, capital, August 1, 1998		$29 0 0 0 00
Net income for the year	$23 1 9 5 00	
Less withdrawals	5 2 0 0 00	
Increase in owner's equity		17 9 9 5 00
T. Roderick, capital, July 31, 1999		$46 9 9 5 00

Harbour Marina
Balance Sheet
July 31, 1999

Assets				Liabilities		
Current assets:				Current liabilities:		
Cash	$3 4 2 5 00			Accounts payable	$ 9 2 5 00	
Accounts receivable	8 0 0 0 00			Unearned revenue	7 5 0 00	
Supplies	3 8 0 00			Wages payable	4 4 0 00	
Prepaid insurance	3 0 5 00			Total liabilities		$ 2 1 1 5 00
Total current assets		$12 1 1 0 00				
Capital assets:				**Owner's Equity**		
Office equipment	$51 6 5 0 00			T. Roderick, capital		46 9 9 5 00
Less accumulated amort.	14 6 5 0 00	37 0 0 0 00	Total liabilities and		
Total assets		$49 1 1 0 00		owner's equity		$49 1 1 0 00

3.

				JOURNAL				PAGE	
	Date		Description	Post. Ref.	Debit		Credit		
1			Adjusting Entries						1
2	July 1999	31	Supplies Expense		8 9 0 00				2
3			Supplies				8 9 0 00		3
4									4
5		31	Insurance Expense		3 1 5 00				5
6			Prepaid Insurance				3 1 5 00		6
7									7
8		31	Amortization Expense		4 9 5 0 00				8
9			Accumulated Amortization				4 9 5 0 00		9
10									10
11		31	Wages Expense		4 4 0 00				11
12			Wages Payable				4 4 0 00		12
13									13
14		31	Accounts Receivable		1 0 0 0 00				14
15			Revenue Earned				1 0 0 0 00		15
16									16
17		31	Unearned Revenue		5 0 0 00				17
18			Revenue Earned				5 0 0 00		18

4.

			JOURNAL			PAGE
Date		Description	Post. Ref.	Debit	Credit	
1		Closing Entries				1
2	July 31	Revenue Earned		60 6 2 5 00		2
3	1999	Income Summary			60 6 2 5 00	3
4						4
5	31	Income Summary		37 4 3 0 00		5
6		Wages Expense			22 8 5 5 00	6
7		Rent Expense			4 2 0 0 00	7
8		Utilities Expense			2 7 1 5 00	8
9		Miscellaneous Expense			1 5 0 5 00	9
10		Supplies Expense			8 9 0 00	10
11		Insurance Expense			3 1 5 00	11
12		Amortization Expense			4 9 5 0 00	12
13						13
14	31	Income Summary		23 1 9 5 00		14
15		T. Roderick, Capital			23 1 9 5 00	15
16						16
17	31	T. Roderick, Capital		5 2 0 0 00		17
18		T. Roderick, Withdrawals			5 2 0 0 00	18
19						19

SELF-EXAMINATION QUESTIONS (ANSWERS AT END OF CHAPTER)

1. Which of the following accounts would you extend from the Adjusted Trial Balance columns of the work sheet to the Balance Sheet columns?
   A. Utilities Expense   C. M. E. Jones, Withdrawals
   B. Rent Income   D. Miscellaneous Expense

2. Which of the following accounts would you classify as a current asset on the balance sheet?
   A. Office Equipment   C. Accumulated Amortization
   B. Land   D. Accounts Receivable

3. Which of the following entries closes the owner's drawing account at the end of the period?
   A. Debit the withdrawals account, credit the income summary account.
   B. Debit the owner's capital account, credit the withdrawals account.
   C. Debit the income summary account, credit the withdrawals account.
   D. Debit the withdrawals account, credit the owner's capital account.

4. Which of the following accounts would not be closed to the income summary account at the end of a period?
   A. Revenue Earned   C. Rent Expense
   B. Wages Expense   D. Accumulated Amortization

5. Which of the following accounts would not be included in a post-closing trial balance?
   A. Cash   C. Accumulated Amortization
   B. Revenue Earned   D. J. C. Smith, Capital

DISCUSSION QUESTIONS

1. Is the work sheet a substitute for the financial statements? Discuss.
2. In the Income Statement columns of the work sheet, the Debit column total is greater than the Credit column total before the amount for the net income or net loss has been included. Would the income statement report a net income or a net loss? Explain.

3. In the Balance Sheet columns of the work sheet for McReynolds Co. for the current year, the Debit column total is $91,500 greater than the Credit column total before the amount for net income or net loss has been included. Would the income statement report a net income or a net loss? Explain.

4. Describe the nature of the assets that compose the following sections of a balance sheet: (a) current assets, (b) long-term assets.

5. What is the difference between a current liability and a long-term liability?

6. What types of accounts are referred to as temporary accounts?

7. Are adjusting and closing entries in the journal dated as of the last day of the fiscal period or as of the day the entries are actually made? Explain.

8. Why are closing entries required at the end of an accounting period?

9. What is the difference between adjusting entries and closing entries?

10. Describe the four entries that close the temporary accounts.

11. What types of accounts are closed by transferring their balances (a) as a debit to Income Summary, (b) as a credit to Income Summary?

12. To what account is the income summary account closed?

13. To what account is the owner's withdrawals account closed?

14. What is the purpose of the post-closing trial balance?

15. What term is applied to the annual accounting period adopted by a business?

16. What is the natural business year?

17. Why might a department store select a fiscal year ending January 31, rather than a fiscal year ending December 31?

18. The fiscal years for several well-known companies were as follows:

Company	Fiscal Year Ending
Mark's Work Warehouse	January 29
Toys "R" Us, Inc.	February 3
Federated Department Stores	February 2

What general characteristic shared by these companies explains why they do not have fiscal years ending December 31?

EXERCISES

EXERCISE 4–1
Extending accounts in a work sheet
Objective 1

The balances for the accounts listed below appeared in the Adjusted Trial Balance columns of the work sheet. Indicate whether each balance should be extended to (a) the Income Statement columns or (b) the Balance Sheet columns.

1. J. C. Laroche, Capital
2. Revenue Earned
3. Accounts Payable
4. Wages Expense
5. Supplies

6. Unearned Revenue
7. Utilities Expense
8. J. C. Laroche, Withdrawals
9. Accounts Receivable
10. Wages Payable

EXERCISE 4–2
Classifying accounts
Objective 1

Balances for each of the following accounts appear in the Adjusted Trial Balance columns of the work sheet. Identify each as (a) asset, (b) liability, (c) revenue, or (d) expense.

1. Unearned Rent
2. Supplies
3. Salary Expense
4. Rent Income
5. Prepaid Advertising
6. Insurance Expense

7. Accounts Receivable
8. Land
9. Revenue Earned
10. Supplies Expense
11. Salary Payable
12. Prepaid Insurance

EXERCISE 4–3
Steps in completing a work sheet
Objective 1

The steps performed in completing a work sheet are listed below in random order.

a. Add or deduct adjusting entry data to trial balance amounts and extend amounts to the Adjusted Trial Balance columns.

b. Extend the adjusted trial balance amounts to the Income Statement columns and the Balance Sheet columns.

c. Enter the amount of net income or net loss for the period in the proper Income Statement column and Balance Sheet column.

d. Add the Debit and Credit columns of the Balance Sheet and Income Statement columns of the work sheet to verify that the totals are equal.

e. Add the Debit and Credit columns of the Adjusted Trial Balance columns of the work sheet to verify that the totals are equal.

f. Add the Debit and Credit columns of the Adjustments columns of the work sheet to verify that the totals are equal.

g. Enter the adjusting entries into the work sheet, based upon the adjustment data.

h. Add the Debit and Credit columns of the unadjusted Trial Balance columns of the work sheet to verify that the totals are equal.

i. Add the Debit and Credit columns of the Balance Sheet and Income Statement columns of the work sheet to determine the amount of net income or net loss for the period.

j. Enter the unadjusted account balances from the general ledger into the unadjusted Trial Balance columns of the work sheet.

Indicate the order in which the preceding steps would be performed in preparing and completing a work sheet.

EXERCISE 4–4

Adjustments data on work sheet

Objective 1

Sanitize Services Co. offers cleaning services to business clients. The trial balance for Sanitize Services Co. has been prepared on the following work sheet for the year ended December 31, 1999.

Sanitize Services Co.
Work Sheet
For the Year Ended December 31, 1999

Account Title	Trial Balance Dr.	Trial Balance Cr.	Adjustments Dr.	Adjustments Cr.	Adjusted Trial Balance Dr.	Adjusted Trial Balance Cr.
Cash	6					
Accounts Receivable	25					
Supplies	4					
Prepaid Insurance	6					
Land	10					
Equipment	12					
Accumulated Amor.—Equip.		1				
Accounts Payable		13				
Wages Payable		0				
Joe Camarillo, Capital		41				
Joe Camarillo, Withdrawals	4					
Revenue Earned		27				
Wages Expense	7					
Rent Expense	4					
Insurance Expense	0					
Utilities Expense	2					
Amortization Expense	0					
Supplies Expense	0					
Miscellaneous Expense	2					
Totals	82	82				

The data for year-end adjustments are as follows:

a. Revenue earned, but not yet billed, $3.
b. Supplies on hand, $3.
c. Insurance premiums expired, $4.
d. Amortization expense, $1.
e. Wages accrued, but not paid, $2.

Enter the adjustments data and extend balances to the Adjusted Trial Balance columns.

EXERCISE 4–5
Completing a work sheet
Objective 1

Sanitize Services Co. offers cleaning services to business clients. The following is a partially completed work sheet for Sanitize Services Co.

Sanitize Services Co.
Work Sheet
For the Year Ended December 31, 1999

Account Title	Adjusted Trial Balance Dr.	Cr.	Income Statement Dr.	Cr.	Balance Sheet Dr.	Cr.
Cash	6				6	
Accounts Receivable	28				28	
Supplies	3				3	
Prepaid Insurance	2				2	
Land	10				10	
Equipment	12				12	
Accumulated Amor.—Equip.		2				2
Accounts Payable		13				13
Wages Payable		2				2
Joe Camarillo, Capital		41				41
Joe Camarillo, Withdrawals	4				4	
Revenue Earned		30		30		
Wages Expense	9		9			
Rent Expense	4		4			
Insurance Expense	4		4			
Utilities Expense	2		2			
Amortization Expense	1		1			
Supplies Expense	1		1			
Miscellaneous Expense	2		2			
Totals	88	88	23	30		
Net Income (Loss)			7			7
			30	30	65	65

Complete the work sheet.

EXERCISE 4–6
Financial statements
Objective 2

Based upon the data in Exercise 4–5, prepare an income statement, statement of owner's equity, and balance sheet for Sanitize Services Co.

EXERCISE 4–7
Adjusting entries
Objective 3

Based upon the data in Exercise 4–4, prepare the adjusting entries for Sanitize Services Co.

EXERCISE 4–8
Closing entries
Objective 4

Based upon the data in Exercise 4–5, prepare the closing entries for Sanitize Services Co.

EXERCISE 4–9
Income statement
Objective 2

The following account balances were taken from the Adjusted Trial Balance columns of the work sheet for The Courier Co., a delivery service firm, for the current fiscal year ended April 30:

Revenue Earned	$112,500
Salaries Expense	47,100
Rent Expense	18,000
Utilities Expense	7,500
Supplies Expense	2,050
Miscellaneous Expense	1,350
Insurance Expense	1,500
Amortization Expense	3,100

Prepare an income statement.

EXERCISE 4–10
Income statement; net loss
Objective 2

The following revenue and expense account balances were taken from the ledger of Custom Services Co. after the accounts had been adjusted on January 31, the end of the current fiscal year:

Amortization Expense	$ 7,500
Insurance Expense	3,900
Miscellaneous Expense	2,250
Rent Expense	34,000
Service Revenue	81,200
Supplies Expense	3,100
Utilities Expense	8,500
Wages Expense	46,750

Prepare an income statement.

EXERCISE 4–11
Statement of owner's equity
Objective 2

Newcomer Services Co. offers its services to new arrivals in the Toronto area. Selected accounts from the ledger of Newcomer Services Co. for the current fiscal year ended December 31 are as follows:

F. Henri, Capital					F. Henri, Withdrawals			
Dec. 31	10,000	Jan. 1	122,500	Mar. 31	2,500	Dec. 31	10,000
		Dec. 31	33,250	June 30	2,500		
				Sep. 30	2,500		
				Dec. 31	2,500		

Income Summary			
Dec. 31	578,150	Dec. 31	611,400
31	33,250		

Prepare a statement of owner's equity for the year.

EXERCISE 4–12
Statement of owner's equity; net loss
Objective 2

Selected accounts from the ledger of News Services Co. for the current fiscal year ended July 31 are as follows:

C. Chang, Capital					C. Chang, Withdrawals			
July 31	20,000	Aug. 1	360,500	Oct. 31	5,000	July 31	20,000
31	10,500			Jan. 31	5,000		
				Apr. 30	5,000		
				July 31	5,000		

Income Summary			
July 31	723,400	July 31	712,900
		31	10,500

Prepare a statement of owner's equity for the year.

EXERCISE 4–13
Classifying assets
Objective 2

Identify each of the following as (a) a current asset or (b) a long-term asset:

1. Supplies
2. Cash
3. Building
4. Accounts receivable
5. Equipment
6. Land

EXERCISE 4–14
Balance sheet classification
Objective 2

At the balance sheet date, a business owes a mortgage note payable of $300,000, the terms of which provide for payments of $5,000 to be paid off the principal each month. Explain how the liability should be classified on the balance sheet.

EXERCISE 4–15
Balance sheet
Objective 2

Shape Up Co. offers personal weight reduction consulting services to individuals. After all the accounts have been closed on April 30, the end of the current fiscal year, the balances of selected accounts from the ledger of Shape Up Co. are as follows:

Accounts Payable	$12,750
Accounts Receivable	29,920
Accumulated Amortization—Equipment	21,100
Cash	6,150
Equipment	80,600
J. Fonda, Capital	87,820
Prepaid Insurance	4,100
Prepaid Rent	2,400
Salaries Payable	3,750
Supplies	4,750
Unearned Revenue	2,500

Prepare a classified balance sheet.

EXERCISE 4–16
Balance sheet
Objective 2

List the errors you can find in the following balance sheet. Prepare a corrected balance sheet.

Healthcare Services Co.
Balance Sheet
For the Year Ended August 31, 1999

Assets			Liabilities		
Current assets:			Current liabilities:		
Cash	$ 6,170		Accounts receivable		$ 5,390
Accounts payable	5,390		Accum. amor.—building		23,525
Supplies	590		Accum. amor.—equipment		17,340
Prepaid insurance	845		Net loss		15,500
Land	20,000		Total liabilities		$ 61,755
Total current assets		$ 32,995			
			Owner's Equity		
Long-term assets:			Wages payable		$ 975
Building		$ 55,500	Wally Olstein, capital		69,515
Equipment		28,250	Total owner's equity		$ 70,490
Total capital assets		$ 99,250	Total liabilities and		
Total assets		$132,245	owner's equity		$132,245

EXERCISE 4–17
Adjusting entries from work sheet
Objective 3

Smog Purifier Co. is a consulting firm specializing in pollution control. The entries in the Adjustments columns of the work sheet for Smog Purifier Co. are shown below.

	Adjustments	
	Dr.	Cr.
Accounts Receivable	1,200	
Supplies		975
Prepaid Insurance		1,100
Accumulated Amortization—Equipment		500
Wages Payable		636
Unearned Rent	2,500	
Revenue Earned		1,200
Wages Expense	636	
Supplies Expense	975	
Rent Income		2,500
Insurance Expense	1,100	
Amortization Expense	500	

Prepare the adjusting journal entries.

EXERCISE 4–18
Identifying accounts to be closed
Objective 4

From the following list, identify the accounts that should be closed to Income Summary at the end of the fiscal year:

a. Accounts Payable
b. Salaries Payable
c. Revenue Earned
d. Salaries Expense
e. Amortization Expense—Buildings
f. Supplies

g. Equipment
h. Supplies Expense
i. H. Schulz, Capital
j. H. Schulz, Withdrawals
k. Land
l. Accumulated Amortization—Buildings

EXERCISE 4–19
Closing entries
Objective 4

Prior to the completion of the closing process, Income Summary had total debits of $257,500 and total credits of $318,000.

◀▬▬▶ Briefly explain the purpose served by the income summary account and the nature of the entries that resulted in the $257,500 and the $318,000.

EXERCISE 4–20
Closing entries
Objective 4

After all revenue and expense accounts have been closed at the end of the fiscal year, Income Summary has a debit of $695,500 and a credit of $787,500. At the same date, Lee Sassier, Capital has a credit balance of $139,500, and Lee Sassier, Withdrawals has a balance of $25,000. (a) Journalize the entries required to complete the closing of the accounts. (b) Determine the amount of Lee Sassier, Capital at the end of the period.

EXERCISE 4–21
Closing entries
Objective 4

Image Services Co. offers its services to individuals desiring to improve their personal images. After the accounts have been adjusted at August 31, the end of the fiscal year, the following balances were taken from the ledger of Image Services Co.

W. J. Sharp, Capital	$795,300
W. J. Sharp, Withdrawals	40,000
Revenue Earned	355,000
Wages Expense	221,500
Rent Expense	39,000
Supplies Expense	15,500
Miscellaneous Expense	2,000

Journalize the four entries required to close the accounts.

EXERCISE 4–22
Identifying permanent account
Objective 4

Which of the following accounts will usually appear in the post-closing trial balance?

a. Accounts Receivable
b. Accumulated Amortization
c. Cash
d. Unearned Revenue
e. Amortization Expense
f. Wages Payable

g. Equipment
h. Wages Expense
i. S. A. McDermott, Capital
j. Revenue Earned
k. S. A. McDermott, Withdrawals

EXERCISE 4–23
Post-closing trial balance
Objective 4

An accountant prepared the following post-closing trial balance:

Cheatham Repairs Co.
Post-Closing Trial Balance
October 31, 20—

Cash	9,400	
Accounts Receivable	11,250	
Supplies		1,800
Equipment		31,500
Accumulated Amortization —Equipment	15,130	
Accounts Payable	7,250	
Salaries Payable		1,500
Unearned Rent	4,000	
Joe Harris, Capital	26,070	
	73,100	34,800

Prepare a corrected post-closing trial balance. Assume that all accounts have normal balances and that the amounts shown are correct.

EXERCISE 4–24
Steps in the accounting cycle
Objective 6

Rearrange the following steps in the accounting cycle in proper sequence:

a. Adjusting entries are journalized and posted to ledger.
b. Post-closing trial balance is prepared.
c. Closing entries are journalized and posted to ledger.
d. Transactions are analyzed and recorded in journal.
e. Financial statements are prepared.
f. Trial balance is prepared, adjustment data are assembled, and work sheet is completed.
g. Transactions are posted to ledger.

APPENDIX EXERCISE 4–25
Adjusting and reversing entries

On the basis of the following data, (a) journalize the adjusting entries at December 31, 1999, the end of the current fiscal year, and (b) journalize the reversing entries on January 1, 2000, the first day of the following year.

1. Sales salaries are uniformly $15,000 for a five-day workweek, ending on Friday. The last payday of the year was Friday, December 24.
2. Accrued fees earned but not recorded at December 31, $5,750.

APPENDIX EXERCISE 4–26
Entries posted to the wages expense account

Portions of the wages expense account of a business are as follows:

ACCOUNT   *Wages Expense*   ACCOUNT NO.   53

Date		Item	Post. Ref.	Dr.	Cr.	Balance	
						Dr.	Cr.
20—							
Dec.	27	(1)	51	15,000		245,500	
	31	(2)	52	9,000		254,500	
	31	(3)	53		254,500	—	—
20—							
Jan.	2	(4)	54		9,000		9,000
	3	(5)	55	15,000		6,000	

a. Indicate the nature of the entry (payment, adjusting, closing, reversing) from which each numbered posting was made.
b. Journalize the complete entry from which each numbered posting was made.

PROBLEMS SERIES A

PROBLEM 4–1A
Work sheet and related items
Objectives 1, 2, 3, 4

The trial balance of The Washboard Laundromat at March 31, 1999, the end of the current fiscal year, and the data needed to determine year-end adjustments are as follows:

The Washboard Laundromat
Trial Balance
March 31, 1999

Cash	6,290	
Laundry Supplies	5,850	
Prepaid Insurance	2,400	
Laundry Equipment	96,750	
Accumulated Amortization		52,700
Accounts Payable		3,950
Lee Cheswick, Capital		37,450
Lee Cheswick, Withdrawals	3,000	
Laundry Revenue		66,900
Wages Expense	22,900	
Rent Expense	14,400	
Utilities Expense	8,500	
Miscellaneous Expense	910	
	161,000	161,000

a. Laundry supplies on hand at March 31 are $1,040.
b. Insurance premiums expired during the year are $1,700.
c. Amortization of equipment during the year is $5,220.
d. Wages incurred but not paid at March 31 are $850.

Instructions

1. Record the trial balance on a 10-column work sheet and complete the work sheet.
2. Prepare an income statement, a statement of owner's equity (no additional investments were made during the year), and a balance sheet.
3. On the basis of the adjustment data in the work sheet, journalize the adjusting entries.
4. On the basis of the data in the work sheet, journalize the closing entries.

PROBLEM 4–2A
Adjusting and closing entries; statement of owner's equity
Objectives 2, 3

Grail Company is an investigative services firm that is owned and operated by S. Launcelot. On November 30, 20—, the end of the current fiscal year, the accountant for Grail Company prepared a trial balance, journalized and posted the adjusting entries, prepared an adjusted trial balance, prepared the financial statements, and completed the other procedures required at the end of the accounting cycle. The two trial balances as of November 30, one before adjustments and the other after adjustments, are as follows:

Grail Company
Trial Balance
November 30, 20—

	Unadjusted		*Adjusted*	
Cash	7,325		7,325	
Accounts Receivable	16,900		20,500	
Supplies	6,920		1,610	
Prepaid Insurance	4,275		1,350	
Equipment	69,750		69,750	
Accumulated Amortization—Equipment		29,395		32,185
Accounts Payable		4,310		5,030
Salaries Payable		—		3,480
Taxes Payable		—		2,200
Unearned Rent		3,750		1,500
S. Launcelot, Capital		31,345		31,345
S. Launcelot, Withdrawals	7,500		7,500	
Service Revenue Earned		181,200		184,800
Rent Income		—		2,250
Salary Expense	116,385		119,865	
Rent Expense	15,600		15,600	
Supplies Expense	—		5,310	
Amortization Expense—Equipment	—		2,790	
Utilities Expense	2,720		3,440	
Taxes Expense	915		3,115	
Insurance Expense	—		2,925	
Miscellaneous Expense	1,710		1,710	
	250,000	250,000	262,790	262,790

Instructions

1. Journalize the eight entries that were required to adjust the accounts at November 30. None of the accounts was affected by more than one adjusting entry.
2. Journalize the entries that were required to close the accounts at November 30.
3. Prepare a statement of owner's equity for the fiscal year ended November 30, 20—. There were no additional investments during the year.
4. ━━▶ If the balance of S. Launcelot, Withdrawals had been $75,000 instead of $7,500, what would the balance of S. Launcelot, Capital have been on November 30, 20—? Explain how this balance would be reported on the balance sheet.

PROBLEM 4–3A
Work sheet and financial statements
Objectives 1, 2

Beacon Company maintains and repairs warning lights, such as those found on radio towers and lighthouses. Beacon Company prepared the following trial balance at May 31, 1998, the end of the current fiscal year:

Beacon Company
Trial Balance
May 31, 1998

Cash	7,500	
Accounts Receivable	16,500	
Prepaid Insurance	2,600	
Supplies	1,950	
Land	60,000	
Building	100,500	
Accumulated Amortization—Building		81,700
Equipment	72,400	
Accumulated Amortization—Equipment		63,800
Accounts Payable		6,100
Unearned Rent		1,500
Iris Cuttner, Capital		60,700
Iris Cuttner, Withdrawals	4,000	
Revenue Earned		161,200
Salaries and Wages Expense	60,200	
Advertising Expense	19,000	
Utilities Expense	18,200	
Repairs Expense	8,100	
Miscellaneous Expense	4,050	
	375,000	375,000

The data needed to determine year-end adjustments are as follows:

a. Revenue accrued at May 31 is $1,200.
b. Insurance expired during the year is $1,250.
c. Supplies on hand at May 31 are $450.
d. Amortization of building for the year is $1,620.
e. Amortization of equipment for the year is $3,160.
f. Accrued salaries and wages at May 31 are $1,450.
g. Unearned rent at May 31 is $500.

Instructions

1. Record the trial balance on a 10-column work sheet and complete the work sheet.
2. Prepare an income statement for the year ended May 31.
3. Prepare a statement of owner's equity for the year ended May 31. No additional investments were made during the year.
4. Prepare a balance sheet as of May 31.
5. Compute the percent of net income to total revenue for the year.

PROBLEM 4–4A
Ledger accounts, work sheet, and related items
Objectives 1, 2, 3, 4

The trial balance of Fix-It Repairs at March 31, 1999, the end of the current year, and the data needed to determine year-end adjustments are as follows:

Fix-It Repairs
Trial Balance
March 31, 1999

Cash	6,950	
Supplies	1,000	
Equipment	40,650	
Accumulated Amortization—Equipment		11,209
Trucks	36,300	
Accumulated Amortization—Trucks		6,400
Accounts Payable		2,015
Jay Hammer, Capital		40,426
Jay Hammer, Withdrawals	5,000	
Service Revenue		89,950
Wages Expense	33,925	
Supplies Expense	3,295	
Rent Expense	9,600	
Truck Expense	8,350	
Insurance Expense	2,735	
Miscellaneous Expense	2,195	
	150,000	150,000

a. Supplies on hand at March 31 are $1,302.
b. Insurance premiums expired during year are $1,050.
c. Amortization of equipment during year is $3,380.
d. Amortization of trucks during year is $4,400.
e. Wages incurred but not paid at March 31 are $650.

Instructions

1. For each account listed in the trial balance, enter the balance in the appropriate Balance column of a four-column account and place a check mark (√) in the Posting Reference column.
2. Record the trial balance on a 10-column work sheet and complete the work sheet.
3. Prepare an income statement, a statement of owner's equity (no additional investments were made during the year), and a balance sheet.
4. Journalize and post the adjusting entries, inserting balances in the accounts affected.
5. Journalize and post the closing entries. Indicate closed accounts by inserting a line in both Balance columns opposite the closing entry.
6. Prepare a post-closing trial balance.

PROBLEM 4–5A
Accounting Concepts Review

Indicate the generally accepted accounting principles or concepts that best justify each of the following accounting practices.

1. The amounts on the financial statements are rounded to the nearest thousand.
2.. A business prepares and posts adjusting entries at the end of the fiscal year.
3. A business prepares monthly financial statements for distribution to owners.
4. The cost of printing sales coupons to be distributed in the next year is reported as an asset at the end of the current year.
5. The transactions for a sole proprietorship are recorded separately from the personal transaction of the owner.
6. At the end of the fiscal period several customers owe money to a business. However, the company only reports one total for *Accounts Receivable* that includes all of the amounts due from different customers.

PROBLEM 4–1B
Work sheet and related items
Objectives 1, 2, 3, 4

The trial balance of Tidal Wave Laundry at August 31, 1998, the end of the current fiscal year, and the data needed to determine year-end adjustments are as follows:

Tidal Wave Laundry
Trial Balance
August 31, 1998

Cash	13,100	
Laundry Supplies	6,560	
Laundry Equipment	100,100	
Accumulated Amortization		45,200
Accounts Payable		6,100
Sylvia Akai, Capital		37,800
Sylvia Akai, Withdrawals	2,000	
Laundry Revenue		140,900
Wages Expense	51,400	
Rent Expense	36,000	
Insurance Expense	4,490	
Utilities Expense	13,650	
Miscellaneous Expense	2,700	
	230,000	230,000

a. Laundry supplies on hand at August 31 are $2,050.
b. Insurance premiums expired during the year are $2,800.
c. Amortization of equipment during the year is $4,600.
d. Wages incurred but not paid at August 31 are $1,750.

Instructions

1. Record the trial balance on a 10-column work sheet and complete the work sheet.
2. Prepare an income statement, a statement of owner's equity (no additional investments were made during the year), and a balance sheet.
3. On the basis of the adjustment data in the work sheet, journalize the adjusting entries.
4. On the basis of the data in the work sheet, journalize the closing entries.

PROBLEM 4–2B
Adjusting and closing entries; statement of owner's equity
Objectives 2, 3

Merlin Company is a financial planning services firm owned and operated by K. Arthur. As of December 31, the end of the current fiscal year, the accountant for Merlin Company prepared a trial balance, journalized and posted the adjusting entries, prepared an adjusted trial balance, prepared the financial statements, and completed the other procedures required at the end of the accounting cycle. The two trial balances as of December 31, one before adjustments and the other after adjustments, are as shown on the following page.

Instructions

1. Journalize the nine entries that were required to adjust the accounts at December 31. None of the accounts was affected by more than one adjusting entry.
2. Journalize the entries that were required to close the accounts at December 31.
3. Prepare a statement of owner's equity for the fiscal year ended December 31. There were no additional investments during the year.
4. ➤ If the balance of K. Arthur, Withdrawals had been $140,000 instead of $10,000, what would the balance of K. Arthur, Capital have been on December 31? Explain how this balance would be reported on the balance sheet.

Merlin Company
Trial Balance
December 31, 20—

	Unadjusted		Adjusted	
Cash	3,650		3,650	
Accounts Receivable	20,380		23,960	
Supplies	11,760		3,380	
Prepaid Insurance	2,400		800	
Land	42,500		42,500	
Buildings	116,000		116,000	
Accumulated Amortization—Buildings		77,600		82,400
Equipment	82,000		82,000	
Accumulated Amortization—Equipment		32,800		50,900
Accounts Payable		7,120		7,640
Salaries Payable		—		1,450
Taxes Payable		—		2,920
Unearned Rent		1,900		300
K. Arthur, Capital		114,900		114,900
K. Arthur, Withdrawals	10,000		10,000	
Service Revenue Earned		140,680		144,260
Rent Income		—		1,600
Salary Expense	71,200		72,650	
Amortization Expense—Equipment	—		18,100	
Rent Expense	9,000		9,000	
Supplies Expense	—		8,380	
Utilities Expense	4,550		5,070	
Amortization Expense—Buildings	—		4,800	
Taxes Expense	600		3,520	
Insurance Expense	—		1,600	
Miscellaneous Expense	960		960	
	375,000	375,000	406,370	406,370

PROBLEM 4–3B

Work sheet and financial statements

Objectives 1, 2

The Office Company offers interior design services for commercial clients. They prepared the following trial balance at April 30, 1999, the end of the current fiscal year:

Office Company
Trial Balance
April 30, 1999

Cash	3,200	
Accounts Receivable	10,500	
Prepaid Insurance	3,800	
Supplies	1,950	
Land	50,000	
Building	137,500	
Accumulated Amortization—Building		51,700
Equipment	90,100	
Accumulated Amortization—Equipment		35,300
Accounts Payable		7,500
Unearned Rent		3,000
Jean Ginsburg, Capital		164,100
Jean Ginsburg, Withdrawals	10,000	
Revenue Earned		198,400
Salaries and Wages Expense	80,200	
Advertising Expense	38,200	
Utilities Expense	19,000	
Repairs Expense	11,500	
Miscellaneous Expense	4,050	
	460,000	460,000

The data needed to determine year-end adjustments are as follows:

a. Accrued revenue at April 30 are $1,500.
b. Insurance expired during the year is $2,600.
c. Supplies on hand at April 30 are $450.
d. Amortization of building for the year is $1,620.
e. Amortization of equipment for the year is $3,500.
f. Salaries and wages in April incurred but not yet paid are $800.
g. Unearned rent at April 30 is $1,000.
h. Utilities used but not recorded at April 30 are $1,000.

Instructions

1. Record the trial balance on a 10-column work sheet and complete the work sheet.
2. Prepare an income statement for the year ended April 30.
3. Prepare a statement of owner's equity for the year ended April 30. No additional investments were made during the year.
4. Prepare a balance sheet as of April 30.
5. Compute the percent of net income to total revenue for the year.

PROBLEM 4–4B
Ledger accounts, work sheet, and related items
Objectives 1, 2, 3, 4

The trial balance of Like-New Repairs at December 31, 1999, the end of the current year, is shown at the top of the next page. The data needed to determine year-end adjustments are as follows:

a. Supplies on hand at December 31 are $1,360.
b. Insurance premiums expired during year are $2,050.
c. Amortization of equipment during year is $6,080.
d. Amortization of trucks during year is $5,500.
e. Wages incurred but not paid at December 31 are $500.

Like-New Repairs
Trial Balance
December 31, 1999

Cash	6,825	
Supplies	4,820	
Prepaid Insurance	3,500	
Equipment	42,200	
Accumulated Amortization—Equipment		9,050
Trucks	45,000	
Accumulated Amortization—Trucks		27,100
Accounts Payable		4,015
S. Driver, Capital		29,885
S. Driver, Withdrawals	3,000	
Service Revenue		99,950
Wages Expense	42,010	
Rent Expense	10,100	
Truck Expense	9,350	
Miscellaneous Expense	3,195	
	170,000	170,000

Instructions

1. For each account listed in the trial balance, enter the balance in the appropriate Balance column of a four-column account and place a check mark (√) in the Posting Reference column.
2. Record the trial balance on a 10-column work sheet and complete the work sheet.
3. Prepare an income statement, a statement of owner's equity (no additional investments were made during the year), and a balance sheet.
4. Journalize and post the adjusting entries, inserting balances in the accounts affected.
5. Journalize and post the closing entries. Indicate closed accounts by inserting a line in both Balance columns opposite the closing entry.
6. Prepare a post-closing trial balance.

PROBLEM 4–5B
Accounting Concepts Review

Fabri-Kate Co. is a wholesaler of prefabricated buildings for use by businesses. Indicate which generally accepted accounting principles or concepts are violated by each of the accounting practices of Fabri-Kate Co. described below.

1. Cash received by the owner of Fabri-Kate for the sale of a personal automobile was recorded by Fabri-Kate as a cash sale.
2. Fabri-Kate recorded $5,500 of office supplies on hand at year end as supplies expense because it was not considered a significant amount. The business reported total assets of $60,000 and net income of $25,000 in its financial statements.
3. In 1998 Fabri-Kate paid $5,000 to produce a television commercial that is to be aired in 1999. The business recorded the $5,000 as advertising expense in its 1998 income statement.
4. Fabri-Kate signed an agreement to rent office space to Lee Co. on a one-year lease. When moving into the premises on December 1, 1998, Lee gave Fabri-Kate $2,000 to cover its first and last month's rent. Fabri-Kate reported this as rent revenue on its income statement for the year ended December 31, 1998.
5. Fabri-Kate purchased a building for $100,000 in 1998. At the end of 1999 it hired an independent outside consultant to assess the market value of the property. Since the company planned to put the building up for sale the next year, it reported the property on its 1999 balance sheet at the appraised value estimated by the consultant of $120,000.

CHALLENGE PROBLEMS

PROBLEM CP4–1

Kathy Lee opened a commercial printing business on July 1, 1998. The business was organized as Lee Enterprises with an investment by the owner of $50,000. Having taken a little bookkeeping in high school, Kathy kept a record of all cash receipts and disbursements for the year. At the end of the year she journalized these and posted them to the general ledger. When you arrive to perform the audit of the business for the year ended June 30, 1999, Kathy gives you the following summary of the year's cash transactions (which have been posted to the general ledger):

Cash receipts:		
Owner's investment	$ 50,000	
Bank loan	20,000	
Cash received from customers	175,000	
	$245,000	

Cash payments:		
Salary Expense	$ 50,000	
Withdrawal by owner	40,000	
Rent Expense	39,000	
Equipment	75,000	
Supplies Expense	20,000	
Insurance Expense	6,000	
Interest Expense	900	
Utilities Expense	7,100	
Advertising Expense	5,000	(243,000)
Cash balance at year-end		$ 2,000

During your audit, you discover the following information:

a. On September 1, 1998 the business borrowed $20,000 from the bank. The bank charges the interest each month on the first day of the following month.
b. The firm purchased equipment with a useful life of five years on July 1, 1998.
c. The rental lease signed July 1, 1998 calls for monthly payments of $3,000.
d. On July 1, 1998 Lee paid $6,000 for a two-year insurance policy.
e. Unpaid salaries at June 30, 1999 are $2,000.
f. $9,000 is owed by customers at June 30, 1999.

g. On June 30, 1999 the following bills for services used to that date have not yet been paid: utilities $500; advertising $400.

h. $4,000 in supplies were on hand at June 30, 1999.

Instructions

1. Prepare any adjusting entries required at June 30, 1999.
2. Prepare an income statement for the year ended June 30, 1999.
3. Prepare a balance sheet at June 30, 1999.
4. Which of the adjusting entries made in question 1 could be reversed on July 1, 1999?

PROBLEM CP4–2

You have been called in to audit the financial statements of JJ's Home Repairs at the end of its first year of operations. When you arrive, the owner, John Jacobs, presents you with the following statements that he has prepared.

John Jacobs
Income Statement
December 31, 1999

Repair service revenue		95,200
Gain on land and building		15,000
Total revenue		110,200
Expenses:		
Repair parts used	15,000	
Wage expense	33,300	
Utilities expense	8,000	
Withdrawals	9,000	
Amortization—Furniture and Equipment	14,000	
Interest expense	8,000	
		87,300
Net income		22,900

John Jacobs
Balance Sheet
December 31, 1999

Debits:		Credits:	
Cash	25,000	Accounts payable	18,000
Accounts receivable	15,000	Note payable	80,000
Supplies (repair parts)	12,500	Accumulated amortization	14,000
Land and building	100,000	Capital	110,500
Furniture and equipment	70,000		
	222,500		222,500

Additional Information:

1. Repair service revenue consists of cash received from customers during the year plus billings sent to customers for services rendered during the year, but which were still unpaid at year end. The $95,200 shown for repair service revenue includes $1,500 in deposits from customers for repair jobs that were started and completed early in 2000. However, it does not include $2,500 billed to customers in January 2000 for work that was completed in December 1999.

2. On January 1, 1999 Jacobs purchased the land and building for $85,000. Jacobs recorded a $15,000 gain on the property after it was appraised for $100,000 by a certified real estate appraiser in November 1999.

3. Jacobs purchased the furniture and equipment for $70,000 at an auction in January 1999. Included in the $70,000 were a few antique pieces worth about $8,000. Since these pieces were not really serviceable in the store, Jacobs had these delivered to his home.

4. The $18,000 in accounts payable was composed of the following:
   - $14,000 bill received for parts delivered December 20 and paid January 15, 2000;

- $3,000 for a purchase order (commitment to buy) that Jacobs had signed in November 1999. The contract obligated Jacobs to buy 50 boxes of repair parts from a German supplier. The parts were expected to arrive in February, 2000.
- $1,000 estimated utility bill for December. The bill has still not yet been received.

Instructions

1. Calculate the following (show all calculations):
   a. Jacobs' initial investment in the business.
   b. Total cash received from customers in 1999.
   c. Estimated useful life of the furniture and equipment.
2. Without preparing a corrected set of statements, identify all the changes that you would make before issuing these financial statements. For each change:
   a. Explain which generally accepted accounting principle or principles have been violated by Jacobs' presentation of the item.
   b. Explain what you believe is the correct treatment of the item. If applicable, list all the balance sheet and income statement accounts that would be affected by your correction and give corrected dollar amounts for these accounts.

PROBLEM CP4–3

The following information represents the unadjusted trial balance for James Service at December 31, 1999:

Utility expense	750	Service revenue	21,000
Cash	3,750	Salary expense	5,000
Capital	23,500	Accounts payable	2,400
Furniture	40,000	Supplies	1,400
Prepaid insurance	1,500	Withdrawals	1,000
Accumulated amortization	8,000	Unearned revenue	1,500
Accounts receivable	3,000		

Additional Information:

1. Furniture with a 10-year life was purchased January 1, 1997.
2. A $1,500 premium was paid July 1, 1999 for a one-year insurance policy.
3. A $90 bill for utilities used in December was received January 15, 2000.
4. Supplies on hand at year-end were $600.
5. By December 31, 1999 the only revenue still unearned was $800.
6. $1,000 wages for the last week of December were paid January 3, 2000.

Instructions

1. Prepare, in good form, an income statement for the year ended December 31, 1999.
2. Prepare a balance sheet for James Service as at December 31, 1999.

CONTINUING PROBLEM

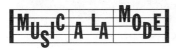

The unadjusted trial balance of Music A La Mode as of December 31, 1999, along with the adjustment data for the two months ended December 31, 1999, are shown in the work sheet that you began preparing at the end of Chapter 3.

Instructions

1. Complete the 10-column work sheet for Music A La Mode.
2. Prepare an income statement, a statement of owner's equity, and a balance sheet. (*Note:* Julian Felipe made investments in Music A La Mode on November 1 and December 1, 1999.)
3. Journalize and post the adjusting entries, inserting balances in the accounts affected.
4. Add the income summary account (#33) to the ledger of Music A La Mode. Journalize and post the closing entries. Indicate closed accounts by inserting a line in both Balance columns opposite the closing entry.
5. Prepare a post-closing trial balance.

COMPREHENSIVE PROBLEM 1

For the past several years, Damon Carnegie has operated a consulting business from his home on a part-time basis. As of September 1, 1999, Damon decided to move to rented quarters and to operate the business, which was to be known as Impact Consulting, on a full-time basis. Impact Consulting entered into the following transactions during September:

Sept. 1. The following assets were received from Damon Carnegie: cash, $5,000; accounts receivable, $1,500; supplies, $1,250; and office equipment, $7,200. There were no liabilities received.

2. Paid three months' rent on a lease rental contract, $2,400.

2. Paid the premiums on property and casualty insurance policies, $1,800.

4. Received cash from clients as an advance payment for services to be performed and recorded them as unearned fees, $3,500.

5. Purchased additional office equipment on account from Payne Company, $1,800.

6. Received cash from clients on account, $800.

10. Paid cash for a newspaper advertisement, $120.

11. Paid Payne Company for part of the debt incurred on September 5, $900.

12. Recorded services performed on account for the period September 1–12, $1,200.

13. Paid part-time receptionist for two weeks' salary, $400.

17. Recorded cash from cash clients for revenue earned during the first half of September, $2,100.

18. Paid cash for supplies, $750.

20. Recorded services performed on account for the period September 13–20, $1,100.

24. Recorded cash from cash clients for revenue earned for the period September 17–24, $1,850.

25. Received cash from clients on account, $1,300.

27. Paid part-time receptionist for two weeks' salary, $400.

29. Paid telephone bill for September, $130.

30. Paid electricity bill for September, $200.

30. Recorded cash from cash clients for revenue earned for the period September 25–30, $850.

30. Recorded services performed on account for the remainder of September, $500.

30. Damon withdrew $1,000 for personal use.

Instructions

1. Journalize each transaction in a two-column journal, referring to the following chart of accounts in selecting the accounts to be debited and credited. (Do not insert the account numbers in the journal at this time.)

11 Cash	31 Damon Carnegie, Capital
12 Accounts Receivable	32 Damon Carnegie, Withdrawals
14 Supplies	41 Revenue Earned
15 Prepaid Rent	51 Salary Expense
16 Prepaid Insurance	52 Rent Expense
18 Office Equipment	53 Supplies Expense
19 Accumulated Amortization	54 Amortization Expense
21 Accounts Payable	55 Insurance Expense
22 Salaries Payable	59 Miscellaneous Expense
23 Unearned Revenue	

2. Post the journal to a ledger of four-column accounts.

3. Prepare a trial balance as of September 30, 1999, on a 10-column work sheet, listing all the accounts in the order given in the ledger. Complete the work sheet, using the following adjustment data:

a. Insurance expired during September is $150.

b. Supplies on hand on September 30 are $1,320.

c. Amortization of office equipment for September is $250.

d. Accrued receptionist salary on September 30 is $100.

e. Rent expired during September is $800.

f. Unearned revenue on September 30 are $1,100.

4. Prepare an income statement, a statement of owner's equity, and a balance sheet.
5. Journalize and post the adjusting entries.
6. Journalize and post the closing entries. (Income Summary is account #33 in the chart of accounts.) Indicate closed accounts by inserting a line in both Balance columns opposite the closing entry.
7. Prepare a post-closing trial balance.

CASES

CASE 4–1
Visual Co.
Classifying account receivable

Visual Co. is a graphics arts design consulting firm. Joel Pazer, its treasurer and vice-president of finance, has prepared a classified balance sheet as of March 31, 1999, the end of its fiscal year. This balance sheet will be submitted with Visual's loan application to Metro Trust & Savings Bank.

In the Current Assets section of the balance sheet, Joel reported a $30,000 receivable from Susan Eisenberg, the pres-

ident of Visual, as a trade account receivable. Susan borrowed the money from Visual Co. in February 1998 for a down payment on a new home. She has verbally assured Joel that she will pay off the account receivable within the next year. Joel reported the $30,000 in the same manner on the preceding year's balance sheet.

Evaluate whether it is ethical for Joel Pazer to prepare the March 31, 1999 balance sheet in the manner indicated above.

CASE 4–2
Ecological Supplies Co.
Financial statements

The following is an excerpt from a telephone conversation between Janice Maple, president of Ecological Supplies Co., and Fred Spruce, who is owner of Cameo Employment Co.

Janice: Fred, you're going to have to do a better job of finding me a new computer programmer. That last guy was great at programming, but he didn't have any common sense.

Fred: What do you mean? The guy had a master's degree with straight A's.

Janice: Yes, well, last month he developed a new financial reporting system. He said we could do away with manually preparing a work sheet and financial statements. The computer would automatically generate our financial statements with "a push of a button."

Fred: So what's the big deal? Sounds to me like it would save you time and effort.

Janice: Right! The balance sheet showed a minus for supplies!

Fred: Minus supplies? How can that be?

Janice: That's what I asked.

Fred: So, what did he say?

Janice: Well, after he checked the program, he said that it must be right. The minuses were greater than the pluses...

Fred: Didn't he know that supplies can't have a credit balance—it must have a debit balance?

Janice: He asked me what a debit and credit were.

Fred: I see your point.

1. Comment on (a) the desirability of computerizing Ecological Supplies Co.'s financial reporting system, (b) the elimination of the work sheet in a computerized accounting system, and (c) the computer programmer's lack of accounting knowledge.
2. Explain to the programmer why supplies could not have a credit balance.

CASE 4–3
Sears Canada Inc.
Financial analysis

The ability of a business to meet its financial obligations (debts) as they come due is called solvency. There are many ways in which financial statement data can be analyzed to provide insight into the solvency of a business. One financial measure that relates to a business's ability to pay its debts is working capital. Working capital is the excess of the current assets of a business over its current liabilities, as follows:

Working capital = Current assets – Current liabilities

Working capital is especially useful in making monthly or other period-to-period comparisons for a company.

1. Determine the working capital for Sears Canada Inc. as of December 31 of the current and preceding years.
2. What conclusions concerning the company's ability to meets its financial obligations can you draw from these data?

CASE 4–4
No-Pest
Financial statements

Assume that you recently accepted a position with the Royal Bank as an assistant loan officer. As one of your first duties, you have been assigned the responsibility of evaluating a loan request for $50,000 from No-Pest, a small sole proprietorship. In support of the loan application, Nancy Roach, owner, submitted the shown "Statement of Accounts" (trial balance) for the first year of operations ended December 31, 1999.

1. ▶ Explain to Nancy Roach why a set of financial statements (income statement, statement of owner's equity, and balance sheet) would be useful to you in evaluating the loan request.

2. In discussing the "Statement of Accounts" with Nancy Roach, you discovered that the accounts had not been adjusted at December 31. Through analysis of the "Statement of Accounts," indicate possible adjusting entries that might be necessary before an accurate set of financial statements could be prepared.

3. ▶ Assuming that an accurate set of financial statements will be submitted by Nancy Roach in a few days, what other considerations or information would you require before making a decision on the loan request?

No-Pest
Statement of Accounts
December 31, 1999

Cash	4,120	
Billings Due from Others	8,740	
Supplies (chemicals, etc.)	14,950	
Trucks	32,750	
Equipment	26,150	
Amounts Owed to Others		5,700
Investment in Business		47,500
Service Revenue		107,650
Wages Expense	60,100	
Utilities Expense	6,900	
Rent Expense	4,800	
Insurance Expense	1,400	
Other Expenses	940	
	160,850	160,850

ANSWERS TO SELF-EXAMINATION QUESTIONS

1. **C** The withdrawals account, M. E. Jones, Withdrawals (answer C), would be extended to the Balance Sheet columns of the work sheet. Utilities Expense (answer A), Rent Income (answer B), and Miscellaneous Expense (answer D) would all be extended to the Income Statement columns of the work sheet.

2. **D** Cash or other assets that are expected to be converted to cash or sold or used up within one year or less, through the normal operations of the business, are classified as current assets on the balance sheet. Accounts Receivable (answer D) is a current asset, since it will normally be converted to cash within one year. Office Equipment (answer A), Land (answer B), and Accumulated Amortization (answer C) are all reported in the plant asset section of the balance sheet under long-term assets.

3. **B** The entry to close the owner's drawing account is to debit the owner's capital account and credit the drawing account (answer B).

4. **D** Since all revenue and expense accounts are closed at the end of the period, Revenue Earned (answer A), Wages Expense (answer B), and Rent Expense (answer C) would all be closed to Income Summary. Accumulated Amortization (answer D) is a contra asset account that is not closed.

5. **B** Since the post-closing trial balance includes only balance sheet accounts (all of the revenue, expense, and drawing accounts are closed), Cash (answer A), Accumulated Amortization (answer C), and J. C. Smith, Capital (answer D) would appear on the post-closing trial balance. Revenue Earned (answer B) is a temporary account that is closed prior to the preparation of the post-closing trial balance.

PART TWO

Advanced Accounting Systems

5

Accounting Systems, Internal Controls, and Special Journals

YOU AND ACCOUNTING

Controls are a part of your everyday life. At one extreme, laws are used to govern your behaviour. However, you are also affected by many informal controls. For example, professors use exams as a control to verify that you have studied the material. Colleges and universities use high school grades as a control to verify a minimum level of academic knowledge prior to your being accepted as a student. Banks give you a personal identification number (PIN) as a control to prevent unauthorized access to your cash from an automated teller machine. Dairies use "freshness dating" on their milk containers as a control to prevent you from buying soured milk.

Just as there are many examples of controls throughout society, businesses must also implement controls to help guide the behaviour of their employees toward enterprise objectives. This is one aspect of accounting systems that we will discuss in this chapter.

In the previous chapter, we discussed completing the accounting cycle and preparing financial statements for Computer King. This is a major part of the accounting system of a business. In this chapter, we will discuss controls that can be used to provide assurance about the reliability of these statements. We will apply the principles of accounting system design to manual systems, using special journals and subsidiary ledgers. We will then conclude the chapter by describing the basic design elements of a computer-based accounting system.

After studying this chapter, you should be able to:

Objective 1
Describe the basic principles of accounting systems.

Objective 2
List and describe the three phases of accounting systems installation and revision.

Objective 3
Define internal control, list the four objectives of internal control, and define and give examples of the five elements of an internal control framework.

Objective 4
Journalize and post transactions, using subsidiary ledgers and the following special journals:

Revenue journal
Cash receipts journal
Purchases journal
Cash payments journal

Objective 5
Describe and give examples of additional subsidiary ledgers and modified special journals.

Objective 6
Describe the basic features of a computerized accounting system.

Principles of Accounting Systems

Objective 1

Describe the basic principles of accounting systems.

The methods and procedures for recording and reporting financial information make up a business's accounting system. The accounting system for most businesses, however, is more complex than we have illustrated in the preceding chapters. One reason for this complexity is that the accounting system is uniquely designed for a business because of differences in management's information needs, the type and number of transactions to be recorded, and the information needs of external users of financial statements. For example, how would an accounting system for a law firm differ from that of a merchandising business? The accounting system for a law firm would emphasize fees earned and expenses incurred. The accounting system for a merchandising business would emphasize sales and cost of goods sold, an inventory system, and related accounts. Accounting systems will also vary, depending on whether a business uses a manual system or a computerized system. However, the basic principles that we discuss in the following paragraphs are applicable to all types of systems.

COST-BENEFIT BALANCE

An accounting system must be designed to meet the specific information needs of a business. However, providing information is costly. Thus, a major consideration in designing an accounting system is balancing the benefits against the cost of the information. In general, the benefits should be greater than or at least equal to the cost of producing the information.

EFFECTIVE REPORTS

To be effective, the reports generated by an accounting system must be timely, clear, and concise. When preparing these reports, we must consider the needs and knowledge of the user. For example, managers may need a variety of detailed reports for planning and controlling operations on a daily or weekly basis. In contrast, regulatory agencies such as the Provincial Securities Commissions and Revenue Canada Taxation often require uniform reports at established intervals, such as quarterly or yearly.

ABILITY TO ADAPT TO FUTURE NEEDS

Businesses operate in a changing environment. This environment may include changes beyond the control of a business, such as new government regulations, changes in accounting principles, or changes in computer technology. An accounting system must be able to adapt to the changing information needs in such an environment. For example, regulatory agencies often change the information, timing, and nature of reports they require of businesses.

Accounting systems also reflect the organizational structure and the information needs of individuals within the business. As individuals or lines of authority and responsibility within a business change, the accounting system must also adapt and change. To be effective, the accounting system must support all levels of management.

ADEQUATE INTERNAL CONTROLS

An accounting system provides information that management reports to owners, creditors, and other interested parties. In addition, the system aids management in planning and controlling operations. **Internal controls** are the detailed policies and procedures used to direct operations toward desired goals, ensure accurate financial reports, and ensure compliance with applicable laws and regulations. We discuss the general principles for an adequate internal control structure later in this chapter.

Accounting Systems Installation and Revision

Objective 2
List and describe the three phases of accounting systems installation and revision.

Designing and installing an accounting system for a business requires a thorough knowledge of the business's operations. In addition, accounting systems must be continually reviewed for possible revisions in order to keep pace with the changing information needs of businesses. For example, some areas of the system, such as the types and design of forms and the number and titles of accounts, continually change as the business grows and adapts to its environment. This process of installing or changing an accounting system consists of three phases: (1) analysis, (2) design, and (3) implementation.

SYSTEMS ANALYSIS

Systems analysis usually begins with a review of the organizational structure and the job descriptions of personnel. This review is followed by a study of the forms, records, procedures, processing methods, and reports used by the business. The source of such information is usually found in the firm's *Systems Manual*.

The goal of systems analysis is to determine information needs, the sources of information, any weaknesses in the procedures, and the data processing methods in use. In addition to analyzing and reviewing the current system, the systems analyst also assesses management's plans for changes in operations (volume, products, territories, etc.). Such changes usually require changes in the current system.

SYSTEMS DESIGN

Accounting systems are changed as a result of the kind of systems analysis described above. Such changes may involve only minor changes from the existing system, such as revision of a particular form and the related procedures and processing methods. In contrast, a business may require a complete revision of the entire system. Many companies are completely revising their systems to be more integrated. For example, **Oracle, SAP**, and **D & B** software companies have developed integrated systems in which data are entered only once into a database that is shared by all system components. A **database** contains the financial and non-financial data needed by a business to satisfy its information needs.

System designers must have a general knowledge of different accounting systems and methods of processing transactions, both manual and computerized. A successful systems design depends upon the creativity, imagination, and ability of the systems designer to evaluate alternatives. The basic principles of accounting systems are also necessary for a successful design.

SYSTEMS IMPLEMENTATION

The final phase of systems installation is to carry out, or implement, the systems design. The business must install new or revised forms, records, procedures, and equipment, and withdraw any that are no longer useful. All personnel responsible for operating the system must be carefully trained and supervised until the system is fully operational.

Major revisions of a system, such as changing from a centralized computer system to a decentralized, micro-computer-based data processing system, require careful planning. Managers must have reasonable assurance that the new system will provide complete and accurate information. Therefore, many companies implement new or revised systems in stages over a period of time. Management can detect weaknesses and conflicting or unnecessary elements in the design more easily when the implementation is gradual rather than all at once. In addition, this approach reduces the chances that essential operating information will be unavailable during the systems implementation.

Another approach to new system implementation is to conduct a parallel test. In a parallel test, we run the old and new systems at the same time. We can then compare the outputs of both systems. Parallel tests are costly, since we are running two systems at once. However, many managers believe this additional cost is worth the assurance that the new system is complete and accurate. In addition, this approach guarantees that essential operating information will be available from the old system if the new system does not function properly.

ACCOUNTING SYSTEMS, PROFIT MEASUREMENT, AND MANAGEMENT

A Greek restaurant owner had his own system of accounting. He kept his accounts payable in a cigar box on the left-hand side of his cash register, his daily cash returns in the cash register, and his receipts for paid bills in another cigar box on the right.

When his youngest son graduated as an accountant, he was appalled by his father's primitive methods. "I don't know how you can run a business that way," he said. "How do you know what your profits are?"

"Well, son," the father replied, "when I got off the boat from Greece, I had nothing but the pants I was wearing. Today, your brother is a doctor. You are an accountant. Your sister is a speech therapist. Your mother and I have a nice car, a city house, and a country home. We have a good business, and everything is paid for...."

"So, you add all that together, subtract the pants, and there's your profit!"

Internal Control

Objective 3

Define internal control and list the four objectives of internal control, and define and give examples of the five elements of an internal control framework.

Managing a lawn care business would require the use of internal controls to guide its operations and achieve desired goals.

One of the key aspects of systems analysis, design, and implementation is a business's internal control. Businesses use internal controls to guide their operations. For example, assume that you own and manage a lawn care service during the summer months. Assume further that your business employs several teams, each with a vehicle and lawn equipment that you provide. What are some of the issues you would face as a manager in controlling the operations of this business? Below are some examples.

- Lawn care needs to be provided on schedule.
- The quality of lawn care services must meet customer expectations.
- Employees must provide work for the hours they are paid.
- Lawn care equipment should be used for business purposes only.
- Customers must be billed and bills collected for services rendered.
- Vehicles should be used for business purposes only.

How would you address some of these control issues? You could, for example, have "surprise" inspections by arriving on site at random times to verify that the teams are working on schedule. You could develop a schedule at the beginning of each day and then inspect the work at the end of the day to verify its completion and quality. You could require the work teams to return the vehicles and equipment to a central location to prevent unauthorized use. You could bill customers after you inspected the work, and you could monitor collection of all receivables. You could keep a log of odometer readings at the end of each day to verify that the vehicle has not been used for "joy riding." All of these are examples of internal control.

OBJECTIVES OF INTERNAL CONTROL

Internal control consists of the policies and procedures established and maintained by management to assist in achieving its objective of ensuring, as far as practical, the orderly and efficient conduct of the entity's business.[1]

Management has specific internal control objectives to provide reasonable assurance that the organization is:

1. Optimizing the use of resources;
2. Preventing and detecting error and fraud;
3. Safeguarding assets;
4. Maintaining reliable control systems.[2]

Internal control can direct an organization towards the achievement of desired goals, preparation of reliable financial reports, and compliance with laws and regulations.

Internal control can prevent loss of resources, provide information about how the business is performing, and help guide it in the planned direction. Unfortunately, internal control cannot eliminate all bad decisions or unexpected events. Internal control provides managers with assurance that their business is complying with external financial reporting standards and applicable laws and regulations. Examples of such standards and laws include generally accepted accounting principles (GAAP), environmental regulations, contract terms, and safety regulations.

---

[1] *CICA Handbook*, Section 5200.
[2] *CICA Handbook*, Section 5220, Appendix C.

ELEMENTS OF INTERNAL CONTROL

How does management achieve internal control? Internal control consists of five major elements: (1) the control environment, (2) risk assessment, (3) control procedures, (4) monitoring, and (5) information and communication. These elements form the internal control framework for achieving the four objectives identified on page 182.

Exhibit 1 illustrates the internal control framework. In this exhibit, the elements of internal control form a pyramid. The base of the pyramid is the business's control environment, upon which the remaining elements are built. Information and communication occur between each element and management, who is responsible for achieving the three internal control objectives. In the following paragraphs, we discuss each of these elements.

Exhibit 1

Elements of Internal Control

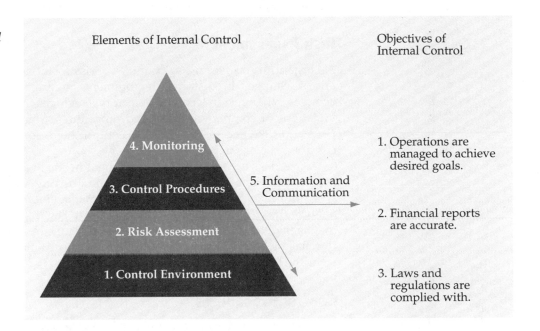

Control Environment

A business's control environment is the overall attitude of management and employees about the importance of controls. One of the factors that influences the control environment is management's philosophy and operating style. A management that overemphasizes operating goals may indirectly encourage employees to overstate or misreport operating data. For example, a car repair company could have a policy of paying bonuses to its automobile department managers, based on the amount of work provided. This bonus arrangement can create incentives for service department managers to overstate the amount of service work customers require. Thus, customers can be charged for work that they do not need.

A management that often deviates from established control policies and procedures may also be indicating to employees that controls are not important. For example, if management routinely ignores a policy requiring that safety glasses be worn in the plant, employees may interpret the policy as "optional," thereby creating an unsafe plant environment. On the other hand, a management that emphasizes the importance of controls and encourages adherence to control policies will create an effective control environment.

Another factor that influences the control environment is the business's organizational structure, which is the framework for planning and controlling operations. For example, a department store chain might organize each of its stores as relatively separate business units. Each store manager is given full authority over pricing and other operating activities. In such a structure, each store manager has the responsibility for establishing an effective control environment.

Personnel policies and procedures also affect the control environment. Personnel policies involve the hiring, training, evaluating, compensating, and promoting of employees. The human resource area also includes the development of job descriptions, employee codes of ethics, and conflict-of-interest policies. For example, **Teledyne Inc.** has developed a code of business conduct that establishes ethical guidelines for governmental contracting, employee hiring and development, environmental management, and international business. Such policies and procedures can enhance the internal control environment if they provide reasonable assurance that only competent, honest employees are hired and retained.

Risk Assessment

All organizations face risks. Examples of risk include the nature of assets and operations, changes in customer requirements, new competitive threats, regulatory changes, changes in economic factors (such as interest rates), and employee violations of company policies and procedures. Management should assess these risks and take necessary actions to control them, so that the objectives of internal control can be achieved.

Once risks are identified, management needs to analyze them to estimate their significance, to assess their likelihood of occurring, and to determine actions that will minimize them. For example, the manager of a warehouse operation may analyze the risk of employee back injuries, which might give rise to lawsuits. If the manager determines that the risk is significant, the company may take action by purchasing back support braces for its warehouse employees and requiring them to wear the braces.

Control Procedures

The results of a survey of members of the American Institute of Certified Public Accountants indicate the importance of control procedures. This survey reported that as many as 38% of the accountants responding witnessed fraud during the past year.[3]

Management establishes control procedures to provide reasonable assurance that enterprise goals will be achieved and fraud will be prevented. In the following paragraphs, we will briefly discuss control procedures that can be integrated throughout the accounting system.

COMPETENT PERSONNEL, ROTATING DUTIES, AND MANDATORY VACATIONS. The successful operation of an accounting system requires procedures to ensure that people are able to perform the duties assigned to them. Hence, it is necessary that all accounting employees be adequately trained and supervised in performing their jobs. It may also be advisable to rotate clerical personnel periodically from job to job. In addition to increasing their understanding of the system, the knowledge that an employee's work may be performed by others encourages adherence to prescribed procedures. For nonclerical personnel such as managers, mandatory vacations normally are used rather than job rotations. During vacation periods, other managers perform the relevant job responsibilities.

---

[3] John P. Rice, et al, "Old Fashioned Fraud Is Alive and Well: Results of a Survey of Practicing CPAs," *CPA Journal*, September 1988, pp. 74–77.

Rotating duties and mandating vacations may prevent errors or detect existing errors and fraud. For example, an accounts receivable clerk should be periodically rotated to another job or required to take a vacation. If the clerk steals customers' cash payments, the thefts will likely be discovered when a new clerk bills customers for amounts they have already paid.

ASSIGNING RESPONSIBILITY. If employees are to work efficiently, management needs to clearly define their responsibilities. Control procedures should provide assurance that no overlapping or undefined areas of responsibility exist and that employees are held accountable for their responsibilities. For example, if two or more salesclerks are to use the same cash register, management should assign the clerks separate cash drawers and register keys. In this way, the clerks are responsible for their individual cash drawers and management can obtain a daily proof of cash for each clerk.

SEPARATING RESPONSIBILITIES FOR RELATED OPERATIONS. To decrease the possibility of inefficiency, errors, and fraud, management should divide responsibility for a sequence of related operations among two or more persons. For example, the responsibilities for purchasing, receiving, and paying for computer supplies should be divided among three persons or departments. If the same person orders supplies, verifies the receipt of the supplies, and pays the supplier, the following abuses are possible:

1. The purchaser may place orders on the basis of friendship with a supplier, rather than on price, quality, and other objective factors.
2. The quantity and quality of supplies received may not be verified.
3. The employee may steal supplies.
4. The validity and accuracy of invoices may be verified carelessly, thus causing the payment of false or inaccurate invoices. For example, studies have estimated that the typical company pays one of every 100 invoices more than once.[4]

The "checks and balances" provided by dividing responsibilities among various departments requires no duplication of effort. The business documents prepared by one department are designed to coordinate and support those prepared by other departments.

SEPARATING ACCOUNTING, CUSTODY OF ASSETS, AND OPERATIONS. Control policies and procedures should establish the responsibilities for various business activities. To reduce the possibility of errors and fraud, management should separate the following functions:

1. Accounting for the business's transactions.
2. Custody of the firm's assets.
3. Engaging in the firm's operating activities.

When these functions are separated, the accounting records serve as an independent check on the individuals who have custody of the assets and who engage in the business operations. For example, the employees entrusted with handling cash receipts from credit customers should not record cash receipts in the accounting records. To do so would allow employees to borrow or steal cash and hide the theft in the records. Likewise, if those engaged in operating activities also record the results of operations, they could distort the accounting reports to show favourable results. For example, a store manager whose year-end bonus is based upon operating profits might record fictitious sales in order to receive a larger bonus.

---

[4] *Checkers, Simon, and Rosner—Client Report*, Spring 1994 (Issue 3).

When responsibilities for the functions above are not separated, a company is more vulnerable to employee theft. For example, one individual, who called himself David Shelton, was hired as a bookkeeper at a number of firms, where he stole thousands of dollars and then disappeared. Shelton's main method was to steal cash receipts, while changing the books to hide the shortage. Separating the cash-handling function from the bookkeeping function would have reduced the likelihood of this type of theft.[5]

PROOFS AND SECURITY MEASURES. Proofs and security measures should be used to safeguard business assets and ensure reliable accounting data. The control procedures use many different techniques, such as authorization, approval, and reconciliation procedures. For example, the firm should require employees who travel on company business to obtain a department manager's approval on a travel request form.

Other examples of control procedures include the use of bank accounts and other measures to ensure the safety of cash and other valuable documents. Using a cash register that displays the amount recorded for each sale and provides a printed receipt for the customer, and an internal record in the machine, can be an effective part of the internal control structure. An all-night convenience store could use the following security measures to deter robberies:

1. Locate the cash register near the door, so that it is fully visible from outside the store; have two employees work late hours, or employ a security guard.
2. Deposit cash in the bank daily before 5 p.m.
3. Keep only small amounts of cash on hand after 5 p.m. by depositing excess cash in a store safe that cannot be opened by employees on duty.
4. Install security cameras and alarm systems.

Companies may obtain insurance to protect against losses from employee fraud. Such insurance, called a **fidelity bond**, normally requires background checks on all employees covered. If a claim is paid, insurance companies normally take legal action against the employees responsible. Such legal action tends to deter employee fraud and enhances the internal control structure.

Monitoring

Monitoring the internal control system locates deficiencies and improves control effectiveness. The internal control system may be monitored through either ongoing efforts by management or separate evaluations. Ongoing monitoring efforts may include observing both employee behaviour and warning signs from the accounting system.[6] The following employee activities may be clues to dishonest behaviour:

1. Abrupt change in lifestyle (without winning the lottery).
2. Close social relationships with suppliers.
3. Refusal to take vacation.
4. Frequent borrowing from other employees.
5. Excessive use of alcohol or drugs.

The following warning signs from the accounting system may indicate the presence of fraud:

1. Missing documents or gaps in transaction numbers (could mean documents are being used for fraudulent transactions).
2. An unusual increase in customer refunds (they may be phony).

---

[5] J. R. Emshwiller, "Looking for a New Bookkeeper? Beware of this One," *Wall Street Journal,* April 19, 1994, pp. B1–B2.
[6] Edwin C. Bliss, "Employee Theft," *Boardroom Reports,* July 15, 1994, pp. 5–6.

3. Discrepancies between daily cash receipts and bank deposits (could mean some receipts are being pocketed).
4. Sudden increase in slow payments (employee may be pocketing the payment).
5. Backlog in recording transactions (possibly an attempt to delay detection of fraud).

Separate evaluations generally occur when there are major changes in strategy, senior management, corporate structure, or operations. In large businesses, internal auditors, who are independent of operations, monitor the internal control system. In addition, external auditors also evaluate internal control as a normal part of their annual financial statement audit.

Often the internal auditor's review will be noted in a company's annual report. The following excerpt is from the "Management's Report" in the Annual Report of Schneider Corporation.

In fulfilling its responsibilities, management has developed internal control systems and procedures designed to provide reasonable assurance that the Corporation's assets are safeguarded, that transactions are executed in accordance with appropriate authorization and that accounting records may be relied upon to properly reflect the Corporation's business transactions. To augment the internal control systems, the Corporation maintains an internal audit department which evaluates company operations, provides control self-assessment training to employees, and formally reports on the adequacy and effectiveness of the controls and procedures to the Audit Committee of the Board of Directors.

USING ACCOUNTING TO UNDERSTAND BUSINESS

Internal Control Failure	*What Happened When Internal Control Failed?*
Recording cash received as revenue, even though future services are required.	**Jiffy Lube** franchises 10-minute automobile oil change centres. Up-front fees paid by franchisees for these centres were recorded immediately by Jiffy Lube as revenue, even though future services to the franchisees were required. The company was forced to restate earnings, causing a 75% reduction in previously reported profits. The stock price dropped by approximately 90% during this period.
Recording revenue before it is earned.	**Datapoint Corporation,** a computer company, recorded revenue before it had been earned. In 1981, the Securities and Exchange Commission charged the company with overstating earnings. This event began a long slide in the company's stock price from $120 per share in 1981 to around $4 per share in 1990.
Improperly recording expenses as assets.	**DeLaurentis Entertainment Group (DEG),** a movie production company, improperly recorded $1.3 million of selling, administrative, and interest costs as assets rather than expenses. This caused the income to be grossly overstated. DEG agreed to settle a government case against it by preparing and adhering to new internal control policies.
Recording a refund from a supplier as revenue.	**L.A. Gear** manufactures and sells athletic sportswear. The SEC charged L.A. Gear with improperly recording $4.7 million of cash received from suppliers for returned merchandise as revenue. The company was forced to restate its reported income and record a loss. As a result, L.A. Gear's stock price decreased from $50 to $20 per share in one year's time.

The examples and categories are from Howard M. Schmilit's book, *Financial Shenanigans*, McGraw-Hill, Inc., New York, 1993.

The Corporation communicates throughout the organization the responsibility for employees to maintain high ethical standards in their conduct of the Corporation's affairs. This responsibility is characterized in the Code of Conduct signed by each management employee which provides for compliance with laws of each jurisdiction in which the Corporation operates and for observance of rules of ethical business conduct.

The Audit Committee of the Board of Directors is comprised of directors who are not employees. The Committee meets periodically and independently with management, the internal auditors and the shareholders' auditors to discuss significant accounting, reporting and internal control matters. The Committee reviews the consolidated financial statements of the Corporation and recommends them to the Board for approval. Both the internal auditors and the independent external auditors have unrestricted access to the Audit Committee.

Information and Communication

Information and communication are essential elements of an organization's internal control. Management needs information about the control environment, risk assessment, control procedures, and monitoring to guide operations and ensure compliance with reporting, legal, and regulatory requirements.

The business can also acquire information from sources outside of the firm. Management can use this information to assess external standards, laws, regulations, events, and conditions that impact decision making and external reporting. For example, management uses information from the CICA Accounting Standards Committee to assess the impact of possible changes in reporting standards.

Subsidiary Ledgers and Special Journals

Objective 4

Journalize and post transactions, using subsidiary ledgers and the following special journals:

Revenue journal
Cash receipts journal
Purchases journal
Cash payments journal

In preceding chapters, we manually recorded all transactions for Computer King in an all-purpose (two-column) journal. We then posted the journal entries individually to the accounts in the ledger. Such manual accounting systems are simple to use and easy to understand. Manually kept records may serve a business reasonably well when the amount of data collected, stored, and used by a business is relatively small. For a large business with a large database, however, such manual processing is too costly and too time-consuming. For example, a large company such as **Bell Canada** earns millions in long distance telephone fees daily. Each telephone fee on account requires an entry debiting Accounts Receivable and crediting Revenue Earned. In addition, the firm needs a record of each customer's receivable. Clearly, a simple manual system would not serve the business needs of Bell Canada.

When a business has a large number of similar transactions, using an all-purpose journal is inefficient and impractical. In such cases, subsidiary ledgers and special journals are useful. In addition, a computerized system can supplement or replace a manual system. Although we illustrate the use of manually prepared special journals and subsidiary ledgers, the basic principles we describe in the following paragraphs also apply to a computerized accounting system.

SUBSIDIARY LEDGERS

We need to design an accounting system to provide information on the amounts due from various customers (accounts receivable) and amounts owed to various creditors (accounts payable). We could add a separate account for each customer and creditor in the ledger. However, as the number of customers and creditors increases, the ledger becomes unwieldy when we include a separate account for each customer and creditor.

When there are a large number of individual accounts with a common characteristic, we can group them together in a separate ledger called a **subsidiary ledger**. The primary ledger, which contains all of the balance sheet and income statement accounts, is then called the **general ledger**. Each subsidiary ledger is represented in the general ledger by a summarizing account, called a **control account**. The sum of the balances of the accounts in a subsidiary ledger must equal the balance of the related control account. Thus, you may think of a subsidiary ledger as a secondary ledger that supports a control account in the general ledger.

We keep the individual accounts with customers in alphabetical or numerical order (if customers and suppliers are identified by number) in a subsidiary ledger called the **accounts receivable subsidiary ledger** or **customers ledger**. The control account in the general ledger that summarizes the debits and credits to the individual customer accounts is Accounts Receivable. We keep the individual accounts with creditors in a subsidiary ledger called the **accounts payable subsidiary ledger** or **creditors ledger**. The related control account in the general ledger is Accounts Payable. The relationship between the general ledger and these subsidiary ledgers is illustrated in Exhibit 2.

SPECIAL JOURNALS

One method of processing data more efficiently in a manual accounting system is to expand the all-purpose two-column journal to a multicolumn journal. We use each column in a multicolumn journal only for recording transactions that affect a

Exhibit 2
*General Ledger and
Subsidiary Ledgers*

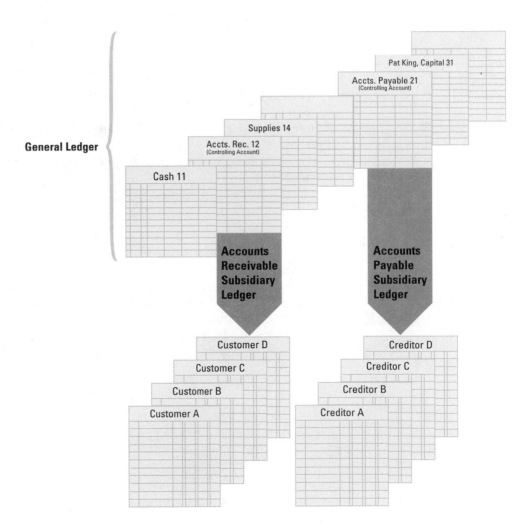

certain account. For example, we might use a special column only for recording debits to the cash account, and another special column only for recording credits to the cash account. The addition of the two special columns would eliminate the writing of *Cash* in the journal for every receipt and payment of cash. Also, there would be no need to post each individual debit and credit to the cash account. Instead, we could total the *Cash Dr.* and *Cash Cr.* columns periodically and post the totals. In a similar way, we could add special columns for recording credits to Revenue Earned, debits and credits to Accounts Receivable and Accounts Payable, and other entries that are often repeated.

An all-purpose multicolumn journal may be adequate for a small business that has many transactions of a similar nature. However, a journal that has many columns for recording many different types of transactions is impractical for larger businesses.

The next logical extension of the accounting system is to replace the single multicolumn journal with several special journals. We design each special journal to record a single kind of transaction that occurs frequently. For example, since most businesses have many transactions in which cash is paid out, they will likely use a special journal for recording cash payments. Likewise, they will use another special journal for recording cash receipts.

The format and number of special journals that a business uses depend upon the nature of the business. A business that renders services to customers on account might use a special journal designed for recording only revenue from services provided on credit. On the other hand, a business that does not give credit would have no need for such a journal. In other cases, we can reduce record-keeping costs by using supporting documents such as serially prenumbered invoices as special journals.

The transactions that occur most often in a medium-sized service business and the special journals in which they are recorded are as follows:

Rendering of services
on account   **recorded in** → Revenue (sales) journal
Receipt of cash
from *any* source   **recorded in** → Cash receipts journal
Purchase of items
on account   **recorded in** → Purchases journal
Payment of cash
for *any* purpose   **recorded in** → Cash payments (disbursements) journal

We use the all-purpose two-column journal, called the general journal or simply the **journal**, for entries that do not fit into any of the special journals. For example, we record adjusting and closing entries in the general journal.

In the following sections, we illustrate the use of special journals and subsidiary ledgers for Computer King. We will use a minimum number of transactions in order to simplify the illustration. We will assume that Computer King had the following selected general ledger balances on March 1, 1999:

Account Number	Account	Balance
11	Cash	$6,200
12	Accounts Receivable	3,400
14	Supplies	2,500
18	Office Equipment	2,500
21	Accounts Payable	1,230
52	Rent Expense	3,200
54	Utilities Expense	2,000

REVENUE JOURNAL

We use the revenue journal (or sales journal) for recording **the sale of goods or rendering of services on account.** *If there were cash sales, we would record them in the cash receipts journal.* We will compare the use of a revenue journal with a general journal by assuming that Computer King recorded the following revenue transactions in a general journal:

2000
Mar.	2	Accounts Receivable—Handler Co.	2,200	
		Revenue Earned		2,200
	6	Accounts Receivable—Jordan Co.	1,750	
		Revenue Earned		1,750
	18	Accounts Receivable—Kenner Co.	2,650	
		Revenue Earned		2,650
	27	Accounts Receivable—Handler Co.	3,000	
		Revenue Earned		3,000

For these four transactions, Computer King recorded eight account titles and eight amounts. In addition, Computer King made 12 postings to the ledgers—four to Accounts Receivable in the general ledger, four to the accounts receivable subsidiary ledger, and four to Revenue Earned in the general ledger. In contrast, we could record these transactions more efficiently in a revenue journal as shown in Exhibit 3.

Exhibit 3
Revenue Journal

			REVENUE JOURNAL			**PAGE 35**
	Date	Invoice No.	Account Debited	Post. Ref.	Accts. Rec. Dr. Revenue Earned Cr.	
1	2000 Mar. 2	615	Handler Co.		2 2 0 0 00	1
2	6	616	Jordan Co.		1 7 5 0 00	2
3	18	617	Kenner Co.		2 6 5 0 00	3
4	27	618	Handler Co.		3 0 0 0 00	4
5	31				9 6 0 0 00	5
6						6

In each revenue transaction, the amount of the debit to Accounts Receivable is the same as the amount of the credit to Revenue Earned. Therefore, only a single amount column is necessary. We enter the date, invoice number, customer name, and amount separately for each transaction.

We must post each transaction recorded in a revenue journal individually to the customer accounts in the accounts receivable subsidiary ledger. We post a single monthly total to Accounts Receivable and Revenue Earned in the general ledger. Exhibit 4 shows the basic procedure of posting from a revenue journal to the accounts receivable subsidiary ledger and the general ledger.

The individual amounts in Exhibit 4, such as the $2,200 debit to Handler Co., are posted frequently to the accounts receivable subsidiary ledger. In this way, management has information on the current balance of each customer's account. Since the balances in the customer accounts are usually debit balances, businesses often use the three-column account form shown in the exhibit.

We indicate the source of the entries posted to the subsidiary ledger in the Posting Reference column of each account by inserting the letter *R* and the page number of the revenue journal. We insert a check mark (✓) instead of a number in the Posting Reference column of the revenue journal, as shown in Exhibit 4.

We maintain the customer accounts in the subsidiary ledger in alphabetical order. If a customer's account has a credit balance, we should indicate this by an

Exhibit 4
Revenue Journal Postings to Ledgers

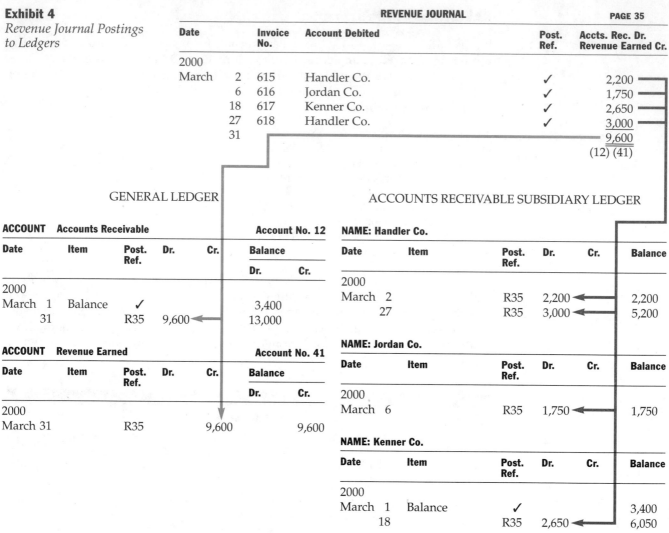

asterisk or parentheses in the Balance column. When an account's balance is zero, a line may be drawn in the Balance column.

At the end of each month, we total the amount column of the revenue journal. This total is equal to the sum of the month's debits to the individual accounts in the subsidiary ledger. We post it in the general ledger as a debit to Accounts Receivable and a credit to Revenue Earned, as shown in Exhibit 4. We then insert account numbers below the total in the revenue journal to indicate that the posting is completed, as shown in Exhibit 4. In this way, we post all of the transactions for revenue earned during the month to the general ledger only once—at the end of the month—greatly simplifying the posting process.

CASH RECEIPTS JOURNAL

We record all transactions that involve the receipt of cash in a cash receipts journal. Thus, the cash receipts journal has a column entitled *Cash Dr.*, as shown in Exhibit 5. All transactions recorded in the cash receipts journal will involve an entry in the Cash Dr. column. For example, on March 28 Computer King received cash of $2,200 from Handler Co. and entered that amount in the Cash Dr. column.

The kinds of transactions in which cash is received and how often they occur determine the titles of the other columns. For Computer King, the most frequent source of cash is collections from customers. Thus, Computer King's cash receipts journal has an *Accounts Receivable Cr.* column.

We use the Other Accounts Cr. column in Exhibit 5 to record credits to any account for which there is no special credit column. For example, Computer King received cash on March 1 for rent. Since no special column exists for Rent Income, we write *Rent Income* in the Account Credited column and enter $400 in the Other Accounts Cr. column.

Exhibit 5 shows the flow of data from the cash receipts journal to the ledgers of Computer King. At regular intervals, we post each amount in the Other Accounts Cr. column to the proper account in the general ledger. The posting is indicated by inserting the account number in the Posting Reference column of the cash receipts journal. We insert the posting reference *CR* and the proper page number in the Posting Reference columns of the accounts.

We post the amounts in the Accounts Receivable Cr. column at frequent intervals to the customer accounts in the accounts receivable subsidiary ledger. These customers are identified in the Account Credited column of the cash receipts journal. We insert the posting reference *CR* and the proper page number in the Posting Reference column of each customer's account. We place a check mark in the Posting Reference

Exhibit 5

Cash Receipts Journal and Postings

CASH RECEIPTS JOURNAL   **PAGE 14**

Date	Account Credited	Post. Ref.	Cash Dr.	Other Accounts Cr.	Accounts Receivable Cr.
2000					
March 1	Rent Income	42	400	400	
19	Kenner Co.	✓	3,400		3,400
28	Handler Co.	✓	2,200		2,200
30	Jordan Co.	✓	1,750		1,750
31			7,750	400	7,350
			(11)	(✓)	(12)

GENERAL LEDGER

ACCOUNT Rent Income   **Account No. 42**

Date	Item	Post. Ref.	Dr.	Cr.	Balance Dr.	Balance Cr.
2000						
March 1		CR14		400		400

ACCOUNT Accounts Receivable   **Account No. 12**

Date	Item	Post. Ref.	Dr.	Cr.	Balance Dr.	Balance Cr.
2000						
March 1	Balance	✓			3,400	
31		R35	9,600		13,000	
31		CR14		7,350	5,650	

ACCOUNT Cash   **Account No. 11**

Date	Item	Post. Ref.	Dr.	Cr.	Balance Dr.	Balance Cr.
2000						
March 1	Balance	✓			6,200	
31		CR14	7,750		13,950	

ACCOUNTS RECEIVABLE SUBSIDIARY LEDGER

NAME: Handler Co.

Date	Item	Post. Ref.	Dr.	Cr.	Balance
2000					
March 2		R35	2,200		2,200
27		R35	3,000		5,200
28		CR14		2,200	3,000

NAME: Jordan Co.

Date	Item	Post. Ref.	Dr.	Cr.	Balance
2000					
March 6		R35	1,750		1,750
30		CR14		1,750	—

NAME: Kenner Co.

Date	Item	Post. Ref.	Dr.	Cr.	Balance
2000					
March 1	Balance	✓			3,400
18		R35	2,650		6,050
19		CR14		3,400	2,650

column of the cash receipts journal to show that we have posted each amount. None of the individual amounts in the Cash Dr. column is posted separately.

At the end of the month, all of the amount columns are totalled and ruled. As a routine check, we verify the equality of the debits and credits. Because we have posted each amount in the Other Accounts Cr. column individually to a general ledger account, we insert a check mark below the column total to indicate that no further action is needed. The totals of the Accounts Receivable Cr. and Cash Dr. columns are posted to the proper accounts in the general ledger, and their account numbers are inserted below the totals to show that the postings have been completed.

ACCOUNTS RECEIVABLE CONTROL AND SUBSIDIARY LEDGER

After we have completed all posting for the month, we should compare the sum of the balances in the accounts receivable subsidiary ledger with the balance of the accounts receivable control account in the general ledger. If the control account and the subsidiary ledger do not agree, we must locate and correct the error or errors. The balances of the individual customer accounts may be summarized in a schedule. The total of Computer King's schedule, $5,650, agrees with the balance of its accounts receivable control account on March 31, 2000, as shown below.

Accounts Receivable (Control Account)		Computer King Schedule of Accounts Receivable March 31, 2000	
Balance, March 1, 2000	$3,400	Handler Co.	$3,000
Debit from R35	9,600	Jordan Co.	0
Credit from CR14	(7,350)	Kenner Co.	2,650
Balance, March 31, 2000	$5,650	Total accounts receivable	$5,650

Internal control is enhanced by separating the function of recording credit sales in the revenue journal from recording cash collections in the cash receipts journal. Thus, for example, one person could not hide the embezzlement of cash collections by not recording the original sale.

PURCHASES JOURNAL

The purchases journal is designed for recording all items purchased on account. Thus, the purchases journal has a column entitled **Accounts Payable Cr.** *We record cash purchases in the cash payments journal.* Exhibit 6 shows the purchases journal used by Computer King, along with postings to the accounts payable subsidiary ledger and general ledger accounts.

The purchases journal also includes special columns for recording debits to accounts most often affected. Since Computer King makes frequent debits to its supplies account, it uses a Supplies Dr. column for these transactions.

We use the Other Accounts Dr. column in Exhibit 6 to record purchases, on account, of any item for which there is no special debit column. We enter the title of the account to be debited in the Other Accounts Dr. column, and enter the amount in the Amount column. We use a separate Posting Reference column for this section of the purchases journal. For Computer King, office equipment purchased on account on March 12 was recorded in the Other Accounts Dr. column.

Exhibit 6 shows the flow of the data from the purchases journal of Computer King to the ledgers. The principles used in posting the purchases journal are similar to those used in posting the revenue and cash receipts journals. We indicate the source of the entries posted to the subsidiary and general ledgers in the Posting Reference column of each account by inserting the letter *P* and the page number of

PURCHASES JOURNAL   PAGE 11

Date	Account Credited	Post. Ref.	Accounts Payable Cr.	Supplies Dr.	Other Accounts Dr.	Post. Ref.	Amount
2000							
March 3	Howard Supplies	✓	600	600			
7	Donnelly Supplies	✓	420	420			
12	Jewett Business Systems	✓	2,800		Office Equipment	18	2,800
19	Donnelly Supplies	✓	1,450	1,450			
27	Howard Supplies	✓	960	960			
31			6,230	3,430			2,800
			(21)	(14)			(✓)

GENERAL LEDGER

ACCOUNTS PAYABLE SUBSIDIARY LEDGER

ACCOUNT   Accounts Payable   Account No. 21

Date	Item	Post. Ref.	Dr.	Cr.	Balance
2000					
March 1	Balance	✓			1,230
31		P11		6,230	7,460

ACCOUNT   Supplies   Account No. 14

Date	Item	Post. Ref.	Dr.	Cr.	Balance
2000					
March 1	Balance	✓			2,500
31		P11	3,430		5,930

ACCOUNT   Office Equipment   Account No. 18

Date	Item	Post. Ref.	Dr.	Cr.	Balance
2000					
March 1	Balance	✓			2,500
12		P11	2,800		5,300

NAME: Donnelly Supplies

Date	Item	Post. Ref.	Dr.	Cr.	Balance
2000					
March 7		P11		420	420
19		P11		1,450	1,870

NAME: Grayco Supplies

Date	Item	Post. Ref.	Dr.	Cr.	Balance
2000					
March 1	Balance	✓			1,230

NAME: Howard Supplies

Date	Item	Post. Ref.	Dr.	Cr.	Balance
2000					
March 3		P11		600	600
27		P11		960	1,560

NAME: Jewett Business Systems

Date	Item	Post. Ref.	Dr.	Cr.	Balance
2000					
March 12		P11		2,800	2,800

Exhibit 6
Purchases Journal and Postings

the purchases journal. We insert a check mark (✓) in the Posting Reference column of the purchases journal after posting each credit to a creditor's account in the accounts payable subsidiary ledger.

At regular intervals, we post the amounts in the Other Accounts Dr. column to the accounts in the general ledger. As we post each amount, we insert the related general ledger account number in the Posting Reference column of the Other Accounts section.

At the end of each month, we total the purchases journal. Before posting the totals to the general ledger, we should compare the sum of the totals of the two debit columns with the total of the credit column to prove their equality.

We post the totals of the Accounts Payable Cr. and Supplies Dr. columns to the appropriate general ledger accounts in the usual manner, with the related account numbers inserted below the column totals. Because we posted each amount in the Other Accounts Dr. column individually, we place a check mark below the $2,800 total to show that no further action is needed.

CASH DISBURSEMENTS JOURNAL

We determine the special columns for the cash disbursements (payments) journal in the same manner as for the revenue, cash receipts, and purchases journals based on the kinds of transactions to be recorded and how often they occur.

Exhibit 7 shows that the cash disbursements journal has a Cash Cr. column. Payments to creditors on account happen often enough to require an Accounts Payable Dr. column. We record debits to creditor accounts for invoices paid in the Accounts Payable Dr. column, and credits for the amounts paid in the Cash Cr. column.

Computer King makes all payments by cheque. As we record each transaction in the cash disbursements journal, we enter the related cheque number in the column at the right of the Date column. The cheque numbers are helpful in controlling cash payments and they provide a useful cross-reference.

We use the Other Accounts Dr. column for recording debits to any account for which there is no special column. For example, Computer King paid $1,600 on March 2 for rent. We record the transaction by writing *Rent Expense* in the space provided and $1,600 in the Other Accounts Dr. and Cash Cr. columns.

Exhibit 7 also shows the flow of data from the cash disbursements journal to the ledgers of Computer King. At frequent intervals during the month, we post the amounts entered in the Accounts Payable Dr. column to the creditor accounts in the accounts payable subsidiary ledger. After each posting, we insert *CP* and the page number of the journal in the Posting Reference column of the account. We place a check mark in the Posting Reference column of the cash payments journal to indicate that we have posted each amount.

We also post the items in the Other Accounts Dr. column to the accounts in the general ledger at regular intervals. We indicate the posting by writing the account numbers in the Posting Reference column of the cash payments journal.

At the end of the month, we total each of the amount columns in the cash payments journal. Then we compare the sum of the two debit totals with the sum of the credit total to determine their equality, and rule the journal. We place a check mark below the total of the Other Accounts Dr. column to indicate that it is not posted. When we have posted each of the totals of the other two columns to a general ledger account, we insert the account numbers below the column totals.

ACCOUNTS PAYABLE CONTROL AND SUBSIDIARY LEDGER

After we have completed all posting for the month, we should compare the sum of the balances in the accounts payable subsidiary ledger with the balance of the accounts payable control account in the general ledger. If the control account and the subsidiary ledger do not agree, we must locate and correct the error or errors. The balances of the individual supplier accounts may be summarized in a schedule. The total of Computer King's schedule, $2,410, agrees with the balance of the accounts payable control account on March 31, 2000, as shown below.

Accounts Payable (Control Account)		Computer King Schedule of Accounts Payable March 31, 2000	
Balance, March 1, 2000	$1,230	Donnelly Supplies	$1,450
Credit from P11	6,230	Grayco Supplies	0
Debit from CP7	(5,050)	Howard Supplies	960
		Jewett Business Systems	0
Balance, March 31, 2000	$2,410	Total	$2,410

Exhibit 7

Cash Payments Journal and Postings

CASH DISBURSEMENTS JOURNAL   PAGE 7

Date	Ch. No.	Account Debited	Post. Ref.	Cash Cr.	Other Accounts Dr.	Accounts Payable Dr.
2000						
March 2	150	Rent Expense	52	1,600	1,600	
15	151	Grayco Supplies	✓	1,230		1,230
21	152	Jewett Business Systems	✓	2,800		2,800
22	153	Donnelly Supplies	✓	420		420
30	154	Utilities Expense	54	1,050	1,050	
31	155	Howard Supplies	✓	600		600
31				7,700	2,650	5,050
				(11)	(✓)	(21)

GENERAL LEDGER

ACCOUNT   Accounts Payable   Account No. 21

Date	Item	Post. Ref.	Dr.	Cr.	Balance
2000					
March 1	Balance	✓			1,230
31		P11		6,230	7,460
31		CD7	5,050		2,410

ACCOUNT   Cash   Account No. 11

Date	Item	Post. Ref.	Dr.	Cr.	Balance
2000					
March 1	Balance	✓			6,200
31		CR14	7,750		13,950
31		CD7		7,700	6,250

ACCOUNT   Rent Expense   Account No. 52

Date	Item	Post. Ref.	Dr.	Cr.	Balance
2000					
March 1	Balance	✓			3,200
2		CD7	1,600		4,800

ACCOUNT   Utilities Expense   Account No. 54

Date	Item	Post. Ref.	Dr.	Cr.	Balance
2000					
March 1	Balance	✓			2,000
30		CD7	1,050		3,050

ACCOUNTS PAYABLE SUBSIDIARY LEDGER

NAME: Donnelly Supplies

Date	Item	Post. Ref.	Dr.	Cr.	Balance
2000					
March 7		P11		420	420
19		P11		1,450	1,870
22		CD7	420		1,450

NAME: Grayco Supplies

Date	Item	Post. Ref.	Dr.	Cr.	Balance
2000					
March 1	Balance	✓			1,230
15		CD7	1,230		—

NAME: Howard Supplies

Date	Item	Post. Ref.	Dr.	Cr.	Balance
2000					
March 3		P11		600	600
27		P11		960	1,560
31		CD7	600		960

NAME: Jewett Business Systems

Date	Item	Post. Ref.	Dr.	Cr.	Balance
2000					
March 12		P11		2,800	2,800
21		CD7	2,800		—

Internal control is enhanced by separating the function of recording purchases in the purchases journal from recording cash payments in the cash payments journal. Separating duties in this way would prevent an individual from recording fictitious purchases and then collecting payments for these purchases that were never delivered.

Adapting Accounting Systems

Objective 5
Describe and give examples of additional subsidiary ledgers and modified special journals.

The preceding sections of this chapter illustrate subsidiary ledgers and special journals that are common for a medium-sized business. Many businesses use subsidiary ledgers for other accounts, in addition to Accounts Receivable and Accounts Payable. Also, special journals are often adapted or modified in practice to meet the specific needs of a business. In the following paragraphs, we describe other subsidiary ledgers and modified special journals.

ADDITIONAL SUBSIDIARY LEDGERS

Generally, subsidiary ledgers are used for accounts that consist of a large number of individual items, each of which has unique characteristics. For example, businesses may use a subsidiary equipment ledger to keep track of each item of equipment purchased, its cost, location, and other data. Such ledgers are similar to the accounts receivable and accounts payable subsidiary ledgers that we illustrated in this chapter.

MODIFIED SPECIAL JOURNALS

A business may modify its special journals by adding one or more columns for recording transactions that occur frequently. For example, a business may collect Provincial Sales Tax (PST), the Goods and Services Tax (GST), or the Harmonized Sales Tax (HST)[7] that must be remitted periodically to a province and the federal government. Thus, the business may add a special column for Sales Taxes Payable in its revenue journal, as shown below.

		REVENUE JOURNAL					PAGE 40
Date	Invoice No.	Account Debited	Post. Ref.	Accts. Rec. Dr.	Revenue Earned Cr.	Provincial Sales Taxes Payable Cr.	Goods and Services Tax Cr.
2000 Nov. 2	842	Litten Co.	✓	5 1 7 5 00	4 5 0 0 00	3 6 0 00	3 1 5 00
3	843	Kauffman Supply Co.	✓	1 2 6 5 00	1 1 0 0 00	8 8 00	7 7 00

In addition, businesses required to collect and remit the Goods and Services Tax are entitled to offset the GST they collect against the GST they incur on purchases. This is called an "input tax credit." To keep track of input tax credits, a special column is added to the purchases journal as shown below.

		PURCHASES JOURNAL						
Date	Account Credited	Post. Ref.	Accts. Payable Cr.	GST Dr.	Supplies Dr.	Other Accounts Dr.	Amount
2000 Nov. 3	Howard Supplies	✓	7 4 9 00	4 9 00	7 0 0 00		
4	Ax Insurance	✓	1 0 7 0 00	7 0 00		Prepaid Insurance	1 0 0 0 00

[7] All provinces except Alberta levy a sales tax on the sale of most goods and services. The federal government levies the Goods and Services Tax on the sale of most goods and services. In some provinces, the PST and GST are blended into the Harmonized Sales Tax (HST).

Each time the business files a GST report with Revenue Canada, the GST billed to customers is combined with the GST incurred on purchases and a net payment or net receivable determined.

To fully implement such a system it is also necessary to modify the column headings in the Cash Receipts and Cash Disbursements Journals in order to keep track of Sales Tax amounts on cash transactions.

Some other examples of how special journals may be modified for a variety of different types of businesses are:

- **Farm**
  The purchases journal may include columns for various types of seeds (corn, wheat), livestock (cows, hogs, sheep), fertilizer, and fuel.

- **Automobile Repair Shop**
  The revenue journal may include columns for each major type of repair service. In addition, columns for warranty repairs, credit card charges, and sales taxes may be added.

- **Hospital**
  The cash receipts journal may include columns for receipts from patients on account, from Green Shield Canada, or other major insurance reimbursers, and provincial health care plans.

- **Movie Theatre**
  The cash receipts journal may include columns for revenues from admissions, gift certificates, and concession sales.

- **Restaurant**
  The purchases journal may include columns for food, linen, silverware and glassware, and kitchen supplies.

Regardless of how a special journal is modified, the basic principles and procedures discussed in this chapter apply. For example, special journals are normally totalled and ruled at periodic intervals. The totals of the debit and credit columns are then compared to verify their equality before the totals are posted to the general ledger accounts.

Computerized Accounting Systems

Objective 6
Describe the basic features of a computerized accounting system.

Computerized accounting systems have become more widely used as the cost of computer hardware and software has declined. Given this wide usage, why do we study manual accounting systems? The reason is that the basic concepts for a manual system also apply to computerized systems.

Computerized accounting systems have three main advantages. First, in a computerized accounting system, transactions are simultaneously recorded in journals and posted electronically to subsidiary ledger accounts. The posting process is done without manual effort, since the original transactions include the required information for posting to the ledger. Thus, computerized accounting systems simplify the record-keeping process. Second, computerized accounting systems are generally more accurate than manual systems. Computer systems will not make common mistakes, such as math errors, posting errors, and journal recording errors. Thus, computerized systems avoid the time lost in correcting common errors. Third, computerized systems provide management current account balance information for customers and suppliers since account balances are posted as the transactions occur. Thus, a computerized accounting system provides management more current information to support decision making.

COMPUTER KING

How do computerized accounting systems work? Computerized accounting systems consist of various subsystems. Examples include the accounts receivable and the accounts payable subsystems. We illustrate a computerized accounts receivable subsystem for Computer King in Exhibit 8.

Assume that Pat King renders services to four customers on May 5. Computer King needs to bill (invoice) these four customers for the services. A computer operator sits at a console and enters billing data for each customer into the computer. The data include the date, customer's account number, and the amount billed. An electronic listing of this information in the computer is termed an **invoice file**. This process is much like recording information in a revenue journal in a manual system. The computer uses the invoice file information to print bills for mailing to the customers. In addition, the computer electronically posts each of the four amounts in the invoice file as debits to the appropriate customer accounts in the subsidiary ledger.

Exhibit 8
*Computerized Accounts
Receivable System*

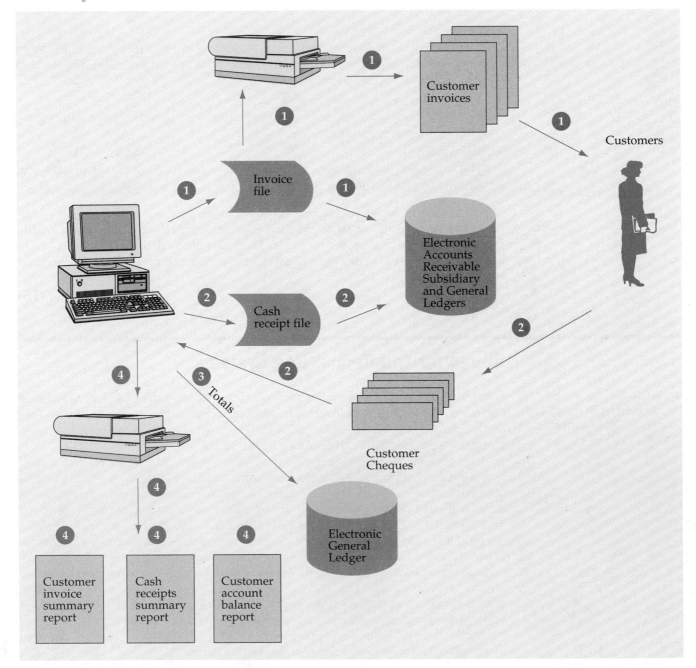

The posting is automatic. The accounting software is programmed to take the information in the invoice file and automatically create the appropriate debits or credits in the electronic ledger. These steps are indicated by the number *1* in Exhibit 8.

Assume that Computer King also received five cheques from customers on May 5 in payment for services rendered in April. The computer operator inputs the cheque information into the computer before depositing the cheques at the bank. The data include the date of receipt, customer's account number, and amount of the cheque. An electronic listing of this information in the computer is termed a cash receipts file. This process is much like recording information in a cash receipts journal in a manual system. The computer uses this information to electronically post each of the five cheques as credits to the appropriate customer accounts in the subsidiary ledger. These steps are indicated by the number *2* in Exhibit 8.

Most computer accounting systems have sub-programs to total the data from individual transaction entries (for example, the invoice file and cash receipts file) and post the totals to the appropriate general ledger accounts in an electronic general ledger. This step is indicated by the number *3* in Exhibit 8. As well, reports can be printed. Three common reports from the accounts receivable system are the customer invoice summary report, cash receipts summary report, and customer account balance report. These reports are indicated by the number *4* in Exhibit 8.

The **customer invoice summary report** is a summary of the invoice files for a period of time. The customer invoice summary report is often similar in format to the revenue journal in a manual system.

The **cash receipts summary report** is a summary of the cash receipts files for a period of time. The cash receipts summary report is similar in format to the cash receipts journal in the manual system.

The **customer account balance report** is a listing of all of the accounts receivable balances from the electronic accounts receivable subsidiary ledger. Since the accounts are posted electronically from the invoice and cash receipts file information, the balances are always current.

If management needs the reports at more frequent intervals, for example, for decision making, the computer programs usually have options for daily, weekly, or bi-weekly generation of reports.

We have illustrated the accounts receivable system in a computerized environment to help you understand how a portion of a computerized accounting system is constructed. Although a description of a complete computerized accounting system is beyond our scope, a thorough understanding of this chapter provides a solid foundation for applying the concepts in either a manual or a computer environment. In addition, an understanding of manual accounting systems assists managers in recognizing the interrelationships that exist between accounting data and accounting reports. This recognition, in turn, enables managers to better anticipate how decisions may affect operations and the financial statements and other reports of a business.

KEY POINTS

Objective 1. Describe the basic principles of accounting systems.

Although accounting systems vary from business to business, the following principles apply to all systems:

1. The cost of the information must be balanced against its benefits.
2. Reports must be prepared with the needs and the knowledge of the user considered.
3. The system must be able to adapt to changing needs.
4. Internal controls must be adequate.

Objective 2. List and describe the three phases of accounting systems installation and revision.

The three phases of accounting systems installation are (1) analysis of information needs, (2) design of the system, and (3) implementation of the systems design.

Objective 3. Define internal control, list the four objectives of internal control, and define and give examples of the five elements of an internal control framework.

Internal control consists of the policies and procedures established and maintained by management to assist in achieving its objective of ensuring, as far as practical, the orderly and efficient conduct of the entity's business. The four objectives of internal control are (1) optimizing the use of resources, (2) preventing and detecting error and fraud, (3) safeguarding assets, and (4) maintaining reliable control systems.

The five elements of an internal control framework are the control environment, risk assessment, control procedures, monitoring, and information and communication. The control environment is the overall attitude of management and employees about the importance of controls. The existence of employee codes of ethics and conflict-of-interest policies contributes to the effectiveness of a control environment. Management must continually assess and attempt to reduce the influence of risk. Risk assessment includes evaluating competitor threats, regulatory changes, and changes in economic factors. Control procedures are established to provide reasonable assurance that enterprise goals will be achieved. Control procedures include rotating duties and mandatory vacations. The internal control system should be monitored periodically. Monitoring can be provided by an internal audit staff or by external auditors. Information and communication provide feedback about internal control. Information includes reports about business operations.

Objective 4. Journalize and post transactions, using subsidiary ledgers and the following special journals:

Revenue journal
Cash receipts journal
Purchases journal
Cash payments journal

Subsidiary ledgers may be used to maintain separate records for each customer (the accounts receivable subsidiary ledger) and creditor (the accounts payable subsidiary ledger). When subsidiary ledgers are used, each subsidiary ledger is repre-

sented in the general ledger by a summarizing account, called a controlling account. The sum of the balances of the accounts in a subsidiary ledger must agree with the balance of the related controlling account.

Special journals may be used to reduce the processing time and expense of recording a large number of similar transactions. The revenue journal is used to record the sale of services on account. The cash receipts journal is used to record all receipts of cash. The purchases journal is used to record purchases on account. The cash payments journal is used to record all payments of cash. The general journal is used for recording transactions that do not fit in any of the special journals. The use of each special journal and the accounts receivable and accounts payable subsidiary ledgers is illustrated in the chapter.

Objective 5. Describe and give examples of additional subsidiary ledgers and modified special journals.

Subsidiary ledgers may be maintained for a variety of accounts, such as plant assets, as well as accounts receivable and accounts payable. Special journals may be modified by adding columns in which to record frequently occurring transactions. For example, an additional column is often added to the revenue journal for recording sales taxes payable.

Objective 6. Describe the basic features of a computerized accounting system.

Computerized accounting systems are similar to manual accounting systems. The main advantages of a computerized accounting system are the simultaneous recording and posting of transactions, the high degree of accuracy, and the timeliness of reporting. An example of an accounts receivable computer subsystem is provided in the chapter.

GLOSSARY OF KEY TERMS

Accounting system. The methods and procedures used by a business to record and report financial data for use by management and external users. *Objective 1*

Accounts payable subsidiary ledger. The subsidiary ledger containing the individual accounts with suppliers (creditors). *Objective 4*

Accounts receivable subsidiary ledger. The subsidiary ledger containing the individual accounts with customers (debtors). *Objective 4*

Cash disbursements journal. The journal in which all cash and cheque payments are recorded. *Objective 4*

Cash receipts file. An electronic listing of customer cash receipts information. *Objective 6*

Cash receipts journal. The journal in which all cash receipts are recorded. *Objective 4*

Control account. The account in the general ledger that summarizes the balances of the accounts in a subsidiary ledger. *Objective 4*

General journal. The two-column form used for entries that do not "fit" in any of the special journals. *Objective 4*

General ledger. The primary ledger, when used in conjunction with subsidiary ledgers, that contains all of the balance sheet and income statement accounts. *Objective 4*

Internal control framework. Consists of five major elements: (1) the control environment, (2) risk assessment, (3) control procedures, (4) monitoring, and (5) information and communication. *Objective 3*

Internal control. The policies and procedures established and maintained by management to assist in achieving its objective of ensuring, as far as practical, the orderly and efficient conduct of the entity's business. *Objective 3*

Invoice file. An electronic listing of customer billing information in a computer. *Objective 6*

Purchases journal. The journal in which all items purchased on account are recorded. *Objective 4*

Revenue journal. The journal in which all sales of goods or services on account are recorded. *Objective 4*

Special journals. Journals designed to be used for recording a single type of transaction. *Objective 4*

Subsidiary ledger. A ledger containing individual accounts with a common characteristic. *Objective 4*

ILLUSTRATIVE PROBLEM

Selected transactions of O'Malley Co. for the month of May are as follows:

May

a.   1. Issued Cheque No. 1001 in payment of rent for May, $1,200.
b.   2. Purchased office supplies on account from McMillan Co., $3,600.
c.   4. Issued Cheque No. 1003 in payment of transportation charges on the supplies pur-
         chased on May 2, $320.
d.   8. Rendered services on account to Waller Co., Invoice No. 51, $4,500.
e.   9. Issued Cheque No. 1005 for office supplies purchased, $450.
f. 10. Received cash for office supplies sold to employees at cost, $120.
g. 11. Purchased office equipment on account from Fender Office Products, $15,000.
h. 12. Issued Cheque No. 1010 in payment of the supplies purchased from McMillan Co.
         on May 2, $3,600.
i. 16. Rendered services on account to Riese Co., Invoice No. 58, $8,000.
j. 18. Received $4,500 from Waller Co. in payment of May 8 invoice.
k. 20. Invested additional cash in the business, $10,000.
l. 25. Rendered services for cash, $15,900.
m. 30. Issued Cheque No. 1040 for withdrawal of cash for personal use, $1,000.
n. 30. Issued Cheque No. 1041 in payment of electricity and water bills, $690.
o. 30. Issued Cheque No. 1042 in payment of office and sales salaries for May, $15,800.
p. 31. Journalized adjusting entries from the work sheet prepared for the fiscal year ended
         May 31.

O'Malley Co. maintains a revenue journal, a cash receipts journal, a purchases journal, a cash disbursements journal, and a general journal and uses accounts receivable and accounts payable subsidiary ledgers.

Instructions

1. Indicate the journal in which you would record each of the preceding transactions, (a) through (p).
2. Indicate whether each of the preceding transactions affects an account in the accounts receivable or accounts payable subsidiary ledgers.
3. Journalize transactions (b), (c), (d), (h), and (j) in the appropriate journals.

Solution

1. *Journal*	2. *Subsidiary Ledger*
a. Cash disbursements journal	
b. Purchases journal	Accounts payable ledger
c. Cash disbursements journal	
d. Revenue journal	Accounts receivable ledger
e. Cash disbursements journal	
f. Cash receipts journal	
g. Purchases journal	Accounts payable ledger
h. Cash disbursements journal	Accounts payable ledger
i. Revenue journal	Accounts receivable ledger
j. Cash receipts journal	Accounts receivable ledger
k. Cash receipts journal	
l. Cash receipts journal	
m. Cash disbursements journal	
n. Cash disbursements journal	
o. Cash disbursements journal	
p. General journal	

3.

Transaction (b):

PURCHASES JOURNAL

Date	Account Credited	Post. Ref.	Accounts Payable Cr.	Office Supplies Dr.	Other Accounts Dr.	Post. Ref.	Amount
May 2	McMillan Co.		3 6 0 0 00	3 6 0 0 00			

Transactions (c) and (h):

CASH DISBURSEMENTS JOURNAL

Date	Ch. No.	Account Debited	Post. Ref.	Cash Cr.	Accounts Payable Dr.	Other Accounts Dr.
May 4	1003	Transportation In		3 2 0 00		3 2 0 00
12	1010	McMillan Co.		3 6 0 0 00	3 6 0 0 00	

Transaction (d):

REVENUE JOURNAL

Date	Invoice No.	Account Debited	Post. Ref.	Accts. Rec. Dr. Fees Earned Cr.
May 8	51	Waller Co.		4 5 0 0 00

Transaction (j):

CASH RECEIPTS JOURNAL

Date	Account Credited	Post. Ref.	Cash Dr.	Accounts Receivable Cr.	Other Accounts Cr.
May 18	Waller Co.		4 5 0 0 00	4 5 0 0 00	

SELF-EXAMINATION QUESTIONS (ANSWERS AT END OF CHAPTER)

1. The final phase of the installation of an accounting system that involves carrying out the proposals for changes in the system is called:
   A. systems analysis
   B. systems design
   C. systems implementation
   D. systems training

2. The detailed procedures used by management to direct operations toward desired goals are called:
   A. internal controls
   B. systems analysis
   C. systems design
   D. systems implementation

3. A payment of cash for the purchase of services should be recorded in the:
   A. purchases journal
   B. cash payments journal
   C. revenue journal
   D. cash receipts journal

4. When there are a large number of individual accounts with a common characteristic, it is common to place them in a separate ledger called:
   A. a subsidiary ledger
   B. a creditors ledger
   C. an accounts payable ledger
   D. an accounts receivable ledger

5. The control account in the general ledger that summarizes the debits and credits to the individual customer accounts in the subsidiary ledger is entitled:
   A. Accounts Payable
   B. Accounts Receivable
   C. Revenue Earned
   D. Rent Expense

DISCUSSION QUESTIONS

1. Why is the accounting system of a business an information system?
2. What are internal controls?
3. What is the objective of systems analysis?
4. What is included in a firm's *Systems Manual*?
5. What are the four objectives of internal control?
6. Name and describe the five elements of the internal control framework.
7. Should management attempt to assess risk associated with embezzlement?
8. How does a policy of rotating clerical employees from job to job aid in strengthening the control procedures within the control environment?
9. Why should the responsibility for a sequence of related operations be divided among different persons?
10. Why should the employee who handles cash receipts not have the responsibility for maintaining the accounts receivable records?
11. Why should the employee who handles cash receipts not be responsible for approving refunds to customers?
12. In an attempt to improve operating efficiency, one employee was made responsible for all purchasing, receiving, and storing of supplies. Is this organizational change wise from an internal control standpoint? Explain.
13. In an attempt to improve operating efficiency, one employee was made responsible for maintaining all personnel records, for timekeeping, for preparing payroll records, and for distributing payroll cheques. Is this organizational change wise from an internal control standpoint? Explain.
14. The ticket seller at a movie theatre doubles as a ticket taker for a few minutes each day while the ticket taker is on a break. Which control procedure of a business's system of internal control is violated in this situation?
15. Why should the responsibility for maintaining the accounting records be separated from the responsibility for operations?
16. How can the use of a fidelity bond aid internal control?
17. How does a periodic review by internal auditors strengthen the internal control framework?
18. How does management use information and communication in the internal control framework?
19. What is the term applied (a) to the ledger containing the individual customer accounts and (b) to the single account summarizing accounts receivable?
20. What are the major advantages of the use of special journals?
21. Environmental Services Co. uses the special journals described in this chapter. Which journal will be used to record fees earned (a) for cash, (b) on account?

22. In recording 250 revenue earned on account during a single month, how many times will it be necessary to write *Revenue Earned* (a) if each transaction, including revenue earned, is recorded individually in a two-column general journal; (b) if each transaction for revenue earned is recorded in a revenue journal?

23. How many individual postings to the ledger account, Revenue Earned, for the month would be needed in Question 22 if the procedure described in (a) had been used; if the procedure described in (b) had been used?

24. As illustrated in this chapter, what does a check mark (✓) in the Posting Reference column of the cash receipts journal signify (a) when the account credited is an account receivable; (b) when the account credited is Revenue Earned?

25. During the current month, the following errors occurred in recording transactions in the purchases journal or in posting from it:
    a. An invoice for $900 of supplies from Hoffman Co. was recorded as having been received from Hoffer Co., another supplier.
    b. A credit of $840 to JPC Company was posted as $480 in the subsidiary ledger.
    c. An invoice for equipment of $6,500 was recorded as $5,500.
    d. The Accounts Payable column of the purchases journal was overstated by $2,000.
    How will each error come to the bookkeeper's attention, other than by chance discovery?

26. The Accounts Payable and Cash columns in the cash disbursements journal were unknowingly overstated by $100 at the end of the month. (a) Assuming no other errors in recording or posting, will the error cause the trial balance totals to be unequal? (b) Will the creditors ledger agree with the accounts payable control account?

27. Assuming the use of a two-column general journal, a purchases journal, and a cash disbursements journal as illustrated in this chapter, indicate the journal in which each of the following transactions should be recorded:
    a. Purchase of supplies for cash.
    b. Purchase of office supplies on account.
    c. Payment of cash on account to creditor.
    d. Purchase of store equipment on account.
    e. Payment of cash for office supplies.

28. In the **Equity Funding** fraud, approximately $2 billion of insurance policies that were claimed to have been sold by the company were bogus. The bogus policies, which were supported by falsified policy applications, were listed along with real policies on Equity Funding's computer tapes (records). These computer tapes were kept in a separate room where they were easily accessible by Equity Funding personnel, including the computer programmers. In addition, computer programmers and other company personnel had access to the computer. What general weaknesses in Equity Funding's internal controls contributed to the occurrence and the size of the fraud?

EXERCISES

EXERCISE 5–1
Internal controls
Objective 3

Karen Byers was recently hired as the manager of Jenny's Deli. Jenny's is a national chain of franchised delicatessens. During her first month as store manager, Karen encountered the following internal control situations:

a. Jenny's has one cash register. Prior to Karen's joining the deli, each employee working on a shift would take a customer order, accept payment, and then prepare the order. Karen made one employee on each shift responsible for taking orders and accepting the customer's payment. Other employees prepare the orders.

b. Since only one employee uses the cash register, that employee is responsible for counting the cash at the end of the shift and verifying that the cash in the drawer matches the amount of cash sales recorded by the cash register. Karen expects each cashier to balance the drawer to the penny **every** time—no exceptions.

c. Karen caught an employee putting a box of 100 single-serving bags of potato chips in his car. Not wanting to create a scene, Karen smiled and said, "I don't think you're putting those chips on the right shelf. Don't they belong inside the deli?" The employee returned the chips to the stockroom.

State whether you agree or disagree with Karen's handling of each situation and explain your answer.

EXERCISE 5–2
Internal controls
Objective 3

Fancy Fashions is a retail store specializing in women's clothing. The store has established a liberal return policy for the holiday season in order to encourage gift purchases. Any item purchased during November and December may be returned through January 31, with a receipt, for cash or exchange. If the customer does not have a receipt, cash will still be refunded for any item under $25. If the item is more than $25, a cheque is mailed to the customer.

Whenever an item is returned, a store clerk completes a return slip, which the customer signs. The return slip is placed in a special box. The store manager visits the return counter approximately once every two hours to authorize the return slips. Clerks are instructed to place the returned merchandise on the proper rack on the selling floor as soon as possible.

This year, returns at Fancy Fashions have reached an all-time high. There are a large number of returns under $25 without receipts.

a. ➤ How could sales clerks employed at Fancy Fashions use the store's return policy to steal money from the cash register?

b. ➤ 1. What internal control weaknesses do you see in the return policy that could make cash thefts easier?

2. Would issuing a store credit in place of a cash refund for all merchandise returned without a receipt reduce the possibility of theft? List some advantages and disadvantages of issuing a store credit in place of a cash refund.

3. Assume that Fancy Fashions is committed to the current policy of issuing cash refunds without a receipt. What changes could be made in the store's procedures regarding customer refunds in order to improve internal control?

EXERCISE 5–3
Internal controls for bank lending
Objective 3

The Provincial Bank provides loans to businesses in the community through its Commercial Lending Department. Small loans (less than $100,000) may be approved by an individual loan officer, while larger loans (greater than $100,000) must be approved by a board of loan officers. Once a loan is approved, the funds are made available to the loan applicant under agreed terms. The president of The Provincial Bank has instituted a policy whereby she has the individual authority to approve loans up to $5,000,000. The president believes that this policy will allow flexibility to approve loans to valued clients much quicker than under the previous policy.

➤ As an internal auditor of The Provincial Bank, how would you respond to this change in policy?

EXERCISE 5–4
Identifying postings from revenue journal
Objective 4

Using the following revenue journal for J. A. Bach Co., identify each of the posting references, indicated by a letter, as representing (1) a posting to a general ledger account, (2) a posting to a subsidiary ledger account, or (3) a posting to two general ledger accounts.

REVENUE JOURNAL

Date	Invoice No.	Account Debited	Post. Ref.	
20—				
Nov. 1	772	Environmental Safety Co.	(a)	$1,700
10	773	Greenberg Co.	(b)	795
20	774	Smith and Smith	(c)	900
27	775	Envirolab	(d)	540
30				$3,935
				(e)

EXERCISE 5–5
Accounts receivable ledger
Objective 4

Based upon the data presented in Exercise 5-4, (a) set up a T account for Accounts Receivable and T accounts for the four accounts needed in the customers ledger, (b) post to the T accounts, (c) determine the balance in the accounts, if necessary, and (d) prepare a schedule of accounts receivable at November 30.

EXERCISE 5–6
Identifying journals
Objective 4

Assuming the use of a two-column (all-purpose) general journal, a revenue journal, and a cash receipts journal as illustrated in this chapter, indicate the journal to use in recording the following transactions:

a. Investment of additional cash in the business by the owner.
b. Receipt of cash refund from overpayment of taxes.
c. Rendering of services for cash.
d. Rendering of services on account.
e. Receipt of cash from sale of office equipment.
f. Receipt of cash on account from a customer.
g. Sale of office supplies on account, at cost, to a neighboring business.
h. Adjustment to record accrued salaries at the end of the year.
i. Closing of drawing account at the end of the year.
j. Receipt of cash for rent.

EXERCISE 5–7
Identifying journals
Objective 4

Assuming the use of a two-column (all-purpose) general journal, a purchases journal, and a cash disbursements journal as illustrated in this chapter, indicate the journal to use in recording the following transactions:

a. Payment of six months' rent in advance.
b. Purchase of office supplies on account.
c. Purchase of an office computer on account.
d. Purchase of office supplies for cash.
e. Advance payment of a one-year fire insurance policy on the office.
f. Adjustment to prepaid rent at the end of the month.
g. Adjustment to record accrued salaries at the end of the period.
h. Adjustment to prepaid insurance at the end of the month.
i. Adjustment to record amortization at the end of the month.
j. Purchase of office equipment for cash.
k. Purchase of services on account.

EXERCISE 5–8
Identifying transactions in accounts receivable ledger
Objective 4

The following customer's account taken from the accounts receivable subsidiary ledger shows the debits and credits from three related transactions.

NAME   *Future Environmental Services*
ADDRESS   *1319 Main Street*

Date	Item	Post. Ref.	Debit	Credit	Balance
20—					
Sept. 3		R50	6,000		6,000
9		J9		700	5,300
13		CR38		5,300	—

Describe each transaction and identify the source of each posting.

EXERCISE 5–9
Identifying postings from purchases journal
Objective 4

Using the following purchases journal to identify each of the posting references, indicated by a letter, as representing (1) a posting to a general ledger account, (2) a posting to a subsidiary ledger account, or (3) that no posting is required.

PURCHASES JOURNAL   **Page 49**

Date	Account Credited	Post. Ref.	Accounts Payable Cr.	Store Supplies Dr.	Office Supplies Dr.	Other Accounts Dr. Account	Post. Ref.	Amount
20—								
June 4	Coastal Insurance Co.	(a)	4,525			Prepaid Insurance	(b)	4,525
6	Porter Supply Co.	(c)	3,000			Office Equipment	(d)	3,000
11	Baker Products	(e)	1,950	1,500	450			
13	Wilson and Wilson	(f)	6,800		6,800			
20	Cowen Supply	(g)	3,775	3,775				
27	Porter Supply Co.	(h)	9,100			Store Equipment	(i)	9,100
30			29,150	5,275	7,250			16,625
			(j)	(k)	(l)			(m)

EXERCISE 5–10

Identifying postings from cash disbursements journal
Objective 4

Using the following cash payments journal to identify each of the posting references, indicated by a letter, as representing (1) a posting to a general ledger account, (2) a posting to a subsidiary ledger account, or (3) that no posting is required.

		CASH DISBURSEMENTS JOURNAL				Page 46
Date	Ch. No.	Account Debited	Post. Ref.	Cash Cr.	Other Accounts Dr.	Accounts Payable Dr.
20—						
July 3	611	Aquatic Systems Co.	(a)	4,000		4,000
5	612	Utilities Expense	(b)	325	325	
10	613	Prepaid Rent	(c)	3,200	3,200	
17	614	Coe Bros.	(d)	2,500		2,500
20	615	Office Equipment	(e)	2,100	2,100	
22	616	Advertising Expense	(f)	400	400	
25	617	Office Supplies	(g)	250	250	
27	618	Evans Co.	(h)	5,500		5,500
31	619	Salaries Expense	(i)	1,750	1,750	
31				20,025	8,025	12,000
				(l)	(j)	(k)

EXERCISE 5–11

Identifying transactions in accounts payable ledger account
Objective 4

The following creditor's account taken from the accounts payable ledger shows the debits and credits from three related transactions.

NAME   *Echo Co.*
ADDRESS   *1717 Kirby Street*

Date	Item	Post. Ref.	Debit	Credit	Balance
20—					
July 6		P34		10,500	10,500
10		J10	500		10,000
16		CD37	10,000		—

Describe each transaction and identify the source of each posting.

EXERCISE 5–12

Error in accounts payable ledger and schedule of accounts payable
Objective 4

After Wittier Company had completed all postings for October in the current year, the sum of the balances in the following accounts payable ledger did not agree with the balance of the appropriate control account in the general ledger.

NAME   *C. D. Cali Co.*
ADDRESS   *1240 W. Main Street*

Date	Item	Post. Ref.	Debit	Credit	Balance
20—					
Oct. 1	Balance	✓			4,750
10		CD22	4,750		—
17		P30		3,250	3,250
25		J7	250		2,000

NAME   *Cutler and Powell*
ADDRESS   *717 Elm Street*

Date	Item	Post. Ref.	Debit	Credit	Balance
20—					
Oct. 1	Balance	✓			6,100
18		CD23	6,100		—
29		P31		9,500	9,500

NAME   *C. D. Greer and Son*
ADDRESS   *972 S. Tenth Street*

Date	Item	Post. Ref.	Debit	Credit	Balance
20—					
Oct. 17		P30		3,750	3,750
27		P31		7,000	10,750

NAME   *Taber Supply*
ADDRESS   *1170 Mattis Avenue*

Date	Item	Post. Ref.	Debit	Credit	Balance
20—					
Oct. 1	Balance	✓			8,250
7		P30		4,900	13,050
12		J7	250		12,800
20		CD23	5,700		7,100

NAME   *L. L. Weiss Co.*
ADDRESS   *915 E. Walnut Street*

Date	Item	Post. Ref.	Debit	Credit	Balance
20—					
Oct. 5		P30		2,750	2,750

Assuming that the control account balance of $33,200 has been verified as correct, (a) determine the error(s) in the preceding accounts and (b) prepare a schedule of accounts payable from the corrected accounts payable subsidiary ledger.

EXERCISE 5–13
Identifying postings from special journals
Objective 4

Tracy Company makes most of its sales and purchases on credit. It uses the five journals described in this chapter (revenue, cash receipts, purchases, cash disbursements, and general journals). Identify the journal most likely used in recording the postings for selected transactions indicated by letter in the following T accounts:

Cash					Prepaid Rent		
a.	9,650	b.	8,325			g.	400

Accounts Receivable					Accounts Payable		
c.	10,950	d.	9,200	h.	7,600	i.	7,790

Office Supplies					Revenue Earned		
e.	7,790					j.	10,950
f.	1,725					k.	450

Rent Expense		
l.	400	

EXERCISE 5–14
Cash receipts journal
Objective 4

The following cash receipts journal headings have been suggested for a small service firm. How many errors can you find in the headings?

			CASH RECEIPTS JOURNAL			PAGE	
Date	Account Credited	Post. Ref.	Revenue Earned Cr.	Accounts Rec. Cr.	Cash Cr.	Other Accounts Dr.	

EXERCISE 5–15
Modified special journals
Objectives 4, 5

Wellguard Testing Services was established on June 15 of the current year. Wellguard collects the 7% Goods and Services Tax on all testing services provided.

June 16. Provided testing services to A. Sommerfeld on account, Invoice No. 1, $160 plus tax.
   19. Provided testing services to B. Lin, Invoice No. 2, $40 plus tax.
   21. Provided testing services to J. Koss, Invoice No. 3, $60 plus tax.
   22. Provided testing services to D. Jeffries, Invoice No. 4, $100 plus tax.
   24. Provided testing services to K. Sallinger in exchange for testing supplies, $200 plus tax.
   26. Provided testing services to J. Koss, Invoice No. 5, $120 plus tax.
   28. Provided testing services to B. Lin, Invoice No. 6, $80 plus tax.
   30. Provided testing services to D. Finnigan, Invoice No. 7, $180 plus tax.

a. Journalize the transactions for June, using a three-column revenue journal and a two-column general journal. Create customer accounts in an accounts receivable subsidiary ledger, post the transactions, and insert the balance immediately after recording each entry.

b. Post the general journal and the revenue journal to the following general ledger accounts, inserting account balances only after the last postings:

   12   Accounts Receivable
   14   Testing Supplies
   22   Sales Tax Payable
   41   Revenue Earned

c. 1. What is the sum of the balances in the accounts receivable subsidiary ledger at June 30?
   2. What is the balance of the control account at June 30?

PROBLEMS SERIES A

PROBLEM 5–1A
Revenue journal; accounts receivable and general ledgers
Objective 4

Horowitz and Sons Co. was established on May 20 of the current year to provide advertising services. It rendered services during the remainder of the month as follows:

May 21. Rendered services on account to Dunlop Co., Invoice No. 1, $1,200.
   22. Rendered services on account to Stark Co., Invoice No. 2, $2,750.
   24. Rendered services on account to Morris Co., Invoice No. 3, $3,175.
   27. Rendered services on account to Mintz Co., Invoice No. 4, $2,500.
   28. Rendered services on account to Benner Co., Invoice No. 5, $1,500.
   28. Received a $3,600 note receivable from Brown Co. for services rendered.
   30. Rendered services on account to Stark Co., Invoice No. 6, $2,925.
   31. Rendered services on account to Morris Co., Invoice No. 7, $995.

Instructions

1. Journalize the transactions for May, using a single-column revenue journal and a two-column general journal. Post to the following customer accounts in the accounts receivable ledger, and insert the balance immediately after recording each entry: Benner Co.; Dunlop Co.; Mintz Co.; Morris Co.; Stark Co.

2. Post the revenue journal and the general journal to the following accounts in the general ledger, inserting the account balances only after the last postings:

   12 Accounts Receivable
   13 Notes Receivable
   41 Revenue Earned

3. a. What is the sum of the balances of the accounts in the subsidiary ledger at May 31?
   b. What is the balance of the controlling account at May 31?

4. ➤ Assume that on June 1, the province in which Horowitz and Sons operates begins requiring that sales tax be collected on advertising services. Briefly explain how the revenue journal may be modified to accommodate sales of services on account that require the collection of a provincial sales tax.

PROBLEM 5–2A
Revenue and cash receipts journals; accounts receivable and general ledgers
Objective 4

Transactions related to revenue and cash receipts completed by Collier Environmental Services during the period June 15–30 of the current year are as follows:

June 15. Issued Invoice No. 793 to Yamura Co., $8,320.
16. Received cheque from AGI Co. for the balance owed on its account.
19. Issued Invoice No. 794 to Hardy Co., $4,210.
20. Issued Invoice No. 795 to Ross and Son, $5,570.
Post all journals to the accounts receivable ledger.
23. Received cheque from Hardy Co. for the balance owed on June 15.
24. Issued Invoice No. 796 to Hardy Co., $3,190.
Post all journals to the accounts receivable ledger.
25. Received cheque from Yamura Co. for the balance due on invoice of June 15.
28. Received cheque from Hardy Co. for invoice of June 19.
28. Issued Invoice No. 797 to AGI Co., $1,890.
30. Received $5,000 of supplies for services rendered to Hang Company.
30. Recorded cash fees received for the second half of the month, $10,400.
Post all journals to the accounts receivable ledger.

Instructions

1. Insert the following balances in the general ledger as of June 1:

11	Cash	$14,380
12	Accounts Receivable	10,440
14	Supplies	8,000
41	Revenue Earned	—

2. Insert the following balances in the accounts receivable ledger as of June 15:

AGI Co.	$ 7,890
Hardy Co.	11,410
Ross and Son	—
Yamura Co.	—

3. In a single-column revenue journal and a cash receipts journal, insert *June 15 Total(s) Forwarded* on the left side of the first line of the journal. Use the following column headings for the cash receipts journal: Other Accounts, Revenue Earned, Accounts Receivable, and Cash. The Revenue Earned column is used to record cash revenue. Insert a check mark (✓) in the Post. Ref. column, and the following dollar figures in the respective amount columns:

    Revenue journal: 28,460
    Cash receipts journal: 3,260; 11,820; 19,600; 34,680.

4. Using the two special journals and the two-column general journal, journalize the transactions for the remainder of June. Post to the accounts receivable ledger, and insert the balances at the points indicated in the narrative of transactions. *Determine the balance in the customer's account before recording a cash receipt.*
5. Total each of the columns of the special journals, and post the individual entries and totals to the general ledger. Insert account balances after the last posting.
6. Determine that the subsidiary ledger agrees with the control account in the general ledger.

PROBLEM 5–3A
Purchases, accounts payable account, and accounts payable ledger
Objective 4

Lee Landscaping Services designs and installs landscaping. Office supplies are used by the landscape designers and office staff, while field supplies (rock, bark, etc.) are used in the actual landscaping. Purchases on account completed by Lee Landscaping during May of the current year are as follows:

May 1. Purchased field supplies on account from Yin Co., $5,430.
4. Purchased office supplies on account from Lapp Co., $2,600.
9. Purchased field supplies on account from Nelson Co., $1,240.

13. Purchased field supplies on account from Yin Co., $980.
14. Purchased office equipment on account from Emerald Computers Co., $8,900.
17. Purchased office supplies on account from J-Mart Supplies Co., $2,040.
20. Purchased office equipment on account from Cencor Co., $9,500.
24. Purchased field supplies on account from Nelson Co., $1,020.
29. Purchased office supplies on account from J-Mart Supplies Co., $3,560.
31. Purchased field supplies on account from Nelson Co., $2,040.

Instructions

1. Insert the following balances in the general ledger as of May 1:

14	Field Supplies	$ 3,120
15	Office Supplies	1,760
18	Office Equipment	28,600
21	Accounts Payable	7,600

2. Insert the following balances in the accounts payable ledger as of May 1:

Cencor Co.	$ 3,250
Emerald Computers Co.	—
J-Mart Supplies Co.	1,780
Lapp Co.	2,570
Nelson Co.	—
Yin Co.	—

3. Journalize the transactions for May, using a purchases journal similar to the one illustrated in this chapter and a two-column general journal. Prepare the purchases journal with columns for Accounts Payable, Field Supplies, Office Supplies, and Other Accounts. Post to the creditor accounts in the accounts payable ledger immediately after each entry.
4. Post the general journal and the purchases journal to the accounts in the general ledger.
5. a. What is the sum of the balances in the subsidiary ledger at May 31?
   b. What is the balance of the control account at May 31?

PROBLEM 5–4A
Purchases and cash disbursements journals; accounts payable and general ledgers
Objective 4

Desai Water Testing Service was established on June 16 of the current year. Desai uses field equipment and field supplies (chemicals and other supplies) to analyze water for unsafe contaminants in streams, lakes, and ponds. Transactions related to purchases and cash disbursements during the remainder of June are as follows:

June 16. Issued Cheque No. 1 in payment of rent for the remainder of June, $1,200.
16. Purchased field equipment on account from Harper Equipment Co., $6,890.
16. Purchased field supplies on account from Heath Supply Co., $12,340.
17. Issued Cheque No. 2 in payment of field supplies, $3,450, and office supplies, $240.
18. Purchased office equipment on account from Chavez Co., $2,090.
19. Purchased office supplies on account from Aztec Supply Co., $980.
   Post the journals to the accounts payable ledger.
23. Issued Cheque No. 3 to Harper Equipment Co. in payment of invoice, $6,890.
24. Issued Cheque No. 4 to Heath Supply Co. in payment of invoice, $12,340.
25. Issued Cheque No. 5 to purchase land, $24,000.
26. Issued Cheque No. 6 to Chavez Co. in payment of the balance owed.
27. Purchased office supplies on account from Aztec Supply Co., $1,340.
   Post the journals to the accounts payable ledger.
30. Purchased the following from Harper Equipment Co. on account: field supplies, $3,400, and field equipment, $11,280.
30. Issued Cheque No. 7 to Aztec Supply Co. in payment of invoice, $980.
30. Purchased field supplies on account from Heath Supply Co., $8,670.
30. Issued Cheque No. 8 in payment of salaries, $5,400.
30. Acquired land in exchange for field equipment having a cost of $10,500.
   Post the journals to the accounts payable ledger.

Instructions

1. Journalize the transactions for June. Use a purchases journal and a cash disbursements journal, similar to those illustrated in this chapter, and a two-column general journal. Refer to the following partial chart of accounts:

11	Cash
14	Field Supplies
15	Office Supplies
17	Field Equipment
18	Office Equipment
19	Land
21	Accounts Payable
61	Salary Expense
71	Rent Expense

   At the points indicated in the narrative of transactions, post to the following accounts in the accounts payable ledger:

   Aztec Supply Co.
   Chavez Co.
   Harper Equipment Co.
   Heath Supply Co.

2. Post the individual entries (Other Accounts columns of the purchases journal and the cash payments journal and both columns of the general journal) to the appropriate general ledger accounts.
3. Total each of the columns of the purchases journal and the cash disbursements journal, and post the appropriate totals to the general ledger. (Because the problem does not include transactions related to cash receipts, the cash account in the ledger will have a credit balance.)
4. Prepare a schedule of accounts payable.

PROBLEM 5–5A
All journals and general ledger; trial balance
Objective 4

The transactions completed by Miles Delivery Company during July, the first month of the current fiscal year, were as follows:

July 1. Issued Cheque No. 610 for July rent, $1,200.
      2. Purchased a vehicle on account from Browning Transportation, $15,680.
      3. Purchased office equipment on account from Gunter Computer Co., $5,360.
      5. Issued Invoice No. 940 to Capps Co., $1,400.
      6. Received cheque from Pease Co. for $3,100 invoice.
      6. Issued Cheque No. 611 for fuel expense, $750.
      9. Issued Invoice No. 941 to Collins Co., $2,570.
     10. Issued Cheque No. 612 for $1,860 to Hoy Enterprises in payment of invoice.
     10. Received cheque from Sokol Co. for $4,450 invoice.
     10. Issued Cheque No. 613 to Burks Co. for $4,400 invoice.
     11. Issued Invoice No. 942 to Joy Co., $4,180.
     11. Issued Cheque No. 614 for $1,030 to Porter Co. in payment of account.
     12. Received cheque from Capps Co. for $1,400 invoice.
     13. Issued Cheque No. 615 to Browning Transportation in payment of $15,680 balance.
     16. Issued Cheque No. 616 for $6,000 for cash purchase of a vehicle.
     16. Cash fees earned for July 1–16, $14,370.
     17. Purchased maintenance supplies on account from Burks Co., $3,200.
     18. Issued Cheque No. 617 for miscellaneous administrative expense, $700.
     18. Received cheque for rental of office space, $1,200.
     19. Purchased the following on account from McClain Co.: maintenance supplies, $3,260; office supplies, $1,540.
     20. Used $3,450 maintenance supplies to repair delivery vehicles.
     20. Issued Cheque No. 618 in payment of advertising expense, $2,250.
     23. Issued Invoice No. 943 to Sokol Co., $3,490.
     24. Purchased office supplies on account from Hoy Enterprises, $1,020.

25. Issued Invoice No. 944 to Collins Co., $8,350.

25. Received cheque for $7,280 from Pease Co. in payment of balance.

26. Issued Cheque No. 619 to Gunter Computer Co. in payment of $5,360 invoice of July 3.

27. Issued Cheque No. 620 to D. D. Miles as a personal withdrawal, $3,000.

30. Issued Cheque No. 621 for monthly salaries as follows: driver salaries, $1,400; office salaries, $2,600.

31. Cash fees earned for July 17–31, $8,300.

31. Issued Cheque No. 622 in payment for office supplies, $360.

Instructions

1. Enter the following account balances in the general ledger as of July 1:

11	Cash	$12,450
12	Accounts Receivable	14,830
14	Maintenance Supplies	3,240
15	Office Supplies	1,430
16	Office Equipment	8,900
17	Accumulated Amortization—Office Equipment	300
18	Vehicles	42,000
19	Accumulated Amortization—Vehicles	4,200
21	Accounts Payable	7,290
31	D. D. Miles, Capital	71,060
32	D. D. Miles, Withdrawals	—
41	Revenue Earned	—
42	Rent Income	—
51	Driver Salaries Expense	—
52	Maintenance Supplies Expense	—
53	Fuel Expense	—
61	Office Salaries Expense	—
62	Rent Expense	—
63	Advertising Expense	—
64	Miscellaneous Administrative Expense	—

2. Journalize the transactions for July, using the following journals similar to those illustrated in this chapter: purchases journal (with columns for Accounts Payable, Maintenance Supplies, Office Supplies, and Other Accounts), cash receipts journal, single-column revenue journal, cash disbursements journal, and two-column general journal. Assume that an assistant makes daily postings to the individual accounts in the accounts payable ledger and the accounts receivable ledger.

3. Post the appropriate individual entries to the general ledger.

4. Total each of the columns of the special journals and post the appropriate totals to the general ledger; insert the account balances.

5. Prepare a trial balance.

6. Verify the agreement of each subsidiary ledger with its control account. The sum of the balances of the accounts in each subsidiary ledger as of July 31 is as follows:

Accounts receivable: $18,590
Accounts payable: $9,020

PROBLEMS SERIES B

PROBLEM 5–1B
Revenue journal; accounts receivable and general ledgers
Objective 4

Durbin Company was established on May 15 of the current year to provide accounting services. It rendered services during the remainder of the month as follows:

May 18. Rendered services on account to Jay Co., Invoice No. 1, $1,500.

20. Rendered services on account to Reese Co., Invoice No. 2, $3,250.

22. Rendered services on account to Innis Co., Invoice No. 3, $3,375.

27. Rendered services on account to D. L. Victor Co., Invoice No. 4, $3,125.

28. Rendered services on account to Bower Co., Invoice No. 5, $500.
28. Received a $5,000 note receivable from Taylor Co. for services rendered.
30. Rendered services on account to Reese Co., Invoice No. 6, $1,800.
31. Rendered services on account to Innis Co., Invoice No. 7, $1,495.

Instructions

1. Journalize the transactions for May, using a single-column revenue journal and a two-column general journal. Post to the following customer accounts in the accounts receivable ledger, and insert the balance immediately after recording each entry: Bower Co.; Innis Co.; Jay Co.; Reese Co.; D. L. Victor Co.

2. Post the revenue journal to the following accounts in the general ledger, inserting the account balances only after the last postings:

   12   Accounts Receivable
   13   Notes Receivable
   41   Revenue Earned

3. a. What is the sum of the balances of the accounts in the subsidiary ledger at May 31?
   b. What is the balance of the control account at May 31?

4. ➤ Assume that on June 1, the province in which Durbin Company operates begins requiring that sales tax be collected on accounting services. Briefly explain how the revenue journal may be modified to accommodate sales of services on account requiring the collection of a provincial sales tax.

PROBLEM 5–2B
Revenue and cash receipts journals; accounts receivable and general ledgers
Objective 4

Transactions related to revenue and cash receipts completed by Jayco Co. during the period June 15–30 of the current year are as follows:

June 15. Issued Invoice No. 717 to Acme Co., $6,780.
     16. Received cheque from AGI Co. for the balance owed on its account.
     17. Issued Invoice No. 718 to Hardy Co., $5,340.
     18. Issued Invoice No. 719 to Ross and Son, $6,500.
          Post all journals to the accounts receivable ledger.
     21. Received cheque from Hardy Co. for the balance owed on June 15.
     24. Issued Invoice No. 720 to Hardy Co., $2,960.
          Post all journals to the accounts receivable ledger.
June 25. Received cheque from Acme Co. for the balance due on invoice of June 15.
     27. Received cheque from Hardy Co. for invoice of June 17.
     29. Issued Invoice No. 721 to AGI Co., $1,600.
     30. Recorded cash sales for the second half of the month, $11,340.
     30. Received $4,000 of supplies for services rendered to Breck Company.
          Post all journals to the accounts receivable ledger.

Instructions

1. Insert the following balances in the general ledger as of June 1:

11	Cash	$13,560
12	Accounts Receivable	8,800
14	Supplies	6,000
41	Revenue Earned	—

2. Insert the following balances in the accounts receivable ledger as of June 15:

AGI Co.	$ 6,340
Hardy Co.	10,680
Ross and Son	—
Acme Co.	—

3. In a single-column revenue journal and a cash receipts journal, insert *June 15 Total(s) Forwarded* on the left side of the first line of the journal. Use the following column headings for the cash receipts journal: Other Accounts, Revenue Earned, Accounts Receivable, and

Cash. The Revenue Earned column is used to record cash revenue. Insert a check mark (✓) in the Post. Ref. column and the following dollar figures in the respective amount columns:

Revenue journal: 26,790
Cash receipts journal: 4,120; 9,980; 18,570; 32,670.

4. Using the two special journals and the two-column general journal, journalize the transactions for the remainder of June. Post to the accounts receivable ledger, and insert the balances at the points indicated in the narrative of transactions. *Determine the balance in the customer's account before recording a cash receipt.*

5. Total each of the columns of the special journals, and post the individual entries and totals to the general ledger. Insert account balances after the last posting.

6. Determine that the subsidiary ledger agrees with the control account in the general ledger.

PROBLEM 5–3B
Purchases, accounts payable account, and accounts payable ledger
Objective 4

Robbins Surveyors provides survey work for construction projects. Office supplies are used by the office staff, while field supplies are used by surveying crews at construction sites. Purchases on account completed by Robbins Surveyors during May of the current year are as follows:

May 1. Purchased field supplies on account from Wendell Co., $4,230.
       3. Purchased office supplies on account from Lassiter Co., $3,120.
       8. Purchased field supplies on account from Trent Supply, $1,640.
      12. Purchased field supplies on account from Wendell Co., $1,890.
      13. Purchased office equipment on account from Gore Computers Co., $7,500.
      15. Purchased office supplies on account from J-Mart Co., $940.
      18. Returned portion of field supplies purchased on May 8 from Trent Supply, $350.
      23. Purchased field supplies on account from Trent Supply, $2,340.
      26. Purchased office supplies on account from J-Mart Co., $1,250.
      30. Purchased field supplies on account from Trent Supply, $6,780.

Instructions

1. Insert the following balances in the general ledger as of May 1:

14	Field Supplies	$ 4,570
15	Office Supplies	2,050
18	Office Equipment	19,500
21	Accounts Payable	8,210

2. Insert the following balances in the accounts payable ledger as of May 1:

Eskew Co.	$ 2,860
Gore Computers Co.	—
J-Mart Co.	1,030
Lassiter Co.	4,320
Trent Supply	—
Wendell Co.	—

3. Journalize the transactions for May, using a purchases journal similar to the one illustrated in this chapter and a two-column general journal. Prepare the purchases journal with columns for Accounts Payable, Field Supplies, Office Supplies, and Other Accounts. Post to the creditor accounts in the accounts payable ledger immediately after each entry.

4. Post the general journal and the purchases journal to the accounts in the general ledger.

5. a. What is the sum of the balances in the subsidiary ledger at May 31?
    b. What is the balance of the controlling account at May 31?

PROBLEM 5–4B
Purchases and cash disbursements journals; accounts payable and general ledgers
Objective 4

Cruz Exploration Co. was established on March 15 of the current year to provide oil-drilling services. Cruz uses field equipment (rigs, pipe, drill bits) and field supplies in its operations. Transactions related to purchases and cash payments during the remainder of March are as follows:

Mar.16. Issued Cheque No. 1 in payment of rent for March, $800.

16. Purchased field equipment on account from Harper Equipment Co., $7,400.

17. Purchased field supplies on account from Culver Supply Co., $4,780.

18. Issued Cheque No. 2 in payment of field supplies, $3,450, and office supplies, $450.

19. Purchased office equipment on account from Lacy Co., $8,950.

20. Purchased office supplies on account from Ange Supply Co., $1,460.
Post the journals to the accounts payable ledger.

24. Issued Cheque No. 3 to Harper Equipment Co. in payment of invoice, $7,400.

26. Issued Cheque No. 4 to Culver Supply Co. in payment of invoice, $4,780.

28. Issued Cheque No. 5 to purchase land from the owner, $19,000.

28. Issued Cheque No. 6 to Lacy Co. in payment of the balance owed.

28. Purchased office supplies on account from Ange Supply Co., $860.
Post the journals to the accounts payable ledger.

30. Purchased the following from Harper Equipment Co. on account: field supplies, $2,300, and office equipment, $7,230.

30. Issued Cheque No. 7 to Ange Supply Co. in payment of invoice, $1,460.

30. Purchased field supplies on account from Culver Supply Co., $7,320.

31. Issued Cheque No. 8 in payment of salaries, $1,750.

31. Acquired land in exchange for field equipment having a cost of $4,800.
Post the journals to the accounts payable ledger.

Instructions

1. Journalize the transactions for March. Use a purchases journal and a cash disbursements journal, similar to those illustrated in this chapter, and a two-column general journal. Refer to the following partial chart of accounts:

   11   Cash
   14   Field Supplies
   15   Office Supplies
   17   Field Equipment
   18   Office Equipment
   19   Land
   21   Accounts Payable
   61   Salary Expense
   71   Rent Expense

   At the points indicated in the narrative of transactions, post to the following accounts in the accounts payable ledger:

   Ange Supply Co.
   Culver Supply Co.
   Harper Equipment Co.
   Lacy Co.

2. Post the individual entries (Other Accounts columns of the purchases journal and the cash payments journal; both columns of the general journal) to the appropriate general ledger accounts.

3. Total each of the columns of the purchases journal and the cash payments journal, and post the appropriate totals to the general ledger. (Because the problem does not include transactions related to cash receipts, the cash account in the ledger will have a credit balance.)

4. Prepare a schedule of accounts payable.

PROBLEM 5–5B
All journals and general ledger; trial balance
Objective 4

The transactions completed by Davis Courier Company during May, the first month of the current fiscal year, were as follows:

May 1. Issued Cheque No. 205 for May rent, $900.

2. Purchased a vehicle on account from Bunting Co., $21,400.

3. Purchased office equipment on account from Gill Computer Co., $6,400.

5. Issued Invoice No. 91 to Carlton Co., $970.

6. Received cheque from Pease Co. for $2,450 invoice.

6. Issued Cheque No. 206 for vehicle fuel, $700.

9. Issued Invoice No. 92 to Collins Co., $1,860.
10. Received cheque from Sing Co. for $5,630 invoice.
10. Issued Cheque No. 207 to Haber Enterprises in payment of $2,140 invoice.
10. Issued Cheque No. 208 to Bastille Co. in payment of $3,420 invoice.
11. Issued Invoice No. 93 to Joy Co., $3,560.
11. Issued Cheque No. 209 to Porter Co. in payment of $1,370 invoice.
12. Received cheque from Carlton Co. for $970 invoice.
13. Issued Cheque No. 210 to Bunting Co. in payment of $21,400 invoice.
16. Cash fees earned for May 1–16, $17,680.
16. Issued Cheque No. 211 for purchase of a vehicle, $8,000.
17. Purchased maintenance supplies on account from Bastille Co., $2,680.
18. Issued Cheque No. 212 for miscellaneous administrative expenses, $1,000.
18. Received cheque for rent income on office space, $1,500.
19. Purchased the following on account from Master Co.: maintenance supplies, $1,250, and office supplies, $3,250.
20. Issued Cheque No. 213 in payment of advertising expense, $3,500.
20. Used maintenance supplies with a cost of $4,580 to overhaul vehicle engines.
23. Issued Invoice No. 94 to Sing Co., $5,400.
24. Purchased office supplies on account from Haber Enterprises, $850.
25. Received cheque from Pease Co. for $1,760 invoice.
25. Issued Invoice No. 95 to Collins Co., $2,780.
26. Issued Cheque No. 214 to Gill Computer Co. in payment of $6,400 invoice.
27. Issued Cheque No. 215 to C. Davis as a personal withdrawal, $2,800.
30. Issued Cheque No. 216 in payment of driver salaries, $1,900.
31. Issued Cheque No. 217 in payment of office salaries, $2,950.
31. Issued Cheque No. 218 for office supplies, $1,850.
31. Cash sales for May 17–31, $21,400.

Instructions

1. Enter the following account balances in the general ledger as of May 1:

11	Cash	$14,680
12	Accounts Receivable	9,840
14	Maintenance Supplies	4,210
15	Office Supplies	2,100
16	Office Equipment	12,400
17	Accumulated Amortization—Office Equipment	2,000
18	Vehicles	62,000
19	Accumulated Amortization—Vehicles	12,400
21	Accounts Payable	6,930
31	C. Davis, Capital	83,900
32	C. Davis, Withdrawals	—
41	Revenue Earned	—
42	Rent Income	—
51	Driver Salaries Expense	—
52	Maintenance Supplies Expense	—
53	Fuel Expense	—
61	Office Salaries Expense	—
62	Rent Expense	—
63	Advertising Expense	—
64	Miscellaneous Administrative Expense	—

2. Journalize the transactions for May, using the following journals similar to those illustrated in this chapter: single-column revenue journal, cash receipts journal, purchases journal (with columns for Accounts Payable, Maintenance Supplies, Office Supplies, and Other Accounts), cash disbursements journal, and two-column general journal. Assume that an assistant makes daily postings to the individual accounts in the accounts payable ledger and the accounts receivable ledger.
3. Post the appropriate individual entries to the general ledger.
4. Total each of the columns of the special journals, and post the appropriate totals to the general ledger; insert the account balances.
5. Prepare a trial balance.

6. Verify the agreement of each subsidiary ledger with its control account. The sum of the balances of the accounts in each subsidiary ledger as of May 31 is as follows:

Accounts receivable: $13,600
Accounts payable: $8,030

CASES

CASE 5–1
Gunthorpe Security Co.
Internal controls

Lee Baskin sells security systems for Gunthorpe Security Co. Baskin has a monthly sales quota of $40,000. If Baskin exceeds this quota, he is awarded a bonus. In measuring the quota, a sale is credited to the salesperson when a customer signs a contract for installation of a security system. Through the 25th of the current month, Baskin has sold $30,000 in security systems.

Vortex Co., a business rumoured to be on the verge of bankruptcy, contacted Baskin on the 26th of the month about having a security system installed. Baskin estimates that the contract would yield about $14,000 of business for Gunthorpe

Security Co. In addition, this contract would be large enough to put Baskin "over the top" for a bonus in the current month. However, Baskin is concerned that Vortex Co. will not be able to make the contract payment after the security system is installed. In fact, Baskin has heard rumours that a competing security services company refused to install a system for Vortex Co. because of these concerns.

Upon further consideration, Baskin concluded that his job is to sell security systems and that it's someone else's problem to collect the resulting accounts receivable. Thus, Baskin wrote the contract with Vortex Co. and received a bonus for the month.

➤ Discuss whether Lee Baskin was acting in an ethical manner. How might Gunthorpe Security Co. use internal controls to prevent this scenario from occurring?

CASE 5–2
Lafont Co.
Manual vs. computerized accounting systems

The following conversation took place between Lafont Co.'s bookkeeper, Gerry Monroe, and the accounting supervisor, Lyn Hargrove.

Lyn: Gerry, I'm thinking about bringing in a new computerized accounting system to replace our manual system. I guess this will mean that you will need to learn how to do computerized accounting.

Gerry: What does computerized accounting mean?

Lyn: I'm not sure, but you'll need to prepare for this new way of doing business.

Gerry: I'm not so sure we need a computerized system. I've been looking at some of the sample reports from the software vendor. It looks to me like the computer will not add much to what we are already doing.

Lyn: What do you mean?

Gerry: Well, look at these reports. This Customer Invoice Summary Report looks like our revenue journal, and the Cash Receipts Summary Report looks like our cash receipts journal. Granted, they are typed by the computer, so they look much neater than my special journals, but I don't see that we're gaining much from this change.

Lyn: Well, surely there's more to it than nice-looking reports. I've got to believe that a computerized system will save us time and effort someplace.

Gerry: I don't see how. We still need to key in transactions into the computer. If anything, there may be more work when it's all said and done.

➤ Do you agree with Gerry? Why might a computerized environment be preferred over the manual system?

CASE 5–3
Hitchcock Company
Internal controls

Like most businesses, when Hitchcock Company renders services to another business, it is typical that the service is rendered "on account," rather than as a cash transaction. As a result, Hitchcock Company has an account receivable for the service provided. Likewise, the company receiving the service has an account

payable for the amount owed for services received. At a later date, Hitchcock Company will receive payment from the customer to satisfy the accounts receivable balance. However, when individuals conduct transactions with each other, it is common for the transaction to be satisfied with cash. For example, when you buy a pizza, you often pay with cash.

➤ Why is it unusual for businesses such as Hitchcock Company to engage in cash transactions, while for individuals it is more common?

CASE 5–4
Sears Canada Inc.
Financial analysis

Corporations generally issue annual reports to their shareholders and other interested parties. These annual reports include a Management Responsibility (or Management Report) section as well as financial statements. The Management Responsibility section discusses responsibility for the financial statements and normally includes an assessment of the company's internal control system.

What does the annual report for Sears Canada Inc. indicate about the internal control system?

CASE 5–5
Rockland Landscaping Services
Design of accounting systems

For the past few years, your client, Rockland Landscaping Services (RLS), has operated a small landscaping business. RLS's current annual revenues are $420,000. Because the accountant has been spending more and more time each month recording all transactions in a two-column journal and preparing the financial statements, RLS is considering improving the accounting system by adding special journals and subsidiary ledgers. RLS has asked you to help with this project and has compiled the following information:

Type of Transaction	Estimated Frequency per Month
Revenue earned on account	240
Purchase of landscaping supplies on account	190
Receipts from customers on account	175
Cash receipts from customers at time services rendered	120
Purchase of office supplies on account	15
Payments to suppliers on account	50
Cash purchases of office supplies	6
Purchase of fuel on account	5
Purchase of landscaping equipment on account	4
Payments for office salaries	3
Payments for utilities expense	3

The Provincial Sales Tax and the Goods and Services Tax are collected on all customer bills, and monthly financial statements are prepared.

1. Briefly discuss the circumstances under which special journals would be used in place of a two-column (all-purpose) journal. Include in your answer your recommendations for RLS's business.
2. Assume that RLS has decided to use a revenue journal and purchases journal. Design the format for each journal, giving special consideration to the needs of the landscaping business.
3. Which subsidiary ledgers would you recommend for the landscaping business?

ANSWERS TO SELF-EXAMINATION QUESTIONS

1. **C** The task of installing an accounting system is composed of three phases. Systems analysis (answer A) is the initial phase of determining the informational needs, sources of such information, and deficiencies in the procedures and data processing methods currently employed. Systems design (answer B) is the phase in which proposals for changes are developed. Systems implementation (answer C) is the final phase involving carrying out or implementing the proposals for changes. Systems training (answer D) is not a separate phase of installing an accounting system but is considered part of the systems implementation.

2. **A** The policies and procedures that are established to provide reasonable assurance that the enterprise's goals will be achieved are called internal controls (answer A).

The three phases of installing or changing an accounting system are (1) analysis (answer B), (2) design (answer C), and (3) implementation (answer D). Systems analysis is determining the informational needs, sources of such information, and deficiencies in the procedures and data processing methods presently used. Systems design refers to the design of a new system or change in the present system based on the systems analysis. The carrying out of proposals for the design of a system is called systems implementation.

3. **B** All payments of cash for any purpose are recorded in the cash payments journal (answer B). Only purchases of services or other items on account are recorded in the purchases journal (answer A). All sales of services on account are recorded in the revenue journal (answer C), and all

receipts of cash are recorded in the cash receipts journal (answer D).

4. **A** The general term used to describe the type of separate ledger that contains a large number of individual accounts with a common characteristic is a subsidiary ledger (answer A). The creditors ledger (answer B), sometimes called the accounts payable ledger (answer C), is a specific subsidiary ledger containing only individual accounts with creditors. Likewise, the accounts receivable ledger (answer D), also called the customers ledger, is a specific subsidiary ledger containing only individual accounts with customers.

5. **B** The control account for the customers ledger (the ledger that contains the individual accounts with customers) is Accounts Receivable (answer B). The accounts payable account (answer A) is the control account for the creditors ledger. There are no subsidiary ledgers for the revenue earned (answer C) and rent expense (answer D) accounts.

6 Accounting for Merchandising Businesses

```
         INGLES #26
      ABBOTSFORD, BC

                      10/02/98

GROCERY              2.99
GROCERY              1.00 TX
FZ FOOD              1.29
SUBTOTAL             5.28
TAX-GST               .07
TOTAL                5.35

CASH                10.00

CHANGE               4.65

# ITEMS    3


THANK YOU C123 R03 T12:38
```

YOU AND ACCOUNTING

Assume that you bought groceries at a store and received the receipt shown here. This receipt indicates that you purchased three items totalling $5.28. The Goods and Services Tax (GST) on the one taxable item purchased for $1.00 was $0.07 (7%). The total due was $5.35, you gave the clerk $10.00, and you received change of $4.65. The receipt also indicates that the sale was made by Store #26 of the Ingles chain, located in Abbotsford, B.C. The receipt also indicates the date and time of the sale and other data used internally by the store.

Whether you are buying groceries, textbooks, school supplies, or an automobile, you are doing business with a retail or merchandising business. As you might imagine, the accounting for a merchandising business is more complex than for a service business. For example, the accounting system for a merchandiser must be designed to record the receipt of goods for resale, keep track of the goods on hand and available for sale, and record the eventual sale and cost of the goods sold. The system must also record any special price reductions to customers who pay their bills early or who return damaged merchandise. Likewise, the accounting system must ensure prompt payments to suppliers and keep a record of the amounts paid.

In this chapter, we will focus on the accounting principles and concepts for merchandising businesses. We begin our discussion by highlighting the basic differences in the activities of such businesses and service businesses. We then describe and illustrate the proper recording of purchases and sales transactions for merchandising businesses. We conclude the chapter by illustrating the preparation of financial statements for merchandisers.

After studying this chapter, you should be able to:

Objective 1
Compare a service business's income statement to a merchandising business's income statement.

Objective 2
Journalize the entries for merchandise transactions, including:

a. Merchandise sales
b. Merchandise purchases

Objective 3
Journalize the entries for merchandise transactions using both the perpetual and periodic methods.

Objective 4
Prepare a chart of accounts for a merchandising business.

Objective 5
Prepare an income statement for a merchandising business.

Objective 6
Describe the accounting cycle for a merchandising business.

Nature of Merchandising Businesses

Objective 1
Compare a service business's income statement to a merchandising business's income statement.

How do the revenue activities of Computer King, a lawyer, and an architect, which are service businesses, differ from those of **Sears** or **Canadian Tire,** which are merchandising businesses? These differences are highlighted in the following condensed income statements:

Service Business			Merchandising Business	
Revenue earned	$XXX		Sales	$XXX
Operating expenses	XXX		Cost of goods sold	XXX
Net income	$XXX		Gross profit	$XXX
			Operating expenses	XXX
			Net income	$XXX

The revenue-generating activities of a service business involve providing services to customers. On the income statement for a service business, we report the revenues from services as revenue earned. We subtract the operating expenses incurred in providing the services from the revenue earned to arrive at net income.

In contrast, the revenue-generating activities of a merchandising business involve the buying and selling of merchandise. A merchandising business must first purchase merchandise to sell to its customers. When this merchandise is sold, we report the revenue as sales, and its cost as an expense called the cost of goods sold (or the cost of merchandise sold). For many merchandising businesses, the cost of goods sold is the largest expense. For example, the approximate percentage of cost of goods sold to sales is 70% for **Toys "R" Us, Inc.,** 63% for **Mark's Work Wearhouse,** and 78% for **Future Shop.**

We subtract the cost of goods sold from sales to arrive at gross profit. We call this amount gross profit because we deduct the operating expenses from it to arrive at net income.

Merchandise that is not sold at the end of an accounting period is called inventory. We report inventory as a current asset on the balance sheet.

In the remainder of this chapter we discuss the transactions that affect the identifying features of a merchandising business's financial statements—sales, cost of goods sold, gross profit on the income statement, and inventory on the balance sheet. We will illustrate these transactions for Computer King, assuming that Computer King opened a retail store in January 2001.

We record merchandise transactions in the accounts, using the rules of debit and credit that we described and illustrated in earlier chapters. Special journals, such as those we described and illustrated for service businesses in the previous chapter, are also used by merchandising businesses. Alternatively, the firm may enter, record, and post transactions to the accounts electronically. For illustrative purposes, we will use a two-column general journal format in the remainder of this chapter in order to simplify the illustrations.

When we report on the operations of a merchandising business, we must indicate both the sales made during the period and the cost of the goods that have been sold. As we will discuss later, businesses may use different accounting methods for keeping track of their inventory and cost of sales. However, the accounting for sales revenue is the same no matter what inventory method is used. Therefore, we begin our discussion by illustrating how firms record revenue from merchandising transactions. Later, we will examine the different methods of accounting for purchases and the cost of the goods sold.

Accounting for Sales

Objective 2a

Journalize the entries for merchandise sales.

We usually identify revenue from merchandise sales in the ledger as *Sales*. Sometimes a business will use a more exact title, such as *Sales of Merchandise*.

A business may sell merchandise for cash. Cash sales are normally rung up (entered) on a cash register. At the end of the day, we can record the sales as follows:

Jan.	3	Cash	1,800
		Sales		1,800
		Cash sales for the day.	

How do retailers record sales made with the use of **MasterCard** or **VISA?** Sales to customers who use such bank credit cards are usually treated as cash sales. The seller deposits the credit card receipts (slips) for these sales directly into the bank. The credit card slips, cash, and cheques received for the sales make up the total deposit.

Normally, banks charge service fees for handling credit card sales. We should debit these service fees to an expense account. An entry at the end of a month to record the payment of service charges on bank credit card sales is shown below.

Jan.	31	Bank Credit Card Expense	48
		Cash		48
		Service charges on bank	
		credit card sales for the month.	

Sales may also be made by accepting a customer's nonbank credit card (such as **American Express**). A business must report these sales directly to the card company before cash is received. Therefore, such sales create a receivable with the card company. Before the card company pays cash, it normally deducts a service fee. For example, assume that a retailer makes nonbank credit card sales of $1,000 and reports this to the card company on January 20. On January 27, the card company deducts a service fee of 5% ($50) and sends $950 to the seller. We record these transactions as follows:

Jan. 20	Accounts Receivable	1,000	
	Sales		1,000
	American Express credit card sales.		
27	Cash	950	
	Nonbank Credit Card Expense	50	
	Accounts Receivable		1,000
	Receipt of cash from American Express		
	for sales reported on January 20.		

A business may sell merchandise on account. Such sales result in a debit to Accounts Receivable and a credit to Sales. An example of an entry for a sale on account of $510 follows.

Jan. 12	Accounts Receivable	510	
	Sales		510
	Invoice No. 7172 to Sims Co.		

SALES DISCOUNTS

The invoice, or bill, that the seller sends to the buyer normally indicates the terms of a sale. Exhibit 1 shows an example of such an invoice.

The terms agreed on by the buyer and the seller as to when payments for merchandise are to be made are called the **credit terms.** If payment is required on delivery, the terms are said to be *cash* or *net cash*. Otherwise, the buyer is allowed an amount of time, known as the **credit period,** in which to pay.

The credit period usually begins with the date of the sale as shown on the invoice. If payment is due within a stated number of days after the date of the invoice, such as 30 days, the terms are said to be *net 30 days*. These terms may be written as *n/30*.[1] If payment is due by the end of the month in which the sale was made, it may be written as *n/eom*.

As a means of encouraging payment before the end of the credit period, the seller may offer a discount to the buyer for the early payment of cash. For example, a seller may offer a buyer a 2% discount if payment is received within 10 days of the invoice date. If the buyer does not take the discount, the total amount is due within 30 days. These terms are expressed as *2/10, n/30* and are read as *2% discount if paid*

Exhibit 1
Invoice

Wallace Electronics Supply	3800 Yonge Street Toronto, Ontario		
SOLD TO Computer King 1000 Portage Avenue Winnipeg, Manitoba		**CUSTOMER'S ORDER NO. & DATE** 412 Jan. 10, 2000 **REFER TO INVOICE NO.** 106-8	
DATE SHIPPED Jan. 12, 2000 **FROM** Toronto	**HOW SHIPPED AND ROUTE** Western Trucking Co. **F.O.B.** Winnipeg	**TERMS** 2/10, n/30 **PREPAID OR COLLECT?** Prepaid	**INVOICE DATE** Jan. 12, 2000
QUANTITY 20	**DESCRIPTION** 33.3k Modems	**UNIT PRICE** 75.00	**AMOUNT** 1,500.00

[1] The word *net* as used here does not have the usual meaning of a number after deductions have been subtracted, as in *net income*.

Exhibit 2
Credit Terms

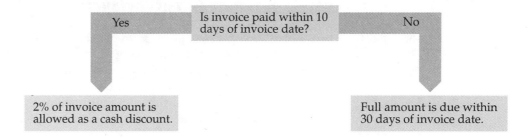

Is invoice paid within 10 days of invoice date?

Yes

No

2% of invoice amount is allowed as a cash discount.

Full amount is due within 30 days of invoice date.

within 10 days, net amount due within 30 days. The credit terms of 2/10, n/30 are summarized in Exhibit 2.

The seller regards such discounts as sales discounts. When a buyer takes advantage of such a discount by paying within the discount period, the seller debits the sales discounts account. For example, if cash is received within the discount period (10 days) from the credit sale of $1,500, shown on the invoice in Exhibit 1, Wallace Electronics Supply, as a seller, would record the transaction as follows:

Jan. 22	Cash	1,470	
	Sales Discounts	30	
	Accounts Receivable		1,500
	Collection on Invoice No. 106–8 to		
	Computer King, less discount.		

Sales discounts are a reduction in the amount initially recorded in Sales. In this sense, the balance of the sales discounts account is viewed as a contra (or offsetting) account to Sales.

If the buyer pays after the discount period, on say, January 30, the buyer must pay the full amount of the invoice. In this case, the seller simply records the entry as:

Jan. 30	Cash	1,500	
	Accounts Receivable		1,500
	Collection on Invoice No. 106-8 to		
	Computer King.		

USING ACCOUNTING TO UNDERSTAND BUSINESS

Have you ever wondered why some retailers accept one type of credit card and not another? For example, a retailer may accept **MasterCard** or **VISA** but not **American Express.** Also, some retailers will offer you a discount if you pay in cash.

The service fees that credit card companies charge retailers is the primary reason why businesses do not accept all credit cards. For example, American Express Co.'s service fees are normally higher than MasterCard's or VISA's. As a result, some retailers choose not to accept American Express cards. The primary disadvantage of this practice for retailers is that they may lose customers to competitors who do accept American Express cards.

SALES RETURNS AND ALLOWANCES

Sometimes, the buyer will return merchandise sold to the seller (sales return). On other occasions, the seller may allow the buyer a reduction from the initial price at which the goods were sold because of defects or for other reasons (sales allowance). If the return or allowance is for a sale on account, the seller usually issues the buyer a credit memorandum. This memorandum shows the amount and the reason for which the buyer's account receivable is to be credited. Exhibit 3 illustrates a credit memorandum.

Exhibit 3
Credit Memorandum

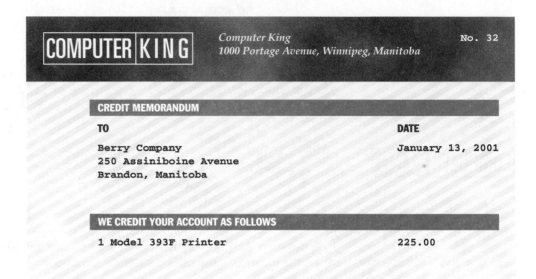

The effect of a sales return or allowance is to reduce sales revenue and cash or accounts receivable. To reduce sales, we could debit the sales account directly. However, the balance of the sales account would then represent net sales for the period. Because of the loss in revenue and the related expense that may result from returns and allowances, management closely monitors the amount of returns and allowances. If it becomes too large, management may take appropriate action to reduce returns and allowances. For this reason, a business will usually keep track of sales returns and allowances in a separate account entitled *Sales Returns and Allowances*. Because sales returns and allowances reduce the amount initially recorded in Sales, the sales returns and allowances account is a contra (or offsetting) account to Sales.

We debit Sales Returns and Allowances for the amount of the return or allowance. If the original sale is on account, we credit Accounts Receivable.

Computer King would record the credit memo in Exhibit 3 as follows:

Jan. 13   Sales Returns and Allowances   225
     Accounts Receivable   225
      Credit Memo No. 32.

What if the buyer pays for the merchandise and later returns it? In this case, the seller may issue a credit and apply it against other accounts receivable owed by the buyer, or may refund the cash. If the credit is to be applied against the buyer's other receivables, we record entries similar to the preceding. If cash is refunded for merchandise returned or for an allowance, we debit Sales Returns and Allowances and credit Cash.

SALES TAXES

Almost all provinces levy a tax on sales of merchandise. Sales taxes (PST) vary from province to province. As well, most merchandise transactions with the exception of food and pharmaceutical products are subject to the Federal Goods and Services Tax (GST).[2] Some provinces have combined the PST with the GST into the Harmonized Sales Tax (HST). The liability for the sales tax and GST is incurred at the time the sale is made.

At the time of a cash sale, the seller collects the sales tax. When a sale is on account, the seller charges the tax to the buyer by debiting Accounts Receivable. The seller credits the sales account for only the amount of the sale and credits the tax to Sales Tax Payable. For example, a sale of $100 on account, subject to a provincial sales tax of 8% and 7% GST is recorded by the following entry:

Aug. 12	Accounts Receivable	115	
	Sales		100
	Provincial Sales Tax Payable		8
	GST Payable		7
	Invoice No. 339.		

The seller normally pays the amount of the sales tax that has been collected to the taxing unit on a regular basis. An entry to record such a payment is as follows:

Sep. 15	Provincial Sales Tax Payable	2,900	
	Cash		2,900
	Payment for sales taxes collected during August.		

TRADE DISCOUNTS

Many wholesalers of merchandise publish periodic catalogues that are used by buyers in ordering merchandise. Rather than updating their catalogues frequently, wholesalers publish price updates, which may involve large discounts from the list prices in their catalogues. In addition, sellers frequently offer certain classes of buyers, such as government agencies or buyers who order large quantities, special discounts. These special discounts or discounts for large quantities purchased are called **trade discounts.**

Sellers and buyers always record sales and purchases after deducting (net of) the related trade discounts. For example, assume that a seller offers for sale an item with a list price of $1,000 and a 40% trade discount. The seller records the sale of the item at $600 [$1,000 less the trade discount of $400 ($1,000 × 40%)]. Likewise, the buyer records the purchase at $600. For accounting purposes, only the final price—$600 in this example—is important.

Transportation Costs

The terms of a sales agreement between a buyer and a seller should indicate when the ownership (title) of the merchandise passes to the buyer. The point at which the title of the merchandise passes to the buyer determines which party, the buyer or the seller, must pay the transportation costs.[3]

---

[2] Businesses that purchase merchandise for resale to others are normally exempt from paying provincial sales taxes on their purchases. Only *final* buyers of merchandise normally pay sales taxes. The Goods and Services Tax is discussed in Chapter 11.

[3] The passage of title also determines whether the buyer or seller must pay other costs, such as the cost of insurance while the merchandise is in transit.

A sales agreement should indicate when the title of the merchandise passes from the seller to the buyer, because that determines who must pay the transportation costs.

The ownership of the merchandise may pass to the buyer when the seller delivers the merchandise to the transportation company or freight carrier. For example, **Chrysler Corp.** records the sale and the transfer of ownership of its vehicles to dealers when the vehicles are shipped. In this case, the terms are said to be **FOB shipping point.** This shipping term means that Chrysler delivers the merchandise *free on board* to the shipping point. The dealer pays the transportation costs to the final destination.

The ownership of the merchandise may pass to the buyer when the merchandise is received by the buyer. In this case, the terms are said to be **FOB destination.** This shipping term means that the seller delivers the merchandise *free on board* to the buyer's final destination. The seller pays the transportation costs to the final destination.

Sometimes FOB shipping point and FOB destination are expressed in terms of the location at which the title to the merchandise passes to the buyer. For example, assume that a seller located in Montreal ships merchandise to a buyer located in Calgary. In this case, the terms FOB shipping point could be expressed as *FOB Montreal.* Likewise, the terms FOB destination could be expressed as *FOB Calgary.*

Shipping terms, the passage of title, and whether the buyer or seller is to pay the transportation costs are summarized as follows:

	FOB Shipping Point	*FOB Destination*
Ownership (title) passes to buyer when merchandise is	delivered to freight carrier	delivered to buyer
Transportation costs are paid by.	buyer	seller

When merchandise is purchased on terms of FOB shipping point, the buyer pays the transportation costs. Such costs are part of the total cost of acquiring inventory. We will discuss accounting for these costs later when we illustrate accounting for purchases.

When the terms of shipment are FOB destination, the seller pays and debits the amounts paid for delivery to **Transportation Out,** Delivery Expense, or a similarly titled account. We report the total of such costs incurred during a period on the seller's income statement as an operating (selling) expense.

As a convenience or courtesy to the buyer, the seller may prepay the transportation costs even though the terms are FOB shipping point. For example, the seller often prepays the transportation costs when shipping the merchandise by parcel post. The seller will then add the transportation costs to the invoice. The buyer will credit Accounts Payable for the total amount of the invoice, including transportation costs.

To illustrate, assume that on June 10, Computer King sells merchandise to Reese Company on account, $900, terms FOB shipping point, n/30. Computer King pays the transportation costs of $50 and adds them to the invoice. Computer King (the seller) makes the following entries:

June 10	Accounts Receivable	900	
	Sales		900
	Sale on account to Reese Company.		
10	Accounts Receivable	50	
	Cash		50
	Paid freight and charged to customer.		

Transportation costs are not subject to sales discounts. Thus, if the terms had been 2/10, n/30 in the preceding illustration, the payment by Reese Company within the discount period would be $932, computed as follows:

Invoice from Computer King, including prepaid transportation of $50		$950
Amount subject to discount	$900	
Rate of discount	× 2%	
Amount of sales discount		18
Amount of payment		$932

Accounting for Purchases

Objective 2b

Journalize the entries for merchandise purchases.

There are two systems for accounting for merchandise purchased for sale: perpetual and periodic. In the perpetual inventory system, the business records each purchase and sale of merchandise in an inventory account. In this way, the inventory records always (perpetually) disclose the amount of merchandise on hand and the amount sold. In the periodic inventory system, the firm makes no attempt to keep detailed inventory records of the amounts on hand throughout the period. Instead, it prepares a detailed listing of the merchandise on hand (called a physical inventory) at the end of the accounting period. We use this physical inventory listing to determine the cost of the inventory on hand at the end of the period and the cost of the goods sold during the period.

Why do some retailers use a perpetual system while others use the periodic method? What are the advantages and disadvantages of each? One advantage of a perpetual system is that it provides better internal control over inventory. Under this method accounting records are always up-to-date, indicating how much inventory is on hand and available for sale. This information is useful for determining when to reorder more inventory, so that stocks do not get too low. A business that deals in high cost items, such as a car dealership or a jewellery retailer, needs a system that keeps close control over every unit of inventory, since the loss of even one item would be very expensive.

Large retailers and many small merchandising businesses use computerized perpetual inventory systems. Such systems normally use bar codes, such as the one on the back of this textbook. An optical scanner reads the bar code to initiate the recording of merchandise purchased for resale and sales of merchandise to customers. Examples of such retailers are **Canadian Tire, Sears,** and **Wal-Mart,** and grocery store chains such as **Safeway** and **Zehrs.**

Obviously, the perpetual method requires very detailed and extensive record-keeping. This would be too time-consuming for a retailer who did not have an optical scanning cash register and who dealt with a high volume of small cost items. For example, a small variety store without this equipment would have to use a periodic inventory system, since it would be impossible to keep track of every small item bought and sold every day. At the end of the fiscal period the business will have to take a physical count of inventory on hand in order to update its inventory account and determine the cost of goods sold during the period. A firm using a periodic system must physically count its inventory before it can prepare its annual financial statements.

Even under a perpetual system where the accounting records indicate the inventory on hand at all times, a business must still conduct a physical count of inventory from time to time to ensure that its books are accurate and that it has not suffered any serious shortages due to theft or wastage. Thus, every firm must conduct a physical count of inventory at least once a year, if not more often. With a perpetual system, this count could occur at any time during the year and does not necessarily have to be taken at the end of the fiscal period.

In the following sections we illustrate how to account for all transactions affecting inventory (both purchases and sales) under both the (1) perpetual and (2) periodic inventory systems.

PERPETUAL INVENTORY SYSTEM

a. Purchases

Under the perpetual inventory system, a business records purchases of merchandise for sale in the inventory account in the ledger. When it makes purchases for cash, it records the following:

Jan.	3	Inventory	2,510	
		Cash		2,510
		Purchases from supplier, Bowen Co.		

Purchases of merchandise on account are recorded as follows:

Jan.	4	Inventory	9,250	
		Accounts Payable		9,250
		Purchases from supplier, Thomas Corporation.		

If the business pays any transportation costs when making a purchase, it adds this amount to the total cost recorded in the Inventory account, with the credit to Accounts Payable or Cash. For example, if the firm pays $100 cash for freight costs incurred on the January 4 purchase, under a perpetual system it will record:

Jan.	4	Inventory	100	
		Cash		100
		Transportation costs on purchase from Thomas Corporation.		

USING ACCOUNTING TO UNDERSTAND BUSINESS

Do you pay your bills, such as utility bills and credit card bills, as soon as you receive them? The terms of payment on each bill (the credit terms) may allow you to delay payment a week or more.

Most bills you receive do not offer discounts for early payment. Rather, the bills normally indicate only a due date and perhaps a penalty for late payment. Many times you receive bills weeks before their due date. In such cases, it is to your advantage to file the bill by its due date in a folder or other organizer, such as a desk calendar, and mail the payment a few days before it is due. In this way, you have the opportunity to earn additional interest on the balance of your chequing or savings account.

Businesses design their accounting systems in much the same way that you might organize your system for paying bills. That is, they design their accounting systems to pay bills at the latest possible date, but yet take advantage of all discounts and avoid late payment penalties. Often businesses computerize their accounting systems so that cheques are automatically created when the bill is scheduled for payment. In more advanced computerized systems, the payments may be electronically transferred from the business's bank account to the supplier's bank account without a cheque even being written.

b. Purchase Discounts

As we illustrated in our discussion of sales transactions, a seller may offer the buyer credit terms that include a discount for early payment, such as 2/10, n/30. The buyer regards such discounts as purchase discounts. Most businesses attempt to pay within the discount date, since the cost of missing a discount represents a high interest charge for the late payment. For example, suppose that a purchaser pays the invoice at the end of 30 days. For paying 20 days after the discount date, the purchaser has missed a 2% savings. This works out to a cost of 0.1% per day (2% divided by 20 days), which is equal to an annual interest rate of 36%. Obviously, the buyer would be better off to make a bank loan, if necessary, in order to pay the invoice in time in order to take advantage of the purchase discount.

To illustrate, suppose that the purchaser buys goods for $10,000 on terms 2/10, n/30. If the purchaser can borrow money from the bank at an interest rate of 10%, we can compare the cost of two alternatives: (1) miss the discount on the invoice and pay the balance in 30 days or (2) make a bank loan in order to pay the invoice on the discount date.

Cost of missing the discount (2% × $10,000)	$200
Interest on bank loan for 20 days (10% × $10,000 × 20/365)	55
Savings by making bank loan to pay within discount period	$120

Let us return to the example in Exhibit 1. We assume that Computer King is using a perpetual inventory system and initially records the purchase at the full amount of the invoice:[4]

Jan. 12	Inventory	1,500	
	Accounts payable		1,500
	Invoice 106-8 from Wallace Electronics Supply.		

If Computer King pays the invoice in time to get the discount, we make the following entry. We debit Accounts Payable for the full amount of the invoice to remove the payable from the books. At the same time, we credit Cash for the amount actually paid (invoice price less the discount) and credit Inventory for the amount of the discount:

Jan. 22	Accounts payable	1,500	
	Cash		1,470
	Inventory		30
	Payment of Invoice 106-8 from Wallace Electronics Supply.		

If Computer King pays after the discount date, we debit Accounts Payable and credit Cash for the full amount:

Jan. 31	Accounts payable	1,500	
	Cash		1,500
	Payment of Invoice 106-8 from Wallace Electronics Supply.		

---

[4] In this chapter we assume that both sellers and buyers initially record invoices at their full amount and later record the discount taken if payment is made by the discount date. This method of recording the sale or purchase is called the **gross method**. An alternative method (the **net method**) is for the seller and/or buyer to initially record the invoice net of the discount. In this case, the discount will only be recorded separately at a later date if it is **not** taken. Because the gross method is simpler and more commonly used, this is the one shown above. We illustrate the net method in the appendix to this chapter.

c. Purchases Returns and Allowances

When we return merchandise (purchases return) or request a price adjustment (purchases allowance), we usually notify the supplier in writing. We may state the details in a letter, or we (debtor) may use a debit memorandum form. This form, shown in Exhibit 4, informs the supplier (creditor) of the amount we propose to debit to the account payable due the seller. It also states the reasons for the return or the request for a price reduction.

Exhibit 4
Debit Memorandum

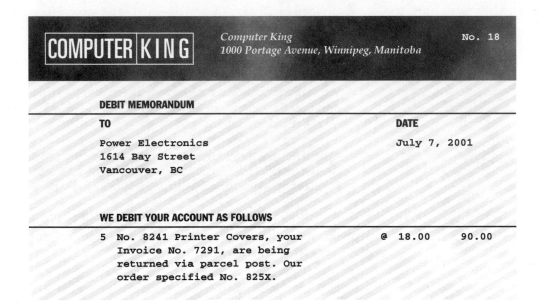

The buyer may use a copy of the debit memorandum as the basis for an entry or may wait for confirmation from the seller. The seller confirms the return or allowance by issuing a **credit memorandum**. In either event, the buyer debits Accounts Payable and credits Inventory. To illustrate, the entry by Computer King to record the return of the merchandise indicated in the debit memo in Exhibit 4 is as follows:

July	7	Accounts Payable	90	
		Inventory		90
		Debit Memo No. 18.		

Suppose that the items returned were part of an order billed on Invoice No. 7291 by Power Electronics on July 1 with a total invoice price of $590, terms 2/10, n/30. On July 10 Computer King pays the amount owing on the invoice after deducting the cost of the items returned ($90) and the discount on the remaining items (2% of $500 = $10):

July	10	Accounts Payable	500	
		Cash		490
		Inventory		10
		Payment of Invoice 7291 from		
		Power Electronics.		

d. Cost of Goods Sold

Under a perpetual inventory system, whenever the business records a sale, at the same time it also records the cost of the goods sold and the reduction in inventory.

In this way, the inventory account is always up to date, indicating the amount of merchandise that should be on hand. To illustrate, suppose that on January 3 the firm sells merchandise that cost $1,200 for $1,800 on account. Under a perpetual system the journal entry must record both the sale and the cost of the goods sold, as follows:

Jan. 3	Accounts Receivable	1,800	
	Sales		1,800
	Cost of Goods Sold	1,200	
	Inventory		1,200
	Sale on account for $1,800 of goods costing $1,200.		

On January 13 the customer returns goods that had a selling price of $225 and a cost of $140. Under a perpetual system the journal entry must record both the sales return and the reduction in the cost of goods sold. Assuming that the items can be resold, we also add them back to the Inventory account, as follows:

Jan. 13	Sales Returns and Allowances	225	
	Accounts Receivable		225
	Inventory	140	
	Cost of Goods Sold		140
	Customer returned for $225 credit goods costing $140.		

PERIODIC INVENTORY SYSTEM

Under a periodic inventory system, no attempt is made to keep the inventory account up to date as purchases and sales are made. When studying the entries for the periodic system, which are illustrated below, remember that under this method *the only time that the business makes an entry to the inventory account is when a physical count of inventory is taken.*

a. Purchases, Purchase Discounts, Purchase Returns and Allowances, and Transportation-in

Under a periodic system, when a business buys inventory, it debits the cost to an account called Purchases. Purchases is a temporary account that appears on the income statement (as we will discuss later), and which is closed at the end of the period. This is clearly a different account from Inventory, which is a permanent account reported on the balance sheet. Under the periodic system the firm records discounts taken in a separate account called **Purchase Discounts** and purchase returns and allowances in an account called **Purchase Returns and Allowances**. These are also temporary accounts that are closed at the end of the period. Both of these accounts have credit balances. They are contra accounts that are deducted from the Purchases account on the income statement.

To illustrate these entries, let us return to the example in Exhibit 1. If Computer King is using a periodic system, we initially record the purchase in the Purchases account:

Jan. 12	Purchases	1,500	
	Accounts Payable		1,500
	Invoice 106-8 from Wallace Electronics Supply.		

If Computer King pays the invoice in time to get the discount, we record the discount in a Purchase Discount account:

Jan. 22	Accounts payable	1,500	
	Cash		1,470
	Purchase Discounts		30
	Payment of Invoice 106-8 from		
	Wallace Electronics Supply.		

If Computer King pays after the discount date, we debit Accounts Payable and credit Cash for the full amount:

Jan. 31	Accounts payable	1,500	
	Cash		1,500
	Payment of Invoice 106-8 from		
	Wallace Electronics Supply.		

To illustrate accounting for purchase returns and allowances, we can return to Exhibit 4. Under a periodic system Computer King debits Purchase Returns and Allowances to record the return of merchandise, which cost $90:

July 7	Accounts Payable	90	
	Purchase Returns and Allowances		90
	Debit Memo No. 18.		

If a business incurs any transportation costs with respect to its purchase of inventory, under a periodic system it will record this cost in another temporary account called Transportation-in **(Freight-in)**. This account is added to Purchases on the income statement at the end of the period. To illustrate, assume that on January 3 Computer King pays $100 cash for the shipment of inventory that it purchased FOB shipping point. To record the freight costs, it makes the following entry:

Jan. 3	Transportation-in	100	
	Cash		100
	Freight cost on inventory purchase.		

The entries that we made to the various accounts for Purchases, Purchase Discounts, Purchase Returns and Allowances, and Transportation-in under the periodic system would all have been made to Inventory under a perpetual system.

b. Cost of Goods Sold

Under a periodic system, at the time that a business sells inventory, the only entry it makes is to record the sale (by crediting Sales and debiting Cash or Accounts Receivable). However, it makes no entry to record the cost of the goods sold or to record a change in the Inventory account. Similarly, if customers return some items, it records only the sales return (debiting Sales Returns and Allowances and crediting Cash or Accounts Receivable), but it makes no entries to Cost of Goods Sold or Inventory.

Under a perpetual system, the normal journal entries that the firm records for purchases and sales will provide it with the current balance of the inventory on hand at the end of the period and the cost of goods sold during the period. Under a periodic system, since we have not kept the inventory account up to date, it is necessary to physically count inventory in order to determine the balance on hand at the end of the period. Also, we need to know the balance of ending inventory in order to compute the cost of goods sold during the period.

How do we compute the cost of goods sold during a period? Basically, we add all of the costs pertaining to the goods that the business had available for sale during the period. Either one of two things happened to the goods on hand: (1) they were sold or (2) they were not sold and are still on hand at the end of the period. We count the inventory to see how much is left on hand at the end of the period. Whatever cost is not left in ending inventory must be the cost of the goods sold during the period.

To illustrate, assume that on January 3, 2000, Computer King opened a merchandising outlet selling microcomputers and software. During 2000, Computer King purchased $340,000 of merchandise. The inventory on December 31, 2000, is $59,700. We calculate the cost of goods sold during 2000 as follows:

Cost of goods sold:	
Purchases	$340,000
Less inventory, December 31, 2000	59,700
Cost of goods sold	$280,300

To continue the example, assume that during 2001 Computer King purchased additional merchandise of $521,980. Computer King also received credit for purchases returns and allowances of $9,100, took purchases discounts of $2,525, and paid transportation costs of $17,400. We deduct the purchases returns and allowances and the purchases discounts from the total purchases to yield the net purchases. We then add the transportation costs to the net purchases to yield the cost of goods purchased:

Purchases		$521,980	
Less: Purchases returns and allowances	$9,100		
Purchases discounts	2,525	11,625	
Net purchases		$510,355	
Add transportation-in		17,400	
Cost of goods purchased			$527,755

The ending inventory of Computer King on December 31, 2000, $59,700, becomes the beginning inventory for 2001. We add this beginning inventory to the cost of goods purchased to yield the goods available for sale. The ending inventory on December 31, 2001, $62,150, is then subtracted from the goods available for sale to yield the cost of goods sold. Exhibit 5 shows the cost of goods sold during 2001.

Exhibit 5

Cost of Goods Sold—Periodic Inventory System

Cost of goods sold:			
Inventory, January 1, 2001			$ 59,700
Purchases		$521,980	
Less: Purchases returns and allowances	$9,100		
Purchases discounts	2,525	11,625	
Net purchases		$510,355	
Add transportation-in		17,400	
Cost of goods purchased			527,755
Goods available for sale			$587,455
Less inventory, December 31, 2001			62,150
Cost of goods sold			$525,305

After counting the ending inventory and computing cost of goods sold, the business needs to make a journal entry to bring these accounts up to date in its ledger. The adjusting entry required at the end of the period under a periodic system does the following:

1. it adjusts the Inventory account to the balance on hand at year end;
2. it closes Purchases and Transportation-in by crediting the balances in these accounts;
3. it closes Purchase Discounts and Purchase Returns and Allowances by debiting the balances in these accounts; and
4. it debits Cost of Goods Sold to reflect the cost incurred during the period.

Based on the example shown above, on December 31, 2001 Computer King must adjust its Inventory account to reflect closing inventory of $62,150. Since the opening balance in Inventory was $59,700, we debit Inventory for the difference of $2,450 ($62,150 − $59,700). At the same time we close the temporary accounts for Purchases, Purchase Discounts, Purchase Returns and Allowances, and Transportation-in and record Cost of Goods Sold:

Dec. 31	Cost of Goods Sold	525,305	
	Inventory	2,450	
	Purchase Discounts	2,525	
	Purchase Returns and Allowances	9,100	
	Purchases		521,980
	Transportation-in		17,400
	To record correct balance of closing inventory and record cost of goods sold for the period.		

In this illustration, we have recorded the Cost of Goods Sold of $525,305 in a separate expense account, which will be closed to Income Summary. When using a periodic system, a firm may choose not to set up a separate account for Cost of Goods Sold, but instead just debit the $525,305 immediately to Income Summary. Also, instead of adjusting the Inventory account for the $2,450 difference between the opening and closing balances, the accountant may debit Ending Inventory for $62,150 and credit Opening Inventory for $59,700. In this case, the journal entry will be:

Dec. 31	Income Summary	525,305	
	Ending Inventory	62,150	
	Purchase Discounts	2,525	
	Purchase Returns and Allowances	9,100	
	Purchases		521,980
	Transportation-in		17,400
	Opening Inventory		59,700

The effect of this entry on Owner's Equity is the same as in the one above, and the business will still report cost of goods sold on its income statement in both cases. In this text we prefer to use the first entry, recording Cost of Goods Sold in a separate ledger account.[5]

Illustration of Accounting for Merchandise Transactions

Objective 3
Journalize the entries for merchandise transactions using both the perpetual and periodic methods.

The following illustration summarizes the principles and concepts of accounting for merchandising transactions by presenting entries for both purchases and sales using both the perpetual and periodic methods.

[5] We believe that using a Cost of Goods Sold account under a periodic system is conceptually neater than the alternative form of the entry for two reasons. (1) It emphasizes that, under the periodic system, all of these temporary accounts (Purchases, Purchase Discounts, Purchase Returns and Allowances, Transportation-in) flow through Cost of Goods Sold at year end and (2) it facilitates a more direct comparison of the perpetual and periodic methods.

Assuming that the business has an opening balance in inventory of $1,000 on January 1 and that it takes a physical count of inventory on January 31, the entries to record the transactions for the month of January are shown below:

Transaction	Perpetual			Periodic		

Jan. 1. Buy goods on account for $5,000, 2/10, n/30.	Inventory
	  Accounts Payable
		5,000	5,000	Purchases
				  Accounts Payable
					5,000	5,000

Jan. 1. Paid $200 freight for goods purchased.	Inventory
	  Cash
		200	200	Transportation-in
				  Cash
					200	200

Jan. 4. Returned for credit goods purchased on Jan. 1 costing $700.	Accounts Payable
	  Inventory
		700	700	Accounts Payable
				  Purchase Returns
					700	700

Jan. 10. Paid invoice for Jan. 1 purchase.	Accounts Payable
	  Cash
	  Inventory
		4,300	4,214
			86
				Accounts Payable
				  Cash
				  Purchase Discounts
					4,300	4,214
						86

Jan. 11. Sold on account goods costing $2,000 for $3,000, 3/10, n/30.	Accounts Receivable
	  Sales
	Cost of Goods Sold
	  Inventory
		3,000
		
		2,000
			3,000
			
			2,000
				Accounts Receivable
				  Sales
					3,000	3,000

Jan. 11. Paid $100 to ship goods sold FOB destination.	Transportation-out
	  Cash
		100	100	Transportation-out
				  Cash
					100	100

Jan. 13. Goods returned by customer that sold for $300 and cost $200.	Sales Returns
	  Account Receivable
	Inventory
	  Cost of Goods Sold
		300
		
		200
			300
			
			200
				Sales Returns
				  Accounts Receivable
					300	300

Jan. 20. Customer paid for Jan. 11 sale.	Cash
	Sales Discounts
	  Accounts Receivable
		2,619
		81
			2,700	Cash
				Sales Discounts
				  Accounts Receivable
					2,619
					81
						2,700

Jan 31. Inventory count determines inventory on hand is $2,614.	No entry.			Inventory
				Cost of Goods Sold
				Purchase Discounts
				Purchase Returns
				  Purchases
				  Transportation-in
					2,614
					1,800
					86
					700
						5,000
						200

Chart of Accounts for a Merchandising Business

Objective 4

Prepare a chart of accounts for a merchandising business.

The chart of accounts for a merchandising business should reflect the types of transactions described in the preceding paragraphs. We will use Computer King as a basis for illustrating a merchandiser's chart of accounts.

When Computer King opened a merchandising outlet selling microcomputers and software on January 1, 2001, it stopped providing consulting services. As a result of this change in the type of its transactions, Computer King's chart of accounts changed. A new chart of accounts for Computer King is shown in Exhibit 6. The accounts related to merchandising transactions are shown in colour. Exhibit 6 assumes that Computer King is using a perpetual inventory system. An appropriate chart of accounts for a periodic system is shown in Exhibit 7.

Computer King is now using three-digit account numbers, which are assigned in a manner that permits the addition of new accounts as they are needed. The first digit indicates the major financial statement classification (1 for assets, 2 for

Exhibit 6
Chart of Accounts for Computer King, Merchandising Business — Perpetual Inventory System

Balance Sheet Accounts	Income Statement Accounts
100 Assets	400 Revenues
110 Cash	410 Sales
111 Notes Receivable	411 Sales Returns and Allowances
112 Accounts Receivable	412 Sales Discounts
113 Interest Receivable	500 Costs and Expenses
115 Inventory	510 Cost of Goods Sold
116 Office Supplies	520 Sales Salaries Expense
117 Prepaid Insurance	521 Advertising Expense
120 Land	522 Amortization Expense—Store Equipment
123 Store Equipment	
124 Accumulated Amortization— Store Equipment	529 Miscellaneous Selling Expense
	530 Office Salaries Expense
125 Office Equipment	531 Rent Expense
126 Accumulated Amortization Office Equipment	532 Amortization Expense—Office Equipment
200 Liabilities	533 Insurance Expense
210 Accounts Payable	534 Office Supplies Expense
211 Salaries Payable	539 Misc. Administrative Expense
212 Unearned Rent	600 Other Income
215 Notes Payable	610 Rent Income
300 Owner's Equity	611 Interest Income
310 Pat King, Capital	700 Other Expense
311 Pat King, Withdrawals	710 Interest Expense
312 Income Summary	

Exhibit 7
Chart of Accounts—Periodic Inventory System

Balance Sheet Accounts	Income Statement Accounts
100 Assets	400 Revenues
110 Cash	410 Sales
111 Notes Receivable	411 Sales Returns and Allowances
112 Accounts Receivable	412 Sales Discounts
113 Interest Receivable	500 Costs and Expenses
115 Inventory	500 Cost of Goods Sold
116 Office Supplies	510 Purchases
117 Prepaid Insurance	511 Purchases Returns and Allowances
120 Land	
123 Store Equipment	512 Purchases Discounts
124 Accumulated Amortization— Store Equipment	513 Transportation-In
	520 Sales Salaries Expenses
125 Office Equipment	521 Advertising Expense
126 Accumulated Amortization— Office Equipment	522 Amortization Expense—Store Equipment
200 Liabilities	529 Miscellaneous Selling Expense
210 Accounts Payable	530 Office Salaries Expense
211 Salaries Payable	531 Rent Expense
212 Unearned Rent	532 Amortization Expense—Office Equipment
215 Notes Payable	
300 Owner's Equity	533 Insurance Expense
310 Pat King, Capital	534 Office Supplies Expense
311 Pat King, Withdrawals	539 Misc. Administrative Expense
312 Income Summary	600 Other Income
	610 Rent Income
	611 Interest Income
	700 Other Expense
	710 Interest Expense

liabilities, and so on). The second digit indicates the subclassification (e.g., 11 for current assets, 12 for noncurrent assets). The third digit identifies the specific account (e.g., 110 for Cash, 123 for Store Equipment).

Computer King is using a more complex numbering system because it has a greater variety of transactions. As a business grows, the types of transactions and the complexities of transactions usually increase. For example, a rapidly growing business may borrow funds to expand its operations by issuing notes payable. It may also accept notes receivable from major customers for sales of merchandise. Interest expense may be incurred on the notes payable, and interest income may be earned on the notes receivable. Thus, such transactions would require including Notes Receivable, Notes Payable, Interest Income, and Interest Expense in the chart of accounts.

The growth of a business also creates a need for more detailed information for use in managing it. For example, a wages expense account may be adequate for managing a small service business with one or two employees. However, a merchandising business normally uses two or more payroll accounts, such as Sales Salaries Expense and Office Salaries Expense.

Income Statement for a Merchandising Business

Objective 5
Prepare an income statement for a merchandising business.

In this section, we emphasize the income statement of a merchandising business because merchandising transactions primarily affect this financial statement. The balance sheet is only affected to the extent that inventory is reported as a current asset. There are two widely used formats for preparing an income statement: multiple step and single step. A survey of the annual reports of 200 large Canadian public companies indicates that no more than 3% used the simple-step format, while the remainder presented some version of a multi-step income statement.[6]

MULTIPLE-STEP FORM

The multiple-step income statement contains several sections, subsections, and subtotals. The amount of detail presented in these sections varies from company to company. For example, instead of reporting gross sales, sales returns and allowances, and sales discounts, some companies just report net sales.

We use Computer King's income statement, shown in Exhibit 8, as a basis for illustrating the multiple-step form for a merchandising business. We discuss each of the sections of the income statement in the following paragraphs.

Revenue from Sales

The total amount charged customers for merchandise sold, for cash and on account, is reported in this section. Sales returns and allowances and sales discounts are deducted from this total to yield net sales.

Cost of Goods Sold

The cost of goods sold during the period may also be called the **cost of goods sold** or the **cost of sales.** Under a periodic inventory system, this section of the income statement may include the calculation of the cost of goods sold as shown on page 237.

---

[6] C. Byrd and I. Chen, *Financial Reporting in Canada (1997)*, 22nd ed., CICA, Toronto, 1997.

Exhibit 8
Multiple-Step Income Statement

Computer King Income Statement For the Year Ended December 31, 2001			
Revenue from sales:			
Sales		$720 1 8 5 00	
Less: Sales returns and allowances	$ 6 1 4 0 00		
Sales discounts	5 7 9 0 00	11 9 3 0 00	
Net sales			$708 2 5 5 00
Cost of goods sold			525 3 0 5 00
Gross profit			$182 9 5 0 00
Operating expenses:			
Selling expenses:			
Sales salaries expense	$60 0 3 0 00		
Advertising expense	10 8 6 0 00		
Amor. expense—store equipment	3 1 0 0 00		
Miscellaneous selling expense	6 3 0 00		
Total selling expenses		$ 74 6 2 0 00	
Administrative expenses:			
Office salaries expense	$21 0 2 0 00		
Rent expense	8 1 0 0 00		
Amor. expense—office equipment	2 4 9 0 00		
Insurance expense	1 9 1 0 00		
Office supplies expense	6 1 0 00		
Misc. administrative expense	7 6 0 00		
Total administrative expenses		34 8 9 0 00	
Total operating expenses			109 5 1 0 00
Income from operations			$ 73 4 4 0 00
Other income:			
Interest income	$ 3 8 0 0 00		
Rent income	6 0 0 00		
Total other income		$ 4 4 0 0 00	
Other expense:			
Interest expense		2 4 4 0 00	1 9 6 0 00
Net income			$ 75 4 0 0 00

Gross Profit

The excess of net sales over cost of goods sold is called **gross profit.** We sometimes call it **gross profit on sales** or **gross margin.**

Operating Expenses

Most merchandising businesses classify operating expenses as either selling expenses or administrative expenses. However, depending on the decision-making needs of managers and other users of the financial statements, other classifications could be used.

Expenses that are incurred directly in the selling of merchandise are selling expenses. They include such expenses as salespersons' salaries, store supplies used, amortization of store equipment, and advertising.

Expenses incurred in the administration or general operations of the business are administrative expenses or **general expenses.** Examples of these expenses are office salaries, amortization of office equipment, and office supplies used. Bank credit card expense is also normally classified as an administrative expense.

We can divide expenses that are related to both administrative and selling functions between the two classifications. In small businesses, however, such expenses as rent, insurance, and taxes are commonly reported as administrative expenses. We report transactions for small, infrequent expenses as Miscellaneous Selling Expense or Miscellaneous Administrative Expense.

Income from Operations

We call the excess of gross profit over total operating expenses income from operations or **operating income.** The relationships of income from operations to total assets and to net sales are important factors in judging the efficiency and profitability of operations. If operating expenses are greater than the gross profit, the excess is called a **loss from operations.**

Other Income and Other Expense

A business classifies revenue from sources other than the primary operating activity of a business as other income or **nonoperating income.** In a merchandising business, these items include income from interest, rent, and gains resulting from the sale of plant assets.

We identify expenses that cannot be traced directly to operations as other expense or **nonoperating expense.** Interest expense that results from financing activities and losses incurred in the disposal of plant assets are examples of these items.

We offset other income and other expense against each other on the income statement. If the total of other income exceeds the total of other expense, we add the difference to income from operations. If the reverse is true, we subtract the difference from income from operations.

Net Income

The final figure on the income statement is called **net income** (or **net loss**). It is the net increase (or net decrease) in the owner's equity as a result of the period's profit-making activities.

SINGLE-STEP FORM

In the single-step income statement, the total of all expenses is deducted *in one step* from the total of all revenues. Exhibit 9 illustrates such a statement for Computer King. The statement has been condensed to focus attention on its primary features. Such condensing is not essential for the single-step form.

The single-step form has the advantage of emphasizing total revenues and total expenses as the factors that determine net income. A criticism of the single-step form is that such amounts as gross profit and income from operations are not readily available for analysis.

Exhibit 9
Single-Step Income Statement

Computer King
Income Statement
For the Year Ended December 31, 2001

Revenues:		
Net sales		$708 2 5 5 00
Interest income		3 8 0 0 00
Rent income		6 0 0 00
Total revenues		$712 6 5 5 00
Expenses:		
Cost of goods sold	$525 3 0 5 00	
Selling expenses	74 6 2 0 00	
Administrative expenses	34 8 9 0 00	
Interest expense	2 4 4 0 00	
Total expenses		637 2 5 5 00
Net income		$ 75 4 0 0 00

The Accounting Cycle for a Merchandising Business

Objective 6

Describe the accounting cycle for a merchandising business.

Earlier in this chapter, we described and illustrated the chart of accounts and the analysis and recording of transactions for a merchandising business. We also illustrated the preparation of an income statement for a merchandiser, Computer King, at the end of an accounting cycle. In the remainder of this chapter, we describe the other elements of the accounting cycle for a merchandising business. In this discussion, we will focus primarily on the elements of this cycle that are likely to differ from those of a service business.

INVENTORY SHRINKAGE

What is merchandise **inventory shrinkage?** Under the perpetual inventory system, a business keeps its inventory account up to date in the ledger. Throughout the accounting period, this account shows the amount of merchandise that should be on hand at any time. However, merchandising businesses may experience some loss of inventory due to shoplifting, employee theft, or errors in recording or counting inventory. As a result, the physical inventory taken at the end of the accounting period may differ from the amount of inventory shown in the inventory records. Normally, the amount of merchandise that should be on hand, as indicated by the balance of the merchandise inventory account, is larger than the total amount of merchandise counted during the physical inventory. For this reason, the difference is often called inventory shrinkage or **inventory shortage.**

To illustrate, under the perpetual system Computer King's inventory records indicate that $63,950 of merchandise should be on hand on December 31, 2001. The physical inventory taken on December 31, 2001, however, indicates that only $62,150 of merchandise is actually on hand. Thus, the inventory shrinkage for the year ending December 31, 2001, is $1,800 ($63,950 − $62,150). This amount is recorded by the following adjusting entry:

Dec. 31	Cost of Goods Sold	1,800	
	Inventory		1,800
	Adjust inventory to agree with physical count.		

After we have recorded and posted this entry, the accounting records agree with the actual physical inventory at the end of the period. Since no system of procedures and safeguards can totally eliminate it, inventory shrinkage is often considered a normal cost of operations. If the amount of the shrinkage is abnormally large, the firm may disclose it separately on the income statement, below the cost of goods sold. In such cases, it may record the shrinkage in a separate account, such as Loss From Inventory Shrinkage.

Under a periodic inventory system, a business must conduct a physical count at the end of period to determine the balance of ending inventory. In the Computer King example discussed above, the physical count indicated $62,150 for inventory on hand at December 31, 2001. We use this balance to calculate the Cost of Goods Sold for 2001. Therefore, any cost for inventory shrinkage will automatically be included in the amount recorded for Cost of Goods Sold. However, the amount of shrinkage will not be noted separately as it is under the perpetual method. By providing more information about the extent of inventory shrinkage, the perpetual method provides a better measure of internal control. An excessively high entry for shrinkage should alert management to a weakness in the firm's inventory control system.

WORK SHEET

Most merchandising businesses use a computerized accounting system. In a computerized system, the adjusting entries are recorded and financial statements prepared without using a work sheet. Therefore, in this chapter, we do not illustrate the preparation of a work sheet. The appendix at the end of the chapter, however, illustrates the work sheet and the adjusting entries for a merchandising business that uses a manual accounting system.

STATEMENT OF OWNER'S EQUITY

Exhibit 10 shows the statement of owner's equity for Computer King. A business prepares this statement in the same manner that we described previously for a service business.

Exhibit 10

Statement of Owner's Equity for Merchandising Business

Computer King Statement of Owner's Equity For the Year Ended December 31, 2001		
Pat King, capital, January 1, 2001		$153 8 0 0 00
Net income for year	$75 4 0 0 00	
Less withdrawals	18 0 0 0 00	
Increase in owner's equity		57 4 0 0 00
Pat King, capital, December 31, 2001		$211 2 0 0 00

BALANCE SHEET

As we discussed and illustrated in previous chapters, a business may present its balance sheet with assets on the left side and the liabilities and owner's equity on the right side. We call this form of the balance sheet the account form. A company may also present its balance sheet in a downward sequence in three sections. The total of the Assets section equals the combined total of the Liabilities and Owner's

Equity sections. We call this form of balance sheet the report form. Exhibit 11 shows the report form of balance sheet for Computer King. In this balance sheet, note that the business reports inventory at the end of the period as a current asset and that the current portion of the note payable is $5,000.

Exhibit 11
Report Form of Balance Sheet

Computer King Balance Sheet December 31, 2001			
Assets			
Current assets:			
Cash		$52 9 5 0 00	
Notes receivable		40 0 0 0 00	
Accounts receivable		60 8 8 0 00	
Interest receivable		2 0 0 00	
Inventory		62 1 5 0 00	
Office supplies		4 8 0 00	
Prepaid insurance		2 6 5 0 00	
Total current assets			$219 3 1 0 00
Plant assets:			
Land		$10 0 0 0 00	
Store equipment	$27 1 0 0 00		
Less accumulated amortization	5 7 0 0 00	21 4 0 0 00	
Office equipment	$15 5 7 0 00		
Less accumulated amortization	4 7 2 0 00	10 8 5 0 00	
Total plant assets			42 2 5 0 00
Total assets			$261 5 6 0 00
Liabilities			
Current liabilities:			
Accounts payable		$22 4 2 0 00	
Note payable (current portion)		5 0 0 0 00	
Salaries payable		1 1 4 0 00	
Unearned rent		1 8 0 0 00	
Total current liabilities			$ 30 3 6 0 00
Long-term liabilities:			
Note payable (final payment due 2002)		25 0 0 0 00	
Less current portion		5 0 0 0 00	20 0 0 0 00
Total liabilities			$ 50 3 6 0 00
Owner's Equity			
Pat King, capital			211 2 0 0 00
Total liabilities and owner's equity			$261 5 6 0 00

CLOSING ENTRIES

The closing entries for a merchandising business are similar to those for a service business. The first entry closes the temporary accounts with credit balances, such as Sales, to the Income Summary account. The second entry closes the temporary accounts with debit balances, including Sales Returns and Allowances, Sales Discounts, and Cost of Goods Sold, to the Income Summary account. The third entry closes the balance of the Income Summary account to the Owner's Capital account. The fourth entry closes the Owner's Withdrawals account to the Owner's Capital account.

In a computerized accounting system, the closing entries are prepared automatically. Therefore, in this chapter, we do not illustrate the closing entries for a merchandising business. The closing entries for Computer King are illustrated in the appendix.

Appendix A: Use of the Net Method for Recording Sales Discounts and Purchase Discounts

In this chapter we assumed that both sellers and buyers initially recorded invoices at their full amount and later recorded the discount taken if the payment was made by the discount date. However, an alternative method is for a business to initially record the invoice **net** of the discount, and to record the discount separately at a later date only if it is **not** taken.

COMPUTER KING

In this case, the seller records the sales discount not taken as other revenue. On the other side, the purchaser records the purchase discount lost as an expense. The following table illustrates the net method for both seller and purchaser using the data from Exhibit 1. In this example Wallace Electronics Supply initially records the $1,500 sale on account net of the 2% discount of $30, while Computer King also records the purchase net of the discount. The entries shown below assume that Computer King is using a perpetual inventory system:

Transaction	Seller's Books (Wallace Electronics Supply)		Purchaser's Books (Computer King)	

Jan. 12. Wallace Electronics Supply sells goods on account for $1,500, 2/10, n/30.	Account Receivable 1,470
	    Sales 1,470
			Inventory 1,470
			    Account Payable 1,470	

If invoice is paid Jan. 22 within discount period.	Cash 1,470
	    Account Receivable 1,470
			Account Payable 1,470
			    Cash 1,470	

If invoice is paid Jan. 31 after discount period.	Cash 1,500
	    Account Receivable 1,470
	    Sales Discount Revenue 30
			Account Payable 1,470
			Purchase Discounts Lost 30
			    Cash 1,500	

If the invoice is not paid until after the discount date, the discount represents interest paid by the buyer for making a late payment. Therefore, the seller could report the Sales Discount Revenue as Interest Revenue on its income statement, and the buyer could report Purchase Discounts Lost as Interest Expense.

Although the use of the net method is not as widespread as the gross method, the former is theoretically preferable to the latter for several reasons. (1) The net method records the original transaction under the assumption that the discount will be taken, and this is what usually happens in practice. (2) Most consistent with the historical cost principle, the net method reports inventory at the amount for which it could have been purchased for cash (its cash equivalent). (3) The net method reports discounts not taken for what they really are, an interest charge for late payment. (4) The net method is a better control mechanism for alerting management if the firm is failing to take advantage of purchase discounts. If the purchaser misses a discount, the net method highlights this by showing Purchase

Discounts Lost as a separate account. Under the gross method, discounts lost are not highlighted, so that management may not be aware that the business is incurring excessive interest charges for not paying its suppliers promptly.

Appendix B: Work Sheet and Adjusting and Closing Entries for a Merchandising Business

A merchandising business that does not use a computerized accounting system may use a work sheet in assembling the data for preparing financial statements and adjusting and closing entries. In this appendix, we illustrate such a work sheet, along with the adjusting and closing entries for a merchandising business under both a perpetual and a periodic inventory system.

The work sheet in Exhibit 12 is for Computer King on December 31, 2001, the end of its first year of operations as a merchandiser. Exhibit 12 assumes that the business uses a perpetual system. Exhibit 13 illustrates the work sheet under a periodic system. In the work sheet, we list all of the accounts, including the accounts that have no balances, in the order that they appear in Computer King's ledger.

The data needed for adjusting the accounts of Computer King are as follows:

Interest accrued on notes receivable on December 31, 2001		$ 200
Physical inventory on December 31, 2001		62,150
Office supplies on hand on December 31, 2001		480
Insurance expired during 2001		1,910
Amortization during 2001 on: Store equipment		3,100
Office equipment		2,490
Salaries accrued on December 31, 2001: Sales salaries	$780	
Office salaries	360	1,140
Rent income earned during 2001		600

There is no specific order in which to analyze the accounts in the work sheet, assemble the adjustment data, and make the adjusting entries.

After entering all the adjustments on the work sheet, total the Adjustments columns to prove the equality of debits and credits. As we illustrated in previous chapters, we extend the balances of the accounts in the Trial Balance columns and the amount of any adjustments to the Adjusted Trial Balance columns.[7] We then total the Adjusted Trial Balance columns to prove the equality of debits and credits.

The process of extending the balances, as adjusted, to the statement columns usually begins with Cash and moves down the work sheet, item by item. After extending all the items to the statement columns, total the four columns and determine the net income or net loss. For Computer King, the difference between the credit and debit columns of the Income Statement section is $75,400, the amount of the net income. The difference between the debit and credit columns of the Balance Sheet section is also $75,400, which is the increase in owner's equity as a result of the net income. Agreement between the two balancing amounts is evidence of debit-credit equality and mathematical accuracy.

After extending all account balances, prepare the income statement, statement of owner's equity, and balance sheet from the work sheet in a manner similar to that of a service business. The Adjustments columns in the work sheet provide the data for journalizing the adjusting entries. Computer King's adjusting entries at the end of 2001 are as follows:

---

[7] Some accountants prefer to eliminate the Adjusted Trial Balance columns and to extend the adjusted balances directly to the statement columns. Such a work sheet is often used if there are only a few adjustment items.

Exhibit 12

Work Sheet for Merchandising Business—
Perpetual Method

Computer King
Work Sheet
For the Year Ended December 31, 2001

Account Title	Trial Balance Dr.	Trial Balance Cr.	Adjustments Dr.	Adjustments Cr.	Adjusted Trial Balance Dr.	Adjusted Trial Balance Cr.	Income Statement Dr.	Income Statement Cr.	Balance Sheet Dr.	Balance Sheet Cr.
Cash	52,950				52,950				52,950	
Notes Receivable	40,000				40,000				40,000	
Accounts Receivable	60,880				60,880				60,880	
Interest Receivable			(a) 200		200				200	
Inventory	63,950			(h)1,800	62,150				62,150	
Office Supplies	1,090			(b) 610	480				480	
Prepaid Insurance	4,560			(c)1,910	2,650				2,650	
Land	10,000				10,000				10,000	
Store Equipment	27,100				27,100				27,100	
Accum. Amor.—Store Equip.		2,600		(d)3,100		5,700				5,700
Office Equipment	15,570				15,570				15,570	
Accum. Amor.—Office Equip.		2,230		(f)2,490		4,720				4,720
Accounts Payable		22,420				22,420				22,420
Salaries Payable				(f)1,140		1,140				1,140
Unearned Rent		2,400	(g) 600			1,800				1,800
Notes Payable (final payment due 2002)		25,000				25,000				25,000
Pat King, Capital		153,800				153,800				153,800
Pat King, Withdrawals	18,000				18,000				18,000	
Sales		720,185				720,185		720,185		
Sales Returns and Allowances	6,140				6,140		6,140			
Sales Discounts	5,790				5,790		5,790			
Cost of Goods Sold	523,505		(h)1,800		525,305		525,305			
Sales Salaries Expense	59,250		(f) 780		60,030		60,030			
Advertising Expense	10,860				10,860		10,860			
Amor. Exp.—Store Equip.			(d)3,100		3,100		3,100			
Miscellaneous Selling Expense	630				630		630			
Office Salaries Expense	20,660		(f) 360		21,020		21,020			
Rent Expense	8,100				8,100		8,100			
Amor. Exp.—Office Equip.			(e)2,490		2,490		2,490			
Insurance Expense			(c)1,910		1,910		1,910			
Office Supplies Expense			(b) 610		610		610			
Misc. Administrative Expense	760				760		760			
Rent Income				(g) 600		600		600		
Interest Income		3,600		(a) 200		3,800		3,800		
Interest Expense	2,440				2,440		2,440			
	932,235	932,235	11,850	11,850	939,165	939,165	649,185	724,585	289,980	214,580
Net Income							75,400			75,400
							724,585	724,585	289,980	289,980

(a) Interest earned but not received on notes receivable, $200.
(b) Office supplies used, $610 ($1,090 – $480).
(c) Insurance expired, $1,910.
(d) Amortization of store equipment, $3,100.
(e) Amortization of office equipment, $2,490.
(f) Salaries accrued but not paid (sales salaries, $780; office salaries, $360), $1,140.
(g) Rent earned from amount received in advance, $600.
(h) Inventory shrinkage for period, $1,800 ($63,950 – $62,150).

Exhibit 13
Work Sheet—Periodic Inventory System

Computer King
Work Sheet
For the Year Ended December 31, 2001

Account Title	Trial Balance Dr.	Cr.	Adjustments Dr.	Cr.	Adjusted Trial Balance Dr.	Cr.	Income Statement Dr.	Cr.	Balance Sheet Dr.	Cr.
Cash	52,950				52,950				52,950	
Notes Receivable	40,000				40,000				40,000	
Accounts Receivable	60,880				60,880				60,880	
Interest Receivable			(a) 200		200				200	
Inventory	59,700		(h) 2,450			62,150			62,150	
Office Supplies	1,090			(b) 610	480				480	
Prepaid Insurance	4,560			(c) 1,910	2,650				2,650	
Land	10,000				10,000				10,000	
Store Equipment	27,100				27,100				27,100	
Accum. Amort.—Store Equipment		2,600		(d) 3,100		5,700				5,700
Office Equipment	15,570				15,570				15,570	
Accum. Amort.—Office Equipment		2,230		(e) 2,490		4,720				4,720
Accounts Payable		22,420				22,420				22,420
Salaries Payable				(f) 1,140		1,140				1,140
Unearned Rent		2,400	(g) 600			1,800				1,800
Notes Payable (final payment, 2002)		25,000				25,000				25,000
Pat King, Capital		153,800				153,800				153,800
Pat King, Withdrawals	18,000				18,000				18,000	
Sales		720,185				720,185		720,185		
Sales Returns and Allowances	6,140				6,140		6,140			
Sales Discounts	5,790				5,790		5,790			
Cost of Goods Sold			(h)525,305		525,305		525,305			
Purchases	521,980			(h)521,980						
Purchases Returns & Allowances		9,100	(h) 9,100							
Purchases Discounts		2,525	(h) 2,525							
Transportation-In	17,400			(h) 17,400						
Sales Salaries Expense	59,250		(f) 780		60,030		60,030			
Advertising Expense	10,860				10,860		10,860			
Amort. Expense—Store Equipment			(d) 3,100		3,100		3,100			
Miscellaneous Selling Expense	630				630		630			
Office Salaries Expense	20,660		(f) 360		21,020		21,020			
Rent Expense	8,100				8,100		8,100			
Amort. Expense—Office Equipment			(e) 2,490		2,490		2,490			
Insurance Expense			(c) 1,910		1,910		1,910			
Office Supplies Expense			(b) 610		610		610			
Misc. Administrative Expense	760				760		760			
Rent Income				(g) 600		600		600		
Interest Income		3,600		(a) 200		3,800		3,800		
Interest Expense	2,440				2,440		2,440			
	943,860	943,860	549,530	549,530	939,165	939,165	649,185	724,585	289,980	214,580
Net Income							75,400			75,400
							724,585	724,585	289,980	289,980

Entries (a) through (g) are the same as in Exhibit 12. Only (h) is different.

(a) Interest earned but not received on notes receivable, $200.

(b) Office supplies used, $610 ($1,090 – $480).

(c) Insurance expired, $1,910.

(d) Amortization of store equipment, $3,100.

(e) Amortization of office equipment, $2,490.

(f) Salaries accrued but not paid (sales salaries, $780; office salaries, $360), $1,140.

(g) Rent earned from amount received in advance, $600.

(h) Adjust ending inventory to $62,150, record cost of goods sold of $525,305, and close the accounts for Purchases, Purchase Discounts, Purchase Returns & Allowances, and Transportation-in.

		JOURNAL			PAGE 28
Date	Description	Post. Ref.	Debit		Credit
2001	Adjusting Entries				
Dec. 31	Interest Receivable	113	2 0 0 00		
	Interest Income	611			2 0 0 00
	Accrue interest on notes receivable.				
31	Office Supplies Expense	534	6 1 0 00		
	Office Supplies	116			6 1 0 00
	Office supplies used during the period.				
31	Insurance Expense	533	1 9 1 0 00		
	Prepaid Insurance	117			1 9 1 0 00
	Insurance expired during the period.				
31	Amortization Expense— Store Equipment	522	3 1 0 0 00		
	Accumulated Amortization— Store Equipment	124			3 1 0 0 00
	Amortization on store equipment.				
31	Amortization Expense— Office Equipment	532	2 4 9 0 00		
	Accumulated Amortization— Office Equipment	126			2 4 9 0 00
	Amortization on office equipment.				
31	Sales Salaries Expense	520	7 8 0 00		
	Office Salaries Expense	530	3 6 0 00		
	Salaries Payable	211			1 1 4 0 00
	Accrue office salaries at the end of the period.				
31	Unearned Rent	212	6 0 0 00		
	Rent Income	610			6 0 0 00
	Rental income earned during the period.				

The only difference in the adjusting entries made in Exhibits 12 and 13 involves the entry for inventory. In Exhibit 12 under the perpetual system we make an entry to reconcile the Inventory account with the physical count of inventory and record inventory shrinkage:

Dec. 31	Cost of Goods Sold	510	1800	
	Inventory	115		1800
	To adjust Inventory to agree with the physical count at year end.			

In Exhibit 13 we make an entry to (1) update the Inventory account to agree with the physical count, (2) close the temporary accounts for Purchases, Purchase Discounts, Purchase Returns and Allowances, and Transportation-in, and (3) record Cost of Goods Sold. We showed this entry earlier when illustrating the periodic system:

Dec. 31	Cost of Goods Sold	500	525,305	
	Inventory	115	2,450	
	Purchase Discounts	512	2,525	
	Purchase Returns and Allowances	511	9,100	
	Purchases	510		521,980
	Transportation-in	13		17,400

The Income Statement columns of the work sheet provide the data for preparing the closing entries. The closing entries for Computer King at the end of 2001 are as follows:

	Date	Description	Post. Ref.	Debit	Credit
					PAGE 29
1	2001	Closing Entries			
2	Dec. 31	Sales	410	720 1 8 5 00	
3		Rent Income	610	6 0 0 00	
4		Interest Income	611	3 8 0 0 00	
5		Income Summary	312		724 5 8 5 00
6					
7	31	Income Summary	312	649 1 8 5 00	
8		Sales Returns and Allowances	411		6 1 4 0 00
9		Sales Discounts	412		5 7 9 0 00
10		Cost of Goods Sold	500		525 3 0 5 00
11		Sales Salaries Expense	520		60 0 3 0 00
12		Advertising Expense	521		10 8 6 0 00
13		Amor. Expense—Store Equipment	522		3 1 0 0 00
14		Miscellaneous Selling Expense	529		6 3 0 00
15		Office Salaries Expense	530		21 0 2 0 00
16		Rent Expense	531		8 1 0 0 00
17		Amor. Expense—Office Equipment	532		2 4 9 0 00
18		Insurance Expense	533		1 9 1 0 00
19		Office Supplies Expense	534		6 1 0 00
20		Misc. Administrative Expense	539		7 6 0 00
21		Interest Expense	710		2 4 4 0 00
22					
23	31	Income Summary	312	75 4 0 0 00	
24		Pat King, Capital	310		75 4 0 0 00
25					
26	31	Pat King, Capital	310	18 0 0 0 00	
27		Pat King, Withdrawals	311		18 0 0 0 00
28					

The balance of Income Summary, after the first two closing entries have been posted, is the net income or net loss for the period. The third closing entry transfers this balance to the owner's capital account. Computer King's income summary account after the closing entries have been posted is as follows:

ACCOUNT *Income Summary*						ACCOUNT NO. *312*	
Date	Item	Post. Ref.	Debit	Credit	Balance Debit		Credit
2001 Dec. 31	Revenues	29		724 5 8 5 00			724 5 8 5 00
31	Expenses	29	649 1 8 5 00				75 4 0 0 00
31	Net income	29	75 4 0 0 00		—		—

After the closing entries have been prepared and posted to the accounts, prepare a post-closing trial balance to verify the debit-credit equality. The only accounts that should appear on the post-closing trial balance are the asset, contra asset, liability, and owner's capital accounts with balances. These are the same accounts that appear on the end-of-period balance sheet.

KEY POINTS

Objective 1. Compare a service business's income statement to a merchandising business's income statement.

The primary differences between a service business and a merchandising business relate to revenue activities. Merchandising businesses purchase merchandise for selling to customers.

On a merchandising business's income statement, we report revenue from selling merchandise as sales. We subtract the cost of the goods sold from sales to arrive at gross profit. We subtract the operating expenses from gross profit to arrive at net income.

We report inventory, which is merchandise not sold, as a current asset on the balance sheet.

Objective 2a. Journalize the entries for merchandise sales.

We record sales of merchandise for cash or on account by crediting Sales. Under a perpetual inventory system we also record the cost of goods sold and the reduction in inventory at the time of the sale.

For sales of merchandise on account, the credit terms may allow sales discounts for early payment. The seller records such discounts as a debit to Sales Discounts. Likewise, when merchandise is returned or a price adjustment is granted, the seller debits Sales Returns and Allowances. Sales Discounts and Sales Returns and Allowances are contra accounts deducted from Sales on the income statement.

We record the liability for sales tax incurred at the time the sale is made as a credit to the sales tax payable account. When we pay the amount of the sales tax to the taxing unit, we debit Sales Tax Payable and credit Cash.

Many wholesalers offer trade discounts, which are discounts off the list prices of merchandise. Neither the seller nor the buyer records the list price and the related trade dis-

count in the accounts. When merchandise is shipped FOB shipping point, the buyer pays the transportation costs, debiting Inventory (perpetual) or Transportation-in (periodic). When merchandise is shipped FOB destination, the seller pays the transportation costs and debits Transportation Out, Delivery Expense, or a similarly titled account. If the seller prepays transportation costs as a convenience to the buyer, the seller debits Accounts Receivable for the costs.

Objective 2b. Journalize the entries for merchandise purchases.

We record purchases of merchandise for cash or on account by debiting the Inventory account (under a perpetual system) or Purchases (under a periodic system). Credit terms may allow the buyer a cash discount for early payment. We credit discounts taken to Inventory (perpetual) or Purchase Discounts (periodic). When we return merchandise to a supplier, we credit Inventory (perpetual) or Purchase Returns and Allowances (periodic). When merchandise is shipped FOB shipping point, the buyer pays the transportation costs, debiting Inventory (perpetual) or Transportation-in (periodic).

Objective 3. Journalize the entries for merchandise transactions from both the buyer's and the seller's point of view using both the perpetual and periodic methods.

The illustration in this chapter summarizes the principles and concepts of accounting for merchandising transactions by presenting the entries for both sale and purchase transactions under both the perpetual and periodic inventory methods.

Objective 4. Prepare a chart of accounts for a merchandising business.

The chart of accounts for a merchandising business is more complex than that for a service business and normally includes accounts such as Sales, Sales Discounts, Sales Returns and Allowances, Cost of Goods Sold, and Inventory. A firm using the periodic method will also have accounts for Purchases, Purchase Discounts, Purchase Returns and Allowances, and Transportation-in.

Objective 5. Prepare an income statement for a merchandising business.

The income statement of a merchandising business reports sales, cost of goods sold, and gross profit. We can prepare the income statement using either the multiple-step form or the single-step form.

Objective 6. Describe the accounting cycle for a merchandising business.

The accounting cycle for a merchandising business is similar to that of a service business. However, a merchandiser is likely to experience inventory shrinkage, which must be recorded. The normal adjusting entry is to debit Cost of Goods Sold and credit Inventory for the amount of the shrinkage.

We may prepare the balance sheet using either the account form or the report form. Regardless of the form used, we should report merchandise inventory as a current asset.

GLOSSARY OF KEY TERMS

Account form of balance sheet. A form of balance sheet with assets on the left side and liabilities and owner's equity on the right side. *Objective 6*

Administrative expenses. Expenses incurred in the administration or general operations of a business. *Objective 5*

Credit memorandum. The form issued by a seller to inform a buyer that a credit has been posted to the buyer's account receivable. *Objective 2a*

Debit memorandum. The form issued by a buyer to inform a seller that a debit has been posted to the seller's account payable. *Objective 2b*

FOB destination. Terms of agreement between buyer and seller whereby ownership passes when merchandise is received by the buyer, and the seller pays the transportation costs. *Objective 2a*

FOB shipping point. Terms of agreement between buyer and seller whereby ownership passes when merchandise is delivered to the freight carrier, and the buyer pays the transportation costs. *Objective 2a*

Gross profit. The excess of net sales over the cost of goods sold. *Objective 1*

Income from operations. The excess of gross profit over total operating expenses. *Objective 5*

Inventory (merchandise inventory). Merchandise on hand and available for sale to customers. *Objective 1*

Inventory shrinkage. Loss of inventory due to shoplifting, employee theft, or errors in recording or counting inventory. *Objective 6*

Invoice. The bill provided by the seller (who refers to it as a *sales invoice*) to a buyer (who refers to it as a *purchase invoice*) for items purchased. *Objective 2a*

Multiple-step income statement. An income statement with several sections, subsections, and subtotals. *Objective 5*

Other expense. An expense that cannot be traced directly to operations. *Objective 5*

Other income. Revenue from sources other than the primary operating activity of a business. *Objective 5*

Periodic inventory system. A system of inventory accounting in which only the revenue from sales is recorded each time a sale is made. The cost of merchandise on hand at the end

of a period is determined by a detailed listing (physical inventory) of the merchandise on hand. *Objective 2b*

Perpetual inventory system. A system of inventory accounting in which both the revenue from sales and the cost of goods sold are recorded each time a sale is made, so that the records continually disclose the amount of the inventory on hand. *Objective 2b*

Physical inventory. The detailed listing of merchandise on hand. *Objective 2b*

Purchases account. Temporary account in which we record purchases of inventory during the period under a periodic inventory system. *Objective 3*

Purchases discounts. An available discount taken by a buyer for early payment of an invoice. *Objective 2b*

Purchases returns and allowances. Reductions in purchases, resulting from merchandise being returned to the seller or from the seller's reduction in the original purchase price. *Objective 2b*

Report form of balance sheet. A form of balance sheet with the liabilities and owner's equity sections below the assets section. *Objective 6*

Sales discounts. An available discount granted by a seller for early payment of an invoice; a contra account to Sales. *Objective 2a*

Sales returns and allowances. Reductions in sales, resulting from merchandise being returned by customers or from the seller's reduction in the original sales price; a contra account to Sales. *Objective 2a*

Selling expenses. Expenses incurred directly in the sale of merchandise. *Objective 5*

Single-step income statement. An income statement in which the total of all expenses is deducted in one step from the total of all revenues. *Objective 5*

Trade discounts. Special discounts from published list prices offered by sellers to certain classes of buyers. *Objective 2b*

Transportation-in. Temporary account in which we record freight costs on inventory purchases under a periodic system. *Objective 2b*

Transportation-out. Selling expense incurred when seller pays freight on a sale. *Objective 2b*

ILLUSTRATIVE PROBLEM

Montrose Company completed the following transactions during May of the current year. Montrose Company uses a perpetual inventory system and records all purchases and sales at the gross invoice price. There was no inventory May 1.

May 3. Purchased merchandise on account from Floyd Co., $4,000, terms FOB shipping point, 2/10, n/30, with prepaid transportation costs of $120 added to the invoice.

5. Purchased merchandise on account from Kramer Co., $8,500, terms FOB destination, 1/10, n/30.

6. Sold merchandise on account to C. F. Howell Co., list price $4,000, trade discount 30%, terms 2/10, n/30. The cost of the merchandise sold was $1,125.

8. Purchased office supplies for cash, $150.

10. Returned merchandise purchased on May 5 from Kramer Co., $1,300.

13. Paid Floyd Co. on account for purchase of May 3, less discount.

14. Purchased merchandise for cash, $10,500.

15. Paid Kramer Co. on account for purchase of May 5, less return of May 10 and discount.

16. Received cash on account from sale of May 6 to C. F. Howell Co., less discount.

19. Sold merchandise on nonbank credit cards and reported accounts to the card company, $2,450. The cost of the merchandise sold was $980.

22. Sold merchandise on account to Comer Co., $3,480, terms 2/10, n/30. The cost of the merchandise sold was $1,400.

24. Sold merchandise for cash, $4,350. The cost of the merchandise sold was $1,750.

25. Received merchandise returned by Comer Co. from sale on May 22, $1,480. The cost of the returned merchandise was $600.

31. Received cash from card company for nonbank credit card sales of May 19, less $140 service fee.

Instructions

1. Journalize the preceding transactions. Explanations may be omitted.
2. A physical count indicates inventory on hand at year end is $5,763, indicating inventory shrinkage of $750. Journalize the adjusting entry for inventory shrinkage.
3. Explain how your entries would change if Montrose used a periodic system.

Solution

1.

Date	Account	Debit	Credit
May 3	Inventory	4,120	
	Accounts Payable		4,120
5	Inventory	8,500	
	Accounts Payable		8,500
6	Accounts Receivable	2,800	
	Sales		2,800
	[$4,000 − (30% × $4,000)]		
6	Cost of Goods Sold	1,125	
	Inventory		1,125
8	Office Supplies	150	
	Cash		150
10	Accounts Payable	1,300	
	Inventory		1,300
13	Accounts Payable	4,120	
	Cash		4,040
	Inventory		80
14	Inventory	10,500	
	Cash		10,500

May 15	Accounts Payable ($8,500 – 1,300)	7,200		
	Cash		7,128	
	Inventory		72	
16	Cash	2,744		
	Sales Discounts	56		
	Accounts Receivable		2,800	
19	Accounts Receivable	2,450		
	Sales		2,450	
19	Cost of Goods Sold	980		
	Inventory		980	
22	Accounts Receivable	3,480		
	Sales		3,480	
22	Cost of Goods Sold	1,400		
	Inventory		1,400	
24	Cash	4,350		
	Sales		4,350	
24	Cost of Goods Sold	1,750		
	Inventory		1,750	
25	Sales Returns and Allowances	1,480		
	Accounts Receivable		1,480	
25	Inventory	600		
	Cost of Goods Sold		600	
31	Cash	2,310		
	Credit Card Collection Expense	140		
	Accounts Receivable		2,450	

2.

May 31	Cost of Goods Sold	750	
	Inventory		750

3. Under a periodic system the entries would have differed from those above in the following respects:

May 3	instead of debiting Inventory $4,120, debit Purchases $4,000 and Transportation-in $120		
5	debit Purchases $8,500 instead of Inventory		
6	no entry for Cost of Goods Sold or Inventory		
10	credit Purchase Returns $1,300 instead of Inventory		
14	credit Purchase Discounts for $80 instead of Inventory		
14	credit Purchase Discounts for $72 instead of Inventory		
19	no entry for Cost of Goods Sold or Inventory		
22	no entry for Cost of Goods Sold or Inventory		
24	no entry for Cost of Goods Sold or Inventory		
25	no entry for Cost of Goods Sold or Inventory		
31	Inventory	5,763	
	Cost of Goods Sold	5,405	
	Purchase Discounts	152	
	Purchase Returns and Allowances	1,300	
	Purchases		12,500
	Transportation-in		120

There is no separate entry for inventory shrinkage.

SELF-EXAMINATION QUESTIONS (ANSWERS AT END OF CHAPTER)

1. If merchandise purchased on account is returned, the buyer may inform the seller of the details by issuing:
   A. a debit memorandum   C. an invoice
   B. a credit memorandum   D. a bill

2. If merchandise is sold on account to a customer for $1,000, terms FOB shipping point, 1/10, n/30, and the seller prepays $50 in transportation costs, the amount of the discount for early payment would be:

A. $0   C. $10.00   A. operating income   C. gross profit
B. $5.00   D. $10.50   B. income from operations D. net income

3. The income statement in which the total of all expenses is deducted from the total of all revenues is termed:
   A. multiple-step form   C. account form
   B. single-step form   D. report form

4. On a multiple-step income statement, the excess of net sales over the cost of goods sold is called:

5. Which of the following expenses would normally be classified as Other expense on a multiple-step income statement?
   A. Amortization expense—   C. Insurance expense
      office equipment   D. Interest expense
   B. Sales salaries expense

DISCUSSION QUESTIONS

1. What distinguishes a merchandising business from a service business?
2. Can a business earn a gross profit but incur a net loss? Explain.
3. In which type of system for accounting for merchandise held for sale is there no attempt to record the cost of goods sold until the end of the period, when a physical inventory is taken?
4. What is the name of the account in which purchases of goods are recorded in a perpetual inventory system? in a periodic system?
5. What is the name of the account in which sales of goods are recorded?
6. How does the accounting for sales to customers using bank credit cards, such as MasterCard and VISA, differ from accounting for sales to customers using nonbank credit cards, such as American Express?
7. The credit period during which the buyer of goods is allowed to pay usually begins with what date?
8. Boyd Company ordered $1,000 of goods from Smith Company on April 1, terms 2/10, n/30. Although Smith Company shipped the goods on April 6, the goods were not received by Boyd Company until April 7. The invoice received with the goods was dated April 6. What is the last date Boyd Company could pay the invoice and still receive the discount?
9. What is the meaning of (a) 1/10, n/60; (b) n/30; (c) n/eom?
10. What is the term applied to discounts for early payment of an invoice (a) by the seller, (b) by the buyer?
11. It is not unusual for a customer to drive into some **Texaco, Mobil,** or **BP** gasoline stations in the United States and discover that the cash price per gallon is 3 or 4 cents less than the credit price per gallon. As a result, many customers pay cash rather than use their credit cards. Why would a gasoline station owner establish such a policy?
12. What is the nature of (a) a credit memorandum issued by the seller of goods, (b) a debit memorandum issued by the buyer of goods?
13. Who bears the transportation costs when the terms of sale are (a) FOB shipping point, (b) FOB destination?
14. Name at least three accounts that would normally appear in the chart of accounts of a merchandising business but would not appear in the chart of accounts of a service business.
15. Differentiate between the multiple-step and the single-step forms of the income statement.
16. What major advantages and disadvantages does the single-step form of income statement have in comparison to the multiple-step statement?
17. What type of revenue is reported in the Other income section of the multiple-step income statement?
18. The Furniture Accessory Co., which uses a perpetual inventory system, experienced a normal inventory shrinkage of $32,000. What accounts would be debited and credited to record the adjustment for the inventory shrinkage at the end of the accounting period?
19. Assume that The Furniture Accessory Co. in Question 18 experienced an abnormal inventory shrinkage of $232,000. The Furniture Accessory Co. has decided to record the abnormal inventory shrinkage so that it would be separately disclosed on the income statement. What account would be debited for the abnormal inventory shrinkage?
20. Differentiate between the account form and the report form of balance sheet.

For all of the following problems and exercises, assume that invoices are recorded at the gross invoice price, unless otherwise stated.

EXERCISES

EXERCISE 6–1
Determining gross profit
Objective 1

During the current year, goods are sold for $230,000 cash and for $415,000 on account. The cost of the goods sold is $430,000.

a. What is the amount of the gross profit?
b. ▬▬▶ Will the income statement necessarily report a net income? Explain.

EXERCISE 6–2
Determining cost of goods sold
Objective 1

Sales were $310,000, and the gross profit was $190,000. What was the amount of the cost of goods sold?

EXERCISE 6–3
Sales-related transactions, including the use of credit cards
Objective 2

Assuming a perpetual system, journalize, in a two-column general journal, the entries for the following transactions:

a. Sold goods for cash, $10,500. The cost of the goods sold was $7,500.
b. Sold goods on account, $9,500. The cost of the goods sold was $6,000.
c. Sold goods to customers who used MasterCard and VISA, $5,750. The cost of the goods sold was $2,850.
d. Sold goods to customers who used American Express, $4,100. The cost of the goods sold was $1,860.
e. Paid an invoice from First National Bank for $350, representing a service fee for processing MasterCard and VISA sales.
f. Received $3,890 from American Express Company after a $210 collection fee had been deducted.

EXERCISE 6–4
Sales returns and allowances
Objective 2

During the year, sales returns and allowances totalled $112,150. The cost of the goods returned was $67,300. The accountant recorded all the returns and allowances by debiting the sales account and crediting Cost of Goods Sold for $112,150.
▬▬▶ Was the accountant's method of recording returns acceptable? Explain. In your explanation, include the advantages of using a sales returns and allowances account. Assume the company uses a perpetual inventory system.

EXERCISE 6–5
Sales-related transactions
Objective 2

After the amount due on a sale of $7,000, terms 2/10, n/eom, is received from a customer within the discount period, the seller consents to the return of the entire shipment. (a) What is the amount of the refund owed to the customer? (b) Journalize the entry made by the seller to record the return and the refund.

EXERCISE 6–6
Sales-related transactions
Objective 2

The debits and credits for three related transactions are presented in the following T accounts. Describe each transaction.

Cash				Sales	
(5)	6,930			(1)	8,000

Accounts Receivable				Sales Discounts	
(1)	8,000	(3)	1,000	(5)	70
		(5)	7,000		

Inventory			Sales Returns and Allowances		
(4)	750	(2)	6,000	(3)	1,000

		Cost of Goods Sold		
(2)	6,000	(4)	750

EXERCISE 6–7
Sales-related transactions
Objective 2

Goods are sold on account to a customer for $20,000, terms FOB shipping point, 3/10, n/30. The seller paid the transportation costs of $500. Determine the following: (a) amount of the sale, (b) amount debited to Accounts Receivable, (c) amount of the discount for early payment, and (d) amount due within the discount period.

EXERCISE 6–8
Sales tax
Objective 2

A sale of goods on account for $500 is subject to an 8% sales tax. (a) Should the sales tax be recorded at the time of sale or when payment is received? (b) What is the amount of the sale? (c) What is the amount debited to Accounts Receivable? (d) What is the title of the account to which the $40 is credited?

EXERCISE 6–9
Sales tax transactions
Objective 2

Journalize, in a two-column general journal, the entries to record the following selected transactions. Assume a perpetual inventory system.

a. Sold $11,500 of goods on account, subject to a provincial sales tax of 8% and 7% GST. The cost of the goods sold was $7,000.
b. Remitted payment for taxes collected.

EXERCISE 6–10
Sales-related transactions
Objectives 2, 3

Coyles Co., a furniture wholesaler, sells goods to Westbury Co. on account, $6,900, terms 2/15, n/30. The cost of the goods sold is $3,900. Coyles Co. issues a credit memorandum for $750 for goods returned and subsequently receives the amount due within the discount period. The cost of the goods returned is $450. Journalize, in a two-column general journal, Coyles Co.'s entries for (a) the sale, (b) the credit memorandum, and (c) the receipt of the cheque for the amount due from Westbury Co. Assume a perpetual inventory system. How would these entries differ under a periodic system?

EXERCISE 6–11
Purchase-related transaction
Objective 2

Blair Company purchased goods on account from a supplier for $3,000, terms 2/10, n/30. Blair Company returned $800 of the merchandise and received full credit.

a. If Blair Company pays the invoice within the discount period, what is the amount of cash required for the payment?
b. Under a perpetual inventory system, what account is credited by Blair Company to record the return? Under a periodic system, what account is credited?

EXERCISE 6–12
Determining amounts to be paid on invoices
Objective 2

Determine the amount to be paid in full settlement of each of the following invoices, assuming that credit for returns and allowances was received prior to payment and that all invoices were paid within the discount period.

	Goods	Transportation Paid by Seller	Terms	Returns and Allowances
a.	$6,000	—	FOB shipping point, 1/10, n/30	$1,500
b.	1,000	$50	FOB shipping point, 2/10, n/30	600
c.	8,000	—	FOB destination, n/30	400
d.	4,000	75	FOB shipping point, 1/10, n/30	100
e.	5,000	—	FOB destination, 2/10, n/30	—

EXERCISE 6–13
Purchase-related transactions
Objective 2

A retailer is considering the purchase of 10 units of a specific item from either of two suppliers. Their offers are as follows:

X: $600 a unit, total of $6,000, 2/10, n/30, plus transportation costs of $375.
Y: $630 a unit, total of $6,300, 1/10, n/30, no charge for transportation.

Which of the two offers, X or Y, yields the lower price?

EXERCISE 6–14
Purchase-related transactions
Objective 2

The debits and credits from four related transactions are presented in the following T accounts. Describe each transaction. Is this firm using a perpetual or a periodic inventory system?

Cash			Accounts Payable			
(2)	200	(3)	1,000	(1)	6,000
(4)	4,900	(4)	5,000		

Inventory			
(1)	6,000	(3)	1,000
(2)	200	(4)	100

EXERCISE 6–15
Purchase-related transactions
Objective 2

Madeline Co., a women's clothing store, purchased $12,000 of goods from a supplier on account, terms FOB destination, 2/10, n/30. Madeline Co. returned $2,500 of the goods, receiving a credit memorandum, and then paid the amount due within the discount period. Journalize Madeline Co.'s entries in a two-column general journal to record (a) the purchase, (b) the goods return, and (c) the payment. Assume a perpetual inventory system.

EXERCISE 6–16
Purchase-related transactions
Objective 2

Journalize, in a two-column general journal, entries for the following related transactions of Restoration Company under (1) a perpetual system and (2) a periodic system.

a. Purchased $20,000 of goods from Veneer Co. on account, terms 2/10, n/30.
b. Paid the amount owed on the invoice within the discount period.
c. Discovered that $5,000 of the goods were defective and returned items, receiving credit.
d. Purchased $4,000 of goods from Veneer Co. on account, terms 2/10, n/30.
e. Received a cheque for the balance owed from the return in (c), after deducting for the purchase in (d).

EXERCISE 6–17
Purchase-related transactions
Objectives 2, 3

Based on the data presented in Exercise 6-10, journalize, in a two-column general journal, Westbury Co.'s entries for (a) the purchase, (b) the return of the goods for credit, and (c) the payment of the invoice within the discount period. Assume Westbury uses a periodic system. How would your entries have differed under a perpetual system?

EXERCISE 6–18
Normal balances of merchandise accounts
Objective 2

What is the normal balance of the following accounts: (a) Sales Returns and Allowances, (b) Inventory, (c) Sales Discounts, (d) Transportation-out, (e) Sales, (f) Cost of Goods Sold, (g) Purchase Discounts, (h) Purchase Returns and Allowances?

EXERCISE 6–19
Purchases-related transactions—periodic inventory system
Objective 2

Journalize entries for the following related transactions, assuming the Sports "R" Us Co. uses the periodic inventory system.

a. Purchased $10,000 of goods from Nikon Co. on account, terms 2/10, n/30.
b. Discovered that some of the goods were defective and returned items with an invoice price of $1,000, receiving credit.
c. Paid the amount owed on the invoice within the discount period.
d. Purchased $6,000 of goods from Shick Co. on account, terms 1/10, n/30.
e. Paid the amount owed on the invoice within the discount period.

EXERCISE 6–20
Sales-related transactions—
periodic inventory system
Objective 2

Journalize entries for the following related transactions, assuming that Suzuki Company uses the periodic inventory system.

Mar. 8 Sold goods to a customer for $12,000, terms FOB shipping point, 2/10, n/30.
      8 Paid the transportation charges of $230, debiting the amounts to Accounts Receivable.
     12 Issued a credit memorandum for $1,800 to a customer for goods returned.
     18 Received a cheque for the amount due from the sale.

EXERCISE 6–21
Chart of accounts
Objective 4

Las Posas Co. is a newly organized business with the following list of accounts, arranged in alphabetical order:

Accounts Payable
Accounts Receivable
Accumulated Amortization—Office Equipment
Accumulated Amortization—Store Equipment
Advertising Expense
A. E. Carmen, Capital
A. E. Carmen, Withdrawals
Cash
Cost of Goods Sold
Amortization Expense—Office Equipment
Amortization Expense—Store Equipment
Income Summary
Insurance Expense
Interest Expense
Interest Income
Interest Receivable
Inventory
Land
Miscellaneous Administrative Expense
Miscellaneous Selling Expense
Notes Payable (short-term)
Notes Receivable (short-term)
Office Equipment
Office Salaries Expense
Office Supplies
Office Supplies Expense
Prepaid Insurance
Rent Expense
Salaries Payable
Sales
Sales Discounts
Sales Returns and Allowances
Sales Salaries Expense
Store Equipment
Store Supplies
Store Supplies Expense

Construct a chart of accounts, assigning account numbers and arranging the accounts in balance sheet and income statement order, as illustrated in Exhibit 6. Each account number is to comprise three digits: the first digit is to indicate the major classification ("1" for assets, and so on); the second digit is to indicate the subclassification ("11" for current assets, and so on); and the third digit is to identify the specific account ("110" for Cash, and so on).

EXERCISE 6–22
Income statement for
merchandiser
Objective 5

For the fiscal year, sales were $1,230,000, sales discounts were $20,100, sales returns and allowances were $60,000, and the cost of goods sold was $825,000. What was the amount of net sales and gross profit?

EXERCISE 6–23
Determining amounts for items omitted from income statement
Objective 5

Two items are omitted in each of the following four lists of income statement data. Determine the amounts of the missing items, identifying them by letter.

Sales	$ (a)	$600,000	$800,000	$757,500
Sales returns and allowances	12,000	17,000	(e)	30,500
Sales discounts	5,000	8,000	10,000	(g)
Net sales	250,000	(c)	765,000	(h)
Cost of goods sold	150,000	345,000	(f)	540,000
Gross profit	(b)	(d)	300,000	170,000

EXERCISE 6–24
Multiple-step income statement
Objective 5

How many errors can you find in the following income statement?

Enclosures Company
Income Statement
For the Year Ended December 31, 20—

Revenue from sales:			
Sales			$1,000,000
Add: Sales returns and allowances		$18,000	
Sales discounts		4,500	22,500
Gross sales			$1,022,500
Cost of goods sold			495,000
Income from operations			$ 527,500
Operating expenses:			
Selling expenses		$ 145,000	
Transportation on merchandise sold		5,300	
Administrative expenses		87,200	
Total operating expenses			237,500
Gross profit			$ 290,000
Other expense:			
Interest expense			27,500
Net loss			$ 262,500

EXERCISE 6–25
Single-step income statement
Objective 5

Summary operating data for Orthodontics Company during the current year ended April 30, 1999, are as follows: cost of goods sold, $825,000; administrative expenses, $125,000; interest expense, $17,500; rent income, $30,000; net sales, $1,600,000; and selling expenses, $200,000. Prepare a single-step income statement.

EXERCISE 6–26
Multiple-step income
Objectives 5, 6

At the end of the year, selected accounts and related amounts appearing in the ledger of Carriage Company, a furniture wholesaler, are listed in alphabetical order as follows:

Administrative Expenses	$ 74,500
Building	512,500
Cash	48,500
Cost of Goods Sold	636,300
J. I. Ford, Capital	$180,000
J. I. Ford, Withdrawals	15,000
Interest Expense	7,500
Inventory	130,000
Notes Payable	25,000
Office Supplies	10,600
Salaries Payable	3,220
Sales	975,000
Sales Discounts	10,200
Sales Returns and Allowances	24,300
Selling Expenses	132,700
Store Supplies	7,700

All selling expenses have been recorded in the account entitled *Selling Expenses,* and all administrative expenses have been recorded in the account entitled *Administrative Expenses.*

a. Prepare a multiple-step income statement for the year ended December 31.
b. ▬▬▶ Compare the major advantages and disadvantages of the multiple-step and single-step forms of income statements.

EXERCISE 6–27
Adjusting entries for inventory—periodic inventory system
Objective 3

Data assembled for preparing the work sheet for T. C. Hardy's Co. for the fiscal year ended December 31, 2000, included the following:

Purchases	$900,000
Inventory as of January 1, 2000	155,000
Inventory as of December 31, 2000	187,500

Journalize the adjusting entry for inventory that would appear on the work sheet, assuming that the periodic inventory system is used.

EXERCISE 6–28
Identification of missing items from income statement— periodic inventory system
Objective 5

For (a) through (i), identify the items designated by "X".

a. Sales – (X + X) = Net sales
b. Purchases – (X + X) = Net purchases
c. Net purchases + X = Cost of goods purchased
d. Inventory (beginning) + cost of goods purchased = X
e. Goods available for sale – X = Cost of goods sold
f. Net sales – cost of goods sold = X
g. X + X = Operating expenses
h. Gross profit – operating expenses = X
i. Income from operations + X – X = Net income

EXERCISE 6–29
Multiple-step income statement—periodic inventory system
Objective 5

Selected data for Cabinet Company for the current year ended December 31 are as follows:

Inventory, January 1	$ 45,000
Inventory, December 31	67,500
Purchases	662,000
Purchases discounts	8,000
Purchases returns and allowances	15,500
Sales	805,000
Sales discounts	6,500
Sales returns and allowances	8,700
Transportation-in	22,500

Prepare a multiple-step income statement through gross profit for Cabinet Company for the current year ended December 31.

EXERCISE 6–30
Adjusting and closing entries—periodic inventory system
Appendix B

Selected account titles and related amounts appearing in the Income Statement and Balance Sheet columns of the work sheet of Las Posas Company for the year ended December 31 are listed in alphabetical order as follows:

Administrative Expenses	$ 69,500
Building	312,500
Cash	58,500
Interest Expense	2,500
J. Sanchez, Capital	472,580
J. Sanchez, Withdrawals	45,000
Inventory (1/1)	325,000
Inventory (12/31)	280,000
Notes Payable	25,000

Office Supplies	$ 10,600
Purchases	750,000
Purchases Discounts	6,000
Purchases Returns and Allowances	7,000
Salaries Payable	4,220
Sales	1,375,000
Sales Discounts	10,200
Sales Returns and Allowances	44,300
Selling Expenses	232,700
Store Supplies	7,700
Transportation-In	21,300

All selling expenses have been recorded in the account entitled Selling Expenses, and all administrative expenses have been recorded in the account entitled Administrative Expenses. Assuming that Las Posas Company uses the periodic inventory system, journalize the adjusting entries for inventory and the closing entries.

EXERCISE 6–31
Adjusting entry for inventory shrinkage
Objective 6

Wilkes Inc. perpetual inventory records indicate that $129,500 of merchandise should be on hand on December 31, 1999. The physical inventory indicates that $127,300 of merchandise is actually on hand. Journalize, in a two-column general journal, the adjusting entry for the inventory shrinkage for Wilkes Inc. for the year ended December 31, 1999.

EXERCISE 6–32
Closing the accounts of a merchandiser
Objective 6

From the following list, identify the accounts that should be closed to Income Summary at the end of the fiscal year: (a) Accounts Receivable, (b) Cost of Goods Sold, (c) Inventory, (d) Sales, (e) Sales Discounts, (f) Sales Returns and Allowances, (g) Supplies, (h) Supplies Expense, (i) Salaries Expense, (j) Salaries Payable, (k) Accumulated Amortization, (l) Purchases.

EXERCISE 6–33
Closing entries

Based on the data presented in Exercise 6–26, journalize the closing entries in a two-column general journal.

EXERCISE 6–34
Net method of accounting for sales
Appendix

Singh Retailing sells goods on terms 3/10, n/30. On January 1, 2000 Singh sold goods on account to Indira Company for $12,000 and goods on account to Kipling Company for $20,000. Indira paid its invoice on January 10 and Kipling paid its account on January 30. Prepare all entries for Singh to account for these sales and collections under:

a. the gross method
b. the net method

EXERCISE 6–35
Net method of accounting for purchases
Appendix

Using the information in Exercise 6–34 above, and assuming that Indira and Kipling both use a perpetual inventory system:

a. Record the purchase and payment for Indira under (i) the gross method and (ii) the net method.
b. Record the purchase and payment for Kipling under i) the gross method and (ii) the net method.
c. Explain which method, net or gross, is theoretically preferable, and why.

PROBLEMS SERIES A

PROBLEM 6–1A
Purchase-related transactions
Objective 2

The following selected transactions were completed by Bizcomp Company during March of the current year:

Mar. 1. Purchased goods from Kohl Co., $6,100, terms FOB destination, n/30.
       4. Purchased goods from Laufer Co., $8,000, terms FOB shipping point, 2/10, n/eom. Prepaid transportation costs of $150 were added to the invoice.

5. Purchased goods from Faber Co., $5,000, terms FOB destination, 2/10, n/30.
8. Issued debit memorandum to Faber Co. for $1,000 of goods returned from purchase on March 5.
14. Paid Laufer Co. for invoice of March 4.
15. Paid Faber Co. for purchase of March 5.
19. Purchased goods from Porcelain Co., $6,250, terms FOB shipping point, n/eom.
19. Paid transportation charges of $120 on March 19 purchase from Porcelain Co.
20. Purchased goods from Hatcher Co., $3,500, terms FOB destination, 1/10, n/30.
30. Paid Hatcher Co. for invoice of March 20.
31. Paid Kohl Co. for invoice of March 1.
31. Paid Porcelain Co. for invoice of March 19.

Instructions

Journalize, in a two-column general journal, the entries to record the transactions of Bizcomp Company for March. Assume that the company uses

(1) a perpetual inventory system.
(2) a periodic inventory system.

PROBLEM 6–2A
Sales-related transactions
Objective 2

The following selected transactions were completed by Mallory Supply Co. Mallory Supply Co. sells office supplies primarily to wholesalers but occasionally sells to retail customers.

Oct. 1. Sold goods on account to Beckman Co., $4,200, terms FOB destination, 2/10, n/30. The cost of the goods sold was $2,400.
1. Paid transportation costs of $125 on goods sold on October 1.
2. Sold goods for $620 plus 5% sales tax to cash customers. The cost of goods sold was $350.
4. Sold goods on account to Atlas Co., $2,400, terms FOB shipping point, n/eom. The cost of goods sold was $1,800.
5. Sold goods for $1,400 plus 5% sales tax to customers who used MasterCard. Deposited credit card receipts into the bank. The cost of goods sold was $750.
9. Sold goods on account to Atlas Co., $1,450, terms FOB shipping point, n/eom. The cost of goods sold was $900.
11. Received cheque for amount due from Beckman Co. for sale on October 1.
14. Sold goods to customers who used American Express cards, $3,600. The cost of goods sold was $2,100.
15. Sold goods on account to Monroe Co., $6,500, terms FOB shipping point, 1/10, n/30. The cost of goods sold was $3,900.
17. Issued credit memorandum for $500 to Monroe Co. for goods returned from sale on October 15. The cost of the goods returned was $300.
17. Sold goods on account to Davis Co., $10,000, terms FOB destination, 2/15, n/30. The cost of goods sold was $6,000.
18. Sold goods on account to Braggs Co., $7,500, terms FOB shipping point, 1/10, n/30. Added $85 to the invoice for transportation costs prepaid. The cost of goods sold was $4,500.
25. Received cheque for amount due from Monroe Co. for sale on October 15.
26. Issued credit memorandum for $250 to Davis Co. for allowance for damaged goods sold on October 17.
26. Received $9,410 from American Express for $10,000 of sales reported during the week of October 11-17.
28. Received cheque for amount due from Braggs Co. for sale of October 18.
31. Received cheque for amount due from Atlas Co. for sales of October 4 and October 9.
31. Paid Fast Delivery Service $770 for merchandise delivered during October to local customers under shipping terms of FOB destination.
Nov. 4. Paid National Bank $480 for service fees for handling MasterCard sales during October.
10. Paid $875 to provincial sales tax division for taxes owed on October sales.
16. Received cheque for amount due from Davis Co. for sale of October 17, less credit memorandum of October 26.

Instructions

Journalize, in a two-column general journal, the entries to record the transactions of Mallory Supply Co. Assume a perpetual inventory system.

PROBLEM 6–3A

Sales-related and purchase-related transactions
Objective 2

The following were selected from among the transactions completed by The Accessories Company during April of the current year:

Apr. 3. Purchased office supplies for cash, $320.

4. Purchased goods on account from Anchor Co., list price $15,000, trade discount 40%, terms FOB destination, 2/10, n/30.

5. Sold goods for cash, $3,950. The cost of the goods sold was $2,450.

7. Purchased goods on account from Mattox Co., $6,400, terms FOB shipping point, 2/10, n/30, with prepaid transportation costs of $190 added to the invoice.

7. Returned $2,500 of goods purchased on April 4 from Anchor Co.

11. Sold goods on account to Bowles Co., list price $2,250, trade discount 20%, terms 1/10, n/30. The cost of the goods sold was $880.

14. Paid Anchor Co. on account for purchase of April 4.

15. Sold goods on nonbank credit cards and reported accounts to the card company, $5,850. The cost of the goods sold was $3,900.

17. Paid Mattox Co. on account for purchase of April 7.

20. Purchased goods for cash, $6,500.

21. Received cash on account from sale of April 11 to Bowles Co.

25. Sold goods on account to Clemons Co., $3,200, terms 1/10, n/30. The cost of the goods sold was $2,025.

28. Received a cheque from card company for nonbank credit card sales of April 15, less $280 service fee.

30. Received goods returned by Clemons Co. from sale on April 25, $1,700. The cost of the returned goods was $810.

Instructions

Journalize the transactions in a two-column general journal. Assume a perpetual inventory system.

PROBLEM 6–4A

Sales-related and purchase-related transactions for seller and buyer
Objectives 2, 3

The following selected transactions were completed during July between Spivey Company and C. K. Barker Co.:

July 3. Spivey Company sold goods on account to C. K. Barker Co., $9,500, terms FOB destination, 2/15, n/eom. The cost of the goods sold was $6,000.

3. Spivey Company paid transportation costs of $400 for delivery of goods sold to C. K. Barker Co. on July 3.

10. Spivey Company sold goods on account to C. K. Barker Co., $12,000, terms FOB shipping point, n/eom. The cost of the goods sold was $9,000.

11. C. K. Barker Co. returned $2,000 of goods purchased on account on July 3 from Spivey Company. The cost of the goods returned was $1,200.

14. C. K. Barker Co. paid transportation charges of $200 on July 10 purchase from Spivey Company.

17. Spivey Company sold goods on account to C. K. Barker Co., $18,000, terms FOB shipping point, 1/10, n/30. Spivey Company paid transportation costs of $1,500, which were added to the invoice. The cost of the goods sold was $10,800.

18. C. K. Barker Co. paid Spivey Company for purchase of July 3.

27. C. K. Barker Co. paid Spivey Company on account for purchase of July 17.

31. C. K. Barker Co. paid Spivey Company on account for purchase of July 10.

Instructions

Journalize, in a two-column general journal, the July transactions for (1) Spivey Company and (2) C. K. Barker Co. Assume a perpetual system.

PROBLEM 6–5A

Sales-related and purchase-related transactions—periodic inventory system
Objectives 2, 3

The following were selected from among the transactions completed by The Accessories Company during April of the current year:

Apr. 3. Purchased office supplies for cash, $320.
4. Purchased goods on account from Anchor Co., list price $15,000, trade discount 40%, terms FOB destination, 2/10, n/30.
5. Sold goods for cash, $3,950.
7. Purchased goods on account from Mattox Co., $6,400, terms FOB shipping point, 2/10, n/30, with prepaid transportation costs of $190 added to the invoice.
7. Returned goods purchased on April 4 from Anchor Co., $2,500.
11. Sold goods on account to Bowles Co., list price $2,250, trade discount 20%, terms 1/10, n/30.
14. Paid Anchor Co. on account for purchase of April 4.
15. Sold goods on nonbank credit cards and reported accounts to the card company, $5,850.
17. Paid Mattox Co. on account for purchase of April 7.
20. Purchased goods for cash, $6,500.
21. Received payment on account from sale of April 11 to Bowles Co.
25. Sold goods on account to Clemons Co., $3,200, terms 1/10, n/30.
28. Received a cheque from card company for nonbank credit card sales of April 15, less $280 service fee.
30. Received goods returned by Clemons Co. from sale on April 25, $1,700.

Instructions

Journalize the transactions for The Accessories Co. in a two-column general journal. Assume a periodic inventory system.

PROBLEM 6–6A

Sales-related and purchase-related transactions for seller and buyer—periodic inventory system
Objectives 2, 3

Using the data in Problem 6–4A, journalize the July transactions for (1) Spivey Company and for (2) C. K. Barker Co. Assume a periodic inventory system.

PROBLEM 6–7A

Multiple-step income statement and report form of balance sheet
Objectives 5, 6

The following selected accounts and their normal balances appear in the ledger of The Attache Co. for the fiscal year ended March 31, 1999:

Cash	$ 18,000
Notes Receivable (short-term)	120,000
Accounts Receivable	92,000
Inventory	100,000
Office Supplies	5,600
Prepaid Insurance	3,400
Office Equipment	55,000
Accumulated Amortization—Office Equipment	12,800
Store Equipment	113,000
Accumulated Amortization—Store Equipment	24,200
Accounts Payable	45,600
Salaries Payable	2,400
Note Payable (final payment due 2012)	56,000
J. Hartmann, Capital	291,000
J. Hartmann, Withdrawals	15,000
Sales	1,400,000
Sales Returns and Allowances	12,100
Sales Discounts	11,900
Cost of Goods Sold	1,050,000
Sales Salaries Expense	113,200
Advertising Expense	32,800
Amortization Expense—Store Equipment	6,400

Miscellaneous Selling Expense	$ 1,600
Office Salaries Expense	51,150
Rent Expense	16,350
Amortization Expense—Office Equipment	12,700
Insurance Expense	3,900
Office Supplies Expense	1,300
Miscellaneous Administrative Expense	1,600
Interest Income	11,000
Interest Expense	6,000

Instructions

1. Prepare a multiple-step income statement.
2. Prepare a statement of owner's equity.
3. Prepare a report form of balance sheet, assuming that the current portion of the note payable is $15,000.
4. ━━━▶ Briefly explain (a) how multiple-step and single-step income statements differ and (b) how report-form and account-form balance sheets differ.

PROBLEM 6–8A
Single-step income statement and account form of balance sheet
Objectives 5, 6

Selected accounts and related amounts for The Attache Co. for the fiscal year ended March 31, 1999, are presented in Problem 6–7A.

Instructions

1. Prepare a single-step income statement in the format shown in Exhibit 9.
2. Prepare a statement of owner's equity.
3. Prepare an account form of balance sheet, assuming that the current portion of the note payable is $15,000.

PROBLEM 6–9A
Work sheet, financial statements, and adjusting and closing entries

The accounts and their balances in the ledger of The Bag Co. on December 31 of the current year are as follows:

Cash	$ 38,175
Accounts Receivable	112,500
Inventory	230,000
Prepaid Insurance	9,700
Store Supplies	4,250
Office Supplies	2,100
Store Equipment	132,000
Accumulated Amortization—Store Equipment	40,300
Office Equipment	50,000
Accumulated Amortization—Office Equipment	17,200
Accounts Payable	66,700
Salaries Payable	—
Unearned Rent	1,200
Note Payable (final payment due 2008)	105,000
C. Tote, Capital	175,510
C. Tote, Withdrawals	40,000
Income Summary	—
Sales	895,000
Sales Returns and Allowances	11,900
Sales Discounts	7,100
Cost of Goods Sold	476,200
Sales Salaries Expense	76,400
Advertising Expense	25,000
Amortization Expense—Store Equipment	—
Store Supplies Expense	—
Miscellaneous Selling Expense	1,335
Office Salaries Expense	44,000
Rent Expense	26,000
Insurance Expense	—

Amortization Expense—Office Equipment		—
Office Supplies Expense		—
Miscellaneous Administrative Expense		1,650
Rent Income		—
Interest Expense		12,600

The data needed for year-end adjustments on December 31 are as follows:

Physical inventory on December 31		$220,000
Insurance expired during the year		6,260
Supplies on hand on December 31:		
Store supplies		1,300
Office supplies		750
Amortization for the year:		
Store equipment		7,500
Office equipment		3,800
Salaries payable on December 31:		
Sales salaries	$3,750	
Office salaries	1,150	4,900
Unearned rent on December 31		400

Instructions

1. Prepare a work sheet for the fiscal year ended December 31. List all accounts in the order given.
2. Prepare a multiple-step income statement.
3. Prepare a statement of owner's equity.
4. Prepare a report form of balance sheet, assuming that the current portion of the note payable is $15,000.
5. Journalize the adjusting entries.
6. Journalize the closing entries.

PROBLEMS SERIES B

EXERCISE 6–1B
Purchase-related transactions
Objective 2

The following selected transactions were completed by Babcock Co. during August of the current year:

Aug. 1. Purchased goods from Pickron Co., $7,750, terms FOB destination, n/30.
     4. Purchased goods from Jones Co., $8,000, terms FOB shipping point, 2/10, n/eom. Prepaid transportation costs of $150 were added to the invoice.
     5. Purchased goods from Rice Co., $5,000, terms FOB destination, 1/10, n/30.
     7. Issued debit memorandum to Rice Co. for $1,000 of goods returned from purchase on August 5.
    14. Paid Jones Co. for invoice of August 4, less discount.
    15. Paid Rice Co. for purchase of August 5.
    18. Purchased goods from Robbins Company, $7,250, terms FOB shipping point, n/eom.
    18. Paid transportation charges of $120 on August 18 purchase from Robbins Company.
    19. Purchased goods from Hatcher Co., $7,500, terms FOB destination, 2/10, n/30.
    29. Paid Hatcher Co. for invoice of August 19.
    31. Paid Pickron Co. for invoice of August 1.
    31. Paid Robbins Company for invoice of August 18.

Instructions

Journalize, in a two-column general journal, the entries to record the transactions of Babcock Co. for August under

(1) a perpetual inventory system
(2) a periodic inventory system

PROBLEM 6–2B
Sales-related transactions
Objective 2

The following selected transactions were completed by Acoustical Supplies Co., which sells electrical supplies primarily to wholesalers but occasionally sells to retail customers.

May 1. Sold goods on account to Boyd Company, $15,000, terms FOB destination, 1/10, n/30. The cost of goods sold was $9,200.

1. Paid transportation costs of $155 on goods sold on May 1.

2. Sold goods for $1,800 plus 6% sales tax to cash customers. The cost of goods sold was $950.

3. Sold goods on account to Cramer Co., $2,500, terms FOB shipping point, n/eom. The cost of goods sold was $1,300.

7. Sold goods for $1,150 plus 6% sales tax to customers who used VISA Cards. Deposited credit card receipts into the bank. The cost of goods sold was $800.

9. Sold goods on account to Cramer Co., $3,500, terms FOB shipping point, n/eom. The cost of goods sold was $2,700.

11. Received cheque for amount due from Boyd Company for sale on May 1.

13. Sold goods to customers who used American Express cards, $4,500. The cost of goods sold was $2,600.

14. Sold goods on account to Monroe Co., $6,500, terms FOB shipping point, 1/10, n/30. The cost of goods sold was $4,000.

16. Issued credit memorandum for $500 to Monroe Co. for goods returned from sale on May 13. The cost of the goods returned was $360.

16. Sold goods on account to Lester Co., $5,400, terms FOB destination, 2/15, n/30. The cost of goods sold was $3,000.

18. Sold goods on account to Stockton Company, $7,500, terms FOB shipping point, 1/10, n/30. Paid $110 for transportation costs and added them to the invoice. The cost of goods sold was $5,000.

24. Received cheque for amount due from Monroe Co. for sale on May 14.

24. Issued credit memorandum for $850 to Lester Co. for allowance for damaged goods sold on May 16.

27. Received $7,680 from American Express for $8,000 of sales reported during the week of May 12–18.

28. Received cheque for amount due from Stockton Company for sale of May 18.

30. Received cheque for amount due from Cramer Co. for sales of May 3 and May 9.

31. Paid Anywhere Delivery Service $1,050 for goods delivered during May to local customers under shipping terms of FOB destination.

June 3. Paid National Bank $425 for service fees for handling MasterCard sales during May.

10. Paid $580 to provincial sales tax division for taxes owed on May sales.

15. Received cheque for amount due from Lester Co. for sale of May 16, less credit memorandum of May 24.

Instructions

Journalize, in a two-column general journal, the entries to record the transactions of Acoustical Supplies Co.

PROBLEM 6–3B
Sales-related and purchase-related transactions
Objective 2

The following were selected from among the transactions completed by Stevens Company during March of the current year:

Mar. 2. Purchased goods on account from Doyle Co., list price $15,000, trade discount 20%, terms FOB shipping point, 2/10, n/30, with prepaid transportation costs of $720 added to the invoice.

4. Purchased goods on account from Annex Co., $6,000, terms FOB destination, 1/10, n/30.

6. Sold goods on account to C. F. Howell Co., list price $4,000, trade discount 30%, terms 2/10, n/30. The cost of the goods sold was $1,125.

7. Purchased office supplies for cash, $350.

9. Returned $1,300 of goods purchased on March 4 from Annex Co.

12. Paid Doyle Co. on account for purchase of March 2, less discount.

13. Purchased goods for cash, $18,000.

14. Paid Annex Co. on account for purchase of March 4.

Mar. 16. Received a cheque on account from sale of Mar. 6 to C. F. Howell Co.
　　19. Sold goods on nonbank credit cards and reported accounts to the card company, $3,450. The cost of the goods sold was $1,950.
　　22. Sold goods on account to Comer Co., $3,480, terms 2/10, n/30. The cost of the goods sold was $1,400.
　　24. Sold goods for cash, $4,350. The cost of the goods sold was $1,750.
　　25. Received goods returned by Comer Co. from sale on March 22, $1,480. The cost of the returned goods was $600.
　　31. Received a cheque from card company for nonbank credit card sales of March 19, less $340 service fee.

Instructions

Journalize the transactions in a two-column general journal. Assume a perpetual system.

PROBLEM 6–4B
Sales-related and purchase-related transactions for seller and buyer
Objectives 2, 3

The following selected transactions were completed during November between Selby Company and Bristol Company:

Nov. 3. Selby Company sold goods on account to Bristol Company, $10,500, terms FOB shipping point, 2/10, n/30. Selby Company paid transportation costs of $600, which were added to the invoice. The cost of the goods sold was $7,500.
　　8. Selby Company sold goods on account to Bristol Company, $12,000, terms FOB destination, 1/15, n/eom. The cost of the goods sold was $9,500.
　　8. Selby Company paid transportation costs of $650 for delivery of goods sold to Bristol Company on November 8.
　　12. Bristol Company returned $4,000 of goods purchased on account on November 8 from Selby Company. The cost of the goods returned was $2,500.
　　13. Bristol Company paid Selby Company for purchase of November 3.
　　23. Bristol Company paid Selby Company for purchase of November 8.
　　24. Selby Company sold goods on account to Bristol Company, $6,000, terms FOB shipping point, n/eom. The cost of the goods sold was $4,000.
　　27. Bristol Company paid transportation charges of $150 on November 24 purchase from Selby Company.
　　30. Bristol Company paid Selby Company on account for purchase of November 24.

Instructions

Journalize, in a two-column general journal, the November transactions for (1) Selby Company and (2) Bristol Company. Assume a perpetual system.

PROBLEM 6–5B
Sales-related and purchase-related transactions—periodic inventory system
Objectives 2, 3

The following were selected from among the transactions completed by Stevens Company during March of the current year:

Mar. 2. Purchased goods on account from Doyle Co., list price $15,000, trade discount 20%, terms FOB shipping point, 2/10, n/30, with prepaid transportation costs of $720 added to the invoice.
　　4. Purchased goods on account from Annex Co., $6,000, terms FOB destination, 1/10, n/30.
　　6. Sold goods on account to C. F. Howell Co., list price $4,000, trade discount 30%, terms 2/10, n/30.
　　7. Purchased office supplies for cash, $350.
　　9. Returned goods purchased on March 4 from Annex Co., $1,300.
　　12. Paid Doyle Co. on account for purchase of March 2.
　　13. Purchased goods for cash, $18,000.
　　14. Paid Annex Co. on account for purchase of March 4.
　　16. Received payment on account from sale of March 6 to C. F. Howell Co.
　　19. Sold goods on nonbank credit cards and reported accounts to the card company, $3,450.
　　22. Sold goods on account to Comer Co., $3,480, terms 2/10, n/30.
　　24. Sold goods for cash, $4,350.

Mar. 25. Received goods returned by Comer Co. from sale on March 22, $1,480.
   31. Received a cheque from card company for nonbank credit card sales of March 19, less $340 service fee.

Instructions

Journalize the transactions for Stevens Co. in a two-column general journal. Assume a periodic inventory system.

PROBLEM 6–6B
Multiple-step income statement and report form of balance sheet
Objectives 5, 6

The following selected accounts and their normal balances appear in the ledger of Renwick Co. for the fiscal year ended June 30, 1999:

Cash	$ 38,000
Notes Receivable	50,000
Accounts Receivable	62,000
Inventory	100,000
Office Supplies	1,600
Prepaid Insurance	6,800
Office Equipment	54,000
Accumulated Amortization—Office Equipment	10,800
Store Equipment	107,500
Accumulated Amortization—Store Equipment	48,900
Accounts Payable	27,000
Salaries Payable	1,700
Note Payable (final payment due 2010)	30,000
J. Lucas, Capital	194,010
J. Lucas, Withdrawals	15,000
Sales	1,257,000
Sales Returns and Allowances	19,000
Sales Discounts	8,500
Cost of Goods Sold	870,300
Sales Salaries Expense	108,000
Advertising Expense	28,300
Amortization Expense—Store Equipment	4,600
Miscellaneous Selling Expense	1,000
Office Salaries Expense	50,900
Rent Expense	22,150
Insurance Expense	12,750
Amortization Expense—Office Equipment	8,700
Office Supplies Expense	900
Miscellaneous Administrative Expense	1,150
Interest Income	5,400
Interest Expense	3,660

Instructions

1. Prepare a multiple-step income statement.
2. Prepare a statement of owner's equity.
3. Prepare a report form of balance sheet, assuming that the current portion of the note payable is $5,000.
4. Briefly explain (a) how multiple-step and single-step income statements differ and (b) how report-form and account-form balance sheets differ.

PROBLEM 6–7B
Single-step income statement and account form of balance sheet
Objectives 5, 6

Selected accounts and related amounts for Renwick Co. for the fiscal year ended June 30, 1999, are presented in Problem 6–6B.

Instructions

1. Prepare a single-step income statement in the format shown in Exhibit 9.
2. Prepare a statement of owner's equity.
3. Prepare an account form of balance sheet, assuming that the current portion of the note payable is $5,000.

PROBLEM 6–8B
Work sheet, financial statements, and adjusting and closing entries

The accounts and their balances in the ledger of The Luggage Co. on December 31 of the current year are as follows:

Cash	$ 49,575
Accounts Receivable	116,100
Inventory	235,000
Prepaid Insurance	10,600
Store Supplies	3,750
Office Supplies	1,700
Store Equipment	125,000
Accumulated Amortization—Store Equipment	40,300
Office Equipment	62,000
Accumulated Amortization—Office Equipment	17,200
Accounts Payable	66,700
Salaries Payable	—
Unearned Rent	1,200
Note Payable (final payment due 2005)	105,000
J. Samsonite, Capital	220,510
J. Samsonite, Withdrawals	40,000
Income Summary	—
Sales	1,007,500
Sales Returns and Allowances	15,500
Sales Discounts	6,000
Cost of Goods Sold	571,200
Sales Salaries Expense	86,400
Advertising Expense	29,450
Amortization Expense—Store Equipment	—
Store Supplies Expense	—
Miscellaneous Selling Expense	1,885
Office Salaries Expense	60,000
Rent Expense	30,000
Insurance Expense	—
Amortization Expense—Office Equipment	—
Office Supplies Expense	—
Miscellaneous Administrative Expense	1,650
Rent Income	—
Interest Expense	12,600

The data needed for year-end adjustments on December 31 are as follows:

Physical inventory on December 31		$220,000
Insurance expired during the year		7,200
Supplies on hand on December 31:		
Store supplies		1,050
Office supplies		750
Amortization for the year:		
Store equipment		8,500
Office equipment		4,500
Salaries payable on December 31:		
Sales salaries	$3,250	
Office salaries	1,550	4,800
Unearned rent on December 31		400

Instructions

1. Prepare a work sheet for the fiscal year ended December 31. List all accounts in the order given.
2. Prepare a multiple-step income statement.
3. Prepare a statement of owner's equity.
4. Prepare a report form of balance sheet, assuming that the current portion of the note payable is $15,000.
5. Journalize the adjusting entries.
6. Journalize the closing entries.

PROBLEM 6–9B

Preparation of work sheet, financial statements, and adjusting and closing entries—periodic inventory system

The accounts and their balances in the ledger of The Bag Co. on December 31 of the current year are as follows:

Cash	$ 38,175
Accounts Receivable	112,500
Inventory	180,000
Prepaid Insurance	9,700
Store Supplies	4,250
Office Supplies	2,100
Store Equipment	132,000
Accumulated Amortization—Store Equipment	40,300
Office Equipment	50,000
Accumulated Amortization—Office Equipment	17,200
Accounts Payable	66,700
Salaries Payable	—
Unearned Rent	1,200
Note Payable (final payment, 2008)	105,000
C. Tote, Capital	175,510
C. Tote, Withdrawals	40,000
Income Summary	—
Sales	895,000
Sales Returns and Allowances	11,900
Sales Discounts	7,100
Cost of Goods Sold	—
Purchases	535,000
Purchases Returns and Allowances	10,100
Purchases Discounts	4,900
Transportation-In	6,200
Sales Salaries Expense	76,400
Advertising Expense	25,000
Amortization Expense—Store Equipment	—
Store Supplies Expense	—
Miscellaneous Selling Expense	1,335
Office Salaries Expense	44,000
Rent Expense	26,000
Insurance Expense	—
Amortization Expense—Office Equipment	—
Office Supplies Expense	—
Miscellaneous Administrative Expense	1,650
Rent Income	—
Interest Expense	12,600

The data needed for year-end adjustments on December 31 are as follows:

Inventory on December 31		$220,000
Insurance expired during the year		6,260
Supplies on hand on December 31:		
Store supplies		1,300
Office supplies		750
Amortization for the year:		
Store equipment		7,500
Office equipment		3,800
Salaries payable on December 31:		
Sales salaries	$3,750	
Office salaries	1,150	4,900
Unearned rent on December 31		400

Instructions

1. Prepare a work sheet for the fiscal year ended December 31, listing all accounts in the order given.
2. Prepare a multiple-step income statement.

3. Prepare a statement of owner's equity.
4. Prepare a report form of balance sheet, assuming that the current portion of the note payable is $15,000.
5. Journalize the adjusting entries.
6. Journalize the closing entries.

CHALLENGE PROBLEMS

PROBLEM CP6–1

The following is a random list of some of the accounts and their December 31, 2000 balances for Valdez Foods. Valdez uses a periodic inventory system and all account balances are normal.

Purchases	$320,000	Sales Revenue	$460,000
Interest Revenue	23,000	Wages Expense	45,000
Transportation-in	17,000	Purchase Discounts	31,000
Sales Returns & Allowances	35,000	Interest Expense	18,000
Freight-out	24,000	Sales Discounts	27,000
Insurance Expense	10,000	Purchase Returns & Allowances	46,000
J. Valdez, Capital	30,000	Utilities Expense	14,000
Amortization Expense	10,000	J. Valdez, Withdrawals	15,000
Rent Expense	6,000	Accumulated Amortization	20,000
Unearned Revenue	6,000		

The beginning and ending amounts for inventory are $58,000 and $65,000, respectively.

Instructions
1. Prepare all adjusting and closing entries required at December 31, 2000.
2. Prepare a multiple-step income statement in good form for the year ended December 31, 2000.
3. Suppose that Valdez had been using a perpetual system. How would the accounts have differed from those shown above? If some of the accounts shown above would not have appeared, what would have appeared instead? Give account name(s) and amount(s) where possible.

PROBLEM CP6–2

The following income statement has been prepared for Henry James Stores.

Henry James Stores
Income Statement
December 31, 1999

Sales		$150,000
Less: Trade discounts	$ 9,500	
Cash discounts	3,000	
Cost of goods sold	51,500	64,000
Net sales		86,000
Other revenue:		
Deposits from customers		5,000
Interest receivable		1,000
Total revenue		92,000
Expenses paid:		
Salaries	20,000	
Rent	1,800	
Sales returns	5,000	
Freight-in	2,200	
Accumulated amortization	20,000	
Dividends	13,000	62,000
Net gain		$ 30,000

Instructions

1. List all of the errors contained in this income statement.
2. Prepare a correct multi-step income statement for this firm.

PROBLEM CP6–3

The following transactions occurred during the month of January, 1999:

Jan. 1. Lapierre Enterprises sold on account 2,000 units of inventory costing $7 each at a selling price of $10 each plus 8% provincial sales tax and 7% GST, terms 2/10, n/30. Manny Merchandiser purchased 1,000 of these items and 1,000 were purchased by Ronnie Retailer. The items were shipped FOB shipping point. Freight charges of $100 were paid in cash by each purchaser when the goods were received.

3. Manny returned 20 items for credit. Whenever items are returned, the purchaser receives credit for any taxes paid on the initial purchase.

5. Ronnie returned 30 items for credit.

10. Manny paid off its account in full.

18. Manny returned 15 more items and Lapierre issued a cheque to Manny for the return.

31. Ronnie paid off its account in full.

31. Lapierre issued cheques to pay the sales tax and GST owing to the government.

Lapierre and Ronnie use the perpetual inventory method. Manny uses the periodic method.

Instructions

Prepare all journal entries required on the books of Lapierre, Ronnie, and Manny to record these transactions for January. Assume that discounts are based on the total invoice, tax included.

PROBLEM CP6–4

For each of the transactions listed below for Drew Diversified Stores, indicate the effect any errors on gross profit reported for the period and assets and liabilities reported at the end of the period. For each item indicate whether the transaction caused the item to be overstated (O) or understated (U) and by what amount. If the transaction did not misstate an item, indicate this by the letters NE. As an example, we have indicated the effects of the first transaction shown. Assume that Drew uses a periodic inventory system.

Error	Gross Profit	Total Assets	Total Liabilities
1. The bookkeeper forgot to report $2,000 amortization of office equipment.	NE	O by 2,000	NE
2. On Feb. 1 Drew recorded sales of $10,000 on account, terms 5/10, n/30. Drew debited Cash and credited Accounts Receivable for $9,500 received on Feb. 10.			
3. Drew made cash sales for $5,000 plus 8% sales tax and 7% GST. These were recorded by a debit to Cash and a credit to Sales of $5,750.			
4. Drew recorded $300 Transportation-in as Transportation-out.			
5. Drew recorded a $500 Purchase Discount as Other Revenue.			
6. When counting ending inventory, the manager forgot to include $6,000 in goods that were stored in a back room.			

COMPREHENSIVE PROBLEM 2

The Bike Co. is a merchandising business. The account balances for The Bike Co. as of May 1, 1999 (unless otherwise indicated) are as follows:

110	Cash	$ 29,160
111	Notes Receivable	—
112	Accounts Receivable	50,220
113	Interest Receivable	—
115	Inventory	123,900
116	Prepaid Insurance	3,750
117	Store Supplies	2,550
123	Store Equipment	54,300
124	Accumulated Amortization	12,600
210	Accounts Payable	38,500
211	Salaries Payable	—
310	F. R. Schwinn, Capital, June 1, 1998	173,270
311	F. R. Schwinn, Withdrawals	25,000
312	Income Summary	—
410	Sales	731,600
411	Sales Returns and Allowances	13,600
412	Sales Discounts	5,200
510	Cost of Goods Sold	497,540
520	Sales Salaries Expense	74,400
521	Advertising Expense	18,000
522	Amortization Expense	—
523	Store Supplies Expense	—
529	Miscellaneous Selling Expense	2,800
530	Office Salaries Expense	29,400
531	Rent Expense	24,500
532	Insurance Expense	—
539	Miscellaneous Administrative Expense	1,650
611	Interest Income	—

During May, the last month of the fiscal year, the following transactions were completed:

May 1. Paid rent for May, $2,400.
 1. Received a $10,000 note receivable from a customer on account.
 2. Purchased goods on account, terms 2/10, n/30, FOB shipping point, $25,000.
 3. Paid transportation charges on purchase of May 2, $750.
 4. Purchased goods on account, terms n/20, FOB destination, $18,200.
 5. Sold goods on account, terms 2/10, n/30, FOB shipping point, $8,500. The cost of the goods sold was $5,000.
 7. Received $16,900 cash from customers on account, no discount.
 10. Sold goods for cash, $18,300. The cost of the goods sold was $11,000.
 11. Paid $12,800 to creditors on account.
 12. Paid for goods purchased on May 2, less discount.
 13. Received goods returned on sale of May 5, $1,000. The cost of the goods returned was $600.
 14. Paid advertising expense for last half of May, $2,500.
 15. Received cash from sale of May 5, less return of May 13 and discount.
 18. Paid sales salaries of $1,500 and office salaries of $500.
 19. Purchased goods for cash, $7,400.
 19. Paid $13,150 to creditors on account.
 20. Sold goods on account, terms 1/10, n/30, FOB shipping point, $16,000. The cost of the goods sold was $9,600.
 21. For the convenience of the customer, paid shipping charges on sale of May 20, $600.

May 21. Received $30,380 cash from customers on account, after discounts of $620 had been deducted.

21. Purchased goods on account, terms 1/10, n/30, FOB destination, $15,000.

22. Paid for goods purchased on May 4.

24. Returned $3,000 of damaged goods purchased on May 21, receiving credit from the seller.

25. Refunded cash on sales made for cash, $750. The cost of the goods returned was $480.

27. Paid sales salaries of $1,200 and office salaries of $400.

28. Sold goods on account, terms 2/10, n/30, FOB shipping point, $25,700. The cost of the goods sold was $15,000.

29. Purchased store supplies for cash, $350.

30. Received cash from sale of May 20, less discount, plus transportation paid on May 21.

31. Paid for purchase of May 21, less return of May 24 and discount.

31. Sold goods on account, terms 2/10, n/30, FOB shipping point, $17,400. The cost of the goods sold was $10,000.

31. Purchased goods on account, terms 1/10, n/30, FOB destination, $15,700.

Instructions

1. Enter the balances of each of the accounts in the appropriate balance column of a four-column account. Write *Balance* in the item section, and place a check mark (✓) in the Posting Reference column. Assume a perpetual inventory system.
2. Journalize the transactions for May in a two-column general journal.
3. Journalize the adjusting entries, using the following adjustment data:

   a. Interest accrued on notes receivable
      on May 31 $ 100
   b. Inventory on May 31   145,000
   c. Insurance expired during the year   1,250
   d. Store supplies on hand on May 31   1,050
   e. Amortization for the current year   8,860
   f. Accrued salaries on May 31:
      Sales salaries $400
      Office salaries   140   540

4. Post the journal to the ledger, extending the month-end balances to the appropriate balance columns after all posting is completed.
5. Prepare a multiple-step income statement, a statement of owner's equity, and a report form of balance sheet.
6. Journalize and post the closing entries. Indicate closed accounts by inserting a line in both balance columns opposite the closing entry. Insert the new balance in the owner's capital account.
7. Prepare a post-closing trial balance.

CASES

CASE 6–1
Field Company
Purchases discounts

On March 1, 1999, Field Company, a garden retailer, purchased $5,000 of corn seed, terms 1/10, n/30, from Dynacorn Co. Even though the discount period had expired on March 15, 1999, Ed Farmer subtracted the discount of $50 when he processed the documents for payment.

◖▬▬▶ Discuss whether Ed Farmer behaved in an ethical manner by subtracting the discount, even though the discount period had expired.

CASE 6–2
The Home Store Co.
Purchases discounts and accounts payable

 The Home Store Co. is owned and operated by Julius Billups. The following is an excerpt from a conversation between Julius Billups and JoAnn Sims, the chief accountant for The Home Store.

Julius: JoAnn, I've got a question about this recent balance sheet.

JoAnn: Sure, what's your question?

Julius: Well, as you know, I'm applying for a bank loan to finance our new store in Kirksville, and I noticed that the accounts payable are listed as $750,000.

JoAnn: That's right. Approximately $720,000 of that represents amounts due our suppliers, and the remainder is miscellaneous payables to creditors for utilities, office equipment, supplies, etc.

Julius: That's what I thought. But as you know, we normally receive a 2% discount from our suppliers for earlier payment, and we always try to take the discount.

JoAnn: That's right. I can't remember the last time we missed a discount.

Julius: Well, in that case, it seems to me the accounts payable should be listed minus the 2% discount. Let's list the accounts payable due suppliers as $705,600, rather than $720,000. We can just debit accounts payable for $14,400 and plug the credit through other revenue. Every little bit helps. You never know. It might make the difference between getting the loan and not. Besides, the bank will never catch us on this.

➤ How would you respond to Julius Billups' request? Is his suggestion ethical?

CASE 6–3
Audio-Tec versus Powerhouse Electronics
Determining cost of purchase

The following is an excerpt from a conversation between Joe Hitachi and Kim Kenwood. Joe is debating whether to buy a stereo system from Audio-Tec, a locally owned electronics store, or Powerhouse Electronics, a mail-order electronics company.

Joe: Kim, I don't know what to do about buying my new stereo.

Kim: What's the problem?

Joe: Well, I can buy it locally at Audio-Tec for $689.95. However, Powerhouse Electronics has the same system listed for $699.99.

Kim: So what's the big deal? Buy it from Audio-Tec.

Joe: It's not quite that simple. Powerhouse said something about not having to pay sales tax, since I was out-of-province.

Kim: Yes, that's a good point. If you buy it at Audio-Tec, they'll charge you 8% sales tax.

Joe: But Powerhouse Electronics charges $15 for shipping and handling. If I have them send it next-day air, it'll cost an additional $20 for shipping and handling.

Kim: I guess it is a little confusing.

Joe: That's not all. Audio-Tec will give an additional 2% discount if I pay cash. Otherwise, they will let me use my MasterCard, or I can pay it off in three monthly installments.

Kim: Anything else???

Joe: Well...Powerhouse says I have to charge it on my MasterCard. They don't accept cheques.

Kim: I am not surprised. Many mail-order houses don't accept cheques.

Joe: I give up. What would you do?

1. Assuming that Powerhouse Electronics doesn't charge sales tax on the sale to Joe, which company is offering the best buy?

2. ➤ What might be some considerations other than price that might influence Joe's decision on where to buy the stereo system?

CASE 6–4
Sears Canada Inc.
Financial analysis

 Profitability refers to a business's ability to earn profits or net income. This ability depends on the efficiency of operations as well as the assets available to the business. Thus, profitability analysis focuses primarily on the relationship between the operating results (the income statement) and the assets used (the balance sheet).

One ratio that may be used to assess how effectively a firm uses its assets is computed as follows:

$$\text{Ratio of net sales to assets} = \frac{\text{Net sales}}{\text{Total assets}}$$

1. Using total assets at the end of each year, determine the ratio of net sales to total assets for Sears Canada Inc. for the current and preceding years.

2. ➤ What conclusions can be drawn from these ratios?

CASE 6–5
Escapade Video Company
Sales discounts

Your sister operates Escapade Video Company, a videotape distributorship that is in its third year of operation. The following income statement was recently prepared for the year ended October 31, 1999:

Escapade Video Company
Income Statement
For the Year Ended October 31, 1999

Revenues:		
Net sales		$450,000
Interest income		2,500
Total revenues		$452,500
Expenses:		
Cost of goods sold	$310,000	
Selling expenses	46,000	
Administrative expenses	24,000	
Interest expense	5,000	
Total expenses		385,000
Net income		$ 67,500

Your sister is considering a proposal to increase net income by offering sales discounts of 2/15, n/30, and by shipping all merchandise FOB shipping point. Currently, no sales discounts are allowed and goods are shipped FOB destination.

It is estimated that these credit terms will increase net sales by 10%. The ratio of the cost of goods sold to net sales is expected to be 70%. All selling and administrative expenses are expected to remain unchanged, except for store supplies, miscellaneous selling, office supplies, and miscellaneous administrative expenses, which are expected to increase proportionately with increased net sales. The amounts of these preceding items for the year ended October 31, 1999, were as follows:

Store supplies expense	$2,000
Miscellaneous selling expense	1,000
Office supplies expense	800
Miscellaneous administrative expense	1,500

The other income and other expense items will remain unchanged. The shipment of all goods FOB shipping point will eliminate all transportation-out expenses, which for the year ended October 31, 2000, were $18,000.

1. Prepare a projected single-step income statement for the year ending October 31, 2000, based on the proposal.
2. a. Based on the projected income statement in (1), would you recommend the implementation of the proposed changes?
   b. Describe any possible concerns you may have related to the proposed changes described in (1).

ANSWERS TO SELF-EXAMINATION QUESTIONS

1. **A** A debit memorandum (answer A), issued by the buyer, indicates the amount the buyer proposes to debit to the accounts payable account. A credit memorandum (answer B), issued by the seller, indicates the amount the seller proposes to credit to the accounts receivable account. An invoice (answer C) or a bill (answer D), issued by the seller, indicates the amount and terms of the sale.

2. **C** The amount of discount for early payment is $10 (answer C), or 1% of $1,000. Although the $50 of transportation costs paid by the seller is debited to the customer's account, the customer is not entitled to a discount on that amount.

3. **B** The single-step form of income statement (answer B) is so named because the total of all expenses is deducted in one step from the total of all revenues. The multiple-step form (answer A) includes numerous sections and subsections with several subtotals. The account form

(answer C) and the report form (answer D) are two common forms of the balance sheet.

4. **C** Gross profit (answer C) is the excess of net sales over the cost of goods sold. Operating income (answer A) or income from operations (answer B) is the excess of gross profit over operating expenses. Net income (answer D) is the final figure on the income statement after all revenues and expenses have been reported.

5. **D** Expenses such as interest expense (answer D) that cannot be associated directly with operations are identified as *Other expense* or *Nonoperating expense*. Amortization expense—office equipment (answer A) is an administrative expense. Sales salaries expense (answer B) is a selling expense. Insurance expense (answer C) is a mixed expense with elements of both selling expense and administrative expense. For small businesses, insurance expense is usually reported as an administrative expense.

PART THREE

Assets and Liabilities

7 Cash

YOU AND ACCOUNTING

When you receive the monthly statement for your chequing account, you may simply accept the bank statement as correct. However, banks can make mistakes. For example, at the bottom right-hand corner of each cheque returned from the bank is a magnetic coding that has been entered by a bank clerk. This coding indicates the amount of the cheque. If the clerk enters the coding incorrectly, then the cheque will be processed for a wrong amount. To illustrate, the following cheque written for $25 was incorrectly processed as $250:

Ed Smith	**7406**
495 Glengyle Ave.	
London, Ontario	7/23 19 98 64-7088/2611

PAY TO THE ORDER OF *C. Jones* .... $ 25 00/100

Twenty-Five Dollars and no/100 _____ DOLLARS

Bank of Montreal
1810 Dundas St. E.
London, Ontario

FOR _____   *Ed Smith*

⑆261170889⑆ 04 33 503662⑈ 7406 ⑈000002500⑈

We are all concerned about controlling our cash. Likewise, businesses need to control cash. Inadequate controls can and often do lead to theft, misappropriation, or otherwise embarrassing situations. For example, in one of the biggest errors in banking history, **Chemical Bank** in the United States incorrectly deducted customer automated teller machine (ATM) withdrawals twice from each customer's account. For instance, if a customer withdrew $100 from his or her account, the bank actually deducted $200 from the account balance. Before the error was discovered, Chemical Bank mistakenly deducted about $15 million from more than 100,000 customer accounts. The error was caused by inadequate controls over the changing of its computer programs. Chemical Bank corrected the error, but it was obviously quite embarrassed by it.[1]

Not only can banks make errors, but so can you. To detect such errors, both the bank and you should use control procedures. In a prior chapter, we described basic internal control concepts and procedures. In this chapter, we will apply these concepts to the control of cash. We begin by describing methods used by businesses to control cash receipts and cash payments. We then illustrate how to apply these methods. For example, we illustrate how businesses reconcile their monthly bank statements as a means of accounting for and controlling cash. You may want to use this illustration as a guide for reconciling your own bank statement to your record of your chequing account.

After studying this chapter, you should be able to:

Objective 1
Describe the nature of cash and the importance of internal control over cash.

Objective 2
Summarize basic procedures for achieving internal control over cash receipts, including the use of cash change funds and the cash short and over account.

Objective 3
Summarize basic procedures for achieving internal control over cash payments, including the use of a voucher system and a petty cash account.

Objective 4
Describe the nature of a bank account and its use in controlling cash.

Objective 5
Prepare a bank reconciliation and journalize any necessary entries.

Objective 6
Summarize how cash is presented on the balance sheet.

Objective 7
Define electronic funds transfers and give an example of how they are used to process cash transactions.

Nature of Cash and Importance of Controls Over Cash

Objective 1
Describe the nature of cash and the importance of internal control over cash.

Cash is the most liquid of all assets. By this we mean that cash can be used immediately to purchase other assets or services or to pay obligations. It takes varying length of time to employ other assets for these purposes. For example, suppose that we have a debt that is coming due. If we have sufficient cash on hand, we can pay it off immediately. If we do not have enough cash, but have receivables due to us, we might have to postpone paying our debt for a few weeks until we have had time to collect amounts owing from our customers. If our funds are tied up in inventory, it could take even longer until we could sell enough inventory to get the cash to pay our obligation. If we had to sell our building or equipment in order to raise the necessary cash, it might be a long time before we could pay off our debt. The **liquidity** of other assets is usually defined by how quickly the asset can be converted to cash.

We define cash as legal tender that is immediately available for payment of current obligations. Cash includes coins, currency (paper money), cheques, money orders, traveller's cheques, and money on deposit that is available for unrestricted withdrawal from banks and other financial institutions. You can think of cash as anything that a bank would accept for deposit in your account. For example, a traveller's cheque, money order, or cheque made payable to you could normally be deposited in a bank and thus is considered cash.

Not included in cash would be items such as postage stamps (which might be found in a petty cash drawer), postdated cheques, or cheques received from customers that have been returned "NSF" (insufficient funds) by the bank. None of these items is cash because none would be immediately accepted by your bank for deposit. Postage stamps are considered a prepaid expense. A cheque that is postdated (dated in the future) is not cash, but instead represents a type of receivable. That is, the party writing the cheque to you is promising to pay you the amount in the future. A bank will not accept a cheque for deposit unless it is due and payable immediately. If you deposit a customer's cheque and there is not enough cash in the customer's bank account to cover the cheque, your bank will refuse to accept the cheque for deposit and will return it to you. In this case, you would no longer include the NSF cheque in cash, but would consider it as an amount still owing (receivable) from the customer.

To be classified as cash, money on deposit in a financial institution must be unrestricted and available for withdrawal to make payments to meet current obligations. Sometimes, a business will place money on deposit in a bank account for a special purpose, possibly in order to fulfil a contractual obligation. For example, a company may have a legal obligation to deposit money into a special account that will be used to make future pension payments to its employees when they retire. In this instance, these funds are restricted. Since the business no longer has access to withdraw cash from this account to pay its current bills, we would not classify this account as cash in the firm's balance sheet.

In practice, a business normally has several cash accounts in its ledger. For example, a business often maintains separate ledger accounts for cash on hand and for cash used for other current needs, such as travel reimbursements. It may maintain a ledger account for each of its bank accounts, such as one for general cash payments and another for payroll. To simplify, we will assume, in this chapter, that the business maintains only one bank account for its current needs, represented in the ledger as *Cash in Bank*. We will introduce other nonbank cash ledger accounts later in the chapter.

Good management of cash is essential to the successful operation of a business. The maintenance of effective internal controls for this asset is essential for two reasons. First, most business transactions affect the receipt or payment of cash, either directly or indirectly. Although the balance of the cash account reported on the balance sheet may not be as large as the amounts shown for other assets, usually a great deal of cash will be flowing in and out of the business each day. Second, because cash is a very liquid asset that can be transferred with ease, it is the most susceptible to being misused or misappropriated by employees.

A business has three basic responsibilities in properly managing its cash resources. (1) Management must maintain cash resources at a level sufficient to meet current needs. A business cannot afford to miss valuable purchase discounts or fail to meet its current obligations because of a shortage of cash. (2) At the same time, management should not hold more cash than is needed, as idle cash will not earn a profit for the business. A short-term excess of cash should be transferred to a temporary, income-generating investment until such time as it is required to pay current obligations. (3) Lastly, management must design and use controls to authorize cash transactions and safeguard cash from embezzlement. We discuss these controls in the following section.

Internal Control of Cash Receipts

Objective 2
Summarize basic procedures for achieving internal control over cash receipts, including the use of cash change funds and the cash short and over account.

To protect cash from theft and misuse, a business must control cash from the time it receives the cash until the business deposits it in a bank. Such procedures are called **protective controls**.

Procedures that are designed to detect theft or misuse of cash are called **detective controls**. In a sense, detective controls are also preventive in nature, since employees are less likely to steal or misuse cash if they know there is a good chance they will be detected.

Retail businesses normally receive cash from two main sources: (1) over the counter from cash customers and (2) by mail from credit customers making payments (usually by cheque) on account. For example, fast-food restaurants such as **Harvey's, Swiss Chalet,** and **Tim Hortons** receive cash primarily from over-the-counter sales to customers. Mail-order retailers such as **Mountain Equipment Co-op** and **L.L. Bean** receive cash primarily through the mail and from credit card companies. Wholesalers receive the majority of their cash through the mail. Regardless of the source of cash receipts, every business must properly safeguard and record its cash receipts.

One control for safeguarding cash receipts is the use of prenumbered sales invoices. If sales staff must account for prenumbered sales invoices, it is more difficult for them to misappropriate cash by not reporting some sales.

One way a retail business such as a fast-food restaurant receives cash is from over-the-counter sales to customers.

Another very important control for protecting cash received in over-the-counter sales is a cash register. You may have noticed that when the clerk (cashier) enters the amount of the sale, the cash register normally displays the amount. You, the customer, usually receive a paper receipt, which helps you verify the accuracy of the purchase and serves as an additional control. The cash register tape is normally locked into the cash register. Usually a supervisor will control the key necessary to unlock the register, so that the cashier has no opportunity to remove the tape or tamper with it.

At the end of the day or work shift, the cashiers count the cash in their cash drawers and record the amounts on cash or sales memorandum forms. The cashiers' supervisor removes the cash register tapes on which total receipts were recorded. The supervisor counts the cash and compares the total with the memorandums and the tapes, noting any differences. Normally, the supervisor then places the cash in a store safe until it can be deposited in the bank. The tapes and memorandums are forwarded to the Accounting Department, where they become the basis for journal entries.

Cash is received in the mail when customers pay their bills. This cash is usually in the form of cheques and money orders. Most companies' invoices are designed so that customers return a remittance advice with these payments. The employee who opens the incoming mail should initially compare the amount of cash received with the amount shown on the remittance advice. As a protective control, the employee should also stamp the cheques and money orders "For Deposit Only."

If a customer does not return a remittance advice, an employee prepares one on a form designed for such use. Like the cash register, this record of cash received establishes the initial accountability for the cash. It also helps ensure that the posting to the customer's account is accurate.

The employee who opens the mail should prepare a list of all cash received and forward a copy of the list, along with the cash, to the Cashier's Department. An employee there combines it with the receipts from cash sales and prepares a bank deposit slip. The remittance advices and their summary totals are delivered to the Accounting Department. An accounting clerk then prepares the journal entries and posts them to the customer accounts in the subsidiary ledger.

Cash sales and customer payments received in the mail should be taken to the bank for deposit at the end of each business day. After the cash is deposited in the bank, the duplicate deposit slips or other bank receipt forms are returned to the Accounting Department. An accounting clerk then compares the total amount deposited with the amount recorded as the cash receipt. This control helps ensure that all the cash is deposited and that no cash is lost or stolen on the way to the bank. Any shortages are thus promptly detected.

The proper handling of cash requires a separation of duties so that no one person has the custody of cash, the authorization for cash transactions, and the responsibility for cash records. The separation of the duties of the Cashier's Department, which handles cash, and the Accounting Department, which records cash, is a preventive control. If Accounting Department employees both handled and recorded cash, an employee could steal cash and change the accounting records to hide the theft. Surprise cash counts should also be made periodically by either the internal or external auditors. The auditor's unexpected appearance can provide a useful check on whether employees are properly following the firm's internal control policies for cash.

CASH CHANGE FUNDS

Retail stores and other businesses that receive cash directly from customers must keep some currency and coins on hand in order to make change. This cash is recorded in a cash change fund account.

A business establishes the cash change fund by drawing a cheque for the required amount, debiting Cash on Hand, and crediting Cash in Bank. No additional charges or credits to the Cash on Hand account are made unless the business increases or decreases the amount of the fund.

The cash on hand may be divided up among the various cash registers. We must record the amount in each cash register for later use in reconciling cash sales for the day. At the end of each day the business should deposit the total amount of cash received during the day, retaining the original amount of the change fund. At the beginning of a work shift, each cashier must verify by a physical count the amount of cash in his or her register, and must have sole access to this cash drawer while on duty. In this way, the cashier can be held responsible for the cash on hand at the end of the shift, which should agree with the opening balance plus the cash sales recorded on the cash register tape during that period.

CASH SHORT AND OVER

The amount of cash on hand at the end of each day should be the beginning amount of cash in each cash register plus the cash sales for the day. However, the amount of actual cash on hand at the end of the day often differs from this amount. This occurs because of errors in recording cash sales or errors in making change.

We record differences in the amount of cash counted and the amount of cash in the records in an account entitled Cash Short and Over. For example, the following entry records one day's cash sales, when the actual cash on hand is less than the amount indicated by the cash register tally:

Cash in Bank	4,592.50	
Cash Short and Over	7.50	
Sales		4,000.00
Sales tax payable (8%)		320.00
GST payable (7%)		280.00

If there is a debit balance in the cash short and over account at the end of a period, we classify it as a miscellaneous administrative expense in the income statement. If there is a credit balance, we list it in the Other Income section. If the balance becomes larger than may be expected from minor errors in making change, management should investigate the cause of the discrepancy and take any necessary corrective measures.

Internal Control of Cash Payments

Objective 3
Summarize basic procedures for achieving internal control over cash payments, including the use of a voucher system and a petty cash account.

Regardless of the size of the company, the control over cash payments often can be improved. Auditors customarily review the cash payments made by their client companies, searching for errors, such as duplicate payments, failures to take discounts, and inaccurate calculations. **Howard Schultz & Associates (HS&A)**, a U.S. firm of auditors, reported that the typical amount recovered for its clients was about one-tenth of one percent of the total payments made to suppliers. This averages to about $300,000 per client. In one case, HS&A recovered over $4.5 million for a client.[2]

Internal control over cash payments should provide reasonable assurance that the business only makes payments for authorized transactions. In addition, controls should ensure that cash is used efficiently. For example, controls should ensure that all available discounts, such as purchase and trade discounts, are taken so that cash is not wasted.

In the following paragraphs, we describe controls that address these issues. We also discuss how controls are often modified for small cash payments when the cost of more elaborate controls is not worthwhile.

[2] Thomas Buell, Jr., "Demand Grows for Auditor," *The Naples Daily News*, January 12, 1992, p. 14F.

BASIC FEATURES OF THE VOUCHER SYSTEM

In a small business, an owner/manager may sign all cheques, based upon personal knowledge of all goods and services purchased. In a large business, however, cheques are prepared by employees who do not likely have such a complete knowledge of the transactions. In such businesses, the duties of issuing purchase orders, inspecting goods received, and verifying invoices are divided among the employees of several departments. These activities must be coordinated with the final issuance of cheques to creditors. One system used for this purpose is the voucher system.

A **voucher system** is a set of methods and procedures for authorizing and recording liabilities and cash payments. A voucher system normally uses (1) vouchers, (2) a file for unpaid vouchers, and (3) a file for paid vouchers.

The term voucher is widely used in accounting. Generally, a voucher is any document that serves as proof of authority to pay cash, such as an invoice approved for payment. In some businesses, a **voucher** is a special form on which is recorded relevant data about a liability and the details of its payment. Exhibit 1 shows an example of such a form.

Vouchers are normally prenumbered for control purposes. Each voucher provides space for the name and address of the creditor, the date, and a summary of the basic details of the supporting document. The voucher includes the invoice number and the amount and terms of the invoice. One half of the back of the voucher is devoted to the account distribution and the other half to summaries of the voucher and the details of payment. Spaces are also provided for the signature or initials of certain employees.

An accounts payable clerk in the Accounting Department normally prepares the voucher based on an invoice or other supporting document. For example, a voucher prepared for the purchase of merchandise should be supported by the supplier's invoice, a purchase order, and a receiving report. In preparing the voucher, the accounts payable clerk should verify the quantity, price, and mathematical accuracy of the supporting documents. This procedure provides reasonable assurance that what is being paid for was properly ordered and received.

After preparing a voucher such as the one shown in Exhibit 1, the accounts payable clerk should attach the invoice or other supporting evidence to the voucher and give the voucher to the proper official for approval.

Exhibit 1
Voucher   *(face)*   *(back)*

COMPUTER KING   VOUCHER

Date July 1, 2001   Voucher No. 451
Payee Allied Manufacturing Company
       6300 Yonge St.
       Toronto, Ontario

Date	Details	Amount
June 28, 2001	Invoice No. 4693-C, FOB Toronto, 2/10, n/30	1,500.00

Attach Supporting Documents

ACCOUNT DISTRIBUTION		
DEBIT	AMOUNT	
MERCHANDISE INVENTORY	1500	00
SUPPLIES		
ADVERTISING EXPENSE		
DELIVERY EXPENSE		
MISC. SELLING EXPENSE		
MISC. ADMIN. EXPENSE		
CREDIT ACCOUNTS PAYABLE	1500	00

DISTRIBUTION APPROVED L. Donnelly

NO. 451
DATE 7/1/01   DUE 7/8/01
PAYEE
Allied Manufacturing Company
6300 Yonge St.
Toronto, Ontario

VOUCHER SUMMARY		
AMOUNT	1500	00
ADJUSTMENT		
DISCOUNT	30	00
NET	1470	00

APPROVED M.C. Leshen CONTROLLER
RECORDED W.B.

PAYMENT SUMMARY	
DATE	7/8/98
AMOUNT	1470.00
CHEQUE NO.	863

APPROVED Pat King
RECORDED L.K.R.   A.S.

After a voucher has been approved, we record it as a credit to Accounts Payable and a debit to the appropriate account or accounts. For example, if we assume a periodic inventory system, Computer King's entry to record the voucher illustrated in Exhibit 1 (No. 451), is as follows:

| Purchases | 1,500 | |
| Accounts Payable | | 1,500 |

After recording the voucher, we file it in an unpaid voucher file by the due date. The amount due on each voucher represents the credit balance of an account payable.

When the voucher is to be paid, we remove it from the unpaid voucher file and prepare a cheque for payment. Cheques should be prenumbered and kept in a secure place to which only authorized employees have access. The cheque with the accompanying voucher file is forwarded to those authorized to sign cheques on the company's account. Most business bank accounts are set up to require the signatures of two authorized employees on every cheque, so that no one employee can issue a payment by him or herself. Before issuing the cheque, we should list the date, the number, and the amount of the cheque written in payment on the back of the voucher. To prevent accidental or intentional repayment of the same voucher, we should immediately cancel paid vouchers and supporting documents.

We record the payment of a voucher in the same manner as the payment of an account payable. For example, Computer King's entry to record the cheque issued in payment of the voucher in Exhibit 1 is as follows:

Accounts Payable	1,500	
Cash in Bank		1,470
Purchase Discounts		30

After payment, we usually file cancelled vouchers in numerical order in a paid voucher file. They are then readily available for examination by employees needing information about a certain expenditure.

A voucher system not only provides effective accounting controls over cash payments but also aids management in fulfilling its responsibilities. For example, management can use a voucher system in predicting future cash requirements in order to make the best use of cash resources.

In practice, companies should use a control system, such as a voucher system, that provides for the timely payment of all invoices within the discount period. However, purchase discounts may be missed due to oversight, errors in recording due dates, or other reasons. Controls should also exist to monitor missed discounts. If the amount of missed discounts becomes large, management may then take corrective action, such as revising the manner in which due dates are recorded or changing personnel.

PETTY CASH

As in your own day-to-day life, most businesses frequently need cash to pay small amounts, such as postage due or for small purchases of urgently needed supplies. Normal control procedures, which might require payment by cheque, could result in unnecessary delay and expense in such cases. Yet, these small payments may occur frequently enough to add up to a significant total amount. Thus, it is desirable to retain some control over such payments. For this purpose, we use a special cash fund called a **petty cash fund.**

We establish a petty cash fund by first estimating the amount of cash needed for payments from the fund during a period, such as a week or a month. If we are using a voucher system, we prepare a voucher for this amount. We record the voucher as a debit to Petty Cash and a credit to Accounts Payable. The cheque drawn to pay the voucher is recorded as a debit to Accounts Payable and a credit to Cash in Bank.

The money obtained from cashing the cheque is placed in the custody of a specific employee who is authorized to disburse monies from the fund. Management may restrict the maximum amount and the nature of fund disbursements. Each time monies are disbursed from the fund, the fund custodian records the essential details on a petty cash receipt form. In addition, the signature of the payee and the initials of the custodian of the fund are written on the form as proof of the payment. Exhibit 2 illustrates a typical petty cash receipt.

The business must replenish the petty cash fund when it is depleted or reaches a minimum amount. It must also replenish the fund at the end of each accounting period, so that the books can be updated to reflect all expenditures made during the period. When replenishing a petty cash fund, we summarize the petty cash receipts in order to determine the accounts to be debited. If a voucher system is used, we record the voucher as a debit to the various expense and asset accounts and a credit to Accounts Payable, and record the cheque in payment of the voucher in the usual manner.

To illustrate the entries in accounting for petty cash, assume the use of a voucher system with a petty cash fund of $100 established on August 1. At the end of August, the petty cash receipts indicate expenditures for the following items: office supplies, $28; postage (office supplies), $22; store supplies, $25; and newspapers (miscellaneous expense), $13.70. The entries to establish and replenish the petty cash fund are as follows:

Aug. 1	Petty Cash	100.00	
	Accounts Payable		100.00
1	Accounts Payable	100.00	
	Cash in Bank		100.00
31	Office Supplies	50.00	
	Store Supplies	25.00	
	Miscellaneous Expense	13.70	
	Accounts Payable		88.70
31	Accounts Payable	88.70	
	Cash in Bank		88.70

Replenishing the petty cash fund restores it to its original amount of $100. You should note that there is no entry to Petty Cash when the fund is replenished. We debit Petty Cash only when the fund is initially set up or when the permanent amount of the fund is increased at some later date.

Exhibit 2
Petty Cash Receipt

PETTY CASH RECEIPT		
No. ____121____		Date ___August 1, 2001___
Paid to ___Globe and Mail___		**Amount**
For ___Daily newspaper___		13 | 70
Charge to ___Miscellaneous Administrative Expense___		
Payment received:		
_____S.O. Hall_____	**Approved by** ___N.E.R.___	

OTHER CASH FUNDS

Businesses may also establish cash funds to meet other special current needs of a business. For example, money may be advanced for travel expenses as needed. Periodically, after employees submit their expense reports, the accountant records the expenses and the fund is replenished. A similar procedure may be used to provide a cash operating fund for a sales office located in another city. The amount of the fund may be deposited in a local bank, and the sales representative may be authorized to draw cheques for payment of rent, salaries, and other operating expenses. Each month, the representative sends the invoices, paid cheques, and other business documents to the home office. The home office audits the data, records the expenditures, and issues a replenishing cheque for deposit in the local bank.

As with petty cash funds, we do not record disbursements from other cash funds in the accounts until the funds are replenished. To bring the accounts up to date, such funds should always be replenished at the end of an accounting period. The amount of monies in these funds will then agree with the balances in the fund accounts. At the same time, the expenses and the assets for which payments have been made will be recorded in the proper period.

Bank Accounts: Their Nature and Use as a Control Over Cash

Objective 4
Describe the nature of a bank account and its use in controlling cash.

Most of you are already familiar with bank accounts if you have a chequing account at a local bank, credit union, or trust company. In this section, we discuss the nature of a bank account maintained by a business. The features of such accounts will be similar to your own bank account. We then discuss the use of bank accounts as an additional control over cash.

BUSINESS BANK ACCOUNTS

As we mentioned earlier in the chapter, a business often maintains several bank accounts. The forms used with such accounts are a signature card, deposit slip, cheque, and record of cheques drawn. We briefly describe each of these forms below.

Signature Card

When you open a chequing account, you sign a **signature card**. This card is used by the bank to verify the signature on cheques that you have written. Also, when you open an account, the bank assigns an identifying number to the account. As mentioned earlier, the signature card on a business account will usually require the presence of two signatures to authorize a payment from the account.

Deposit Slip

When making a deposit, the depositor usually lists the details of the deposit on a printed form supplied by the bank. These **deposit slips** may be prepared in duplicate. The bank teller stamps or initials a copy of the deposit slip and gives it to the depositor as a receipt. The bank may also use other types of receipts to give the depositor written proof of the date and the total amount of the deposit.

Cheque

A **cheque** is a written instrument signed by the depositor, ordering the bank to pay a sum of money to an individual or entity. There are three parties to a cheque—the drawer, the drawee, and the payee. The **drawer** is the one who signs the cheque, ordering payment by the bank. The **drawee** is the bank on which the cheque is drawn. The **payee** is the recipient of the payment.

When a business issues cheques to pay bills, we record them as credits to Cash on the day issued. The credit to Cash is recorded, even though the payee will not present the cheque to the drawer's bank until a later date. Likewise, when the business receives cheques from customers, we record them as debits to Cash.

The name and the address of the depositor are often printed on each cheque. In addition, cheques are normally prenumbered, so that we can easily keep track of them, as an aid to internal control. Most banks use automatic sorting and posting equipment that requires that the bank's identification number and the depositor's account number be printed on each cheque. These numbers are usually printed along the lower margin in machine-readable magnetic ink. When the payee presents the cheque for payment, the amount for which it is drawn is inserted next to the account number, which is also in magnetic ink. At the beginning of this chapter, we illustrated a cheque that had been processed by a bank.

Record of Cheques Drawn

You should prepare a record of the basic details of a cheque at the time the cheque is written. You could use a copy of each cheque written or a stub from which the cheque is detached as the basis for recording cash payments. A small booklet called a **transactions register** may also be used.

We may insert the invoice number or other data in spaces provided on the cheque or on an attachment to the cheque. Normally, cheques issued to a creditor on account are sent with a form that identifies the specific invoice being paid. The purpose of this form, sometimes called a **remittance advice,** is to make sure that proper credit is recorded in the accounts of the creditor. In this way, mistakes are less likely to occur. Exhibit 3 illustrates a cheque and remittance advice.

Exhibit 3
Cheque and Remittance Advice

COMPUTER KING   **363**

1000 Portage Avenue   Winnipeg, Manitoba   April 12, 2001   9-42 / 720

Pay to the Order of _____ Hammond Office Products _____ $ 921.20

Nine hundred twenty-one 20/100----------------------------- Dollars

Canadian Imperial Bank of Commerce   K.R. Simons _____ Treasurer
333 Portage Ave., Winnipeg, Manitoba   Earl M. Hartman _____ Vice President

⑈072000423⑈ 162704 2 363⑈

DETACH THIS PORTION BEFORE CASHING

Date	Description	Gross Amount	Deductions	Net Amount
4/12/01	Invoice No. 529482	940.00	18.80	921.20

COMPUTER KING

Before depositing the cheque at the bank, the payee removes the remittance advice. The payee may then use the remittance advice as written proof of the details of the cash receipt.

BANK STATEMENT

Banks usually maintain a record of all chequing account transactions. The bank mails a summary of all transactions, called a **statement of account**, to the depositor, usually once each month. Like any account with a customer or a creditor, the bank statement shows the beginning balance, additions, deductions, and the balance at the end of the period.

The depositor's cheques cleared by the bank during the period may accompany the bank statement, arranged in the order of payment. The paid or cancelled cheques are perforated, stamped "Paid," or stamped with the name of the bank in which they were deposited, together with the date of payment. Debit or credit memorandums describing other entries in the depositor's account may also be enclosed with the statement. For example, the bank may have debited the depositor's account for service charges or for deposited cheques returned because of insufficient funds. It may have credited the account for receipts from notes receivable left for collection, for loans to the depositor, or for interest. Exhibit 4 illustrates a typical bank statement.

BANK ACCOUNTS AS A CONTROL OVER CASH

A bank account is one of the primary tools a business can use to control cash. For example, businesses often require that all cash receipts be initially deposited in a bank account. Likewise, all cash payments are often disbursed from one or more

Exhibit 4
Bank Statement

```
                                                                    PAGE      1

   CANADIAN IMPERIAL                     ACCOUNT NUMBER    1627042
   BANK OF COMMERCE
   333 Portage Ave., Winnipeg, Manitoba  FROM   6/30/01      TO      7/31/01
                                         BALANCE                    4,218.60
                                      22 DEPOSITS                  13,749.75
                                      52 WITHDRAWALS               14,698.57

                                       3 OTHER DEBITS                 90.00CR
                                         AND CREDITS
   COMPUTER KING
   1000 PORTAGE AVE.
   WINNIPEG, MANITOBA                     NEW BALANCE              3,359.78


   *--CHEQUES AND OTHER DEBITS---*---DEPOSITS--*--DATE--*--BALANCE--*

    819.40      122.54                    585.75    07/01    3,862.41
    369.50      732.26      20.15         421.53    07/02    3,162.03
    600.00      190.70      52.50         781.30    07/03    3,100.13
     25.93      160.00                    662.50    07/05    3,576.70
     36.80  NSF 300.00                    503.18    07/07    3,743.08

     32.26      535.09                    932.00    07/29    3,404.40
     21.10      126.20                    705.21    07/30    3,962.31
             SC  18.00                 MS 408.00    07/30    4,352.31
     26.12    1,615.13                    648.72    07/31    3,359.78


    EC--ERROR CORRECTION                OD--OVERDRAFT
    MS--MISCELLANEOUS                   PS--PAYMENT STOPPED
    NSF--NOT SUFFICIENT FUNDS           SC--SERVICE CHARGE

    ***                      ***                              ***
   THE RECONCILEMENT OF THIS STATEMENT WITH YOUR RECORDS IS ESSENTIAL.
         ANY ERROR OR EXCEPTION SHOULD BE REPORTED IMMEDIATELY.
```

If a depositor uses the night depository, there will probably be a time lag between the date of the deposit and the date that it is recorded by the bank

bank accounts. When such a system is used, there is a double record of cash transactions—one by the business and the other by the bank.[3]

A bank statement allows a business to compare the cash transactions recorded in the accounting records to those recorded by the bank. The cash balance shown by a bank statement is usually different from the Cash in Bank balance shown in the accounting records of the business. The difference may be the result of a delay by either party in recording transactions. For example, there is a time lag of one day or more between the date a cheque is written and the date on which the cheque clears the bank for payment. If the depositor mails deposits to the bank or uses the night depository, the date of the deposit on the depositor's records will likely be earlier than the date that is recorded by the bank. Conversely, the bank may debit or credit the depositor's account for transactions about which the depositor will not be informed until later. Examples are service or collection fees charged by the bank and the proceeds of notes receivable sent to the bank for collection.

The difference may also be the result of errors by either party in recording transactions. For example, a depositor may incorrectly post to Cash in Bank a cheque written for $4,500 as $450. Likewise, a bank may incorrectly enter the amount of a cheque, as we illustrated at the beginning of this chapter.

To enhance internal control, a business must reconcile the difference between the bank statement and the ledger account for cash in the bank. An employee who does not take part in or record cash transactions should prepare this reconciliation. Without a proper separation of these duties, mistakes are likely to occur and it is more likely that cash could be stolen or otherwise misapplied. For example, if a single employee performed all these duties, he or she could prepare and cash an unauthorized cheque, omit it from the accounts, and omit it from the reconciliation.

Bank Reconciliation

Objective 5

Prepare a bank reconciliation and journalize any necessary entries.

A **bank reconciliation** is a listing of items and amounts that cause the cash balance reported in the bank statement to differ from the Cash in Bank account balance. It is usually divided into two sections. The first section begins with the cash balance according to the bank statement and ends with the adjusted balance. The second section begins with the cash balance according to the depositor's records and ends with the adjusted balance. The two amounts designated as the adjusted balance must be equal. The form and the content of the bank reconciliation are shown below:

Cash balance according to **bank statement**			$XXX
Add:	Additions by depositor not on bank statement	$XX	
	Bank errors	XX	XX
			$XXX
Deduct:	Deductions by depositor not on bank statement	$XX	
	Bank errors	XX	XX
Adjusted balance			$XXX
Cash balance according to **depositor's records**			$XXX
Add:	Additions by bank not recorded by depositor	$XX	
	Depositor errors	XX	XX
			$XXX
Deduct:	Deductions by bank not recorded by depositor	$XX	
	Depositor errors	XX	XX
Adjusted balance			$XXX

[3] The Cash in Bank account in the business's (the depositor's) ledger is an asset account with a debit balance. This same account is shown in the bank's records as a liability.

The following steps are useful in finding the reconciling items and determining the adjusted balance of Cash in Bank:

1. Compare individual deposits listed on the bank statement with outstanding deposits (deposits recorded in the company's books, but not recorded by the bank by the end of the period) appearing in the preceding period's reconciliation and with deposit receipts or other records of deposits. *Add deposits not recorded by the bank to the balance according to the bank statement.*

2. Compare paid cheques with outstanding cheques appearing on the preceding period's reconciliation and with cheques recorded this period. *Deduct cheques outstanding that have not been paid by the bank from the balance according to the bank statement.*

3. Compare bank credit memorandums to entries in the journal. For example, a bank would issue a credit memorandum for a note receivable and interest that it collected for a customer. *Add credit memorandums that have not been recorded by the business to the balance according to the depositor's records.*

4. Compare bank debit memorandums to entries recording cash payments. For example, a bank normally issues debit memorandums for service charges and cheque printing charges. A bank also issues debit memorandums for not-sufficient-funds cheques. A **not-sufficient-funds (NSF) cheque** is a customer's cheque that was recorded and deposited but was not paid when it was presented to the customer's bank for payment. NSF cheques are normally charged back to the customer's account receivable. *Deduct debit memorandums that have not been recorded by the business from the balance according to the depositor's records.*

5. List separately on the reconciliation any errors discovered during the preceding steps. For example, if the business has recorded an amount incorrectly, adjust the cash balance according to the depositor's records to correct the error. Similarly, adjust the cash balance according to the bank statement for any errors made by the bank.

To illustrate a bank reconciliation, we will use the bank statement for Computer King shown in Exhibit 4. This bank statement shows a balance of $3,359.78 as of July 31. The balance in Cash in Bank in Computer King's ledger as of the same date is $2,549.99. The following reconciling items are revealed by using the steps outlined above:

Deposit of July 31 not recorded on bank statement	$ 816.20
Cheques outstanding: No. 812, $1,061.00; No. 878, $435.39; No. 883, $48.60	1,544.99
Note plus interest of $8 collected by bank (credit memorandum), not recorded in the journal	408.00
Cheque from customer (Thomas Ivey) returned by bank because of insufficient funds (NSF)	300.00
Bank service charges (debit memorandum) not recorded in the journal	18.00
Cheque No. 879 for $732.26 to Taylor Co. on account, recorded in the journal as $723.26	9.00

The bank reconciliation based on the bank statement and the reconciling items is as follows:

Computer King
Bank Reconciliation
July 31, 2001

Cash balance according to bank statement				$3 3 5 9 78
Add deposit of July 31, not recorded by bank				8 1 6 20
				$4 1 7 5 98
Deduct outstanding cheques:				
No. 812	$1 0 6 1 00			
No. 878	4 3 5 39			
No. 883	4 8 60		1 5 4 4 99	
Adjusted balance				$2 6 3 0 99
Cash balance according to depositor's records				$2 5 4 9 99
Add note and interest collected by bank				4 0 8 00
				$2 9 5 7 99
Deduct: Cheque returned because of				
insufficient funds	$ 3 0 0 00			
Bank service charges	1 8 00			
Error in recording Cheque No. 879	9 00		3 2 7 00	
Adjusted balance				$2 6 3 0 99

No entries are necessary on the depositor's records as a result of the informa-tion included in the first section of the bank reconciliation. This section begins with the cash balance according to the bank statement. However, the bank should be notified of any errors that need to be corrected on its records.

USING ACCOUNTING TO UNDERSTAND BUSINESS

Many of us reconcile our bank accounts each month after we receive our bank state-ments. In reconciling our accounts, most of us first scan the bank statement for any bank entries that we have not yet recorded. Examples of such entries include service charges (a debit entry) and interest earned (a credit entry). We then enter these amounts in our cheque book (register) and determine the balance of our account. Many individuals stop at this point. If you do so, you are assuming that the bank hasn't made any errors.

If you decide to continue and fully reconcile your account, you then must examine your cheque book to determine items that the bank has not yet recorded. Such items nor-mally include (1) deposits in transit and (2) outstanding cheques. You must add deposits in transit to the bank balance and subtract outstanding cheques from the bank balance. The result is an adjusted bank balance that should agree with the balance of your cheque book. If the two are not equal, either you or the bank has made an error.

The depositor must record any addition or deduction items in the second section of the bank reconciliation in its accounts. This section begins with the cash balance according to the depositor's records. We must record entries for bank memorandums not previously recorded by the depositor and for any depositor's errors.

The entries for Computer King, based on its bank reconciliation, are as follows:

July	31	Cash in Bank	408	
		Notes Receivable		400
		Interest Income		8
		Note collected by bank.		
	31	Accounts Receivable—Thomas Ivey	300	
		Miscellaneous Administrative Expense	18	
		Accounts Payable—Taylor Co.	9	
		Cash in Bank		327
		NSF cheque, bank service charges,		
		and error in recording Cheque No. 879.		

After the above entries have been posted, Cash in Bank will have a debit balance of $2,630.99. This balance agrees with the adjusted cash balance shown on the bank reconciliation. It is the amount of cash available as of July 31 and the amount that would be reported on the balance sheet on that date.

Although businesses may reconcile their bank accounts in a slightly different format from what we described above, the objective is the same: to control cash by reconciling the company's records to the records of an independent outside source—the bank. By so doing, the business may detect any errors or misappropriations of cash.

Presentation of Cash on the Balance Sheet

Objective 6
Summarize how cash is presented on the balance sheet.

We present assets in the Current Assets section of the balance sheet in order of their liquidity. Since cash is the most liquid asset, it is listed first. Most companies combine all their cash accounts and present only a single cash amount on the balance sheet. This amount will include the balance held in various bank accounts, as well as petty cash and change funds.

Sometimes a business may write cheques in excess of the money that it has on deposit in its account. If the bank clears these payments, the bank account will be overdrawn and the company's ledger account for Cash in Bank may have a negative (credit) balance. How should this be reported on the balance sheet? If the company has other accounts at the same branch of the bank with a positive balance, we can group the accounts together and report the net positive balance reported as Cash. If not, we must report the credit balance for the overdrawn bank account not as an asset, but as a Bank Overdraft under Current Liabilities (since the amount is owed by the firm to the bank).

A company may have cash in excess of its immediate operating needs. In such cases, it may temporarily invest in highly liquid investments in order to earn interest. These investments are called **cash equivalents.** Cash equivalents "are short-term, highly liquid investments that are readily convertible to known amounts of cash and which are subject to an insignificant risk of changes in value."[4] Examples of cash equivalents include Treasury Bills, notes issued by major corporations (referred to as commercial paper), and money market funds. Companies that have invested excess cash in cash equivalents usually report *Cash and cash equivalents* as one amount on the balance sheet.

---

[4] CICA *Handbook*, Section 1540, paragraph .06.

The components of cash and cash equivalents normally require disclosures in the notes to the financial statements.[5] However, if the ability to withdraw cash is restricted, the entity should disclose these restrictions. For example, companies with foreign operations often have cash deposits in foreign banks. These deposits may be subject to foreign laws that limit withdrawals to certain amounts. Such limitations should be disclosed in the notes to the financial statements. A survey of financial reporting by Canadian companies indicated that approximately 38% presented "Cash" separately in the balance sheet. The remainder reported cash grouped with other items such as cash equivalents, temporary investments, or term deposits,[6] such as the following:

Lafarge Canada Inc.

	1994	1993
Balance Sheet - current assets		
Cash and cash equivalents	$126,161	$135,574

Notes to financial statements
Note 1 - Summary of Accounting Policies
Cash and cash equivalents

Cash and cash equivalents consist primarily of commercial paper and deposits with an original maturity date at date of purchase of three months or less. Because of the short-term maturity of these investments, their carrying amount approximates fair value.

A bank often requires a business to maintain in a bank account a minimum cash balance. Such a balance is called a **compensating balance**. The bank may impose this requirement as a part of a loan agreement or line of credit. A line of credit is a pre-approved amount the bank is willing to lend to a customer upon request. Compensating balance requirements should be disclosed in notes to the financial statements.

Electronic Funds Transfer

Objective 7
Define electronic funds transfers and give an example of how they are used to process cash transactions.

Rapidly changing technology has created new systems to more efficiently record and transfer cash among companies. Such systems often use electronic funds transfer (EFT). In an EFT system, computerized information, rather than paper (money, cheques, etc.), is used to effect cash transactions. For example, a business may pay its employees by means of EFT. Under such a system, employees may authorize the deposit of their net pay directly into their chequing accounts. Each pay period, the business electronically transfers the employees' net pay to their chequing accounts through the use of computer systems and telephone lines.

More and more companies are using EFT systems to process cash transactions. For example, in 1994 the treasurer for **Chevron U.S.A.** reported that Chevron was making more than 5,800 electronic payments a month to suppliers, nearly 14% of the cheques it once wrote.[7] EFT systems are also now common in retailing. For example, in a point-of-sale (POS) system, a customer pays for goods at the time of purchase by presenting a plastic debit card. The card authorizes the transfer of cash from the customer's chequing account to the retailer's bank account at the time of the sale.

---

[5] *CICA Handbook*, Section 1540, paragraph 48.
[6] CICA, *Financial Reporting in Canada 1995*, 21st edition, Toronto, p. 89.
[7] Fred R. Bleakley, "Fast Money: Electronic Payments Now Supplant Checks at More Large Firms," *The Wall Street Journal*, April 3, 1994.

Exhibit 5 indicates the rapid growth in the usage of debit cards in Canada since their introduction in 1992. By 1996 debit cards were used for 530 million point-of-sale transactions in Canada, accounting for $30 billion (13%) of total retail sales, as compared to $67 billion (29%) for Visa and Mastercard.[8] In Canada the market for debit cards is run by **Interac,** a co-operative owned by the big banks and trust companies. Another advance in EFT is Internet electronic currency, which allows consumers to make retail purchases and payments over the Internet. With Digicash, for example, banks sell electronic tokens to consumers who can load these into their own computers, and later use them to make purchases from participating retailers.

The benefits of EFT include reduced transaction costs for financial institutions and retailers, as well as convenience for consumers. However, EFT has also raised some concerns among consumer groups over issues such as the loss of information privacy, the potential for fraud, the degree of cost savings that will be passed on to consumers, and the impact on low-income Canadians who may not have access to the benefits of the new technology.[9]

Exhibit 5

Number of Interac Direct Payment Transactions by Month in Canada (millions)

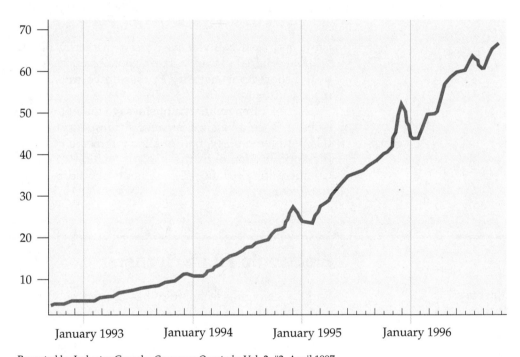

Reported by Industry Canada, *Consumer Quarterly,* Vol. 2, #2, April 1997.

[8] Industry Canada, *Consumer Quarterly*, Vol.2, #2, April 1997.
[9] *Ibid.*

KEY POINTS

Objective 1. Describe the nature of cash and the importance of internal control over cash.

Cash includes coins, currency (paper money), cheques, traveller's cheques, money orders, and money on deposit that is available for unrestricted withdrawal from banks and other financial institutions. Because of the ease with which money can be transferred, businesses should design and use controls that safeguard cash and authorize cash transactions.

Objective 2. Summarize basic procedures for achieving internal control over cash receipts, including the use of cash change funds and the cash short and over account.

One of the most important controls to protect cash received in over-the-counter sales is a cash register. A remittance advice is a protective control for cash received through the mail. The separation of the duties of handling cash and recording cash is also a protective control.

Retail stores and other businesses that receive cash directly from customers must keep some currency and coins in a cash change fund in order to make change. Differences in the amount of cash counted and the amount of cash in the records are normally recorded in Cash Short and Over.

Objective 3. Summarize basic procedures for achieving internal control over cash payments, including the use of a voucher system and a petty cash account.

A voucher system is a set of methods and procedures for authorizing and recording liabilities and cash payments. A voucher system uses vouchers, a file for unpaid vouchers, and a file for paid vouchers.

Businesses should take advantage of all purchases discounts. A business may use a petty cash fund to make small payments that occur frequently. The money in a petty cash fund is placed in the custody of a specific employee, who authorizes payments from the fund. Periodically or when the amount of money in the fund is depleted or reduced to a minimum amount, the fund is replenished. The business must replenish the fund at the end of each accounting period in order to update the company's records for all expenditures made during the period.

Objective 4. Describe the nature of a bank account and its use in controlling cash.

The forms used with bank accounts are a signature card, deposit slip, cheque, and record of cheques drawn. Each month, the bank usually sends a bank statement to the depositor, summarizing all of the transactions for the month. The bank statement allows a business to compare the cash transactions recorded in the accounting records to those recorded by the bank.

Objective 5. Prepare a bank reconciliation and journalize any necessary entries.

The first section of the bank reconciliation begins with the cash balance according to the bank statement. This balance is adjusted for the depositor's changes in cash that do not appear on the bank statement and for any bank errors. The second section begins with the cash balance according to the depositor's records. This balance is adjusted for the bank's changes in cash that do not appear on the depositor's records and for any depositor errors. The adjusted balances for the two sections must be equal.

No entries are necessary on the depositor's records as a result of the information included in the first section of the bank reconciliation. However, the items in the second section must be journalized on the depositor's records.

Objective 6. Summarize how cash is presented on the balance sheet.

Cash is listed as the first asset in the Current Assets section of the balance sheet. Companies that have invested excess cash in highly liquid investments usually report *Cash and cash equivalents* as a single item on the balance sheet.

Objective 7. Define electronic funds transfers and give an example of how they are used to process cash transactions.

Electronic funds transfer (EFT) is a payment system that uses computerized information rather than paper (money, cheques, etc.) to effect cash transactions. EFT may be used in processing cash payments and cash receipts and in processing retail sales.

GLOSSARY OF KEY TERMS

Bank reconciliation. The analysis that details the items responsible for the difference between the cash balance reported in the bank statement and the balance of the cash account in the ledger. *Objective 5*

Cash. Coins, currency (paper money), cheques, traveller's cheques, money orders, and money on deposit that is available for unrestricted withdrawal from banks or other financial institutions. *Objective 1*

Cash equivalents. Highly liquid investments that are usually reported on the balance sheet with cash. *Objective 6*

Electronic funds transfer (EFT). A payment system that uses computerized information rather than paper (money, cheques, etc.) to effect a cash transaction. *Objective 7*

Petty cash fund. A special cash fund used to pay relatively small amounts. *Objective 3*

Voucher. A document that serves as evidence of authority to pay cash. *Objective 3*

Voucher system. Records, methods, and procedures used in verifying and recording liabilities and paying and recording cash payments. *Objective 3*

ILLUSTRATIVE PROBLEM

The bank statement for Urethane Company for June 30 indicates a balance of $9,143.11. Urethane Company uses a voucher system in controlling cash payments. All cash receipts are deposited each evening in a night depository after banking hours. The accounting records indicate the following summary data for cash receipts and payments for June:

Cash balance as of June 1	$ 3,943.50
Total cash receipts for June	28,971.60
Total amount of cheques issued in June	28,388.85

Comparison of the bank statement and the accompanying cancelled cheques and memorandums with the records reveals the following reconciling items:

a. The bank had collected for Urethane Company $1,030 on a note left for collection. The face of the note was $1,000.
b. A deposit of $1,852.21, representing receipts of June 30, had been made too late to appear on the bank statement.
c. Cheques outstanding totalled $5,265.27.
d. A cheque drawn for $157 had been erroneously charged by the bank as $175.
e. A cheque for $30 returned with the statement had been recorded in the depositor's records as $240. The cheque was for the payment of an obligation to Avery Equipment Company for the purchase of office supplies on account.
f. Bank service charges for June amounted to $18.20.

Instructions

1. Prepare a bank reconciliation for June.
2. Journalize the entries that should be made by Urethane Company.

Solution

1.

Urethane Company
Bank Reconciliation
June 30, 20—

Cash balance according to bank statement		$ 9,143.11
Add: Deposit of June 30 not recorded by bank	$1,852.21	
Bank error in charging cheque as $175		
instead of $157	18.00	1,870.21
		$11,013.32
Deduct: Outstanding cheques		5,265.27
Adjusted balance		$ 5,748.05
Cash balance according to depositor's records		$ 4,526.25*
Add: Proceeds of note collected by bank, including		
$30 interest	$1,030.00	
Error in recording cheque	210.00	1,240.00
		$ 5,766.25
Deduct: Bank service charges		18.20
Adjusted balance		$ 5,748.05

*$3,943.50 + $28,971.60 − $28,388.85

2.

Cash in Bank	1,240.00	
Notes Receivable		1,000.00
Interest Income		30.00
Accounts Payable		210.00
Miscellaneous Expense	18.20	
Cash in Bank		18.20

SELF-EXAMINATION QUESTIONS (ANSWERS AT END OF CHAPTER)

1. A voucher system is used and the company uses a periodic system. When a purchase of merchandise is made for $500 under terms 1/10, n/30:
   A. Inventory would be debited for $500.
   B. Purchase Discounts would be debited for $5 if the voucher is paid within the discount period.
   C. Cash would be credited for $495 when the voucher is initially recorded.
   D. none of the above.

2. A petty cash fund is:
   A. used to pay relatively small amounts.
   B. established by estimating the amount of cash needed for disbursements of relatively small amounts during a specified period.
   C. reimbursed when the amount of money in the fund is reduced to a predetermined minimum amount.
   D. all of the above.

3. The bank erroneously charged Tropical Services' account for $450.50 for a cheque that was correctly written and recorded by Tropical Services as $540.50. To reconcile the bank account of Tropical Services at the end of the month, you would:
   A. add $90 to the cash balance according to the bank statement.
   B. add $90 to the cash balance according to Tropical Services' records.
   C. deduct $90 from the cash balance according to the bank statement.
   D. deduct $90 from the cash balance according to Tropical Services' records.

4. In preparing a bank reconciliation, the amount of cheques outstanding would be:
   A. added to the cash balance according to the bank statement.
   B. deducted from the cash balance according to the bank statement.
   C. added to the cash balance according to the depositor's records.
   D. deducted from the cash balance according to the depositor's records.

5. Journal entries based on the bank reconciliation are required for:
   A. additions to the cash balance according to the depositor's records.
   B. deductions from the cash balance according to the depositor's records.
   C. both A and B.
   D. neither A nor B.

DISCUSSION QUESTIONS

1. Why is cash the asset that often warrants the most attention in the design of an effective internal control structure?
2. Most retail businesses maintain cash change funds. (a) What is the purpose of such funds, and (b) what entry is made to establish a cash change fund?
3. The combined cash count of all cash registers at the close of business is $4 less than the cash sales indicated by the cash register tapes. (a) In what account is the cash shortage recorded? (b) Are cash shortages debited or credited to this account?
4. In which section of the income statement would you report a credit balance in Cash Short and Over?
5. What is meant by the term *voucher* as applied to the voucher system?
6. Before approving a voucher for the purchase of merchandise for payment, you should compare supporting documents to verify the accuracy of the liability. Name an example of a supporting document for the purchase of merchandise.
7. After approving a voucher for payment, you record it as a credit to what account?
8. The controller approves all vouchers before they are submitted to the treasurer for payment. What procedure can the controller add to the system to ensure that the documents accompanying the vouchers and supporting the payments are not "reused" to support future vouchers improperly?
9. The accounting clerk pays all obligations by prenumbered cheques. What are the strengths and weaknesses in the internal control over cash payments in this situation?
10. In what order are vouchers ordinarily filed (a) in the unpaid voucher file and (b) in the paid voucher file? Give reasons for the answers.
11. As a general rule, all payments should be made by cheque. Explain why some cash payments are made in coins and currency from a petty cash fund.

12. What account or accounts do you debit when recording the voucher (a) establishing a petty cash fund and (b) replenishing a petty cash fund?

13. The petty cash account has a debit balance of $500. At the end of the accounting period, there is $93 in the petty cash fund, along with petty cash receipts totalling $407. Should you replenish the fund as of the last day of the period? Discuss.

14. Distinguish between the drawer and the payee of a cheque.

15. What name is often given to the notification, attached to a cheque, that indicates the specific invoice being paid?

16. The balance of Cash in Bank is likely to differ from the cash balance reported by the bank statement. What two factors are likely to be responsible for the difference?

17. What is the purpose of preparing a bank reconciliation?

18. Do items reported on the bank statement as credits represent (a) additions made by the bank to the depositor's balance, or (b) deductions made by the bank from the depositor's balance?

19. What entry should you make if a cheque received from a customer and deposited is returned by the bank for lack of sufficient funds (an NSF cheque)?

20. a. What is meant by the term *cash equivalents?*
    b. How do you report cash equivalents in financial statements?

21. a. What is meant by the term *compensating balance* as applied to the chequing account of a firm?
    b. How do you report the compensating balance in financial statements?

22. What is meant by *electronic funds transfer?*

EXERCISES

EXERCISE 7–1
Internal control of cash receipts
Objective 2

The procedures used for over-the-counter receipts are as follows. At the close of each day's business, the sales clerks count the cash in their respective cash drawers, after which they determine the amount recorded by the cash register and prepare the memorandum cash form, noting any discrepancies. An employee from the cashier's office counts the cash, compares the total with the memorandum, and takes the cash to the cashier's office.

a. ▭▬► Indicate the weak link in internal control.
b. ▭▬► How can the weakness be corrected?

EXERCISE 7–2
Internal control of cash receipts
Objective 2

Ed Pinto works at the drive-through window of Dominick's Burgers. Occasionally, when a drive-through customer orders, Ed fills the order and pockets the customer's money. He does not ring up the order on the cash register.

▭▬► Identify the internal control weaknesses that exist at Dominick's Burgers, and discuss what can be done to prevent this theft.

EXERCISE 7–3
Internal control of cash receipts
Objective 2

The mailroom employees send all remittances and remittance advices to the cashier. The cashier deposits the cash in the bank and forwards the remittance advices and duplicate deposit slips to the Accounting Department.

a. ▭▬► Indicate the weak link in internal control in the handling of cash receipts.
b. ▭▬► How can the weakness be corrected?

EXERCISE 7–4
Entry for cash sales
Objective 2

The actual cash received from cash sales was $12,839.79, and the amount indicated by the cash register total was $12,853.16. Journalize the entry, in general journal form, to record the cash receipts and cash sales.

EXERCISE 7–5
Internal control of cash payments
Objective 3

Montclair Co. is a medium-size merchandising company. A review of vouchers paid indicated that the amount of purchases discounts lost was disproportionately large in comparison with earlier periods. Further investigation revealed that in spite of a sufficient bank balance, a significant amount of available cash discounts had been lost because of failure to make timely payments. In addition, it was discovered that several purchases invoices had been paid twice.

▸ Outline procedures for the payment of vendors' invoices, so that the possibilities of losing available cash discounts and of paying an invoice a second time will be minimized.

EXERCISE 7–6
Internal control of cash payments
Objective 3

NYCOM Company, a communications equipment manufacturer, recently fell victim to an embezzlement scheme masterminded by one of its employees. To understand the scheme, it is necessary to review NYCOM's procedures for the purchase of services.

The purchasing agent is responsible for ordering services (such as repairs to a photocopy machine or office cleaning) after receiving a service requisition from an authorized manager. However, since no tangible goods are delivered, a receiving report is not prepared. When the Accounting Department receives an invoice billing NYCOM for a service call, the accounts payable clerk calls the manager who requested the service in order to verify that it was performed.

The embezzlement scheme involves Judy Bell, the manager of plant and facilities. Judy arranged for her uncle's company, Advo Industrial Supply and Service, to be placed on NYCOM's approved vendor list. Judy did not disclose the family relationship.

On several occasions, Judy would submit a requisition for services to be provided by Advo's Industrial Supply and Service. However, the service requested was really not needed, and it was never performed. Advo would bill NYCOM for the service and then split the cash payment with Judy.

▸ Explain what changes should be made to NYCOM's procedures for ordering and paying for services in order to prevent such occurrences in the future.

EXERCISE 7–7
Internal control of cash
Objectives 1, 3

Between September 3 and September 22, 17 prenumbered cheques totalling $1,129,232.39 were forged and cashed on the accounts of **Perini Corporation,** a construction company based in the Boston suburb of Framingham. Perini Corporation kept its supply of blank prenumbered cheques in an unlocked storeroom with items such as styrofoam coffee cups. Every clerk and secretary had access to this storeroom. It was later discovered that someone had apparently stolen two boxes of prenumbered cheques. The numbers of the missing cheques matched the numbers of the out-of-sequence cheques cashed by the banks.

▸ What fundamental principle of control over cash was violated in this case?

EXERCISE 7–8
Purchases discounts
Objective 3

Journalize the entries to record the following transactions by Dill Inc.:

a. Purchased merchandise on October 1, terms 3/10, n/30, $10,000.
b. Paid the invoice on October 9.

EXERCISE 7–9
Borrowing to take a purchases discount
Objective 3

From the data in Exercise 7–8, compute the following:

a. The net savings to Dill Inc. from borrowing at 12% to take the discount.
b. The approximate interest rate earned on taking a discount on a purchase with credit terms of 3/10, n/30.

EXERCISE 7–10
Petty cash fund entries
Objective 3

Journalize the entries to record the following:

a. Voucher No. 10002 is prepared to establish a petty cash fund of $450.
b. Cheque No. 2511 is issued in payment of Voucher No. 10002.
c. The amount of cash in the petty cash fund is now $87.30. Voucher No. 10127 is prepared to replenish the fund, based on the following summary of petty cash receipts: office supplies, $115.83; miscellaneous selling expense, $125.60; miscellaneous expense, $118.10. (Since the amount of the cheque to replenish the fund plus the balance in the fund do not equal $450, record the discrepancy in the Cash Short and Over account.)
d. Cheque No. 2555 is issued by the disbursing officer in payment of Voucher No. 10127. The cheque is cashed, and the money is placed in the fund.

EXERCISE 7–11
Cash change fund entries with voucher system
Objectives 2, 3

Journalize the entries for the following transactions:

a. Voucher No. 130 is prepared to establish a change fund of $800.
b. Cheque No. 1170 is issued in payment of Voucher No. 130.
c. Cash sales for the day, according to the cash register tapes, were $7,358.10, and cash on hand is $8,162.90. A bank deposit slip was prepared for $7,362.90.

EXERCISE 7–12
Bank reconciliation
Objective 5

Identify each of the following reconciling items as: (a) an addition to the cash balance according to the bank statement, (b) a deduction from the cash balance according to the bank statement, (c) an addition to the cash balance according to the depositor's records, or (d) a deduction from the cash balance according to the depositor's records. (None of the transactions reported by bank debit and credit memorandums has been recorded by the depositor.)

1. Cheque for $36 charged by bank as $63.
2. Cheque drawn by depositor for $25 but recorded as $250.
3. Outstanding cheques, $6,515.50.
4. Deposit in transit, $5,279.12.
5. Note collected by bank, $5,200.00.
6. Cheque of a customer returned by bank to depositor because of insufficient funds, $712.50.
7. Bank service charges, $20.10.

EXERCISE 7–13
Entries based on bank reconciliation
Objective 5

Which of the reconciling items listed in Exercise 7–12 necessitate an entry in the depositor's accounts?

EXERCISE 7–14
Bank reconciliation
Objective 5

The following data were accumulated for use in reconciling the bank account of The Skin Care Co. for May:

a. Cash balance according to the depositor's records at May 31, $8,530.20.
b. Cash balance according to the bank statement at May 31, $11,100.50.
c. Cheques outstanding, $4,276.20.
d. Deposit in transit, not recorded by bank, $1,780.40.
e. A cheque for $230 in payment of a voucher was erroneously recorded in the cheque register as $320.
f. Bank debit memorandum for service charges, $15.50.

Prepare a bank reconciliation.

EXERCISE 7–15
Entries for bank reconciliation
Objective 5

Using the data presented in Exercise 7–14, journalize, in general journal form, the entry or entries that should be made by the depositor.

EXERCISE 7–16
Entries for note collected by bank
Objective 5

Accompanying a bank statement for Profumeria Company is a credit memorandum for $12,255, representing the principal ($12,000) and interest ($255) on a note that had been collected by the bank. The depositor had been notified by the bank at the time of the collection, but had made no entries. In general journal form, journalize the entry that should be made by the depositor to bring the accounting records up to date.

EXERCISE 7–17
Bank reconciliation
Objective 5

An accounting clerk for The Emporium Co. prepared the following bank reconciliation:

The Emporium Co.
Bank Reconciliation
January 31, 2000

Cash balance according to depositor's records		$12,100.75
Add: Outstanding cheques	$3,557.12	
Error by the Emporium Co. in recording Cheque		
No. 345 as $760 instead of $670	90.00	
Note for $1,500 collected by bank, including		
interest	1,620.00	5,267.12
		$17,367.87
Deduct: Deposit in transit on January 31	$1,150.00	
Bank service charges	25.60	1,175.60
Cash balance according to bank statement		$16,192.27

a. Using the data in the above bank reconciliation, prepare a bank reconciliation for The Emporium Co. in the format shown in the chapter.

b. If a balance sheet were prepared for The Emporium Co. on January 31, 2000, what amount should be reported for cash in bank?

EXERCISE 7–18
Using bank reconciliation to determine cash receipts stolen
Objective 5

Desktop Co. records all cash receipts on the basis of its cash register tapes. Desktop Co. discovered during June 1999 that one of its sales clerks had stolen an undetermined amount of cash receipts when he took the daily deposits to the bank. The following data have been gathered for June:

Cash in bank according to the general ledger	$10,773.22
Cash according to the June 30, 1999 bank statement	12,271.14
Outstanding cheques as of June 30, 1999	1,889.37
Bank service charge for June	18.60
Note receivable, including interest collected by bank in June	1,060.00

No deposits were in transit on June 30, which fell on a Sunday.

a. Determine the amount of cash receipts stolen by the sales clerk.

b. What accounting controls would have prevented or detected this theft?

EXERCISE 7–19
Bank reconciliation
Objective 5

How many errors can you find in the following bank reconciliation prepared as of the end of the current month?

Abracadabra Co.
Bank Reconciliation
For the Month Ended June 30, 20—

Cash balance according to bank statement			$13,767.76
Add outstanding cheques:			
No. 3721		$ 345.95	
3739		172.75	
3743		359.60	
3744		601.50	1,479.80
			$15,247.56
Deduct deposit of June 30, not recorded by bank			1,010.06
Adjusted balance			$10,237.50
Cash balance according to depositor's records			$10,739.32
Add: Proceeds of note collected by bank:			
Principal	$2,500.00		
Interest	75.00	$2,575.00	
Service charges		19.50	2,594.50
			$13,333.82
Deduct: Cheque returned because of			
insufficient funds		$ 266.80	
Error in recording May 15			
deposit of $1,859 as $1,589		270.00	536.80
Adjusted balance			$12,797.02

PROBLEMS SERIES A

PROBLEM 7–1A
Evaluating internal control of cash
Objectives 1, 2, 3

The following procedures were recently installed by Kato Company:

a. The bank reconciliation is prepared by the cashier, who works under the supervision of the treasurer.

b. All mail is opened by the mail clerk, who forwards all remittances to the cashier. The cashier prepares a listing of the cash receipts and forwards a copy of the list to the accounts receivable clerk for recording in the accounts.

c. At the end of each day, an accounting clerk compares the duplicate copy of the daily cash deposit slip with the deposit receipt obtained from the bank.

    d. The accounts payable clerk prepares a voucher for each disbursement. The voucher along with the supporting documentation is forwarded to the treasurer's office for approval.

    e. After necessary approvals have been obtained for the payment of a voucher, the treasurer signs and mails the cheque. The treasurer then stamps the voucher and supporting documentation as paid and returns the voucher and supporting documentation to the accounts payable clerk for filing.

    f. Along with petty cash expense receipts for postage, office supplies, etc., several postdated employee cheques are in the petty cash fund.

    g. At the end of each day, any deposited cash receipts are placed in the bank's night depository.

    h. At the end of the day, cash register clerks are required to use their own funds to make up any cash shortages in their registers.

Instructions

Indicate whether each of the procedures of internal control over cash represents (1) a strength or (2) a weakness. For each weakness, indicate why it exists.

PROBLEM 7–2A
Transactions for petty cash, advances to salespersons fund; cash short and over
Objectives 2, 3

Hamilton Company has just adopted the policy of depositing all cash receipts in the bank and of making all payments by cheque in conjunction with the voucher system. The following transactions were selected from those completed in August of the current year:

Aug. 2. Recorded Voucher No. 1 to establish a petty cash fund of $400 and a change fund of $500.

      2. Issued Cheque No. 719 in payment of Voucher No. 1.

      3. Recorded Voucher No. 5 to establish an advances to salespersons fund of $2,000.

      5. Issued Cheque No. 722 in payment of Voucher No. 5.

    17. The cash sales for the day, according to the cash register tapes, totalled $2,970.60. The combined count of all cash on hand (including the change fund) totalled $3,473.20.

    29. Recorded Voucher No. 44 to reimburse the petty cash fund for the following disbursements, each evidenced by a petty cash receipt:

        Aug. 3. Store supplies, $21.50.

            5. Express charges on merchandise sold, $16.00.

            8. Office supplies, $12.75.

          11. Office supplies, $9.20.

          17. Postage stamps, $52 (Office Supplies).

          19. Repair to office calculator, $37.50 (Miscellaneous Expense).

          22. Postage due on special delivery letter, $1.05 (Miscellaneous Expense).

          23. Express charges on merchandise sold, $35.

          27. Office supplies, $11.10.

    29. Issued Cheque No. 752 in payment of Voucher No. 44.

    30. The cash sales for the day, according to the cash register tapes, totalled $3,055.50. The count of all cash on hand (including the change fund) totalled $3,551.60.

    31. Recorded Voucher No. 49 to replenish the advances to salespersons fund for the following expenditures for travel: Mark May, $312.50; Joe Wolf, $556.50; Tony Sacca, $372.10.

    31. Issued Cheque No. 760 in payment of Voucher No. 49.

Instructions

Journalize the transactions.

PROBLEM 7–3A
Entries for voucher system, petty cash
Objective 3

The following selected transactions were completed by a company that uses a voucher system and a perpetual inventory system.

Sept. 3. Recorded Voucher No. 540 for $800, payable to Patel Supply Co., for office supplies purchased, terms n/eom.

      8. Recorded Voucher No. 542 for $9,000, payable to Cox Co., for merchandise purchased, terms 1/10, n/30.

      9. Recorded Voucher No. 548 for $1,400, payable to Collins Co., for merchandise purchased, terms 2/10, n/30.

    19. Issued Cheque No. 264 in payment of Voucher No. 548.

Sept. 29. Recorded Voucher No. 560 for $255.14 to replenish the petty cash fund for the following disbursements: store supplies, $92.88; office supplies, $84.95; miscellaneous expense, $42.45; miscellaneous selling expense, $34.86.
    30. Issued Cheque No. 270 in payment of Voucher No. 560.
    30. Issued Cheque No. 277 in payment of Voucher No. 542.
    30. Issued Cheque No. 289 in payment of Voucher No. 540.

Instructions

Journalize the transactions.

PROBLEM 7–4A

Bank reconciliation and entries
Objective 5

The Cash in Bank account for Zashy Carpets at November 30 of the current year indicated a balance of $15,100.30. The bank statement indicated a balance of $21,016.30 on November 30. Comparison of the bank statement and the accompanying cancelled cheques and memorandums with the records revealed the following reconciling items:

a. Cheques outstanding totalled $8,169.75.
b. A deposit of $3,917.75, representing receipts of November 30, had been made too late to appear on the bank statement.
c. The bank had collected $3,150 on a note left for collection. The face of the note was $3,000.
d. A cheque for $1,500 returned with the statement had been incorrectly recorded by Zashy Carpets as $1,050. The cheque was for the payment of an obligation to Morgan Co. for the purchase of office equipment on account.
e. A cheque drawn for $600 had been erroneously charged by the bank as $1,600.
f. Bank service charges for June amounted to $36.00.

Instructions

1. Prepare a bank reconciliation.
2. Journalize the necessary entries. The accounts have not been closed. The voucher system is used.

PROBLEM 7–5A

Bank reconciliation and entries
Objective 5

The Cash in Bank account for Conner Co. at August 1 of the current year indicated a balance of $18,443.90. During August, the total cash deposited was $30,650.75, and cheques written totalled $31,770.25. The bank statement indicated a balance of $26,465.50 on August 31. Comparison of the bank statement, the cancelled cheques, and the accompanying memorandums with the records revealed the following reconciling items:

a. Cheques outstanding totalled $8,003.84.
b. A deposit of $2,148.21, representing receipts of August 31, had been made too late to appear on the bank statement.
c. The bank had collected for Conner Co. $3,650 on a note left for collection. The face of the note was $3,500.
d. A cheque for $470 returned with the statement had been incorrectly charged by the bank as $740.
e. A cheque for $84.20 returned with the statement had been recorded by Conner Co. as $8.42. The cheque was for the payment of an obligation to Bartles Co. on account.
f. Bank service charges for August amounted to $18.75.

Instructions

1. Prepare a bank reconciliation as of August 31.
2. Journalize the necessary entries. The accounts have not been closed.

PROBLEM 7–6A

Bank reconciliation and entries
Objective 5

The Vanier Company uses the voucher system in controlling cash payments. All cash receipts are deposited each Wednesday and Friday in a night depository, after banking hours. The data required to reconcile the bank statement as of June 30 have been taken from various documents and records and are reproduced as follows. The sources of the data are printed in capital letters.

CASH IN BANK ACCOUNT:
    Balance as of June 1 $7,317.40

CASH RECEIPTS FOR MONTH OF JUNE: 7,579.58

DUPLICATE DEPOSIT SLIPS:
  Date and amount of each deposit in June:

Date	Amount	Date	Amount	Date	Amount
June 1	$908.50	June 10	$ 896.61	June 22	$897.34
3	854.17	15	882.95	24	942.71
8	840.50	17	1,046.74	29	310.06

CHEQUES WRITTEN:
  Number and amount of each cheque issued in June:

Cheque No.	Amount	Cheque No.	Amount	Cheque No.	Amount
740	$237.50	747	Void	754	$249.75
741	495.15	748	$450.90	755	172.75
742	501.90	749	640.13	756	113.95
743	671.30	750	276.77	757	407.95
744	506.88	751	299.37	758	359.60
745	117.25	752	537.01	759	701.50
746	298.66	753	380.95	760	486.39

Total amount of cheques issued in June: $7,905.66

JUNE BANK STATEMENT:

BANK OF MONTREAL

PAGE   1

ACCOUNT NUMBER

FROM 6/01/20—	TO	6/30/20—
BALANCE		7,447.20
9 DEPOSITS		10,944.77
20 WITHDRAWALS		7,145.91
4 OTHER DEBITS AND CREDITS		326.30
NEW BALANCE		10,919.76

THE VANIER COMPANY

```
*----CHEQUES AND OTHER DEBITS---*---DEPOSITS-*-DATE-*--BALANCE--*

No.731  162.15    No.738  251.40        690.25   06/01   7,723.90
No.739   60.55    No.740  237.50        908.50   06/02   8,334.35
No.741  495.15    No.742  501.90        854.17   06/04   8,191.47
No.743  671.30    No.744  506.88        840.50   06/09   7,853.79
No.745  117.25    No.746  298.66   MS 2,500.00   06/09   9,937.88
No.748  450.90    No.749  640.13   MS   125.00   06/09   8,971.85
No.750  276.77    No.751  299.37        896.61   06/11   9,292.32
No.752  537.01    No.753  380.95        882.95   06/16   9,257.31
No.754  249.75    No.756  113.95      1,406.74   06/18  10,300.35
No.757  407.95    No.760  486.39        897.34   06/23  10,303.35
                                        942.71   06/25  11,246.06
                         NSF  291.90             06/28  10,954.16
                         SC    34.40             06/30  10,919.76


    EC--ERROR CORRECTION              OD--OVERDRAFT
    MS--MISCELLANEOUS                 PS--PAYMENT STOPPED
    NSF--NOT SUFFICIENT FUNDS         SC--SERVICE CHARGE

    ***                      ***                         ***

  THE RECONCILEMENT OF THIS STATEMENT WITH YOUR RECORDS IS ESSENTIAL.
      ANY ERROR OR EXCEPTIONS SHOULD BE REPORTED IMMEDIATELY.
```

BANK RECONCILIATION FOR PRECEDING MONTH:

The Vanier Company
Bank Reconciliation
May 31, 20—

Cash balance according to bank statement		$7,447.20
Add deposit for May 31, not recorded by bank		690.25
		$8,137.45
Deduct outstanding cheques:		
No. 731	$162.15	
736	345.95	
738	251.40	
739	60.55	820.05
Adjusted balance		$7,317.40
Cash balance according to depositor's records		$7,352.50
Deduct service charges		35.10
Adjusted balance		$7,317.40

Instructions

1. Prepare a bank reconciliation as of June 30. If you discover errors in recording deposits or cheques, assume that the errors were made by the company. Assume that all deposits are from cash sales. All cheques are in payment of vouchers.
2. Journalize the necessary entries. The accounts have not been closed.
3. What is the amount of Cash in Bank that should appear on the balance sheet as of June 30?
4. ◖▬▬▶ If in preparing the bank reconciliation you note that a cancelled cheque for $250 has been incorrectly recorded by the bank as $520, briefly explain how the error would be included in the bank reconciliation and how it should be corrected.

PROBLEMS SERIES B

PROBLEM 7–1B
Evaluating internal control of cash
Objectives 1, 2, 3

The following procedures were recently installed by Jafra Company:

a. The bank reconciliation is prepared by the accountant.
b. Each cashier is assigned a separate cash register drawer, to which no other cashier has access.
c. All sales are rung up on the cash register, and a receipt is given to the customer. All sales are recorded on a tape locked inside the cash register.
d. At the end of a shift, each cashier counts the cash in his or her cash register, unlocks the tape, and compares the amount of cash with the amount on the tape to determine cash shortages and overages.
e. Cheques received through the mail are given daily to the accounts receivable clerk for recording collections on account and for depositing in the bank.
f. Disbursements are made from the petty cash fund only after a petty cash receipt has been completed and signed by the payee.
g. Vouchers and all supporting documents are perforated with a PAID designation after being paid by the treasurer.

Instructions

◖▬▬▶ Indicate whether each of the procedures of internal control over cash represents (1) a strength or (2) a weakness. For each weakness, indicate why it exists.

PROBLEM 7–2B
Transactions for petty cash, advances to salespersons fund; cash short and over
Objectives 2, 3

Physical Dynamics Company has just adopted the policy of depositing all cash receipts in the bank and of making all payments by cheque in conjunction with the voucher system. The following transactions were selected from those completed in April of the current year:

April 1. Recorded Voucher No. 1 to establish a petty cash fund of $350 and a change fund of $500.
      1. Issued Cheque No. 299 in payment of Voucher No. 1.

April 5. Recorded Voucher No. 5 to establish an advances to salespersons fund of $1,500.
      6. Issued Cheque No. 302 in payment of Voucher No. 5.
    15. The cash sales for the day, according to the cash register tapes, totalled $1,995.60. The combined count of all cash on hand (including the change fund) totalled $2,498.20.
    26. Recorded Voucher No. 38 to reimburse the petty cash fund for the following disbursements, each evidenced by a petty cash receipt:
      April 4. Store supplies, $26.50.
           6. Express charges on merchandise purchased, $15.50.
           8. Office supplies, $14.75.
           9. Office supplies, $9.20.
         12. Postage stamps, $52.00 (Office Supplies).
         16. Repair to adding machine, $39.50 (Miscellaneous Expense).
         20. Repair to typewriter, $31.50 (Miscellaneous Expense).
         22. Postage due on special delivery letter, $1.05 (Miscellaneous Expense).
         24. Express charges on merchandise purchased, $19.50.
    26. Issued Cheque No. 337 in payment of Voucher No. 38.
    30. The cash sales for the day, according to the cash register tapes, totalled $2,009.50. The count of all cash on hand (including the change fund) totalled $2,505.60.
    30. Recorded Voucher No. 43 to replenish the advances to salespersons fund for the following expenditures for travel: Susan Hilgenberg, $119.50; Al Del Greco, $433.40; Alice McKyer, $375.10.
    30. Issued Cheque No. 340 in payment of Voucher No. 43.

Instructions

Journalize the transactions.

PROBLEM 7–3B

Entries for voucher system, petty cash
Objective 3

The following selected transactions were completed by a company that uses a voucher system and a periodic inventory system.

Jan. 3. Recorded Voucher No. 1015 for $2,500, payable to Edwards Supply Co., for office supplies purchased, terms n/30.
     5. Recorded Voucher No. 1020 for $8,000, payable to Fair Co., for merchandise purchased, terms 2/10, n/eom.
   10. Recorded Voucher No. 1028 for $2,500, payable to Clinton Co., for merchandise purchased, terms 1/10, n/30.
   20. Issued Cheque No. 795 in payment of Voucher No. 1028.
   30. Recorded Voucher No. 1040 for $239.84 to replenish the petty cash fund for the following disbursements: store supplies, $92.88; office supplies, $69.95; miscellaneous expense, $42.45; miscellaneous selling expense, $34.56.
   31. Issued Cheque No. 806 in payment of Voucher No. 1040.
   31. Issued Cheque No. 821 in payment of Voucher No. 1020.
   31. Issued Cheque No. 835 in payment of Voucher No. 1015.

Instructions

Journalize the transactions.

PROBLEM 7–4B

Bank reconciliation and entries
Objective 5

The Cash in Bank account for Intercom Systems at March 31 of the current year indicated a balance of $17,460. The bank statement indicated a balance of $23,391.40 on March 31. Comparison of the bank statement and the accompanying cancelled cheques and memorandums with the records reveals the following reconciling items:

a. Cheques outstanding totalled $3,943.90.
b. A deposit of $1,215.50, representing receipts of March 31, had been made too late to appear on the bank statement.
c. The bank had collected $2,600 on a note left for collection. The face of the note was $2,500.
d. A cheque for $180 returned with the statement had been incorrectly recorded by Intercom Systems as $810. The cheque was for the payment of an obligation to Optel Co. for the purchase of office supplies on account.
e. A cheque drawn for $75 had been incorrectly charged by the bank as $57.
f. Bank service charges for March amounted to $45.

Instructions

1. Prepare a bank reconciliation.
2. Journalize the necessary entries. The accounts have not been closed. The voucher system is used.

PROBLEM 7–5B
Bank reconciliation and entries
Objective 5

The cash in bank account for Powlen Co. at June 1 of the current year indicated a balance of $12,881.40. During June, the total cash deposited was $40,500.40, and cheques written totalled $38,850.47. The bank statement indicated a balance of $18,880.45 on June 30. Comparison of the bank statement, the cancelled cheques, and the accompanying memorandums with the records revealed the following reconciling items:

a. Cheques outstanding totalled $4,180.27.
b. A deposit of $2,481.70, representing receipts of June 30, had been made too late to appear on the bank statement.
c. A cheque for $190 had been incorrectly charged by the bank as $100.
d. A cheque for $570.45 returned with the statement had been recorded by Powlen Co. as $750.45. The cheque was for the payment of an obligation to Scott and Son on account.
e. The bank had collected for Powlen Co. $2,400 on a note left for collection. The face of the note was $2,000.
f. Bank service charges for June amounted to $19.45.

Instructions

1. Prepare a bank reconciliation as of June 30.
2. Journalize the necessary entries. The accounts have not been closed.

PROBLEM 7–6B
Bank reconciliation and entries
Objective 5

Trevino Interiors uses the voucher system in controlling cash payments. All cash receipts are deposited each Wednesday and Friday in a night depository, after banking hours. The data required to reconcile the bank statement as of August 31 have been taken from various documents and records and are reproduced as follows. The sources of the data are printed in capital letters.

CASH IN BANK ACCOUNT:
  Balance as of August 1 $10,578.00

CASH RECEIPTS FOR MONTH OF AUGUST   6,132.60

DUPLICATE DEPOSIT SLIPS:
  Date and amount of each deposit in August:

Date	Amount	Date	Amount	Date	Amount
Aug. 2	$619.50	Aug. 12	$780.70	Aug. 23	$731.45
5	701.80	16	600.10	26	601.50
9	819.24	19	701.26	31	577.05

CHEQUES WRITTEN:
  Number and amount of each cheque issued in August:

Cheque No.	Amount	Cheque No.	Amount	Cheque No.	Amount
614	$243.50	621	$409.50	628	$ 737.70
615	650.10	622	Void	629	329.90
616	279.90	623	Void	630	882.80
617	395.50	624	707.01	631	1081.56
618	535.40	625	658.63	632	62.40
619	230.10	626	550.03	633	310.08
620	238.87	627	318.73	634	203.30

Total amount of cheques issued in August: $8,825.01

```
                                                              PAGE       1
   NIAGARA CREDIT UNION              ACCOUNT NUMBER

                                 FROM   8/01/20—    TO    8/31/20—
                                 BALANCE            10,422.80
                              9  DEPOSITS           11,436.35
                             20  WITHDRAWALS         8,514.11

   TREVINO INTERIORS          4  OTHER DEBITS           249.50
                                 AND CREDITS

                                 NEW BALANCE        13,095.54


   *-----CHEQUES AND OTHER DEBITS-------------*--DEPOSITS-*-DATE-*-BALANCE-*

   No.580  310.10   No.612   92.50           780.80  08/01  10,801.00
   No.613  137.50   No.614  243.50           619.50  08/03  11,039.50
   No.615  650.10   No.616  279.90           701.80  08/06  10,811.30
   No.617  395.50   No.618  535.40           819.24  08/11  10,699.64
   No.619  320.10   No.620  238.87           780.70  08/13  10,921.37
   No.621  409.50   No.624  707.01    MS  5000.00  08/14  14,804.86
   No.625  658.63   No.626  550.03    MS   100.00  08/14  13,696.20
   No.627  318.73   No.629  329.90           600.10  08/17  13,647.67
   No.630  882.80   No.631 1081.56  NSF 225.40  08/20  11,457.91
   No.632   62.40   No.633  310.08           701.26  08/21  11,786.69
                                             731.45  08/24  12,518.14
                                             601.50  08/28  13,119.64
                         SC    24.10                 08/31  13,095.54


       EC--ERROR CORRECTION           OD--OVERDRAFT
       MS--MISCELLANEOUS              PS--PAYMENT STOPPED
       NSF--NOT SUFFICIENT FUNDS      SC--SERVICE CHARGE

       ***                      ***                      ***

   THE RECONCILEMENT OF THIS STATEMENT WITH YOUR RECORDS IS ESSENTIAL.
   ANY ERROR OR EXCEPTIONS SHOULD BE REPORTED IMMEDIATELY.
```

BANK RECONCILIATION FOR PRECEDING MONTH:

Trevino Interiors Company
Bank Reconciliation
July 31, 20—

Cash balance according to bank statement		$10,422.80
Add deposit of July 31, not recorded by bank		780.80
		$11,203.60
Deduct outstanding cheques:		
No. 580	$310.10	
No. 602	85.50	
No. 612	92.50	
No. 613	137.50	625.60
Adjusted balance		$10,578.00
Cash balance according to depositor's records		$10,605.70
Deduct service charges		27.70
Adjusted balance		$10,578.00

Instructions

1. Prepare a bank reconciliation as of August 31. If you discover errors in recording deposits or cheques, assume that the errors were made by the company. Assume that all deposits are from cash sales. All cheques are in payment of vouchers.
2. Journalize the necessary entries. The accounts have not been closed.

3. What is the amount of Cash in Bank that should appear on the balance sheet as of August 31?
4. ◀━━▶ Assume that in preparing the bank reconciliation, you note that a cancelled cheque for $570 has been incorrectly recorded by the bank as $750. Briefly explain how the error would be included in the bank reconciliation and how it should be corrected.

CHALLENGE PROBLEMS

PROBLEM CP7–1

Kutsey Kloz is a children's clothing store that first opened its doors for business on January 1, 1999. At the end of January 2000, owner, Karen Kutsey, engages you to perform an audit of the business's first year of operations. When you arrive to perform your audit, Karen appears upset:

"I really don't know what I'm going to do. Two weeks ago I lost my best cashier and bookkeeper, Lily White. And now I hear that she's moved out of town. I don't know how we'll ever manage without Lily! She used to take care of everything. Before she left, Lily prepared the bank reconciliation for December 31, 1999 and so that should be of some help to you. I was kind of surprised that we didn't have more cash in the bank at the end of December. It was a very good month for Christmas sales, and I thought that our bank balance would have been higher than it was at the end of the year."

The bank reconciliation that Lily prepared is shown below:

Kutsey Kloz
Bank Reconciliation
December 31, 1999

Balance per Bank	$ 8,660.10	Balance per Books	$11,499.60
Add: Deposits in transit	2,940.50		
	$11,600.60		
Less Outstanding cheques:		Less:	
No. 840 $350.55		Unrecorded credit $660.00	
No. 845 150.00		Bank charges 20.00	680.00
No. 846 280.45	781.00		
Correct Balance per Bank	$10,819.60	Correct Balance per Books	$10,819.60

During your audit you discover the following:

1. A cheque for $390 that cleared the bank on December 14 was recorded in the books as $930. This error has never been corrected.
2. The bank confirmed that the deposit in transit was entered into the bank's records on January 2, 2000. However, the amount of the deposit was $2,440.50 rather than the amount indicated on the bank reconciliation.
3. Cheque No. 720 in the amount of $300.00 was recorded in the books on November 28. This appeared as an outstanding cheque on the November 30 bank reconciliation, but did not clear the bank until January 10, 2000.
4. The $660 unrecorded credit shown on the bank reconciliation represents an electronic funds transfer from one of Kutsey's customers. The bank statement shows that this amount was deposited to Kutsey's bank account on December 21.

Instructions

1. During your audit you conclude that Lily White may have absconded with some of the company's funds. Calculate the cash that appears to be missing from Kutsey's bank account.
2. How do you think Lily managed to misappropriate cash from the business? Suggest how the company might improve its internal control procedures regarding cash.

PROBLEM CP7–2

On June 30, before replenishing its petty cash, Chen Consultants showed the following balances in its general ledger:

Cash	$4,525.05
Petty Cash	$ 125.00

At the end of the day, the petty cash was replenished. At that time the petty cash drawer contained the following: $29.50 in cash and receipts for $16.00 in postage, $30.00 in miscellaneous expenses, $43.15 in office supplies, and a $15 IOU from the cashier. A week later Chen received a bank statement showing a balance of $5,468.50. During the month, the bank had collected a note for Chen totalling $688.50, including $18.50 interest. Included with the statement was an NSF cheque for $42.38, which had been received from a customer, D. Welsh. The bank statement showed service charges of $5.50 and a $25 charge for a safety deposit box. The safety deposit box actually belonged to another client of the bank and should not have been charged to Chen's account. In recording a deposit for $160 received on account from customer A. Roubi, Chen's accountant had erroneously listed the collection as $16. The cheque was shown for the correct amount among the deposits listed on the June bank statement. Outstanding cheques at the end of June (before replenishment of petty cash) totalled $502.12 and outstanding deposits were $318.29.

Instructions

a. Prepare all journal entries (ignoring closing entries) required to correct and update the books at June 30.
b. What amount should you record under the heading of "Cash" on the June 30 balance sheet?

CASES

CASE 7–1
The Cosmetics Co.
Bank reconciliation

During the preparation of the bank reconciliation for The Cosmetics Co., Karen Kay, the assistant controller, discovered that the Bank of Montreal erroneously recorded a $1,700 cheque written by The Cosmetics Co. as $700. Karen has decided not to notify the bank, but to wait for the bank to detect the error. Karen plans to record the $1,000 error as Other Income if the bank fails to detect the error within the next three months.

➤ Discuss whether Karen is behaving in an ethical manner.

CASE 7–2
Regents Computer Co.
Internal controls

The following is an excerpt from a conversation between two sales clerks, Carol Morrow and Will Fleming. Both Carol and Will are employed by Regents Computer Co., a locally owned and operated computer retail store.

Carol: Did you hear the news?
Will: What news?
Carol: Agatha and Bailey were both arrested this morning.
Will: What? Arrested? You're putting me on!
Carol: No, really! The police arrested them first thing this morning. Put them in handcuffs, read them their rights—the whole works. It was unreal!

Will: What did they do?
Carol: Well, apparently they were filling out merchandise refund forms for fictitious customers and then taking the cash.
Will: I guess I never thought of that. How did they catch them?
Carol: The store manager noticed that returns were twice that of last year and seemed to be increasing. When he confronted Agatha, she became flustered and admitted to taking the cash, apparently over $2,000 in just three months. They're going over the last six months' transactions to try to determine how much Bailey stole. He apparently started stealing first.

➤ Suggest appropriate control procedures that would have prevented or detected the theft of cash.

CASE 7–3
Friendly Grocery Stores
Internal controls

The following is an excerpt from a conversation between the store manager of Friendly Grocery Stores, Kim Hennsley, and Myles Cockren, president of Friendly Grocery Stores.

Myles: Kim, I'm concerned about this new scanning system.

Kim: What's the problem?

Myles: Well, how do we know the clerks are ringing up all the merchandise?

Kim: That's one of the strong points about the system. The scanner automatically rings up each item, based on its bar code. We update the prices daily, so we're sure that the sale is rung up for the right price.

Myles: That's not my concern. What keeps a clerk from pretending to scan items and then simply not charging his friends? If his friends were buying 10 to 15 items, it would be easy for the clerk to pass through several items with his finger over the bar code or just pass the merchandise through the scanner with the wrong side showing. It would look normal for anyone observing. In the old days, we at least could hear the cash register ringing up each sale.

Kim: I see your point.

➤ Suggest ways that Friendly Grocery Stores could prevent or detect the theft of merchandise as described.

CASE 7–4
Sunrise Markets
Internal controls

Leo Reckler and Deborah Getman are both cash register clerks for Sunrise Markets. Jo Calloway is the store manager for Sunrise Markets. The following is an excerpt of a conversation between Leo and Deborah:

Leo: Debbie, how long have you been working for Sunrise Markets?

Deborah: Almost five years this September. You just started two weeks ago . . . right?

Leo: Yes. Do you mind if I ask you a question?

Deborah: No, go ahead.

Leo: What I want to know is, have they always had this rule that if your cash register is short at the end of the day you have to make up the shortage out of your own pocket?

Deborah: Yes, as long as I've been working here.

Leo: Well, it's the pits. Last week I had to pay in almost $60.

Deborah: It's not that big a deal. I just make sure that I'm not short at the end of the day.

Leo: How do you do that?

Deborah: I just short-change a few customers early in the day. There are a few jerks that deserve it anyway. Most of the time, their attention is elsewhere and they don't think to check their change.

Leo: What happens if you're over at the end of the day?

Deborah: Jo lets me keep it as long as it doesn't get to be too large. I've not been short in over a year. I usually clear about $10 to $40 extra per day.

➤ Discuss the ethics of this case from the viewpoints of Deborah, Leo, and Jo.

CASE 7–5
Sears Canada Inc.
Financial analysis

Corporations generally issue annual reports to their shareholders and other interested parties. These annual reports include a Management Responsibility (or Management Report) section as well as financial statements. The Management Responsibility section discusses responsibility for the financial statements and normally includes an assessment of the company's internal control system. The financial statements also report the company's cash and cash equivalents.

1. What does the annual report for Sears Canada Inc. indicate about the internal control system?
2. What is Sears's amount of cash and cash equivalents at the end of the current year?
3. What is the makeup of cash equivalents at the end of the current year?
4. In which financial statement are the major inflows and outflows of cash and cash equivalents reported?

CASE 7–6
Interscope Company
Bank reconciliation and internal control

The records of Interscope Company indicate a May 31 cash in bank balance of $22,631.05, which includes undeposited receipts for May 30 and 31. The cash balance on the bank statement as of May 31 is $20,004.95. This balance includes a note of $3,000 plus $150 interest collected by the bank but not recorded in the journal. Cheques outstanding on May 31 were as follows: No. 470, $950.20; No. 479, $510; No. 490, $616.50; No. 796, $127.40; No. 797, $520; and No. 799, $351.50.

On May 3, the cashier resigned, effective at the end of the month. Before leaving on May 31, the cashier prepared the following bank reconciliation:

Cash balance per books, May 31		$22,631.05
Add outstanding cheques:		
No. 796	$127.40	
797	520.00	
799	351.50	798.90
		$24,129.95
Less undeposited receipts		3,425.00
Cash balance per bank, May 31		$20,004.95
Deduct unrecorded note with interest		3,150.00
True cash, May 31		$16,854.95

Calculator Tape of Outstanding Cheques

```
      0.00 *
    127.40 +
    520.00 +
    351.50 +
    798.90 *
```

Subsequently, the owner of Interscope Company discovered that the cashier had stolen all undeposited receipts in excess of the $3,425 on hand on May 31. The owner, a close family friend, has asked your help in determining the amount that the former cashier has stolen.

1. Determine the amount the cashier stole from Interscope Company. Show your computations in good form.
2. How did the cashier attempt to conceal the theft?
3. a. Identify two major weaknesses in internal controls, which allowed the cashier to steal the undeposited cash receipts.
   b. ◀▬▬▬ Recommend improvements in internal controls, so that similar types of thefts of undeposited cash receipts can be prevented.

ANSWERS TO SELF-EXAMINATION QUESTIONS

1. **D**   When the voucher is recorded initially under a periodic system, we debit Purchases for $500, not Inventory (answer A is incorrect). When the voucher is *paid* within the discount period, we *credit* Purchase Discounts for $5 (not answer B) and we credit Cash for $495 (not answer C).

2. **D**   To avoid the delay, annoyance, and expense that is associated with paying all obligations by cheque, relatively small amounts (answer A) are paid from a petty cash fund. The fund is established by estimating the amount of cash needed to pay these small amounts during a specified period (answer B), and it is then reimbursed when the amount of money in the fund is reduced to a predetermined minimum amount (answer C).

3. **C**   The error was made by the bank, so the cash balance according to the bank statement needs to be adjusted. Since the bank deducted $90 ($540.50 − $450.50) too little, the error of $90 should be deducted from the cash balance according to the bank statement (answer C).

4. **B**   On any specific date, the cash in bank account in a depositor's ledger may not agree with the account in the bank's ledger because of delays and/or errors by either party in recording transactions. The purpose of a bank reconciliation, therefore, is to determine the reasons for any differences between the two account balances. All errors should then be corrected by the depositor or the bank, as appropriate. In arriving at the adjusted (correct) cash balance according to the bank statement, outstanding cheques must be deducted (answer B) to adjust for cheques that have been written by the depositor but that have not yet been presented to the bank for payment.

5. **C**   All reconciling items that are added to and deducted from the cash balance according to the depositor's records on the bank reconciliation (answer C) require that journal entries be made by the depositor to correct errors made in recording transactions or to bring the cash account up to date for delays in recording transactions.

8

Receivables and Temporary Investments

YOU AND ACCOUNTING

Assume that you have decided to sell your car to a neighbour for $7,500. Your neighbour agrees to pay you $1,500 immediately and the remaining $6,000 in a year. How much should you charge your neighbour for interest?

You could determine an appropriate interest rate by asking some financial institutions what they currently charge their customers. Using this information as a starting point, you could then negotiate with your neighbour and agree upon a rate. Assuming that the agreed-upon rate is 8%, you will receive interest totalling $480 for the one-year loan.

In this chapter, we will describe and illustrate how interest is computed. In addition, we will discuss the accounting for receivables, including uncollectible receivables. Most of these receivables result from a business rendering services or selling merchandise on account. We conclude this chapter with a discussion of temporary investments of excess cash.

Classification of Receivables

Objective 1
List the common classifications of receivables.

The term **receivables** includes all money claims against other entities, including individuals, business firms, and other organizations. We normally classify receivables as accounts receivable, notes receivable, or other receivables. These receivables are usually a significant portion of the total current assets. For example, the 1997 annual report of **La-Z-Boy Chair Company** reports that receivables make up over 55% of La-Z-Boy's current assets.

ACCOUNTS RECEIVABLE

The most common transaction giving rise to a receivable is selling merchandise or services on credit. We record this as a debit to the Accounts Receivable account and normally expect to collect such accounts within a relatively short period, such as 30 or 60 days. **Accounts receivable** are classified on the balance sheet as a current asset.

NOTES RECEIVABLE

A business may grant credit to customers on the basis of a formal instrument of credit, called a promissory note. A promissory note, often simply called a note, is a written promise to pay a sum of money on demand or at a definite time. Notes are often used for credit periods of more than 60 days, such as an installment plan for equipment sales. Notes may also be used to settle a customer's account receivable. The acceptance of a note is recorded as a debit to the Notes Receivable account. As long as a note is expected to be collected within a year we normally classify it on the balance sheet as a current asset.

Notes and accounts receivable that originate from sales transactions are sometimes called **trade receivables.** Unless otherwise described, we will assume that accounts and notes receivable have originated from credit sales in the usual course of business.

OTHER RECEIVABLES

Other receivables include interest receivable, dividends receivable, taxes receivable, and receivables from officers or employees. Other receivables are normally listed separately on the balance sheet. If we expect to collect such receivables within one year, we classify them as a current asset on the balance sheet. If collection is expected beyond one year, we classify them as a noncurrent asset.

Internal Control of Receivables

Objective 2

Summarize and provide examples of internal control procedures that apply to receivables.

The principles of internal control discussed in prior chapters are applicable in establishing procedures to safeguard receivables. These controls include separating the business operations from the accounting for receivables. In this way, the accounting records can serve as an independent check on operations. Thus, the employee who handles the accounting for notes and accounts receivables should not be involved with the operating aspects of approving credit or collecting receivables. Separating these functions reduces the possibility of errors and misuse of funds. For example, if the accounts receivable billing clerk has access to cash receipts from customers, the clerk could steal the cash but report the receipt only on the customer's monthly statement and not in the ledger account. The customer would not complain and the theft would go undetected.

To further illustrate the internal control principle of separating related operating functions, assume that salespersons have authority to approve credit. If the salespersons are paid commissions, say 10% of sales, they can increase their commissions by approving poor credit risks. Thus, we would normally assign the credit approval function to an individual outside the sales area.

Within the accounting function, we also separate related functions. In this way, the work of one employee serves as a check on the work of another employee. For example, a business should separate the responsibilities for maintaining the accounts receivable customers' (subsidiary) ledger and the general ledger. The work of the accounts receivable clerk is checked by comparing the total of the individual account balances in the customers' (subsidiary) ledger with the balance of the accounts receivable control account maintained by the general ledger clerk. If one individual performs both functions, this control will be lacking.

For most businesses, the primary receivables are notes receivable and accounts receivable. As we mentioned in the preceding section, we normally record notes receivable in a single general ledger account. If there are many notes, the general ledger account can be supported by a notes receivable register or a subsidiary ledger. The register would contain details of each note, such as the name of the maker, place of payment, amount, term, interest rate, and due date. When a note is due for payment, the business should notify the maker of the note to minimize the risk that the maker will overlook the due date.

Control over accounts receivable begins with the proper credit approval of the sale by an authorized company official. The business needs to develop clear procedures for granting credit. Likewise, procedures for authorizing adjustments of accounts receivable, such as for sales returns and allowances and sales discounts, should be developed. The business also needs collection procedures to ensure timely collection of accounts receivable and to minimize losses from uncollectible accounts.

Uncollectible Receivables

In prior chapters, we described and illustrated the accounting for transactions involving sales of merchandise or services on credit. The primary accounting issue that we have not yet discussed is uncollectible receivables.

As we discussed in the preceding section, companies attempt to limit the number and amount of uncollectible accounts by using control procedures. The primary focus of controls in this area is the credit-granting function. These controls normally involve investigating customer credit-worthiness, using references, and running background checks. For example, most of us have completed credit application forms requiring such information. Companies may also impose credit limits on new customers. For example, you may have been limited to a maximum of $1,000 when your credit card was first issued to you. Such limits are designed to control potentially uncollectible amounts.

Once an account is past due, companies should use procedures to maximize the collection of the account. After repeated attempts at collection, such procedures may include turning over an account to a collection agency.

Retail businesses often attempt to shift the risk of uncollectible accounts to other companies. For example, some retailers do not accept sales on account, but will only accept cash or credit cards. Such policies effectively shift the risk to the credit card companies. Other retailers, such as **Sears, Eaton's,** and **Canadian Tire,** have developed their own credit cards. However, these retailers often sell their credit card receivables to other companies.

The selling of a company's receivables is called **factoring** the receivables, and the purchaser of the receivable is called a **factor.** One advantage of factoring its receivables is that the company receives immediate cash for operations and other needs. In addition, depending upon the factoring agreement, the business may shift some of the risk of uncollectible accounts to the factor.[1]

Regardless of the care used in granting credit and the collection procedures used, a part of the claims from sales to customers on credit will normally not be collectible. The operating expense incurred because of the failure to collect receivables is called an expense or a loss from **uncollectible accounts, doubtful accounts,** or **bad debts.**[2]

When does an account or a note become uncollectible? There is no general rule for determining when an account becomes uncollectible. The fact that a debtor fails to pay an account according to a sales contract or dishonours a note on the due date does not necessarily mean that the amount will be uncollectible. Bankruptcy of the debtor is one of the most significant indications of partial or complete uncollectibility. Other indications include the closing of the customer's business and the failure of repeated attempts to collect.

There are two methods of accounting for receivables that appear to be uncollectible. The **allowance method** provides an expense for uncollectible receivables in advance of their write-off. The other procedure, called the **direct write-off method** or **direct charge-off method,** recognizes the expense only when certain accounts are judged to be worthless. We will discuss each of these methods in the following paragraphs.

Some retailers such as Eaton's have developed their own credit cards to minimize the risk of uncollectible receivables.

---

[1] The accounting for the factoring of accounts receivable, with and without recourse, is beyond the scope of our discussion in this chapter. The accounting for such transactions is discussed in advanced accounting texts.

[2] If both notes and accounts are involved, both may be included in the expense account title, as in *Uncollectible Notes and Accounts Expense,* or *Uncollectible Receivables Expense.* Because of its wide usage and simplicity, we will use *Uncollectible Accounts Expense* in this text.

Allowance Method of Accounting for Uncollectibles

Generally accepted accounting principles require that businesses estimate and provide an allowance for the uncollectible portion of their trade receivables. An adjusting entry at the end of a fiscal period records the expense for future uncollectibility. As with all periodic adjustments, this entry serves two purposes. First, it reduces the value of the receivables to the amount of cash expected to be realized in the future, called the **net realizable value.** Second, it matches the uncollectible expense of the current period with the related revenues of the period.

To illustrate the allowance method, we will assume the following data for a new business, Richards Company. The business began in August and uses the calendar year as its fiscal year. The accounts receivable control account, shown below, has a balance of $105,000 at the end of the period.

ACCOUNT *Accounts Receivable*					ACCOUNT NO. *114*	
Date	**Item**	**Post. Ref.**	**Debit**	**Credit**	**Balance**	
					Debit	**Credit**
20— Aug. 31			20 0 0 0 00		20 0 0 0 00	
Sept. 30			25 0 0 0 00		45 0 0 0 00	
30				15 0 0 0 00	30 0 0 0 00	
Oct. 31			40 0 0 0 00		70 0 0 0 00	
31				25 0 0 0 00	45 0 0 0 00	
Nov. 30			38 0 0 0 00		83 0 0 0 00	
30				23 0 0 0 00	60 0 0 0 00	
Dec. 31			75 0 0 0 00		135 0 0 0 00	
31				30 0 0 0 00	105 0 0 0 00	

The customer accounts making up the $105,000 balance in Accounts Receivable include some that are past due. No specific accounts are believed to be totally uncollectible at this time. However, it seems likely that some will be collected only in part and that others will not pay at all. Based on a careful study, Richards estimates that a total of $3,000 will eventually be uncollectible. The net realizable value of the accounts receivable is therefore $102,000 ($105,000 − $3,000). The $3,000 reduction in value is the uncollectible accounts expense for the period.

Because the $3,000 reduction in accounts receivable is an estimate, we cannot credit it to specific customer accounts or to the accounts receivable control account. Instead, we credit a contra asset account entitled Allowance for Doubtful Accounts. The adjusting entry to record the expense and the reduction in the asset is as follows:

```
                Adjusting Entry
Dec. 31    Uncollectible Accounts Expense      717    3,000
               Allowance for Doubtful Accounts  115             3,000
```

The two accounts to which the entry is posted are as follows:

ACCOUNT *Uncollectible Accounts Expense*					ACCOUNT NO. *717*	
Date	**Item**	**Post. Ref.**	**Debit**	**Credit**	**Balance**	
					Debit	**Credit**
20— Dec. 31	Adjusting		3 0 0 0 00		3 0 0 0 00	

ACCOUNT *Allowance for Doubtful Accounts*						ACCOUNT NO. *115*
Date	Item	Post. Ref.	Debit	Credit	Balance	
					Debit	Credit
Dec.²⁰⁻ 31	Adjusting			3 0 0 0 00		3 0 0 0 00

The debit balance of $105,000 in Accounts Receivable is the amount of the total claims against customers on open account. The credit balance of $3,000 in Allowance for Doubtful Accounts is the amount to be deducted from Accounts Receivable to determine the net realizable value.

A business normally reports uncollectible accounts expense on the income statement as an administrative expense because the credit-granting and collection duties are the responsibilities of departments within the administrative area. At the end of the period, we close the $3,000 balance in Uncollectible Accounts Expense to Income Summary.

We present the accounts receivable as shown below in the Current Assets section of the balance sheet. Alternatively, the accounts receivable may be listed on the balance sheet at the net amount of $102,000, with or without a notation in parentheses or in the end notes showing the amount of the allowance.

Current assets:		
Cash		$ 21,600
Accounts receivable	$105,000	
Less allowance for doubtful accounts	3,000	102,000

WRITE-OFFS TO THE ALLOWANCE ACCOUNT

When a business determines that a specific account is uncollectible, we write it off against the allowance account as follows:

Jan. 21	Allowance for Doubtful Accounts	610	
	Accounts Receivable—John Parker		610
	To write off the uncollectible account.		

Authorization for write-offs should originate with the credit manager or other designated officer. The authorizations, which should be written, serve as support for the accounting entry.

The total amount written off against the allowance account during a period will rarely be equal to the amount in the account at the beginning of the period. The allowance account will have a credit balance at the end of the period if the write-offs during the period are less than the beginning balance. It will have a debit balance if the write-offs exceed the beginning balance. After the year-end adjusting entry is recorded, the allowance account must have a credit balance.

An account receivable that has been written off against the allowance account may later be collected. In such cases, we reinstate the account by an entry that is the exact reverse of the write-off entry. For example, assume that the account of $610 written off in the preceding entry is later collected. The entry to reinstate the account would be as follows:

June 10	Accounts Receivable—John Parker	610	
	Allowance for Doubtful Accounts		610
	To reinstate account written off on January 21.		

We record the cash received in payment as a receipt on account as follows:

June 10   Cash   610
          Accounts Receivable—John Parker   610

The two preceding entries can be combined. However, recording two separate entries in the customer's account, with proper notation, provides useful credit information.

ESTIMATING UNCOLLECTIBLES

How do you estimate the amount of uncollectible accounts expense? We base the estimate of uncollectibles at the end of a fiscal period on past experience and forecasts of future business activity. When the general economic environment is favourable, the amount of the expense should normally be less than when the trend is in the opposite direction. We usually base the estimate of uncollectibles on either (1) the amount of credit sales for the period or (2) the balance and the age of the receivable accounts at the end of the period.

Estimate Based on Sales (Income Statement Method)

Accounts receivable result from sales on account. The amount of such credit sales during the year may therefore be used to estimate the amount of uncollectible accounts. We add the amount of this estimate to whatever balance exists in Allowance for Doubtful Accounts. For example, assume that the allowance account has a credit balance of $700 before adjustment. The business estimates from past experience that 1% of credit sales will be uncollectible. If credit sales for the period are $300,000, the adjusting entry for uncollectible accounts at the end of the period is as follows:

Dec. 31   Uncollectible Accounts Expense   3,000
          Allowance for Doubtful Accounts   3,000

After the adjusting entry has been posted, the balance in the allowance account is $3,700. If there had been a debit balance of $200 in the allowance account before the year-end adjustment, the amount of the adjustment would still have been $3,000. The balance in the allowance account, after the adjusting entry has been posted, would be $2,800 ($3,000 – $200).

Instead of credit sales, some businesses use total sales (including those made for cash) in estimating the percentage of uncollectible accounts. Using total sales is less costly, since total sales is available in the sales account in the ledger. In contrast, a separate analysis may be required to determine credit sales. If the ratio of credit sales to cash sales does not change very much from year to year, estimates using total sales will be acceptable. In the above example, if ¾ of 1% is used to estimate uncollectibles, based upon total sales of $400,000, the same estimate of $3,000 would result.

The estimate-based-on-sales method is widely used due to its simplicity. Because this method emphasizes the matching of uncollectible accounts expense with the related sales of the period, it is known as the income statement method of estimating uncollectible accounts expense. Large corporations with many smaller accounts use this method.

Estimate Based on Analysis of Receivables (Balance Sheet Method)

The other method of determining uncollectibles account expense is called the **balance sheet method,** because it emphasizes the importance of reporting accounts receivable at no more than their net realizable value. Here, the focus is on adjusting the balance in the allowance account to equal the amount of expected uncollectibles, so that net accounts receivable (accounts receivable minus the allowance) represents the amount of cash that the business will actually collect in the future.

The easiest way of estimating the uncollectible accounts at the end of the period would be to simply approximate a certain percentage of closing receivables as uncollectible. Some companies may determine the appropriate balance for the allowance based on the relationship between the allowance and the receivables balance reported in prior years. However, a more accurate method of estimating the correct balance needed in the allowance requires a closer analysis of the specific accounts outstanding at the end of the current period.

The longer an account receivable remains outstanding, the less likely that it will be collected. For example, the *Annual Collectibility Survey* conducted by the Commercial Collection Agency Section of the **Commercial Law League of America** reported the following statistics on collection rates:[3]

Number of Months Past Due	Collection Rate
1	93.4%
2	84.6
3	72.9
6	57.0
9	41.9
12	25.4
24	12.5

We can base the estimate of uncollectible accounts on how long the accounts have been outstanding. For this purpose, we can use a process called aging the receivables.

The beginning point for determining the age of a receivable is its due date. Exhibit 1 shows an example of a typical aging of accounts receivable.

Exhibit 1
Aging of Accounts Receivable

Customer	Balance	Not Due	Days Past Due 1-30	31-60	61-90	91-180	181-365	over 365
Ashby & Co.	$ 150			$ 150				
B.T. Barr	610					$ 350	$260	
Brock Co.	470	$ 470						
J. Zimmer Co.	160							160
Total	$86,300	$75,000	$4,000	$3,100	$1,900	$1,200	$800	$300

We complete the aging schedule by adding the columns to determine the total amount of receivables in each age group. A sliding scale of percentages, based on industry or company experience, is used to estimate the amount of uncollectibles in each group. The data are presented as shown in Exhibit 2.

The estimate of uncollectible accounts is $3,390 in Exhibit 2. This amount is deducted from accounts receivable to yield the accounts receivable net realizable value. It is also the amount of the desired balance of the allowance account at the end of the period. The excess of this amount over the balance of the allowance account before adjustment is the amount of the uncollectible accounts expense for the period.

[3] *Boardroom Reports*, May 1994, p. 12.

Exhibit 2
Estimate of Uncollectible Accounts

Age Interval	Balance	Estimated Uncollectible Accounts Percent	Amount
Not due	$75,000	2%	$1,500
1–30 days past due	4,000	5	200
31–60 days past due	3,100	10	310
61–90 days past due	1,900	20	380
91–180 days past due	1,200	30	360
181–365 days past due	800	50	400
Over 365 days past due	300	80	240
Total	$86,300		$3,390

To continue the example, assume that the allowance account has a credit balance of $510 before adjustment. We need to add $2,880 ($3,390 – $510) to the balance to attain the required balance in the allowance account. The adjusting entry is as follows:

Dec. 31   Uncollectible Accounts Expense   2,880
                  Allowance for Doubtful Accounts   2,880

After the adjusting entry has been posted, the credit balance in the allowance account is $3,390, the desired amount. If there had been a debit balance of $300 in the allowance account before the year-end adjustment, the amount of the adjustment would have been $3,690 ($3,390 desired balance + $300 debit balance).

Estimates of uncollectible accounts expense based on analyzing receivables are less common than estimates based on sales volume. The primary advantage of analyzing receivables is that it emphasizes the current net realizable value of the receivables. Smaller businesses with a smaller number of accounts often use this method.

Direct Write-Off Method of Accounting for Uncollectibles

Objective 5
Journalize the entries for the direct write-off of uncollectible receivables.

The allowance method emphasizes reporting uncollectible accounts expense in the period in which the sales occur and reporting receivables on the balance sheet at their net realizable value. This emphasis on matching expenses with related revenue and not overstating assets is the generally accepted method of accounting for uncollectible receivables. However, you may encounter a business that sells most of its goods or services on a cash basis and the amount of its expense from uncollectible accounts is very small in relation to its revenue. The amount of its receivables at any time is also likely to represent a relatively small part of its total current assets. Examples of such a business are a veterinarian or a small retail store such as a hardware store. In such cases, the owners may delay recognizing uncollectible expense until the accounts are determined to be worthless. Thus, under the direct write-off method, the business does not use an allowance account and an adjusting entry at the end of the period. This method writes off an account when it is determined to be uncollectible as follows:

May 10   Uncollectible Accounts Expense   420
                  Accounts Receivable—D. L. Ross   420
                        To write off uncollectible account.

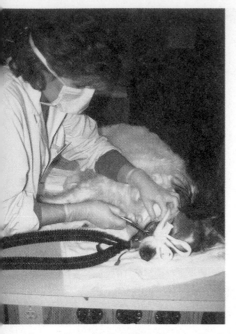

For veterinarians, the amount of receivables is typically small in relation to the total current assets of the business.

What if a customer later pays on an account that has been written off? If this happens, the account should be reinstated. If the recovery is in the same period as the write-off, the earlier entry should be reversed to reinstate the account. For example, assume that the account written off in the May 10 entry is collected in November of the same fiscal year. The entry to reinstate the account is as follows:

Nov. 21	Accounts Receivable—D. L. Ross	420	
	Uncollectible Accounts Expense		420
	To reinstate account written		
	off on May 10.		

We record the receipt of cash in payment of the reinstated amount in the usual manner by debiting Cash and crediting Accounts Receivable.

When an account that has been written off is collected in a later fiscal year, the business may reinstate the account by debiting Accounts Receivable and crediting Uncollectible Accounts Expense. An alternative is to credit some other appropriately titled account, such as Recovery of Uncollectible Accounts Written Off. The credit balance in such an account at the end of the period may then be reported on the income statement as a deduction from Uncollectible Accounts Expense. In either case, only the net uncollectible expense is reported.

Although you may find some small businesses using the direct write-off method, it is not really an acceptable method of accounting for uncollectibles. This method has two weaknesses: (1) it overstates receivables at the end of the period; and (2) it does not attempt to match uncollectibles expense in the same period as the revenue to which it relates. The *CICA Handbook* requires that receivables should be shown at "the best possible estimate of the amount for which reasonable assurance of collection exists."[4]

Characteristics of Notes Receivable

Objective 6

State the accounting implications of promissory notes.

The typical retail business makes most of its sales for cash or on credit. If the account of a customer is past due, the business may insist that the customer convert the account receivable into a note receivable.

A claim supported by a note has some advantages over a claim in the form of an account receivable. By signing a note, the debtor recognizes the debt and agrees to pay it according to the terms listed. A note is therefore a stronger legal claim if there is a court action. A note is also normally more liquid than an open account. That is, if the business needs cash, it is usually easier to convert a note receivable to cash than an account receivable.

Retail firms that sell merchandise on long-term credit may also accept notes receivable as a form of payment. For example, a dealer in automobiles or furniture may require a down payment at the time of sale and accept a note or a series of notes for the remainder. Such arrangements usually provide for monthly payments.

As we stated earlier in the chapter, a note is a written promise to pay a sum of money on demand or at a definite time. It must be payable to the order of a certain person or firm or to the bearer. It must be signed by the person or firm that makes the promise. The one to whose order the note is payable is called the **payee**, and the one making the promise is called the **maker**. In the example in Exhibit 3, Pearland Company is the payee and Selig Company is the maker.

Notes have several characteristics that have accounting implications. We describe these characteristics in the following paragraphs.

[4] *CICA Handbook*, Section 3020, paragraph 12.

Exhibit 3
Promissory Note

$ __2,500.00__	Thunder Bay, Ontario __March 16__ 19 __99__

__Ninety days__ AFTER DATE __We__ PROMISE TO PAY TO

THE ORDER OF __Pearland Company__

__Two thousand five hundred 00/100----------------------__ DOLLARS

PAYABLE AT __The Bank of Nova Scotia__

VALUE RECEIVED WITH INTEREST AT __10%__

NO. __14__ DUE __June 14, 1999__

H.B. Lane

TREASURER, *SELIG COMPANY*

DUE DATE

The due date or maturity date is the date a note is to be paid. The period of time between the issuance date and the due date of a short-term note may be stated in either days or months. When the term of a note is stated in days, the due date is the specified number of days after its issuance. To illustrate, the due date of the 90-day note in Exhibit 3 is determined as follows:

Term of the note		90
March (days)	31	
Date of note	16	15
Number of days remaining		75
April (days)		30
		45
May (days)		31
Due date, June		14

When the term of a note is stated as a certain number of months after the issuance date, we determine the due date by counting the number of months from the issuance date. For example, a three-month note dated June 5 would be due on September 5. In those cases in which there is no date in the month of maturity that corresponds to the issuance date, the due date becomes the last day of the month. For example, a two-month note dated July 31 would be due on September 30.

INTEREST

A note normally specifies that interest be paid for the period between the issuance date and the due date.[5] Notes covering a period of time longer than one year normally provide that the interest be paid semiannually, quarterly, or at some other stated interval. The time involved in business credit transactions is usually less than one year, and the interest provided for by a note is usually payable at the time the note is paid.

The interest rate on such notes is normally stated in terms of a year, regardless of the actual period of time involved. Thus, the interest on $2,000 for one year at 12% is $240 (12% of $2,000). The interest on $2,000 for one-fourth of one year at 12% is $60 (¼ of $240).

It is important for consumers to understand how interest is computed on credit or installment purchases because slight variations in interest rates can mean significant savings.

[5] You may occasionally see references to non-interest-bearing notes receivable. Such notes are not widely issued and normally include an implicit interest rate. For example, you may purchase $10,000 worth of merchandise in exchange for a non-interest-bearing note of $10,200 due in 60 days. Although there is no interest rate stated on the note, you are paying $200 extra (implicit interest) for the privilege of delaying your payment for 60 days.

USING ACCOUNTING TO UNDERSTAND BUSINESS

Whenever a business borrows money or enters into a credit agreement that requires the payment of interest, it is important for the business to understand how the interest will be computed. For example, the difference in 180 days' interest computed on the basis of a 365-day year versus a 360-day year is shown below for a loan of $40,000 at an interest rate of 12%:

$40,000 \times 12\% \times {}^{180}\!/_{365} = \$2,367.12$
$40,000 \times 12\% \times {}^{180}\!/_{360} = \$2,400.00$

The difference of $32.88 may seem relatively small, but for a business that might enter into thousands of such transactions for millions of dollars, the difference between computing interest on a 360-day year versus a 365-day year can be significant.

The basic formula for computing interest is as follows:

Face Amount (or Principal) × Rate × Time = Interest

To illustrate the formula, the $62.50 interest for the $2,500, 10%, 90-day note in Exhibit 3 is computed as follows:

$$\$2,500 \times 10\% \times \frac{90}{360} = \$62.50 \text{ interest}$$

In computing interest for a period of less than one year, many financial institutions use the actual number of days in the year. For example, 90 days is ${}^{90}\!/_{365}$ of one year. However, some businesses use 360 days rather than 365. To simplify computations, we will use 360 days. Thus, 90 days is considered to be ${}^{90}\!/_{360}$, or one-fourth of a year.

When the term of a note is stated in months instead of in days, each month may be considered $\frac{1}{12}$ of a year. Alternatively, the actual number of days in the term may be counted. For example, you could compute the interest on a three-month note dated June 1 on the basis of $\frac{3}{12}$ of a year or on the basis of ${}^{92}\!/_{360}$ of a year. To simplify, we will treat a month as $\frac{1}{12}$ of a year.

Understanding interest is also useful to you. For example, credit card balances that remain unpaid at the end of the month incur an interest charge expressed in terms of a percent per month. Interest charges of 1½% per month are common. Such charges approximate an annual interest rate of 18% per year (1½% × 12). Thus, if you can borrow money at less than 18%, you are better off borrowing the money and paying off the credit card balance than incurring the monthly interest charges on the unpaid balance. Likewise, many companies charge penalties for late payment of bills. For example, a utility bill might be due on the 15th of the month, with a late charge of 5% if paid after the 15th. If the bill remains unpaid after 30 days, the utility stops services. If you pay late and incur the 5% late charge, you are, in effect, borrowing the amount of the bill for an extra 15 days. But the extra 15 days cost you 5%, which approximates an annual rate of 120% [(360 days ÷ 15 days) × 5%]. Again, you would be better off borrowing to avoid the late charge.

MATURITY VALUE

The maturity value is the amount due at the maturity or due date. The maturity value of a note is the sum of the face amount and the interest. In the note in Exhibit 3, the maturity value is $2,562.50 ($2,500 face amount plus $62.50 interest).

Accounting for Notes Receivable

Objective 7
Journalize the entries for notes receivable transactions. (The appendix includes the accounting for discounted notes receivable and dishonoured notes receivable.)

When a customer presents a note to apply on account, we record the event by debiting the notes receivable account and crediting Accounts Receivable and the account of the customer from whom the note is received. To illustrate, assume that we accept a 30-day, 12% note dated November 21, 1999, in settlement of the account of W. A. Bunn Co., which is past due and has a balance of $6,000. The entry to record the transaction is as follows:

Nov. 21	Notes Receivable	6,000	
	Accounts Receivable—W. A. Bunn Co.		6,000
	Received 30-day, 12% note dated November 21, 1999.		

At the time the note matures, the entry to record the receipt of $6,060 ($6,000 principal plus $60 interest) is as follows:

Dec. 21	Cash	6,060	
	Notes Receivable		6,000
	Interest Income		60

If a note matures in a later fiscal period, we must accrue the interest in the correct period. For example, assume that a 90-day, 12% note dated December 1 is received from Crawford Company to settle its account, which has a balance of $4,000. The entry to record the receipt of the note is similar to the November 21 entry above. If the business has a December 31 fiscal year end we must make the following adjusting entry to record the $40 interest earned for 30 days in December ($4,000 × 12% × $\frac{30}{360}$):

Dec. 31	Interest Receivable	40	
	Interest Income		40

The interest income account is closed at December 31. The amount of interest income is reported in the Other Income section of the income statement for the year ended December 31, 1999.

DISHONOURED NOTES RECEIVABLE

If the maker of a note fails to pay the debt on the due date, the note is said to be dishonoured. A **dishonoured note receivable** is no longer negotiable. For this reason, the holder usually transfers the claim, including any interest due, to the accounts receivable account. For example, assume that the $6,000, 30-day, 12% note received from W. A. Bunn Co. and recorded on November 21 is dishonoured at maturity. The entry to charge the note, including the interest, back to the customer's account is as follows:

Dec. 21	Accounts Receivable—W. A. Bunn Co.	6,060	
	Notes Receivable		6,000
	Interest Income		60
	Dishonoured note and interest.		

Temporary Investments (Short Term)

Objective 8
Define temporary investments and account for the acquisition, sale, and valuation of such investments.

A business may have excess cash that it does not need immediately for operations. Rather than allow this excess cash to be idle until it is needed, a business may invest all or a part of it in income-yielding marketable securities. Since these investments can be quickly sold and converted to cash as needed, they are called temporary investments or marketable securities. Although such investments may be retained for a number of years, we continue to classify them as temporary, provided they meet two conditions. First, the securities are readily marketable and can be sold for cash at any time. Second, management intends to sell the securities when the business needs more cash for operations.

Temporary investments are either debt securities or equity securities. A debt security represents a creditor relationship between the entity issuing the security and the individuals or entities holding the security. Debt securities called bonds or debentures are issued by corporations and government agencies. An equity security represents ownership in a business. The most common example of an equity security is shares in a corporation. Debt securities generate interest income for the holder, while equity securities may pay dividends to holders as a return on their investment.

Investors purchase investments in shares and bonds by using the services of investment brokers. The securities are traded on the stock exchanges or, occasionally, on the less formal over-the-counter market. Canada has stock exchanges in Toronto, Montreal, Winnipeg, Calgary, and Vancouver. Investors must usually pay brokerage commission fees and government taxes when buying or selling securities.

TEMPORARY INVESTMENTS IN BONDS

We record temporary bond investments at acquisition cost, which includes any brokers' commissions and transfer taxes. A bond is a debt security and the bondholder receives periodic interest payments from the bond issuer. Interest accrues daily on a bond and usually is paid semi-annually.

The **face value,** or **maturity value,** of a bond is the amount of principal to be repaid at the maturity date. The annual rate of interest paid on a bond is stated in the bond agreement. To determine the amount of interest paid semi-annually on such bonds, we multiply the face value by one-half the coupon rate of interest. We call the interest rate that is stated on the bond the **coupon rate** or **nominal rate** of interest.

Bonds trade on the stock exchange at their market value, which is determined by various economic factors, including current market interest rates. The market price of a bond is quoted as a percentage of its face value. Thus, a bond with a face value of $1,000 that is trading at 97½ will sell for $975 (97.5% × $1,000).

Assume that on September 1, 2000 Computer King buys $10,000 face value Beco 9% bonds as a temporary investment when the bonds are trading at 98. The bonds pay semi-annual interest every August 31 and February 28. If Computer King pays a brokerage commission of $80 to purchase the investment, the entry to record the purchase is as follows:

Sept. 1	Temporary Investment in Beco Bonds	9,880*	
	Cash		9,880
	* ($10,000 × 98%) + $80 commission fee		

Computer King has a December 31 fiscal year end and will need to accrue interest earned on the bonds, but not yet received by year end. The adjusting entry to debit Interest Receivable and credit Interest Income for $300 to record the four months of interest earned by year end is as follows:

Dec. 31	Interest receivable	300*	
	Interest Income		300

* ($10,000 × 9% × $\frac{4}{12}$)

On February 28, 2001 Computer King will receive the semi-annual interest payment of $450 ($10,000 × 9% × $\frac{6}{12}$). At that time, we will debit Cash for $450, credit Interest Receivable for the $300 accrued at December 31, and credit Interest Income for $150 to record the two months of interest earned for January and February:

Feb. 28	Cash	450	
	Interest Receivable		300
	Interest Income		150

On an interest payment date, the bondholder receives the full amount of interest due since the last payment date. As a result, the price paid for a bond that is sold between interest payment dates includes not only the current market price and any brokerage commission, but also any interest accrued since the last interest payment date. The bond seller, therefore, receives the interest income earned, but not yet paid, up to the date of sale. The bond investor debits the accrued interest purchased to an Interest Receivable account and will receive this back in the next interest payment.

To illustrate this, assume the same information as the above example except that Computer King does not purchase the Beco bonds until October 1, 2000. In this case, Computer King will have to pay the bond seller an additional $75 for one month of interest due on the bonds since the last interest payment date of August 31 ($10,000 × 9% × $\frac{1}{12}$). We will record this amount as Interest Receivable, and the entry to record the purchase is as follows:

Oct. 1	Temporary Investment in Beco Bonds	9,880	
	Interest Receivable	75	
	Cash		9,955

Since it has already accrued this one month of interest receivable, at its December 31 fiscal year end Computer King will only accrue $225 for the additional interest three months of interest receivable since October 1:

December 31	Interest Receivable	225	
	Interest Income		225

The total interest receivable at December 31 is $300 for the period accruing since the last interest date. Whether it purchased the bonds on September 1 or October 1, Computer King's records will show Interest Receivable of $300 at December 31, and this is the amount that it will report on its balance sheet. However, the amount of Interest Income reported on the 2000 income statement will vary, depending on the date of the purchase. If Computer King purchased the bonds on September 1, it has earned $300 of interest income by holding the investment for four months. If the company purchased the bonds on October 1, it has only held the bonds for three months, and therefore has only earned $225 of interest income, as recorded in the above entry.

When Computer King liquidates (sells) the bond, the transaction will usually result in a gain or loss on disposal. The gain or loss equals the difference between the net proceeds on the sale (selling price less any commission and taxes) and the book value of the investment. For example, assume that the company sells the investment on March 1, 2001 when the bonds are trading at 101 and pays a brokerage commission of $85. The book value of the investment is $9,880 and the net proceeds on the sale are $10,015 [($10,000 × 101%) − $85]. Therefore, the gain on the sale is $135 ($10,015 − $9,880) and the entry to record the sale is as follows:

Mar. 1	Cash	10,015	
	Temporary Investment in Beco Bonds		9,880
	Gain on Sale of Investment		135

TEMPORARY INVESTMENTS IN SHARES

We record temporary share investments in the investment account at cost (the total purchase price including charges for such items as brokers' commission and transfer taxes). Assume that Computer King purchases 100 shares of Alberta Energy Company common stock as a temporary investment on October 1 at a cost of $2,350, including commissions and taxes. We record the investment as follows:

| Oct. 1 | Temporary Investment in Alberta Energy Shares | 2,350 | |
| | Cash | | 2,350 |

A corporation's Board of Directors may declare a dividend as a distribution of the corporation's income to shareholders. We do not automatically accrue dividend income on shares each period (as we do for interest on bonds), since a corporation has no legal obligation to pay a dividend until it is declared by the Board. Assume Alberta Energy Corporation declares a dividend of $2.00 per share on December 20, 2000 payable January 10, 2001. On December 20 Computer King can debit Dividend Receivable and credit Dividend Income for $200 (100 shares × $2):

| Dec. 20 | Dividend Receivable | 200 | |
| | Dividend Income | | 200 |

When the dividend is paid, Computer King records:

| Jan. 10 | Cash | 200 | |
| | Dividend Receivable | | 200 |

When Computer King sells its investment in shares, the transaction will likely result in a gain or loss, which is calculated as the difference between the net proceeds (selling price less commissions and taxes) and the book value of the investment. Assume Computer King sells all of its Alberta Energy shares February 28 for $25 per share less total commissions of $48. The entry to record the sale is as follows:

Feb. 28	Cash ($2,500 – $48)	2,452	
	Temporary Investment in Alberta Energy Shares		2,350
	Gain on Sale of Investments		102

YEAR END REPORTING—LOWER OF COST AND MARKET

Temporary investments are initially recorded at cost and classified as current assets. However, generally accepted accounting principles require that we recognize any decline in the market value below cost and include the loss in the determination of income. This principle is known as the lower of cost and market (LCM) and is an application of the general principle of conservatism. This accounting principle requires that we anticipate no profits before they are realized, and that we provide for all possible losses as soon as they are apparent. When uncertainty exists, we should ensure that assets and revenues are not overstated, and that liabilities and losses are not understated. However, adhering to the principle of conservatism does not mean that we should deliberately understate our net assets or income.[6]

---

[6] *CICA Handbook*, "Financial Statement Concepts," Section 1000, paragraph. .21.

There are two ways to apply the LCM principle to temporary investments: on a portfolio wide (aggregate) basis or on an individual security basis. If the market value is less than cost, we debit the difference to Unrealized Loss on Temporary Investments and credit Allowance to Reduce Temporary Investments (contra asset) account.

To illustrate the LCM rule, assume Computer King has the following portfolio of temporary investments in shares at the end of its first year of operations.

Stock	Total Cost	Total Market Value	LCM Item-by-Item
Alberta Energy	$30,000	$25,000	$25,000
Bell Canada	15,000	16,200	15,000
Stelco	10,000	8,900	8,900
	$55,000	$50,100	$48,900

If we apply the LCM rule on the aggregate basis, we write down the investments from their total cost ($55,000) to the market value of the total portfolio ($50,100) and make the following journal entry:

| Dec. 31 | Unrealized Loss on Temporary Investments | 4,900 | |
| | Allowance to Reduce Temporary Investments to Market | | 4900 |

If we apply the LCM rule to each individual security (item-by-item), we would define market value as $48,900, the total of the last column shown above. Using this method, we would require $6,100 in the allowance to reduce the balance of the investments from cost ($55,000) to market ($48,900). This represents a loss of $1,200 more than that determined under the portfolio method. This occurs because the portfolio method allows unrealized losses to be netted with unrealized gains ($1,200 on the Stelco shares). Thus, the individual security basis of applying the LCM principle is more conservative than the portfolio method. However, generally accepted accounting principles permit the use of either method.

We report the unrealized loss as an expense in the current year's income statement. The credit to the allowance account: (1) maintains the original cost in the individual investment accounts and (2) reduces the total book value of the investments to market value on the balance sheet. Assuming that Computer King applied the LCM rule on the portfolio basis, it would report its temporary investments in shares on the balance sheet under current assets as follows:

Temporary Share Investments (cost)	$55,000
Less Allowance to Reduce Temporary Investments to Market	4,900
Temporary Investments in Shares at Market	$50,100

Alternatively, the balance sheet may report the investments in condensed form:

| Temporary Share Investments, at lower of Cost and Market (cost $55,000) | $50,100 |

The LCM rule is applied to all temporary investments, including investments in debt as well as equity securities. If market value exceeds cost, application of the LCM rule will result in the investments being reported at cost with no allowance account required. However, financial statement users will still be interested in knowing the market value of the temporary investments, since this is relevant information for an asset that is held for its liquidity, and that management intends to sell in the near future. Therefore, even when temporary investments are reported at cost, we should still disclose market value on the balance sheet in parentheses.[7]

[7] *CICA Handbook*, Section 3010, paragraph .05.

At the end of each fiscal year, we must compute the current market value of the investments and compare it to the cost recorded in the investment account. We then make the adjusting entry necessary to adjust the allowance to the correct balance so that the net carrying value of the investment (Temporary Investments Minus Allowance) is equal to the LCM at year end.

To illustrate this, assume that in the above example Computer King applies the LCM rule on the portfolio basis and holds the same portfolio of Temporary Investments in Shares at the end of its second year of operations. The investment account still shows the cost of these shares at $55,000. If the current market value of the shares is now $50,000, the balance required in the allowance should be $5,000. Since the balance in the allowance is $4,900 (carried forward from last year), Computer King needs to credit the allowance for an additional $100 at the end of the second year, as follows:

Dec. 31	Unrealized Loss on Temporary Investments	100	
	Allowance to Reduce Temporary Investments to Market		100

However, suppose that the current market value of the shares at the end of the second year has risen to $53,000. In this case, we need to ensure that the ending balance in the allowance is $2,000 to reduce the cost of the investments ($55,000) to their market value. To do this, we need to debit the allowance by $2,900 to reduce it from $4,900 to $2,000. We record the offsetting credit as an Unrealized Gain on Temporary Investment as:

Dec. 31	Allowance to Reduce Temporary Investments to Market	2,900	
	Unrealized Gain on Temporary Investments		2,900

Suppose the current market value of the investments at the end of the second year was, say, $56,000, exceeding their original cost. In this case, we would eliminate the allowance completely, with the credit recorded as an Unrealized Gain on Temporary Investment. However, we would not write up the investments above their original cost, as this would violate the principle of conservatism.

Temporary Investments and Receivables in the Balance Sheet

Objective 9

Prepare the Current Assets section of the balance sheet that includes temporary investments and receivables.

We present temporary investments and all receivables that are expected to be realized in cash within a year in the Current Assets section of the balance sheet. It is customary to list the assets in the order of their liquidity. This is the order in which they are expected to be converted to cash during normal operations. Exhibit 4 presents an example of the presentation of temporary investments and receivables in the partial balance sheet for Crabtree Co.

Exhibit 4 reports the balances of Crabtree's notes receivable, accounts receivable, and interest receivable accounts. The allowance for doubtful accounts is subtracted from the accounts receivable. When the allowance account includes provision for doubtful notes as well as accounts, it should be deducted from the total of Notes Receivable and Accounts Receivable.

Other disclosures related to receivables are presented either on the face of the financial statements or in the accompanying notes. Such disclosures include the

Exhibit 4

Temporary Investments and Receivables in Balance Sheet

Crabtree Co.
Balance Sheet
December 31, 20—

Assets		
Current assets:		
Cash		$119 5 0 0 00
Temporary investments in		
marketable equity securities (at cost)	$690 0 0 0 00	
Less unrealized loss	30 0 0 0 00	660 0 0 0 00
Notes receivable		250 0 0 0 00
Accounts receivable	$445 0 0 0 00	
Less allowance for doubtful accounts	15 0 0 0 00	430 0 0 0 00
Interest receivable		14 5 0 0 00

market (fair) value of the receivables.[8] Generally, the market value of receivables approximates their carrying value.[9] In addition, a business must report details related to credit risk if, for example, the majority of receivables are due from one customer, customers located in one area of the country, or one industry.[10] An example of note disclosure related to credit risk for **Air Canada** from the 1996 financial statements is as follows:

Note 14 Financial Instruments and Risk Management

Concentration of Credit Risk

The corporation does not believe it is subject to any significant concentration of credit risk. Cash and short-term investments are in place with major financial institutions, Canadian Governments, and major corporations. Accounts receivable are generally the result of sales of tickets to individuals through geographically dispersed travel agents, corporate outlets, or other airlines, often through the use of major credit cards.

Source: *Financial Reporting in Canada*, 22nd Edition, CICA, 1997, Toronto, p. 393.

Appendix: Discounting Notes Receivable

Although it is not a common transaction, a company in need of cash may transfer its notes receivable to a bank by endorsement. The discount (interest) charged by the bank is computed on the maturity value of the note for the period that the bank must hold the note. This period, called the **discount period,** is the time that will pass between the date of the transfer and the due date of the note. The amount of the proceeds paid to the endorser is the excess of the maturity value over the discount.

For example, assume that a 90-day, 12%, $1,800 note receivable from Pryor & Co., dated April 8, is discounted at the payee's bank on May 3 at the rate of 14%. The data used in determining the effect of the transaction are as follows:

[8] Financial Instruments: Disclosure and Presentation, *CICA Handbook*, Section 3860, paragraph .78.
[9] *Ibid.*, paragraph .87.
[10]*Ibid.*, paragraphs .76 and .77.

Face value of note dated April 8	$1,800.00
Interest on note (90 days at 12%)	54.00
Maturity value of note due July 7	$1,854.00
Discount on maturity value (65 days from	
May 3 to July 7, at 14%)	46.87
Proceeds	$1,807.13

The excess of the proceeds from discounting the note, $1,807.13, over its face value, $1,800, is recorded as interest income. The entry for the transaction is as follows:

May 3	Cash	1,807.13	
	Notes Receivable		1,800.00
	Interest Income		7.13

What if the proceeds from discounting a note receivable are less than the face value? When this situation occurs, the excess of the face value over the proceeds is recorded as interest expense. The length of the discount period and the difference between the interest rate and the discount rate determines whether interest expense or interest income will result from discounting.

Without a statement limiting responsibility, the endorser of a note is committed to paying the note if the maker defaults. Such potential obligations will become actual liabilities only if certain events occur in the future. These potential obligations are called contingent liabilities. Thus, the endorser of a note that has been discounted has a contingent liability until the due date. If the maker pays the promised amount at maturity, the contingent liability is removed without any action on the part of the endorser. If, on the other hand, the maker defaults and the endorser is notified according to legal requirements, the liability becomes an actual one.

Significant contingent liabilities should be disclosed on the balance sheet or in an accompanying note. In a later chapter, we will discuss disclosure requirements for contingent liabilities.

When a discounted note receivable is dishonoured, the holder usually notifies the endorser of that fact and asks for payment. If the request for payment and notification of dishonour are timely, the endorser is legally obligated to pay the amount due on the note. The entire amount paid to the holder by the endorser, including the interest, should be debited to the account receivable of the maker. For example, assume that the $1,800, 90-day, 12% note discounted on May 3 is dishonoured at maturity by the maker, Pryor & Co. The entry to record the payment by the endorser is as follows:

July 7	Accounts Receivable—Pryor & Co.	1,854	
	Cash		1,854

In some cases, the holder of a dishonoured note gives the endorser a notarized statement of the facts of the dishonour. The fee for this statement, known as a protest fee, is charged to the endorser, who in turn charges it to the maker of the note. For example, if the bank charges a protest fee of $12 in connection with the dishonoured Pryor & Co. note, the entry to record the payment by the endorser is as follows:

July 7	Accounts Receivable—Pryor & Co.	1,866	
	Cash		1,866

KEY POINTS

Objective 1. List the common classifications of receivables.

The term receivables includes all money claims against other entities, including individuals, business firms, and other organizations. They are normally classified as accounts receivable, notes receivable, or other receivables.

Objective 2. Summarize and provide examples of internal control procedures that apply to receivables.

The internal controls that apply to receivables include the separation of responsibilities for related functions. In this way, the work of one employee can serve as a check on the work of another employee. Other controls are the use of subsidiary ledgers and authorization procedures for credit approval and adjustments of accounts.

Objective 3. Describe the nature of and the accounting for uncollectible receivables.

Regardless of controls in granting credit and in collection procedures, some sales to customers on account will not be collected. The allowance method requires a business to estimate its uncollectible receivables at the end of each period and report its receivables at their net realizable value. Generally accepted accounting principles require the use of this method where receivables and/or uncollectible amounts are of a material amount. The direct write-off method recognizes the expense only when the account is judged to be uncollectible. This is not generally an accepted practice in most cases.

Objective 4. Journalize the entries for the allowance method of accounting for uncollectibles, and estimate uncollectible receivables based on sales and on an analysis of receivables.

The business should make an adjusting entry made at the end of the fiscal period to provide for (1) the reduction of the value of the receivables to the amount of cash expected to be realized from them in the future and (2) the allocation to the current period of the expected expense resulting from such reduction. The adjusting entry debits Uncollectible Accounts Expense and credits Allowance for Doubtful Accounts. When an account is believed to be uncollectible, we write it off against the allowance account.

When the estimate of uncollectibles is based upon the amount of sales for the fiscal period, we make the adjusting entry at the end of the period without regard to the balance of the allowance account. When the estimate of uncollectibles is based upon the amount and the age of the receivable accounts at the end of the period, we make the adjusting entry so that the balance of the allowance account will equal the estimated uncollectibles at the end of the period.

The allowance account, which will have a credit balance after we post the adjusting entry, is a contra asset account. We generally report the uncollectible accounts expense on the income statement as an administrative expense.

Objective 5. Journalize the entries for the direct write-off of uncollectible receivables.

Under the direct write-off method, a business makes no estimate in advance of the portion of its receivables that are likely to prove uncollectible. It writes off specific amounts only when they are determined to be uncollectible by debiting Uncollectible Accounts Expense and crediting Accounts Receivable. This method is not generally acceptable because it overstates assets and violates the matching principle.

Objective 6. State the accounting implications of promissory notes.

The accounting implications of a promissory note include recognizing interest and determining the due date and the maturity value of the note. The basic formula for computing interest on a note is: Principal × Rate × Time = Interest. The maturity (due) date is the date a note is to be paid, and the period of time between the issuance date and the due date is normally stated in either days or months. The maturity value of a note is the sum of the face amount and the interest.

Objective 7. Journalize the entries for notes receivable transactions. (The appendix includes the accounting for discounted notes receivable and dishonoured notes receivable.)

A note received in settlement of an account receivable is recorded as a debit to Notes Receivable and a credit to Accounts Receivable. When a note matures, we debit Cash and credit Notes Receivable and Interest Income.

Objective 8. Define temporary investments and account for the acquisition, sale, and valuation of such investments.

Temporary investments or marketable securities are either debt securities or equity securities. A debt security is an obligation between a creditor and a business issuing the obligation. Equity securities represent ownership in a business, such as stock in a corporation.

We account for temporary investments by recording acquisitions at cost. When they are sold, we record the difference between the proceeds of the sale and acquisition cost as a gain or loss on the income statement. We apply a lower of cost and market test to equity investments at the end of each reporting period. This test can be applied to the portfolio in total or on an individual security basis. In either case, we record an allowance (contra asset) to reduce the book value to the lower of cost or market and recognize the unrealized loss as an expense on the income statement.

Objective 9. Prepare the Current Assets section of the balance sheet that includes temporary investments and receivables.

We report temporary investments and all receivables that are expected to be realized in cash within a year in the current assets section of the balance sheet. We normally list the assets in the order of their liquidity, which is the order in which they can be converted to cash in normal operations.

GLOSSARY OF KEY TERMS

Aging the receivables. The process of analyzing the accounts receivable and classifying them according to various age groupings, with the due date being the base point for determining age. *Objective 4*

Allowance method. A method of accounting for uncollectible receivables, whereby we make advance provision for the estimated uncollectibles. *Objective 3*

Conservatism. The concept that requires accountants, when uncertainty exists, to select the alternative that ensures that assets and revenues are not overstated, and that liabilities and losses are not understated. *Objective 8*

Contingent liabilities. Potential obligations that will materialize only if certain events occur in the future. *Objective 7*

Debt security. A security that represents an obligation between a creditor and the business issuing the obligation. *Objective 8*

Direct write-off method. A method of accounting for uncollectible receivables, which recognizes an expense only when specific accounts are judged to be uncollectible. *Objective 3*

Discount. The interest deducted from the maturity value of a note receivable. *Objective 7*

Equity security. A security that represents ownership in a business, such as shares in a corporation. *Objective 8*

Lower of cost and market method. A method of valuing temporary investments at the lower of their cost or current market value. *Objective 8*

Marketable securities. Investments in securities that can be readily sold when cash is needed. *Objective 8*

Maturity value. The amount due (face value plus interest) at the maturity or due date of a note or bond. *Objective 6*

Note receivable. A written promise to pay, representing an amount to be received by a business. *Objective 1*

Proceeds. The net amount available from discounting a note. *Objective 7*

Promissory note. A written promise to pay a sum in money on demand or at a definite time. *Objective 1*

Temporary investments. Investments in securities that can be readily sold when cash is needed. *Objective 8*

ILLUSTRATIVE PROBLEM

Ditzler Company, a construction supply company, uses the allowance method of accounting for uncollectible accounts receivable. Selected transactions completed by Ditzler Company are as follows:

Feb. 1. Sold merchandise on account to Ames Co., $8,000.

Mar. 15. Accepted a 60-day, 12% note for $8,000 from Ames Co. on account.

Apr. 9. Wrote off a $2,500 account from Dorset Co. as uncollectible.

21. Loaned $7,500 cash to Jill Klein, receiving a 90-day, 14% note.

May 14. Received the interest due from Ames Co. and a new 90-day, 14% note as a renewal of the loan. (Record both the debit and the credit to the notes receivable account.)

June 13. Reinstated the account of Dorset Co., written off on April 9, and received $2,500 in full payment.

July 20. Received from Jill Klein the amount due on the note of May 14.

Aug.12. Received from Ames Co. the amount due on its note of May 14.

Dec. 16. Accepted a 60-day, 12% note for $12,000 from Global Company on account.

31. It is estimated that 3% of the credit sales of $1,375,000 for the year ended December 31 will be uncollectible.

Instructions

1. Journalize the transactions.
2. Journalize the adjusting entry to record the accrued interest on December 31 on the Global Company note.

Solution

1.

Feb. 1	Accounts Receivable—Ames Co.	8,000.00	
	Sales		8,000.00
Mar. 15	Notes Receivable—Ames Co.	8,000.00	
	Accounts Receivable—Ames Co.		8,000.00

Apr. 9	Allowance for Doubtful Accounts		2,500.00	
	Accounts Receivable—Dorset Co.			2,500.00
21	Notes Receivable—Jill Klein		7,500.00	
	Cash			7,500.00
May 14	Notes Receivable—Ames Co.		8,000.00	
	Cash		160.00	
	Notes Receivable—Ames Co.			8,000.00
	Interest Income			160.00
June 13	Accounts Receivable—Dorset Co.		2,500.00	
	Allowance for Doubtful Accounts			2,500.00
13	Cash		2,500.00	
	Accounts Receivable—Dorset Co.			2,500.00
July 20	Cash		7,762.50	
	Notes Receivable —Jill Klein			7,762.50
	($7,500)			
	Interest Revenue			
	($262.50)			
Aug. 12	Cash		8,280.00	
	Notes Receivable—Ames Co.			8,000.00
	Interest Income			280.00
Dec. 16	Notes Receivable—Global Company		12,000.00	
	Accounts Receivable—Global Company			12,000.00
31	Uncollectible Accounts Expense		41,250.00	
	Allowance for Doubtful Accounts			41,250.00

2.

Dec. 31	Interest Receivable		60.00	
	Interest Income			60.00
	($12,000 \times 12\% \times {}^{15}\!/_{360}$)			

SELF-EXAMINATION QUESTIONS (ANSWERS AT END OF CHAPTER)

1. At the end of the fiscal year, before the accounts are adjusted, Accounts Receivable has a balance of $200,000 and Allowance for Doubtful Accounts has a credit balance of $2,500. If the estimate of uncollectible accounts determined by aging the receivables is $8,500, the current provision to be made for uncollectible accounts expense is:

A. $2,500
B. $6,000
C. $8,500
D. $11,000

2. At the end of the fiscal year, Accounts Receivable has a balance of $100,000 and Allowance for Doubtful Accounts has a balance of $7,000. The expected net realizable value of the accounts receivable is:

A. $7,000
B. $93,000
C. $100,000
D. $107,000

3. What is the maturity value of a 90-day, 12% note for $10,000?

A. $8,800
B. $10,000
C. $10,300
D. $11,200

4. Under what caption would a temporary investment in shares be reported in the balance sheet?

A. Current assets
B. Capital assets
C. Investments
D. Current liabilities

DISCUSSION QUESTIONS

1. What are the three classifications of receivables?
2. What types of transactions give rise to accounts receivable?
3. Describe the nature of a promissory note.
4. In what section of the balance sheet should a note receivable be listed if its term is (a) 90 days, (b) five years?

5. Give two examples of other receivables.

6. The accounts receivable clerk is also responsible for handling cash receipts. Which principle of internal control is violated in this situation?

7. Which of the two methods of accounting for uncollectible accounts provides for the recognition of the expense at the earlier date?

8. What kind of an account (asset, liability, etc.) is Allowance for Doubtful Accounts, and is its normal balance a debit or a credit?

9. After the accounts are adjusted and closed at the end of the fiscal year, Accounts Receivable has a balance of $201,250 and Allowance for Doubtful Accounts has a balance of $12,250. Describe how the accounts receivable and the allowance for doubtful accounts are reported on the balance sheet.

10. A firm has consistently adjusted its allowance account at the end of the fiscal year by adding a fixed per cent of the period's net sales on account. After five years, the balance in Allowance for Doubtful Accounts has become disproportionately large in relationship to the balance in Accounts Receivable. Give two possible explanations.

11. Which of the two methods of estimating uncollectibles, when advance provision for uncollectible receivables is made, provides for the most accurate estimate of the current net realizable value of the receivables?

12. For a business, what are the advantages of a note receivable in comparison to an account receivable?

13. Fess Company issued a promissory note to Hubble Company. (a) Who is the payee? (b) What is the title of the account used by Hubble Company in recording the note?

14. If a note provides for payment of principal of $10,000 and interest at the rate of 10%, will the interest amount to $1,000? Explain.

15. Collins Co. accepted a 60-day, 9% note for $5,000, dated June 1, from one of its customers. (a) What is the face value of the note? (b) What is the due date of the note?

16. Why do corporations make temporary investments in securities? Where are temporary investments classified in the balance sheet?

17. Interest on bond investments is accrued, but dividends on share investments are not accrued. Why?

18. At what amount are temporary investments in shares reported on the balance sheet? Where are unrealized losses on such investments reported?

19. Under what caption should securities held as a temporary investment be reported on the balance sheet?

20. A company has two equity securities that it holds as a temporary investment. If they have a total cost of $210,000 and a fair market value of $202,750, at what amount should these securities be reported in the Current Assets section of the company's balance sheet?

Appendix

21. Lemke Co. accepted a 60-day, 9% note for $5,000, dated April 20, from one of its customers. Instead of waiting for receipt of the maturity value of $5,075.00 on June 19, Lemke Co. endorses it to a bank on May 10. The bank discounts the note at 10% and pays Lemke Co. $5,018.61. Why would Lemke Co. be willing to accept less from the bank than from the customer?

22. DeLong Co. received a 90-day note dated August 7 from a customer on account. DeLong Co. discounted the note at the bank August 22. (a) Did DeLong Co. have a contingent liability on August 22 after the note was discounted? (b) If the answer in (a) is "yes," when does the contingent liability expire?

23. During the year, a business discounted notes receivable of $160,000 at a bank. By the end of the year, $112,500 of these notes have matured. How should the business report the contingent liability for notes discounted at the end of the year?

24. The maker of a $6,000, 8%, 90-day note receivable failed to pay the note on the due date. What accounts should be debited and credited by the payee to record the dishonoured note receivable?

25. A discounted note receivable is dishonoured by the maker, and the endorser pays the bank the face of the note, $10,000, the interest, $500, and a protest fee of $150. What entry should be made in the accounts of the endorser to record the payment?

EXERCISES

EXERCISE 8–1
Internal control procedures
Objective 2

Omar Carpet Company sells carpeting. Over 85% of all carpet sales are on credit. The following procedures are used by Omar to process this large number of credit sales and the subsequent collections.

a. All credit sales to a first-time customer must be approved by the Credit Department. Salespersons will assist the customer in filling out a credit application, but an employee in the Credit Department is responsible for verifying employment and checking the customer's credit history before granting credit.

b. Omar's standard credit period is 45 days. The Credit Department may approve an extension of this repayment period of up to one year. Whenever an extension is granted, the customer signs a promissory note. Up to 30% of the credit sales in any one year are for repayment periods exceeding 45 days.

c. A formal ledger is not maintained for customers who sign promissory notes. Omar simply keeps a copy of each signed note in a file cabinet. These unpaid notes are filed by due date.

d. Omar employs an accounts receivable clerk. The clerk is responsible for recording customer credit sales (based on sales tickets), receiving cash from customers, giving customers credit for their payments, and handling all customer billing complaints.

e. The general ledger control account for Accounts Receivable is maintained by the General Accounting Department at Omar. This department records total credit sales, based on credit sale information from the store's electronic cash register, and total customer receipts, based on the bank deposit slip.

State whether each of these procedures is appropriate or inappropriate, considering the principles of internal control. If inappropriate, state which internal control procedure is violated.

EXERCISE 8–2
Nature of uncollectible accounts
Objective 3

Hilton Hotels Corporation owns and operates casinos at several of its hotels, located primarily in Nevada. At the end of a recent fiscal year, the following accounts and notes receivable were reported (in thousands):

Hotel accounts and notes receivable	$75,796	
Less: Allowance for doubtful accounts	3,256	
		$72,540
Casino accounts receivable	$26,334	
Less: Allowance for doubtful accounts	6,654	
		19,680

a. Compute the percentage of allowance for doubtful accounts to the gross hotel accounts and notes receivable for the end of the fiscal year.

b. Compute the percentage of the allowance for doubtful accounts to the gross casino accounts receivable for the end of the fiscal year.

c. Discuss possible reasons for the difference in the two ratios computed in (a) and (b).

EXERCISE 8–3
Estimating doubtful accounts
Objective 4

The aging of accounts receivable for Wyckoff Co., a wholesaler of office supplies, revealed the following balances on December 31, 1999:

Age Interval	Balance
Not due	$215,500
1–30 days past due	86,000
31–60 days past due	17,000
61–90 days past due	12,000
91–180 days past due	8,400
Over 180 days past due	3,500
	$342,400

A historical analysis indicates the following percentage of uncollectible accounts in each age category:

Age Interval	Percent Uncollectible
Not due	2%
1–30 days past due	4
31–60 days past due	9
61–90 days past due	15
91–180 days past due	60
Over 180 days past due	90

Estimate what the proper balance of the allowance for doubtful accounts should be as of December 31, 1999.

EXERCISE 8–4
Entry for uncollectible accounts
Objective 4

Using the data in Exercise 8–3, assume that the allowance for doubtful accounts for Wyckoff Co. had a debit balance of $1,280 as of December 31, 1999.
    Journalize the adjusting entry for uncollectible accounts as of December 31, 1999.

EXERCISE 8–5
Provision for doubtful accounts
Objective 4

At the end of the current year, the accounts receivable account has a debit balance of $450,000, and net sales for the year total $4,100,000. Determine the amount of the adjusting entry to record the provision for doubtful accounts under each of the following assumptions:

a. The allowance account before adjustment has a credit balance of $2,750. Uncollectible accounts expense is estimated at ¼ of 1% of net sales.
b. The allowance account before adjustment has a credit balance of $2,750. Analysis of the accounts in the customer's ledger indicates doubtful accounts of $18,350.
c. The allowance account before adjustment has a debit balance of $1,050. Uncollectible accounts expense is estimated at ½ of 1% of net sales.
d. The allowance account before adjustment has a debit balance of $1,050. Analysis of the accounts in the customer's ledger indicates doubtful accounts of $21,400.

EXERCISE 8–6
Entries for write-off of accounts receivable
Objectives 4, 5

Martin Company, a computer consulting firm, has decided to write off the $1,050 balance of an account owed by a customer. Journalize the entry to record the write-off (a) assuming that the allowance method is used, and (b) assuming that the direct write-off method is used.

EXERCISE 8–7
Entries for uncollectible receivables using allowance method
Objective 4

Journalize the following transactions in the accounts of Bella Company, a restaurant supply company that uses the allowance method of accounting for uncollectible receivables and a perpetual inventory system:

Feb. 20. Sold merchandise on account to J. Harrey, $3,500. The cost of the goods sold was $1,400.
May 19. Received $1,000 from J. Harrey and wrote off the remainder owed on the sale of February 20 as uncollectible.
Sept. 30. Reinstated the account of J. Harrey that had been written off on May 19 and received $2,500 cash in full payment.

EXERCISE 8–8
Entries for uncollectible accounts using direct write-off method
Objective 5

Journalize the following transactions in the accounts of Webster Co., a hospital supply company that uses the direct write-off method of accounting for uncollectible receivables and a perpetual inventory system:

Mar. 11. Sold merchandise on account to E. Dodge, $3,200. The cost of the goods sold was $1,250.
May 1. Received $1,800 from E. Dodge and wrote off the remainder owed on the sale of March 11 as uncollectible.
Nov. 15. Reinstated the account of E. Dodge that had been written off on May 1 and received $1,400 cash in full payment.

EXERCISE 8–9
Effect of doubtful accounts on net income
Objectives 4, 5

During its first year of operations, Waterloo Automotive Supply Co. had net sales of $1,250,000, wrote off $12,800 of accounts as uncollectible, using the direct write-off method, and reported net income of $72,600. If the allowance method of accounting for uncollectibles had been used, 1.5% of net sales would have been estimated as uncollectible. Determine what the net income would have been if the allowance method had been used.

EXERCISE 8–10
Effect of doubtful accounts on net income
Objectives 4, 5

Using the data in Exercise 8–9, assume that during the second year of operations Waterloo Automotive Supply Co. had net sales of $1,800,000, wrote off $24,500 of accounts as uncollectible, using the direct write-off method, and reported net income of $112,300.

a. Determine what net income would have been in the second year if the allowance method (using 1.5% of net sales) had been used in both the first and second years.
b. Determine what the balance of the allowance for doubtful accounts would have been at the end of the second year if the allowance method had been used in both the first and second years.

EXERCISE 8–11
Determining due date and interest on notes
Objective 6

Determine the due date and the amount of interest due at maturity on the following notes:

	Date of Note	Face Amount	Term of Note	Interest Rate
a.	March 3	$ 5,000	45 days	8%
b.	May 20	6,000	60 days	10%
c.	May 31	10,000	75 days	14%
d.	June 9	15,000	90 days	10%
e.	July 1	17,500	120 days	12%

EXERCISE 8–12
Estimating the rate of interest on notes
Objective 6

Muscatine Co. borrowed $100,000 from The Royal Bank, signing a 90-day note. The bank deducted interest of $2,900 and deposited the proceeds of $97,100 in Muscatine Co.'s account. Estimate (to the nearest whole per cent) the interest rate that the bank charged Muscatine Co. on the note.

EXERCISE 8–13
Entries for notes receivable
Objectives 6, 7

Burke Interior Decorators issued a 60-day, 9% note for $15,000, dated March 3, to Loree Furniture Company on account.

a. Determine the due date of the note.
b. Determine the maturity value of the note.
c. Journalize the entries to record the following: (1) receipt of the note by the payee, and (2) receipt by the payee of payment of the note at maturity.

EXERCISE 8–14
Entries for notes receivable
Objective 7, Appendix

The series of six transactions recorded in the following T accounts were related to a sale to a customer on account and the receipt of the amount owed. Briefly describe each transaction.

	Cash					Sales		
(4)	27,305	(5)	28,000	(2)	2,500	(1)		30,000
(6)	28,300							

	Notes Receivable					Interest Income		
(3)	27,500	(4)	27,500			(6)		300

	Accounts Receivable					Interest Expense	
(1)	30,000	(2)	2,500	(4)	195	
(5)	28,000	(3)	27,500			
		(6)	28,000			

EXERCISE 8–15
Entries for notes receivable, including year-end entries
Objective 7

The following selected transactions were completed during the current year by Elastic Co., a supplier of elastic bands for clothing:

Dec. 15. Received from Dino Co., on account, an $18,000, 90-day, 10% note dated December 15.
   31. Recorded an adjusting entry for accrued interest on the note of December 15.
   31. Closed the interest income account. The only entry in this account originated from the December 31 adjustment.

Journalize the transactions.

EXERCISE 8–16
Bond investment
Objective 8

As a temporary investment, Smith Company purchased 20 $1,000, 10% bonds at 97 plus accrued interest and commission of $120 on April 1, 1999. The bonds pay interest semi-annually June 30 and December 31. Prepare journal entries to record the following:

1. The purchase of the bonds April 1.
2. The receipt of the semi-annual interest payment June 30.
3. The receipt of the semi-annual interest payment December 31.

EXERCISE 8–17
Bond investments
Objective 8

Prepare the journal entry to record the sale of the bonds described in Exercise 8–16 at 101 plus accrued interest less a 2% commission on March 1, 2000.

EXERCISE 8–18
Share investments
Objective 8

During 1999 Jetty Company had the following transactions related to temporary share investments. On March 31 the company bought 500 shares of Company A at $52 per share plus a 2% commission. On July 23 the company bought 400 shares of Company B at $40 per share plus a 2% commission. On December 2 the company received a dividend of $2.20 per share from Company A. On December 15 the company sold 400 shares of Company B at $39 per share less 2% commission. Journalize the entries to record these transactions.

EXERCISE 8–19
Temporary investments in financial statements
Objective 9

As of December 31, 1999, the end of its first year of operations, Mason Oil Supply Company has the following portfolio of marketable securities held as temporary investments:

	Cost	Market
Security A	$65,500	$68,000
Security B	21,000	18,100
Security C	39,250	35,000
Security D	40,250	41,300

Assuming the company applies LCM using the aggregate method, describe how the portfolio of securities would be reported on the December 31, 1999 balance sheet and the income statement for the year ended December 31, 1999.

EXERCISE 8–20
Temporary investments in financial statements
Objective 9

Using the data from Exercise 8–19, assume that as of December 31, 2000, Mason Oil Supply Company has the following portfolio of temporary investments:

	Cost	Market
Security A	$65,500	$71,000
Security B	21,000	17,100
Security D	40,250	44,000
Security E	18,000	19,500
Security F	7,500	7,200

During 2000, Mason Oil Supply Company sold Security C for $36,000.

Describe how the selling of Security C and how the remaining portfolio of securities would be reported on the December 31, 1999 balance sheet and the income statement for the year ended December 31, 1999.

EXERCISE 8–21
Receivables and temporary investments in the balance sheet
Objective 9

List any errors you can find in the following partial balance sheet.

Thomas Company
Balance Sheet
December 31, 20—

Assets

Current assets:		
Cash		$ 95,000
Marketable equity securities (cost)	$460,000	
Deduct unrealized gain	30,000	430,000
Notes receivable		250,000
Accounts receivable	$445,000	
Plus allowance for doubtful accounts	15,000	460,000
Interest receivable		9,000

APPENDIX EXERCISE 8–22
Discounting notes receivable

Woodbridge Co., a building construction company, holds a 90-day, 8% note for $25,000, dated July 18, which was received from a customer on account. On August 21, the note is discounted at the bank at the rate of 12%.

a. Determine the maturity value of the note.
b. Determine the number of days in the discount period.
c. Determine the amount of the discount.
d. Determine the amount of the proceeds.
e. Journalize the entry to record the discounting of the note on August 21.

APPENDIX EXERCISE 8–23
Entries for receipt and discounting of note receivable and dishonoured notes

Journalize the following transactions in the accounts of Les Mis Theatre Productions:

Aug. 1. Received a $50,000, 90-day, 10% note dated August 1 from Revolt Company on account.
      16. Discounted the note at the Bank of Montreal at 11%.
Oct. 30. The note is dishonoured by Revolt Company; paid the bank the amount due on the note, plus a protest fee of $100.
Nov. 29. Received the amount due on the dishonoured note plus interest for 30 days at 15% on the total amount charged to Revolt Company on October 30.

EXERCISE 8–24
Entries for receipt and dishonour of notes receivable

Journalize the following transactions in the accounts of Davenport Co., which operates a riverboat casino:

Mar. 1. Received a $10,000, 30-day, 12% note dated March 1 from Moline Co. on account.
      21. Received a $15,000, 60-day, 10% note dated March 10 from Walcott Co. on account.
      31. The note dated March 1 from Moline Co. is dishonoured, and the customer's account is charged for the note, including interest.
May 20. The note dated March 21 from Walcott Co. is dishonoured, and the customer's account is charged for the note, including interest.
June 29. Cash is received for the amount due on the dishonoured note dated March 1 plus interest for 90 days at 12% on the total amount debited to Moline Co. on March 31.
Aug. 31. Wrote off against the allowance account the amount charged to Walcott Co. on May 20 for the dishonoured note dated March 21.

PROBLEMS SERIES A

PROBLEM 8–1A
Entries related to uncollectible accounts
Objective 4

The following transactions, adjusting entries, and closing entries were completed by The Etching Art Gallery during the current fiscal year ended December 31:

Jan. 21. Reinstated the account of Jon Hillis, which had been written off in the preceding year as uncollectible. Journalized the receipt of $2,025 cash in full payment of Hillis' account.
      28. Wrote off the $8,500 balance owed by D'Arrigo Co., which is bankrupt.
June 7. Received 40% of the $8,000 balance owed by Lombard Co., a bankrupt business, and wrote off the remainder as uncollectible.
Aug. 29. Reinstated the account of Louis Estes, which had been written off two years earlier as uncollectible. Recorded the receipt of $900 cash in full payment.
Dec. 30. Wrote off the following accounts as uncollectible (compound entry): Channel Co., $1,050; Engel Co., $1,260; Loach Furniture, $1,775; Briana Parker, $820.
      31. Based on an analysis of the $435,500 of accounts receivable, it was estimated that $22,000 will be uncollectible. Journalized the adjusting entry.
      31. Journalized the entry to close the appropriate account to Income Summary.

Instructions

1. Record the following January 1 credit balance in the account indicated:

115 Allowance for Doubtful Accounts $18,955
313 Income Summary   —
718 Uncollectible Accounts Expense   —

2. Journalize the transactions and the adjusting and closing entries described. After it has been journalized, post each entry to the three selected accounts affected and extend the new balances.
3. Determine the expected net realizable value of the accounts receivable as of December 31.
4. Assuming that, instead of basing the provision for uncollectible accounts on an analysis of receivables, the adjusting entry on December 31 had been based on an estimated expense of ¾ of 1% of the net sales of $3,500,000 for the year, determine the following:
   a. Uncollectible accounts expense for the year.
   b. Balance in the allowance account after the adjustment of December 31.
   c. Expected net realizable value of the accounts receivable as of December 31.

PROBLEM 8–2A
Comparing two methods of accounting for uncollectible receivables
Objectives 4, 5

Ananda Company, which operates a chain of 10 electronics supply stores, has just completed its fourth year of operations. The direct write-off method of recording uncollectible accounts expense has been used during the entire period. Because of substantial increases in sales volume and amount of uncollectible accounts, the firm is considering the possibility of changing to the allowance method. Information is requested as to the effect an annual provision of 1% of sales would have had on the amount of uncollectible accounts expense reported for each of the past four years. It is also considered desirable to know what the balance of Allowance for Doubtful Accounts would have been at the end of each year. The following data have been obtained from the accounts:

Year	Sales	Uncollectible Accounts Written Off	Year of Origin of Accounts Receivable Written Off as Uncollectible			
			1st	2nd	3rd	4th
1st	$ 650,000	$2,600	$2,600			
2nd	720,000	3,500	1,950	$1,550		
3rd	850,000	8,600	2,200	3,400	$3,000	
4th	1,050,000	9,550	6 750	2,300	2,950	$4,300

Instructions

1. Assemble the desired data, using the following columnar captions:

Year	Uncollectible Accounts Expense			Balance of Allowance Account, End of Year
	Expense Actually Reported	Expense Based on Estimate	Increase (Decrease) in Amount of Expense	

2. ➤ Experience during the first four years of operations indicated that the receivables were either collected within two years or had to be written off as uncollectible. Does the estimate of 1% of sales appear to be reasonably close to the actual experience with uncollectible accounts originating during the first two years? Explain.

PROBLEM 8–3A
Accounts receivable and uncollectible accounts
Objective 4

At December 31 of the current year, the Lander Company had a balance of $80,000 in its Accounts Receivable account and a credit balance of $900 in the Allowance for Uncollectible Accounts. The Accounts Receivable subsidiary ledger consisted of $82,400 in debit balances and $2,400 in credit balances. The following schedule shows the aging of the company's accounts and the percentages of each age group that have proven uncollectible in the past. The company bases its provision for credit losses on the aging analysis.

	Amount	Percent Doubtful
Current	$65,000	2
0–60 Days Past Due	10,000	6
61–180 Days Past Due	3,800	15
Over Six Months Past Due	3,600	30
Total Past Due	$82,400	

Instructions

1. Prepare the adjusting journal entry to record the uncollectible accounts expense for the year.
2. Show how Accounts Receivable (including the credit balances) and Allowance for Uncollectible Accounts would appear in the December 31 balance sheet.

PROBLEM 8–4A

Sales, notes receivable
Objective 7

The following were selected from among the transactions completed during the current year by Nash Co., an appliance wholesale company:

Jan. 11. Sold merchandise on account to Atlas Co., $15,000. The cost of goods sold was $10,000.
Mar. 12. Accepted a 60-day, 10% note for $15,000 from Atlas Co. on account.
May 11. Received from Atlas Co. the amount due on the note of March 12.
June 1. Sold merchandise on account to Kohl's for $5,000. The cost of goods sold was $3,500.
     5. Loaned $7,500 cash to Frank Gary, an employee, receiving a 30-day, 12% note.
    11. Received from Kohl's the amount due on the invoice of June 1, less 2% discount.
July 5. Received the interest due from Frank Gary and a new 60-day, 14% note as a renewal of the loan of June 5. (Record both the debit and the credit to the notes receivable account.)
Sept. 3. Received from Frank Gary the amount due on his note of July 5.
     4. Sold merchandise on account to Hanover Co., $4,000. The cost of goods sold was $2,500.
Oct. 4. Accepted a 60-day, 12% note for $4,000 from Hanover Co. on account.
Dec. 3. Received from Hanover Co. the amount owed on the note of October 4 plus interest.

Instructions

Journalize the transactions. Assume Nash uses a perpetual inventory system.

PROBLEM 8–5A

Details of notes receivable
Objective 7

During the last six months of the current fiscal year, Lite-Up Co. received the following notes. Lite-Up Co. produces advertising videos.

	Date	Face Amount	Term	Interest Rate
1.	Apr. 1	$20,000	90 days	8%
2.	June 10	12,000	60 days	12%
3.	July 11	15,000	90 days	8%
4.	Sept. 1	20,000	90 days	7%
5.	Dec. 1	24,000	60 days	9%
6.	Dec. 16	36,000	30 days	13%

Instructions

1. Determine for each note (a) the due date and (b) the amount of interest due at maturity, identifying each note by number.
2. Journalize the adjusting entry to record the accrued interest on Notes (5) and (6) on December 31.

PROBLEM 8–6A

Notes receivable entries
Objective 7

The following data relate to notes receivable and interest for Barth Co., a financial services company. (All notes are dated as of the day they are received.)

Mar. 1. Received a $20,000, 9%, 60-day note on account.
    21. Received an $18,000, 9%, 90-day note on account.
Apr. 30. Received $20,300 on note of March 1.
May 16. Received a $12,000, 12%, 90-day note on account.
    31. Received a $7,500, 8%, 30-day note on account.
June 19. Received $18,405 on note of March 21.
    30. Received $7,550 on note of May 31.

July   1.   Received a $10,000, 12%, 30-day note on account.
     31.   Received $10,100 on note of July 1.
Aug.14.   Received $12,360 on note of May 16.

Instructions

1. Journalize the entries to record the transactions.
2. If Barth Co. has a June 30 year end, prepare any adjusting entry required for notes receivable as of June 30.

PROBLEM 8–7A
Investment in shares
Objective 7

The Sharma Corporation began operations on January 1 of the current year and selected a December 31 fiscal year end. During the year it entered a number of transactions related to temporary investments in shares as follows:

Mar.   8.   Purchased 3,000 common shares of Canadian Tire Ltd. for a total cost of $49,000.
Apr. 15.   Purchased 1,200 common shares of Ford Canada Ltd. for a total cost of $32,100.
July 28.   Purchased 2,000 common shares of Alberta Energy Corporation for a total cost of $41,200.
Sept.29.   Sold 500 shares of Ford Canada at a price of $28 per share less a commission of 2%.
Nov. 30.   Received a dividend of $1.10 per share from Ford Canada Ltd.
Dec. 15.   Received a dividend of $0.30 per share from Alberta Energy Corporation.

On December 31, the market prices for the shares were: Alberta Energy–$21.50, Canadian Tire–$17.00, and Ford–$23.00. Sharma has decided to use the individual security method (item by item) to apply lower of cost and market to temporary share investments.

Instructions

1. Prepare journal entries to record the transactions.
2. Prepare any adjusting entries necessary at December 31.

PROBLEMS SERIES B

PROBLEM 8–1B
Entries related to
uncollectible accounts
Objective 4

The following transactions, adjusting entries, and closing entries were completed by Johnson Contractors Co. during the current fiscal year ended December 31:

Mar. 10.   Received 65% of the $12,000 balance owed by Agnew Co., a bankrupt business, and wrote off the remainder as uncollectible.
June   3.   Reinstated the account of B. Bush, which had been written off in the preceding year as uncollectible. Journalized the receipt of $1,050 cash in full payment of Bush's account.
Sept.19.   Wrote off the $7,250 balance owed by Larkin Co., which has no assets.
Oct. 30.   Reinstated the account of Giles Co., which had been written off in the preceding year as uncollectible. Journalized the receipt of $3,500 cash in full payment of the account.
Dec. 31.   Wrote off the following accounts as uncollectible (compound entry): Huang Co., $2,950; Nance Co., $1,600; Powell Distributors, $9,500; J. J. Stevens, $5,200.
     31.   Based on an analysis of the $795,000 of accounts receivable, it was estimated that $42,700 will be uncollectible. Journalized the adjusting entry.
     31.   Journalized the entry to close the appropriate account to Income Summary.

Instructions

1. Record the following January 1 credit balance in the account indicated:

    115   Allowance for Doubtful Accounts $19,050
    313   Income Summary   —
    718   Uncollectible Accounts Expense   —

2. Journalize the transactions and the adjusting and closing entries described. After it has been journalized, post each entry to the three selected accounts affected and extend the new balances.

3. Determine the expected net realizable value of the accounts receivable as of December 31.
4. Assuming that, instead of basing the provision for uncollectible accounts on an analysis of receivables, the adjusting entry on December 31 had been based on an estimated expense of ¾ of 1% of the net sales of $6,100,000 for the year, determine the following:
   a. Uncollectible accounts expense for the year.
   b. Balance in the allowance account after the adjustment of December 31.
   c. Expected net realizable value of the accounts receivable as of December 31.

PROBLEM 8–2B
Comparing two methods of accounting for uncollectible receivables
Objectives 4, 5

WBC Company, a telephone service and supply company, has just completed its fourth year of operations. The direct write-off method of recording uncollectible accounts expense has been used during the entire period. Because of substantial increases in the sales volume and amount of uncollectible accounts, the firm is considering the possibility of changing to the allowance method. Information is requested as to the effect that an annual provision of 1% of sales would have had on the amount of uncollectible accounts expense reported for each of the past four years. It is also considered desirable to know what the balance of Allowance for Doubtful Accounts would have been at the end of each year. The following data have been obtained from the accounts:

Year	Sales	Uncollectible Accounts Written Off	Year of Origin of Accounts Receivable Written Off as Uncollectible			
			1st	2nd	3rd	4th
1st	$ 450,000	$2,500	$2,500			
2nd	660,000	3,950	1,900	$2,050		
3rd	950,000	5,700	700	2,600	$2,400	
4th	1,000,000	6,800	*5100*	2,200	2,550	$2,050

6850

Instructions

1. Assemble the desired data, using the following columnar captions:

	Uncollectible Accounts Expense			Balance of
Year	Expense Actually Reported	Expense Based on Estimate	Increase (Decrease) in Amount of Expense	Allowance Account, End of Year

2. ▬▬▬ Experience during the first four years of operations indicated that the receivables were either collected within two years or had to be written off as uncollectible. Does the estimate of 1% of sales appear to be reasonably close to the actual experience with uncollectible accounts originating during the first two years? Explain.

PROBLEM 8–3B
Accounts receivable and uncollectible accounts
Objective 4

On December 31 of the current year, the Jackson Company had a balance of $250,000 in its Accounts Receivable account and a credit balance of $1,700 in its Allowance for Uncollectible Accounts. The Accounts Receivable subsidiary ledger consisted of $251,500 in debit balances and $1,500 in credit balances. The following schedule shows the company's analysis of Accounts Receivable balances at December 31, and the percentages of each age group that have proven uncollectible in the past.

	Amount	Percent Doubtful
Current	$194,000	1
0–60 Days Past Due	35,000	5
61–180 Days Past Due	18,000	15
Over Six Months Past Due	4,500	40
Total Past Due	$251,500	

Instructions

1. Prepare the adjusting journal entry to record the provision for credit losses for the year.
2. Show how Accounts Receivable (including the credit balances) and Allowance for Uncollectible Accounts would appear in the December 31 balance sheet.

PROBLEM 8–4B
Sales, notes receivable
Objective 7

The following were selected from among the transactions completed by Beverly Co. during the current year. Beverly Co. sells and installs home and business security systems.

Jan. 10. Loaned $20,000 cash to Joyce Curtis, receiving a 90-day, 8% note.
Feb. 1. Sold merchandise on account to Peabody and Son, $9,000. The cost of the goods sold was $4,800.
    20. Sold merchandise on account to C. D. Connors Co., $8,000. The cost of the goods sold was $5,000.
Mar. 2. Received from C. D. Connors Co. the amount of the invoice of February 20, less 1% discount.
     3. Accepted a 60-day, 10% note for $9,000 from Peabody and Son on account.
Apr. 10. Received the interest due from Joyce Curtis and a new 90-day, 12% note as a renewal of the loan of January 10. (Record both the debit and the credit to the notes receivable account.)
May 2. Received from Peabody and Son the amount due on the note of March 3.
July 9. Received from Joyce Curtis the amount due on her note of April 10.
    10. Sold merchandise on account to Song Yu and Co., $30,000. The cost of goods sold was $20,000.
Aug. 9. Accepted a 60-day, 12% note for $30,000 from Song Yu and Co. on account.
Oct. 8. Received from Song Yu and Co. the amount owed on the note of Aug. 9 plus interest.

Instructions
Journalize the transactions. Assume the company uses a perpetual inventory system.

PROBLEM 8–5B
Details of notes receivable
Objective 7

During the current fiscal year, Flushing Co. received the following notes. Flushing Co. wholesales bathroom fixtures. Notes (1) and (2) were discounted on the dates and at the rates indicated.

	Date	Face Amount	Term	Interest Rate
1.	May 1	$18,000	60 days	8%
2.	June 11	10,000	30 days	12%
3.	Aug. 20	7,200	90 days	7%
4.	Oct. 31	12,000	60 days	9%
5.	Nov. 28	15,000	60 days	8%
6.	Dec. 26	18,000	30 days	12%

Instructions

1. Determine for each note (a) the due date and (b) the amount of interest due at maturity, identifying each note by number.
2. Journalize the adjusting entry to record the accrued interest on Notes (5) and (6) on December 31.

PROBLEM 8–6B
Notes receivable entries
Objective 7

The following data relate to notes receivable and interest for Fibre Optic Co., a cable manufacturer and supplier. (All notes are dated as of the day they are received.)

July 1. Received an $8,000, 9%, 60-day note on account.
Aug. 16. Received a $30,000, 10%, 120-day note on account.
    30. Received $8,120 on note of July 1.
Sept. 1. Received a $15,000, 8%, 60-day note on account.
Oct. 31. Received $15,200 on note of September 1.
Nov. 8. Received a $24,000, 7%, 30-day note on account.
    30. Received a $3,000, 10%, 30-day note on account.
Dec. 8. Received $24,140 on note of November 8.

Dec. 14. Received $31,000 on note of August 16.
   30. Received $3,025 on note of November 30.

Instructions

1. Journalize entries to record the transactions.
2. If Fibre Optic's year end is October 31, prepare any adjusting entries required in relation to notes receivable as of October 31.

PROBLEM 8–7B
Temporary investments in shares and bonds
Objective 7

The Lachance Company had the following short-term investment transactions during 1999, its first year of operations. The company adopted December 31 as its fiscal year end.

Mar. 26. Purchased 2,000 common shares of Alberta Energy Corporation at a total cost of $42,380.
July 1. Purchased 30 $1,000, 10% Government of Canada Bonds at 102 plus accrued interest and commission of $200. The bonds pay interest May 31 and November 30.
Sept.15. Purchased 3,500 common shares of Philips Environmental Services Inc. at a total cost of $105,000.
Nov. 30. Received semi-annual interest payment on Government of Canada Bonds.
Nov. 30. Alberta Energy declared a cash dividend of $0.30 per common share payable December 15.
Dec. 17. Received the cash dividend from Alberta Energy.

On December 31 the market prices for the share investments were Alberta Energy–$21.50 and Philips–$29, and $101 for the bonds. Lachance has decided to use the portfolio basis of valuing temporary investments at the lower of cost and market.

Instructions

1. Prepare journal entries to record the transactions.
2. Prepare any adjusting entries required on December 31.

CHALLENGE PROBLEMS

PROBLEM CP8–1

Greeta Co. sells merchandise that have a unit selling price of $100 and credit terms of 2/10, n/30. On December 31, 1999 the firm showed accounts receivable of $33,900 and allowance for doubtful accounts of $1,500. Transactions for the year ended December 31, 2000 were as follows:

1. Collected $29,400 cash from 1999 credit sales, all within the discount period.
2. Collected $2,100 cash from 1999 credit sales after discount period.
3. Wrote off an account of $900.
4. Collected $600 on an account written off in 1998.
5. Sold merchandise for $45,600 cash. All other sales for 2000 were on account.
6. Sold merchandise to B.P.; invoice price $3,600. Two days later, B.P. returned one defective unit for credit. Paid off account within nine days.
7. Sold merchandise to P.Z.; invoice price $5,200. Paid in full after 20 days. Two weeks later P.Z. returned three defective units for a full refund.
8. Sold merchandise to A.F.; invoice price, $25,000.

Instructions

a. Give entries for the above transactions.
b. Prepare the entry to record bad debt expense under each of the following independent assumptions:
 i. bad debt expense is estimated as 4% of gross credit sales.
 ii. based on an aging schedule, you determine that $1,500 of the receivables outstanding on December 31, 1999 are likely uncollectible.
 iii. you estimate uncollectibles as 5% of the receivables outstanding at year end.
c. Assuming bad debts are estimated under part i. above, prepare (in good form) all sections of the 2000 financial statements (except cash) related to the above transactions.

PROBLEM CP8–2

The following accounts appeared in the ledger of Rizzo Co. on December 31, 1999 and December 31, 2000.

	Dec. 31, 1999*	Dec. 31, 2000**
Accounts receivable	$220,000	$300,000
Allowance for uncollectibles (cr)	16,000	2,200
Sales	600,000	800,000

*adjusted pre-closing balance   **unadjusted balance

During the year 2000, sales on account amounted to 80% of total sales and one account for $4,200, which had been written off in 1999, was collected. It is estimated that 2% of the current year's credit sales will prove to be uncollectible.

Instructions

a. Prepare journal entries that were made during the year 2000 regarding these accounts.
b. Prepare the adjusting journal entry required on December 31, 2000.

PROBLEM CP8–3

Cool Co. makes all of its sales on account, with terms 5/10, n/30, and records all sales gross of the sales discount. On January 1, 1999, Cool Co. showed a balance in accounts receivable of $80,000 and a balance in the allowance for uncollectibles of $3,000. During 1999 credit sales were $240,000. Cash collections totalled $250,000 and sales discounts taken by customers were $7,000. During the year, $3,500 of accounts were written off as uncollectible, and the company collected $300 on an account written off in 1998 (this amount was in addition to the $250,000 cash collections mentioned above). On November 1, Cool accepted a $5,000, 10% note receivable due in three months in settlement for an account receivable that was one month overdue. On January 1, 2000, Cool discounted the note at the bank at 12%. After doing an aging of receivables, you estimate that $5,000 of the accounts receivables outstanding at December 31, 1999 will likely prove uncollectible.

Instructions

Prepare all journal entries required by the above information. Closing entries are *not* required. Cool Co. has a December 31 year end.

PROBLEM CP8–4

Presented below is information related to the Accounts Receivable accounts of Kushner, Inc. during the current year.

1. An aging schedule of the accounts receivable as of December 31 (before adjustment) is as follows:

Age	Net Debit Balance	% to be applied after correction made
Under 60 days	$172,342	1%
61 – 90 days	136,490*	3%
91 – 120 days	39,924	6%
Over 120 days	23,644	$4,200 definitely uncollectible; estimated
	$372,400	remainder collectible is 75%

* Includes a credit balance of $4,840.

2. The Accounts Receivable control account has a debit balance of $372,400 on December 31.
3. Two entries were made in the Bad Debt Expense account during the year: (1) a debit on December 31 for the amount credited to Allowance for Doubtful Accounts (see 4 below), and (2) a credit for $2,520 on November 3 to write off a two-year-old account.
4. A T-account representation of the Allowance for Doubtful Accounts account is as follows for the year.

Allowance for Doubtful Accounts				
Nov. 3	Uncollectible accounts written off	2,520	Jan. 1 Beginning balance	8,750
			Dec. 31 5% of $375,600	18,780

5. A credit exists in the Accounts Receivable (61–90 days) of $4,840, which represents an advance on a sales contract.

Instructions

Assuming that the books have not been closed for the year, make the necessary correcting entries.

CASES

CASE 8–1
National Bank of Canada
Calculating interest

Nataline Smith, vice-president of operations for the National Bank of Canada, has instructed the bank's computer programmer to program the bank's computers to calculate interest on deposi-tory accounts (payables) using a 365-day year. Nataline also instructed the programmer to use a 360-day year to compute interest on loans (receivables).

Discuss whether Nataline is behaving in an eth-ical manner.

CASE 8–2
Do-Rite Construction Supplies Co.
Collecting accounts receivable

The following is an excerpt from a conversation between the office manager, Valerie Cook, and the president of Do-Rite Construction Supplies Co., Marvin Howard. Do-Rite sells building supplies to local contractors.

Valerie: Marvin, we're going to have to do something about these overdue accounts receivable. One-third of our accounts are over 60 days past due, and I've had accounts that have stayed open for almost a year!

Marvin: I didn't realize it was that bad. Any ideas?

Valerie: Well, we could stop giving credit. Make everyone pay with cash or a credit card. We accept MasterCard and Visa already, but only the walk-in customers use them. Almost all of the contractors put purchases on their bills.

Marvin: Yes, but we've been allowing credit for years. As far as I know, all of our competitors allow contractors credit. If we stopped giving credit, we'd lose many of our contrac-tors. They'd just go elsewhere. You know, some of these guys run up bills as high as $40,000 or $50,000. There's no way they could put that kind of money on a credit card.

Valerie: That's a good point. But we've got to do something.

Marvin: How many of the contractor accounts do you actu-ally end up writing off as uncollectible?

Valerie: Not many. Almost all eventually pay. It's just that they take so long!

Suggest one or more solutions to Do-Rite Construction Supplies Co.'s problem concerning the collec-tion of accounts receivable.

CASE 8–3
Sears Canada Inc.
Financial analysis

Businesses that grant long credit terms usually have larger accounts receivable balances than those granting short credit terms. In either case, it is desirable to collect receivables as promptly as possible. The cash collected from receivables improves sol-vency, and prompt collection also lessens the risk of loss from uncollectible accounts.

There are two financial measures that are especially useful in evaluating the efficiency in collecting accounts receivable: (1) accounts receivable turnover and (2) number of days' sales in receivables. The accounts receivable turnover is computed as follows:

$$\text{Accounts receivable turnover} = \frac{\text{Net sales on account}}{\text{Average accounts receivable}}$$

The average accounts receivable can be determined by adding the beginning and ending accounts receivable bal-ances and dividing by two.

The number of days' sales in receivables is an estimate of the length of time the accounts receivable have been out-standing and is computed as follows:

$$\text{Number of days' sales in receivables} = \frac{\text{Accounts receivable, end of year}}{\text{Average daily sales on account}}$$

Average daily sales on account is determined by dividing net sales on account by 365 days.

An improvement in the efficiency in collecting accounts receivable is indicated by an increase in the accounts receivable turnover and a decrease in the number of days' sales in receivables.

1. For Sears Canada Inc., assume that all sales are credit sales and that the accounts receivable were $1,033,000,000 at the beginning of last year.

a. Compute the accounts receivable turnover for the current and preceding year.

b. Compute the number of days' sales in receivables at December 31 of the current and preceding year.

2. ━━━━▶ What conclusions can be drawn from these analyses regarding Sears's efficiency in collecting receivables?

CASE 8–4
Sports Rehab Co.
Estimating uncollectible accounts

For several years, sales have been on a "cash only" basis. On January 1, 1996, however, Sports Rehab Co. began offering credit on terms of n/30. The amount of the adjusting entry to record the estimated uncollectible receivables at the end of each year has been ½ of 1% of credit sales, which is the rate reported as the average for the industry. Credit sales and the year-end credit balances in Allowance for Doubtful Accounts for the past four years are as follows:

Year	Credit Sales	Allowance for Doubtful Accounts
1996	$5,800,000	$ 5,800
1997	6,000,000	8,200
1998	6,100,000	15,400
1999	6,050,000	19,000

Joe Johnson, president of Sports Rehab Co., is concerned that the method used to account for and write off uncollectible receivables is unsatisfactory. He has asked for your advice in the analysis of past operations in this area and for recommendations for change.

1. Determine the amount of (a) the addition to Allowance for Doubtful Accounts and (b) the accounts written off for each of the four years.

2. a. ━━━━▶ Advise Joe Johnson as to whether the estimate of ½ of 1% of credit sales appears reasonable.

   b. ━━━━▶ Assume that after discussing (a) with Joe Johnson, he asked you what action might be taken to determine what the balance of Allowance for Doubtful Accounts should be at December 31, 1999, and what possible changes, if any, you might recommend in accounting for uncollectible receivables. How would you respond?

ANSWERS TO SELF-EXAMINATION QUESTIONS

1. **B** The estimate of uncollectible accounts, $8,500 (answer C), is the amount of the desired balance of Allowance for Doubtful Accounts after adjustment. The amount of the current provision to be made for uncollectible accounts expense is thus $6,000 (answer B), which is the amount that must be added to the Allowance for Doubtful Accounts credit balance of $2,500 (answer A), so that the account will have the desired balance of $8,500.

2. **B** The amount expected to be realized from accounts receivable is the balance of Accounts Receivable, $100,000, less the balance of Allowance for Doubtful Accounts, $7,000, or $93,000 (answer B).

3. **C** Maturity value is the amount that is due at the maturity or due date. The maturity value of $10,300 (answer C) is determined as follows:

Face amount of note	$10,000
Plus interest ($10,000 × 12% × 90/360)	300
Maturity value of note	$10,300

4. **A** Securities held as temporary investments are classified on the balance sheet as current assets (answer A).

9 Inventories

YOU AND ACCOUNTING

Assume that you purchased a compact disc (CD)/receiver in June. You planned on attaching pairs of speakers to the system. Initially, however, you could afford only one pair of speakers, which cost $160. In October, you purchased the second pair of speakers at a cost of $180.

Over the holidays, someone broke into your home and stole one pair of speakers. Luckily, your renters/homeowners insurance policy will cover the theft, but the insurance company needs to know the cost of the speakers that were stolen.

All of the speakers are identical. To respond to the insurance company, however, you will need to identify which pair of speakers was stolen. Was it the first pair, which cost $160? Or was it the second pair, which cost $180? Whichever assumption you make may determine the amount that you receive from the insurance company.

Merchandising businesses make similar assumptions when identical merchandise is purchased at different costs. At the end of a period, some of the inventory will be on hand and some will have been sold. But which costs relate to the sold inventory and which costs relate to the inventory on hand? The business's assumption can involve large dollar amounts and thus can have a significant impact on the financial statements. For example, **Sears Canada Inc.'s** financial statements for the year ending 1996 report inventories that are over $490 million and a cost of goods sold of over $3 billion. The company's operating income for this same period was just over $70 million.

In this chapter, we will discuss such issues as how to determine the cost of inventory on hand and the cost of goods sold. However, we begin this chapter by discussing internal controls over inventory.

After studying this chapter, you should be able to:

Objective 1
Summarize and provide examples of internal control procedures that apply to inventories.

Objective 2
List the procedures for determining the actual quantities in inventory.

Objective 3
Compute the cost of inventory under the perpetual inventory system, using the following costing methods:

First-in, first-out
Last-in, first-out
Average cost

Objective 4
Compute the cost of inventory under the periodic inventory system, using the following costing methods:

First-in, first-out
Last-in, first-out
Average cost

Objective 5
Compare the use of the three inventory costing methods.

Objective 6
Compute the proper valuation of inventory at other than cost, using the lower of cost and market concept.

Objective 7
Prepare a balance sheet presentation of inventory.

Objective 8
Estimate the cost of inventory, using the retail method and the gross profit method.

Internal Control of Inventories

Objective 1
Summarize and provide examples of internal control procedures that apply to inventories.

What is included in inventory? The term **inventory** indicates (1) merchandise held for sale in the normal course of business and (2) materials in the process of production or held for production. In this chapter, we focus primarily on inventory of goods purchased for resale.

Inventory is a significant item in many businesses' financial statements. For example, **Sears Canada Inc.'s** inventory represents over 25% of its current assets and over 20% of its total assets. Likewise, the cost of goods sold represents over 70% of its net sales. Companies such as Sears must maintain good internal control over inventory.

The objective of internal controls over inventory is to ensure that the inventory is safeguarded and is properly reported in the financial statements. These internal controls can be either preventive or detective in nature, as we discuss in the following paragraphs. A preventive control is designed to prevent errors or misstatements from occurring. A detective control is designed to detect an error or misstatement after it has occurred.

Control over inventory should begin as soon as the inventory is received. The business's receiving department should complete prenumbered receiving reports in order to establish the initial accountability for the inventory. To make sure the inventory received is what was ordered, a clerk needs to match each receiving report to the company's original purchase order for the merchandise. Likewise, the clerk should compare the price at which the inventory was ordered, as shown on the purchase order, to the price at which the vendor billed the company, as shown on the vendor's invoice. After the receiving report, purchase order, and vendor's invoice have been reconciled, the business should record the inventory and related account payable in the accounting records.

Internal controls for safeguarding inventory include developing and using security measures to prevent inventory damage or employee theft. For example, the company should store inventory in a warehouse or other area to which access is restricted to authorized employees. The business should control the removal of

In order to safeguard inventory, retail clothing stores often place plastic alarm tags on merchandise.

goods from the warehouse by using properly authorized requisition forms. The storage area should also be climate controlled to prevent inventory damage from heat or cold. Further, when the business is not operating or is not open, it should lock the storage area.

When you have been shopping, you may have noticed how retail stores protect inventory from customer theft. Retail stores often use such devices as two-way mirrors, cameras, and security guards. High-priced items are often displayed in locked cabinets. For example, notebook computers and jewellery at **CostCo Wholesale** stores are kept in locked glass cases to prevent theft of these small, portable items. An employee also checks the customer's cash receipts against the items in their possession as they leave the store. Likewise, retail clothing stores often place plastic alarm tags on valuable items such as leather coats. Sensors at the exit doors set off alarms if the tags have not been removed by the cash register clerk. These controls are designed to prevent customers from taking merchandise without paying (shoplifting).

Using a perpetual inventory system for goods also provides an effective means of control over inventory. The amount of each type of merchandise on hand is always readily available in a subsidiary **inventory ledger.** In addition, the subsidiary ledger can be an aid in maintaining inventory quantities at optimum levels. Frequently comparing balances with predetermined maximum and minimum levels allows for the timely reordering of inventory and prevents the ordering of excess inventory.

To ensure the accuracy of the amount of inventory reported in the financial statements, a merchandising business should take a physical inventory (i.e., count the inventory on hand). In a perpetual inventory system, the physical inventory, which can be taken at any time during the year, is compared to the recorded inventory in order to determine the amount of shrinkage or shortage. If the inventory shrinkage is unusually large, management can investigate further and take any necessary corrective action. Knowledge that a physical inventory will be taken also serves to deter (prevent) employee thefts or misuses of inventory. If a business uses a periodic system it must count inventory at the end of its fiscal year in order to prepare accurate financial statements.

Determining Actual Quantities in the Inventory

Objective 2

List the procedures for determining the actual quantities in inventory.

In the preceding section, we discussed the importance of taking a physical inventory as part of a company's controls over inventory. In this section, we describe the procedures for taking a physical inventory. We then illustrate how errors in taking a physical inventory affect the financial statements.

PROCEDURES FOR TAKING A PHYSICAL INVENTORY

How do you "take" a physical inventory? The first step in this process is to determine the quantity of each kind of inventory the business owns. The specific procedures for determining inventory quantities and assembling the data differ among companies. A common practice is to use teams made up of two persons. One person counts, weighs, or otherwise determines quantity, and the other lists the description and the quantity on inventory count sheets. A second count team may check the quantities indicated for high-cost items during the inventory-taking process. The second count team should also check quantities of other items selected at random from the inventory count sheets.

All the inventory owned by the business on the inventory date, and only such inventory, should be included. For goods in transit, the party (the seller or the buyer) who has title on the inventory date must be determined. To determine who has title, it may be necessary to examine purchases and sales invoices of the last few days of the current period and the first few days of the following period.

As we discussed in a previous chapter, shipping terms are often helpful in determining when title passes. When goods are purchased or sold **FOB shipping point,** title usually passes to the buyer as soon as the goods are shipped. When the terms are **FOB destination,** title usually does not pass to the buyer until the goods are received.

To illustrate, assume that goods purchased FOB shipping point are shipped by the seller on the last day of the buyer's fiscal period. The goods do not arrive until the following period and thus are not available for counting by the inventory crew. However, such goods should be included in the buyer's inventory because title has passed. The buyer should record a debit to Inventory (or Purchases) and a credit to Accounts Payable as of the end of the current period.

Another example, though less common, further illustrates the importance of carefully examining transactions involving shipments of goods. Manufacturers sometimes ship goods to retailers who act as the manufacturer's agent when selling the goods. The manufacturer retains title until the goods are sold. Such goods are said to be *on consignment* to the retailers. The unsold goods are a part of the manufacturer's (consignor's) inventory, even though the goods are in the hands of the retailers. Likewise, the consigned goods should not be included in the retailer's (consignee's) inventory.

EFFECT OF INVENTORY ERRORS ON FINANCIAL STATEMENTS

Any errors in the inventory count will affect both the balance sheet and the income statement. For example, an error in the physical inventory will misstate the inventory, current assets, and total assets on the balance sheet. Also, an error in taking the physical inventory misstates the cost of goods sold, gross profit, and net income on the income statement. In addition, because net income is closed to the owner's equity at the end of the period, owner's equity will also be misstated on the balance sheet. This misstatement of owner's equity will equal the misstatement of the ending inventory, current assets, and total assets.

To illustrate, assume that in taking the physical inventory on December 31, 1998, Sapra Company incorrectly records its physical inventory as $115,000 instead of the correct amount of $125,000. As a result, the inventory, current assets, and total assets reported on the December 31, 1998 balance sheet are understated by $10,000 ($125,000 − $115,000). Because the ending physical inventory is understated, the inventory shrinkage and the cost of goods sold are overstated by $10,000. Thus, the gross profit and the net income for the year are understated by $10,000. Since the net income is closed to owner's equity at the end of the period, the owner's equity on the December 31, 1998 balance sheet is also understated by $10,000. The effects on Sapra Company's financial statements are summarized below:

	Balance Sheet
Inventory	$10,000 understated
Current assets	$10,000 understated
Total assets	$10,000 understated
Owner's equity	$10,000 understated

	Income Statement
Cost of goods sold	$10,000 overstated
Gross profit	$10,000 understated
Net income	$10,000 understated

Assume that in the preceding example the physical inventory was overstated on December 31, 1998, by $10,000. That is, Sapra Company erroneously recorded its inventory as $135,000. In this case, the effects on the balance sheet and income statement would be just the opposite of those indicated.

The ending inventory of one period becomes the opening inventory of the next period. Thus, any errors in recording ending inventory of a given year will also have an effect on the following year's net income. In the Sapra Company example, where inventory is understated at the end of December 31, 1998 by $10,000 and cost of goods sold for the year overstated by $10,000, the error will reverse itself in 1999. Because the 1999 opening inventory is understated, the 1999 cost of goods sold will be understated by $10,000. At the same time the gross profit and net income for 1999 will be overstated by $10,000. However, this error will not affect the ending inventory reported at December 31, 1999. Assuming that the business does not make an error in counting its 1999 inventory, it will report the correct ending inventory balance. Owner's equity will also be correct, since the 1998 understatement of $10,000 in net income has been cancelled out by the 1999 overstatement of $10,000 in net income.

If a business detects that it has made an error in reporting inventory in a prior period, it must correct the financial statements of that prior period thereby eliminating the reversing effect in the current year.

The effect of misstated inventory on the financial statements has been used to defraud investors and others. For example, during the 1980s, **Crazy Eddie Inc.** reported rapid gains in sales and earnings due to what the company claimed was expansion of its electronics stores, adept sales-floor techniques, and catchy commercials. However, it now appears that the rapid growth was due to a fraudulent scheme by Crazy Eddie's founder, Eddie Antar, and others. This scheme resulted in the reporting of misstated inventory and income. In part, Crazy Eddie overstated inventory counts at one warehouse by $10 million, drafted phony inventory count sheets, and included $4 million of goods in inventory when, in fact, the goods were being returned to suppliers. As a result, income was overstated. The apparent purpose of the scheme was to "artificially inflate the net worth of the company" and the value of stock owned by Mr. Antar and others.[1]

Inventory Costing Methods Under a Perpetual Inventory System

Objective 3

Compute the cost of inventory under the perpetual inventory system, using the following costing methods:

First-in, first-out
Last-in, first-out
Average cost

As we described in an earlier chapter, all inventory increases and decreases in a perpetual system are recorded in a manner similar to the recording of increases and decreases in cash. The inventory account at the beginning of an accounting period indicates the quantity on hand on that date. We record purchases by debiting Inventory and crediting Cash or Accounts Payable. On the date of each sale, we record the cost of the goods sold by debiting Cost of Goods Sold and crediting Inventory. Thus, the inventory account constantly (perpetually) discloses the balance of inventory on hand. At the end of the period, the balance in the inventory account, adjusted for any shrinkage, is reported on the balance sheet. The balance in the cost of goods sold account is reported on the income statement.

What costs should be included in inventory? The purchase price of goods, less any purchases discounts taken, is part of the cost of inventory. In addition, we normally include costs incurred in acquiring the goods, such as transportation,

[1] Jeffrey A. Tannenbaum, "Filings by Crazy Eddie Suggest Founder Led Scheme to Inflate Company's Value," *The Wall Street Journal*, May 31, 1988, p. 28.

customs duties, and insurance against losses in transit. However, some costs of acquiring goods, such as the salaries of Purchasing Department employees and other administrative costs, are not easily allocated to the inventory. Therefore, we treat these costs as operating expenses of the period.

A major accounting issue arises when a business acquires identical units of a commodity at different unit costs during a period. In such cases, when an item is sold, we have to determine its unit cost so we can make the proper accounting entry. To illustrate, assume that three identical units of Commodity X are available for sale during the first 10 days in January. One of these units was in the inventory at the beginning of the year, and the business purchased the other two on January 4 and January 9. The costs per unit are as follows:

	Commodity X	Units	Cost
Jan. 1	Inventory	1	$ 9
4	Purchase	1	13
9	Purchase	1	14
Total		3	$36
Average cost per unit			$12

Assume that one unit is sold on January 10. If we can identify this unit with a specific purchase, we can use the **specific identification method** to determine the cost of the unit sold. For example, if the unit sold was purchased on January 4, we would assign a cost of $13 to the unit.

The specific identification method is not practical unless each unit can be identified accurately. An automobile dealer, for example, may be able to use this method. For businesses that buy and sell units that are identical, however, we must make an assumption as to which unit was sold and which units are still on hand. The three most common cost flow assumptions are as follows:

1. Cost flow is in the order in which the costs were incurred—first-in, first-out.
2. Cost flow is in the reverse order in which the costs were incurred—last-in, first-out.
3. Cost flow is an average of the costs.

The cost of the unit of Commodity X sold on January 10 and the cost of the two remaining units are shown here for each of the cost flow assumptions.

	Cost of Units Available		Cost of Unit Sold		Cost of Units Remaining
1. In order in which costs were incurred (first-in, first-out)	$36	–	$ 9	=	$27
2. In reverse order in which costs were incurred (last-in, first-out)	36	–	14	=	22
3. In accordance with average costs	36	–	12	=	24

The three most widely used inventory costing methods (which correspond to the three assumptions of cost flows) are:

1. **First-in, first-out (FIFO)**
2. **Last-in, first-out (LIFO)**
3. **Average cost**

The chart in Exhibit 1 shows the frequency with which various costing methods are used in practice in Canada.

Exhibit 1
Inventory Costing Methods

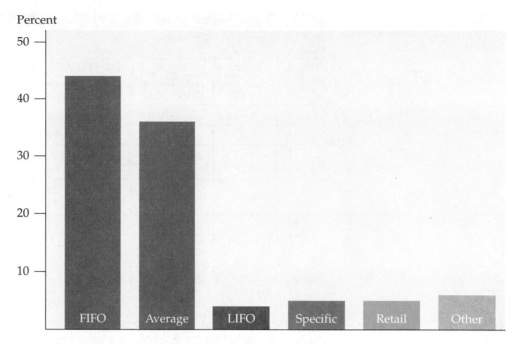

Percent

Source: *Financial Reporting in Canada 1995,* Canadian Institute of Chartered Accountants, Toronto, 1996.

Exhibit 1 indicates that 44% of the Canadian companies surveyed use FIFO, while 36% use average cost, and only 5% use LIFO. A similar survey conducted in the United States reported that approximately 38% of companies use FIFO, 37% use LIFO, and 18% use the average method. We discuss the reasons for these different rates of use of the methods under Objective 5 of this chapter. Although only a small number of Canadian companies use the LIFO method, we study it in this chapter so that you will be able to understand the implications of this method for the many companies in the United States and other countries that choose to use it.

FIRST-IN, FIRST-OUT METHOD

When the first-in, first-out (FIFO) method of costing inventory is used, costs are assumed to be charged against revenue in the order in which they were incurred. Hence, the inventory remaining is assumed to be made up of the most recent costs. We illustrate the FIFO method under a perpetual inventory system using the following data for inventory identified as Commodity 127B:

		Commodity 127B	Units	Unit Cost
Jan.	1	Inventory	10	$20
	4	Sale	7	
	10	Purchase	8	21
	22	Sale	4	
	28	Sale	2	
	30	Purchase	10	22

Exhibit 2 shows the inventory ledger account for Commodity 127B. The number of units on hand after each transaction, together with total costs and unit costs, appear in the inventory section of the account.

Note that after the seven units of the commodity were sold on January 4, there was an inventory of three units at $20 each. The eight units purchased on January 10 were acquired at a unit cost of $21. Therefore, the inventory after the January 10

Exhibit 2
Perpetual Inventory Account (FIFO)

Commodity 127B

Date	Purchases			Cost of Goods Sold			Inventory		
	Quantity	Unit Cost	Total Cost	Quantity	Unit Cost	Total Cost	Quantity	Unit Cost	Total Cost
Jan. 1							10	20	200
4				7	20	140	3	20	60
10	8	21	168				3	20	60
							8	21	168
22				3	20	60			
				1	21	21	7	21	147
28				2	21	42	5	21	105
30	10	22	220				5	21	105
							10	22	220

purchase is reported on two lines, three units at $20 each and eight units at $21 each. Next, note that the $81 cost of the four units sold on January 22 consists of the remaining three units at $20 each and one unit at $21. At this point, seven units are in inventory at a cost of $21 per unit. The remainder of the illustration can be explained in a similar manner.

Most businesses dispose of goods in the order in which the goods are purchased. This would be especially true of perishables and goods whose styles or models often change. For example, grocery stores stock their shelves with goods such as milk products by their expiration dates. Likewise, men's and women's clothing stores stock their clothes by season. At the end of a season, they often have sales to clear their stores of off-season or out-of-style clothing. Thus, the FIFO method is often consistent with the physical movement of merchandise. To the extent that this is the case, the FIFO method provides results that are about the same as those obtained by identifying the specific costs of each item sold and in inventory.

LAST-IN, FIRST-OUT METHOD

When the last-in, first-out (LIFO) method is used in a perpetual inventory system, the cost of the units sold is the cost of the most recent purchases. To illustrate, Exhibit 3 shows the ledger account for Commodity 127B, prepared on a LIFO basis.

Comparing the ledger accounts for the FIFO perpetual system and the LIFO perpetual system indicates that the accounts are the same through the January 10 purchase. Under the LIFO perpetual system, however, the cost of the four units sold on January 22 is the cost of the units from the January 10 purchase ($21 per unit). The cost of the seven units in inventory after the sale on January 22 is the cost of the three units remaining from the beginning inventory and the cost of the four units remaining from the January 10 purchase. The remainder of the LIFO illustration can be explained in a similar manner.

AVERAGE COST METHOD

When the average cost method is used in a perpetual inventory system, an average unit cost for each type of commodity is computed each time the business makes a purchase. We use this unit cost to determine the cost of each sale until another purchase is made and a new average is computed. This averaging technique is called a

Exhibit 3
Perpetual Inventory Account (Lifo)

Commodity 127B

Date	Purchases			Cost of Goods Sold			Inventory		
	Quantity	Unit Cost	Total Cost	Quantity	Unit Cost	Total Cost	Quantity	Unit Cost	Total Cost
Jan. 1							10	20	200
4				7	20	140	3	20	60
10	8	21	168				3	20	60
							8	21	168
22				4	21	84	3	20	60
							4	21	84
28				2	21	42	3	20	60
							2	21	42
30	10	22	220				3	20	60
							2	21	42
							10	22	220

moving weighted average. To illustrate, Exhibit 4 shows the ledger account for Commodity 127B, prepared on an average basis.

Exhibit 4
Perpetual Inventory Account (Average)

Commodity 127B

Date	Purchases			Cost of Goods Sold			Inventory		
	Quantity	Unit Cost	Total Cost	Quantity	Unit Cost	Total Cost	Quantity	Unit Cost	Total Cost
Jan. 1							10	20.00	200.00
4				7	20.00	140.00	3	20.00	60.00
10	8	21.00	168.00				11	20.73[1]	228.00
22				4	20.73	82.92	7	20.73	145.09 [2]
28				2	20.73	41.46	5	20.73	103.64 [3]
30	10	22.00	220.00				15	21.58[4]	323.64

(1) $\dfrac{60.00 + 168.00}{3 + 8} = 20.727$ (rounded to 20.73)

(2) adjusted for rounding.

(3) adjusted for rounding.

(4) $\dfrac{103.64 + 220.00}{5 + 10} = 21.576$ (rounded to 21.58)

The average cost of the opening inventory is $20 per unit and we record this as the unit cost of the seven items sold on January 4. The purchase of an additional eight units on January 10 changes the cost per unit to $20.73. Under a perpetual system, the average cost per unit is always calculated as the total costs in inventory divided by the total units on hand at a particular point in time ($128 ÷ 11 units = $20.73). We use this new cost per unit for recording the items sold on January 22 and 28. The cost per unit changes again when 10 more items are purchased on January 30.

COMPUTERIZED PERPETUAL INVENTORY SYSTEMS

We can maintain a perpetual inventory system by using manually kept records. However, such a system is often too costly and too time consuming for businesses with a large number of inventory items or many purchase and sales transactions. In such cases, the record keeping is often computerized.

An example of using computers in maintaining perpetual inventory records for retail stores is described as follows:

1. Store the relevant details for each inventory item, such as a description, quantity, and unit size, in an inventory record. The individual inventory records make up the computerized inventory file, the total of which agrees with the balance of the inventory ledger account.
2. Record the inventory data in the computer's inventory records and files each time an item is purchased or returned by a customer.
3. Each time an item is sold, a sales clerk scans the item's bar code with an optical scanner. The scanner *reads* the magnetic code, rings up the sale on the cash register, and updates the inventory records and files.
4. After taking a physical inventory, clerks enter the inventory count data into the computer. The computer is programmed to compare these data with the current balances, and print a listing of the overages and shortages. The inventory balances are then adjusted to the quantities determined by the physical count.

By entering additional data, we can extend this system to aid in maintaining inventory quantities at optimal levels. For example, we can enter data on the most economical quantity to be purchased in a single order and the minimum quantity to be maintained for each item into the computer records. The computer software is then programmed to compare these data with the quantities in the inventory records. As necessary, the computer program begins the purchasing activity by preparing purchase orders.

Retail store managers can use scanned sales data to develop and fine-tune their marketing strategies. For example, such data can determine the effectiveness of advertising campaigns, sales promotions, and sales patterns of products.

We can also extend the system to aid in processing the related accounting transactions. For example, as cash sales are entered on an electronic cash register, the computer can accumulate the sales data used for the daily accounting entries. These entries debit Cash and credit Sales as well as debiting Cost of Goods Sold and crediting Inventory.

Inventory Costing Methods Under a Periodic Inventory System

Objective 4

Compute the cost of inventory under the periodic inventory system, using the following costing methods:

First-in, first-out
Last-in, first-out
Average cost

When a business uses the periodic inventory system, it only records revenue each time a sale is made. No entry is made at the time of the sale to record the cost of the goods sold. At the end of the accounting period, a physical inventory must be taken to determine the cost of the inventory on hand and the cost of the goods sold.

As with the perpetual inventory system, we must make a cost flow assumption when identical units of a commodity are acquired at different unit costs during a period. In such cases, the FIFO, LIFO, or average cost method is normally used.

FIRST-IN, FIRST-OUT METHOD

We illustrate the use of FIFO in a periodic inventory system using the same data for Commodity 127B as was used above to illustrate the perpetual system. We calculate the cost of goods available for sale as follows:

Jan.	1	Inventory:	10	units at $20	$200
Jan.	10	Purchase:	8	units at 21	168
Jan.	30	Purchase:	10	units at 22	220
		Available for sale during January	28		$588

The physical count on January 31 shows 15 units on hand. Using FIFO, we determine the cost of these units as follows:

Most recent costs, Jan. 30:	10	units at $22	$220
Next most recent costs, Jan. 10:	5	units at 21	105
Inventory, Jan. 31:	15		$325

Deducting the cost of ending inventory of **$325** from the **$588** cost of goods available for sale yields **$263** as the cost of goods sold. The $263 cost of goods sold is made up of the earliest costs incurred for this commodity.

LAST-IN, FIRST-OUT METHOD

Using LIFO, we assume that the ending inventory is composed of the earliest costs available during the period. We illustrate LIFO in a periodic system based on the same data for Commodity 127B, and compute the cost of the 15 units of ending inventory as follows:

Earliest costs, Jan. 1:	10	units at $20	$200
Next earliest costs, Jan. 10:	5	units at 21	105
Inventory, Jan. 31:	15		$305

Deducting the cost of ending inventory of **$305** from the **$588** cost of goods available for sale yields **$283** as the cost of goods sold. The $283 cost of goods sold is made up of the most recent costs incurred for this commodity.

AVERAGE COST METHOD

We sometimes call the average cost method the **weighted average method.** When using this method, we determine ending inventory using a weighted average cost. We compute the weighted average unit cost by dividing the total cost of each commodity available for sale during the period by the number of units available for sale during the period. Using the same data as in the FIFO and LIFO examples, we compute the weighted average cost and ending inventory as follows:

Average unit cost:	$588 ÷ 28 units = $21
Inventory, Jan. 31:	15 units at $21 = **$315**

Deducting the cost of ending inventory of **$315** from the **$588** cost of goods available for sale yields **$273** as the cost of goods sold.

Comparing Inventory Costing Methods

Objective 5
Compare the use of the three inventory costing methods.

We assumed a different cost flow for each of the three alternative methods of costing inventories. You should note that if the cost of units had remained stable, all three methods would have yielded the same results. Since prices do change, however, the three methods will normally yield different amounts for (1) the ending inventory, (2) the cost of the goods sold for the period, and (3) the gross profit (and net income) for the period. Using the preceding examples for the perpetual periodic inventory system and assuming that net sales were $390, the following partial income statements indicate the effects of each method in this particular example:

Perpetual System	FIFO		Average Cost		Lifo	
Net sales		$390		$390		$390
Cost of goods sold:						
Beginning inventory	$200		$200		$200	
Purchases	388		388		388	
Cost of goods available	$588		$588		$588	
Less ending inventory	325		323		322	
Cost of goods sold		263		265		266
Gross profit		$127		$125		$124

Periodic System	FIFO		Average Cost		Lifo	
Net sales		$390		$390		$390
Cost of goods sold:						
Beginning inventory	$200		$200		$200	
Purchases	388		388		388	
Cost of goods available	$588		$588		$588	
Less ending inventory	325		315		305	
Cost of goods sold		263		273		283
Gross profit		$127		$117		$107

An examination of the comparative income statements presented above reveals the following:

1. The FIFO statements are identical under both the perpetual and periodic systems. However, under both LIFO and average cost, the computation for ending inventory and cost of goods sold can vary, depending on whether or not we are using a perpetual or periodic system.
2. In this example, where inventory costs and quantities on hand are rising, FIFO reported the highest amount for ending inventory, the lowest cost of goods sold, and the highest income. On the other hand, LIFO reported the lowest ending inventory, the highest cost of goods sold, and the lowest income. The average cost method always yielded results between FIFO and LIFO. Moreover, these relationships are the same regardless of whether a perpetual or periodic system is used.

USE OF THE FIRST-IN, FIRST-OUT METHOD

When using the FIFO method, we assume that the costs of the units sold are the earliest costs available during the period. During a period of inflation or rising prices, the earlier unit costs are lower than the more recent unit costs, as shown in the preceding example. Much of the benefit of the larger amount of gross profit reported under FIFO is lost, however, because the business must replace its inventory at everhigher prices. For this reason the larger gross profits that result from the FIFO method are often called *inventory profits* or *illusory profits*.

You should note that in a period of deflation or declining prices, this effect is just the opposite. The FIFO method, compared to the other methods, reports the lowest amount of gross profit. A major criticism of the FIFO method is its tendency to pass through the effects of inflationary and deflationary trends to gross profit. An advantage of the FIFO method, however, is that the balance sheet will report the ending inventory at an amount that is about the same as its current replacement cost.

USE OF THE LAST-IN, FIRST-OUT METHOD

When the LIFO method is used during a period of inflation or rising prices, the results are opposite those of the other two methods. As shown in the preceding example, the LIFO method will report a lower amount of inventory at the end of the period, a higher amount of cost of goods sold, and a lower amount of gross profit than the other two methods. The reason for these effects is that the cost of the most recently acquired units most nearly approximates the cost of their replacement. In a period of inflation, the more recent unit costs are higher than the earlier unit costs. In this example, the LIFO method more nearly matched current costs with current revenues. This latter point was one reason that **Chrysler Corporation** changed from the FIFO method to the LIFO method, as stated in the following footnote that accompanied Chrysler's financial statements:

Chrysler changed its method of accounting from first-in, first-out (FIFO) to last-in, first-out (LIFO) for substantially all of its domestic productive inventories. The change to LIFO was made to more accurately match current costs with current revenues.

Tax laws in the United States permit the use of LIFO for calculating cost of goods sold and determining taxable income. In periods of rising prices, using LIFO offers an income tax savings in the United States because LIFO usually results in the lowest reported net income of all of the inventory cost flow assumptions. During the double-digit inflationary period of the 1970s, many businesses in the United States switched to the LIFO method to take advantage of such tax savings. In Canada, however, the Income Tax Act does not permit businesses to use the LIFO method for calculating cost of goods sold and determining taxable income. This is probably the main reason that few Canadian companies use the LIFO method.

Again, you should note that in a period of deflation or falling price levels, this effect is just the opposite. The LIFO method usually reports the highest amount of gross profit. The major argument for using LIFO is its tendency to minimize the effect of price trends on gross profit. A criticism of using LIFO, however, is that the ending inventory on the balance sheet consists of old costs that may be quite different from current replacement cost.

We also need to take note that the comparison between FIFO and LIFO in terms of the impact on reported income cannot be overgeneralized. In periods where the number of units sold exceeds the number purchased (that is, the ending inventory quantity is less than opening inventory) and prices are changing, the effect of LIFO on reported income will be the opposite of what you might expect. Remember that the amount reported for opening inventory under LIFO consists of older costs than under FIFO. If prices have been rising, the LIFO opening inventory balance will be lower than the dollar amount had FIFO been used. If inventory quantities decrease during a period, some of the older costs in opening inventory will flow through to cost of goods sold. In this case, if prices have been rising, cost of goods sold under LIFO is likely to be *less* than cost of goods sold under FIFO.

The possibility of such an effect creates what may be seen as a disadvantage of the LIFO method. Skilled managers can manipulate reported income by carefully timing the replenishment of inventory in comparison to the flow of sales.

Consider the following example, assuming a LIFO periodic inventory system. At the beginning of the current period a firm holds 1,000 units of inventory costing $10 per unit. During the period the company purchases 1,200 units at $12 each and sells 1,500 units. At the end of the period the replacement cost of the inventory is $14 per unit. If management makes no additional purchases during the current period, cost of goods sold under LIFO is as follows:

Most recent costs	1,200 units at $12	$14,400
Next most recent costs	300 units at 10	3,000
Cost of goods sold	1,500	$17,400

On the other hand, what if management decides to purchase an additional 1,000 units before the end of the period? In this case, LIFO cost of goods sold will be:

Most recent costs	1,000	units at $14	$14,000
Next most recent costs	500	units at 12	6,000
Cost of goods sold	1,500		$20,000

Thus, under LIFO, management can manipulate the amount reported for cost of sales (and hence net income) simply by delaying or accelerating purchases of inventory at year end. Could this happen under FIFO? No! Under FIFO cost of goods sold always consist of the earliest costs available during the period. Additional purchases cannot affect this amount.

USE OF THE AVERAGE COST METHOD

The average cost method of inventory costing is, in a sense, a compromise between FIFO and LIFO. The effect of price trends is averaged in determining the cost of goods sold and the ending inventory. For a series of purchases, the average cost will be the same, regardless of the direction of price trends. For example, a complete reversal of the sequence of unit costs presented in the preceding illustration would not affect the reported cost of goods sold, gross profit, or ending inventory. The average cost method smooths out the effects of fluctuating prices and avoids the extremes of FIFO and LIFO.

SELECTION OF AN INVENTORY COSTING METHOD

The preceding comparisons show the importance attached to the selection of the inventory costing method. Often enterprises apply one method to one class of inventory and a different method to another class. For example, a computer retailer might use the FIFO method for its microcomputer inventory and the LIFO method for software and other inventory. The selection of the most appropriate method or methods "will depend upon the particular circumstances of each enterprise and the industry in which it is engaged."[2] Cost of goods sold, like other expenses, is related to revenues, and thus the **matching** principle should influence the selection of a cost flow assumption. The method chosen should "be one which results in the fairest matching of costs against revenues regardless of whether or not the method corresponds to the physical flow of goods."[3] Current accounting practice does not require a business to choose a cost flow assumption that reflects the physical flow of inventory.

The fact that various accounting methods (such as FIFO, LIFO, and weighted average) are permitted for financial reporting can make it difficult to compare the financial results of companies that use different accounting procedures. The generally accepted accounting principle of **comparability** requires financial reports to be presented in a way that "enables users to identify similarities in and differences between the information provided by two sets of financial statements."[4]

Does the comparability principle require that all companies use the same accounting method? No. It may be quite appropriate for different businesses that face different economic circumstances to adopt different accounting procedures. However, each company should **fully disclose** the method it is using in its financial statements, so that users can take this into account in making comparisons among different firms.

---

[2] *CICA Handbook,* Section 3030, paragraph 8.
[3] *Ibid.,* Section 3030, paragraph 9.
[4] *Ibid.,* Section 1000, paragraph 22.

Besides comparing the business with other companies, investors, creditors, and other users also need to measure the current operations of the firm against its performance in prior years. Comparability is enhanced if the firm uses the same accounting methods consistently from period to period.[5] The generally accepted accounting principle of **consistency** states that financial statement users should be able to expect that an entity will employ the same policies in accounting for similar events from year to year. Thus, if a company employed FIFO last year, we would expect it to use FIFO again this year.

Does the consistency principle imply that a firm can never change its accounting policies? No. But it does mean that a firm should have a valid reason for adopting a new method. If the business changes its accounting policy (from say, FIFO to LIFO), it should fully disclose: (1) the fact that there has been a change; (2) the reason for the change; and (3) the effects of the change on the financial statements in the period in which the new principle is first adopted.

Valuation of Inventory at Other Than Cost

Objective 6

Compute the proper valuation of inventory at other than cost, using the lower of cost and market concept.

As we discussed earlier in the chapter, cost is the primary basis for recording inventories. However, the reported value for inventory should be written down below cost if there is evidence that the inventory's value has declined below cost. Two such cases may arise when (1) the cost of replacing inventory items is below the recorded cost, or (2) the inventory is not saleable at normal sales prices due to imperfections, style or technology changes, or other causes. This departure from the historical cost basis is required by the generally accepted accounting principle of conservatism, which requires that we not overstate net assets and recognize losses as soon as they are apparent, rather than waiting for the eventual sale transaction. Thus, we must apply a "lower of cost and market" test to inventory and adjust the records as necessary.

VALUATION AT LOWER OF COST AND MARKET

For inventory, the definition of the term "market" can be ambiguous. One could define market to be the wholesale cost to replace the inventory as of the balance sheet date using quotes and data from suppliers. This is known as the **replacement cost.** Alternatively, market could be the estimated selling price less any direct costs of completion and disposal (e.g., sales commissions). This is known as the **net realizable value.** Some enterprises will use one definition of market for a certain type of inventory and another definition for another type of inventory. For example, a firm might use replacement cost for raw materials, and net realizable value for goods held for sale. In Canada, the majority of companies use net realizable value as their definition of market for inventory. For damaged or obsolete inventory, market is always defined as net realizable value.

The **lower of cost and market method** can be applied to inventory in three different ways: (1) on a line-by-line (item-by-item) basis, (2) to major classes or categories, or (3) to the inventory as a whole. The table in Exhibit 5 illustrates a common way to organize data for applying the lower of cost and market method.

The far right-hand column indicates the amount to be included in inventory applying the method line-by-line. Inventory would be written down $470 from a total of $15,520 at cost to $15,020 at the lower of cost and market. Note that each item is in the final total at the lower of its cost and market. The line-by-line basis is

Exhibit 5
Determining Inventory at Lower of Cost or Market

Commodity	Inventory Quantity	Unit Cost Price	Unit Market Price	Total Cost	Market	Lower of C or M item-by-item
A	400	$10.25	$ 9.50	$ 4,100	$ 3,800	$ 3,800
B	120	22.50	24.10	2,700	2,892	2,700
C	600	8.00	7.75	4,800	4,650	4,650
D	280	14.00	14.75	3,920	4,130	3,920
Total				$15,520	$15,472	$15,070

the most conservative application of the method, since it does not net items whose market is greater than cost with the items whose cost is greater than market.

If we apply the method to the inventory as a whole, we would report the inventory at its aggregate market value of $15,472. Inventory would be written down $48 from the total cost of $15,520. In this case, the comparison of cost to market is on a net basis for the inventory as a whole. This minimizes the write-down since the excess of market over cost from some items is used to offset the excess of cost over market on others. This method is less conservative than applying the comparison line-by-line, but is permitted under generally accepted accounting principles.

Regardless of the method used, we usually include the amount of the write-down in the cost of goods sold, although we could show it separately if desired.

Presentation of Inventory on the Balance Sheet

Objective 7
Prepare a balance sheet presentation of inventory.

As we discussed in an earlier chapter, we usually present inventory in the Current Assets section of the balance sheet, following receivables. Both the method of determining the cost of the inventory (FIFO, LIFO, or average) and the method of valuing the inventory (the lower of cost and market) should be shown. A description of the method of determining market is a preferred disclosure. These details may be disclosed in parentheses on the balance sheet or in a footnote to the financial statements. Exhibit 6 shows how parentheses may be used.

As we noted previously, it is not unusual for large businesses with varied activities to use different costing methods for different segments of their inventories. The following note taken from the financial statements of **Haley Industries Limited** illustrates how this information may be disclosed:

Exhibit 6
Inventory on the Balance Sheet

Afro-Arts
Trial Balance
December 31, 1999

Assets		
Current assets:		
Cash		$ 19 4 0 0 00
Accounts receivable	$80 0 0 0 00	
Less allowance for doubtful accounts	3 0 0 0 00	77 0 0 0 00
Inventory—at lower of cost (first-in, first-out method) and net realizable value		216 3 0 0 00

Notes to financial statements

1. *Significant Accounting Policies (in part)*

   c) *Inventory valuation*

   Inventories are valued at the lower of cost and market. For finished goods and work in process, cost is calculated on an average cost basis and market is determined as net realizable value. For patterns, cost is determined on a specific item basis and market is determined as net realizable value. For raw materials and supplies, cost is calculated on the first in, first out basis and market is determined as replacement cost.

2. *Inventories*

	1994	1993
	(In thousands)	
Finished goods	$ 577	$ 937
Work in process	1,916	1,380
Raw materials and supplies	1,714	1,468
Patterns	1,584	1,461
	$5,791	$5,246

Source: *Financial Reporting in Canada 1995*, CICA, Toronto 1996, p. 109.

Estimating Inventory Cost

Objective 8

Estimate the cost of inventory, using the retail method and the gross profit method.

When a disaster such as a fire has destroyed the inventory, its cost can be estimated using either the retail or the gross profit method.

In practice, a business may need to know the amount of inventory when perpetual inventory records are not maintained and it is impractical to count the inventory. For example, a business that uses a periodic inventory system may need monthly income statements, but taking a physical inventory each month may be too costly. Moreover, when a disaster such as a fire has destroyed the inventory, the business must determine the amount of the loss. In this case, taking a physical inventory is impossible, and even if perpetual inventory records have been kept, these records may also have been destroyed. In such cases, we can estimate the inventory cost by using (1) the retail method or (2) the gross profit method.

RETAIL METHOD OF INVENTORY COSTING

The **retail inventory method** of estimating inventory cost is based on the relationship of the cost of goods available for sale to the retail price of the same goods. To use this method, we must accumulate the retail prices of all goods acquired. Next, we determine the inventory at retail by deducting sales for the period from the retail price of the goods that were available for sale during the period. The estimated inventory cost is then calculated by multiplying the inventory at retail by the ratio of cost to selling (retail) price for the goods available for sale, as we illustrate in Exhibit 7.

When using the cost to selling price ratio, we assume that the *mix* of the items in the ending inventory is the same as the entire stock of goods available for sale. In Exhibit 7, for example, it is unlikely that the retail price of every item comprised exactly 62% cost and 38% gross profit. We assume, however, that the weighted average of the cost percentages of the goods in the inventory ($30,000) is the same as in the goods available for sale ($100,000). When the inventory consists of different classes of goods with very different gross profit rates, the cost to retail percentages can be developed for each class of inventory.

One of the major advantages of the retail method is that it provides inventory figures for use in preparing monthly or quarterly statements when the periodic system is used. Department stores and similar merchandisers like to determine gross profit and operating income each month but take a physical inventory only

Exhibit 7
Determining Inventory by the Retail Method

	Cost	Retail
Inventory, January 1	$ 19,400	$ 36,000
Purchases in January (net)	42,600	64,000
Goods available for sale	$ 62,000	$100,000

Ratio of cost to retail price: $\dfrac{\$ 62,000}{\$100,000} = 62\%$

	Cost	Retail
Sales for January (net)		70,000
Inventory, January 31, at retail		$ 30,000
Inventory, January 31, at estimated cost ($30,000 × 62%)		$ 18,600

once a year. In addition, even if we are taking a physical inventory we can use the estimated inventory to help identify inventory shortages resulting from shoplifting and other causes. Management can then take appropriate actions.

The retail method may also be used to facilitate taking a physical inventory at the end of the year. In this case, the items counted are recorded on the inventory sheets at their retail (selling) prices instead of their cost prices. The physical inventory at selling price is then converted to cost by applying the ratio of cost to selling (retail) price for the goods available for sale.

To illustrate, assume that the data in Exhibit 7 are for an entire fiscal year rather than for only January. If the physical inventory taken at the end of the year totalled $29,000, priced at retail, this amount rather than the $30,000 would be converted to cost. Thus, the inventory at cost would be $17,980 ($29,000 × 62%) instead of $18,600 ($30,000 × 62%). The $17,980 would be used for the year-end financial statements and for income tax purposes.

This is a simplified illustration in that it does not, for example, consider accounting for special sales (markdowns and subsequent markdown cancellations). These complexities are beyond the scope of this book.

GROSS PROFIT METHOD OF ESTIMATING INVENTORIES

The **gross profit method** uses the gross profit estimated for the period to estimate the inventory at the end of the period. The gross profit is usually estimated from the actual rate for preceding years, adjusted for any known changes in the cost and sales prices during the current period. By using the gross profit rate, the dollar amount of sales for a period can be divided into its two components: (1) gross profit and (2) cost of goods sold. The latter amount may then be deducted from the cost of goods available for sale to yield the estimated cost of inventory on hand.

Exhibit 8 illustrates the gross profit method for estimating a company's inventory on January 31. In this example, the inventory on January 1 is assumed to be

Exhibit 8
Estimating Inventory by Gross Profit Method

Inventory, January 1		$ 57,000
Purchases in January (net)		180,000
Cost of goods available for sale		$237,000
Sales in January (net)	$250,000	
Less estimated gross profit ($250,000 × 30%)	75,000	
Estimated cost of goods sold		175,000
Estimated inventory, January 31		$ 62,000

$57,000, the net purchases during the month are $180,000, and the net sales during the month are $250,000. In addition, the historical gross profit was 30% of net sales.

The gross profit method is useful for estimating inventories for monthly or quarterly financial statements in a periodic inventory system. It is also useful in estimating the cost of goods destroyed by fire or other disaster.

KEY POINTS

Objective 1. Summarize and provide examples of internal control procedures that apply to inventories.

Internal control procedures for inventories include those developed to protect the inventories from damage, employee theft, and customer theft. In addition, a physical inventory count should be taken periodically to detect shortages as well as to deter employee thefts.

Objective 2. List the procedures for determining the actual quantities in inventory.

The first step in "taking" a physical inventory is to count the goods on hand. Count teams are often made up of two persons—one who counts and the other who records the quantities and descriptions on inventory count sheets. Care must be used to include all goods in transit that is owned. Consigned goods should be included in the consignor's inventory, not the consignee's.

Any errors in reporting inventory based upon the physical inventory will misstate the ending inventory, current assets, total assets, and owner's equity on the balance sheet. In addition, the cost of goods sold, gross profit, and net income will be misstated on the income statement. Errors will also cause the income of the subsequent year to be misstated, but in the opposite direction.

Objective 3. Compute the cost of inventory under the perpetual inventory system, using the following costing methods:

First-in, first-out
Last-in, first-out
Average cost

In a perpetual inventory system, the number of units and the cost of each type of inventory are recorded in a subsidiary inventory ledger, with a separate account for each type of merchandise. Inventory costs and the amounts charged against revenue are illustrated using the FIFO, LIFO, and average cost methods.

Objective 4. Compute the cost of inventory under the periodic inventory system, using the following costing methods:

First-in, first-out
Last-in, first-out
Average cost

In a periodic inventory system, a physical inventory is taken to determine the cost of the inventory and the cost of goods sold. Inventory costs and the amounts charged against revenue are illustrated using FIFO, LIFO, and average cost methods.

Objective 5. Compare the use of the three inventory costing methods.

The three inventory costing methods will normally yield different amounts for (1) the ending inventory, (2) the cost of the goods sold for the period, and (3) the gross profit (and net income) for the period. During periods of inflation, if inventory quantities do not decrease, the FIFO method yields the lowest amount for the cost of goods sold, the highest amount for gross profit (and net income), and the highest amount for the ending inventory. The LIFO method yields the opposite results. During periods of deflation, the preceding effects are reversed. The average cost method yields results that are between those of FIFO and LIFO.

Objective 6. Compute the proper valuation of inventory at other than cost, using the lower of cost and market concept.

If the market price of inventory is lower than its cost, the lower market price is used to compute the value of inventory. Market price is the cost to replace the goods on the inventory date or net realizable value, which is the estimated selling price less any direct costs of disposal. We can apply the lower of cost or market to each item in the inventory, to major classes or categories, or to the inventory as a whole.

Objective 7. Prepare a balance sheet presentation of inventory.

Inventory is usually presented in the Current Assets section of the balance sheet, following receivables. Both the method of determining the cost of the inventory (FIFO, LIFO, or average) and the method of valuing the inventory (the lower of cost and market) should be shown.

Objective 8. Estimate the cost of inventory, using the retail method and the gross profit method.

In using the retail method to estimate inventory, we accumulate the retail prices of all goods acquired. The inventory at retail is determined by deducting sales for the period from the retail price of the goods that were available for sale during the period. We convert the inventory at retail to cost on the basis of the ratio of cost to selling (retail) price for the goods available for sale.

In using the gross profit method to estimate inventory, we deduct the estimated gross profit from the sales to determine the estimated cost of goods sold. We then deduct this amount from the cost of goods available for sale to determine the estimated ending inventory.

GLOSSARY OF KEY TERMS

Average cost method. A method of inventory costing that is based on the assumption that costs should be charged against revenue in accordance with the weighted average unit costs of the items sold. *Objective 3*

Comparability principle. Financial reports should be presented in a way that enables users to identify similarities in and differences between the information provided by different financial statements. *Objective 5*

Consistency principle. A firm is normally expected to employ the same accounting policies from year to year. *Objective 5*

First-in, first-out (FIFO) method. A method of inventory costing based on the assumption that the costs of goods sold should be charged against revenue in the order in which the costs were incurred. *Objective 3*

Gross profit method. A means of estimating inventory based on the relationship of gross profit to sales. *Objective 8*

Last-in, first-out (LIFO) method. A method of inventory costing based on the assumption that the most recent goods costs incurred should be charged against revenue. *Objective 3*

Lower of cost and market method. A method of valuing inventory that reports the inventory at the lower of its cost or current market value. *Objective 6*

Net realizable value. A market value determined as the estimated selling price less any direct cost of disposal. *Objective 6*

Physical inventory. The detailed counting and listing of inventory on hand. *Objective 1*

Replacement cost. The current cost to replace inventory at the inventory date. *Objective 6*

Retail inventory method. A means of estimating inventory based on the relationship of the cost and the retail price of goods. *Objective 8*

ILLUSTRATIVE PROBLEM

Stewart Co.'s beginning inventory and purchases during the year ended December 31, 1998, were as follows:

		Units	Unit Cost	Total Cost
January 1	Inventory	1,000	$50.00	$ 50,000
March 10	Purchase	1,200	52.50	63,000
June 25	Sold 800 units			
August 30	Purchase	800	55.00	44,000
October 5	Sold 1,500 units			
November 26	Purchase	2,000	56.00	112,000
December 31	Sold 1,000 units			
Total		5,000		$269,000

Instructions

1. Determine the cost of inventory on December 31, 1998, using the perpetual inventory system and each of the following inventory costing methods:
   a. first-in, first-out
   b. last-in, first-out
   c. average cost
2. Determine the cost of inventory on December 31, 1998, using the periodic inventory system and each of the following inventory costing methods:
   a. first-in, first-out
   b. last-in, first-out
   c. average cost
3. Assume that during the fiscal year ended December 31, 1998, sales were $290,000 and the estimated gross profit rate was 40%. Estimate the ending inventory at December 31, 1998, using the gross profit method.

Solution

1. a. First-in, first-out method: $95,200

Date	Purchases			Cost of Goods Sold			Inventory		
	Quantity	Unit Cost	Total Cost	Quantity	Unit Cost	Total Cost	Quantity	Unit Cost	Total Cost
Jan. 1							1,000	50	50,000
Mar. 10	1,200	52.50	63,000				1,000	50	50,000
							1,200	52.50	63,000
June 25				800	50	40,000	200	50	10,000
							1,200	52.50	63,000
Aug. 30	800	55	44,000				200	50	10,000
							1,200	52.50	63,000
							800	55	44,000
Oct. 5				200	50	10,000			
				1,200	52.50	63,000			
				100	55	5,500	700	55	38,500
Nov. 26	2,000	56	112,000				700	55	38,500
							2,000	56	112,000
Dec. 31				700	55	38,500			
				300	56	16,800	1,700	56	95,200

b. Last-in, first-out method: $91,000 ($35,000 + $56,000)

Date	Purchases			Cost of Goods Sold			Inventory		
	Quantity	Unit Cost	Total Cost	Quantity	Unit Cost	Total Cost	Quantity	Unit Cost	Total Cost
Jan. 1							1,000	50	50,000
Mar. 10	1,200	52.50	63,000				1,000	50	50,000
							1,200	52.50	63,000
June 25				800	52.50	42,000	1,000	50	50,000
							400	52.50	21,000
Aug. 30	800	55	44,000				1,000	50	50,000
							400	52.50	21,000
							800	55	44,000
Oct. 5				800	55	44,000			
				400	52.50	21,000			
				300	50	15,000	700	50	35,000
Nov. 26	2,000	56	112,000				700	50	35,000
							2,000	56	112,000
Dec. 31				1,000	56	56,000	700	50	35,000
							1,000	56	56,000

c. Average method: $93,739

Date	Purchases			Cost of Goods Sold			Inventory		
	Quantity	Unit Cost	Total Cost	Quantity	Unit Cost	Total Cost	Quantity	Unit Cost	Total Cost
Jan. 1							1,000	50.00	50,000
Mar. 10	1,200	52.50	63,000				2,200	51.364 [1]	113,000
June 25				800	52.364	41,891	1,400	51.364	71,909
Aug. 30	800	55.00	44,000				2,200	52.686 [2]	115,909
Oct. 5				1,500	52.686	79,029	700	52.686	36,880
Nov. 26	2,000	56.00	112,000				2,700	55.141 [3]	148,880
Dec. 31				1,000	55.141	55,141	1,700	55.141	93,739

(1) $\dfrac{50,000 + 63,000}{1,000 + 1,200} = 51.364$ (2) $\dfrac{71,909 + 44,000}{1,400 + 800} = 52.686$ (3) $\dfrac{36,880 + 112,000}{700 + 2,000} = 55.141$

All total cost figures are rounded to nearest dollar for convenience.

2. a. First-in, first-out method:

       1,700 units at $56 = $95,200

    b. Last-in, first-out method:

1,000 units at $50	$ 50,000
700 units at $52.50	36,750
1,700 units	$ 86,750

    c. Average cost method:

Average cost per unit:	$269,000 ÷ 5,000 units = $53.80
Inventory, December 31, 1998:	1,700 units at $53.80 = $ 91,460

3.

Inventory, January 1, 1998		$ 50,000
Purchases (net)		219,000
Goods available for sale		$269,000
Sales (net)	$290,000	
Less estimated gross profit ($290,000 × 40%)	116,000	
Estimated cost of goods sold		174,000
Estimated inventory, December 31, 1998		$ 95,000

SELF-EXAMINATION QUESTIONS (ANSWERS AT END OF CHAPTER)

1. If the inventory shrinkage at the end of the year is overstated by $7,500, the error will cause an:
   A. understatement of cost of goods sold for the year by $7,500.
   B. overstatement of gross profit for the year by $7,500.
   C. overstatement of inventory for the year by $7,500.
   D. understatement of net income for the year by $7,500.

2. The inventory costing method that is based on the assumption that costs should be charged against revenue in the order in which they were incurred is:
   A. FIFO   C. average cost
   B. LIFO   D. perpetual inventory

3. The following units of a particular item were purchased and sold during the period:

Beginning inventory	40 units at $20
First purchase	50 units at $21
Second purchase	50 units at $22
First sale	110 units
Third purchase	50 units at $23
Second sale	45 units

What is the unit cost of the 35 units on hand at the end of the period as determined under the perpetual inventory system by the LIFO costing method?
   A. $20 and $23   C. $20
   B. $20 and $21   D. $23

4. The following units of a particular item were available for sale during the period:

Beginning inventory	40 units at $20
First purchase	50 units at $21
Second purchase	50 units at $22
Third purchase	50 units at $23

What is the unit cost of the 35 units on hand at the end of the period, as determined under the periodic inventory system by the FIFO costing method?
   A. $20   C. $22
   B. $21   D. $23

5. If inventory is being valued at cost, the price level is steadily rising, and quantities have not declined, the method of costing that will report the highest net income is:
   A. LIFO   C. average
   B. FIFO   D. periodic

DISCUSSION QUESTIONS

1. What security measures may retailers use to protect inventory from customer theft?
2. Which inventory system provides the more effective means of controlling inventories (perpetual or periodic)? Why?

3. Before inventory purchases are recorded, the receiving report should be reconciled to what documents?

4. What document should be presented by an employee requesting the release of inventory items from the company's warehouse?

5. Why is it important to periodically take a physical inventory if the perpetual system is used?

6. The inventory shrinkage at the end of the year was understated by $10,000. (a) Did the error cause an overstatement or an understatement of the gross profit for the year? (b) Which items on the balance sheet at the end of the year were overstated or understated as a result of the error? (c) What will be the effect on the income next year?

7. When does title to goods pass from the seller to the buyer if the terms of shipment are (a) FOB shipping point, (b) FOB destination?

8. Bradley Co. sold goods to Midland Company on December 31, FOB shipping point. If the goods are in transit on December 31, the end of the fiscal year, which company would report it as inventory in its financial statements? Explain.

9. A manufacturer shipped goods to a retailer on a consignment basis. If the goods are unsold at the end of the period, which business should include the goods as inventory?

10. What are the two most widely used inventory costing methods?

11. Which of the three methods of inventory costing—FIFO, LIFO, or average cost—is based on the assumption that costs should be charged against revenue in the reverse order in which they were incurred?

12. Do the terms *FIFO* and *LIFO* refer to techniques used in determining quantities of the various classes of goods on hand? Explain.

13. Does the term *last-in* in the LIFO method mean that the items in the inventory are assumed to be the most recent (last) acquisitions? Explain.

14. Under which method of cost flow are (a) the earliest costs assigned to inventory, (b) the most recent costs assigned to inventory, (c) average costs assigned to inventory?

15. If inventory is being valued at cost and both the price level and quantity are steadily rising, which of the three methods of costing—FIFO, LIFO, or average cost—will report (a) the highest inventory cost, (b) the lowest inventory cost, (c) the highest gross profit, (d) the lowest gross profit?

16. Which of the three methods of inventory costing—FIFO, LIFO, or average cost—will in general report an inventory cost most nearly approximating current replacement cost?

17. Can a company change its method of costing inventory? Explain.

18. In the phrase *lower of cost and market*, what is meant by *market*?

19. The cost of a particular inventory item is $410, the market value is $400, and the selling price is $525. At what amount should the item be included in the inventory according to the lower of cost and market?

20. Because of imperfections, an item cannot be sold at its normal selling price. How should this item be valued for financial statement purposes?

21. How is the method of determining the cost of the inventory and the method of valuing it disclosed in the financial statements?

22. What uses can be made of the estimate of the cost of inventory determined by the gross profit method?

EXERCISES

EXERCISE 9–1
Internal control of inventories
Objective 1

Easy-Does-It Hardware Store currently uses a periodic inventory system. Phil Strand, the owner, is considering the purchase of a computer system that would make it feasible to switch to a perpetual inventory system.

Phil is unhappy with the periodic inventory system because it does not provide timely information on inventory levels. Phil has noticed on several occasions that the store runs out of good-selling items, while too many poor-selling items are on hand.

Phil is also concerned about lost sales while a physical inventory is being taken. Easy-Does-It Hardware currently takes a physical inventory twice a year. To minimize distractions, the store is closed on the day inventory is taken. Phil believes closing the store is the only way to get an accurate inventory count.

➤ Will switching to a perpetual inventory system strengthen Easy-Does-It Hardware's control over inventory items? Will switching to a perpetual inventory system eliminate the need for a physical inventory count? Explain.

EXERCISE 9–2
Internal control of inventories
Objective 1

Jamaica Luggage Shop is a small retail establishment located in a large shopping mall. This shop has implemented the following procedures regarding inventory items:

a. Since the shop carries mostly high-quality, designer luggage, all inventory items are tagged with a control device that activates an alarm if a tagged item is removed from the store.

b. Since the display area of the store is limited, only a sample of each piece of luggage is kept on the selling floor. Whenever a customer selects a piece of luggage, the sales clerk gets the appropriate piece from the store's stockroom. Since all sales clerks need access to the stockroom, it is not locked. The stockroom is adjacent to the break room used by all mall employees.

c. Whenever Jamaica receives a shipment of new inventory, the items are taken directly to the stockroom. Jamaica's accountant uses the vendor's invoice to record the amount of inventory received.

State whether each of these procedures is appropriate or inappropriate, considering the principles of internal control. If it is inappropriate, state which internal control procedure is violated.

EXERCISE 9–3
Identifying items to be included in inventory
Objective 2

Ednia Co., which is located in Halifax, Nova Scotia, has identified the following items for possible inclusion in its December 31, 1999 year-end inventory.

a. Ednia has segregated $15,800 of goods ordered by one of its customers for shipment on January 3, 2000.

b. Ednia has in its warehouse $21,000 of goods on consignment from Mannex Co.

c. Goods Ednia shipped FOB shipping point on December 31, 1999, was picked up by the freight company at 11:50 p.m.

d. Goods Ednia shipped to a customer FOB shipping point was picked up by the freight company on December 26, 1999, but had still not arrived at its destination as of December 31, 1999.

e. Ednia has $35,000 of goods on hand, which were sold to customers earlier in the year, but which have been returned by customers to Ednia for various warranty repairs.

f. Ednia has sent $100,000 of goods to various retailers on a consignment basis.

g. On December 21, 1999, Ednia ordered $85,000 of goods, FOB Halifax. The goods were shipped from the supplier on December 28, 1999, but had not been received by December 31, 1999.

h. On December 27, 1999, Ednia ordered $15,000 of goods from a supplier in Toronto. The goods were shipped FOB Toronto on December 30, 1999, but had not been received by December 31, 1999.

i. On December 31, 1999, Ednia received $28,000 of goods that had been returned by customers because the wrong items had been shipped. The replacement order is to be shipped overnight on January 3, 2000.

Indicate which items should be included (I) and which should be excluded (E) from the inventory.

EXERCISE 9–4
Effect of errors in physical inventory
Objective 2

The Rivers Edge sells canoes, kayaks, whitewater rafts, and other boating supplies. During the taking of its physical inventory on December 31, 1999, The Rivers Edge incorrectly counted its inventory as $72,500 instead of the correct amount of $98,300.

a. State the effect of the error on the December 31, 1999 balance sheet of The Rivers Edge.

b. State the effect of the error on the income statement of The Rivers Edge for the year ended December 31, 1999.

EXERCISE 9–5
Effect of errors in physical inventory
Objective 2

Curly's Motorcycle Shop sells motorcycles, jet skis, and other related supplies and accessories. During the taking of its physical inventory on December 31, 1999, Curly's Motorcycle Shop incorrectly counted its inventory as $112,800 instead of the correct amount of $96,900.

a. State the effect of the error on the December 31, 1999 balance sheet of Curly's Motorcycle Shop.

b. State the effect of the error on the income statement of Curly's Motorcycle Shop for the year ended December 31, 1999.

c. State the effect of the error on Curly's financial statements prepared for the year ending December 31, 2000.

EXERCISE 9–6

Error in inventory shrinkage

Objective 2

During 1999, it was discovered that the inventory shrinkage at the end of 1998 had been overstated by $60,000. Instead of correcting the error, the accountant decided to understate the inventory shrinkage of 1999 by $60,000. The accountant reasoned that the error in 1998 would be balanced out by the error in 1999.

Are there any flaws in the accountant's reasoning? Explain.

EXERCISE 9–7

Perpetual inventory using FIFO

Objective 3

Beginning inventory, purchases, and sales data for Commodity TC19 are as follows:

Mar.	1	Inventory	20 units at $40
	7	Sale	15 units
	12	Purchase	18 units at $42
	20	Sale	12 units
	22	Sale	3 units
	30	Purchase	10 units at $45

The business maintains a perpetual inventory system, costing by the first-in, first-out method. Determine the cost of the goods sold for each sale and the inventory balance after each sale, presenting the data in the form illustrated in Exhibit 2.

EXERCISE 9–8

Perpetual inventory using LIFO

Objective 3

Assume that the business in Exercise 9–7 maintains a perpetual inventory system, costing by the last-in, first-out method. Determine the cost of goods sold for each sale and the inventory balance after each sale, presenting the data in the form illustrated in Exhibit 3.

EXERCISE 9–9

Perpetual inventory using average

Objective 3

Assume that the business in Exercise 9–7 maintains a perpetual inventory system, costing by the average method. Determine the cost of goods sold for each sale and the inventory balance after each sale, presenting the data in the form illustrated in Exhibit 4.

EXERCISE 9–10

Perpetual inventory using LIFO

Objective 3

Beginning inventory, purchases, and sales data for Commodity M343 for October are as follows:

Inventory:		Purchases:		Sales:	
Oct. 1	40 units at $15	Oct. 8	10 units at $18	Oct. 11	9 units
		21	15 units at $20	17	25 units
				29	12 units

Assuming that the perpetual inventory system is used, costing by the LIFO method, determine the cost of the inventory balance at October 31, presenting data in the form illustrated in Exhibit 3.

EXERCISE 9–11

Perpetual inventory using FIFO

Objective 3

Assume that the business in Exercise 9–9 maintains a perpetual inventory system, costing by the first-in, first-out method. Determine the cost of goods sold for each sale and the inventory balance after each sale, presenting the data in the form illustrated in Exhibit 2.

EXERCISE 9–12

Perpetual inventory using average

Objective 3

Assume that the business in Exercise 9–10 maintains a perpetual inventory system, costing by the average method. Determine the cost of goods sold for each sale and the inventory balance after each sale, presenting the data in the form illustrated in Exhibit 4.

EXERCISE 9–13
FIFO, LIFO, average costs under perpetual inventory system
Objective 3

The following units of a particular item were available for sale during the year:

Beginning inventory	20 units at $50
Sale	15 units at $90
First purchase	30 units at $54
Sale	25 units at $93
Second purchase	40 units at $65
Sale	35 units at $98

The firm uses the perpetual system, and there are 15 units of the item on hand at the end of the year. What is the total cost of the ending inventory according to (a) FIFO, (b) LIFO, (c) average cost?

EXERCISE 9–14
Periodic inventory by three methods
Objective 4

The units of an item available for sale during the year were as follows:

Jan.	1	Inventory	35 units at $25
Mar.	4	Purchase	10 units at $24
Aug.	20	Purchase	30 units at $28
Nov.	30	Purchase	25 units at $30

There are 45 units of the item in the physical inventory at December 31. The periodic inventory system is used. Determine the inventory cost by (a) the first-in, first-out method, (b) the last-in, first-out method, and (c) the average cost method.

EXERCISE 9–15
Periodic inventory by three methods; cost of goods sold
Objective 4

The units of an item available for sale during the year were as follows:

Jan.	1	Inventory	25 units at $60
Feb.	4	Purchase	10 units at $62
July	7	Purchase	30 units at $65
Oct.	15	Purchase	15 units at $70

There are 30 units of the item in the physical inventory at December 31. The periodic inventory system is used. Determine the inventory cost and the cost of goods sold by three methods, presenting your answers in the following form:

	Cost	
Inventory Method	Inventory	Goods Sold
a. First-in, first-out	$	$
b. Last-in, first-out		
c. Average cost		

EXERCISE 9–16
Lower of cost and market inventory
Objective 6

On the basis of the following data, determine the value of the inventory at the lower of cost and market (a) on a total inventory basis, and (b) on a line-by-line basis. Assemble the data in the form illustrated in Exhibit 5.

Commodity	Inventory Quantity	Unit Cost Price	Unit Market Price
4HU	5	$300	$320
153T	17	110	115
Z10	12	275	260
CW2	30	51	45
SAW1	20	95	100

EXERCISE 9–17
Inventory on the balance sheet
Objective 7

Based on the data in Exercise 9–16 and assuming that cost was determined by the FIFO method, show how the inventory would appear on the balance sheet.

EXERCISE 9–18
Retail method inventory
Objective 8

A business using the retail method of inventory costing determines that inventory at retail is $500,000. If the ratio of cost to retail price is 65%, what is the amount of inventory you would report on the financial statements?

EXERCISE 9–19
Retail inventory method
Objective 8

On the basis of the following data, estimate the cost of the inventory at April 30 by the retail method:

		Cost	Retail
April 1	Inventory	$444,500	$ 670,500
April 1–30	Purchases (net)	608,500	949,500
April 1–30	Sales (net)		1,140,000

EXERCISE 9–20
Gross profit inventory method
Objective 8

The whole inventory was destroyed by fire on July 20. The following data were obtained from the accounting records:

Jan. 1	Inventory	$ 172,250
Jan. 1–July 20	Purchases (net)	812,250
	Sales (net)	1,080,000
	Estimated gross profit rate	35%

a. Estimate the cost of the goods destroyed.
b. Briefly describe the situations in which the gross profit method is useful.

EXERCISE 9–21
Accounting concepts
Objective 5

Ari Department Stores has been reporting inventory by the lower of cost and market method. However, the replacement cost of its inventory has risen significantly during the current year. Therefore, Ari Department Stores elected to report the inventory at the end of the current year at current market prices. The change in method was disclosed in a note to the financial statements that fully reported the effect of the use of market prices on the balance sheet and income statement.

➤ Is there anything wrong with the reporting? Discuss.

EXERCISE 9–22
Accounting concepts
Objective 5

The cost of inventory at the end of the first fiscal year of operations, according to three different methods, is as follows: FIFO, $90,000; average, $76,500; LIFO, $68,000. If the average cost method is used, the net income reported will be $125.00.

a. What will be the amount of net income reported if the LIFO method is adopted?
b. What will be the amount of net income reported if the FIFO method is adopted?
c. Which of the three methods is the most conservative in terms of net income?
d. Is the particular method adopted of sufficient materiality to require disclosure in the financial statements?

PROBLEMS SERIES A

PROBLEM 9–1A
FIFO perpetual inventory
Objective 3

The beginning inventory of C109 at Red Eye Co. and data on purchases and sales for a three-month period are as follows:

Date	Transaction	Number of Units	Per Unit	Total
July 1	Inventory	20,000	$6.10	$122,000
8	Purchase	75,000	6.15	461,250
20	Sale	40,000	7.00	280,000
31	Sale	35,000	7.00	245,000
Aug. 8	Sale	5,000	7.10	35,500
10	Purchase	50,000	6.20	310,000
27	Sale	40,000	7.20	288,000
30	Sale	20,000	7.15	143,000
Sept. 5	Purchase	70,000	6.05	423,500
13	Sale	40,000	7.00	280,000
22	Purchase	30,000	6.00	180,000
30	Sale	55,000	7.00	385,000

Instructions

1. Record the inventory, purchases, and cost of goods sold data in a perpetual inventory record similar to the one illustrated in Exhibit 2, using the first-in, first-out method.
2. Determine the total sales and the total cost of C109 sold for the period. Journalize the entries in the sales and cost of goods sold accounts. Assume that all sales were on account.
3. Determine the gross profit from sales for the period.

PROBLEM 9–2A
Lifo perpetual inventory
Objective 3

The beginning inventory of C109 at Red Eye Co. and data on purchases and sales for a three-month period are shown in Problem 9–1A.

Instructions

1. Record the inventory, purchases, and cost of goods sold data in a perpetual inventory record similar to the one illustrated in Exhibit 3, using the last-in, first-out method.
2. Determine the total sales, the total cost of units sold, and the gross profit from sales for the period.

PROBLEM 9–3A
Average perpetual inventory
Objective 3

The beginning inventory of C109 at Red Eye Co. and data on purchases and sales for a three-month period are shown in Problem 9–1A.

Instructions

1. Record the inventory, purchases, and cost of goods sold data in a perpetual inventory record similar to the one illustrated in Exhibit 4, using the average method.
2. Determine the total sales, total cost of units sold, and the gross profit from sales for the period.

PROBLEM 9–4A
Periodic inventory by three methods
Objective 4

Colour-Tron Television uses the periodic inventory system. Details regarding the inventory of television sets at July 1, 1999, purchases invoices during the year, and the inventory count at June 30, 2000, are summarized as follows:

Model	Inventory, July 1	Purchases Invoices			Inventory Count, June 30
		1st	2nd	3rd	
A37	6 at $240	4 at $250	8 at $260	10 at $262	12
E15	6 at 80	5 at 82	8 at 89	8 at 90	10
L10	2 at 108	2 at 110	3 at 128	3 at 130	3
O18	8 at 88	4 at 79	3 at 85	6 at 92	8
K72	2 at 250	2 at 260	4 at 271	4 at 272	4
S91	5 at 160	4 at 170	4 at 175	7 at 180	8
V17	—	4 at 150	4 at 200	4 at 202	5

Instructions

1. Determine the cost of the inventory on June 30, 2000, by the first-in, first-out method. Present data in columnar form, using the following headings:

Model	Quantity	Unit Cost	Total Cost

If the inventory of a particular model comprises one entire purchase plus a portion of another purchase acquired at a different unit cost, use a separate line for each purchase.
2. Determine the cost of the inventory on June 30, 2000, by the last-in, first-out method, following the procedures indicated in (1).
3. Determine the cost of the inventory on June 30, 2000, by the average cost method, using the columnar headings indicated in (1).

PROBLEM 9–5A
Retail method; gross profit method
Objective 8

Selected data on inventory, purchases, and sales for Cashin Co. and Apex Co. are as follows:

	Cost	Retail
Cashin Co.		
Inventory, August 1	$ 159,800	$270,000
Transactions during August:		
Purchases (net)	658,450	821,000
Sales		890,000
Sales returns and allowances		9,000
Apex Co.		
Inventory, April 1	$ 117,500	
Transactions during April and May:		
Purchases (net)	725,000	
Sales	1,212,000	
Sales returns and allowances	12,000	
Estimated gross profit rate	40%	

Instructions

1. Determine the estimated cost of the inventory of Cashin Co. on August 31 by the retail method, presenting details of the computations.
2. a. Estimate the cost of the inventory of Apex Co. on May 31 by the gross profit method, presenting details of the computations.
   b. Assume that Apex Co. took a physical inventory on May 31 and discovered that $118,000 of inventory was on hand. What was the estimated loss of inventory due to theft or damage during April and May?

PROBLEM 9–6A
Accounting concepts review

Discuss the propriety of each of the following in the context of generally accepted accounting principles.

1. You have just been employed by a relatively small merchandising business that records its revenues only when it receives cash and its expenses only when it pays cash. You suggest that the business should record its revenues and expenses on an accrual basis, but the owner feels that this would violate the accounting principle of consistency.
2. The accountant for a large department store charged the acquisition of various office items, such as an electric pencil sharpener, to an expense account, even though the asset had a useful life of 10 years.
3. A business changed its method of costing inventory from LIFO to FIFO. The company disclosed this change in the notes to its financial statements and reported that the current year's income was $10,000 higher as a result of the switch to FIFO.
4. In estimating its allowance for doubtful accounts, a business always selects the estimation method that results in the lowest balance for the allowance account.

PROBLEMS SERIES B

PROBLEM 9–1B
FIFO perpetual inventory
Objective 3

The beginning inventory of Commodity F3C and data on purchases and sales for a three-month period are as follows:

Date	Transaction	Number of Units	Per Unit	Total
April 1	Inventory	10	$220	$2,200
7	Purchase	25	225	5,625
18	Sale	10	300	3,000
22	Sale	8	300	2,400
May 4	Purchase	15	230	3,450
10	Sale	10	310	3,100
21	Sale	5	310	1,550
31	Purchase	20	235	4,700
June 5	Sale	15	315	4,725
13	Sale	10	315	3,150
21	Purchase	15	240	3,600
28	Sale	11	320	3,520

Instructions

1. Record the inventory, purchases, and cost of goods sold data in a perpetual inventory record similar to the one illustrated in Exhibit 2, using the first-in, first-out method.
2. Determine the total sales and the total cost of Commodity F3C sold for the period. Journalize the entries in the sales and cost of goods sold accounts. Assume that all sales were on account.
3. Determine the gross profit from sales of Commodity F3C for the period.

PROBLEM 9–2B
Lifo perpetual inventory
Objective 3

The beginning inventory of Commodity F3C and data on purchases and sales for a three-month period are shown in Problem 9–1B.

Instructions

1. Record the inventory, purchases, and cost of goods sold data in a perpetual inventory record similar to the one illustrated in Exhibit 3, using the last-in, first-out method.
2. Determine the total sales, the total cost of Commodity F3C sold, and the gross profit from sales for the period.

PROBLEM 9–3B
Average perpetual inventory
Objective 3

The beginning inventory of Commodity F3C and data on purchase and sales for the three-month period are shown in Problem 9–1B.

Instructions

1. Record the inventory, purchases, and cost of goods sold data in a perpetual inventory record similar to the one illustrated in Exhibit 4, using the average method.
2. Determine the total sales, the total cost of Commodity F3C sold, and the gross profit for the period.

PROBLEM 9–4B
Periodic inventory by three methods
Objective 4

Denny's Television uses the periodic inventory system. Details regarding the inventory of television sets at January 1, purchases invoices during the year, and the inventory count at December 31 are summarized as follows:

Model	Inventory, January 1	Purchases Invoices			Inventory Count, December 31
		1st	2d	3d	
B91	4 at $149	6 at $151	8 at $157	7 at $156	5
F10	3 at 208	3 at 212	5 at 213	4 at 225	3
H21	2 at 520	2 at 527	2 at 530	2 at 535	3
J39	6 at 520	8 at 531	4 at 549	6 at 542	8
P80	9 at 213	7 at 215	6 at 222	6 at 225	8
T15	6 at 305	3 at 310	3 at 316	4 at 317	5
V11	—	4 at 222	4 at 232	—	2

Instructions

1. Determine the cost of the inventory on December 31 by the first-in, first-out method. Present data in columnar form, using the following headings:

Model	Quantity	Unit Cost	Total Cost

If the inventory of a particular model comprises one entire purchase plus a portion of another purchase acquired at a different unit cost, use a separate line for each purchase.
2. Determine the cost of the inventory on December 31 by the last-in, first-out method, following the procedures indicated in (1).
3. Determine the cost of the inventory on December 31 by the average cost method, using the columnar headings indicated in (1).

PROBLEM 9–5B
Retail method; gross profit method
Objective 8

Selected data on inventory, purchases, and sales for Adirondack Co. and Trailways Co. are as follows:

	Cost	Retail
Adirondack Co.		
Inventory, February 1	$ 177,100	$ 227,000
Transactions during February:		
Purchases (net)	986,300	1,435,000
Sales		1,460,000
Sales returns and allowances		43,000
Trailways Co.		
Inventory, July 1	$ 317,900	
Transactions during July and August:		
Purchases (net)	1,532,100	
Sales	2,330,000	
Sales returns and allowances	57,000	
Estimated gross profit rate	35%	

Instructions

1. Determine the estimated cost of the inventory of Adirondack Co. on February 28 by the retail method, presenting details of the computations.
2. a. Estimate the cost of the inventory of Trailways Co. on August 31 by the gross profit method, presenting details of the computations.
   b. Assume that Trailways Co. took a physical inventory on August 31 and discovered that $350,000 of inventory was on hand. What was the estimated loss of inventory due to theft or damage during July and August?

PROBLEM 9–6B
Accounting concepts review

Discuss the propriety of each of the following items in relation to generally accepted accounting principles.

1. The last three sets of financial statements prepared by Flush Enterprises covered 9 months, 8½ months, and 14 months.
2. The manager of a small variety store counted inventory at the end of the fiscal period. The amount recorded for ending inventory was calculated by multiplying the quantity of each item on hand by the retail price marked on the item in the store.
3. On January 12 of the current year, Ideal Realty acquired a 10-acre tract of land for $500,000. Before the end of the year, it spent $125,000 on subdividing the tract and paving streets. The market value of the property at the end of the year was $700,000. Although no lots were sold during the year, the income statement reported revenue of $200,000, expenses of $125,000, and net income of $75,000 on the project.
4. A business reports its inventory at FIFO cost of $50,000 on the balance sheet. In the notes to the financial statements the business discloses that the market value of the inventory is $45,000.

CHALLENGE PROBLEMS

PROBLEM CP9–1

Uzup Company opened for business on January 1 of year 1 and closed three years later. Its inventory transactions for its first three years of operation were as follows:

	Year 1	Year 2	Year 3
Purchases:	10,000 units @ $10 each 10,000 units @ $11 each	15,000 units @ $12 each 10,000 units @ $13 each	10,000 units @ $14 each
Sales:	10,000 units @ $15 each	25,000 units @ $18 each	20,000 units @ $20 each

Instructions

a. Assuming a periodic inventory system, compute gross profit for each year under FIFO.
b. Assuming a periodic inventory system, compute gross profit for each year under LIFO.
c. Compare the total income reported for the three year period under FIFO and LIFO. Why does FIFO report a higher income in the first two years? Why does LIFO report a higher income in the third year?
d. What is the gross profit for year 1 under both FIFO and LIFO, assuming that the first purchase is at $11 per unit and the second purchase at $10 per unit. What conclusion could you draw from this example?

PROBLEM CP9–2

The following information pertains to Supply Co. for 2000:

January 1	Opening inventory	1,000 units @ $10 each
March	Purchased on account	550 units @ $11 each
	Returned	50 defective units @ $11 each
June	Sold on account	1,200 units @ $15 each
October	Purchased on account	1,000 units @ $12 each

Instructions

a. Assume that Supply uses a FIFO periodic inventory system. If an inventory count indicates 1,300 units on hand at year end, prepare all journal entries related to inventory and cost of goods sold for 2000.
b. Assuming that an inventory count indicates 1,300 units on hand at year end, calculate the cost of goods sold for 2000 using a LIFO periodic inventory system.
c. Calculate December 31, 2000 cost of goods sold and ending inventory using a weighted average perpetual inventory system. Assume that a physical count indicates that 1,300 units are on hand at year-end.

PROBLEM CP9–3

Martinello Company uses the LIFO method for inventory. In a recent annual report, Martinello reported (in millions)

	December 31, 2000	December 31, 1999
Inventories at LIFO cost	$2,168	$2,298

A note to the financial statements indicated that if FIFO had been used, inventory would have been higher by $152 million at the end of 2000 and by $16 million at the end of 1999. The income statement reported sales revenue of $14,740 million and cost of goods sold of $9,786 million for the 2000 fiscal year.

Instructions

a. Show the computation of Martinello's cost of goods sold and gross profit for the fiscal year 2000 by the LIFO method as actually reported.
b. Compute cost of goods sold for 2000 using FIFO.
c. Did the quantity of inventory increase or decrease during 2000? How can you tell?
d. Were inventory costs increasing or decreasing during 2000? How can you tell?

PROBLEM CP9–4

Indicate the effect of each of the following errors on the following items listed in the 1999 financial statements of Dimand Company. Indicate the amount of the error and whether the error will cause the item to be understated (U), overstated (O), or will have no effect (NE) on the item.

Inventory Error	1999 Net Income	1999 Ending Assets	1999 Ending Owners' Equity
a. 1999 ending inventory overstated by $2,000			
b. 1998 ending inventory overstated by $5,000			
c. Goods costing $10,000 were on consignment with a retailer. Dimand did not include these goods in ending inventory.			
d. Dimand included in ending inventory and purchases $15,000 goods that were in transit at year end. Dimand's supplier had shipped these goods FOB destination.			
e. Dimand had on hand some obsolete inventory with an estimated net realizable value of $2,000. Dimand reported this inventory in its balance sheet at its historical cost of $3,000.			

CASES

CASE 9–1
Hanley Co.
Determining quantities in inventory

Hanley Co. is experiencing a decrease in sales and operating income for the fiscal year ending December 31, 1999. Jill Rizzoli, controller of Hanley Co., has suggested that all orders received before the end of the fiscal year be shipped by midnight, December 31, 1999, even if the shipping department must work overtime. Since Hanley Co. ships all goods FOB shipping point, it would record all such shipments as sales for the year ending December 31, 1999, thereby offsetting some of the decreases in sales and operating income.

➤ Discuss whether Jill Rizzoli is behaving in an ethical manner.

CASE 9–2
Oakey Wholesale Co.
Lifo and inventory flow

The following is an excerpt from a conversation between Leo Kagle, the warehouse manager for Oakey Wholesale Co., and its accountant, Megan Goodman. Oakey Wholesale operates a large regional warehouse that supplies grocery stores in smaller communities with produce and other grocery products.

Leo: Megan, can you explain what's going on here with these monthly statements?
Megan: Sure, Leo. How can I help you?
Leo: I don't understand this last-in, first-out inventory procedure. It just doesn't make sense.

Megan: Well, what it means is that we assume that the last goods we receive are the first ones sold. So the inventory is made up of the items we purchased first.
Leo: Yes, but that's my problem. It doesn't work that way! We always distribute the oldest produce first. Some of that produce is perishable! We can't keep any of it very long or it'll spoil.
Megan: Leo, you don't understand. We only *assume* that the products we distribute are the last ones received. We don't actually have to distribute the goods in this way.
Leo: I always thought that accounting was supposed to show what really happened. It all sounds like "make believe" to me! Why not report what really happens?

➤ Respond to Leo's concerns.

CASE 9–3
Sears Canada Inc.
Financial analysis

 A merchandising business should keep enough inventory on hand to meet the needs of its customers. At the same time, however, too much inventory reduces solvency by tying up funds, and it increases expenses such as storage expense. Moreover, excess inventory increases the risk of losses due to prices declining or the inventory becoming obsolete.

As with many types of financial analyses, it is possible to determine more than one measure to express the relationship between the cost of goods sold (cost of sales) and inventory. Two such goods are the inventory turnover and the number of days' sales in inventory. The inventory turnover is computed as follows:

$$\text{Inventory turnover} = \frac{\text{Cost of goods sold}}{\text{Average inventory}}$$

The average inventory can be determined by dividing the sum of the inventories at the beginning and end of the year by two.

Generally, an increase in the turnover indicates an improvement in managing inventory. However, differences in companies and industries are too great to allow a more specific statement as to what is a good inventory turnover. For example, a firm selling food should have a higher turnover than a firm selling furniture. However, for each business, there is a reasonable turnover rate. A turnover lower than this rate could mean that inventory is not being managed properly. In such cases, management should investigate to determine the causes of the lower inventory rate.

The number of days' sales in inventory is computed as follows:

$$\text{Number of days' sales in inventory} = \frac{\text{Inventory, end of year}}{\text{Average daily cost of goods sold}}$$

The average daily cost of goods sold is determined by dividing the cost of goods sold by 365.

The number of days' sales in inventory is a rough measure of the length of time it takes to acquire, sell, and replace the inventory. Generally, a decrease in the number of days' sales in inventory indicates an improvement in managing the inventory.

a. Sears Canada Inc. reported inventories of $507,000,000, $491,000,000, and $640,000,000 for the years ended 1995, 1996, and 1997. Cost of goods sold were $3,712,100 and $4,204,100 for 1996 and 1997 respectively. For the years ended December 31, 1997 and 1996, determine: (1) the inventory turnover, and (2) the number of days' sales in inventory.

b. ▅▅▅▶ What conclusions can be drawn from these analyses concerning Sears' efficiency in managing inventory?

CASE 9–4
Gant Company
Costing inventory

Gant Company began operations in 1999 by selling a single product. Data on purchases and sales for the year were as follows:

Purchases:

Date	Units Purchased	Unit Cost	Total Cost
April 8	4,875	$13.20	$ 64,350
May 10	5,125	14.00	71,750
June 4	5,000	14.20	71,000
July 10	5,000	15.00	75,000
August 7	3,400	15.25	51,850
October 5	1,600	15.50	24,800
November 1	1,000	15.75	15,750
December 10	1,000	17.00	17,000
	27,000		$391,500

Sales:

April	2,000 units
May	2,000
June	3,500
July	4,000
August	3,500
September	3,500
October	2,250
November	1,250
December	1,000
Total sales	$434,000

On January 3, 2000, the president of the company, Laura Gant, asked for your advice on costing the 4,000-unit physical inventory that was taken on December 31, 1999. Moreover, since the firm plans to expand its product line, she asked for your advice on the use of a perpetual inventory system in the future.

1. Determine the cost of the December 31, 1999 inventory under the periodic system, using the (a) first-in, first-out method, (b) last-in, first-out method, and (c) average cost method.
2. Determine the gross profit for the year under each of the three methods in (1).

3. a. ▬▬▶ Explain varying viewpoints why each of the three inventory costing methods may best reflect the results of operations for 1999.
   b. ▬▬▶ Which of the three inventory costing methods may best reflect the replacement cost of the inventory on the balance sheet as of December 31, 1999?
   c. ▬▬▶ Discuss the advantages and disadvantages of using a perpetual inventory system. From the data presented in this case, is there any indication of the adequacy of inventory levels during the year?

CASE 9–5
Carquest Co.
Accounting concepts

Carquest Co. operates 10 cash-and-carry auto parts stores. In an effort to expand sales, the company has decided to offer two additional sales plans:

1. Credit sales to commercial businesses, such as body and repair shops, with free 24-hour delivery.
2. Installment sales of major dollar items, with payments spread over 24 months.

   The company president has asked you when the revenue from each of the two new plans would be recognized in the accounting records and statements.

a. ▬▬▶ Indicate to the president when the revenue from each type of sale should be journalized in the accounting records.

b. ▬▬▶ While discussing the concepts in (a), the president raised the following questions related to various accounting concepts. How would you respond to each?
   1. "Many businesses cease operating each year; so why do accountants assume a going concern concept when preparing the financial statements?"
   2. "To assume that the value of the dollar does not change and that we don't have inflation is wrong! An automatic transmission that cost $600 five years ago costs $900 today. Why wouldn't it be better to use current dollars, at least for the inventory?"
   3. "With so many different accounting methods that can be used, why can't I switch methods to improve net income this year?"
   4. "Our annual bonuses to store managers are based on store profits. It's not fair to 'anticipate no profits and provide for all losses.'"

ANSWERS TO SELF-EXAMINATION QUESTIONS

1. **D** The overstatement of inventory shrinkage by $7,500 at the end of the year will cause the cost of goods sold for the year to be overstated by $7,500, the gross profit for the year to be understated by $7,500, the inventory to be understated by $7,500, and the net income for the year to be understated by $7,500 (answer D).
2. **A** The FIFO method (answer A) is based on the assumption that costs are charged against revenue in the order in which they were incurred. The LIFO method (answer B) charges the most recent costs incurred against revenue, and the average cost method (answer C) charges a weighted average of unit costs of items sold against revenue. The perpetual inventory system (answer D) is a system that continuously discloses the amount of inventory.
3. **A** The LIFO method of costing is based on the assumption that costs should be charged against revenue in the

reverse order in which costs were incurred. Thus, the oldest costs are assigned to inventory. Thirty of the 35 units would be assigned a unit cost of $20 (since 10 of the beginning inventory units were sold on the first sale), and the remaining five units would be assigned a cost of $23 (answer A).
4. **D** The FIFO method of costing is based on the assumption that costs should be charged against revenue in the order in which they were incurred (first-in, first-out). Thus, the most recent costs are assigned to inventory. The 35 units would be assigned a unit cost of $23 (answer D).
5. **B** When the price level is steadily rising, the earlier unit costs are lower than recent unit costs. Under the FIFO method (answer B), these earlier costs are matched against revenue to yield the highest possible net income. The periodic inventory system (answer D) is a system and not a method of costing.

10   Capital Assets

YOU AND ACCOUNTING

Assume that you are a certified flight instructor and you would like to earn a little extra money by teaching people how to fly. Unfortunately, you don't own an airplane. However, one of the pilots at the Fredericton airport is willing to let you use her airplane for a fixed fee per year. You will also have to pay your share of the annual operating costs, based on hours flown. The owner will consider your request for upgrading the plane's equipment. At the end of the year, the owner has the right to cancel the agreement.

One of your friends is an airplane mechanic. He is familiar with the plane and has indicated that it needs its annual inspection. There is some structural damage on the right aileron. In addition to this repair, you would like to equip the plane with another radio and a better navigation system.

Since you will not have any ownership in the airplane, it is important for you to distinguish between normal operating costs and costs that add future value or worth to the airplane. These latter costs should be the responsibility of the owner. In this case, you should be willing to pay for part of the cost of the annual inspection. The cost of repairing the structural damage and upgrading the navigation system should be the responsibility of the owner.

Businesses also distinguish between the cost of a physical capital asset and the cost of operating the asset. In this chapter, we discuss how to determine the portion of a capital asset's cost that becomes an expense over a period of time. We also discuss accounting for the disposal of capital assets and accounting for intangible capital assets, such as patents and copyrights.

After studying this chapter, you should be able to:

Objective 1
Define physical capital assets and describe the accounting for their cost.

Objective 2
Compute amortization, using the following methods: straight-line method, units-of-production method, and declining-balance method.

Objective 3
Classify capital asset costs as either capital expenditures or revenue expenditures.

Objective 4
Journalize entries for the disposal of capital assets.

Objective 5
Define a lease and summarize the accounting rules related to the leasing of capital assets.

Objective 6
Describe internal controls over physical capital assets and provide examples of such controls.

Objective 7
Define natural resources, compute depletion, and journalize the entry for depletion.

Objective 8
Journalize the entries for acquiring and amortizing intangible assets, such as patents, copyrights, and goodwill.

Objective 9
Describe how amortization expense is reported in an income statement and prepare a balance sheet that includes physical capital assets and intangible assets.

Nature of Physical Capital Assets

Objective 1
Define physical capital assets and describe the accounting for their cost.

Capital assets are long-term assets owned by a business that possess three characteristics: (1) they are used in normal business operations; (2) management intends to use them on a continuing basis; and (3) they are not intended for sale in the ordinary course of business.[1] Tangible capital assets are called physical capital assets. Other descriptive titles for such assets are **fixed assets** or **property, plant, and equipment.** We may also describe these assets in more specific terms, such as equipment, tools, furniture, machinery, buildings, and land.

Capital assets must be capable of providing repeated use or benefit, and have an expected useful life of more than a year. Sometimes we classify an asset as a capital asset even though the business may not be using it on an ongoing basis or even often. For example, capital assets include items of standby equipment held for use in the event of a breakdown of regular equipment or for use only during peak periods of activity.

However, we do not classify long-term assets acquired for resale in the normal course of business as capital assets, regardless of their permanent nature or the length of time they are held. We consider these assets to be investments, not capital assets. For example, we list undeveloped land or other real estate acquired for resale on the balance sheet in the asset section entitled *Investments*.

We report the normal costs of using or operating a physical capital asset as Operating Expenses on a company's income statement. The costs of acquiring such an asset also become expenses over a period of time. In the following paragraphs, we discuss these latter costs and the nature of this periodic expense.

COSTS OF ACQUIRING PHYSICAL CAPITAL ASSETS

When you incur a cost with respect to a capital asset, you can treat the expenditure in either one of two ways. Either (1) debit an expense account immediately or (2)

---

[1] Canadian Institute of Chartered Accountants, *CICA Handbook*, Section 3060, paragraph .04.

debit the amount to an asset account. When you record the cost as a capital asset, we say that you have **"capitalized"** the expenditure. What determines whether or not you should record the expenditure as an asset or as an expense? The general rule is as follows: If you believe that the expenditure will result in future benefits for the business, record it as an asset; otherwise, expense it immediately.

We record physical capital assets at their acquisition cost. What expenditures should you include in computing the acquisition cost of the asset? Acquisition cost includes all amounts spent to get the asset in place and ready for use. For example, freight costs and the costs of installing equipment are part of the acquisition cost. However, you should not include in acquisition cost any expenditures that are not necessary for getting an asset ready for use and that do not increase the asset's usefulness. For example, you should expense immediately any costs incurred due to vandalism or due to errors made in installing equipment. These costs are expensed because they were unnecessary, and did not contribute to the asset's usefulness.

One guideline for determining whether to capitalize a cost incurred at acquisition is to ask the following question: When purchasing the asset, did management plan to make this expenditure in order to get the asset ready for use? If the cost was anticipated *before* the asset was purchased, include it in the acquisition cost. If it was unexpected, you should probably expense it. For example, suppose that you purchase a used truck, intending to repaint it and overhaul the engine before putting it into service. In this case, you should include the costs of the repainting and the overhaul as part of the acquisition cost of the truck. However, suppose that you purchase a truck that you believe is in good running order, and the next day you discover that the transmission is no good. In this case, you should expense the cost of repairing the transmission, since you did not anticipate this as part of your acquisition cost of the asset. Exhibit 1 summarizes how to treat some of the common costs associated with acquiring a physical capital asset such as equipment.

The costs related to acquiring land and buildings often require careful analysis. For example, the cost of land includes not only its negotiated price, but also the broker's commissions, title fees, surveying fees, and other costs of obtaining entitlement to it.[2] If delinquent real-estate taxes are paid by the buyer, they are also part of the cost of the land. If unwanted buildings are located on land acquired for a future building site, the cost of their razing or removal, less the proceeds from any

Exhibit 1
Costs of Acquiring Physical Capital Assets

The cost of physical capital assets includes costs of:

Sales taxes	Insurance while asset is in transit
Freight	Assembling
Installation	Modifying for use
Repairs (used assets)	Testing for use
Reconditioning (used assets)	Permits from government agencies

The cost of plant assets excludes costs of:
Vandalism
Mistakes in installation
Uninsured theft
Damage during unpacking and installing
Fines for not obtaining proper permits from government agencies
Unexpected repairs

[2] In this section we assume that land is to be used only as a location or site. We will consider land acquired for its mineral deposits or other natural resources later in the chapter.

salvage, is a cost of the land. The cost of grading, levelling, or otherwise changing the contour of land is also properly included as a cost of the land. Again, we include all of these expenditures in acquisition cost because, before making the purchase, management would have expected to incur all of these costs in order to get the land ready for its intended use.

The cost of constructing a building includes the fees paid to architects and engineers for plans and supervision. In addition, we should capitalize to the building account the costs of insurance incurred during construction and all other necessary costs related to the project. Canadian accounting practice also allows a business to include in the cost of the building interest incurred during the construction period on money borrowed to finance construction.[3]

You must always separate the acquisition cost of the land from the cost of the building. This is because land is considered a "permanent" asset, which will continue to be useful indefinitely into the future. However, a building will eventually "wear out" with use, so that its usefulness will decline over time. Therefore, the cost of the land must be kept in a separate asset account from that of the building. In future years the account for land will continue to reflect the acquisition cost of the asset. However, as you gradually "use up" the benefits of the building in future years, you will periodically transfer the cost of this asset to an expense account.

Often a business will purchase land and a building for a lump-sum price. How do you know how much to record for the acquisition cost of each separate asset? When a company makes a **lump-sum acquisition** (also called a **basket purchase**), you should allocate the total cost to different assets purchased in proportion to their relative fair market values. For example, suppose that the business buys land and a building for a total payment of $500,000. A real estate appraiser estimates that, if purchased separately, the fair value of the land would be $110,000 and the value of the building would be $440,000. Here, the total value is $550,000 ($110,000 + $440,000), of which the land represents 20% (110,000/550,000) and the building 80% (440,000/550,000). Following the **historical cost principle,** we still record the assets at their total acquisition cost (regardless of their appraisal value), but we can allocate the $500,000 cost based on their relative fair market values, as follows:

Land (20% × $500,000)	100,000	
Building (80% × $500,000)	400,000	
Cash		500,000

In some cases, it may be difficult to determine whether an expenditure is part of the cost of the land or building. For instance, a business may have to pay for the initial cost of paving a public street bordering its land, either by direct payment or by special tax assessment. In this case, the costs related to the paving are normally added to the cost of the land. As another example, the costs incurred in constructing walkways to and around a building may be considered part of the cost of the building, if they are expected to last only as long as the building.

We may also incur costs for items that are neither as permanent as land nor directly related to a building. Examples of such items include the costs of trees and shrubs, fences, outdoor lighting, and paved parking areas. We record these items in a separate asset account called **land improvements.** A general guideline for determining whether to include an item in land or land improvements is to consider whether the firm will have to incur any future costs to replace the asset if it "wears out." For example, a business may have to pay initially for the cost of installing sewers on its property. To which asset account should you capitalize this cost, to land or to land improvements? If the municipality will pay for future repair and replacement of the sewers, capitalize this cost to land, since it is a "permanent" asset to business. However, if the firm is responsible for the future upkeep of the

---

[3] Canadian Institute of Chartered Accountants, *CICA Handbook*, Section 3850.

asset, record the initial cost under land improvements, a physical capital asset like buildings, whose benefits to the business will be "used up" over time.

NATURE OF AMORTIZATION

As we have discussed in earlier chapters, land has an unlimited life and therefore can provide unlimited services. On the other hand, other capital assets such as equipment, buildings, and land improvements lose their ability, over time, to provide services. As a result, we must transfer (or allocate) the costs of equipment, buildings, and land improvements to expense accounts in a rational and systematic manner during their expected useful lives. This periodic cost expiration is called amortization (often called **depreciation**).[4]

Factors that cause a decline in the ability of a physical asset to provide services fall into two categories. First, *physical* decline caused by wear and tear from use and from the action of the elements decreases usefulness. Second, *functional* decline caused by inadequacy and obsolescence decreases usefulness. A physical asset becomes inadequate if its capacity is not able to meet the demands of increased production. A physical asset is obsolete if the item that it produces is no longer in demand or if a newer machine can produce an item of better quality at the same or lower cost. Advances in technology during this century have made obsolescence an increasingly important cause of decline in usefulness.

Many people misunderstand the meaning of the term *amortization* (or *depreciation*) as used in accounting. This occurs because in common usage the term "depreciation" often refers to a decline in the market value of an asset. However, in accounting, amortization is simply a method of charging part of the cost of a long-term asset to expense each period over its useful life, *without regard to the market value of the asset*. When a business uses a capital asset (other than land), it consumes some of the benefits of that asset. Therefore, we record amortization expense to indicate the decline in the future usefulness of the asset to the firm. It is unlikely that the portion of the asset's cost charged to amortization expense during a year will reflect the actual change in the market value of the asset during the period. This occurs because many factors can affect market value besides the usage of the

USING ACCOUNTING TO UNDERSTAND BUSINESS

When a business acquires a capital asset, it often makes an outlay of cash. This outlay affects the cash flows of the business. Although the subsequent amortization is a major expense for many businesses, it does not require a cash outlay. Therefore, in evaluating a business's cash-generating ability, many creditors and investment analysts must add back amortization expense to the reported net income of the business in order to obtain a rough estimate of cash generated from operations. Thus, both amortization and capital asset replacements are important considerations in evaluating the earnings and cash flows of a business.

---

[4] The *CICA Handbook* defines amortization as "the charge to income which recognizes that life is finite and that the cost less salvage value or residual value of a capital asset is allocated to the periods of service provided by the asset" (Section 3060, paragraph 33).

asset. For example, if construction costs are rising quickly because of inflation, the market value of a building may actually *increase* during a period. However, regardless of an increase in market value, the business must still record amortization expense to indicate that it "consumed" some of the asset during the period, and to match the cost of the asset used up against the revenues that the asset helped to generate during the period.

We could define market value as the amount that we would receive if we sold the asset. As explained above, it is unlikely that the amount of a physical asset's unexpired cost reported in the balance sheet will equal the amount that could be realized from its sale. However, remember that a defining characteristic of a capital asset is that it is being held for use, rather than for resale. If we assume that the business will continue as a **going concern,** it will be using its capital assets in its operations, not selling them. In that case, the market value of these assets may not be particularly relevant to users of the financial statements.

Another common misunderstanding is that amortization accounting provides cash needed to replace capital assets as they wear out. However, the cash account is neither increased nor decreased by the periodic entries that transfer the cost of capital assets to amortization expense accounts. The misunderstanding probably occurs because amortization, unlike many expenses, does not require an outlay of cash in the period in which it is recorded.

Accounting for Amortization

Objective 2
Compute amortization, using the following methods: straight-line method, units-of-production method, and declining-balance method.

We consider three factors in determining the amount of amortization expense to be recognized each period. These three factors are (a) the capital asset's initial cost, (b) its expected useful life, and (c) its estimated value at the end of its useful life. This third factor is called the residual value, **scrap value, salvage value,** or **trade-in value.** Exhibit 2 shows the relationship among the three factors and the periodic amortization expense.

The cost to be charged to amortization expense over the asset's useful life is called its **amortizable** (or **depreciable**) cost. If we expect a capital asset to have no residual value at the time that it is taken out of service, then we must allocate its initial acquisition cost over its expected useful life as amortization expense each period. Similarly, if the estimated residual value is very small compared to the cost of the asset, we may ignore this value and spread the entire acquisition cost over the asset's expected useful life. However, if we expect the asset to have a significant residual value, we should amortize only the difference between the acquisition cost and the residual value over the asset's useful life. Thus, where the residual value is significant:

Exhibit 2
Factors that Determine Amortization Expense

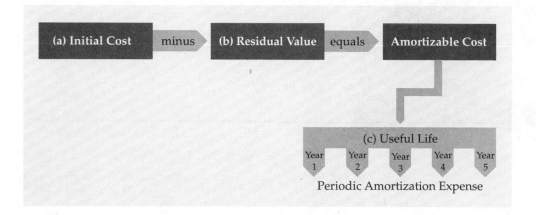

Amortizable Cost = Acquisition Cost – Residual Value

Until an asset is actually taken out of service, we cannot know, *with certainty*, the exact period of its useful life nor its precise residual value at the end of that period. However, we must estimate these two factors at the time the asset is placed into service in order to determine the amount of the periodic amortization. Publications by various trade associations may be helpful in estimating residual values and the useful life of physical capital assets. However, there are no set rules for estimating either factor, and both may be affected by management policies. For example, a company that provides its salespersons with a new automobile every year will have different estimates than a company that keeps its cars for five years. Such variables as climate, use, and maintenance will also affect the estimates.

In addition to the many factors that may affect the useful life of an asset, you will find that firms use various degrees of accuracy in making the computations. For example, companies vary in how they treat a capital asset that was purchased part way through a fiscal year. Some firms adopt a policy of taking no amortization in the year they acquire an asset and a full year's amortization in the year in which they retire it. Others may take one-half year's amortization in both the year of acquisition and the year of retirement. Still others may compute amortization based on the number of months that they used the asset during the year. A month is normally the smallest unit of time used in computing amortization. In this case, the business may account for all assets placed in or taken out of service during the first half of a month as if the event occurred on the first day of that month. Likewise, all capital asset additions and deductions during the second half of a month are treated as if the event occurred on the first day of the next month. In the absence of any statement to the contrary, we will assume this practice throughout this text.

It is not necessary for a business to use a single method of computing amortization for all its physical assets. The amortization methods used in the accounts and financial statements may also differ from the amortization methods used in determining income taxes. The three methods used most often are (1) straight-line, (2) units-of-production, and (3) declining-balance.[5] Exhibit 3 indicates the results of a survey of the use of these methods by Canadian companies which use a single method only.

Exhibit 3
Use of Amortization Methods

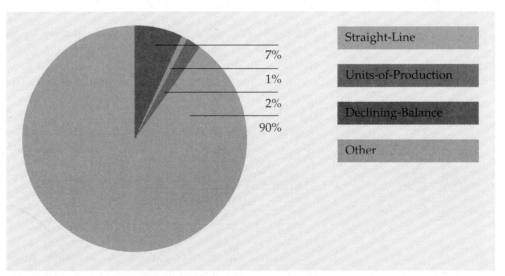

Source: *Financial Reporting in Canada in 1997*, 22nd ed. Canadian Institute of Chartered Accountants, Toronto, 1997.

[5] These methods were used in approximately 98% of 200 annual reports of Canadian public companies surveyed by the Canadian Institute of Chartered Accountants in *Financial Reporting in Canada in 1997*. Although there are other amortization methods, such as the sum-of-the-years digits and sinking fund method, we do not discuss them in this text, since they are so rarely used in Canada.

A considerable number of other companies in this survey reported using more than one method, for example, both straight line and declining balance or straight line and units of production, in recognition of the different characteristics of different types of assets.

STRAIGHT-LINE METHOD

The straight-line method provides for equal amounts of periodic expense over the estimated useful life of the asset. We calculate annual amortization expense by dividing the amortizable cost by the number of years of useful life. For example, assume that the cost of a capital asset is $16,000, its estimated residual value is $1,000, and its estimated life is five years. The annual amortization is computed as follows:

$$\frac{\$16,000 \text{ cost} - \$1,000 \text{ estimated residual value}}{5 \text{ years estimated life}} = \$3,000 \text{ annual amortization}$$

When we use an asset for only part of a year, we should prorate the annual amortization. For example, assume that the fiscal year ends on December 31 and that the asset in the above example is first used on October 5. The amortization for the first fiscal year of use is $750 ($3,000 × $\frac{3}{12}$), computed on the basis of three months usage. If usage begins in the second half of October, the amortization for the year is $500 ($3,000 × $\frac{2}{12}$).

For ease in applying the straight-line method, we can convert the annual amortization rate to a percentage of amortizable cost by dividing 100% by the number of years of useful life. For example, a useful life of 20 years converts to a 5% (100% ÷ 20) rate, 8 years converts to a 12.5% (100% ÷ 8) rate, and so on.[6] The straight-line rate in the above example is 20% (100% ÷ 5). The annual amortization of $3,000 can be computed by multiplying the amortizable cost of $15,000 by this rate.

The straight-line method is simple and is widely used. It provides a reasonable allocation of costs to periodic expense when the usage of the asset and the related revenues from its use are about the same from period to period.

UNITS-OF-PRODUCTION METHOD

The units-of-production amortization method yields amortization expense that varies with the asset's usage. To apply this method, we must express the useful life of the asset in terms of units of productive capacity such as hours or kilometres. We compute amortization per unit of production by dividing amortizable cost by the total productive capacity. We then determine the amortization for each accounting period by multiplying the unit amortization rate by the number of productive units used during the period. For example, assume that a machine with a cost of $16,000 and an estimated residual value of $1,000 is expected to have an estimated life of 10,000 operating hours. The amortization per hour of usage is:

$$\frac{\$16,000 \text{ cost} - \$1,000 \text{ estimated residual value}}{10,000 \text{ estimated hours}} = \$1.50 \text{ hourly amortization}$$

If the machine were in operation for 2,200 hours during a year, the amortization for that year would be $3,300 ($1.50 × 2,200 hours).

When the amount of use of a capital asset varies substantially from year to year, the units-of-production method is more appropriate than the straight-line method. In such cases, the units-of-production method better matches the allocation of cost (amortization expense) with the related revenue. However, it may be difficult to

---

[6] The amortization rate may also be expressed as a fraction. For example, the annual straight-line rate for an asset with a three-year useful life is $\frac{1}{3}$.

estimate the productive capacity of some physical assets, such as a building. Also, this method will be inappropriate if the usefulness of an asset is significantly affected by obsolescence, rather than just usage. For example, we would not amortize a computer on the basis of hours used, since the asset would likely lose its usefulness to the business long before it was physically "worn out."

DECLINING-BALANCE METHOD

The **declining-balance amortization method** generates a pattern of amortization that results in the highest expense in the early years with decreasing charges from year to year over the useful life of the asset. To compute amortization expense each period, we multiply the amortization rate times the **net book value** (also called carrying value) of the asset (acquisition cost minus accumulated amortization) at the beginning of each period. As accumulated amortization increases, the net book value (NBV) decreases, so that the rate is being multiplied by a declining balance each period. This results in decreasing amortization charges each year.

Various amortization rates could be used with the declining-balance method. Different rates may be appropriate for different types of assets, depending on the pattern of benefits that the asset will produce over its useful life. One commonly used method is the **double-declining method**. This method employs an amortization rate that is twice the rate that would be used if the asset were amortized over its useful life on a straight-line basis expressed on a percentage basis.

Let us consider the example that we used earlier in illustrating the straight-line method. The asset cost $16,000 with a residual value of $1,000 and an estimated life of five years. Under the straight-line method we amortized $\frac{1}{5}$ (or 20%) of the amortizable cost each year. Therefore, under the double-declining method we use an amortization rate of 40%, which is double the straight-line rate (2 × 20%). We then multiply this rate by the asset's net book value at the beginning of the year. For the first year we multiply 40% times the acquisition cost of $16,000. After the first year, we multiply the rate times the declining net book value (cost minus accumulated amortization) of the asset:

Year	Cost	Accum. Amor. at Beginning of Year	Book Value at Beginning of Year	Rate	Amortization for Year	Book Value at End of Year
1	$16,000	—	$16,000.00	40%	**$6,400.00**	$9,600.00
2	16,000	$ 6,400.00	9,600.00	40%	**3,840.00**	5,760.00
3	16,000	10,240.00	5,760.00	40%	**2,304.00**	3,456.00
4	16,000	12,544.00	3,456.00	40%	**1,382.40**	2,073.60
5	16,000	13,926.40	2,073.60	40%	**829.44**	1,244.16

You should note that, unlike the straight-line and units-of-production methods, you do not consider the residual value when you compute amortization expense each period using the declining-balance method. However, even under this method, you should not amortize the asset below its estimated residual value. In the above example, suppose we assume that the estimated residual value is $1,500 instead of $1,000. Then we could not record $829.44 for amortization expense in year 5, as this would reduce the net book value below the expected residual value of $1,500. In this case, we would charge amortization for the fifth year of only $573.60 ($2,073.60 – $1,500.00), so that the year-end carrying value of the asset would not be less than its residual value.

In the above illustration, we assumed that the business began to use the asset at the beginning of the fiscal year. This is often not the case in practice, however, and amortization for the first partial year of use must be computed. For example, assume that we placed the asset in service at the end of the third month of the fiscal year.

In this case, we allocate only a portion (⁹⁄₁₂) of the first full year's amortization of $6,400 to the first fiscal year. Thus, we record amortization of $4,800 (⁹⁄₁₂ × $6,400) for the first partial year of use. Thereafter, we compute the amortization for each succeeding year in the usual manner, by multiplying the amortization rate times the net book value at the beginning of the year. Thus, the amortization for the second fiscal year would be $4,480 [40% × ($16,000 − $4,800)].

COMPARING AMORTIZATION METHODS

The straight-line method provides for uniform periodic amounts of amortization expense over the life of the asset. The units-of-production method provides for periodic amounts of amortization expense that vary, depending upon the amount of usage of the asset each period.

The declining-balance method provides for a higher amortization amount in the first year of use of the asset, followed by a gradually declining amount each year. For this reason, the declining-balance method is often called an accelerated amortization method. It is most appropriate for situations in which the decline in an asset's productivity or earning power is greater in the early years of its use than in later years. Accountants sometimes justify using this method because repairs tend to increase with the age of the asset, so that the asset's *net* contribution to earnings declines as the asset gets older. Amortization is a process for expensing the cost of an asset in the periods in which it renders benefits to the business. In this case, the matching principle would suggest that we should record higher amortization expense in the early years because we are receiving more *net* benefits (after deducting repairs) from the asset when it is newer than when it is older.

The periodic amortization amounts for the straight-line method and the double-declining-balance method are compared in Exhibit 4. This comparison is based on an asset cost of $16,000, an estimated life of five years, and an estimated residual value of $1,000.

Exhibit 4
Comparing Amortization Methods

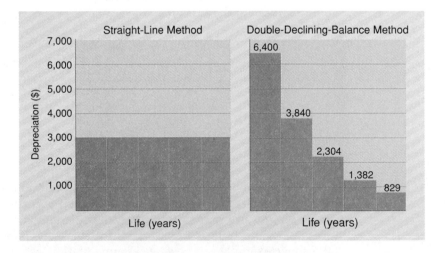

AMORTIZATION AND INCOME TAX

A business maintains its accounting records and reports its financial statements in accordance with generally accepted accounting principles. However, it must prepare its income tax returns in accordance with income tax laws. Quite often the regulations determining the measurement of taxable income will differ from the methods we have used to record transactions for financial accounting purposes.

In Canada, the Income Tax Act specifies that amortization (or depreciation) expense as reflected in financial statements is not an allowable deduction in determining taxable income for businesses. Instead, the Tax Act and related regulations set out an alternative system for determining a deduction from income for the use of capital assets. This deduction is called capital cost allowance (CCA). In many ways, CCA is similar to the declining-balance amortization method discussed above. Tax regulations set out how amortizable assets are to be grouped into various categories (called classes) and specify a maximum amortization rate for each asset group. Some examples of the rates for specific classes are shown below:

Class 1: Brick Buildings—4%
Class 8: Furniture, Equipment, and Machinery—20%
Class 10: Automobiles and Other Vehicles—30%

Often the tax rules change with each budget issued by the federal government. The government will sometimes offer higher rates for specific classes in order to provide incentives for businesses to invest in certain kinds of assets or in certain industries, such as the oil and gas industry.

A study of this system is beyond the scope of this text. For our purposes, it is sufficient to note that the amortization expense reported in a firm's financial statements will often differ from the CCA deducted in computing taxable income. This means that a business will have to maintain a separate set of records to keep track of the **undepreciated capital cost** (UCC) of its physical assets for tax purposes.

REVISION OF PERIODIC AMORTIZATION (CHANGE IN ESTIMATES)

Earlier in this chapter, we indicated that two of the factors used in computing the periodic amortization of a capital asset are (1) its estimated residual value and (2) its estimated useful life. We must estimate these factors at the time the asset is placed into service. Revisions of these estimates are normal and tend to be recurring. When such revisions occur, we use the revised estimates to determine the amortization expense in future periods.

To illustrate, assume management originally estimated that a capital asset purchased for $130,000 would have a useful life of 30 years and a residual value of $10,000. The asset has been amortized for 10 years by the straight-line method. At the end of 10 years, the asset's book value (unamortized cost) is $90,000, determined as follows:

Asset cost	$130,000
Less accumulated amortization ($4,000 per year × 10 years)	40,000
Net book value (unamortized cost), end of tenth year	**$ 90,000**

Early in the eleventh year, management estimates that the remaining useful life is 25 years (instead of 20) and that the residual value is $5,000 (instead of $10,000). The amortization expense for each of the remaining 25 years (beginning with year 11) is $3,400, computed as follows:

Net book value (unamortized cost), end of tenth year	**$90,000**
Less revised estimated residual value	5,000
Revised remaining amortizable cost	$85,000
Revised annual amortization expense ($85,000 ÷ 25)	**$ 3,400**

You should note that the revisions of the estimates used in determining amortization do not affect the amounts of amortization expense recorded in earlier years. Therefore, revisions only affect the current and future years' amortization expense.

RECORDING AMORTIZATION

We may record an adjusting entry for amortization at the end of each month or at the end of the year. As we discussed in an earlier chapter, the entry to record amortization is a debit to Amortization Expense and a credit to a contra asset account entitled Accumulated Amortization. The use of a contra asset account allows the original cost to remain unchanged in the capital asset account.

An exception to recording amortization only monthly or annually is made when a capital asset is sold, traded in, or scrapped. As we will illustrate, we record a disposal by removing from the accounts both the cost of the asset and its related accumulated amortization as of the date of the disposal. Therefore, we must ensure that we record amortization for the current period up to the date of the disposal before recording the disposal of the asset.

SUBSIDIARY LEDGERS FOR CAPITAL ASSETS

When we have to compute amortization on a large number of individual assets, we usually maintain a subsidiary ledger for the physical assets. For example, assume that a business owns 200 items of office equipment with a total cost of $100,000. Unless the business is new, it would have acquired the equipment over a number of years. The individual cost, estimated residual value, and estimated useful life may be different in each case. In addition, the makeup of the assets will continually change because of acquisitions and disposals.

We could maintain the subsidiary records for such assets using either a manual system or a computerized system. In either case, the business would keep a separate ledger account for each asset. The subsidiary ledger account, shown in Exhibit 5, provides spaces for recording the acquisition and the disposal of the asset, the amortization charged each period, the accumulated amortization to date, and the net book value. It may also include other relevant data useful to management.

The number assigned to the account in Exhibit 5 is made up of the number of the controlling account in the general ledger, Office Equipment (123), followed by the number assigned to the specific item of office equipment purchased (215). The business should attach a tag or plaque with the account number to the asset for control purposes. Amortization for the year in which the asset was acquired, computed for nine months on a straight-line basis, is $180. Amortization for the following year is $240. The subsidiary ledger provides the data for the adjusting entries for amortization at the end of each year.

When the firm disposes of an asset, we credit the asset section of the subsidiary account and debit the accumulated amortization section to reduce the balances of

Exhibit 5
An Account in the Office Equipment Ledger

PHYSICAL CAPITAL ASSET RECORD

Account No.: 123–215   **General Ledger Account:** Office Equipment
Item: SF 490 Copier   **Amortization Method:** Straight-Line
Serial No.: AT 47–3926
From Whom Purchased: Hamilton Office Machines Co.
Estimated Useful Life: 10 Years   **Estimated Residual Value:** $500   **Amor. per Year:** $240

| | Asset | | | Accumulated Amortization | | | Book |
Date	Debit	Credit	Balance	Debit	Credit	Balance	Value
04/08/98	2,900		2,900				2,900
12/31/98					180	180	2,720
12/31/98					240	420	2,480

both sections to zero. We then remove the account from the ledger and file for future reference.

Subsidiary ledgers for physical capital assets are useful to accountants for: (1) determining periodic amortization expense, (2) recording the disposal of individual items, (3) preparing tax returns, and (4) preparing insurance claims in the event of insured losses. We can also expand the subsidiary account forms to accumulate data regarding the number of breakdowns, length of time out of service, and cost of repairs. Such information may be useful to management in assessing the operating efficiency of the asset and in making decisions about which size or model to acquire when making future purchases.

AMORTIZATION OF CAPITAL ASSETS OF LOW UNIT COST

Businesses do not usually maintain subsidiary ledgers for classes of physical capital assets consisting of small individual items of low unit cost, such as hand tools, spare parts, or dishes and silverware for a restaurant. Because of hard usage, breakage, and pilferage, such assets may be relatively short-lived and may require frequent replacement.

For capital assets with a low unit cost, the usual amortization methods are generally not practical. One method of accounting for such assets is to expense them immediately when they are acquired. However, this treatment is not appropriate if the total cost of individual assets in this group is significant. Another method of accounting for assets with a low unit cost is to record them as assets when they are acquired. Then, at the end of the year, an inventory of the items on hand is taken, and their current value is estimated. The accountant then adjusts the asset account to the current value at the year end, by crediting the asset and debiting Amortization Expense.

COMPOSITE-RATE METHOD

In the preceding examples, we computed amortization for each individual asset. Another method, called the **composite-rate method,** determines amortization for groups of assets, using a single rate. The basis for grouping may be estimates of useful lives or other common traits. For example, a group may include all assets within a class, such as office equipment or vehicles.

The procedures for computing the composite rate are complex and the entries for recording asset disposals under this method differ from those used for individual assets. We do not cover these topics here, as they are included in more advanced accounting texts.

Capital and Revenue Expenditures

Objective 3
Classify capital asset costs as either capital expenditures or revenue expenditures.

Costs incurred to acquire physical capital assets, or to extend or improve the useful life of such assets, are called capital expenditures. We debit such expenditures to the asset account, although sometimes expenditures made after the original acquisition of the asset are debited to the related accumulated amortization account. Costs that benefit only the current period or costs incurred in order to maintain normal operating efficiency are called revenue expenditures. We debit these costs to expense accounts immediately in the period in which they are incurred.

It is important for a business to distinguish between capital and revenue expenditures in order to properly match expenses to revenues. Capital expenditures affect the amortization expense of more than one period, whereas revenue expenditures affect the expenses of only the current period.

CAPITAL EXPENDITURES

We discussed accounting for the initial costs of acquiring capital assets earlier in the chapter. In the following paragraphs, we discuss accounting for capital expenditures after a plant asset has been acquired. Two types of expenditures after acquisition are (1) additions and (2) betterments.

Additions to Capital Assets

An expenditure for an addition to a physical capital asset should be debited to an asset account. If the addition has the same remaining useful life as the original asset, we could debit the new cost to the original asset account. For example, we would debit the cost of adding a new wing to a building to the building account. If the addition has a different useful life than the original asset, we should record it in a separate asset account and amortize it over its useful life. For example, suppose we purchase a new air conditioning unit with an expected life of 10 years for a building that we expect to use for another 20 years. In this case, we would record the air conditioning unit in a separate asset account that would be amortized over a different period than we are amortizing the building.

Betterments

An expenditure that increases the operating efficiency or remaining useful life of a capital asset is called a **betterment**. We usually debit this capital expenditure to the related asset account. For example, suppose we replace the power unit attached to a machine by one of greater capacity. If we debit the cost of the new power unit to the machine account, we will amortize the expenditure over the remaining useful life of the machine. What if we estimate that the power unit will not last as long as the machine? Then we should debit its cost to a separate asset account and amortize it over its expected useful life.

At the same time that we capitalize the cost of the betterment, we should also remove the cost and the accumulated amortization related to the old power unit. But sometimes we may not know the cost of the old power unit (perhaps because it was attached to the machine when we made the original purchase). In this case, we might use an alternative accounting treatment for recording the betterment. Instead of debiting the cost of the new expenditure to the asset account, we could debit the amount to the related accumulated amortization account. The rationale for doing this is that the betterment has restored some of the benefits that we had amortized in prior years. The amortization for future periods will be computed on the basis of the revised net book value of the asset (original cost minus the revised accumulated amortization) and the revised estimate of the remaining useful life if this has changed.

For example, assume that a machine costing $50,000 has no estimated residual value and an estimated useful life of 10 years. Assume also that the machine has been amortized for six years by the straight-line method ($5,000 annual amortization). At the beginning of the seventh year, an $11,500 expenditure for a new motor increases the remaining useful life of the machine to seven years (instead of the four years originally anticipated). If we debit the $11,500 to Accumulated Amortization, the annual amortization for the remaining seven years of use would be $4,500, computed as follows:

Cost of machine		$50,000
Less Accumulated Amortization balance:		
Amortization for first six years ($5,000 × 6)	$30,000	
Deduct debit for betterment	11,500	
Balance of Accumulated Amortization		18,500
Revised book value of machine after betterment		$31,500
Annual amortization ($31,500 ÷ 7 years remaining useful life)		$ 4,500

REVENUE EXPENDITURES

We classify expenditures for normal maintenance and repairs as revenue expenditures. For example, we debit the cost of replacing tires on an automobile or the cost of repainting a building to expense accounts.

We usually also debit to expense accounts small expenditures that are insignificant in amount, even though they may have the qualities of capital expenditures. The saving in time and record-keeping effort justifies the small loss of accuracy. Some businesses establish a minimum dollar amount required to classify an item as a capital expenditure.

SUMMARY OF CAPITAL AND REVENUE EXPENDITURES

Exhibit 6 summarizes the accounting for capital and revenue expenditures related to capital assets.

Expenditures for normal maintenance, such as the cost of repainting a building, are debited to expense accounts.

Exhibit 6
Capital and Revenue Expenditures

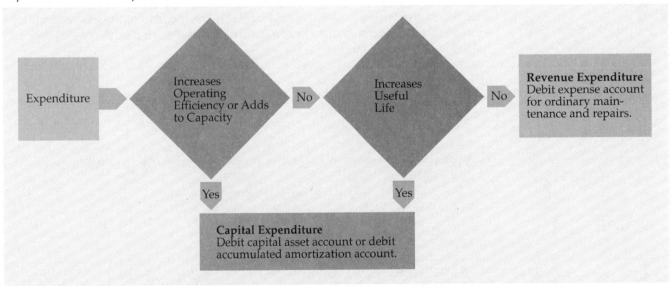

Disposal of Capital Assets

Objective 4
Journalize entries for the disposal of capital assets.

Physical capital assets that are no longer useful may be discarded, sold, or traded for other assets. The details of the entry to record a disposal will vary. In all cases, however, we must remove the net book value of the asset from the accounts by crediting the asset account for the cost of the asset and debiting the asset's accumulated amortization account for its balance on the date of disposal. As noted earlier, we must ensure that we have recorded amortization to the date of disposal before making these entries.

We do not remove a physical capital asset from the accounts just because it has been fully amortized. If the business is still using the asset, its cost and accumulated amortization should remain in the ledger. If we were to remove the asset from the ledger, the accounts would contain no evidence of its continued existence. In addition, we may still need to keep track of the cost and accumulated amortization for property tax and income tax reports.

DISCARDING CAPITAL ASSETS

When physical capital assets are no longer useful to the business and have no residual or market value, they are discarded. If the asset has been fully amortized and there are no costs for removing and disposing of the asset, no loss is realized. For example, assume that an item of equipment acquired at a cost of $25,000 is fully amortized at December 31, 1998. On February 14, 1999, the equipment is discarded. The entry to record this is as follows:

Feb. 14   Accumulated Amortization—Equipment   25,000
                 Equipment   25,000
                     To write off equipment discarded.

If an asset has not been fully amortized, we must record the amortization to date prior to removing it from service and from the accounting records. For example, assume that equipment costing $6,000 is amortized at an annual straight-line rate of 10%. On December 31, 1998, the accumulated amortization balance, after adjusting entries, is $4,750. On March 24, 1999, the firm removes the asset from service. First, we must record the amortization for the three months of 1999 prior to the asset's removal from service:

Mar. 24   Amortization Expense—Equipment   150
                 Accumulated Amortization—Equipment   150
                     To record current amortization on
                     equipment discarded. ($600 × $\frac{3}{12}$)

Then we record the disposal of the equipment by the following entry:

Mar. 24   Amortization Amortization—Equipment   4,900
                 Loss on Disposal of Plant Assets   1,100
                     Equipment   6,000
                         To write off equipment discarded.

In the preceding example, we recorded a loss of $1,100. This loss occurs because the balance of the accumulated amortization account ($4,900) is less than the balance in the equipment account ($6,000). Losses on the discarding of capital assets are non-operating items and are normally reported in the Other Expense section of the income statement.

SALE OF CAPITAL ASSETS

The entry to record the sale of a capital asset is similar to the entries illustrated above, except that we must also record the cash or other asset received when the asset is sold. If the selling price is more than the net book value of the asset, the transaction results in a gain. If the selling price is less than the net book value, there is a loss.

To illustrate, assume that equipment acquired January 1, year 1, at a cost of $10,000 is being amortized at an annual straight-line rate of 10%. The company has a December 31 fiscal year end and sells the equipment for cash on October 1, year 8. The balance of the accumulated amortization account as of December 31, year 7, is $7,000. The entry to update the amortization for the nine months of the current year is as follows:

Oct. 12	Amortization Expense—Equipment	750	
	Accumulated Amortization —Equipment		750
	To record current amortization on equipment sold.		
	($10,000 × 10% × 9/12)		

After we record the current amortization, the carrying value of the asset is $2,250 ($10,000 – $7,750). The entries to record the sale, assuming three different selling prices, are as follows:

Sold at book value, for $2,250. No gain or loss.

Oct. 12	Cash	2,250	
	Accumulated Amortization—Equipment	7,750	
	Equipment		10,000

Sold below book value, for $1,000. Loss of $1,250.

Oct. 12	Cash	1,000	
	Accumulated Amortization—Equipment	7,750	
	Loss on Disposal of Capital Assets	1,250	
	Equipment		10,000

Sold above book value, for $3,000. Gain of $750.

Oct. 12	Cash	3,000	
	Accumulated Amortization—Equipment	7,750	
	Equipment		10,000
	Gain on Disposal of Capital Assets		750

EXCHANGES OF CAPITAL ASSETS

Sometimes a business will dispose of a physical asset by trading it in for another capital asset. In such cases, the seller allows the buyer an amount for the old asset traded in. This amount, which may be either greater or less than the net book value of the old asset, is called the trade-in allowance. If the fair market value of the new asset exceeds the trade-in allowance for the old asset, the buyer will have to pay cash and/or incur a liability for the difference. This additional amount due from the buyer is called the **monetary consideration** given in the exchange of assets.

How should you account for such an exchange transaction? At what amount should you record the new asset? If the trade-in allowance is not equal to the net book value of the old asset, should you record a gain or loss on the disposal of the old asset? There are basically two ways of accounting for the transaction. Which one is correct depends on whether or not the exchange is considered equivalent to a sale of the old asset. (1) If the exchange is regarded as similar to a sale *in which the earnings process is complete,* we should record the new asset at its fair market value and recognize any gain or loss on disposal of the asset. (2) If not, we should record the new asset at the book value (rather than the market value) of the transaction with no gain or loss recorded.

The *CICA Handbook* Section 3830 outlines when it is appropriate to use each of these methods of accounting for exchange transactions. We should consider the earnings process complete and use method (1) if either (a) the assets exchanged are dissimilar or (b) the monetary consideration involved in the exchange represents at least 10% of the fair value of the total transaction. Thus, we use method (2) only when an asset is exchanged for a similar asset with little or no cash involved in the transaction.

We can illustrate these rules using the following examples involving a business that exchanges equipment with an original acquisition cost of $100,000 and accumulated amortization of $25,000.

Situation (1): Earnings Process Considered Complete

(a) Exchange Involving Dissimilar Assets

The equipment is exchanged for land with a fair value of $90,000. The required journal entry removes the old asset from the books by crediting the asset for its original cost ($100,000) and debiting accumulated amortization ($25,000). We debit Land for its fair market value ($90,000) and recognize the gain on disposal for the difference between the fair value of the new asset received and the net book value of the asset given up ($90,000 – $75,000 = $15,000).

Land	90,000	
Accumulated amortization	25,000	
Equipment		100,000
Gain on disposal of equipment		15,000

(b) Exchange Involving Similar Assets and Significant Monetary Consideration

The business buys similar new equipment with a fair value of $90,000 in exchange for the old equipment and a cash payment of $10,000. Similar to the situation above, the required journal entry removes the original cost and accumulated amortization of the old asset from the books and records the new asset at its fair market value. We credit cash for the payment to and recognize the gain on disposal for the difference between the fair value of the new asset received and the net book value of the assets given up ($90,000 – $75,000 – $10,000 = $5,000).

Equipment (new)	90,000	
Accumulated amortization	25,000	
Equipment (old)		100,000
Cash		10,000
Gain on disposal of equipment		5,000

In this example, we have recorded the new asset at its fair value. You should be aware that the fair value of the new asset often differs from its **list price.** For example, purchasers rarely pay the list or "sticker" price for a new car. The list price is set above what the dealer will accept in order to "leave room" for negotiation and bargaining. In the case illustrated above, assume that the new equipment had a list price of $92,000. However, the dealer would sell it for $90,000 cash. Here, the cash amount that the seller is willing to accept represents the fair value of the vehicle. The dealer might tell you that she was allowing you a trade-in allowance for your old equipment of $82,000 off the list price of $92,000 by asking you to pay the remaining $10,000 in cash. Should you record the new equipment at $92,000 and recognize a gain of $7,000 on disposal of the old equipment? No! You should not record the new equipment at more than its cash value of $90,000. You should ignore the list price and use the fair value for recording the new asset.

Situation (2): Earnings Process Not Considered Complete

Exchange of Similar Assets With Little or No Monetary Consideration

This situation is the same as (1) (b) above, except that the cash payment involved in the transaction is only $5,000 (less than 10% of the fair value of the new equipment being acquired). Following the *CICA Handbook,* we record the new equipment at the net book value of the assets given up ($5,000 cash plus $75,000 net book value of the old equipment), recognizing no gain on the disposal of the old equipment.

Equipment (new)	80,000	
Accumulated amortization	25,000	
Equipment (old)		100,000
Cash		5,000

Leasing Capital Assets

Objective 5
Define a lease and summarize the accounting rules related to the leasing of plant assets.

A business may acquire the use of a capital asset through a lease. A **lease** is a contract for the use of an asset for a stated period of time. The two parties to a lease contract are the lessor and the lessee. The **lessor** is the party who is the legal owner of the asset. The **lessee** is the party to whom the rights to use the asset are granted by the lessor. The lessee is obligated to make periodic rent payments for the lease term. Companies often lease assets such as automobiles, computers, medical equipment, buildings, and airplanes. Of the companies surveyed in the 1995 edition of *Financial Reporting in Canada*, 77% reported some type of lease arrangements.

For accounting purposes we classify leases into two categories. One type of lease, which we call an operating lease, represents a true rental arrangement, permitting the lessee temporary use of an asset that will ultimately be returned to its owner, the lessor. For example, you might lease a car for a week when you are out of town. The other type of lease, which we call a capital lease, is really similar to a purchase agreement, whereby the lessee assumes substantially all of the benefits and risks of ownership of the leased property.[7] Suppose you sign a five-year contract to lease a new car from a Ford dealership. During the term of the lease you are responsible for all maintenance and insurance on the vehicle, and you have the right to purchase the car at the end of the lease term for a nominal amount. In this case, the lease arrangement is really no different than purchasing the vehicle under a long-term payment plan.

We consider that a lease has transferred the benefits and risks of ownership to the lessee and classify it as a capital lease if it includes at least one of the following elements:

1. The lessee will likely obtain ownership of the asset at the end of the lease term.
2. The lease term extends over most of the economic life of the asset.
3. The value of the rental payments approximate the fair market value of the asset.[8]

We account for a capital lease as if the lessee has, in fact, purchased the asset. The lessee debits a capital asset account for the approximate fair market value of the asset (based on the lease payments) and credits a long-term lease liability account. We amortize the leased property over its useful life in the same manner as for other capital assets. Each lease payment consists of interest on the liability and a partial payment of the principal of the obligation. The accounting for capital leases is discussed in detail in more advanced accounting texts.

We classify leases that do not meet the preceding criteria as **operating leases.** The rentals of assets described in the earlier chapters of this text were accounted for as operating leases. Here, the lessee simply records the lease payments as rent expense, recognizing neither the leased asset nor the lease liability in the accounts. However, the lessee must disclose future lease commitments in footnotes to the financial statements.[9]

---

[7] *CICA Handbook,* Section 3065, paragraph .09.
[8] *Ibid.,* paragraph .06.
[9] *Ibid.,* paagraph .32.

Internal Control of Physical Capital Assets

Objective 6
Describe internal controls over physical capital assets and provide examples of such controls.

Because of the dollar value and the long-term nature of physical capital assets, it is important to design and implement effective internal controls over them. Such controls should begin with authorization and approval procedures for the purchase of these assets. Procedures should also exist to ensure that capital assets are acquired at the lowest possible costs. One procedure to achieve this objective is to require competitive bids from preapproved vendors.

Like the assets we discussed in earlier chapters, the business must safeguard capital assets from possible theft, misuse, or other damage. For example, those assets that are highly marketable and susceptible to theft, such as computers, should be locked or otherwise safeguarded when not in use. For computers, safeguarding includes proper consideration of climate controls and special fire-extinguishing equipment. Procedures should also exist for training employees to properly operate assets such as equipment and machinery. The company should also insure these assets against theft, fire, flooding, or other disasters.

As soon as a physical capital asset is received, it should be inspected and tagged for control purposes, and an entry should be made in the plant asset subsidiary ledger. A company that maintains a computerized subsidiary ledger may use bar-coded tags, similar to the one on the back of this textbook, so that plant asset data can be directly scanned into computer records.

The company should take a physical inventory of tangible capital assets periodically in order to verify the accuracy of the accounting records. Such an inventory would detect missing, obsolete, or idle plant assets. In addition, capital assets should be inspected periodically in order to determine their state of repair.

The company must also exercise careful control over the disposal of capital assets. All disposals should be properly authorized and approved. Fully amortized assets should be retained in the accounting records until disposal has been authorized and they are removed from service. In this way, the business can maintain accountability for the asset throughout the period of ownership.

Natural Resources and Depletion

Objective 7
Define natural resources, compute depletion, and journalize the entry for depletion.

Natural resources include items such as timber, oil, gas, and metal ores that are removed from the ground. These are also called **wasting assets,** because their removal results in the physical consumption of the natural resource. The amount that is capitalized in the natural resource account includes the costs of (1) acquiring the property; (2) exploring the property to locate the natural resource; and (3) developing the property.

As the natural resource is removed from the property, we must record the amortization of this capital asset. The amortization of a natural resource is called depletion. Computing depletion is similar to determining amortization using the units-of-production method. We calculate a depletion rate by dividing the total costs recorded in the natural resource account by the estimated units we expect to produce from the asset. The amount of periodic depletion is determined by multiplying the units extracted during the period by the depletion rate.

Unlike the amortization of other capital assets, we do not record depletion directly to an expense account. This occurs because, when the natural resource is extracted, it will usually be held in inventory until it is sold. We will record the cost as an expense on the income statement (as cost of goods sold) in the period when the inventory is sold.

To illustrate, we assume that a mining company paid $200,000 to purchase a property. The company incurred $300,000 in exploration and development costs to locate and prepare the mineral deposit for extraction. The entries to record these costs are as follows:

Natural resource	200,000	
Cash		200,000
To record the purchase of the property.		

Natural resource	300,000	
Cash		300,000
To record the exploration and development costs.		

The company estimated that the property contains 1,000,000 tons of ore. Therefore, the depletion rate is $0.50 per ton ($500,000 ÷ 1,000,000 tons). If 100,000 tons are mined during the year, the company would record:

Ore Inventory	50,000	
Accumulated Depletion—Natural Resource		50,000
To record the depletion of the natural resource		
(100,000 tons @ $0.50 per ton).		

Like the accumulated amortization account, the Accumulated Depletion account is a contra asset account. We report it on the balance sheet as a deduction from the cost of the Natural Resources. Note that Inventory is a current asset, whereas Natural Resources is a noncurrent asset. When the inventory is sold, we will make an entry to credit Inventory and debit Cost of Goods Sold.

Intangible Capital Assets

Objective 8
Journalize the entries for acquiring and amortizing intangible assets, such as patents, copyrights, and goodwill.

Long-term assets that are without physical attributes and not held for sale but are useful in the operations of a business are intangible assets. Intangible assets include such items as patents, copyrights, and goodwill.

The basic principles of accounting for intangible assets are like those described earlier for physical capital assets. The major concerns are (1) determining the initial cost and (2) recognizing the periodic cost expiration. Amortization results from the passage of time or a decline in the usefulness of the intangible asset.

PATENTS

Manufacturers may acquire exclusive rights to produce and sell goods with one or more unique features. Such rights are granted by **patents,** which the federal government issues to inventors. These rights continue in effect for 17 years. A business may purchase patent rights from others, or it may obtain patents developed by its own research and development efforts.

We debit the initial cost of a purchased patent to an asset account. We amortize the cost (usually on a straight-line basis) over the years of the patent's expected usefulness. This period of time may be less than the remaining legal life of the patent.

The estimated useful life of the patent may also change as technology or consumer tastes change.

We do not usually use a separate contra asset account to record the accumulated amortization of patents. We normally record the credit directly in the patents account. This practice is common for all intangible assets.

To illustrate, assume that at the beginning of its fiscal year a business acquires patent rights for $100,000. The patent had been granted six years earlier by the Federal Patent Office. Although the patent will not expire for 11 years, we estimate that its remaining useful life is five years. The entry to amortize the patent at the end of the fiscal year is as follows:

The exclusive right to sell a creative work like "The Lion King" is granted by a copyright issued by the federal government.

	Adjusting Entry		
Dec. 31	Amortization Expense—Patents	20,000	
	Patents		20,000

Assume that after two years of use it appears that this patent will have only two years of remaining usefulness. The cost to be amortized in the third year is $30,000, which is the balance of the asset account, $60,000 ($100,000 – $40,000), divided by two years.

Rather than purchase patent rights, a business may incur significant costs in developing patents through its own research and development efforts. The *CICA Handbook* sets out detailed recommendations for determining what expenditures should be defined in research and development costs, and which of these costs may be capitalized as intangible assets.[10] The study of these recommendations and procedures is the subject of more advanced accounting texts.

Whether patent rights are purchased or developed internally, a business often incurs significant legal fees related to patents. For example, legal fees may be incurred in filing for patents or in defending the legal rights to patents. We debit such fees to the asset account and then amortize them over the remaining years of usefulness of the patents.

COPYRIGHTS

The exclusive right to publish and sell a literary, artistic, or musical composition is granted by a **copyright.** Copyrights are issued by the federal government and extend for 50 years beyond the author's death. The costs of a copyright include all costs of creating the work plus any administrative or legal costs of obtaining the copyright. A copyright that is purchased from another should be recorded at the price paid for it. Because of the uncertainty regarding the useful life of a copyright, we normally amortize it over a short period of time. For example, the copyright costs of this text are amortized over three years.

GOODWILL

In business, goodwill refers to an intangible asset of a business that is created from such favourable factors as location, product quality, reputation, and managerial skill. Goodwill allows a business to earn a rate of return on its investment that is often in excess of the normal rate for other firms in the same business.

Generally accepted accounting principles permit the recording of goodwill in the accounts only if its value can be objectively determined by an exchange transaction. This means that a company cannot record goodwill that it has built up for itself. However, it may record goodwill acquired when it purchases another business.

[10]*CICA Handbook*, Section 3450.

Goodwill is sometimes called the **unidentifiable intangible asset.** Unlike, say, a patent that we can buy or sell, goodwill cannot be identified or purchased separately from the business as a whole. If a business is worth more than the fair value of the net assets that we can identify, then the excess amount must be due to goodwill.

For example, suppose that we pay $100,000 to purchase a business whose balance sheet reports assets of $120,000 and liabilities of $50,000. Since the net book value of the business is only $70,000 ($120,000 − $50,000), why would we pay $100,000 for it? One reason might be that the fair value of some assets is really higher than their cost, which is shown on the balance sheet. Another reason might be that the business has very good personnel and has a good reputation, valuable qualities that are not included on its balance sheet.

In the above example, assume that the business owns land with a fair value of $50,000 that is reported at cost on its balance sheet at $35,000. We can then calculate the amount that we are paying for the company's goodwill as follows:

Purchase price of business acquired	$100,000
Less net book value of business ($120,000 − $50,000)	(70,000)
Excess paid over net book value	$ 30,000
Due to fair value of land in excess of cost ($50,000 − $35,000)	(15,000)
Amount paid for goodwill (unidentifiable intangible)	$ 15,000

As for other intangible assets, we must record purchased goodwill as an asset and amortize it over its useful life. Generally accepted accounting practice requires that goodwill be amortized over a period of not more than 40 years.[11] The 1997 edition of *Financial Reporting in Canada* indicates that goodwill was by far the most commonly reported intangible asset, with almost half of the companies surveyed reporting this asset.

Financial Reporting for Physical Capital Assets and Intangible Capital Assets

Objective 9
Describe how amortization expense is reported in an income statement and prepare a balance sheet that includes physical capital assets and intangible assets.

How should a business report its capital assets in its financial statements? The firm should disclose the amount of amortization expense for a period, along with a description of the method(s) and rates used in computing this expense.[12] The business may present this information either in the income statement or in the notes accompanying the financial statements. The company should also disclose, either on the balance sheet or the notes, the amount of each major class of capital assets and the related accumulated amortization.[13]

The cost and accumulated depletion of natural resources is normally presented in the physical capital assets section of the balance sheet. In some cases, the balance sheet reports these net of depletion, with the accumulated depletion shown in the notes.

Companies usually report their intangible assets on the balance sheet in a separate section immediately following physical capital assets. The business should disclose, either on the balance sheet or in the notes, each major class of intangible assets net of amortization taken to date.

Exhibit 7 illustrates how Torstar Corporation reports both its physical capital assets and its intangible assets in its financial statements:

[11]*CICA Handbook*, Section 1580, paragraph 58.
[12]*CICA Handbook*, Section 3060, paragraph 60.
[13]*Ibid.*, Section 3060, paragraph 58.

Exhibit 7
*Capital and Intangible Assets
in the Balance Sheet*

Balance Sheet Disclosure

December 31, 1996 and 1995
(thousands of dollars)

	1996	1995
Assets		
Property, plant, and equipment (net) (Note 3)	433,566	436,342
Goodwill and other assets (Note 4)	498,577	373,018

Notes to Financial Statements

Note 1   Accounting Policies (in part)

(g) Property, plant, and equipment
These assets are recorded at cost and depreciated over their estimated useful lives. The rates and methods used for the major depreciable assets are:

Buildings:
 • straight-line over 25 years or 5% diminishing balance

Leasehold Improvements:
 • straight-line over the life of the lease

Machinery and Equipment:
 • straight-line over 10 to 20 years or 20% diminishing balance

(h) Goodwill and other assets
Goodwill is amortized on a straight-line basis primarily over a period of 40 years from the date of acquisition of operations. The company assesses whether there has been a permanent impairment in the carrying value of goodwill by determining whether the unamortized goodwill balance can be recovered based on the fair value of the operation. The cost of a distribution services agreement is amortized on a straight-line basis over the 10-year term of the agreement.

Note 3   Property, Plant, and Equipment

	Cost	Accumulated Depreciation	Net
1996			
Land	$ 12,983	–	$ 12,983
Buildings and leasehold improvements	190,095	$ 47,729	142,366
Machinery and equipment	487,723	209,506	278,217
Total	$690,801	$257,235	$433,566
1995			
Land	$ 8,962	–	$ 8,962
Buildings and leasehold improvements	181,606	$ 39,817	141,789
Machinery and equipment	462,886	177,295	285,591
Total	$653,454	$217,112	$436,342

Note 4   Goodwill and Other Assets

	1996	1995
Goodwill at amortized cost	$438,064	$340,349
Deferred pension charges	16,553	11,072
Distribution Services Agreement (Note 9)	21,260	–
Investment in associated business	–	4,771
Non-interest bearing executive stock loans (Note 6(a)(i))	1,075	2,456
Other Torstar	4,583	6,995
Other Hebdo Mag	17,042	7,375
	$498,577	$373,018

Source: CICA, *Financial Reporting in Canada 1997*, 22nd ed., Toronto, 1997, pp. 211–12.

KEY POINTS

Objective 1. Define physical capital assets and describe the accounting for their cost.

Physical capital assets are long-term tangible assets that are owned by the business and are used in the normal operations of the business. Examples are equipment, buildings, and land. The initial cost of the asset includes all amounts spent to get the asset in place and ready for use. For example, sales tax, freight, insurance in transit, and installation costs are all included in the cost of the asset. As time passes, all such assets except land lose their ability to provide services. As a result, we must transfer the cost of the asset to an expense account, in a systematic manner, during the asset's expected useful life. This periodic cost expiration is called amortization.

Objective 2. Compute amortization, using the following methods: straight-line method, units-of-production method, and declining-balance method.

In computing amortization, we need to consider three factors: (1) the asset's initial cost, (2) the useful life of the asset, and (3) the residual value of the asset.

The straight-line method spreads the initial cost less the residual value equally over the useful life. The units-of-production method spreads the initial cost less the residual value equally over the units produced by the asset during its useful life. The declining-balance method is applied by multiplying the declining net book value of the asset by the amortization rate.

Objective 3. Classify capital asset costs as either capital expenditures or revenue expenditures.

We classify costs for additions to physical capital assets and other costs related to improving efficiency or capacity as capital expenditures. Expenditures that benefit only the current period or that maintain normal operating efficiency are debited to expense accounts and are classified as revenue expenditures.

Objective 4. Journalize entries for the disposal of physical capital assets.

Before recording the disposal of a capital asset, first ensure that amortization has been recorded for the current period up to the disposal date. In accounting for the disposal: (1) debit cash or the appropriate asset account for any other assets received as proceeds, and (2) remove the net book value of the asset from the books by crediting the asset account for the cost of the asset and debiting the asset's accumulated amortization account. If (1) the proceeds received, exceed (2), the net book value of the old asset, the difference is credited to a revenue account (gain on disposal). If (1) is less than (2), the difference is debited to an expense account (loss on disposal). When the old asset is exchanged for another capital asset, the new asset is usually recorded at its fair market value. The only exception is where similar assets are exchanged with little or no monetary consideration involved. In this case, record the new asset at the book value of the exchange.

Objective 5. Define a lease and summarize the accounting rules related to the leasing of capital assets.

A lease is a contract for the use of an asset for a period of time. A capital lease is accounted for as if the lessee has purchased the asset. The lease payments under an operating lease are accounted for as rent expense for the lessee.

Objective 6. Describe internal controls over physical capital assets and provide examples of such controls.

Internal controls over capital assets should include procedures for authorizing the purchase of assets. Once acquired, plant assets should be safeguarded from theft, misuse, or damage. A physical inventory of plant assets should be taken periodically.

Objective 7. Define natural resources, compute depletion, and journalize the entry for depletion.

Natural resources are wasting assets such as timber, oil, gas, and mineral deposits, which are physically consumed as they are removed from the ground. Compute the depletion rate by dividing the total cost of the asset by the total estimated units of output in the natural resource property. Record periodic depletion by multiplying the depletion rate by the units extracted from the property during the period. To record depletion, credit accumulated depletion and debit inventory. When the inventory is sold, the cost will be recorded through the income statement.

Objective 8. Journalize the entries for acquiring and amortizing intangible assets, such as patents, copyrights, and goodwill.

Long-term assets that are without physical attributes but are used in the business are classified as intangible assets. Examples of intangible assets are patents, copyrights, and goodwill. We debit the initial cost of an intangible asset to an asset account. This cost should be amortized over the years of the asset's expected usefulness by debiting an expense account and crediting the intangible asset account.

Objective 9. Describe how amortization expense is reported in an income statement and prepare a balance sheet that includes physical capital assets and intangible assets.

The financial statements should disclose the amount of amortization expense and the method or methods used in computing amortization. In addition, each major class of physical capital assets should be disclosed, along with the related accumulated amortization. Intangible assets are usually presented in the balance sheet in a separate section immediately following physical capital assets. Each major class of intangible assets should be disclosed at an amount net of the amortization recorded to date.

GLOSSARY OF KEY TERMS

Accelerated amortization method. An amortization method that provides for a high amortization expense in the first year of use of an asset and a gradually declining expense thereafter. *Objective 2*

Amortization. The periodic expense attributed to the decline in usefulness of a capital asset. *Objective 2*

Betterment. An expenditure that increases operating efficiency, productive capacity, and/or useful life of a capital asset. *Objective 3*

Capital asset. Long-term assets (tangible and intangible) controlled by a business that are used in normal business operations and not intended for resale. *Objective 2*

Capital cost allowance (CCA). Deduction allowed for amortization expense of physical capital assets in computing taxable income. Rates and methods of computing CCA are specified by the Income Tax Act. *Objective 2*

Capital expenditures. Costs that add to the usefulness of capital assets for more than one accounting period and increase the operating efficiency, productive capacity, and/or useful life of the asset. *Objective 3*

Capital leases. Leases that transfer substantially all of the benefits and risks of ownership of the leased property from the lessor to the lessee. *Objective 5*

Declining-balance amortization method. A method of amortization that provides declining periodic amortization expense over the estimated life of an asset. *Objective 2*

Depletion. The cost of natural resources removed from the earth. *Objective 7*

Double-declining-balance amortization method. Declining-balance amortization method using twice the straight-line rate. *Objective 2*

Goodwill. An intangible asset of a business due to such favorable factors as location, product superiority, reputation, and managerial skill. May only be recorded when a business is purchased. *Objective 8*

Intangible assets. Long-lived assets that are useful in the operations of a business, are not held for sale, and are without physical qualities. *Objective 8*

Natural resources. Wasting assets such as timber, oil, gas, and mineral deposits, which are physically consumed as they are removed from the ground. *Objective 7*

Net book value. The cost of a capital asset minus the accumulated amortization on the asset. *Objective 2*

Operating leases. Leases that do not meet the criteria for capital leases and are accounted for as rent expenses. *Objective 5*

Physical capital assets. Long-lived tangible assets used in the operations of a business and not held for resale. *Objective 1*

Residual value. The estimated recoverable cost of a capital asset as of the time of its removal from service. *Objective 2*

Revenue expenditures. Expenditures that do not increase the productive capacity or useful life of a capital asset. *Objective 3*

Straight-line amortization method. A method that provides for equal periodic amortization expense over the estimated life of an asset. *Objective 2*

Trade-in allowance. The amount a seller grants a buyer for a capital asset that is traded in for another asset. *Objective 4*

Units-of-production amortization method. A method that provides for amortization expense based on the productive output of the asset during a period proportionate to the total expected productive capacity of the asset over its lifetime. *Objective 2*

ILLUSTRATIVE PROBLEM

McCollum Company, a furniture wholesaler, acquired new equipment at a cost of $150,000 at the beginning of the fiscal year. The equipment has an estimated life of five years and an estimated residual value of $12,000. Ellen McCollum, the president, has requested information regarding alternative amortization methods.

Instructions

1. Determine the annual amortization for each of the five years of estimated useful life of the equipment, the accumulated amortization at the end of each year, and the net book value of the equipment at the end of each year by (a) the straight-line method and (b) the double declining-balance method.

2. Assume that the equipment was amortized under the double-declining-balance method. In the first week of the fifth year, the equipment was traded in for similar equipment with a list price of $180,000 and a fair market value of $175,000. The trade-in allowance on the old equipment was $10,000, and cash was paid for the balance. Journalize the entry to record the exchange.

Solution

1.

Year	Amortization Expense	Accumulated Amortization, End of Year	Net Book Value, End of Year
a. 1	$27,600*	$ 27,600	$122,400
2	27,600	55,200	94,800
3	27,600	82,800	67,200
4	27,600	110,400	39,600
5	27,600	138,000	12,000

*$27,600 = ($150,000 − $12,000) ÷ 5

b. 1	$60,000**	$ 60,000	$90,000
2	36,000	96,000	54,000
3	21,600	117,600	32,400
4	12,960	130,560	19,440
5	7,440***	138,000	12,000

**$60,000 = $150,000 × 40%
***The asset is not amortized below the estimated residual value of $12,000.

2.

a.			
Accumulated Amortization—Equipment		130,560	
Equipment (new)		175,000	
Loss on Disposal of Equipment		9,440	
Equipment (old)			150,000
Cash			165,000

SELF-EXAMINATION QUESTIONS (ANSWERS AT END OF CHAPTER)

1. Which of the following expenditures incurred in connection with the acquisition of machinery is a proper charge to the asset account?
   A. Freight
   B. Installation costs
   C. Both A and B
   D. Neither A nor B

2. What is the amount of amortization, using the double-declining-balance method for the second year of use for equipment costing $9,000, with an estimated residual value of $600 and an estimated life of three years?
   A. $6,000
   B. $3,000
   C. $2,000
   D. $400

3. An example of an accelerated amortization method is:
   A. Straight-line
   B. Declining-balance
   C. Units-of-production
   D. Depletion

4. A physical capital asset priced at $100,000 is acquired by trading in a similar asset that has a net book value of $25,000. Assuming that the trade-in allowance is $30,000 and that $70,000 cash is paid for the new asset, what is the cost of the new asset for financial reporting purposes?
   A. $100,000
   B. $95,000
   C. $70,000
   D. $30,000

5. Which of the following is an example of an intangible asset?
   A. Patents
   B. Goodwill
   C. Copyrights
   D. All of the above

DISCUSSION QUESTIONS

1. Which of the following qualities are characteristic of physical capital assets? (a) tangible, (b) capable of repeated use in the operations of the business, (c) held for sale in the normal course of business, (d) long-lived.
2. Buckner Office Equipment Co. has a fleet of automobiles and trucks for use by salespersons and for delivery of office supplies and equipment. Ellsworth Auto Sales Co. has automobiles and trucks for sale. Under what caption would we report the automobiles

and trucks on the balance sheet of (a) Buckner Office Equipment Co., (b) Ellsworth Auto Sales Co.?

3. T. Camarillo Co. acquired an adjacent vacant lot with the hope of selling it in the future at a gain. The lot is not intended to be used in Camarillo's business operations. Where should such real estate be listed in the balance sheet?

4. Terminix Company solicited bids from several contractors to construct an addition to its office building. The lowest bid received was for $140,000. Terminix Company decided to construct the addition itself at a cost of $125,000. What amount should be recorded in the building account?

5. Are the amounts at which capital assets are reported in the balance sheet their approximate market values as of the balance sheet date? Discuss.

6. a. Does the recognition of amortization in the accounts provide a special fund for the replacement of plant assets? Explain.
   b. Describe the nature of amortization as the term is used in accounting.

7. Name the three factors that need to be considered in determining the amount of periodic amortization.

8. Nordhoff Company purchased a machine that has a manufacturer's suggested life of 15 years. The company plans to use the machine on a special project that will last six years. At the completion of the project, the machine will be sold. Over how many years should the company amortize the machine?

9. Is it necessary for a business to use the same method of computing amortization (a) in the financial statements, and (b) in determining income taxes?

10. Of the three common amortization methods, which is most widely used?

11. a. Under what conditions is the use of an accelerated amortization method most appropriate?
    b. What is meant by the terms "Capital Cost Allowance" and "Undepreciated Capital Cost"?

12. A revision of amortized capital asset lives resulted in an increase in the remaining lives of certain capital assets. The company would like to include, as income of the current period, the cumulative effect of the changes, which reduce the amortization expense of past periods. Is this in accordance with generally accepted accounting principles? Discuss.

Source: "Q's and A's Technical Hotline," *Journal of Accountancy*, December 1991, p. 89.

13. a. Differentiate between capital expenditures and revenue expenditures.
    b. Why are some items that have the characteristics of capital expenditures treated as revenue expenditures?

14. Immediately after acquiring a used truck, a company installed a new motor and replaced the tires at a total cost of $3,950. Is this a capital expenditure or a revenue expenditure? Explain.

15. For some of the capital assets of a business, the balance in Accumulated Amortization is exactly equal to the cost of the asset. (a) Is it permissible to record additional amortization on the assets if they are still useful to the business? Explain. (b) When should you make an entry to remove the cost and the accumulated amortization from the accounts?

16. In what sections of the income statement should you report gains and losses from the disposal of capital assets?

17. Differentiate between a capital lease and an operating lease.

18. The financial statements of **La-Z-Boy Chair Company** contain the following footnote:

The Company has several long-term leases covering manufacturing facilities. The lease agreements require the Company to insure and maintain the facilities and provide for annual payments, which include interest. These leases give the Company the option to purchase the facilities for nominal amounts, or in some instances to renew the leases for extended periods at nominal annual rentals.

Would these leases be classified as operating or capital leases? Discuss.

19. Describe the internal controls for acquiring physical capital assets.

20. Why is a physical count of physical capital assets necessary?

21. What is the term applied to the periodic charge for ore removed from a mine?

22. a. Over what period of time should the cost of a patent acquired by purchase be amortized?
    b. In general, what is the required treatment for goodwill?

23. How should (a) physical capital assets and (b) intangible assets be reported in the balance sheet?

EXERCISES

EXERCISE 10–1
Costs of acquiring capital assets
Objective 1

Marie Alfuri owns and operates Quality Print Co. During July, Quality Print Co. incurred the following costs in acquiring two printing presses. One printing press was new, and the other was used by a business that recently filed for bankruptcy.

Costs related to new printing press:

1. Sales tax on purchase price
2. Freight
3. Insurance while in transit
4. Special foundation
5. New parts to replace those damaged in unloading
6. Fee paid to factory representative for installation

Costs related to secondhand printing press:

7. Freight
8. Installation
9. Repair of vandalism during installation
10. Replacement of worn-out parts
11. Repair of damage incurred in reconditioning the press
12. Fees paid to attorney to review purchase agreement

a. Indicate which costs incurred in acquiring the new printing press you should debit to the asset account.
b. Indicate which costs incurred in acquiring the secondhand printing press you should debit to the asset account.

EXERCISE 10–2
Determining cost of land
Objective 1

A company has developed a tract of land into a ski resort. The company has cut the trees, cleared and graded the land and hills, and constructed ski lifts. (a) Should the tree cutting, land clearing, and grading costs of constructing the ski slopes be debited to the land account? (b) If such costs are debited to Land, should they be amortized?

Source: "Technical Issues Feature," *Journal of Accountancy,* December 1987, p. 82.

EXERCISE 10–3
Determining cost of land
Objective 1

Same-Day Delivery Company acquired an adjacent lot to construct a new warehouse, paying $20,000 and giving a short-term note for $80,000. Legal fees paid were $3,500, delinquent taxes assumed were $7,500, and fees paid to remove an old building from the land were $12,100. Materials salvaged from the demolition of the building were sold for $3,000. A contractor was paid $212,500 to construct a new warehouse. Determine the cost of the land to be reported on the balance sheet.

EXERCISE 10–4
Lump-sum acquisition
Objective 1

On January 1, Mamet Company acquired land and a building for $295,000 cash. In addition, Mamet paid $5,000 in legal costs related to the purchase. At the time, a real-estate appraiser appraised the value of the land at $80,000 and the value of the building at $240,000. Prepare the journal entry to record the acquisition of the land and the building.

EXERCISE 10–5
Nature of amortization
Objective 1

Millefleurs Metal Casting Co. reported $425,000 for equipment and $110,000 for accumulated amortization—equipment on its balance sheet.
Does this mean (a) that the replacement cost of the equipment is $425,000 and (b) that $110,000 is set aside in a special fund for the replacement of the equipment? Explain.

EXERCISE 10–6
Straight-line amortization rates
Objective 2

Convert each of the following estimates of useful life to a straight-line amortization rate, stated as a percentage, assuming that the residual value of the plant asset is to be ignored: (a) 4 years, (b) 5 years, (c) 10 years, (d) 20 years, (e) 25 years, (f) 40 years, (g) 50 years.

EXERCISE 10–7
Straight-line amortization
Objective 2

A refrigerator used by a meat processor has a cost of $113,500, an estimated residual value of $5,500, and an estimated useful life of eight years. What is the amount of the annual amortization computed by the straight-line method?

EXERCISE 10–8
Amortization by units-of-production method
Objective 2

A diesel-powered generator with a cost of $670,000 and estimated residual value of $50,000 is expected to have a useful operating life of 50,000 hours. During August, the generator was operated 1,250 hours. Determine the amortization for the month.

EXERCISE 10–9
Amortization by units-of-production method
Objective 2

Prior to adjustment at the end of the year, the balance in Trucks is $139,600, and the balance in Accumulated Amortization Trucks is $62,800. Details of the subsidiary ledger are as follows:

Truck No.	Cost	Estimated Residual Value	Estimated Useful Life	Accumulated Amortization at Beginning of Year	Kilometres Operated During Year
1	$65,000	$5,000	250,000 kilometres	$22,500	28,000 kilometres
2	37,600	3,600	170,000	31,000	20,000
3	18,000	3,000	150,000	9,300	34,500
4	19,000	1,000	200,000	—	12,000

a. Determine the amortization rates per kilometre and the amount to be credited to the accumulated amortization section of each of the subsidiary accounts for the kilometres operated during the current year.
b. Journalize the entry to record amortization for the year.

EXERCISE 10–10
Amortization by two methods
Objective 2

A boiler acquired on January 2 at a cost of $315,000 has an estimated useful life of 20 years. Assuming that it will have no residual value, determine the amortization for each of the first two years (a) by the straight-line method and (b) by the double-declining-balance method.

EXERCISE 10–11
Amortization by two methods
Objective 2

A dairy storage tank acquired at the beginning of the fiscal year at a cost of $75,200 has an estimated residual value of $3,200 and an estimated useful life of eight years. Determine the following: (a) the amount of annual amortization by the straight-line method and (b) the amount of amortization for the first and second year computed by the double-declining-balance method using a rate of 30%.

EXERCISE 10–12
Partial-year amortization
Objective 2

Sandblasting equipment acquired at a cost of $95,000 has an estimated residual value of $5,000 and an estimated useful life of 5 years. It was placed in service on April 1 of the current fiscal year, which ends on December 31. Determine the amortization for the current fiscal year and for the following fiscal year by (a) the straight-line method and (b) the double-declining-balance method.

EXERCISE 10–13
Revision of amortization
Objective 2

X-ray equipment with a cost of $310,000 has an estimated residual value of $10,000, an estimated useful life of 40 years, and is amortized by the straight-line method. (a) What is the amount of the annual amortization? (b) What is the net book value at the end of the 25th year of use? (c) If at the start of the 26th year management estimates that the remaining life is 15 years and that the residual value is $8,500, what is the amortization expense for each of the remaining 15 years?

EXERCISE 10–14
Revision of amortization
Objective 2

Mobile communications equipment acquired on January 5, 1996, at a cost of $92,500, has an estimated residual value of $7,500 and an estimated useful life of 10 years. Amortization has been recorded for the first four years ended December 31, 1999, by the straight-line method. Determine the amount of amortization for the current year ended December 31, 2000, if the revised estimated residual value is $3,300 and the revised estimated remaining useful life (including the current year) is six years.

EXERCISE 10–15
Capital and revenue
expenditures
Objective 3

Baggio Co. incurred the following costs related to trucks and vans used in operating its delivery service:

1. Installed a hydraulic lift to a van.
2. Changed the oil and greased the joints of all the trucks and vans.
3. Removed a two-way radio from one of the trucks and installed a new radio with greater range of communication.
4. Overhauled the engine on one of the trucks that had been purchased four years ago.
5. Replaced the shock absorbers on two of the trucks with new shock absorbers that allow for the delivery of heavier loads.
6. Replaced the brakes and alternator on a truck that had been in service for the past five years.
7. Installed security systems on three of the newer trucks.
8. Repaired a flat tire on one of the vans.
9. Tinted the back and side windows of one of the vans to discourage theft of contents.
10. Rebuilt the transmission on one of the vans that had been driven only 25,000 kilometres. The van was no longer under warranty.

Classify each of the costs as a capital expenditure or a revenue expenditure.

EXERCISE 10–16
Capital and revenue
expenditures
Objective 3

Freddie McGriff Co. owns and operates Home Run Transport Co. During the past year, Freddie incurred the following costs related to his 18-wheel truck.

1. Replaced the hydraulic brake system that had begun to fail during his latest trip through the Rocky Mountains.
2. Replaced a headlight that had burned out.
3. Removed the old CB radio and replaced it with a newer model with greater range.
4. Overhauled the engine.
5. Replaced a shock absorber that had worn out.
6. Installed fog lights.
7. Installed a television in the sleeping compartment of the truck.
8. Replaced the old radar detector with a newer model that detects the KA frequencies now used by many of the provincial police radar guns. The detector is wired directly into the cab, so that it is partially hidden. In addition, Freddie fastened the detector to the truck with a locking device that prevents its removal.
9. Modified the factory-installed turbo charger with a special-order kit designed to add 30 more horsepower to the engine performance.
10. Installed a wind deflector on top of the cab to increase fuel mileage.

Classify each of the costs as a capital expenditure or a revenue expenditure.

EXERCISE 10–17
Major repair to capital asset
Objective 3

Dirksen Company completed a number of major structural repairs on a building at the beginning of the current fiscal year at a cost of $79,000. The repairs are expected to extend the life of the building six years beyond the original estimate. The original cost of the building was $650,000, and it is being amortized by the straight-line method for 25 years. The residual value is expected to be negligible and has been ignored. The balance of the related accumulated amortization account after the amortization adjustment at the end of the preceding year is $286,000.

a. What has the amount of annual amortization been in past years?
b. To what account should the cost of repairs ($79,000) be debited?
c. What is the net book value of the building after the repairs have been recorded?
d. What is the amount of amortization for the current year, using the straight-line method (assuming that the repairs were completed at the very beginning of the year)?

EXERCISE 10–18
Entries for sale of capital
asset
Objective 4

Metal recycling equipment acquired on January 3, 1998, at a cost of $77,500, has an estimated useful life of six years, an estimated residual value of $5,500, and is amortized by the straight-line method.

a. What is the net book value of the equipment at December 31, 2000, the end of the fiscal year?

b. Assuming that the equipment is sold on July 1, 2001, for $20,000, journalize the entries to record (1) amortization for the six months of the current year ending December 31, 2001 and (2) the sale of the equipment.

EXERCISE 10–19
Disposal of capital asset
Objective 4

Millinery equipment acquired on January 3, 1997, at a cost of $42,000, has an estimated useful life of four years and an estimated residual value of $2,500.

a. What was the annual amount of amortization for the years 1997, 1998, and 1999, using the straight-line method?
b. What was the net book value of the equipment on January 1, 2000?
c. Assuming that the equipment was sold on January 2, 2000, for $10,500, journalize the entry to record the sale.
d. Assuming that the equipment was sold on January 2, 2000, for $14,500 instead of $10,500, journalize the entry to record the sale.

EXERCISE 10–20
Asset traded for similar asset
Objective 4

A printing press priced at $158,000 is acquired by trading in a similar press and paying cash for the difference between the trade-in allowance and the price of the new press. (a) Assuming that the trade-in allowance is $28,000, what is the amount of cash given? (b) Assuming that the net book value of the press traded in is $23,000, what is the cost of the new press for financial reporting purposes?

EXERCISE 10–21
Asset traded for similar and dissimilar assets
Objective 4

Assume the same facts as in Exercise 10–20, except that the price of the new press is $30,000. (a) What is the amount of cash given? (b) What is the cost of the new press for financial reporting purposes? (c) Would your answer to (b) change if the asset being traded for the new press were a used vehicle? Explain.

EXERCISE 10–22
Entries for trade of capital asset
Objective 4

On April 1, Danavox Co., a water distiller, acquired new bottling equipment with a list price and fair value of $235,000. Danavox received a trade-in allowance of $30,000 on the old equipment of a similar type, paid cash of $50,000, and gave a series of five notes payable for the remainder. The following information about the old equipment is obtained from the account in the equipment ledger: cost, $112,500; accumulated amortization on December 31, the end of the preceding fiscal year, $75,000; annual amortization, $7,500. Journalize the entries to record (a) the current amortization of the old equipment to the date of trade-in and (b) the transaction on April 1 for financial reporting purposes.

EXERCISE 10–23
Entries for trade of capital asset
Objective 4

On October 1, Quota Co. acquired a new truck with a list price of $90,000 and a fair value of $85,000. Quota received a trade-in allowance of $20,000 on an old truck of similar type, paid cash of $10,000, and gave a series of five notes payable for the remainder. The following information about the old truck is obtained from the account in the equipment ledger: cost, $62,500; accumulated amortization on December 31, the end of the preceding fiscal year, $37,500; annual amortization $12,500. Journalize the entries to record (a) the current amortization of the old truck to the date of trade-in and (b) the transaction on October 1 for financial reporting purposes.

EXERCISE 10–24
Amortizable cost of asset acquired by exchange
Objective 4

On the first day of the fiscal year, Chasse Company acquired a delivery truck with a list price of $45,000 and fair value of $43,000 in exchange for an old delivery truck and $3,000 cash. The old truck had a net book value of $36,000 at the date of the exchange. At what amount should you record the new truck?

EXERCISE 10–25
Internal control of capital assets
Objective 6

PCNet Co. is a computer software company marketing products in the United States and Canada. While PCNet Co. has over 60 sales offices, all accounting is handled at the company's headquarters in Calgary, Alberta.

PCNet Co. keeps all its capital asset records on a computerized system. The computer maintains a subsidiary ledger of all plant assets owned by the company and calculates amortization automatically. Whenever a manager at one of the 60 sales offices wants to purchase a capital asset, he or she submits a purchase request to headquarters for approval. Upon approval, the asset is purchased and the invoice is sent back to headquarters so that the asset can be entered into the capital asset system.

A manager who wants to dispose of a capital asset simply sells or disposes of the asset and notifies headquarters to remove the asset from the system. Employees frequently purchase company cars and personal computers when the company retires the asset. Most pieces of office equipment are traded in when new assets are acquired.

What internal control weakness exists in the procedures used to acquire and dispose of capital assets at PCNet Co.?

EXERCISE 10–26
Depletion entries
Objective 7

Bosch Co. acquired mineral rights for $15,000,000. The mineral deposit is estimated at 60,000,000 tons. During the current year, 11,500,000 tons were mined and 5,000,000 tons were sold.

a. Determine the amount of depletion for the current year.
b. Journalize the adjusting entries to record the tons mined and sold.

EXERCISE 10–27
Patents
Objective 8

Cigna Company acquired patent rights on January 3, 1995, for $1,020,000. The patent has a legal life of 17 years. When acquired, its useful life was estimated to be 10 years. On January 5, 1999, Cigna successfully defended the patent in a lawsuit at a cost of $105,000.

Journalize the adjusting entry to recognize amortization expense for the year ended December 31, 1999.

EXERCISE 10–28
Balance sheet presentation
Objective 9

How many errors can you find in the following partial balance sheet?

Isaacsen Company
Balance Sheet
For the year ended December 31, 20—

Assets

Current assets:

Fixed assets:

	Replacement Cost	Accumulated Depletion	Net Book Value
Land	$ 65,000	$ 20,000	$ 45,000
Buildings	160,000	76,000	84,000
Factory equipment	450,000	192,000	258,000
Office equipment	120,000	77,000	43,000
Patents	60,000	—	60,000
Goodwill	45,000	—	45,000
Total capital assets	$900,000	$365,000	535,000

EXERCISE 10–29
Accounting concepts
Objective 1

Explain how you would treat each of the following, giving reasons for your answers.

a. Materials and supplies costing $5,500 were purchased for the construction of a display case. An additional $2,500 was paid to hire a carpenter to build the display case. A similar case would cost $10,000 if purchased from a manufacturer.
b. An adjacent tract of land was acquired for $60,000 to provide additional parking for customers. The structures on the land were removed at a cost of $10,500. The salvaged material from the structures was sold for $1,200. The cost of grading the land was $1,750. $20,000 was paid to an asphalt company to pave the lot.
c. Equipment was purchased for $50,000 under terms of n/30, FOB shipping point. The freight charge amounted to $815, and installation costs totalled $1,050. $1,050 includes $300 for repairs when the equipment was dropped during installation.

EXERCISE 10–30
Accounting concepts
Objective 2

For many years, Douglas Transportation Company has used the declining-balance method of computing amortization. For the current year, the straight-line method was used, amortization expense amounted to $175,000, and net income amounted to $80,000. Amortization computed by the declining-balance method would have been $205,000.

a. What is the quantitative effect of the change in method on the net income for the current year?
b. Is the effect of the change material? Discuss.
c. Should the effect of the change in method be disclosed in the financial statements? Discuss.

EXERCISE 10–31
Accounting concepts
Objective 9

A machine with a cost of $75,000 and accumulated amortization of $65,000 will soon need to be replaced by a similar machine that will cost $120,000. (a) At what amount should the machine presently owned be reported on the balance sheet? (b) What amount should management use in planning for the cash required to replace the machine? Explain.

PROBLEMS SERIES A

PROBLEM 10–1A
Allocating payments and receipts to capital asset accounts
Objective 1

The following payments and receipts are related to land, land improvements, and buildings acquired for use in a ceramic wholesale business. The receipts are shown in brackets.

a.	Cost of real estate acquired as a plant site: Land	$250,000
	Building	75,000
b.	Delinquent real estate taxes on property, assumed by purchaser	18,750
c.	Cost of razing and removing building	5,800
d.	Fee paid to lawyer for title search	900
e.	Cost of filling and grading land	29,700
f.	Architect's and engineer's fees for plans and supervision	60,000
g.	Premium on one-year insurance policy during construction	6,600
h.	Payment to building contractor for new building	850,000
i.	Cost of repairing windstorm damage during construction	1,500
j.	Cost of paving parking lot to be used by customers	12,500
k.	Cost of trees and shrubbery planted	15,000
l.	Special assessment paid to city for extension of water main to the property	3,500
m.	Cost of repairing vandalism damage during construction	500
n.	Interest incurred on building loan during construction	48,000
o.	Cost of floodlights installed on parking lot	13,500
p.	Proceeds from sale of salvage materials from old building	(2,100)
q.	Money borrowed to pay building contractor	(600,000)
r.	Proceeds from insurance company for windstorm damage	(4,000)
s.	Refund of premium on insurance policy (g) cancelled after 11 months	(550)

Instructions

1. Assign each payment and receipt to Land, Land Improvements, Building, or Other Accounts. Indicate receipts by brackets. Identify each item by letter and list the amounts in columnar form, as follows:

Item	Land		Land	Building	Other
	Improvements			*Accounts*	

2. ➤ The costs assigned to the land, which is used as a plant site, will not be amortized, while the costs assigned to land improvements will be amortized. Explain this seemingly contradictory application of the concept of amortization.

PROBLEM 10–2A
Comparing three amortization methods
Objective 2

NIFO Company purchased packaging equipment on January 3, 1998, for $315,000. The equipment was expected to have a useful life of three years, or 12,000 operating hours, and a residual value of $15,000. The equipment was used for 3,000 hours during 1998, 5,800 hours in 1999, and 3,200 hours in 2000.

Instructions

Determine the amount of amortization expense for the years ended December 31, 1998, 1999, and 2000 by (a) the straight-line method, (b) the units-of-production method, and (c) the double-declining-balance method. Also determine the total amortization expense for the three years by each method. The following columnar headings are suggested for recording the amortization expense amounts:

	Amortization Expense		
Year	Straight-Line Method	Units-of-Production Method	Declining-Balance Method

PROBLEM 10–3A

Amortization by three methods; partial years
Objective 2

Gotham Company purchased plastic laminating equipment on July 1, 1998, for $108,000. The equipment was expected to have a useful life of three years, or 17,000 operating hours, and a residual value of $6,000. The equipment was used for 2,400 hours during 1998, 7,600 hours in 1999, 4,800 hours in 2000, and 2,200 hours in 2001.

Instructions

Determine the amount of amortization expense for the years ended December 31, 1998, 1999, 2000, and 2001 by (a) the straight-line method, (b) the units-of-production method, and (c) the declining-balance method, using a rate of 50%.

PROBLEM 10–4A

Amortization by two methods; trade of capital asset
Objectives 2, 4

New lithographic equipment, acquired at a cost of $175,000 at the beginning of a fiscal year, has an estimated useful life of five years and an estimated residual value of $15,000. The manager requested information regarding the effect of alternative methods on the amount of amortization expense each year. On the basis of the data presented to the manager, the double-declining-balance method was selected.

In the first week of the fifth year, the equipment was traded in for similar equipment priced at $205,000. The trade-in allowance on the old equipment was $26,000, cash of $35,000 was paid, and a note payable was issued for the balance.

Instructions

1. Determine the annual amortization expense for each of the estimated five years of use, the accumulated amortization at the end of each year, and the net book value of the equipment at the end of each year by (a) the straight-line method and (b) the double-declining-balance method (at twice the straight-line rate). The following columnar headings are suggested for each schedule:

Year	Amortization Expense	Accumulated Amortization, End of Year	Book Value, End of Year

2. For financial reporting purposes, determine the cost of the new equipment acquired in the exchange.
3. Journalize the entry to record the exchange.
4. Journalize the entry to record the exchange, assuming that the trade-in allowance was $15,000 instead of $26,000.

PROBLEM 10–5A

Correcting entries
Objectives 1, 3, 4

The following recording errors occurred and were discovered during the current year. No entries for amortization have been made as yet for the current year.

a. The $1,050 cost of repairing equipment damaged in the process of installation was charged to Equipment.
b. Store equipment with a net book value of $38,200 was traded in for similar equipment with a list price of $46,000 and a fair value of $45,000. The trade-in allowance on the old equipment was $44,000, and $2,000 cash was given for the balance. A gain on the disposal of capital assets of $5,800 was recorded.

c. Property taxes of $5,000 were paid on real estate acquired during the year and were debited to Property Tax Expense. Of this amount, $3,000 was for taxes that were delinquent at the time the property was acquired.

d. The sale of a computer for $1,750 was recorded by a $1,750 credit to Office Equipment. The original cost of the computer was $7,800, and the related balance in Accumulated Amortization at the beginning of the current year was $6,000. Amortization of $800 accrued during the current year, prior to the sale, had not been recorded.

e. The $3,750 cost of a major motor overhaul expected to prolong the life of a truck three years beyond the original estimate was debited to Delivery Expense. The truck was acquired new four years earlier.

f. The $4,500 cost of repainting several interior rooms of a building was debited to Building. The building had been owned and occupied for 20 years.

g. The cost of a razed building, $35,000, was debited to Loss on Disposal of Capital Assets and credited to Building. The building and the land on which it was located had been acquired at a total cost of $110,000 ($75,000 debited to Land, $35,000 debited to Building) as a parking area for the adjacent plant.

h. The fee of $6,100 paid to the wrecking contractor to raze the building in (g) was debited to Miscellaneous Expense.

i. A $350 charge for incoming transportation on an item of store equipment was debited to Transportation In.

Instructions

Journalize the entries to correct the errors during the current year. Identify each entry by letter. Do not prepare the entries to record amortization expense for the current year.

PROBLEM 10–6A

Transactions for plant assets, including trade

Objectives 1, 3, 4

The following transactions, adjusting entries, and closing entries were completed by Elm Furniture Co. during a three-year period. All are related to the use of delivery equipment. The double declining-balance method of amortization is used.

1997

Jan. 2. Purchased a used delivery truck for $18,800, paying cash.

  7. Paid $1,200 for major repairs to the truck. Management anticipated these when purchasing the truck.

Sep. 17. Paid garage $325 for miscellaneous repairs to the truck.

Dec. 31. Recorded amortization on the truck for the fiscal year. The estimated useful life of the truck is four years, with a residual value of $3,000.

  31. Closed the appropriate accounts to the income summary account.

1998

June 30. Traded in the used truck for a new truck with a list price of $37,000 and fair value of $35,000, receiving a trade-in allowance of $12,500 off list price and paying the balance in cash. (Record amortization to date in 1998.)

Oct. 9. Paid garage $305 for miscellaneous repairs to the truck.

Dec. 31. Recorded amortization on the truck. It has an estimated trade-in value of $18,000 and an estimated life of five years.

  31. Closed the appropriate accounts to the income summary account.

1999

Oct. 1. Purchased a new truck for $42,000, paying cash.

  2. Sold the truck purchased June 30, 1998, for $20,000. (Record amortization for the year to date.)

Dec. 31. Recorded amortization on the remaining truck. It has an estimated residual value of $5,000 and an estimated useful life of eight years.

  31. Closed the appropriate accounts to the income summary account.

Instructions

Journalize the transactions and the adjusting and closing entries. Post to t-accounts.

PROBLEM 10–7A

Amortization and depletion entries

Objectives 7, 8

Data related to the acquisition of timber rights and intangible assets during the current year ended December 31 are as follows:

a. Timber rights on a tract of land were purchased for $180,000 on March 5. The stand of timber is estimated at 900,000 board feet. During the current year, 350,000 board feet of timber were cut.

b. On January 3, the company purchased Desiri Company for $2,000,000. At the time, Desiri's financial statements reported assets of $2,100,000 and liabilities of $800,000. At the time, the fair value of Desiri's capital assets was estimated to be $200,000 higher than their net book value.

c. Governmental and legal costs of $75,000 were incurred on July 1 in obtaining a patent with an estimated economic life of 10 years and a legal life of 17 years.

Instructions

1. Determine the amount of the amortization or depletion for the current year arising from each of the foregoing transactions. Assume that management amortizes intangible assets over the maximum period allowable.
2. Journalize the adjusting entries required to record the amortization or depletion for each item.

PROBLEM 10–8A
Accounting concepts review

Indicate the generally accepted principles or concepts that have been violated by each of the accounting practices described below.

1. A business reports its capital assets in the balance sheet at their fair market value.
2. A set of financial statements does not indicate what amortization method a business is using for amortizing its capital assets.
3. At the end of the current year, the fair market value of a firm's capital assets are worth more than their net book value at the beginning of the year. Management decides that, since the assets have not depreciated during the year, no amortization should be recorded for the current year.
4. Net income for the current year is greater than expected. Therefore, the accountant uses the declining-balance method for determining amortization for the current year to reduce income to a more reasonable amount. The firm has used the straight-line method in the past, and the accountant intends to use the straight-line method again next year, if income is at a more normal level.

PROBLEMS SERIES B

PROBLEM 10–1B
Allocating payments and receipts to capital asset accounts
Objective 1

The following payments and receipts are related to land, land improvements, and buildings acquired for use in a wholesale apparel business. The receipts are identified in brackets.

a.	Cost of real estate acquired as a plant site: Land	$ 275,000
	Building	30,000
b.	Finder's fee paid to real estate agency	15,000
c.	Fee paid for title search	1,500
d.	Delinquent real estate taxes on property, assumed by purchaser	18,500
e.	Cost of razing and removing building	21,250
f.	Proceeds from sale of salvage materials from old building	(3,500)
g.	Cost of filling and grading land	23,500
h.	Architect's and engineer's fees for plans and supervision	105,000
i.	Premium on one-year insurance policy during construction	5,700
j.	Cost of paving parking lot	17,500
k.	Payment to Floral Gardens Landscaping	20,000
l.	Special assessment paid to city for sewers	6,500
m.	Cost of repairing windstorm damage during construction	3,500
n.	Cost of repairing vandalism damage during construction	800
o.	Proceeds from insurance company for windstorm and vandalism damage	(5,300)
p.	Interest incurred on building loan during construction	85,000
q.	Money borrowed to pay building contractor	(1,000,000)
r.	Payment to building contractor for new building	1,250,000
s.	Refund of premium on insurance policy (i) cancelled after 10 months	(950)

Instructions

1. Assign each payment and receipt to Land, Land Improvements, Building, or Other Accounts. Indicate receipts by brackets. Identify each item by letter and list the amounts in columnar form, as follows:

Item	Land	Land Improvements	Building	Other Accounts

2. ▬▬▶ Explain the basis used for deciding if an item should be classified as land or land improvements.

PROBLEM 10–2B
Comparing three amortization methods
Objective 2

Klass Company purchased waterproofing equipment on January 2, 1998, for $130,000. The equipment was expected to have a useful life of four years, or 8,000 operating hours, and a residual value of $10,000. The equipment was used for 1,200 hours during 1998, 2,800 hours in 1999, 2,200 hours in 2000, and 1,800 hours in 2001.

Instructions

Determine the amount of amortization expense for the years ended December 31, 1997, 1998, 1999, and 2000 by (a) the straight-line method, (b) the units-of-production method, and (c) the double-declining-balance method. Also determine the total amortization expense for the four years by each method. The following columnar headings are suggested for recording the amortization expense amounts:

	Amortization Expense		
Year	Straight-Line Method	Units-of-Production Method	Declining-Balance Method

PROBLEM 10–3B
Amortization by three methods; partial years
Objective 2

Afco Company purchased tool sharpening equipment on July 1, 1997, for $75,000. The equipment was expected to have a useful life of three years, or 8,000 operating hours, and a residual value of $3,000. The equipment was used for 1,700 hours during 1997, 3,800 hours in 1998, 1,500 hours in 1999, and 1,000 hours in 2000. The equipment was sold for $3,000 on July 1, 2000.

Instructions

Determine the amount of amortization expense for the years ended December 31, 1997, 1998, 1999, and 2000 by (a) the straight-line method, (b) the units-of-production method, and (c) the double-declining-balance method.

PROBLEM 10–4B
Amortization by two methods; trade of capital asset
Objectives 2, 4

New tire retreading equipment, acquired at a cost of $120,000 at the beginning of a fiscal year, has an estimated useful life of four years and an estimated residual value of $10,000. The manager requested information regarding the effect of alternative methods on the amount of amortization expense each year. On the basis of the data presented to the manager, the declining-balance method was selected.

In the first week of the fourth year, the equipment was traded in for similar equipment with a list price of $185,000 and fair value of $180,000. The trade-in allowance on the old equipment was $30,000, cash of $30,000 was paid, and a note payable was issued for the balance.

Instructions

1. Determine the annual amortization expense for each of the estimated four years of use, the accumulated amortization at the end of each year, and the net book value of the equipment at the end of each year by (a) the straight-line method and (b) the double-declining-balance method. The following columnar headings are suggested for each schedule:

Year	Amortization Expense	Accumulated Amortization, End of Year	Net Book Value, End of Year

2. For financial reporting purposes, determine the cost of the new equipment acquired in the exchange.

3. Journalize the entry to record the exchange.

4. Journalize the entry to record the exchange, assuming that the trade-in allowance was $5,000 instead of $25,000.

PROBLEM 10–5B
Correcting entries
Objectives 1, 3, 4

The following recording errors occurred and were discovered during the current year. No entries for amortization have been made as yet for the current year.

a. At the beginning of the year, the $1,850 cost of purchasing equipment with a five-year useful life and no salvage was charged to Repairs Expense.

b. The sale of a personal computer for $575 was recorded by a $575 credit to Office Equipment. The original cost of the computer was $1,850, and the related balance in Accumulated Amortization at the beginning of the current year was $1,200. Amortization of $150 accrued during the current year, prior to the sale, had not been recorded.

c. The $7,750 cost of repainting several interior rooms of a building was debited to Building. The building had been owned and occupied for 20 years.

d. Office equipment with a net book value of $11,200 was traded in for similar equipment with a list price of $15,000. The trade-in allowance on the old equipment was $14,000, and a note payable was given for the balance. A gain on the disposal of capital assets of $2,800 was recorded.

e. A $450 charge for incoming transportation on an item of factory equipment was debited to Delivery Expense.

f. The cost of a razed building, $25,000, was debited to Loss on Disposal of Capital Assets and credited to Building. The building and the land on which it was located had been acquired at a total cost of $150,000 ($125,000 debited to Land, $25,000 debited to Building) as a lot for a new warehouse.

g. The fee of $6,500 paid to the wrecking contractor to raze the building in (f) was debited to Miscellaneous Expense. $2,000 received for sale of salvage materials was credited to Miscellaneous Income.

h. The $5,100 cost of a major motor overhaul expected to prolong the life of a truck two years beyond the original estimate was debited to Delivery Expense. The truck was acquired new four years earlier.

i. Property taxes of $5,000 were paid on real estate acquired during the year and were debited to Property Tax Expense. Of this amount, $4,000 was for taxes that were delinquent at the time the property was acquired.

Instructions

Journalize the entries to correct the errors during the current year. Identify each entry by letter. Do not prepare the entries to record amortization expense.

PROBLEM 10–6B
Transactions for capital assets, including trade
Objectives 1, 3, 4

The following transactions, adjusting entries, and closing entries were completed by Old World Furniture Co. during three fiscal years ending on June 30. All are related to the use of delivery equipment. The company uses the straight-line method of amortization.

1997–1998 Fiscal Year

July 2. Purchased a used delivery truck for $21,000, paying cash.

6. Paid $3,000 to replace the automatic transmission and instal new brakes on the truck. This expenditure had not been anticipated.

Dec. 7. Paid garage $275 for changing the oil, replacing the oil filter, and tuning the engine on the delivery truck.

June 30. Recorded amortization on the truck for the fiscal year. The estimated useful life of the truck is eight years, with a residual value of $4,000.

30. Closed the appropriate accounts to the income summary account.

1998–1999 Fiscal Year

Sep. 29. Paid garage $310 to tune the engine and make other minor repairs on the truck.

Oct. 31. Traded in the used truck for a new truck priced at $40,000, receiving a trade-in allowance of $17,500 and paying the balance in cash. The new truck could have been purchased for $38,000 cash. No amortization had been recorded since the fiscal year end.

June 30. Recorded amortization on the truck. It has an estimated trade-in value of $3,000 and an estimated life of 10 years.

30. Closed the appropriate accounts to the income summary account.

1999–2000 Fiscal Year

Apr. 1. Purchased a new truck for $45,000, paying cash.

2. Sold the truck purchased October 31, 1999, for $30,000. No amortization had been recorded since the fiscal year end.

June 30. Recorded amortization on the remaining truck. It has an estimated residual value of $4,500 and an estimated useful life of 10 years.

30. Closed the appropriate accounts to the income summary account.

Instructions

Journalize the transactions and the adjusting and closing entries. Post to the following accounts in the ledger and extend the balances after each posting:

122	Delivery Equipment
123	Accumulated Amortization—Delivery Equipment
616	Amortization Expense—Delivery Equipment
617	Truck Repair Expense
812	Loss on Disposal of Capital Assets

PROBLEM 10–7B
Amortization and depletion entries
Objectives 7, 8

Data related to the acquisition of mineral rights and intangible assets during the current year ended December 31 are as follows:

a. Mineral rights on a tract of land were purchased for $150,000 on March 3. $100,000 was spent on exploring and developing the site. The ore deposit is estimated at 2,000,000 tonnes. During the current year, 750,000 tonnes of ore were extracted.

b. Governmental and legal costs of $74,800 were incurred on July 10 in obtaining a patent with an estimated economic life of eight years and legal life of 17 years.

c. On September 1, the company purchased a business for $500,000 that had assets with a net book value of $650,000 and liabilities with a book value of $300,000. The fair value of assets acquired was estimated to be $50,000 more than their net book value. The company's policy is to amortize goodwill over 20 years.

Instructions

1. Determine the amount of the amortization or depletion for the current year for each of the foregoing items.
2. Journalize the adjusting entries to record the amortization or depletion for each item.

PROBLEM 10–8B
Accounting concepts review

Discuss the propriety of each of the following in the context of generally accepted accounting principles.

1. A business purchased land with an old building on it. The company immediately paid a wrecking firm $2,000 to tear down the old building, so that it could construct a new building on the property. The accountant recorded the $2,000 as a loss on the disposal of the old building.

2. A business reports total assets of $50,000, owner's equity of $20,000, and net income of $30,000. Its policy is to expense immediately any expenditure under $3,000 that is related to property, plant, and equipment.

3. A company decides to change its amortization policy from straight-line to double-declining balance in order to conform to the method used by other firms in the same industry.

4. At the beginning of the current year, management decides that an asset purchased for $60,000 three years ago, which was being amortized straight-line over 10 years, will only last for another three years. Management decides to revise the accumulated amortization account at the beginning of the current year from $18,000 to $30,000 to reflect the change in estimate.

CHALLENGE PROBLEMS

PROBLEM CP10–1

On January 1, year 1, Cyr Company erroneously recorded a $3,500 capital expenditure as a revenue expenditure. The asset has a three-year useful life and a salvage value of $500. Assuming that this error is not detected, explain the effect of this error on the financial statements prepared for years 1 and 2.

PROBLEM CP10–2

You have just been appointed auditor of Lafleur Company. During your first examination of the records of the company, you discover that the company charges all of its repairs and maintenance costs to their respective asset accounts. Management indicates that regular maintenance increases the life of an asset; therefore, the maintenance cost is added to the asset account and reflected as increased amortization charges as the asset is being used. In addition, the company owns a building that was purchased five years ago at a cost of $100,000. A real-estate appraisal indicates that, due to inflation, the building has a value of $150,000 at the end of the current year. Since the value of the building has risen during the period, management feels that it would be improper to record any amortization expense for the current year, as this would only tend to further understate the asset in the financial statements.

Instructions

Evaluate the company's policies with respect to generally accepted accounting principles, explaining why their policies are correct or incorrect.

PROBLEM CP10–3

Journalize entries to record each of the following events related to Scarborough Company, which has a December 31 fiscal year end. The company's policy is to record amortization for partial years to the nearest month each year.

a. July 1, 1999: Scarborough Company purchased from a company that was going out of business a machine with a 10-year life and estimated salvage of $5,000 and a vehicle with an estimated four-year life and $4,000 salvage. Because this was a bankruptcy sale, Scarborough was able to purchase these items for $50,000 plus 8% provincial sales tax. This was less than their market values, estimated to be $40,000 for the machine and $20,000 for the used vehicle. Upon making the purchase, Scarborough immediately paid $500 to install new tires and $1,000 to have the vehicle repainted with the company's logo. It cost the company $800 to have the machine installed and $200 to repair a part which was accidentally damaged during the installation. The firm decided to use straight-line amortization for the machine and double-declining-balance for the vehicle.

b. December 31, 2000: Before recording the year's amortization, management determined that the machine would only last another five years, at which time it would likely have a salvage of $8,000. Record amortization for 2000 on both the machine and the vehicle.

c. April 1, 2002: The company traded the machine in for a similar machine with a list price of $50,000. The dealer allowed Scarborough $12,000 off the list price as a trade-in allowance for the old machine. Scarborough paid the balance in cash. Scarborough could have purchased the new machine for $48,000 cash.

d. August 1, 2002: Scarborough paid $3,000 in legal costs to defend a patent that it had purchased on January 1, 1999 for $10,000. The patent was being amortized over a five-year life from its acquisition date.

e. December 31, 2002: Record the amortization on the patent for the current year.

CASES

CASE 10–1
Kaslow Co.
Using plant assets

Louetta Westphal, CMA, is an assistant to the controller of Kaslow Co. In her spare time, Louetta also prepares tax returns and performs general accounting services for clients. Frequently, Louetta performs these services after her normal working hours, using Kaslow Co.'s microcomputers and laser printers. Occasionally, Louetta's clients will call her at the office during regular working hours.

➤ Discuss whether Louetta Westphal is performing her duties in an ethical manner.

CASE 10–2
Laminall Co.
Financial vs. tax accounting

The following is an excerpt from a conversation between two employees of Laminall Co., Wendy Webb and Alan Drexler. Wendy is the accounts payable clerk, and Alan is the cashier.

Wendy: Alan, could I get your opinion on something?

Alan: Sure, Wendy.

Wendy: Do you know Erin, the capital assets clerk?

Alan: I know who she is, but I don't know her real well. Why?

Wendy: Well, I was talking to her at lunch last Monday about how she liked her job, etc. You know, the usual . . . and she mentioned something about having to keep two sets of books . . . one for taxes and one for the financial statements. That can't be good accounting, can it? What do you think?

Alan: Two sets of books? It doesn't sound right.

Wendy: It doesn't seem right to me either. I was always taught that you had to use generally accepted accounting principles. How can there be two sets of books? What can be the difference between the two?

➤ How would you respond to Alan and Wendy if you were Erin?

CASE 10–3
Sears Canada Inc.
Financial analysis

Long-term liabilities (debt) are often secured by mortgages on capital assets. The ratio of total capital assets to long-term liabilities (debt) is a solvency measure that indicates the margin of safety to the creditors. It also indicates the ability of the business to borrow additional funds on a long-term basis. The ratio of capital assets to long-term liabilities (debt) is computed as follows:

$$\text{Ratio of capital assets to long-term liabilities (debt)} = \frac{\text{Capital assets (net)}}{\text{Long-term liabilities (debt)}}$$

a. For **Sears Canada Inc.** compute the ratio of capital assets (property, plant, and equipment) to long-term liabilities (debt) as of the current and previous year.

b. ➤ What conclusions can be drawn from these ratios concerning Sear's ability to borrow additional funds on a long-term basis?

ANSWERS TO SELF-EXAMINATION QUESTIONS

1. **C** All amounts spent to get a capital asset (such as machinery) in place and ready for use are proper charges to the asset account. In the case of machinery acquired, the freight (answer A) and the installation costs (answer B) are both (answer C) proper charges to the machinery account.

2. **C** The periodic charge for amortization under the double-declining-balance method for the second year is determined by first computing the amortization charge for the first year. The amortization for the first year of $6,000 (answer A) is computed by multiplying the cost of the equipment, $9,000, by ⅔ (the straight-line rate of ⅓ multiplied by 2). The amortization for the second year of $2,000 (answer C) is then determined by multiplying the book value at the end of the first year, $3,000 (the cost of $9,000 minus the first-year amortization of $6,000), by ⅔. The third year's amortization is $400 (answer D). It is determined by multiplying the book value at the end of the second year, $1,000, by ⅔, thus yielding $667. However, the equipment cannot be amortized below its residual value of $600; thus, the third-year amortization is $400 ($1,000 – $600).

3. **B** An amortization method that provides for a higher amortization amount in the first year of the use of an asset and a gradually declining periodic amount thereafter is called an accelerated amortization method. The declining-balance method (answer B) is an example of such a method.

4. **A** Since the monetary consideration ($70,000) involved in the exchange is more than 10% of the total value of the exchange ($100,000), the new asset should be recorded at its fair value ($100,000).

5. **D** Long-lived assets that are useful in operations, not held for sale, and without physical qualities are called intangible assets. Patents, goodwill, and copyrights are examples of intangible assets (answer D).

11   Current Liabilities

YOU AND ACCOUNTING

Have you ever gone shopping, and left a deposit with a retailer for some item that you will pick up at a later date? Or you may have bought or received a gift certificate that could be redeemed for merchandise in the future. No doubt, you have purchased some products, such as a watch or CD player, which came with a one- or two-year warranty. All of these situations would give rise to a liability for the business with which you were dealing—a liability for customer deposits, for gift certificates, or for product warranties.

If you are employed, you know that your employer has a liability to you for your earnings until you are paid by cheque or cash. You also know that your "take-home" pay is normally less than the total amount you earned because of deductions for items such as income tax, Canada Pension Plan (CPP), and Employment Insurance (EI). Your employer has a liability to send to the government any amounts withheld from your pay cheque for income taxes, CPP, and EI. In addition, you know that your employer will owe you some vacation pay in the future.

In this chapter, we will discuss the accounting and reporting for several types of current liabilities that firms incur in the normal course of business, such as those described above.

After studying this chapter, you should be able to:

Objective 1
List the characteristics of a liability and
define current liabilities.

Objective 2
Identify and journalize entries for various
current liabilities that are definitely mea-
sureable.

Objective 3
Identify and journalize entries for estimated current liabilities including: (a) warranties and (b) promotional "giveaways."

Objective 4
Identify and journalize entries for current
liabilities dependent on operating results.

Objective 5
Define a contingency and describe
accounting and reporting for contingent
liabilities.

Objective 6
Describe reporting for future obligations.

Objective 7
Describe the presentation of current liabilities in financial statements.

Liabilities: Definition and Classification

Objective 1
List the characteristics of a
liability and define current
liabilities.

According to the *CICA Handbook,* a liability has three essential characteristics.[1] It is
an obligation that:

- will require a future outflow of economic benefits (assets or services);
- the entity has little or no discretion to avoid;
- is due to a transaction or event that has already occurred.

In analyzing the financial position of a business, investors, creditors, and other
users of financial statements are particularly interested in two crucial pieces of
information about the firm's liabilities. First, what amounts does the firm owe?
And second, when does it have to pay them? In order to stay in business, a company will need sufficient current assets to pay any debts that will be coming due
shortly. The ability of a firm to meet its short-term obligations is called **liquidity.** To
assist users in assessing the liquidity of the business, we divide liabilities into two
classifications on the balance sheet: (1) current and (2) long-term.

Current liabilities are debts that the business expects to pay out of current
assets or through the creation of another current liability. These include amounts
payable within one year or within the normal operating cycle, whichever is longer.[2]
We defined the operating cycle earlier in Chapter 7 as the period that elapses
between the time cash flows out of the firm to acquire inventory until the inventory
is sold and cash flows back into the firm when the accounts receivables are collected. Thus, the definition of current liabilities is closely related to that of current
assets. The 1997 edition of *Financial Reporting in Canada* indicates that approximately 93% of Canadian public companies surveyed segregate both current assets
and current liabilities in their balance sheets.[3]

There are many different types of obligations the business may face in the near
future. We will discuss these under the following headings:

1. Current liabilities that are definitely measurable.
2. Current liabilities that must be estimated.
3. Current liabilities that depend on operating results.
4. Contingent liabilities.
5. Future obligations.

---

[1] *CICA Handbook,* Section 1000, paragraph 33.
[2] *Ibid.,* Section 1510, paragraph 3.
[3] C. Byrd and I. Chen, *Financial Reporting in Canada 1997,* 22nd ed., CICA: Toronto, p. 74.

1. Definitely Measurable Current Liabilities

Objective 2
Identify and journalize entries for various current liabilities that are definitely measurable.

In most cases where obligations arise from contracts or from federal or provincial statutes, a business can determine the amount of the debt and its due date with reasonable certainty. Once the firm ascertains that such an obligation exists, it should measure it as accurately as possible and record the liability. In this section we discuss the following examples of these types of current liabilities:

a. trade accounts payable,
b. short-term notes payable,
c. current maturities of long-term debt,
d. unearned revenue,
e. refundable deposits,
f. property taxes payable,
g. PST and GST payable,
h. liabilities related to payrolls, and
i. other accrued liabilities.

1. A) TRADE ACCOUNTS PAYABLE

Trade accounts payable are amounts owed for goods and services purchased on credit. Usually the creditor's invoice clearly indicates the amount and due date of such payables. Chapter 6 illustrated accounting for purchases of inventory and cash discounts on accounts payable. Most accounting systems for recording and controlling payments on trade payables are designed so that the existence, amount, and due date of such liabilities are readily determinable. At the end of the fiscal period the accountant must be especially careful to record all payables related to goods or services received before the end of the period, even though the invoice for some of these items may not arrive until early in the next period.

1. B) SHORT-TERM NOTES PAYABLE

Chapter 8 discussed the nature of promissory notes and accounting for them from the receiver's point of view. Accounting for notes payable is the reverse of accounting for notes receivable.

A note payable is a written promise to pay a stated amount of money at a specific date. Sometimes a business issues a note payable to a supplier in exchange for goods or services or to settle an account payable. Other times a business may obtain cash by signing a note payable to a bank or other financial institution. We will classify the note as current or long-term depending on its due date. Just as a business holding a note receivable must record interest revenue earned at the end of each fiscal period, so too, the issuer of a note payable must accrue interest expense to date at the end of each period.

A promissory note may state an interest rate or not; in the latter case, the note is called non-interest bearing. Does this mean that sometimes a firm can borrow funds without paying any interest? No. There is no such thing as a "free" loan. The holder of a promissory note will *always* demand a return for extending credit to the debtor. However, instead of stating the interest rate separately, the lender may include the (unstated) interest in the amount to be repaid at maturity. Thus, the maturity value of a non-interest-bearing note will be different than the fair value of the consideration received when it is originally issued. In other words, a non-interest-bearing note will be issued at a discount. The discount on a note payable represents the "real" interest being charged to maturity (even though the stated interest is zero). Hence, the issuer must accrue interest on *both* interest and non-interest-bearing notes, as shown below.

When we compute interest using a rate that differs from that stated on a note, we say that we have recorded the expense using an *imputed rate of interest*. The interest stated on the note is called the **nominal** rate, while that used to record the real interest expense is called the **effective** or **market** rate. Non-interest-bearing notes have a nominal rate of zero. Some other notes may have a stated rate that is not zero, but that is still significantly different from the market rate. For example, a car dealership may offer to sell you a car in exchange for a 1.9% note payable when the market rate is 6%. In this case, although the nominal rate on the note is 1.9%, we should impute a rate of 6% when recording interest expense. The accounting for these types of transactions is covered in more detail in the discussion of long-term notes and bonds payable in Chapter 14.

We will illustrate accounting for both interest and non-interest-bearing short-term notes payable using the following example. Vintage Winery receives $10,000 from the bank on September 1, 1999 in exchange for a note payable due March 1, 2000. Vintage has a December 31 fiscal year end. The table illustrates accounting for the note under two different assumptions:

a.   the note has a maturity value of $10,000 and a stated interest rate of 8% (remember interest is always stated as an annual rate);
b.   the note is non-interest bearing and has a maturity value of $10,400.

The table below shows the journal entries required under both (a) and (b) over the life of the note:

1.   to record the issuance of the note on September 1;
2.   to accrue interest expense at the firm's fiscal year end on December 31; and
3.   to record payment of the note on March 1.

	(a) Stated Rate on Note = 8%			(b) Non-interest-bearing Note		
(1) Sept. 1, 1999 Note issued for $10,000.	Cash	10,000		Cash	10,000	
	Note Payable		10,000	Discount on Note Payable	400	
				Note Payable		10,400
(2) Dec. 31, 1999 Accrue interest at year-end.	Interest Expense	267*		Interest Expense	267*	
	Interest Payable		267	Discount on Note Payable		267
	*$10,000 × 8% × $\frac{4}{12}$			*$400 × $\frac{4}{6}$ months		
(3) March 1, 2000 Payment of note and interest.	Note Payable	10,000		Interest Expense	133*	
	Interest Payable	267		Discount on Note Payable		133
	Interest Expense	133*				
	Cash		10,400	Note Payable	10,400	
				Cash		10,400
	*$10,000 × 8% × $\frac{2}{12}$			*$400 × $\frac{2}{6}$ months		

The Discount on Notes Payable is a contra account deducted from the liability on the balance sheet. At December 31, 1999, the balance sheet of Vintage Wineries would appear as follows under situations (a) and (b):

(a)		(b)	
Current liabilities:		Current liabilities:	
8% Note Payable due March 1, 2000	$10,000	Note Payable due March 1, 2000	$10,400
		Less Discount	133
Interest Payable	267	Note Payable, net	$10,267

1. C) CURRENT MATURITIES OF LONG-TERM DEBT

We report, as a current liability, the portion of long-term debt that matures within the next fiscal year. For example, some long-term notes payable may be paid in installments over several periods. In this case, we record the **principal** portion, due in the next year, as a current liability. However, we do not include the interest, due in the next period, as a liability in the current period.

To illustrate, suppose that at December 31, 1999 Reynolds Paint Store has a $15,000 10% long-term note payable. The note is to be repaid in equal installments of blended principal and interest of $3,957 on December 31 of each of the next five years, beginning December 31, 2000. The interest for the year 2000 will be $1,500 ($15,000 × 10%). Thus, the installment payment of $3,957 to be made within the next year consists of:

Total installment due in 2000	$3,957
Less interest portion	1,500
Principal portion maturing next year	$2,457

Therefore, on its December 31, 1999 balance sheet Reynolds Paint Store will report $2,457 as a current liability and the remainder of the note payable under long-term liabilities, as follows:

Current liabilities:	
Current portion of long-term note payable	$ 2,457
Long-term liabilities:	
10% Note Payable	$15,000
(due in five equal installments of $3,957, beginning December 31, 2000)	
Less principal portion due next year, reported above	2,457
	$12,543

We usually classify the portion of long-term liabilities coming due next year as current because we expect that the business will pay this amount by using working capital (decreasing current assets or increasing current liabilities). However, sometimes this is not the case. For example, management may be planning to pay the debt by using a fund (classified as a long-term asset) especially set aside for this purpose or by using the proceeds from a new issuance of owners' equity or new long-term debt. In such cases, if there is evidence that the firm has made contractual arrangements to settle the liability by such means, the obligation is not classified as a current liability.[4] Instead, the business should disclose its plans for repayment of the debt in its financial statements.

1. D) UNEARNED REVENUES

When customers pay in advance for goods or services to be delivered in the future, the business records the advance as a current liability. In Chapters 3 and 4 we used Computer King to illustrate the accounting for unearned (deferred) rent revenue, where the tenant had paid for several months rent in advance. Other circumstances giving rise to unearned revenue might include deposits on sales orders and tickets or magazine subscriptions sold in advance. As the goods or services are delivered, the liability diminishes and is transferred to earned revenue.

Suppose that a publisher issues a monthly magazine that sells a number of two-year subscriptions for $3,600 on November 1, 1999. At that date the publisher records:

[4] *CICA Handbook,* Section 1510, paragraph .06.

Nov. 1, 1999   Cash   3,600
                      Unearned Revenue   3,600
                      Cash received for two-year subscriptions.

Assuming that delivery begins in November, at the company's year end on December 31, 1999 it should reduce the liability for the revenue earned to date:

Dec. 31, 1999   Unearned Revenue   300
                      Earned Subscription Revenue   300
                      Revenue earned for November and December.

Although the subscription extends over more than the next fiscal year, firms usually report the entire amount of the Unearned Revenue as a current liability (rather than attempting to separate the long-term portion). This practice may be justified using the principle of **materiality**, assuming that the cost of differentiating the current and long-term portions of the liability may exceed its benefits. Another possible explanation for disclosing all of the unearned revenue as current is that the amount would become payable immediately, if for some reason the firm stopped publication of the magazine.

1. E) REFUNDABLE DEPOSITS

Sometimes firms will require their customers to pay a deposit that will be refunded at a later date. For example, **Bell Canada** may require a security deposit from new customers, to be returned when the customer discontinues the service. Alternatively, a company that sells large bottles of purified water for water coolers may require a deposit on returnable bottles. The business should record these refundable deposits as current liabilities, not as revenue.

For example, suppose that in 1999 Rocky Mountain Beverages sells for cash 100,000 bottles of water at $9 each, which includes a $4 refundable deposit per bottle (for simplicity, we will ignore sales taxes). In this case, the business should record only $500,000 as sales revenue and set up a liability for the refundable deposits, as follows:

Cash   900,000
  Sales   500,000
  Liability for container deposits   400,000
    Sales of 100,000 bottles of water with returnable deposits.

If 30,000 bottles are returned in 1999, the business will record:

Liability for customer deposits   120,000
  Cash   120,000
    30,000 bottles returned for deposit of $4 each.

At the end of 1999, the business will report a current liability of $280,000 ($400,000 − $120,000).

1. F) PROPERTY TAXES PAYABLE

Property taxes are a major source of revenue for local governments. Often, the exact amount of taxes for a year will not be known until the government sets the tax rate part way through the year. However, a business will usually record the expense each month, using an estimate until the final bill is known.

To illustrate, suppose that Rhonda Burak owns two apartment buildings and prepares income statements on a monthly basis. In 1999 property taxes were

$60,000. In April, 2000 Rhonda receives the current year's tax bill of $61,800 payable on June 1. From January to March, Rhonda may accrue the monthly property expense based on last year's bill, making the following entry each month.

Property tax expense ($60,000 ÷ 12)	5,000	
Property taxes payable		5,000
Accrue property tax expense for the month.		

In April, when Rhonda receives the bill, she calculates her monthly expense for April to December as follows:

Total property tax expense for year	$61,800
Less amount expensed to March 31 (3 × $5,000)	15,000
Expense over rest of year	$46,800
	÷ 9
Monthly expense April through December	$ 5,200

For April and May, Rhonda will record each month:

Property tax expense	5,200	
Property taxes payable		5,200
Accrue property tax expense for the month.		

In June, the entry to record the monthly expense and the payment of the year's taxes will be:

Property tax expense	5,200	
Property tax payable	25,400*	
Prepaid property tax	31,200**	
Cash		61,800
Record property tax expense for June and payment of		
1999 tax bill on June 1.		

* Accrued January 1 to March 31 ($5,000 × 3)	15,000
Accrued April 1 to May 31 ($5,200 × 2)	10,400
	25,400

**Expense July through December ($5,200 × 6 months)

The taxes prepaid in June will be written off to expense each month from July through December as follows:

Property tax expense	5,200	
Prepaid property tax		5,200
Record property tax expense for the month.		

1. G) PST AND GST PAYABLE

All of the provinces, except Alberta, impose a provincial sales tax (PST) on sales to final consumers of products. The amount of PST varies from province to province. In addition, the federal government charges a goods and service tax (GST) on most transactions involving the delivery of merchandise or services to consumers. Sales of certain items, such as most food and pharmaceutical products, are exempt from GST.[5] Some provinces have signed agreements with Ottawa combining the PST

---

[5] The rules detailing the levying of GST and GST exemptions are complex and beyond the scope of this text. Revenue Canada has established different classes of suppliers with different GST obligations. For simplicity, we illustrate only one of several methods for calculating and remitting this tax.

and GST into a single harmonized sales tax (HST), while in other regions the taxes are levied separately. In any case, the two levels of government require businesses to act as collection agents for these taxes. When a firm sells goods or services to a customer, it must add to the sales price any provincial or federal sales taxes that are applicable, and has a liability to remit these taxes to the government in the future.

Assume that during the month of January, 1999, Battista Enterprises made $30,000 in sales on account, subject to 8% PST and a separately levied 7% GST. The entry to record the sales is as follows:

Accounts receivable	34,500	
Sales		30,000
PST Payable		2,400
GST Payable		2,100
Record sale on account.		

When a business buys supplies, inventory, or capital assets, it will usually have to pay GST on these purchases. However, the government allows the firm to claim a refund for these amounts. When the firm makes expenditures on which it may recover the GST, it can debit the GST payable account for the amount that is refundable. In this way the liability account will reflect the net amount to be remitted to the government, which is the difference between the GST collected from customers less the GST refundable on the firm's purchases. For example, suppose that during January, 1999 Battista buys inventory for $20,000 plus 7% GST and is using a periodic system. It would record:

Purchases	20,000	
GST Payable	1,400	
Accounts Payable		21,400
Record purchase of inventory and refundable GST.		

At the end of January Battista records the payment of $2,400 to the provincial government for PST and $700 ($2,100 – $1,400) to the federal government for GST:

PST Payable	2,400	
Cash		2,400
Remit PST payment to government.		

GST Payable	700	
Cash		700
Remit GST payment to government.		

1. H) LIABILITIES RELATED TO PAYROLLS[6]

A business will often report a current liability for salaries or wages owed to employees at the end of an accounting period. In addition, the firm will record liabilities for various payroll deductions and taxes and its obligations to employees for compensated absences (such as vacation pay) and for post-retirement benefits. Accountants must be familiar with the general provisions of payroll tax legislation.

We are all familiar with the term payroll. In accounting, the term payroll refers to the amount paid to employees for services provided during a period. A business's payroll is usually significant for several reasons. First, employees are sensitive to payroll errors and irregularities. Maintaining good employee morale requires that the payroll be paid on a timely, accurate basis. Second, payroll

---

[6] For a more in-depth coverage of payroll accounting, see end-of-chapter Appendix A.

expenditures are subject to various federal and provincial regulations. Finally, payroll expenditures and related payroll taxes have a significant effect on the net income of most businesses. Although the amount of such expenses varies widely, it is not unusual for a business to expend nearly a third of its revenue for payroll and payroll-related expenses.

Liability for Employee Earnings

The term **salary** usually refers to payment for managerial, administrative, or similar services. The rate of salary is normally expressed in terms of a month or a year. The term **wages** usually refers to payment for manual labour, both skilled and unskilled. The rate of wages is normally stated on an hourly or weekly basis. In practice, the terms salary and wages are often used interchangeably.

The basic salary or wage of an employee may be increased by commissions, profit sharing, or cost-of-living adjustment. Although payment is usually made in cash, it may take such forms as securities, notes, lodging, or other property or services. Generally, the form of payment has no effect on how salaries and wages are treated by either the employer or the employee.

Many businesses pay managers an annual bonus in addition to a regular salary. The amount of the bonus is often based on some measure of productivity, such as income or profit of the business. Therefore, managers have a personal interest in selecting accounting principles and determining accounting estimates. For example, a chief executive officer (CEO) who plans to retire in the near future might select accounting principles that tend to increase reported income, such as straight-line amortization and the first-in, first-out inventory costing method, so as to increase the bonus. Likewise, such managers might tend to bias accounting estimates, such as uncollectible accounts expense, in favour of reporting more income.

Salary and wage rates are determined by agreement between the employer and the employees. Provincial statutes regulate employment standards, establishing minimum wage rates and minimum requirements for overtime pay and vacation pay. The statutes specify that after a certain number of hours in a week, an hourly employee must be paid an overtime premium for all subsequent hours.

To illustrate computing an employee's earnings, assume that John T. McGrath is employed by McDermott Supply Co. at the rate of $25 per hour. Any hours in excess of 40 hours per week are paid at a rate of 1½ times the normal rate, or $37.50 ($25 + $12.50) per hour. For the week ended December 27, McGrath's time card indicates that he worked 44 hours. His earnings for that week are computed as follows:

Earnings at base rate (40 × $25)	$1,000
Earnings at overtime rate (4 × $37.50)	150
Total earnings	$1,150

Payroll Deductions

The total earnings of an employee for a payroll period, including bonuses and overtime pay, are called gross pay. From this amount is subtracted one or more **deductions** to arrive at the net pay. Net pay is the amount the employer must pay the employee. The deductions for income taxes are usually the largest deduction. Deductions are also required for Canada Pension Plan and Employment Insurance. Other deductions may be made for group life insurance, contributions to pensions, and for items authorized by individual employees.

INCOME TAX WITHHOLDING. The federal government requires employers to withhold from the employee's pay the approximate income taxes due on those wages. The amount withheld from each worker depends on the employee's pay and

USING ACCOUNTING TO UNDERSTAND BUSINESS

In many companies, the chairman, or vice chairman and chief executive officer (CEO) have the highest salaries of all employees in the business. There are wide differences in the salaries and bonuses earned by such people. The following are some salaries and bonuses of senior officers of banking and investment firms for 1997:

CEO	Company	Salary	Bonus
Matthew Barrett	**Bank of Montreal**	$900,000	$1,400,000
Gordon Cheesbrough	**Scotia Capital**	250,000	2,950,000
John Cleghorn	**Royal Bank**	835,000	1,600,000
Anthony Fell	**RBC Dominion Securities**	300,000	6,000,000

personal income tax exemptions. Revenue Canada provides businesses with income tax formulas and tables for computing the amount of the deductions.[7] Once the firm has withheld income taxes from its employees' pay cheques, it has a liability to remit this amount to the government.

CANADA PENSION PLAN. The federal government requires both employers and employees to contribute to the Canada Pension Plan (CPP), the purpose of which is to provide retirement, disability, and similar benefits. The amount withheld from each worker depends on the employee's pay, although the government sets a ceiling on the maximum CPP contribution required from an individual each year.[8] The business must withhold the employee's share of CPP from the employee's pay cheque, and is then liable to remit both the employee's contribution and its own contribution to the government. The firm's cost for CPP is equal to the sum required from its employees. The Canada Pension Plan applies to all provinces except Quebec, which has its own similar plan.

EMPLOYMENT INSURANCE. The federal government also requires, with a few exceptions, both employers and employees to contribute to the federal Employment Insurance (EI) plan. As with CPP, the amount required from each worker depends on the employee's pay and there is a ceiling on the contribution that can be deducted from an individual each year.[9] The business must withhold the employee's share of the employment insurance premium from the employee's pay cheque, and is then liable to remit both the employee's contribution and its own contribution to the government. The employer's share of EI is 1.4 times the amount required from its employees.

OTHER PAYROLL DEDUCTIONS. A business will often withhold other deductions from its employees' pay cheques for items such as employee contributions to union dues, group life insurance, company pension plans, Canada Savings Bonds, and the United Way. The firm must report the amounts withheld as current liabilities until it remits them to the appropriate payees.

To illustrate accounting for payroll deductions, assume that a business has a weekly payroll of $20,000. From the employees' pay cheques the firm withholds the following: $4,800 for income taxes, $600 for employee contributions to CPP, $800 for EI, and $200 for union dues. The entry to record the payroll accrual would be as follows:

---

[7] The government also provides formulas and tables for computing Canada Pension Plan and Employment Insurance contributions for employees at various pay levels.
[8] For example, in 1998 the maximum CPP contribution was $1,068.80. Once an employee reaches the maximum, the employer will cease taking CPP deductions off the worker's pay cheque.
[9] In 1998 the maximum EI contribution was $1,053.00.

Salaries Expense	20,000	
Employee Income Tax Payable		4,800
CPP Payable		600
EI Payable		800
Union Dues Payable		200
Salaries Payable		13,600
Accrue weekly payroll.		

Exhibit 1 below illustrates an individual employee's payroll cheque and cheque stub showing deductions made from gross pay.

Exhibit 1

Employee's payroll cheque

In addition to the entry made above, the firm needs to record the liability for its own contributions to CPP of $600 and EI of $1,120 (1.4 × employees' contribution of $800):

Payroll Expenses	1,720	
CPP Payable		600
EI Payable		1,120
Accrue employer's share of CPP and EI.		

When the firm issues pay cheques to employees, it will record the cash disbursement as follows:

Salaries Payable	13,600	
Cash		13,600
Disbursement for monthly payroll.		

Similarly, as it remits payments for the other payroll liabilities, it will record those cash disbursements. For example, the entries to record the remittance to the government for employee income taxes, CPP, and EI are as follows:

Employee Income Tax Payable	4,800	
CPP Payable ($600 + $600)	1,200	
EI Payable ($800 + $1,120)	1,920	
Cash		7,920
Remit CPP and EI contributions to the government.		

Other Payroll Liabilities

WORKERS' COMPENSATION. Government programs to provide assistance to employees injured at work fall under provincial jurisdiction. Each province has its own Workers' Compensation Board governed by its own legislation. Employees do not pay for this coverage; these programs are funded through premiums levied on employers. Different rates apply to firms in different industries, with the highest premiums for workers' compensation (WC) charged to those businesses involving the highest risks for worker injuries. For example, in 1998 the Ontario Workers' Compensation Board exempted some industries from this tax, while requiring other businesses to pay premiums varying from 0.21% to 18.5% of the company's total gross payroll.

EMPLOYMENT HEALTH TAX. Some provinces impose a payroll tax on businesses to help pay for the health care system, which falls under provincial jurisdiction. For example, Ontario legislation requires non-public sector employers with annual payrolls in excess of $400,000 to pay an Employment Health Tax (EHT) of 1.95% of the firm's gross payroll. In order to ease the tax burden on smaller businesses, employers with payrolls under $400,000 are exempt from this tax.

COMPENSATED ABSENCES. Businesses pay employees when they are absent from work for statutory holidays, vacations, and illness. Provincial legislation makes employers liable to pay employees a minimum amount of vacation pay, calculated as a proportion of their earned salary. The business's obligation to pay benefits to employees when they are sick varies from firm to firm, depending on the terms of the employment contract at a particular company. The issues involved in determining the exact amounts a business should accrue for compensated absences are complex and beyond the scope of this text. For our purposes, it is sufficient to note that the firm should record some expense and related liability for compensated absences in the period in which they are earned by employees.

To illustrate the accounting for these various payroll expenses, assume that a company with a $20,000 weekly payroll is liable for workers' compensation of 5%, an employment health tax of 1.95%, and 4% vacation pay. At the time that the business records its payroll, it will make the following entry:

Employee vacations and the cost of other fringe benefits are recorded as expenses.

Payroll Expenses	2,190	
WC Payable		1,000
EHT Payable		390
Vacation Pay Payable		800
Accrue expense for workers' compensation, EHT, and vacation pay.		

PENSION AND OTHER POST-RETIREMENT BENEFITS. When employees retire, they are often entitled to receive benefits from a company pension plan, and may also be entitled to post-retirement health care and insurance benefits. The **matching principle** requires that the cost of pension benefits be recorded as an expense during the years in which the employee works for the business.[10] As of the date of writing this text, there are no *CICA Handbook* Recommendations specifying a method of accounting for other post-retirement benefits. Some companies treat them like pen-

---

[10]*CICA Handbook*, Section 3460, paragraph .07.

sion benefits, recording the expense and accruing them as a liability during the years in which the employee works for the business. Alternatively, they may be accrued as a liability at the time the employee retires, or recorded only when they are paid out during the retirement period. The business should provide a general description of these benefits in its financial statements, along with a description of the accounting policies followed for those benefits.[11] Since most post-retirement benefits are not payable in the next year, any obligations reported in this regard are usually classified as long-term, rather than current, liabilities. The calculation of these expenses and the reporting of the related liabilities are complex issues that are covered in more advanced accounting textbooks.

1. I) OTHER ACCRUED LIABILITIES

As illustrated in earlier chapters, a business must set up accruals for any expenses that have been incurred by the end of the fiscal period, but that have not yet been paid. For instance, the firm will often set up a payable for utilities consumed in the current period, but which will not be paid until the next period. Other examples might include accruals for legal services or repairs and maintenance that have been performed but not yet billed.

2. Estimated Current Liabilities

Objective 3
Identify and journalize entries for estimated current liabilities including: (a) warranties and (b) promotional "giveaways."

An estimated liability is an obligation that definitely exists but that is uncertain as to its amount and due date. Here the accountant must make a reasonable estimate of the amount of the liability and then record it. We discuss two common examples of this type of liability below: warranties and promotional "giveaways."

2. A) WARRANTIES

In order to promote sales, many businesses offer their customers guarantees regarding the quality of their products. A warranty is a seller's promise to provide parts and/or labour to fix a product that proves to be defective during some specified period of time. The warranty may also serve the purpose of limiting the seller's legal liability from what the courts might otherwise impose. Thus, for example, Bits and Bytes, a computer company, might offer a two-year warranty on its products.

The **matching principle** requires that a business record all costs associated with a sale in the same period that it records the sales revenue. Therefore, the firm should record warranty expense and a warranty liability in the same period that it records the sale. When a company sells a single item, it does not know for certain that it will incur any warranty costs in relation to that particular item. However, the business can be sure that out of all the units it sells, some will be returned for warranty work. How does the firm know what amount to record as a liability for these future expenditures when the sale is made? The company must *estimate* this amount based on its experience in prior years or on industry averages.

For example, suppose that Bits and Bytes makes product sales of $300,000 in 1999 and $360,000 in the year 2000, and estimates that warranty costs will average 3% of gross sales. During 1999 the company uses $1,000 in parts and incurs $2,000 in labour costs doing warranty work. In 2000 it uses $4,000 in parts and incurs $6,500 in labour costs for warranty work. The following table shows the journal

[11]*CICA Handbook*, Emerging Issues Committee Abstract 5, "Post Retirement Benefits Other Than Pensions."

entries that the business would make for both years to record (1) the accrual for warranty expense and (2) the costs for warranty work performed each year.

	1999			2000		

Record warranty expense related to the year's sales.	Warranty Expense
	   Warranty Liability
	   ($300,000 × 3%)
		9,000	9,000	Warranty Expense
				   Warranty Liability
				   ($360,000 × 3%)
					10,800	10,800

Record costs incurred for warranty work performed during year.	Warranty Liability
	   Parts Supplies
	   Wages Payable
		3,000	1,000
			2,000
				Warranty Liability
				   Parts Supplies
				   Wages Payable
					10,500	4,000
						6,500

At the end of 1999, Bits and Bytes would report a current liability for warranties of $6,000 ($9,000 – $3,000). At the end of 2000, the balance for warranty liabilities is $6,300 ($6,000 + $10,800 – $10,500). Although warranties may extend for several years, accountants usually report the obligation as a current liability. This may be justified on the basis that the customer could bring the product back at any time for the work to be done.

Occasionally, you may encounter a business that does not accrue a warranty liability at the time of sale, but simply records the expense when the warranty work is performed. This is acceptable only if warranty costs are insignificant or the warranty period is very short. In this case, the company could cite the **materiality** principle on the grounds that the financial statements would not be materially different whether warranty costs were treated on a cash or an accrual basis.

2. B) PROMOTIONAL "GIVEAWAYS"

Sometimes businesses may offer promotional "giveaways" as an incentive for customers to buy their products or services. These "giveaways" can take various forms. A company may offer customers cash rebates, coupons for cash discounts, or premiums in exchange for box tops or labels. Another popular promotional scheme is the offer of free air miles to frequent fliers or to customers making purchases from certain retailers or using designated credit cards.

Since companies offer these types of promotions in order to increase current sales, GAAP requires that the promotion expense be matched against current revenue. In all of these cases, the business must estimate the cost of its liability for meeting customer claims for such items in the future. Since not all possible discounts, premiums, rebates, or air miles will be presented for redemption, the firm must *estimate* the amount of the obligation based on past experience. The entries made would be similar to those illustrated above for warranties. The promotion expense and liability would be recorded in the same period as the sale, with the liability written off in the periods when the expenditures were actually incurred.

---

3. Current Liabilities Dependent on Operating Results

Objective 4
Identify and journalize entries for current liabilities dependent on operating results.

The amounts owing for certain liabilities, such as income taxes,[12] management bonuses, and royalties are dependent on operating results. For example, a senior manager may have an employment contract that entitles her to a year-end bonus of 3% of the firm's annual operating income that is in excess of $300,000. If the busi-

---

[12]Only corporations (not proprietorships or partnerships) are taxed separately from their owners. Therefore, only corporations will report income tax expense and income tax liabilities.

ness earns operating income of $500,000, it should accrue a liability for the management bonus, as follows:

Management bonus expense	6,000	
Liability for management bonus		6,000
Accrue management bonus at 3% of $200,000 ($500,000 – $300,000).		

Sometimes a business has a contractual obligation to pay a share of its proceeds to a proprietor, author, or inventor in exchange for the right to use some asset in its business. For example, a publishing company may pay an author a 5% royalty on annual revenue earned from sales of his book. If sales are $200,000, the publisher will record the following entry:

Royalties expense	10,000	
Liability for royalties		10,000

When royalties are calculated on sales revenue, a business will be able to measure the liability with certainty at any particular point in time. If royalties are based on annual operating income, it will not be able to determine the exact amount of the obligation until the year end, when all expenses are known.

Those liabilities that are dependent on operating results can be easily measured at the end of the period. However, it is sometimes difficult to estimate these for interim reports. This topic is covered in more advanced accounting texts.

4. Contingent Liabilities

Objective 5

Define a contingency and describe accounting and reporting for contingent liabilities.

A contingency is "an existing condition or situation involving uncertainty as to possible gain or loss to an enterprise that will ultimately be resolved when one or more future events occur or fail to occur."[13] Resolution of the event in the future will confirm if the past transaction has given rise to either an asset or a liability for the business. A contingent loss may be associated with either impairment (loss in value) of an asset or existence of a liability. The following discussion is limited to accounting for contingent liabilities.

A contingent liability is different from an estimated liability. With an estimated liability, such as warranties, the firm knows with certainty that it will have an outflow of net assets in the future as a result of a past transaction; it just does not know the exact amount or due date of the liability. With a contingent liability, the firm is not certain at the present time whether or not there will be any outflow of net assets in the future.

An example of a contingent liability would be a court case in which the firm is being sued for damages. While the event giving rise to the litigation occurred in the past, the outcome of the event will not be known for certain until a judgment is rendered in the future. Another example of a contingent liability occurs when a business guarantees a bank loan for another entity. If the other party pays the loan when it comes due in the future, the business that guaranteed the loan will suffer no loss. However, if the borrower defaults, the business will have to pay the debt. Again, the outcome of a past transaction (signing as a loan guarantor) will not be known until the future.

How should a firm treat a contingent liability? Should it record an estimated amount for the liability and report it on its balance sheet? Or should it just disclose

---

[13]*CICA Handbook,* Section 3290, paragraph .02.

the possible contingent loss in the notes to the financial statements? The *CICA Handbook* recommends recording the liability in the balance sheet only if *both* of the following conditions hold:

- it is **likely** that a future event will confirm that a loss exists, and
- the amount of the **loss can be reasonably estimated.**

If either of these conditions is missing, the business will not record the contingent loss as a liability, but should report it in the notes to the financial statements in accordance with the **full disclosure principle.**

For example, suppose that Lamb Company had guaranteed a $10,000 loan that is due on March 1, 2000 for a partnership, Oullette Enterprises. At the end of 1999, Oullette is in serious financial difficulty and its owners have filed for bankruptcy. Since it appears very likely that Lamb Company will have to pay the $10,000 loan in two months, Lamb should make the following journal entry at its fiscal year end of December 31, 1999:

Estimated loss on loan guarantee	10,000	
Liability for contingent loss		10,000
Record expected loss on loan guarantee for Oullette Enterprises.		

A survey of large Canadian companies indicates that approximately 65% disclosed contingent losses either as a liability or in the notes to their financial statements.[14] An example of such a note disclosure made by **Canada Post Corporation** for the reporting period ended March 30, 1996 is shown below.

Note 10 Contingencies
(a) Two complaints have been filed with the Canadian Human Rights Commission alleging discrimination by the Corporation concerning work of equal value. The Corporation is presenting its evidence before the Tribunal with respect to one complaint and the Commission has not begun its investigation of the second. The outcome of these complaints is not currently determinable. Settlement, if any, arising from the resolution of these matters, will be recovered in future postal rates (as determined in accordance with the Canada Post Corporation Act) and/or from the Government of Canada.

In practice, businesses are very careful about how they disclose contingencies related to matters that are currently under litigation. The firm will usually try to avoid admitting guilt or disclosing to a plaintiff what amount of damages it expects to pay. Sometimes, companies will disclose various contingencies together in a group, in order to meet reporting requirements without giving away too much information to any particular litigant.

In accordance with the **conservatism principle,** the *CICA Handbook* recommends that a firm should never record contingent gains as assets.[15] However, the firm may disclose these in the notes to the financial statements.

5. Future Obligations

Objective 6
Describe reporting for future obligations.

Sometimes businesses make contractual commitments that can result in substantial future liabilities. For example, a firm may sign a contract to purchase a large quantity of inventory that will be delivered at a future date. Or a business may sign a labour contract with its employees agreeing to pay certain salaries and benefits in

[14]C. Byrd and I. Chen, *Financial Reporting in Canada*, CICA: Toronto, 1997, p. 276.
[15]*CICA Handbook*, Section 3290, paragraph .20.

exchange for future services from those employees. Should the firm record a liability when it signs such a contract? No, because the definition of a liability requires that the obligation results from a *past transaction*. However, in this case there is no obligation until the other party to the contract delivers goods or services *in the future*. If the supplier should fail to deliver the inventory or the employee quit the firm, the business would be under no obligation to pay. For the sake of **full disclosure,** the firm should disclose commitments that can result in substantial future obligations in the notes to its financial statements, but it should not record the amount as a liability until the goods or services have been received.

Presentation of Current Liabilities in the Balance Sheet

Objective 7
Describe the presentation of current liabilities in the financial statements.

Some firms present current liabilities in their balance sheet in the order of maturity. Others present them by order of size (from largest amount to smallest). The main classes should be shown separately: bank loans, trade creditors and accrued liabilities, loans payable, taxes payable, dividends payable, deferred revenues, current payments on long-term debt, and future income tax liabilities.[16] A business should disclose separately any loans owing to the firm's owners, directors, officers, or related companies.[17] If the firm has pledged some of its assets to secure a liability (so that the creditor could seize the asset if the company defaults on the debt), this should also be disclosed.[18]

Exhibit 2 illustrates the presentation of current liabilities by **Shaw Communications Inc.** for the year ended August 31, 1997, in thousands of dollars:

Liabilities and Shareholders' Equity
Current

Bank indebtedness (note 8)	20,876
Accounts payable and accrued liabilities	116,740
Income taxes payable	17,536
Unearned subscriber revenue	35,779
Current portion of long-term debt	70,192
	261,123

Note 8 to the financial statements describes the type of operating loan that the company has, and indicates that it is secured by the firm's accounts receivable.

Appendix A: Accounting Systems for Payroll and Payroll Taxes

As an employee, you expect and are entitled to be paid at regular intervals at the end of each payroll period. Regardless of the number of employees, a business must design its payroll system to process payroll data quickly and accurately.

Good payroll records are essential to defend the firm if one of its employees makes a claim to the Provincial "Employments Standards Commissions" that he or

---

[16]*CICA Handbook,* Section 1510, paragraph 7. Dividends payable and future income tax liabilities will be discussed in a later chapters.
[17]*Ibid.*
[18]*Ibid.*

she was not paid overtime, holiday pay, etc. In the absence of good records, such commissions tend to side with employees.

In designing payroll systems, the business must consider the requirements of various government agencies for payroll data. Payroll data must not only be maintained for each payroll period, but also for each employee. The firm must submit periodic reports using payroll data to the appropriate governmental agencies. The payroll data itself must be retained for possible inspection by government authorities.

Payroll systems should also be designed to provide useful data for management decision-making needs. Such needs might include settling employee grievances and negotiating retirement or other benefits with employees.

Although payroll systems differ among businesses, the major components common to most payroll systems are the payroll register, employee's earnings record, and payroll cheques. We discuss and illustrate each of these major components below. We have kept the illustrations relatively simple, and they may be modified in practice to meet the needs of each individual business.

PAYROLL REGISTER

The **payroll register** is a multicolumn form used in assembling and summarizing the data needed for each payroll period. Its design varies according to the number and classes of employees and the extent to which computers are used. Exhibit 2 shows a form suitable for a small number of employees.

The nature of the data appearing in the payroll register is evident from the column headings. The payroll clerk inserts the number of hours worked and the earnings and deduction data in their proper columns. The sum of the deductions for each employee is then subtracted from the total earnings to yield the amount to be paid. The clerk records the cheque numbers in the payroll register as evidence of payment.

The last two columns of the payroll register accumulate the total wages or salaries to be debited to the various expense accounts. This process is usually called **payroll distribution.** If a large number of accounts are to be debited, the data may be accumulated on a separate payroll distribution sheet.

The format of the payroll register in Exhibit 2 aids in determining the mathematical accuracy of the payroll before cheques are issued to employees. All column totals should be cross-verified, as shown on the next page.

Exhibit 2
Payroll Register

		EARNINGS		
Employee Name	Total Hours	Regular	Overtime	Total
Abrams, Julie S.	40	500.00		500.00
Elrod, Fred G.	44	392.00	58.80	450.80
Gomez, Jose C.		840.00		840.00
McGrath, John T.	**44**	**1,000.00**	**150.00**	**1,150.00**
Wilkes, Glenn K.	40	480.00		480.00
Zumpano, Michael W.		600.00		600.00
Total		13,328.00	574.00	13,902.00

Earnings:

Regular	$13,328.00	
Overtime	574.00	
Total		$13,902.00

Deductions:

CPP	$ 385.75	
EI	465.85	
Income tax	3,332.00	
Canada Savings Bonds	680.00	
United Way	470.00	
Accounts receivable	50.00	
Total		5,383.60
Paid—net amount		$ 8,518.40

Accounts debited:

Sales Salaries Expense		$11,122.00
Office Salaries Expense		2,780.00
Total (as above)		$13,902.00

Recording Employees' Earnings

The accountant may post amounts in the payroll register directly to the accounts. An alternative is to use the payroll register as a supporting record for a journal entry. The entry based on the payroll register in Exhibit 2 follows.

Dec. 27	Sales Salaries Expense	11,122.00	
	Office Salaries Expense	2,780.00	
	CPP Payable		385.75
	EI Payable		465.85
	Employees Income Tax Payable		3,332.00
	Bond Deductions Payable		680.00
	United Way Deductions Payable		470.00
	Accounts Receivable—Fred G. Elrod		50.00
	Salaries Payable		8,518.40
	Payroll for week ended December 27.		

We record the total expense incurred for the services of employees by the debits to the salary expense accounts. Amounts withheld from employees' earnings have no effect on the debits to these accounts. Six of the credits in the preceding entry increase liability accounts and one credit decreases the accounts receivable account.

Exhibit 2 (concluded)

DEDUCTIONS							PAID		ACCOUNTS DEBITED	
CPP	EI	Income Tax	Canada Savings Bonds	Miscel-laneous		Total	Net Amount	Cheque No.	Sales Salaries Expense	Office Salaries Expense
13.85	13.50	119.15	20.00	UW	10.00	176.50	323.50	6857	500.00	
12.27	12.17	107.30		AR	50.00	181.74	269.06	6858		450.80
–	–	236.00	25.00	UW	10.00	271.00	569.00	6859	840.00	
–	–	331.45	20.00	UW	5.00	356.45	793.55	6860	1,150.00	
13.21	12.96	113.45	10.00			149.62	330.38	6880	480.00	
12.05	16.20	145.60	5.00	UW	2.00	180.85	419.15	6881		600.00
385.75	465.85	3,332.00	680.00	UW	470.00	5,383.60	8,518.40		11,122.00	2,780.00
				AR	50.00					

Miscellaneous Deductions UW—United Way; AR—Accounts Receivable

Recording and Paying Payroll Taxes

It is important for you to note that all employer's payroll taxes become liabilities when the related payroll is *paid* to employees. In addition, employers are required to compute and report payroll taxes on a *calendar-year* basis. The business must use the calendar year for payroll taxes, even if it uses a different fiscal year for financial reporting purposes.

Each time the payroll is prepared, the company must determine the amount of employer payroll taxes. The accountant then debits the payroll tax expense accounts and credits the related liability accounts.

To illustrate, the payroll register in Exhibit 2 indicates that the amount of CPP and EI contributions withheld is $385.75 and $465.85, respectively. Since the employer must match the employees' CPP contributions and contribute 1.4 times the employees' EI contribution, the employer owes the federal government an additional $1,037.94 ($385.75 + [$465.85 × 1.4]) for these payroll taxes. Further, assume that the business is liable for employment health tax (.98%) and workers' compensation (3%) on its payroll. The total payroll taxes owed by the firm is as follows:

Employer's share of CPP	$ 385.75
Employer's share of EI	652.19
Employment Health Tax ($13,902 × .98%)	136.24
Workers' Compensation ($13,902 × 3%)	417.06
	$1,591.24

The entry to journalize the payroll tax expense for the week and the liability for the taxes accrued is shown below. Payment of the liabilities for payroll taxes is recorded in the same manner as the payment of other liabilities.

Dec. 27	Payroll Tax Expense	1,591.24	
	CPP Payable		385.75
	EI Payable		652.19
	EHT Payable		136.24
	WC Payable		417.06
	Payroll taxes for week ended December 27.		

EMPLOYEE'S EARNINGS RECORD

The amount of each employee's earnings to date must be readily available at the end of each payroll period. This cumulative amount is required in order to compute each employee's earnings subject to CPP, EI, and income taxes. It is essential that a detailed payroll record be maintained for each employee. This record is called an **employee's earnings record.**

Exhibit 3 shows a portion of the employee's earnings record for John T. McGrath. The relationship between this record and the payroll register can be seen by tracing the amounts entered on McGrath's earnings record for December 27 back to its source—the fourth line of the payroll register in Exhibit 2. McGrath's earnings record shows no deductions for CPP or EI in the fourth quarter because the maximum deductions for these were reached earlier in the year.

In addition to spaces for recording data for each payroll period and the cumulative total of earnings, the employee's earnings record has spaces for quarterly totals and the yearly total. These totals are used in various reports for tax and other purposes. For example, by the last day of February a business must issue to each of its employees a T4 slip showing the renumeration paid to, and taxes withheld from, the employee in the previous calendar year. Employees use T4 slips in preparing

Exhibit 3
Employee's Earnings Record

John T. McGrath
130 Lakeshore Road
St. Catharines, ON

PHONE: 646-0019

MARRIED	NUMBER OF WITHHOLDING ALLOWANCES: 1	PAY RATE: $1,000.00 Per Week
OCCUPATION: Salesperson		EQUIVALENT HOURLY RATE: $25

EARNINGS

Period Ending	Total Hours	Regular Earnings	Overtime	Total Earnings	Cumulative Total
SEP. 27	51	1,000.00	412.50	1,412.50	52,800.00
THIRD QUARTER		13,000.00	4,800.00	17,800.00	
OCT. 4	50	1,000.00	375.00	1,375.00	54,175.00
NOV. 15	48	1,000.00	300.00	1,300.00	62,200.00
NOV. 22	50	1,000.00	375.00	1,375.00	63,575.00
NOV. 29	52	1,000.00	450.00	1,450.00	65,025.00
DEC. 6	50	1,000.00	375.00	1,375.00	66,400.00
DEC. 13	48	1,000.00	300.00	1,300.00	67,700.00
DEC. 20	52	1,000.00	450.00	1,450.00	69,150.00
DEC. 27	44	1,000.00	150.00	1,150.00	70,300.00
FOURTH QUARTER		13,000.00	4,500.00	17,500.00	
YEARLY TOTAL		52,000.00	18,300.00	70,300.00	

their personal tax returns. The business must also file a T4 summary with Revenue Canada each year. The amounts reported in the example of the T4 slip shown below were taken from John T. McGrath's employee's earnings record.

Revenue Canada / Revenu Canada		
T4 Short / Abrégé 1998	STATEMENT OF REMUNERATION PAID / ÉTAT DE LA RÉMUNÉRATION PAYÉE	Notice to Employers — **Important** — Avis aux employeurs. You can use this form if you do not provide any kind of taxable benefit or allowance to your employees. Vous pouvez utiliser ce formulaire si vous n'accordez aucun avantage ni aucune allocation imposable à vos employés. [S]

Employer's name – Nom de l'employeur
→ McDermott Supply Co.

Business Number – Numéro d'entreprise
[54] 887 211190

| Province of employment / Province d'emploi [10] Ontario | Social insurance number / Numéro d'assurance sociale [12] 426-810-410 |

Employee's name and address – Nom et adresse de l'employé

Surname – Nom de famille	First name – Prénom	Initials – Initiales
McGrath	John	T.

130 Lakeshore Rd.
St. Catharines, ON

Employment income – Revenus d'emploi [14] 70 300 00 [101]	Income tax deducted / Impôt sur le revenu retenu [22] 22 131 20 [437]
Employee's CPP contributions / Cotisations de l'employé au RPC [16] 1 068 80 [308]	EI insurable earnings – Gains assurables d'AE [24] 39 000 00
Employee's QPP contributions / Cotisations de l'employé au RRQ [17] [308]	CPP/QPP pensionable earnings / Gains donnant droit à pension – RPC/RRQ [26]
Employee's EI premiums / Cotisations de l'employé à l'AE [18] 1 053 00 [312]	Exempt – Exemption [28] CPP/QPP RPC/RRQ [ ] [ ] EI/AE

Employment commissions / Commissions d'emploi [42] [102]	Union dues – Cotisations syndicales [44] [212]
Pension adjustment – Facteur d'équivalence [52] 8 860 00 [206]	Charitable donations – Dons de bienfaisance [46] 100 00 [340]
RPP contributions – Cotisations à un RPA [20] [207]	RPP or DPSP registration no. / N° d'agrément d'un RPDB ou RPA [50]

T4 Short - Abrégé (98)   0667

Return with T4 Summary return
À retourner avec la déclaration T4 *Sommaire*   **1**

SOC. INS. NO.: 426810410   EMPLOYEE NO.: 814

DATE OF BIRTH: February 15, 1974

DATE EMPLOYMENT TERMINATED:

| DEDUCTIONS | | | | | | PAID | |
CPP	EI	Income Tax	Canada Savings Bonds	Other		Total	Net Amount	Cheque No.
		456.15	20.00			476.15	936.35	6175
		5,625.20	260.00	UW	40	5,925.20	11,874.80	
		437.80	20.00			457.80	917.20	6225
		401.20	20.00			421.20	878.80	6530
		437.80	20.00			457.80	917.20	6582
		480.55	20.00			500.55	949.45	6640
		437.80	20.00	UW	5	462.80	912.20	6688
		401.20	20.00			421.20	878.80	6743
		480.55	20.00			500.55	949.45	6801
		331.45	20.00	UW	5	356.45	793.55	6860
		5,532.80	260.00	UW	15	5,807.80	11,692.20	
1,068.80	1,053.00	22,131.20	1,040.00	UW	100	25,393.00	44,907.00	

Exhibit 3 (concluded)

PAYROLL CHEQUES

At the end of each pay period, one of the major outputs of the payroll system is a series of **payroll cheques.** These cheques are prepared from the payroll register, in which each line applies to an employee. Normally, the payroll cheque includes a detachable statement showing the details of how the net pay was computed. Exhibit 4 is a payroll cheque for John T. McGrath.

When the business uses a voucher system, it prepares a voucher for the net amount to be paid to the employees. The voucher is then recorded as a debit to Salaries Payable and a credit to Accounts Payable. The payment of the voucher is recorded in the usual manner. If the business does not use a voucher system, it records the payment by a debit to Salaries Payable and a credit to Cash.

The amount paid to employees is normally recorded as a single amount, regardless of the number of employees. There is no need to record each payroll cheque separately in the journal, since all of the details are available in the payroll register.

For paying their payroll, most employers use payroll cheques drawn on a special bank account. After the data for the payroll period have been recorded and summarized in the payroll register, a single cheque for the total amount to be paid is written on the firm's regular bank account. This cheque is then deposited in the special payroll bank account. Individual payroll cheques are written from the payroll account, and the numbers of the payroll cheques are inserted in the payroll register.

An advantage of using a separate payroll bank account is that the task of reconciling the bank statements is simplified. The bank returns paid payroll cheques with a bank statement for the payroll account. If all employees have cashed their

Exhibit 4
Payroll Cheque

MS **McDermott Supply Co.**
445 Geneva St.
St. Catharines, ON

John T. McGrath
130 Lakeshore Rd.
St. Catharines, ON

Cheque Number: 6860
Pay Period Ending: 12/27/98

HOURS & EARNINGS		TAXES & DEDUCTIONS		
DESCRIPTION	**AMOUNT**	**DESCRIPTION**	**CURRENT AMOUNT**	**Y-T-D AMOUNT**
Rate of Pay Reg.	25	CPP	–	1,068.80
Rate of Pay O.T.	37.50	EI	–	1,053.00
Hours Worked	40	Income Tax	331.45	22,131.20
Reg.	4	Canada Savings Bonds	20.00	1,040.00
Hours Worked O.T.		United Way	5.00	100.00
	793.55			
Net Pay				
	1,150.00	Total	356.45	25,393.00
Total Gross Pay	70,300.00			

STATEMENT OF EARNINGS. DETACH AND KEEP FOR YOUR RECORDS

MS **McDermott Supply Co.**
445 Geneva St.
St. Catharines, ON

Royal Bank
380 Scott St.
St. Catharines, ON

Pay Period Ending: 12/27/98   6860

PAY SEVEN HUNDRED AND NINETY THREE AND 55/100. . . . .**DOLLARS**

To the
Order of
JOHN T. MCGRATH
130 Lakeshore Rd.
St. Catharines, ON

$***793.55

Franklin D. McDermott

⑈6860⑈ ⑆153111123⑈ ⑈9385402⑈

payroll cheques, the balance of the payroll account should be zero or the amount initially required by the bank to open the account. This is because the amount of each deposit is equal to the total amount of payroll cheques written. Any payroll cheques not cashed by employees will appear as outstanding cheques on the bank reconciliation. After a payroll cheque is stale-dated (six months), the company should cancel it and transfer the funds back to the general account with a corresponding liability established to the employee. This establishes control over these items and prevents the theft or misuse of uncashed payroll cheques.

Currency may be used to pay payroll. For example, currency is often used for paying part-time workers or for employees, such as construction workers, who are paid at remote locations where cashing cheques is difficult. In such cases, the company writes a single cheque, payable to Payroll, for the entire amount to be paid. The cheque is then cashed at the bank and the money is inserted in individual pay envelopes. The employees should be asked for identification and should be required to sign a receipt when picking up their pay envelopes. Where a relative or friend picks up the payroll cheque, the employee should pre-authorize that transfer in a signed written note or form. Journalizing the payroll is the same as if the business used payroll cheques.

Many employees have their net pay deposited directly in a bank. In these cases, funds are transferred electronically.

PAYROLL SYSTEM DIAGRAM

You may find Exhibit 5 useful in following the flow of data within the payroll segment of an accounting system. The diagram indicates the relationships among the primary components of the payroll system we described in this chapter. The need to update the employee's earnings record is indicated by the dotted line.

Our focus in the preceding discussion has been on the outputs of a payroll system: the payroll register, payroll cheques, the employee's earnings record, and

Exhibit 5
Flow of Data in a Payroll System

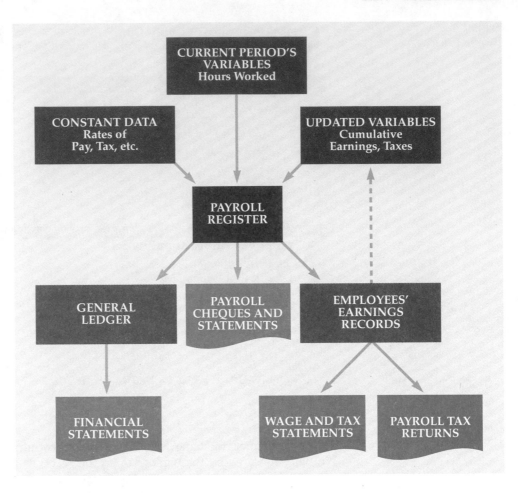

tax and other reports. As shown in the diagram in Exhibit 5, the inputs into a payroll system may be classified as either constants or variables.

Constants are data that remain unchanged from payroll to payroll and thus do not need to be input into the system each pay period. Examples of constants include such data as each employee's name and social insurance number, marital status, rate of pay, payroll category (office, sales, etc.), and department where employed. The CPP, EI, and income tax tables are also constants that apply to all employees. In a computerized accounting system, the business stores constants within its database.

Variables are data that change from payroll to payroll and thus must be input into the system each pay period. Examples of variables include such data as the number of hours or days worked by each employee during the payroll period, days of sick leave with pay, vacation credits, and cumulative earnings and taxes withheld. If salespersons are paid commissions, the amount of their sales would also vary from period to period.

INTERNAL CONTROLS FOR PAYROLL SYSTEMS

Payroll processing, as we discussed above, requires the input of a large amount of data, along with numerous and sometimes complex computations. These factors, combined with the large dollar amounts involved, require controls to ensure that payroll payments are timely and accurate. In addition, the system must also provide adequate safeguards against theft or other misuse of funds.

One scheme to misuse payroll funds was portrayed in the movie *Superman III*. In this movie, actor Richard Pryor played a computer programmer, Gus Gorman,

Internal controls for payroll systems will help avert schemes to misuse funds like that portrayed in "Superman III."

who embezzled payroll funds. Gus programmed the computer to round down each employee's payroll amount to the nearest penny. The amount "rounded out" was then added to Gus's payroll cheque. For example, if an employee's total payroll was $458.533, the payroll program would pay the employee $458.53 and add the $.003 to a special account. The total in this special account would be transferred to Gus's paycheque at the end of the processing of the payroll. In this way, Gus's cheque increased from $143.80 to $85,000 in one pay period.

The cash payment controls we discussed in the cash chapter also apply to payrolls. Thus, it is normally desirable to use a voucher system that includes procedures for proper authorization and approval of payroll. When a cheque-signing machine is used, it is important for the business to carefully control blank payroll cheques and access to the machine in order to prevent the theft or misuse of payroll funds.

It is especially important to authorize and approve in writing employee additions and deletions and changes in pay rates. For example, numerous payroll frauds have occurred where a supervisor has added fictitious employees to the payroll. The supervisor then cashes the fictitious employees' cheques. Similar frauds have occurred where employees have been fired but the Payroll Department is not notified. As a result, payroll cheques to the fired employees are prepared and cashed by a supervisor.

To prevent or detect frauds such as those we described above, the business must carefully control employees' attendance records. For example, you may have used an "In and Out" card on which your time of arrival to and departure from work was recorded when you inserted the card into a time clock. A Payroll Department employee may be stationed near the time clock during normal arrival and departure times in order to verify that employees only "clock in" once and only for themselves. Employee identification cards or badges may also be used to verify that only authorized employees are clocking in and are permitted to enter work areas. When the company distributes payroll cheques, it may require employee identification cards to deter one employee from picking up another's cheque.

Other controls include verifying and approving all payroll rate changes. In addition, in a computerized system, all program changes should be properly approved and tested by employees who are independent of the payroll system. This would prevent or detect any changes such as those portrayed in the movie mentioned above. The use of a special payroll bank account, as we discussed earlier in the chapter, also enhances control over payroll.

KEY POINTS

Objective 1. List the characteristics of a liability and define current liabilities.
A liability is an obligation that: (1) will require a future outflow of economic benefits, (2) the entity has little or no discretion to avoid, and (3) is due to a transaction or event that has already occurred. Current liabilities are debts that the firm expects to pay out of current assets or through the creation of another current liability. These include amounts payable within one year or the normal operating cycle of the business, whichever is longer.

Objective 2. Identify and journalize entries for various current liabilities that are definitely measurable.
Definitely measurable current liabilities are those for which the amount and due date can be determined with reasonable certainty. The accountant must be careful to record all such payables related to goods or services received by the end of the period, and must accrue interest expense on short-term notes payable, whether the notes have a stated interest rate or not. The principal portion of any long-term debt maturing in the next fiscal year is reported as a current liability. The business must also record as current liabilities customer advances for goods or services not yet delivered and for refundable deposits. Businesses often accrue property tax expense each month, recording the appropriate payable until payment has been made. When sales are subject to PST and/or GST, the firm must record a liability that is reversed when the tax is paid to the government. Businesses are allowed to recover GST that they pay on purchases of supplies, inventory, or capital assets, by offsetting these amounts against the GST payments that they remit to the government. Businesses must withhold income taxes, CPP, and UI from employees' pay

cheques, and often withhold other deductions such as union dues. Until these are remitted to the appropriate payee, they represent current liabilities for the business. The firm is also liable to remit payments for the employer's own share of CPP and UIC, and may also incur additional obligations for workers' compensation, employment health tax, and compensated absences.

Objective 3. Identify and journalize entries for estimated current liabilities including: (a) warranties and (b) promotional "giveaways."

An estimated liability is an obligation that definitely exists, but that is uncertain as to amount and due date. Examples include liabilities incurred with respect to warranties and promotional "giveaways." In both cases, the matching principle requires that the business record the expense and accrue the liability in the same period as it records the revenue from the related sale. The liability will be written off in the period(s) in which the business incurs the cost of fulfiling its obligations to its customers.

Objective 4. Identify and journalize entries for current liabilities dependent on operating results.

Some liabilities, such as income taxes, royalties, and management bonuses, are dependent on operating results. The amount of these obligations will be known with certainty at the end of the period, but may have to be estimated if the firm prepares interim reports.

Objective 5. Define a contingency and describe accounting and reporting for contingent liabilities.

A contingency is an existing situation involving uncertainty as to possible gain or loss, the outcome of which will ultimately be resolved when future events occur. A business should accrue a contingent loss as a current liability only if both (1) it is likely to occur and (2) its amount can be reasonably estimated. If either condition is missing, the business should not record a liability, but must disclose the contingency in the notes to its financial statements. A business may also report a contingent gain in the notes, but in accordance with the principle of conservatism, it cannot accrue an asset for the gain.

Objective 6. Describe reporting for future obligations.

If a business makes a commitment that may result in a substantial future liability, it should disclose the commitment in the notes to its financial statements. However, it should not accrue a liability on the balance sheet.

Objective 7. Describe the presentation of current liabilities in the financial statements.

Firms may present their current liabilities in order of maturity or in order of size. The business should disclose separately the main classes of current liabilities, any loans to the firm's owners, directors, officers or related companies, and whether any assets have been pledged to secure the liabilities.

GLOSSARY OF KEY TERMS

Canada Pension Plan (CPP). Federal program for providing retirement, disability, and similar benefits. Requires employers to withhold employee's contribution from employee's pay and to remit this to the government along with matching contribution from employer. *Objective 2*

Compensated absences. Periods when employers are obligated to pay employees for time off work due to statutory holidays, vacations, and illness. Accrued during periods when worker renders service to employer. *Objective 2*

Contingency. Existing situation involving uncertainty as to possible gain or loss, the outcome of which will ultimately be resolved when future events occur. *Objective 5*

Contingent liability. A liability arising from an existing situation involving uncertainty as to possible loss arising from a past event whose outcome will not be resolved until the future. *Objective 5*

Contractual commitment. Contract that may obligate firm to undertake substantial future liabilities. *Objective 6*

Current liabilities. Debts that a business expects to pay out of current assets or through the creation of another current liability. Includes amounts payable within one year or the operating cycle of the firm, whichever is longer. *Objective 1*

Discount on note payable. Difference between the maturity value of the note and the fair value of the consideration received for the note when issued. Represents the "real" interest being charged on a non-interest-bearing note. *Objective 2*

Employment Health Tax (EHT). Payroll tax levied on employers by some provinces to help pay for health care system. *Objective 2*

Employment Insurance (EI). Federal program for providing benefits to unemployed workers. Requires employers to withhold employee's contribution from employee's pay and to remit this to the government along with employer's contribution, calculated at 1.4 times employees' contributions. *Objective 2*

Estimated liability. Obligation that definitely exists, but that is uncertain as to its amount and due date. *Objective 3*

Goods and Services Tax (GST). Federal tax levied on most transactions involving delivery of products or services to customers. Businesses are required to act as agents to collect these taxes and remit them to the government, but may claim a refund for GST paid on its own purchases and capital assets. *Objective 2*

Gross pay. The total earnings of an employee for a payroll period. *Objective 2*

Liability. An obligation that (1) will require a future outflow of economic benefits, (2) the entity has little or no discretion to avoid, and (3) is due to a transaction or event that has already occurred. *Objective 1*

Net pay. Gross pay less payroll deductions; the amount the employer is obligated to pay the employee. *Objective 2*

Note payable. A written promise to pay a stated amount at a specific date. May have an interest rate stated on the note or be non-interest bearing. *Objective 2*

Payroll. The total amount paid to employees for a certain period. *Objective 2*

Provincial Sales Tax (PST). Tax imposed by most provinces on sales to final consumers of products. Businesses are required to act as agents to collect these taxes and remit them to the government. *Objective 2*

Refundable deposits. Security or container deposits that the business intends to return to customers in the future. *Objective 2*

Trade accounts payable. Amounts owed for goods or services purchased on credit. *Objective 2*

Warranty. A seller's promise to provide parts and/or labour to fix a product that proves to be defective during some specified period of time. *Objective 3*

Workers' Compensation (WC). Provincial program to provide assistance to employees injured on the job. Employers pay premiums based on payroll at rates set according to industry risk for worker injuries. *Objective 2*

ILLUSTRATIVE PROBLEM

Taylor Company began operations on December 1, 1999. Selected transactions during its first month of operations are as follows:

1. On December 1 Taylor issued a 10%, 60-day note payable to Canada Trustco for $4,000 cash.

2. On December 2 Taylor purchased inventory on account from Kelvin Co. for $15,000 plus 7% GST. Taylor can claim a refund from the government for any GST it pays on its purchases. Taylor uses a perpetual FIFO inventory system and paid the invoice on December 12.

3. During December Taylor sold merchandise with a cost of $10,000 for cash of $22,000 plus 8% PST and 7% GST. Taylor offers a two-year warranty on any item that it sells. It expects that the cost of servicing these warranties will amount to approximately 2% of gross sales.

4. On December 15 Taylor purchased inventory from Rheamer Co. with a fair value of $3,000 plus 7% GST. In exchange for the inventory Taylor gave Rheamer a three-month, non-interest-bearing note with a maturity value of $3,350.

5. During December Taylor sold gift certificates for $1,200, none of which had been redeemed by the end of December.

6. On December 29 the bookkeeper prepared the monthly payroll based on the following data:

Gross pay	$3,450
Income tax withheld	925
CPP withheld	104
EI withheld	93

The employer is liable for matching the employees' contributions to CPP and for contributing 1.4 times the employees' deductions for EI. In addition, Taylor must accrue 2% of gross payroll for vacation pay and 1% for Workers' Compensation. The payroll cheques were actually issued on December 31.

7. On December 31 Taylor accrued interest on its notes payable. In January, 2000 Taylor used $50 in supplies repairing defective products that were returned for warranty work. During January, Taylor also issued separate cheques to various government agencies to make payments for each of the following December accruals: (1) PST, (2) GST, (3) employees' income tax, CPP, and EI (all paid on one cheque to Revenue Canada), and (4) Workers' Compensation.

Instructions

Journalize the preceding transactions.

Solution

Dec. 1	Cash	4,000	
	Note Payable - Canada Trustco		4,000
	Issued note payable for cash.		
Dec. 2	Inventory	15,000	
	GST Payable	1,050	
	Accounts Payable		16,050
	Purchased inventory on account from Kelvin Co.		
Dec. 12	Accounts Payable	16,050	
	Cash		16,050
	Paid account owed to Kelvin Co.		
Dec.	Cash	25,300	
	Sales		22,000
	PST Payable		1,760
	GST Payable		1,540
	Sold merchandise for cash.		
	Cost of Goods Sold	10,000	
	Inventory		10,000
	Record cost of goods sold.		
	Warranty Expense	440	
	Warranty Liability		440
	Accrue warranty expense at 2% of gross sales (2% × $22,000).		
Dec. 15	Inventory	3,000	
	GST Payable	210	
	Discount on Note Payable	140	
	Note Payable - Rheamer Co.		3,350
	Purchased inventory in exchange for non-interest-bearing		
	note payable.		
Dec.	Cash	1,200	
	Unearned Revenue		1,200
	Sold gift certificates.		
Dec. 29	Salaries Expense	3,450	
	Employees Income Tax Payable		925
	CPP Payable		104
	EI Payable		93
	Salaries Payable		2,328
	Accrue payroll for December.		
	Payroll Expenses	338	
	CPP Payable		104
	EI Payable ($93 × 1.4)		130
	Vacation Pay Payable (2% × $3,450)		69
	WC Payable (1% × $3,450)		35
	Accrue payroll expenses.		
Dec. 31	Salaries Payable	2,328	
	Cash		2,328
	Issued payroll cheques.		
Dec. 31	Interest Expense	33	
	Interest Payable		33
	Accrue interest on Canada Trustco note payable.		
	($4,000 × 10% × $\frac{1}{12}$)		

	Interest Expense	23	
	Discount on Note Payable		23
	Accrue interest on Rheamer note payable. ($140 × ⅓ × ½)		
Jan.	Warranty Liability	50	
	Supplies		50
	Incurred warranty costs.		
	PST Payable	1,760	
	Cash		1,760
	Remitted payment for PST.		
	GST Payable ($1,540 – $1,050 – $210)	280	
	Cash		280
	Remitted payment for GST.		
	Employees' Income Tax Payable	925	
	CPP Payable ($104 + $104)	208	
	EI Payable ($93 + $130)	223	
	Cash		1,356
	Remitted payment for employees' income tax, CPP, and EI for December payroll.		
	WC Payable	35	
	Cash		35
	Remitted payment for WC for December.		

SELF-EXAMINATION QUESTIONS (ANSWERS AT END OF CHAPTER)

1. On November 1, 2000 Zelka Company issued a non-interest-bearing note payable for $20,000 due May 1, 2001 in exchange for equipment that could have been purchased for $19,100 cash. At its fiscal year end of December 31, 2000 Zelka should record interest expense of:
   A. zero
   B. $300
   C. $600
   D. $900

2. Roland Company, which began operations in 1999, sells products that carry a three-year warranty. Roland estimates that warranty costs will be approximately 3% of gross sales. Sales were $150,000 for 1999 and $200,000 for 2000. Warranty costs incurred were $1,800 in 1999 and $3,000 in 2000. At the end of 2000, Roland should report warranty liability of:
   A. $3,000
   B. $4,800
   C. $5,700
   D. $6,000

3. On January 1, 1999 Donnelly Company estimated that its property tax for the calendar year 1999 would be $36,000. On May 15 Donnelly received a property tax bill for 1999 totalling $37,200, which was due June 1. If Donnelly prepares interim financial statements for the three months ended March 31, 1999, it should report:
   A. Property Taxes Payable of $9,000
   B. Property Taxes Payable of $9,300
   C. Prepaid Property Taxes of $9,000
   D. Property Tax Expense of $9,300

4. An employee is paid $600 salary per week. Income tax is $145 and union dues are $10. The employee's contribution to CPP is $17, which must be matched by the employer. The employee's share of EI is $16, and the employer must contribute 1.4 times this amount. The amount of the employee's pay cheque (rounded to the nearest dollar) is:
   A. $600
   B. $445
   C. $412
   D. $373

5. Which of the following statements is true regarding (1) estimated liabilities, (2) contingent liabilities, and (3) future obligations for purchase commitments?
   A. All three should be reported as liabilities on the balance sheet.
   B. Since the exact amount of the obligation is not known for certain, none of these is accrued in the accounts, but all three should be reported in the notes to the financial statements.
   C. (1) and (2) should always be reported on the balance sheet as current liabilities, (3) is only reported in the notes to the financial statements.
   D. (1) is always reported as a liability on the balance sheet, but (3) never is. (2) is reported as a liability only if it is likely and its amount can be estimated.

DISCUSSION QUESTIONS

1. How are liabilities defined?
2. How do you determine if a liability should be reported as current or long-term?
3. In borrowing money from a bank, a business issued a $50,000, 90-day non-interest-bearing note. Will the business receive $50,000 cash from the bank? Explain.
4. Explain what is meant by the term "Discount on Note Payable"? Where is this account reported in the financial statements?
5. A $10,000 note payable issued by Federici Company to the **Toronto-Dominion Bank** three years ago is coming due in two months. Federici has signed a contract with **National Trust Company** to put a new, five-year $50,000 mortgage on its building, with the condition that it use $10,000 of these proceeds to pay off the note payable. Should Federici report the note payable as a current or a long-term liability? Explain.
6. "Unearned Revenue" and "Refundable Deposits" both represent amounts of cash that a firm has received from its customers. Why are these amounts recorded as liabilities, rather than as income? Discuss.
7. Should a firm always wait until it receives a bill for its property taxes before recording any amount for this expense? Discuss.
8. A firm collects both PST and GST from its customers. It remits the entire amount of PST collected to the provincial government, but is not required to send the full amount of GST to the federal government. Explain.
9. What is (a) gross pay and (b) net pay? What items might make up the difference between these two amounts?
10. Why are deductions from employees' earnings classified as liabilities for the employer?
11. For each of the following payroll taxes, indicate whether they generally apply to (a) employees only, (b) employers only, or (c) both employees and employers.
    1. Workers' Compensation
    2. Canada Pension Plan
    3. Income Tax Withheld
    4. Employment Health Tax
    5. Employment Insurance
12. Should the employer record vacation pay expense during the period when an employee is on vacation or during the period when the employee is working? What accounting principle determines when the expense should be recorded? Discuss.
13. What are some examples of post-retirement benefits?
14. "Our business will record warranty expense in the period in which we perform the warranty work. If our products never prove to be defective, we will never have to record any warranty expense on them." Discuss the possible weakness of this accounting policy.
15. **Canadian Airlines** awards flier points to customers who purchase tickets and travel with the airline. When a customer has accumulated enough points, he or she may redeem them for a free trip with Canadian. Discuss the issues involved in accounting for the "free" flights that the airline is offering its customers.
16. Give three examples of liabilities that depend on the operating results of the business.
17. Explain the difference between an estimated liability and a contingent liability. List two examples of contingent liabilities.
18. How should you treat a contingent liability in the financial statements? How should you treat contingent gains? What accounting principle justifies treating these differently?
19. Explain what a purchase commitment is. Should these be recorded as liabilities? Explain.
20. Discuss the general guidelines for presenting current liabilities in the financial statements.

EXERCISES

EXERCISE 11–1
Entries for notes payable
Objective 2

A business issued a 90-day, 10% note for $15,000 to a creditor on account. Journalize the entries to record (a) the issuance of the note and (b) the payment of the note at maturity, including interest. For simplicity, assume a 360-day year.

EXERCISE 11–2
Calculating interest on notes issued
Objective 2

In negotiating a 90-day loan, a business has the option of either (1) issuing a $500,000, non-interest-bearing note in exchange for $487,500 cash or (2) issuing a $500,000 note that bears interest at the rate of 10% and that will be accepted at face value. For simplicity, assume a 360-day year.

a. Calculate the amount of the interest expense for each option.
b. ◀▬▬▶ Which option is more favourable to the borrower? Explain.

EXERCISE 11–3
Evaluating alternative note receivables
Objective 2

A bank has two alternatives in making a loan: (1) accepting a $60,000, 60-day, 10% note in exchange for $60,000 cash or (2) accepting a 60-day, $60,000 non-interest-bearing note in exchange for $59,000 cash. For simplicity, assume a 360-day year.

a. Determine the amount of interest earned in each situation.
b. ◀▬▬▶ Which alternative is more favourable to the bank? Explain.

EXERCISE 11–4
Entries for discounted notes
Objective 2

On December 1, Zelda Co. issues a 60-day, non-interest-bearing note for $200,000 to **Royal Bank** in exchange for $196,000 cash. For simplicity, assume a 360-day year.

a. Journalize the borrower's entries to record:
   1. the issuance of the note.
   2. accrual of interest on December 31.
   3. the payment of the note at maturity.
b. Journalize the creditor's entries to record:
   1. the receipt of the note.
   2. accrual of interest on December 31.
   3. the receipt of payment of the note at maturity.

EXERCISE 11–5
Refundable deposits
Objective 2

The Pop Company sells bottled pop and collects a $0.10 per bottle refundable deposit on all bottles sold. During its first year of operations, the business sold 200,000 bottles and accepted 120,000 returned bottles. The Pop Company estimates that 15% of all bottles will never be returned. Journalize the entries related to refundable deposits. (*Hint:* Record deposits for bottles that will never be returned as Container Revenue.)

EXERCISE 11–6
Property tax
Objective 2

The Smart Clothing Company prepares monthly financial statements and has a fiscal year end of December 31. Property taxes for the current year are estimated at $36,000. The Company makes an interim payment to the city on account of $9,000 on April 30. Journalize the entries related to the property taxes for each month from January through May.

EXERCISE 11–7
Property tax
Objective 2

The Smart Clothing Company (continuing from Exercise 11–6) receives its property tax bill from the city for the current year on June 15 in the amount of $38,000 and pays the balance owing on June 30. Journalize the entry related to the payment, and determine the amount of the monthly entry to be made for property tax expense for July through December.

EXERCISE 11–8
GST and PST
Objective 2

The Brown Shoe Store buys merchandise in January for $8,000 plus GST. Sales (all cash) for January, subject to GST (7%) and PST (8%), were $14,000. Journalize the entries to record these events in January, and the subsequent payment of the GST and PST in February.

EXERCISE 11–9
Summary payroll data
Objective 2

In the following summary of data for a payroll period, some amounts have been intentionally omitted:

Earnings:
1.	At regular rate	?
2.	At overtime rate	$ 6,100
3.	Total earnings	?

Deductions:

4.	CPP and EI withheld	8,600
5.	Income tax withheld	15,500
6.	Group life insurance	1,050
7.	Union dues	1150?
8.	Total deductions	26,300
9.	Net amount paid	92,620

Accounts debited:

10.	Factory Wages	86,250
11.	Sales Salaries	?
12.	Office Salaries	7,500

a. Calculate the amounts omitted in lines (1), (3), (7), and (11).
b. Journalize the entry to record payroll.
c. Journalize the entry to record the payment of the payroll.

EXERCISE 11–10
Payroll
Objective 2

The monthly totals from the payroll register of the Regis Construction Company for March of the current year are as follows:

Gross pay	$25,500
Income tax withheld	7,500
CPP deducted	1,080
EI deducted	1,120
Union dues	400

a. Journalize the entry to record the payroll summary for the month.
b. Journalize the entry to record the payment to employees.
c. Journalize the entry to record the employer portions of CPP and EI for the month.

EXERCISE 11–11
Payroll
Objective 2

Suppose that the Regis Construction Company in Exercise 11-10 is required to make a contribution to Workers' Compensation (WC) of 15% of gross payroll and to remit an Employment Health Tax (EHT) of 0.98%. Journalize the entry to record the liability for the WC and EHT.

EXERCISE 11–12
Accrued vacation pay
Objective 2

A business provides its employees with varying amounts of vacation per year, depending on the length of employment. The average amount of the current year's vacation pay is estimated at 4% of the gross payroll. Journalize the adjusting entry required in January to record the accrued vacation pay if January's gross payroll is $60,800.

EXERCISE 11–13
Accrued product warranty
Objective 3

Park Company warrants its products for one year. The estimated product warranty is 2% of sales. Assuming that sales were $500,000 for January, journalize the adjusting entry required in January to record the accrued product warranty.

EXERCISE 11–14
Product warranty
Objective 3

Assume that the Park Company in Exercise 11–13 has sales of $7,000,000 during the current year and has recorded the appropriate estimate for product warranty at 2% of sales. During the year, $65,000 was paid for parts and labour for warranty repairs and accounted for properly. Determine the balance in the accrued warranty liability at the end of the current year.

EXERCISE 11–15
Promotional giveaways
Objective 3

The All Oats Cereal Company includes a cut-out coupon on each cereal box it sells. Ten coupons can be redeemed for a toy that costs the company $0.80. During the year the company sold 1,000,000 boxes of cereal. It is estimated that only 10% of the coupons will be redeemed. During the year, 60,000 coupons were sent in and 6,000 toys sent out. Journalize the entries to record the liability for coupon redemption and the redemptions during the year. Indicate the balance that will appear on All Oats' balance sheet for estimated coupon redemptions outstanding at the end of the year.

EXERCISE 11–16
Royalties
Objective 4

The Axis Manufacturing Company makes a product under licence from its inventor who holds the patent requiring a royalty of 3% of the revenue from annual sales of the product to be paid within the first quarter of the following year. If sales of the product during the current year are $2,500,000, journalize the entry for the royalty to be accrued at year end.

EXERCISE 11–17
Contingencies
Objective 5

In October of the current year, The Tacky Shop was sued for $500,000 by a customer who tripped over boxes stored on the floor of the store and broke her ankle. The Tacky Shop's lawyer is certain that the customer will win the lawsuit but that the damages awarded will only be $50,000. Explain how the business should treat this contingency. Give reasons for your answer.

EXERCISE 11–18
Commitments
Objective 6

A review of information available when preparing the financial statements for Genesis Computers at the beginning of December, 2000 indicates that the business has signed a contract to purchase $150,000 in inventory that is to be delivered over the next three months. By December 31 $50,000 of this inventory had been received from the supplier, although no payments had been made on the invoice. A second contract for the purchase of a new fax machine for $1,000 was signed on the last day of the year with expectation of delivery within four weeks. Explain how the business should treat these contracts in preparing its financial statements at December 31, 2000.

EXERCISE 11–19
Internal control procedures
Appendix

Memphis Sounds is a retail store specializing in the sale of jazz compact discs and cassettes. The store employs three full-time and 10 part-time workers. The store's weekly payroll averages $1,800 for all 13 workers.

Memphis Sounds uses a personal computer to assist in preparing pay cheques. Each week the store's accountant collects employee time cards and enters the hours worked into the payroll program. The payroll program calculates each employee's pay and prints a pay cheque. The accountant uses a cheque-signing machine to sign the pay cheques. Next, a voucher is prepared to transfer funds from the store's regular bank account to the payroll account. This voucher is authorized by the store's owner.

For the week of May 10, the accountant accidentally recorded 400 hours worked instead of 40 hours for one of the full-time employees. Does Memphis Sounds have internal controls in place to catch this error? If so, how will this error be detected?

EXERCISE 11–20
Internal control procedures
Appendix

Taylor Tools is a small manufacturer of home workshop power tools. The company employs 30 production workers and 10 administrative persons. The following procedures are used to process the company's weekly payroll:

a. Whenever a salaried employee is terminated, Personnel authorizes Payroll to remove the employee from the payroll system. However, this procedure is not required when an hourly worker is terminated. Hourly employees only receive a pay cheque if their time card shows hours worked. The computer automatically drops an employee from the payroll system when that employee has six consecutive weeks with no hours worked.

b. Whenever an employee receives a pay raise, the supervisor must fill out a wage adjustment form, which is signed by the company president. This form is used to change the employee's wage rate in the payroll system.

c. All employees are required to record their hours worked by clocking in and out on a time clock. Employees must clock out for lunch break. Due to congestion around the time clock area at lunch time, management has not objected to having one employee clock in and out for an entire department.

d. Pay cheques are signed by using a cheque-signing machine. This machine is located in the main office, so that it can be easily accessed by anyone needing a cheque signed.

e. Taylor maintains a separate chequing account for payroll cheques. Each week, the total net pay for all employees is transferred from the company's regular bank account to the payroll account.

State whether each of the procedures is appropriate or inappropriate after considering the principles of internal control. If a procedure is inappropriate, state what action must be taken to correct it.

PROBLEM 11–1A
Various current liabilities
Objectives 1, 2, 3, 4, 5, 6

Indicate whether each of the following situations would give rise to reporting a current liability on the balance sheet of Cheng Company at December 31, 1999. In each case explain why a liability should or should not be reported, and indicate the amount that would appear on the balance sheet, if any.

a. Cheng received a shipment of inventory on December 30. An invoice for the inventory, which totalled $5,000, was not received until January 3, 2000.
b. One of Cheng's competitors has filed a $50,000 lawsuit against the company for patent infringement. Cheng's lawyers believe that there is little chance that the claim will be successful.
c. Cheng began selling a new product this year that carries a two-year warranty. The business estimates that the total cost of servicing the warranty for sales in 1999 will be $2,000. During 1999 it incurred $300 in warranty costs.
d. Cheng has signed an agreement to purchase a new machine in January, 2000 at a cost of $15,000.
e. Cheng provides a profit-sharing bonus for its manager equal to 4% of operating income. The 1999 operating income before the bonus is $200,000 (after making all appropriate adjusting entries).

PROBLEM 11–2A
Accounts payable, GST, notes payable, unearned revenue
Objective 2

Imam Company began operations on January 1, year 1. Selected transactions during its first three months of operations are as follows:

a. Purchased inventory on account for $10,000 on terms 2/10, n/30. Assume that there was no sales tax charged on these purchases. One-quarter of these amounts are still unpaid at March 31. Imam paid the remainder of these accounts within the discount date, except for one invoice of $2,000, which was paid after the discount date. Imam uses a FIFO perpetual inventory system, and records purchases gross of purchase discounts.
b. Received $15,000 from the **Canadian Imperial Bank of Commerce (CIBC)** on January 1 in exchange for a note payable with a maturity value of $16,000 due October 1, year 1.
c. Purchased equipment costing $8,000 plus 7% GST on January 1. Imam can claim a refund from the government for any GST it pays on such purchases. The equipment has a useful life of five years and no residual value. In exchange for the equipment, Imam gave an 8%, one-year note payable.
d. During its first quarter Imam made cash sales of $12,000 plus 7% GST and 8% PST. The cost of the goods sold was $6,000.
e. Signed a one-year lease on February 1 to rent out the upper floor of its building to Koustas Consultants for $800 per month. Koustas gave Imam a cheque for $1,600 to cover the February rent and a last month's rent deposit.
f. Made adjusting entries on March 31 to record interest expense and amortization for the first quarter.

Instructions

a. Journalize the entries required to record the above transactions.
b. Prepare the current liabilities section of Imam's balance sheet at March 31, year 1.

PROBLEM 11–3A
Entries for payroll and payroll taxes
Objective 2

The following information relative to the payroll for the week ended January 30 was obtained from the records of Giles Co.:

Salaries:		Deductions:	
Sales salaries	$21,000	Income tax withheld	$32,890
Warehouse salaries	60,600	CPP withheld	2,750
Office salaries	16,100	EI withheld	2,665
	$97,700	Canada Savings Bonds	2,000
		Group insurance	520

Employer obligations:
Match employees' CPP contribution
1.4 times employees' EI contribution
1.5% gross payroll for Workers' Compensation
0.98% gross payroll for Employment Health Tax

Instructions

Prepare journal entries to record the payroll and all payroll obligations on January 30.

PROBLEM 11–4A
Warranties, coupons
Objective 3

The following data relate to Mercier Company, which has a December 31 fiscal year end.

a. In 1999 Mercier began offering a three-year warranty on all products that it sold. Industry experience suggests that warranty expense will amount to 6% of sales revenue.

b. At the beginning of 2000 Mercier introduced a promotional campaign to promote sales and build up customer loyalty. Every time a customer makes a purchase, the customer receives a coupon worth 20% of the value of the purchase, which can be applied as a credit against another purchase made within the next 12 months. The company estimates that only 10% of these coupons will ever be redeemed. Mercier's accounting policy is to set up the expected cost of the promotion in the period that the original sale is made.

Data regarding Mercier's sales, warranty costs incurred, and coupons redeemed over a three-year period are shown below:

	Net Sales	Warranty Costs Incurred	Coupons Redeemed
1999	$ 400,000	$ 3,000	
2000	1,000,000	15,000	$12,000
2001	1,400,000	45,000	21,000
	$2,800,000	$63,000	$33,000

Instructions

a. Calculate the amount that Mercier should report as a warranty liability at the end of 1999, 2000, and 2001.

b. Calculate the amount that Mercier should report as a premium liability at the end of 2000 and 2001.

PROBLEM 11–5A
Contingencies, royalties, commitments
Objectives 4, 5, 6

While auditing the financial statements of Jaeger Company for the fiscal year ended December 31, 1999, you find the following items that have not been entered in the accounting records:

1. A former employee sues Jaeger for $200,000 alleging racial discrimination. Jaeger's lawyer does not think that the suit has merit, but advises Jaeger to agree to an out-of-court settlement of $10,000 to avoid the legal costs of defending the suit. Both Jaeger and the former employee agree to this and sign the appropriate settlement papers.

2. Jaeger is suing a competitor for industrial espionage. A lower court awarded Jaeger $100,000 in damages, but the case has been appealed to a higher court, which is expected to make a decision within the next 12 months.

3. In 1997 Jaeger purchased a patent to manufacture a new product. The patent agreement required Jaeger to pay a royalty of 2% of the sales revenue from the product to the original inventor at the end of each year for five years. Payments are due 30 days after the end of the year. No royalty payments have been made on account of 1999 product sales totalling $300,000.

4. In December, 1999 Jaeger signs a $100,000 employment contract with a television celebrity, who will appear in five commercials promoting the company's products over the next two years.

Instructions

Journalize any entries required by the above information. In any case where a journal entry is not required, explain why not.

PROBLEM 11–6A
Balance sheet presentation of current liabilities
Objective 7

The records of Computer Systems Experts show the following selected account balances for the year ended December 31, 2000:

Notes payable, due April 1, 2001	$40,000
Accounts payable (includes $10,000 short-term loan from owner)	80,000
Note receivable, due August 1, 2001	15,000
Liability for coupons outstanding	9,000
Payroll taxes payable	2,500
8% Note payable, due February 1, 2004	30,000
Interest payable on 8% note payable	2,000
Discount on note payable, due April 1, 2001	800
Payroll payable	3,200
PST and GST Payable	3,500
Unearned revenue	1,500
7% Loan payable ($5,000 installment of principal due on June 1 of each of next three years)	15,000

On December 1, 2000 Computer Systems Experts signed a noncancellable contract to purchase merchandise in March, 2001 for $12,000. The business has also guaranteed a debt of $25,000 issued by a related company, which is in a strong financial position.

Instructions

a. Prepare the current liabilities section of the balance sheet for Computer Systems Experts at December 31, 2000.
b. Prepare any notes to the financial statements required by the information presented above.

PROBLEM 11–7A
Wage and tax statement data and employer payroll taxes
Appendix

Jerico Company began business on January 2 of last year. Salaries were paid to employees on the last day of each month, and income tax, CPP, and EI were withheld in the required amounts. An employee who is hired in the middle of the month receives half the monthly salary for that month. All required payroll tax reports were filed, and the correct amount of payroll taxes was remitted by the company for the calendar year. Before the T4 slips could be prepared for distribution to employees, the employees' earnings records were inadvertently destroyed.

None of the employees resigned or was discharged during the year, and there were no changes in salary rates. Data on dates of employment, salary rates, and employees' payroll taxes withheld, which are summarized as follows, were obtained from personnel records and payroll records. The maximum contribution that could be withheld from an employee for the year was $1,068.80 for CPP and $1,053.00 for EI.

Employee	Date First Employed	Monthly Salary	Monthly Income Tax Withheld	Monthly CPP Withheld	Monthly EI Withheld
Albright	June 2	$3,000	$ 779	$ 86.67	$59.02
Charles	Jan. 2	6,000	1,913	182.68	59.02
Given	Mar. 1	3,200	855	93.08	59.02
Nelson	Jan. 2	4,000	1,160	119.00	59.02
Quinn	Nov. 15	3,600	877	105.88	59.02
Ramsey	Apr. 15	2,000	476	54.67	54.00
Wu	Jan. 16	5,400	1,596	163.48	59.02

Instructions

1. Calculate the amounts to be reported on each employee's T4 slip for the year, arranging the data in the following form:

Employee	Gross Earnings	Income Tax Withheld	CPP Withheld	EI Withheld

2. Calculate the following employer payroll taxes for the year: (a) CPP to match employees' contributions; (b) EI at 1.4 times employee contributions; (c) Workers' Compensation at 2% of gross payroll; (d) total.

PROBLEM 11–1B
Liability transactions
Objectives 2, 3

The following items were selected from among the transactions completed by Shukla Co. during the current year. Assume that Shukla uses a periodic FIFO system for inventory and that there was no sales tax on inventory purchases. Shukla records purchases gross of purchase discounts.

Mar. 2. Purchased inventory on account from Charest Co., $6,000, terms 2/10, n/30.
8. Purchased inventory on account from Mautz Co., $10,000, terms 2/10, n/30.
12. Paid Charest Co. for the invoice of March 2.
Apr. 7. Issued a 60-day, 12% note for $10,000 to Mautz Co., on account.
May 10. Issued a 120-day, non-interest-bearing note for $90,000 to **National Trust** in exchange for $85,800 cash.
June 6. Paid Mautz Co. the amount owed on the note of April 7.
Aug. 5. Borrowed $7,500 from First Financial Corporation, issuing a 60-day, 14% note for that amount.
Sep. 7. Paid National Trust the amount due on the note of May 10.
Oct. 4. Paid First Financial Corporation the interest due on the note of August 5 and renewed the loan by issuing a new 30-day, 16% note for $7,500. (Record both the debit and credit to the notes payable account.)
Nov. 3. Paid First Financial Corporation the amount due on the note of October 4.
15. Purchased store equipment from Singer Equipment Co. for $100,000, paying $16,000 and issuing a series of seven 12% notes for $12,000 each, coming due at 30-day intervals.
Dec. 15. Paid the amount due Singer Equipment Co. on the first note in the series issued on November 15.

Instructions

1. Journalize the transactions. Assume a 360-day year for computing interest.
2. Journalize the adjusting entries for the following accrued expenses for the current year:
   a. Vacation pay, $18,300.
   b. Product warranty cost, $14,000.
3. Journalize the adjusting entry for the accrued interest at December 31 on the six notes owed to Singer Equipment Co.
4. Assume that a single note for $84,000 had been issued on November 15 instead of the series of seven notes and that its terms required principal payments of $12,000 each 30 days, with interest at 12% on the principal balance before applying the $12,000 payment. Calculate the amount that would have been due and payable on December 15.

PROBLEM 11–2B
Property taxes
Objective 2

Yee Company prepares monthly financial statements and has a December 31 fiscal year end. The property tax on its office buildings for the calendar year 1999 was $23,600. Yee estimates that its taxes for the year 2000 will be $24,000. On April 29, 2000 Yee receives its annual tax bill of $25,400, which is due on May 31. Yee records its monthly property tax expense on the last day of each month.

Instructions

a. Journalize the entries that Yee will make on each of the following dates in the year 2000: February 28, April 30, May 31 (show the entries to record both property tax expense and the payment of the tax bill on this date), July 31.
b. Suppose that, instead of all due in one payment, Yee's tax bill of $25,400 is due in two installments: $12,700 is payable on May 31 and $12,700 is payable on August 31. Assuming that Yee pays its taxes on these two dates, prepare the journal entries that the company should make on each of the following dates: February 28, April 30, May 31, July 31, August 31, October 31. On May 31 and August 31 show the entries to record both property tax expense and the payment of the tax bill on these dates.

PROBLEM 11–3B
Payroll accounts and entries
Objective 2

The following accounts, with the balances indicated, appear in the ledger of B & B Co. on December 1 of the current year:

212	Salaries Payable	—
213	CPP Payable	$ 1,220
214	EI Payable	1,180
215	Employees Income Tax Payable	14,586
216	Employment Health Tax Payable	430
217	United Way Payable	396
218	Bond Deductions Payable	850
611	Sales Salaries Expense	694,430
711	Officers Salaries Expense	342,980
712	Office Salaries Expense	94,050
719	Payroll Taxes Expense	101,673

The following transactions relating to payroll, payroll deductions, and payroll taxes occurred during December:

Dec. 2. Issued Cheque No. 728 to purchase Canada Savings Bonds for employees.

3. Issued Cheque No. 729 to Revenue Canada to pay employees' income tax, CPP, and EI payable.

14. Journalized the entry to record the biweekly payroll. A summary of the payroll record follows:

Salary distribution:

Sales	$36,230	
Officers	16,720	
Office	4,180	$57,130

Deductions:

CPP withheld	$ 1,110	
EI withheld	1,060	
Income tax withheld	18,200	
Savings bond deductions	375	
United Way deductions	228	20,973
Net amount		$36,157

14. Issued Cheque No. 738 payable to Payroll Bank Account, for the net amount of the biweekly payroll.

14. Journalized the entry to record payroll taxes on employees' earnings of December 14: match employees' CPP contribution; 1.4 times employees' EI contribution; 0.98% gross payroll for Employment Health Tax.

17. Issued Cheque No. 744 in payment of balance in Employment Health Tax Payable.

19. Issued Cheque No. 750 in payment of balance in United Way payable.

Instructions
Journalize the transactions.

PROBLEM 11–4B
Flier points, returnable containers
Objective 3

During your first two years working in a public accounting firm, you encounter the following situations:

a. Flylite Airlines is a new economy airline that began serving the North American market in early 1999. In order to compete with the larger airlines, Flylite is offering a frequent flier program that works as follows: for every 100 miles flown on a regular fare ticket with the airline, a traveller receives frequent flier points equivalent to 10 free air miles on a future trip. Based on industry experience, Flylite estimates that only 25% of flier points awarded will ever be redeemed. During the years 1999 and 2000 Flylite made regular ticket sales of $8,000,000 and $10,000,000, and redeemed flier points for trips valued at $50,000 and $150,000, respectively.

b. Clearwater Beverage Company sells soft drinks in returnable containers. The beverages sell for $0.70 each plus 6% PST and 7% GST plus $0.10 deposit for the container (no tax is charged on the returnable container). Clearwater began operations in 1999. During that year it made sales of $560,000 (before sales tax) and refunded $23,000 on containers returned by customers. The following year's sales were up 10% and the business refunded $40,000 for returnable containers.

Instructions

a. Journalize all of the entries required by each of the above situations for 1999 and 2000.
b. Determine the balances in the current liabilities accounts at the end of 1999 and 2000 for each of the above situations.

PROBLEM 11–5B
Accounting concepts review

Indicate the generally accepted accounting principles or concepts that best justify each of the accounting practices described below.

1. A liability for future warranty costs related to the current year's sales is recorded in the year that the sale is made.
2. A business indicates in a footnote that it is the defendant in a lawsuit brought by a competitor for patent infringement.
3. In recording a probable liability for a lawsuit involving a violation of environmental laws, a business obtains an estimate from an independent lawyer who specializes in environmental litigation.
4. In preparing the balance sheet, a business does not report detailed information as to each amount due to dozens of trade creditors. The firm presents the total amount under the caption *Accounts Payable*.

PROBLEM 11–6B
Balance sheet presentation of current liabilities
Objective 7

The records of Innovative Design Company show the following account balances at December 31, 2000:

Container deposits	$ 4,000
Wages payable	8,500
Accounts payable	80,000
Bank overdraft	2,000
6% Notes payable, due February 1, 2001	60,000
8% Note payable, due July 1, 2004	10,000
10% Note payable ($1,000 installment of principal due on March 1 and September 1 of each of the next five years)	10,000
Interest payable on 6% note payable	3,300
Interest payable on 8% note payable	2,000
Interest payable on 10% note payable	333
CPP and EI Payable	3,200
PST Payable	5,000

The 6% note payable is due to **Royal Bank**. Innovative Design has signed a contract with the Royal Bank to place a five-year $60,000 mortgage on its office building on February 1, 2001. The bank will apply the cash from the mortgage to pay off the 6% note payable coming due on that date. A customer is suing Innovative Design for $20,000 for false representation of their products. Innovative's lawyers think that there is about a 20% chance that the customer will win the lawsuit.

Instructions

a. Prepare the current liabilities section of the balance sheet for Innovative Design Company at December 31, 2000.
b. Prepare any notes to the financial statements required by the information presented above.

PROBLEM 11–7B
Payroll register
Appendix

The following data for Wang Co. relate to the payroll for the week ended December 7:

Employee	Hours Worked	Hourly Rate	Weekly Salary	Income Tax	CPP	EI	Canada Savings Bonds	Accumulated Earnings, Nov. 30
A	44	$24.00		$344	–	–	$37.50	$51,640
B	40	20.00		220	–	–	25.00	39,900
C			$1,425	463	–	–	50.00	69,825
D	48	12.75		169	19.06	17.90		15,300
E	40	12.00		113	13.21	12.96	25.00	24,000
F			400	95	10.65	10.80		3,200

Employees C and F are office staff, and all of the other employees are sales personnel. All sales personnel are paid 1½ times the regular rate for all hours in excess of 40 hours per week. The next payroll cheque to be used is No. 981.

Instructions

1. Prepare a payroll register for Wang Co. for the week ended December 7.
2. Journalize the entry to record the payroll for the week.

CHALLENGE PROBLEMS

PROBLEM CP11–1

Schuele Company just completed its first year of operations on December 31, year 1. The business uses a periodic inventory system. For each of the transactions listed below, indicate the effect of any errors on year 1's revenues, expenses, and total liabilities reported at year end. For each item indicate whether the transaction caused the item to be overstated (O) or understated (U) and by what amount. If the transaction did not misstate an item, indicate this by the letters NE. As an example, we have indicated the effects of the first transaction shown.

Transaction	Revenues	Expenses	Total Liabilities
1. The bookkeeper forgot to accrue a utility bill for $2,000 at the end of year 1.	NE	U by $2,000	U by $2,000
2. In December Schuele signed a contract to buy $20,000 of inventory to be delivered in January. This was recorded in year 1 by a debit to Purchases and a credit to Accounts Payable for $20,000.			
3. A cash sale for $10,000 plus 8% sales tax and 7% GST was recorded by a debit to Cash and a credit to Sales of $11,500.			
4. In year 1 Schuele sold $60,000 of products carrying a two-year warranty. It estimates warranty work on these items will cost 2% in year 1, 2% in year 2, and 1% in year 3. $1,200 was recorded for warranty expense in year 1.			
5. The year end inventory count included $5,000 of merchandise received December 30. The purchase and account payable were recorded when the purchase invoice was received in January, year 2.			
6. Schuele sells some products in returnable containers. The correct entry was made when the products were sold. When containers were returned, the bookkeeper debited Container Expense and credited Cash for $800.			

PROBLEM CP11–2

In January, year 2 you are called upon to perform an audit of Nicky's Nik-Naks Store, which has just completed its first year of operations on December 31, year 1. The owner, Nicky Nola, has been keeping the books herself, but admits that she knows little about accounting. During the course of your audit you discover that Nicky has lumped several items into a single account called Current Liabilities, which includes the following:

1.	GST and PST payable	$ 3,000
2.	10% promissory note payable due in three equal annual installments, every September 1. No interest has been accrued on this note.	30,000
3.	Trade accounts payable (includes $2,000 due to Nicky)	22,000
4.	Liability for new equipment (payment to be made when equipment is delivered on February 1)	8,000
5.	Employees' Withholdings for CPP ($330), EI ($300), and income tax ($3,200) – No amounts have been recorded for the related employer's share of CPP or EI.	3,830
6.	Unearned Revenue	6,000
	On November 1 Nicky received $6,000 from a tenant who is renting the upper floor of Nicky's store. The $6,000 covered rent from the period from November 1 to April 1, year 2.	

Instructions

a. Prepare any journal entries necessary to correct Nicky's books at the end of year 1. In making your entries, you should clear out the account called Current Liabilities and allocate amounts to the correctly named accounts (with adjustments, as appropriate). For example, the entry to correct item 1 would record GST and PST Payable in a separate account, as follows:

Current Liabilities	3,000	
GST and PST Payable		3,000

b. Prepare the current liabilities section of the balance sheet at December 31, year 1.

PROBLEM CP11–3

Salespersons for Select Realty receive a commission of 5% of sales, the amount of commissions due on sales of one month being paid in the middle of the following month. At the end of each of the first three years of operations, the accountant failed to record accrued sales commissions expense as follows: first year, $30,000; second year, $47,500; third year, $33,500. In each case, the commissions were paid during the first month of the succeeding year and were charged as an expense of that year. Accrued sales commissions expense was properly recorded at the end of the fourth year.

a. Determine the amount by which net income was overstated or understated for each of the four years.
b. Determine the items on the balance sheet that would have been overstated or understated at the end of each of the four years and the amount of overstatement or understatement.

COMPREHENSIVE PROBLEM 3

Selected transactions completed by Gold Co. during its first fiscal year ending December 31 were as follows:

a. Prepared a voucher to establish a petty cash fund of $200 and issued a cheque in payment of the voucher. (Journalize two entries.)
b. Prepared a voucher to replenish the petty cash fund, based on the following summary of petty cash receipts: office supplies, $46; miscellaneous selling expense, $54; miscellaneous administrative expense, $64.
c. Prepared a voucher for the purchase of $5,000 of merchandise, 1/10, n/30. Purchase invoices are recorded at the gross amount using a perpetual inventory system.
d. Paid the invoice in (c) after the discount period had passed.

e. Received cash from daily cash sales for $9,460. The amount indicated by the cash register was $9,500.

f. Received a 60-day, 10% note for $60,000 on account.

g. Received amount owed on note in (f).

h. Received $800 on account and wrote off the remainder owed on a $1,400 accounts receivable balance. (The allowance method is used in accounting for uncollectible receivables.)

i. Reinstated the account written off in (h) and received $600 cash in full payment.

j. Traded office equipment on May 31 for new equipment with a list price of $120,000. A trade-in allowance of $25,000 was received on the old equipment that had cost $100,000 and had accumulated amortization of $65,000 as of May 31. A voucher was prepared for the amount owed of $95,000.

k. Journalized the monthly payroll for November, based on the following data:

Salaries:		Deductions:	
Sales salaries	$13,500	Income tax withheld	$3,960
Office salaries	4,500	CPP withheld	680
	$18,000	EI withheld	620

l. Journalized the employer's payroll taxes on the payroll in (k). The employer must match the employees' contribution to CPP and contribute 1.4 times the employees' deduction for EI. In addition, the employer accrues 4% vacation pay.

m. Issued a 90-day, non-interest-bearing note for $25,000 to the bank in exchange for $24,250.

n. Journalized voucher for payment of the note in (m) at maturity.

Instructions

1. Journalize the selected transactions. Assume a 360-day year for computing interest.

2. Based on the following data, prepare a bank reconciliation for November of the current year:
    a. Balance according to the bank statement at November 30, $94,240.
    b. Balance according to the ledger at November 30, $74,390.
    c. Cheques outstanding at November 30, $42,350.
    d. Deposit in transit, not recorded by bank, $22,300.
    e. Bank debit memorandum for service charges, $65.
    f. A cheque for $150 in payment of a voucher was erroneously recorded in the accounts as $15.

3. Based on the bank reconciliation prepared in (2), journalize the entry or entries to be made by Gold Co.

4. Based on the following selected data, journalize the adjusting entries as of December 31 of the current year:
    a. Estimated uncollectible accounts from aging the accounts receivable at December 31, $5,510. The balance of Allowance for Doubtful Accounts at December 31 was $900 (debit).
    b. Gold Co. uses a perpetual inventory system. The physical inventory on December 31 indicated an inventory shrinkage of $2,000.
    c. Prepaid insurance expired during the year, $16,200.
    d. Office supplies used during the year, $4,800.
    e. Amortization is computed as follows:

Asset	Cost	Residual Value	Acquisition Date	Useful Life in Years	Amortization Method Used
Buildings	$275,000	$ 0	January 2	50	Straight-line
Office Equip.	120,000	12,000	July 1	5	Straight-line
Store Equip.	60,000	10,000	January 3	8	Declining-balance (at twice the straight-line rate)

f. A patent costing $24,000 when acquired on January 2 has a remaining legal life of nine years, and was expected to have value for six years.

g. The cost of mineral rights was $50,000. Of the estimated deposit of 25,000 tons of ore, 4,000 tons were mined and sold during the year.

h. Total vacation pay expense for the year, $5,000.

i. A product warranty was granted beginning December 1 and covering a one-year period. The estimated cost is 3% of sales, which totalled $180,000 in December.

5. Based on the following post-closing trial balance and other data, prepare a balance sheet in account form at December 31 of the current year:

Gold Co.
Post-Closing Trial Balance
December 31, 20—

Petty Cash	200	
Cash	39,250	
Marketable Securities	40,000	
Allowance for decline in market value of Marketable Securities		5,210
Notes Receivable	50,000	
Accounts Receivable	152,300	
Allowance for Doubtful Accounts		5,510
Inventory	220,250	
Prepaid Insurance	12,950	
Office Supplies	2,300	
Land	50,000	
Buildings	275,000	
Accumulated Amortization—Buildings		5,500
Office Equipment	120,000	
Accumulated Amortization—Office Equipment		10,800
Store Equipment	60,000	
Accumulated Amortization—Store Equipment		15,000
Mineral Rights	50,000	
Accumulated Depletion		8,000
Patents	20,000	
CPP Payable		3,000
Employee Income Tax Payable		3,960
EI Payable		1,870
Salaries Payable		14,000
Accounts Payable		88,000
Product Warranty Payable		5,400
Vacation Pay Payable		5,000
Notes Payable		450,000
J. Gold, Capital		471,000
	1,092,250	1,092,250

The following information relating to the balance sheet accounts at December 31 is obtained from supplementary records:

Notes receivable is a current asset.
The inventory is stated at cost by the FIFO method.
The product warranty payable is a current liability.
Notes payable:
   Current liability $ 50,000
   Long-term liability   400,000

6. On February 7 of the following year, the inventory was destroyed by fire. Based on the following data obtained from the accounting records, estimate the cost of the goods destroyed:

Jan. 1 Inventory	$220,250
Jan. 1–Feb. 7 Purchases (net)	194,250
Sales (net)	340,000
Estimated gross profit rate	40%

CASES

CASE 11–1
Cranfield and Co., CA
Payroll ethical issues

Ellen Burks is a staff assistant for Cranfield and Co., Chartered Accountants, a local CA firm. It had been the policy of the firm to provide a holiday bonus equal to two weeks' salary to all employees. The firm's new management team announced on November 25 that a bonus equal to only one week's salary would be made available to employees this year. Ellen thought that this policy was unfair because she and her co-workers planned on the full two-week bonus. The two-week bonus had been given for 10 straight years, so it seemed as though the firm had breached an implied commitment. Thus, Ellen decided that she would make up the lost bonus week by working an extra six hours of overtime per week over the next five weeks until the end of the year. Cranfield's policy is to pay overtime at 150% of straight time.

Ellen's supervisor was surprised to see overtime being reported, since there is generally very little additional or unusual client service demands at the end of the calendar year. However, the overtime was not questioned, since firm employees are on the "honour system" in reporting their overtime.

► Discuss whether Ellen is behaving in an ethical manner. Is the firm acting in an ethical manner?

CASE 11–2
Stevens' Trucking Company
Executive bonuses and accounting methods

Bill Stevens, the owner of Stevens' Trucking Company, initiated an executive bonus plan for his chief executive officer (CEO). The new plan provides a bonus to the CEO equal to 3% of operating income. Upon learning of the new bonus arrangement, the CEO issued instructions to change the company's accounting for trucks. The CEO has asked the controller to make the following two changes:

a. Change from the double-declining-balance method to the straight-line method of amortization.
b. Add 50% to the useful lives of all trucks.

► Why would these changes favour the CEO? How would you respond to the CEO's request?

CASE 11–3
Sears Canada Inc.
Financial analysis

Several measures can be used to assess the ability of a business to pay its current liabilities. Two such analyses that are of special interest to short-term creditors are the current ratio and the acid-test ratio.

The current ratio is computed by dividing current assets by current liabilities, as indicated below:

$$\text{Current ratio} = \frac{\text{Current assets}}{\text{Current liabilities}}$$

The acid-test ratio, or quick ratio, is the ratio of the total quick assets to the total current liabilities. Quick assets are cash and other current assets that can be quickly converted to cash. Quick assets normally include cash, marketable securities, and receivables. The ratio is computed as follows:

$$\text{Acid-test ratio} = \frac{\text{Quick assets}}{\text{Current liabilities}}$$

The current ratio does not consider the makeup of the current assets. The acid-test ratio measures the "instant" debt-paying ability of the company and focuses on the assets that can generally be converted to cash rather quickly to meet current liabilities.

a. For Sears Canada Inc., compute as of December 31 of the current and preceeding years:
    1. the current ratio, and
    2. the acid-test ratio.
b. ► What conclusions can be drawn from these data as to Sears' ability to meet its current liabilities?

CASE 11–4
Royal Co.
Income adjustment for expense accruals

In 1998, your mother retired as president of the family-owned business, Royal Co., and a new president was recruited by an executive search firm. The new president's contract called for an annual base salary of $80,000 plus a bonus of 12% of income before deducting the bonus and income taxes.

In 1999, the first full year under the new president, Royal Co. reported income of $630,000 before deducting the bonus and income taxes. After being fired on January 3, 2000, the new president demanded immediate payment of a $75,600 bonus for 1999.

Your mother was concerned about the accounting practices used during 1999, and she has asked you to help her in reviewing the accounting records before the bonus is paid. Upon investigation, you have discovered the following facts:

1. The payroll for December 27–31, 1999, was not accrued at the end of the year. The salaries for the five-day period and the applicable payroll taxes are as follows:

Sales salaries	$9,000
Office salaries	3,000
Employer portion of payroll taxes	10%

The payroll was paid on January 9, 2000, for the period December 27, 1999, through January 7, 2000.

2. The semiannual pension cost of $56,200 was not accrued for the last half of 1999. The pension cost was paid to Reliance Insurance Company on January 12, 2000, and

was journalized by a debit to Pension Expense and a credit to Cash for $56,200.

3. The estimated product warranty liability of $12,000 for products sold during the year ended December 31, 1999, was not journalized.

4. On July 1, 1999, a one-year insurance policy was purchased for $10,640, debiting the cost to Prepaid Insurance. No adjusting entry was made for insurance expired at December 31, 1999.

5. The vacation pay liability of $12,000 for the year ended December 31, 1999, was not journalized.

    a. What accounting errors were made in 1999 that would affect the amount of the president's bonus?

    b. Based on the employment contract and your answer to (a), what is the correct amount of the president's bonus for 1999?

    c. How much did the president's demand for a $75,600 bonus exceed the correct amount of the bonus under the employment contract?

    d. ◀▬▬▶ Describe the major advantage and disadvantage of using income-sharing bonuses in employment contracts.

ANSWERS TO SELF-EXAMINATION QUESTIONS

1. **B** The $900 difference between the $20,000 maturity value of the note payable and the $19,100 cash proceeds received for the note when issued represents the total interest expense on the note over the six-month period from November 1, 2000 until May 1, 2001. By December 31, two months of this interest should be accrued as interest expense by the borrower. Thus, the interest expense to December 31 is $300 ($900 × ²/₆ months).

2. **C** We calculate the warranty liability at the end of the year 2000 as follows:

Warranty expense for 1999 (3% × $150,000)		$ 4,500
Warranty expense for 2000 (3% × $200,000)		6,000
		$10,500
Less: warranty costs incurred in 1999	$1,800	
warranty costs incurred in 2000	3,000	4,800
Liability for warranty work at the end of 2000.		$ 5,700

3. **A** At the end of each its first quarter, Donnelly should accrue property tax expense equal to one quarter of the total amount of property taxes estimated for the year (¼ × $36,000 = $9,000). Thus, it will make the following entry on March 31:

Property tax expense	9,000	
Property taxes payable		9,000

Although the actual property tax for the year turns out to be greater than $36,000, at March 31 Donnelly does not know the actual tax bill. Therefore the amount recorded on March 31 is only an estimated amount.

4. **C** We calculate the net pay that the employee receives as follows:

Gross pay		$600
Less: Income tax withheld	$145	
Union dues withheld	10	
CPP withheld	17	
EI withheld	16	188
Net pay		$412

The employer's share of CPP and EI are paid by the employer and not deducted from the employee's pay cheque.

5. **D** (1) Estimated liabilities are always accrued on the balance sheet, since these represent obligations (such as warranties) that the firm knows that it owes due to past transactions, although the exact amounts and payment dates are uncertain. (2) Contingent liabilities represent possible losses arising from past events whose outcome will not be known until the future. These amounts are recorded as liabilities only if they are likely and their amount can be estimated. If either or both of these conditions is missing, these are not recorded as liabilities, but are disclosed in notes to the financial statements. (3) Purchase commitments are disclosed in the notes to the financial statements, but are never recorded as liabilities, since no obligation exists unless some future event occurs.

APPENDICES

A. *Accounting Concepts*

B. *Interest Tables*

C. *Annual Report for Sears Canada*

D. *The Basics*

E. *Abbreviations and Acronyms Commonly Used in Business and Accounting*

F. *Classification of Accounts*

G. *A Classified Balance Sheet*

Appendix A: Accounting Concepts

A. CONCEPTUAL FRAMEWORK

Overview

The Accounting Standards Board (AcSB) of the Canadian Institute of Chartered Accountants is responsible for setting accounting standards in Canada. The standards are contained in the *CICA Handbook* and form the basis for Generally Accepted Accounting Principles (GAAP). The conceptual framework of financial accounting embodies the financial statement concepts that guide the AcSB in development of generally accepted accounting principles.

Section 1000 of the *CICA Handbook* outlines the basic components of the financial statement concepts:

1. objectives of financial statements;
2. qualitative characteristics;
3. elements of financial statements;
4. criteria for recognition and measurement; and
5. generally accepted accounting principles.

The notes that follow are a summary of the conceptual framework as set out in Section 1000 of the *CICA Handbook*. These notes were prepared by the Society of Management Accountants of Ontario for a Professional Examination Orientation review manual. We thank the Society for permitting us to reproduce that material here.

1. Objectives of Financial Statements

The objective of financial statements is to communicate information that is useful to investors, members, contributors, creditors, and other users in making their **resource allocation decisions and/or assessing management stewardship.**

Consequently, financial statements provide information about:

a. an entity's economic resources, obligations, and equity/new assets;
b. changes in an entity's economic resources, obligations, and equity/net assets; and
c. the economic performance of the entity.

(Section 1000.15)

2. Qualitative Characteristics

The financial statements identify and define the qualities of accounting information. These qualities are illustrated in Exhibit 1.

A. UNDERSTANDABILITY For the information provided in financial statements to be useful, it must be capable of being understood by users. Users are assumed to have a reasonable understanding of business and economic activities and accounting, together with a willingness to study the information with reasonable diligence. (Section 1000.19)

B. RELEVANCE For the information provided in financial statements to be useful, it must be relevant to the decisions made by users. Information is relevant by its nature when it can influence the decisions of users by helping them evaluate the financial impact of past, present, or future transactions and events or confirm, or correct, previous evaluations. Relevance is achieved through information that has predictive value or feedback value and by its timeliness.

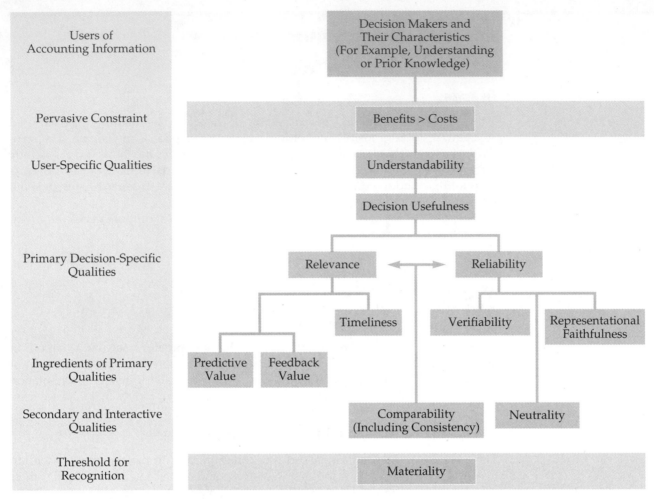

Exhibit 1
A Hierarchy of Accounting Qualities

i. Predictive value and feedback value Information that helps users to predict an entity's future income and cash flows has predictive value. Although information provided in the financial statements will not normally be a prediction in itself, it may be useful in making predictions. The predictive value of the income statement, for example, is enhanced if abnormal items are disclosed separately. Information that confirms or corrects previous prediction has feedback value. Information often has both predictive value and feedback value.

ii. Timeliness For information to be useful for decision making, it must be received by the decision maker before it loses its capacity to influence decisions. The usefulness of information for decision making declines as time elapses. (Section 1000.20)

C. RELIABILITY For the information provided in financial statements to be useful, it must be reliable. Information is reliable when it is in agreement with the actual underlying transactions and events, the agreement is capable of independent verification, and the information is reasonably free from error and bias. Reliability is achieved through representational faithfulness, verifiability, and neutrality. Neutrality is affected by the use of conservatism in making judgments under conditions of uncertainty.

i. Representational faithfulness Representational faithfulness is achieved when transactions and events affecting the entity are presented in financial statements in a manner that is in agreement with the actual underlying transactions or events.

Thus, transactions and events are accounted for and presented in a manner that conveys their substance rather than necessarily their legal or other form.

The substance of transactions and events may not always be consistent with that apparent from their legal or other form. To determine the substance of a transaction or event it may be necessary to consider a group of related transitions and events as a whole. The determination of the substance of a transaction or event will be a matter of professional judgment in the circumstances.

ii. Verifiability The financial statement presentation of a transaction or event is verifiable if knowledgeable and independent observers would concur that it is in agreement with the actual underlying transactions or event with a reasonable degree of precision. Verifiability focuses on the correct application of a basis of measurement rather than its appropriateness.

iii. Neutrality Information is neutral when it is free from bias that would lead users towards making decisions that are influenced by the way the information is measured or presented. Bias in measurement occurs when a measure tends to consistently overstate or understate the items being measured. In the selection of accounting principles, bias may occur when the selection is made with the interests of particular users or with particular economic or political objectives in mind.

Financial statements that do not include everything necessary for faithful representation of transactions and events affecting the entity would be incomplete and, therefore, potentially biased.

iv. Conservatism Use of conservatism in making judgments under conditions of uncertainty affects the neutrality of financial statements in an acceptable manner. When uncertainty exists, estimates of a conservative nature attempt to ensure that assets, revenues, and gain are not overstated and, conversely, that liabilities, expenses, and losses are not understated. However, conservatism does not encompass the deliberate understatement of assets, revenues, and gains or the deliberate overstatement of liabilities, expenses, and losses. (Section 1000.21)

D. COMPARABILITY Comparability is a characteristic of the relationship between two pieces of information rather than of a particular piece of information by itself. It enables users to identify similarities in and differences between the information provided by two sets of financial statements. Comparability is important when comparing the financial statements of two different entities and when comparing the financial statements of the same entity over two periods or at two different points in time. (Section 1000.22)

Comparability in the financial statements of an entity is enhanced when the same accounting policies are used consistently from period to period. Consistency helps prevent misconceptions that might result from the application of different accounting policies in different periods. When a change in accounting policy is deemed to be appropriate, disclosure of the effects of the change may be necessary to maintain comparability. (Section 1000.23)

E. CONSTRAINTS

i. Benefit Versus Cost Constraint The benefits expected to arise from providing information in financial statements should exceed the cost of doing so. This constraint applies to the development of accounting standards by the Committee. It is also a consideration in the preparation of financial statements in accordance with those standards, for example, in considering disclosure of information beyond that required by the standards. The Committee recognizes that the benefits and costs may accrue to different parties and that the evaluation of the nature and amount of benefits and costs is substantially a judgmental process. (Section 1000.16)

It is recognized that costs are incurred whenever a new accounting standard is introduced. These costs may be tangible–collection and presentation of information;

Trade-off: Relevance versus Reliability

In practice, a trade-off between qualitative characteristics is often necessary, particularly between relevance and reliability. For example, there is often a trade-off between the timeliness of producing financial statements and the reliability of the information reported in the statements. Generally, the aim is to achieve an appropriate balance among the characteristics in order to meet the objective of financial statements. The relative importance of the characteristics in different cases is a matter of professional judgment. (Section 1000.24)

or intangible–disclosure. The benefits of introducing a new standard are mainly intangible–the availability of the information to users of the financial statements. A careful balancing is required whenever a new standard is considered, to ensure the costs of introducing such a standard do not outweigh the benefits.

ii. Materiality Users are interested in information that may affect their decision making. Materiality is the term used to describe the significance of financial statement information to decision makers. An item of information, or an aggregate of items, is material if it is probable that its omission or misstatement would influence or change a decision. Materiality is a matter of professional judgment in the particular circumstances. (Section 1000.17)

The threshold for recognition is materiality. An item that is not material need not be reported.

iii. Industry Practice In order for accounting information to be useful, any selective exceptions to GAAP regularly followed by industry participants would be permitted provided there is clear precedent in the industry. Often differences result from differing legal requirements.

3. Elements of Financial Statements

The *CICA Handbook* also contains some definitions of the various elements of financial statements.

A. ASSETS Assets are economic resources controlled by an entity as a result of past transactions or events and from which future economic benefits may be obtained. (Section 1000.29)

Assets have three essential characteristics:

i.   they embody a future benefit that involves a capacity, singly or in combination with other assets, in the case of profit-oriented enterprises, to contribute directly or indirectly to future net cash flows, and, in the case of not-for-profit organizations, to provide services;
ii. the entity can control access to the benefits; and
iii. the transaction or event giving rise to the entity's right to, or control of, the benefit has already occurred.

It is not essential for control of access to the benefit to be legally enforceable for a resource to be an asset, provided the entity can control its use by other means. (Section 1000.31)

B. LIABILITIES Liabilities are obligations of an entity arising from past transactions or events, the settlement of which may result in the transfer or use of assets, provision of services, or other yielding of economic benefits in the future. (Section 1000.32)

Liabilities have three essential characteristics:

i. they embody a duty or responsibility to others that entails settlement by future transfer of use of assets, provision of services, or other yielding of economic benefits, at a specified or determinable date, on occurrence of a specified event, or on demand;

ii. the duty or responsibility obligates the entity, leaving it little or no discretion to avoid it; and

iii. the transaction or event obligating the entity has already occurred. (Section 1000.33)

Liabilities do not have to be legally enforceable provided that they otherwise meet the definition of liabilities; they can be based on equitable or constructive obligations. An equitable obligation is a duty based on ethical or moral considerations. A constructive obligation is one that can be inferred from the facts in a particular situation as opposed to a contractually based obligation. (Section 1000.34)

C. EQUITY/NET ASSETS Equity is the ownership interest in the assets of a profit-oriented enterprise after deducting its liabilities. While equity of a profit-oriented enterprise in total is residual, it includes specific categories of items, for example, types of share capital, contributed surplus, and retained earnings. (Section 1000.35)

In the case of a not-for-profit organization, net assets, sometimes referred to as equity or fund balances, is the residual interest in its assets after deducting its liabilities. Net assets may include specific categories of items that may be either restricted or unrestricted as their use. (Section 1000.36)

D. REVENUES Revenues are increases in economic resources, either by way of inflows or enhancements of assets or reductions of liabilities, resulting from the ordinary activities of an entity. Revenues of entities normally arise from the sale of goods, the rendering of services, or the use by others of entity resources yielding rent, interest, royalties, or dividends. In addition, many not-for-profit organizations receive a significant proportion of their revenues from donation, government grants, and other contributions. (Section 1000.37)

E. EXPENSES Expenses are decreases in economic resources, either by way of outflows or reductions of assets or incurrences of liabilities, resulting from an entity's ordinary revenue generating or service delivery activities. (Section 1000.38)

F. GAINS Gains are increases in equity/net assets from peripheral or incidental transactions and events affecting an entity and from all other transactions, events, and circumstances affecting the entity except those that result from expenses or distributions of equity/net assets. (Section 1000.39)

G. LOSSES Losses are decreases in equity/net assets from peripheral or incidental transactions, events, and circumstances affecting the entity except those that result from expenses or distributions of equity/net assets. (Section 1000.40)

4. Recognition and Measurement Criteria

A. RECOGNITION CRITERIA Recognition is the process of including an item in the financial statements of an entity. Recognition consists of the addition of the amount involved into statement totals together with a narrative description of the item (e.g., "inventory," "sales," or "donations") in a statement. Similar items may be grouped together in the financial statements for the purpose of presentation. (Section 1000.41)

Recognition means inclusion of an item within one or more individual statements and does not mean disclosure in the notes of the financial statements. Notes either provide further details about items recognized in the financial statements, or provide information about items that do not meet the criteria for recognition and thus are not recognized in the financial statements. (Section 1000.42)

The recognition criteria below provide general guidance on when an item is recognized in the financial statements. Whether any particular item is recognized or not will require the application of professional judgment in considering whether the specific circumstances meet the recognition criteria. (Section 1000.43)

The recognition criteria are as follows:

i.   the item has an appropriate basis of measurement and a reasonable estimate can be made of the amount involved: and
ii. for items involving obtaining or giving up future economic benefits, it is probable that such benefits will be obtained or given up. (Section 1000.44)

It is possible that an item will meet the definition of an element but still not be recognized in the financial statements because it is not probable that future economic benefits will be obtained or given up or because a reasonable estimate cannot be made of the amount involved. It may be appropriate to provide information about items that do not meet the recognition criteria in the notes to the financial statements. (Section 1000.45)

B. BASES OF MEASUREMENT Measurement is the process of determining the amount at which an item is recognized in the financial statements. There are a number of bases on which an amount can be measured. However, financial statements are prepared primarily using the historical cost basis of measurement whereby transactions and events are recognized in financial statements at the amount of cash equivalents paid or received or the fair value ascribed to them when they took place. (Section 1000.53)

Other bases of measurement are also used but only in limited circumstances. They include:

i.   **Replacement cost**—the amount that would be needed currently to acquire an equivalent asset. This may be used, for example, when inventories are valued at the lower of historical cost and replacement cost.
ii. **Realizable value**—the amount that would be received by selling an asset. This may be used, for example, to value temporary and portfolio investments. Market value may be used to estimate realizable value when a market for an asset exists.
iii. **Present value**—the discounted amount of future cash flows expected to be received from an asset or required to settle a liability. This is used, for example, to estimate the cost of pension benefits. (Section 1000.54)

C. REVENUE RECOGNITION Items recognized in the financial statements are accounted for in accordance with the accrual basis of accounting. The accrual basis of accounting recognizes the effect of transactions and events in the period in which the transactions and events occur, regardless of whether there has been a receipt of payment of cash or its equivalent. Accrual accounting encompasses deferrals that occur when a cash receipt or payment occurs prior to the criteria for recognition of revenue or expense being satisfied. (Section 1000.46)

Revenues are generally recognized when performance is achieved and reasonable assurance regarding measurement and collectibility of the consideration exists. (Section 1000.47)

Unrestricted contributions to not-for-profit organizations do not normally arise from the sale of goods or the rendering of services and consequently performance achievement is generally not relevant to the recognition of unrestricted contributions; such revenues, since they are not linked with specific expenses, are generally recognized when received or receivable. Other contributions are recognized based on the nature of the related restriction. (Section 1000.48)

Gains are generally recognized when realized. (Section 1000.49)

D. MATCHING Expenses and losses are generally recognized when an expenditure or previously recognized asset does not have future economic benefit. Expenses that are not linked with specific revenues are related to a period on the basis of transactions or events occurring in that period or by allocation. The cost of assets that benefit more than one period is normally allocated over the periods benefited. (Section 1000.50)

Expenses that are linked to revenue generating activities in a cause-and-effect relationship are normally matched with the revenue in the accounting period in which the revenue is recognized. (Section 1000.52)

Expenses incurred by not-for-profit organizations for service delivery activities, as opposed to revenue generating activities, would normally be recognized when the service is delivered. (Section 1000.52)

E. FULL DISCLOSURE All relevant accounting information should be disclosed in either the body of the financial statements, the notes thereto, or supplementary schedules.

A clear and concise description of the significant accounting policies of an enterprise should be included as an integral part of the financial statements. (Section 1505.04)

F. ECONOMIC ENTITY For accounting purposes, accounting information is accumulated from the viewpoint of a single entity. For example, a corporation, a partnership, or a sole proprietorship would constitute a separate accounting unit apart from its owners or other entities. The identifiable business entity need not be a separate legal entity.

G. GOING CONCERN ASSUMPTION Financial statements are prepared on the assumption that the entity is a going concern, meaning it will continue in operation for the foreseeable future and will be able to realize assets and discharge liabilities in the normal course of operations. Different bases of measurement may be appropriate when the entity is not expected to continue in operation for the foreseeable future. (Section 1000.58)

H. MONETARY UNIT Financial statements are prepared with capital maintenance measured in financial terms and with no adjustment being made for the effect on capital of a change in the general purchasing power of the currency during the period. (Section 1000.55)

The concept of capital maintenance used by profit-oriented enterprises in preparing financial statements affects measurement because income in an economic sense exists only after the capital of an enterprise has been maintained. Thus, income is the increase or decrease in the amount of capital at the end of the period over the amount at the beginning of the period, excluding the effects of capital contributions and distributions. (Section 1000.56)

I. PERIODICITY Accounting information is reported on a periodic basis recognizing that decision makers need timely financial information and that accruals and deferrals are a necessary part of preparing the information.

5. Generally Accepted Accounting Principles (GAAP)

Generally accepted accounting principles is the term used to describe the basis on which financial statements are normally prepared. There are special circumstances where a different basis of accounting may be appropriate, for example, in financial statements prepared in accordance with regulator legislation or contractual requirements. (Section 1000.59)

The term generally accepted accounting principles encompasses not only specific rules, practices, and procedures relating to particular circumstances but also broad principles and conventions of general application, including the underlying concepts described in this Section. Specifically, generally accepted accounting principles comprise the Accounting Recommendations in the Handbook and, when a matter is not covered by a Recommendation, other accounting principles that either:

a. are generally accepted by virtue of their use in similar circumstances by a significant number of entities in Canada; or
b. are consistent with the Recommendations in the Handbook and are developed through the exercise of professional judgment, including consultation with other informed accountants where appropriate, and the application of the concepts described in this Section.

In exercising professional judgment, established principles for analogous situations dealt with in the Handbook would be taken into account and reference would be made to:

i. other relevant matters dealt within the Handbook;
ii. practice in similar circumstances;
iii. Accounting Guidelines;
iv. Abstracts of Issues Discussed by the CICA Emerging Issues Committee;
v. International Accounting Standards published by the International Accounting Standards committee;
vi. standards published by bodies authorized to establish financial accounting standards in other jurisdictions;
vii. CICA research studies; and
viii. other sources of accounting literature such as textbooks and journals.

The relative importance of these various sources is a matter of professional judgment in the circumstances. (Section 1000.60)

Appendix B: Interest Tables

Future Amount of $1 at Compound Interest Due in n Periods: $a_{\overline{n}|i} = (1 + i)^n$						
$n \diagdown i$	3%	4%	5%	5.5%	6%	6.5%
1	1.0300	1.0400	1.0500	1.0550	1.0600	1.0650
2	1.0609	1.0816	1.1025	1.1130	1.1236	1.1342
3	1.0927	1.1249	1.1576	1.1742	1.1910	1.2079
4	1.1255	1.1699	1.2155	1.2388	1.2625	1.2865
5	1.1593	1.2167	1.2763	1.3070	1.3382	1.3701
6	1.1941	1.2653	1.3401	1.3788	1.4185	1.4591
7	1.2299	1.3159	1.4071	1.4547	1.5036	1.5540
8	1.2668	1.3686	1.4775	1.5347	1.5938	1.6550
9	1.3048	1.4233	1.5513	1.6191	1.6895	1.7626
10	1.3439	1.4802	1.6289	1.7081	1.7908	1.8771
11	1.3842	1.5395	1.7103	1.8021	1.8983	1.9992
12	1.4258	1.6010	1.7959	1.9012	2.0122	2.1291
13	1.4685	1.6651	1.8856	2.0058	2.1329	2.2675
14	1.5126	1.7317	1.9799	2.1161	2.2609	2.4149
15	1.5580	1.8009	2.0789	2.2325	2.3966	2.5718
16	1.6047	1.8730	2.1829	2.3553	2.5404	2.7390
17	1.6528	1.9479	2.2920	2.4848	2.6928	2.9170
18	1.7024	2.0258	2.4066	2.6215	2.8543	3.1067
19	1.7535	2.1068	2.5270	2.7656	3.0256	3.3086
20	1.8061	2.1911	2.6533	2.9178	3.2071	3.5236
21	1.8603	2.2788	2.7860	3.0782	3.3996	3.7527
22	1.9161	2.3699	2.9253	3.2475	3.6035	3.9966
23	1.9736	2.4647	3.0715	3.4262	3.8197	4.2564
24	2.0328	2.5633	3.2251	3.6146	4.0489	4.5331
25	2.0938	2.6658	3.3864	3.8134	4.2919	4.8277
26	2.1566	2.7725	3.5557	4.0231	4.5494	5.1415
27	2.2213	2.8834	3.7335	4.2444	4.8223	5.4757
28	2.2879	2.9987	3.9201	4.4778	5.1117	5.8316
29	2.3566	3.1187	4.1161	4.7241	5.4184	6.2107
30	2.4273	3.2434	4.3219	4.9840	5.7435	6.6144
31	2.5001	3.3731	4.5380	5.2581	6.0881	7.0443
32	2.5751	3.5081	4.7649	5.5473	6.4534	7.5022
33	2.6523	3.6484	5.0032	5.8524	6.8406	7.9898
34	2.7319	3.7943	5.2533	6.1742	7.2510	8.5092
35	2.8139	3.9461	5.5160	6.5138	7.6861	9.0623
40	3.2620	4.8010	7.0400	8.5133	10.2857	12.4161
45	3.7816	5.8412	8.9850	11.1266	13.7646	17.0111
50	4.3839	7.1067	11.4674	14.5420	18.4202	23.3067

Future Amount of $1 at Compound Interest Due in n Periods: $a_{\overline{n}|i} = (1 + i)^n$

$n \diagdown i$	7%	8%	9%	10%	11%	12%
1	1.0700	1.0800	1.0900	1.1000	1.1100	1.1200
2	1.1449	1.1664	1.1881	1.2100	1.2321	1.2544
3	1.2250	1.2597	1.2950	1.3310	1.3676	1.4049
4	1.3108	1.3605	1.4116	1.4641	1.5181	1.5735
5	1.4026	1.4693	1.5386	1.6105	1.6851	1.7623
6	1.5007	1.5869	1.6771	1.7716	1.8704	1.9738
7	1.6058	1.7138	1.8280	1.9487	2.0762	2.2107
8	1.7182	1.8509	1.9926	2.1436	2.3045	2.4760
9	1.8385	1.9990	2.1719	2.3579	2.5580	2.7731
10	1.9672	2.1589	2.3674	2.5937	2.8394	3.1058
11	2.1049	2.3316	2.5804	2.8531	3.1518	3.4785
12	2.2522	2.5182	2.8127	3.1384	3.4985	3.8960
13	2.4098	2.7196	3.0658	3.4523	3.8833	4.3635
14	2.5785	2.9372	3.3417	3.7975	4.3104	4.8871
15	2.7590	3.1722	3.6425	4.1772	4.7846	5.4736
16	2.9522	3.4259	3.9703	4.5950	5.3109	6.1304
17	3.1588	3.7000	4.3276	5.0545	5.8951	6.8660
18	3.3799	3.9960	4.7171	5.5599	6.5436	7.6900
19	3.6165	4.3157	5.1417	6.1159	7.2633	8.6128
20	3.8697	4.6610	5.6044	6.7275	8.0623	9.6463
21	4.1406	5.0338	6.1088	7.4002	8.9492	10.8038
22	4.4304	5.4365	6.6586	8.1403	9.9336	12.1003
23	4.7405	5.8715	7.2579	8.9543	11.0263	13.5523
24	5.0724	6.3412	7.9111	9.8497	12.2392	15.1786
25	5.4274	6.8485	8.6231	10.8347	13.5855	17.0001
26	5.8074	7.3964	9.3992	11.9182	15.0799	19.0401
27	6.2139	7.9881	10.2451	13.1100	16.7386	21.3249
28	6.6488	8.6271	11.1671	14.4210	18.5799	23.8839
29	7.1143	9.3173	12.1722	15.8631	20.6237	26.7499
30	7.6123	10.0627	13.2677	17.4494	22.8923	29.9599
31	8.1451	10.8677	14.4618	19.1943	25.4104	33.5551
32	8.7153	11.7371	15.7633	21.1138	28.2056	37.5817
33	9.3253	12.6760	17.1820	23.2252	31.3082	42.0915
34	9.9781	13.6901	18.7284	25.5477	34.7521	47.1425
35	10.6766	14.7853	20.4140	28.1024	38.5749	52.7996
40	14.9745	21.7245	31.4094	45.2593	65.0009	93.0510
45	21.0025	31.9204	48.3273	72.8905	109.5302	163.9876
50	29.4570	46.9016	74.3575	117.3909	184.5648	289.0022

Future Amount of Ordinary Annuity of $1 per Period: $A_{\overline{n}|i} = \dfrac{(1 + i)^n - 1}{i}$

$n \diagdown i$	3%	4%	5%	5.5%	6%	6.5%
1	1.0000	1.0000	1.0000	1.0000	1.0000	1.0000
2	2.0300	2.0400	2.0500	2.0550	2.0600	2.0650
3	3.0909	3.1216	3.1525	3.1680	3.1836	3.1992
4	4.1836	4.2465	4.3101	4.3423	4.3746	4.4072
5	5.3091	5.4163	5.5256	5.5811	5.6371	5.6936
6	6.4684	6.6330	6.8019	6.8881	6.9753	7.0637
7	7.6625	7.8983	8.1420	8.2669	8.3938	8.5229
8	8.8923	9.2142	9.5491	9.7216	9.8975	10.0769
9	10.1591	10.5828	11.0266	11.2563	11.4913	11.7319
10	11.4639	12.0061	12.5779	12.8754	13.1808	13.4944
11	12.8078	13.4864	14.2068	14.5835	14.9716	15.3716
12	14.1920	15.0258	15.9171	16.3856	16.8699	17.3707
13	15.6178	16.6268	17.7130	18.2868	18.8821	19.4998
14	17.0863	18.2919	19.5986	20.2926	21.0151	21.7673
15	18.5989	20.0236	21.5786	22.4087	23.2760	24.1822
16	20.1569	21.8245	23.6575	24.6411	25.6725	26.7540
17	21.7616	23.6975	25.8404	26.9964	28.2129	29.4930
18	23.4144	25.6454	28.1324	29.4812	30.9057	32.4101
19	25.1169	27.6712	30.5390	32.1027	33.7600	35.5167
20	26.8704	29.7781	33.0660	34.8683	36.7856	38.8253
21	28.6765	31.9692	35.7193	37.7861	39.9927	42.3490
22	30.5368	34.2480	38.5052	40.8643	43.3923	46.1016
23	32.4529	36.6179	41.4305	44.1118	46.9958	50.0982
24	34.4265	39.0826	44.5020	47.5380	50.8156	54.3546
25	36.4593	41.6459	47.7271	51.1526	54.8645	58.8877
26	38.5530	44.3117	51.1135	54.9660	59.1564	63.7154
27	40.7096	47.0842	54.6691	58.9891	63.7058	68.8569
28	42.9309	49.9676	58.4026	63.2335	68.5281	74.3326
29	45.2189	52.9663	62.3227	67.7114	73.6398	80.1642
30	47.5754	56.0849	66.4388	72.4355	79.0582	86.3749
31	50.0027	59.3283	70.7608	77.4194	84.8017	92.9892
32	52.5028	62.7015	75.2988	82.6775	90.8898	100.0335
33	55.0778	66.2095	80.0638	88.2248	97.3432	107.5357
34	57.7302	69.8579	85.0670	94.0771	104.1838	115.5255
35	60.4621	73.6522	90.3203	100.2514	111.4348	124.0347
40	75.4013	95.0255	120.7998	136.6056	154.7620	175.6319
45	92.7199	121.0294	159.7002	184.1192	212.7435	246.3246
50	112.7969	152.6671	209.3480	246.2175	290.3359	343.1797

Future Amount of Ordinary Annuity of \$1 per Period: $A_{\overline{n}|i} = \dfrac{(1+i)^n - 1}{i}$

$n \diagdown i$	7%	8%	9%	10%	11%	12%
1	1.0000	1.0000	1.0000	1.0000	1.0000	1.0000
2	2.0700	2.0800	2.0900	2.1000	2.1100	2.1200
3	3.2149	3.2464	3.2781	3.3100	3.3421	3.3744
4	4.4399	4.5061	4.5731	4.6410	4.7097	4.7793
5	5.7507	5.8666	5.9847	6.1051	6.2278	6.3528
6	7.1533	7.3359	7.5233	7.7156	7.9129	8.1152
7	8.6540	8.9228	9.2004	9.4872	9.7833	10.0890
8	10.2598	10.6366	11.0285	11.4359	11.8594	12.2997
9	11.9780	12.4876	13.0210	13.5795	14.1640	14.7757
10	13.8164	14.4866	15.1929	15.9374	16.7220	17.5487
11	15.7836	16.6455	17.5603	18.5312	19.5614	20.6546
12	17.8885	18.9771	20.1407	21.3843	22.7132	24.1331
13	20.1406	21.4953	22.9534	24.5227	26.2116	28.0291
14	22.5505	24.2149	26.0192	27.9750	30.0949	32.3926
15	25.1290	27.1521	29.3609	31.7725	34.4054	37.2797
16	27.8881	30.3243	33.0034	35.9497	39.1899	42.7533
17	30.8402	33.7502	36.9737	40.5447	44.5008	48.8837
18	33.9990	37.4502	41.3013	45.5992	50.3959	55.7497
19	37.3790	41.4463	46.0185	51.1591	56.9395	63.4397
20	40.9955	45.7620	51.1601	57.2750	64.2028	72.0524
21	44.8652	50.4229	56.7645	64.0025	72.2651	81.6987
22	49.0057	55.4568	62.8733	71.4027	81.2143	92.5026
23	53.4361	60.8933	69.5319	79.5430	91.1479	104.6029
24	58.1767	66.7648	76.7898	88.4973	102.1742	118.1552
25	63.2490	73.1059	84.7009	98.3471	114.4133	133.3339
26	68.6765	79.9544	93.3240	109.1818	127.9988	150.3339
27	74.4838	87.3508	102.7231	121.0999	143.0786	169.3740
28	80.6977	95.3388	112.9682	134.2099	159.8173	190.6989
29	87.3465	103.9659	124.1354	148.6309	178.3972	214.5828
30	94.4608	113.2832	136.3075	164.4940	199.0209	241.3327
31	102.0730	123.3459	149.5752	181.9434	221.9132	271.2926
32	110.2182	134.2135	164.0370	201.1378	247.3236	304.8477
33	118.9334	145.9506	179.8003	222.2515	275.5292	342.4294
34	128.2588	158.6267	196.9823	245.4767	306.8374	384.5210
35	138.2369	172.3168	215.7108	271.0244	341.5896	431.6635
40	199.6351	259.0565	337.8824	442.5926	581.8261	767.0914
45	285.7493	386.5056	525.8587	718.9048	986.6386	1358.2300
50	406.5289	573.7702	815.0836	1163.9085	1668.7712	2400.0182

Present Value of $1 at Compound Interest Due in n Periods: $p_{\overline{n}|i} = \dfrac{1}{(1 + i)^n}$

$n \diagdown i$	3%	4%	5%	5.5%	6%	6.5%
1	0.9709	0.9615	0.9524	0.9479	0.9434	0.9390
2	0.9426	0.9246	0.9070	0.8985	0.8900	0.8817
3	0.9151	0.8890	0.8638	0.8516	0.8396	0.8278
4	0.8885	0.8548	0.8227	0.8072	0.7921	0.7773
5	0.8626	0.8219	0.7835	0.7651	0.7473	0.7299
6	0.8375	0.7903	0.7462	0.7252	0.7050	0.6853
7	0.8131	0.7599	0.7107	0.6874	0.6651	0.6435
8	0.7894	0.7307	0.6768	0.6516	0.6274	0.6042
9	0.7664	0.7026	0.6446	0.6176	0.5919	0.5674
10	0.7441	0.6756	0.6139	0.5854	0.5584	0.5327
11	0.7224	0.6496	0.5847	0.5549	0.5268	0.5002
12	0.7014	0.6246	0.5568	0.5260	0.4970	0.4697
13	0.6810	0.6006	0.5303	0.4986	0.4688	0.4410
14	0.6611	0.5775	0.5051	0.4726	0.4423	0.4141
15	0.6419	0.5553	0.4810	0.4479	0.4173	0.3888
16	0.6232	0.5339	0.4581	0.4246	0.3936	0.3651
17	0.6050	0.5134	0.4363	0.4024	0.3714	0.3428
18	0.5874	0.4936	0.4155	0.3815	0.3503	0.3219
19	0.5703	0.4746	0.3957	0.3616	0.3305	0.3022
20	0.5537	0.4564	0.3769	0.3427	0.3118	0.2838
21	0.5375	0.4388	0.3589	0.3249	0.2942	0.2665
22	0.5219	0.4220	0.3418	0.3079	0.2775	0.2502
23	0.5067	0.4057	0.3256	0.2919	0.2618	0.2349
24	0.4919	0.3901	0.3101	0.2767	0.2470	0.2206
25	0.4776	0.3751	0.2953	0.2622	0.2330	0.2071
26	0.4637	0.3607	0.2812	0.2486	0.2198	0.1945
27	0.4502	0.3468	0.2678	0.2356	0.2074	0.1826
28	0.4371	0.3335	0.2551	0.2233	0.1956	0.1715
29	0.4243	0.3207	0.2429	0.2117	0.1846	0.1610
30	0.4120	0.3083	0.2314	0.2006	0.1741	0.1512
31	0.4000	0.2965	0.2204	0.1902	0.1643	0.1420
32	0.3883	0.2851	0.2099	0.1803	0.1550	0.1333
33	0.3770	0.2741	0.1999	0.1709	0.1462	0.1252
34	0.3660	0.2636	0.1904	0.1620	0.1379	0.1175
35	0.3554	0.2534	0.1813	0.1535	0.1301	0.1103
40	0.3066	0.2083	0.1420	0.1175	0.0972	0.0805
45	0.2644	0.1712	0.1113	0.0899	0.0727	0.0588
50	0.2281	0.1407	0.0872	0.0688	0.0543	0.0429

Present Value of $1 at Compound Interest Due in n Periods: $p_{\overline{n}|i} = \dfrac{1}{(1+i)^n}$

$n \diagdown i$	7%	8%	9%	10%	11%	12%
1	0.9346	0.9259	0.9174	0.9091	0.9009	0.8929
2	0.8734	0.8573	0.8417	0.8264	0.8116	0.7972
3	0.8163	0.7938	0.7722	0.7513	0.7312	0.7118
4	0.7629	0.7350	0.7084	0.6830	0.6587	0.6355
5	0.7130	0.6806	0.6499	0.6209	0.5935	0.5674
6	0.6663	0.6302	0.5963	0.5645	0.5346	0.5066
7	0.6227	0.5835	0.5470	0.5132	0.4817	0.4523
8	0.5820	0.5403	0.5019	0.4665	0.4339	0.4039
9	0.5439	0.5002	0.4604	0.4241	0.3909	0.3606
10	0.5083	0.4632	0.4224	0.3855	0.3522	0.3220
11	0.4751	0.4289	0.3875	0.3505	0.3173	0.2875
12	0.4440	0.3971	0.3555	0.3186	0.2858	0.2567
13	0.4150	0.3677	0.3262	0.2897	0.2575	0.2292
14	0.3878	0.3405	0.2992	0.2633	0.2320	0.2046
15	0.3624	0.3152	0.2745	0.2394	0.2090	0.1827
16	0.3387	0.2919	0.2519	0.2176	0.1883	0.1631
17	0.3166	0.2703	0.2311	0.1978	0.1696	0.1456
18	0.2959	0.2502	0.2120	0.1799	0.1528	0.1300
19	0.2765	0.2317	0.1945	0.1635	0.1377	0.1161
20	0.2584	0.2145	0.1784	0.1486	0.1240	0.1037
21	0.2415	0.1987	0.1637	0.1351	0.1117	0.0926
22	0.2257	0.1839	0.1502	0.1228	0.1007	0.0826
23	0.2109	0.1703	0.1378	0.1117	0.0907	0.0738
24	0.1971	0.1577	0.1264	0.1015	0.0817	0.0659
25	0.1842	0.1460	0.1160	0.0923	0.0736	0.0588
26	0.1722	0.1352	0.1064	0.0839	0.0663	0.0525
27	0.1609	0.1252	0.0976	0.0763	0.0597	0.0469
28	0.1504	0.1159	0.0895	0.0693	0.0538	0.0419
29	0.1406	0.1073	0.0822	0.0630	0.0485	0.0374
30	0.1314	0.0994	0.0754	0.0573	0.0437	0.0334
31	0.1228	0.0920	0.0691	0.0521	0.0394	0.0298
32	0.1147	0.0852	0.0634	0.0474	0.0355	0.0266
33	0.1072	0.0789	0.0582	0.0431	0.0319	0.0238
34	0.1002	0.0730	0.0534	0.0391	0.0288	0.0212
35	0.0937	0.0676	0.0490	0.0356	0.0259	0.0189
40	0.0668	0.0460	0.0318	0.0221	0.0154	0.0107
45	0.0476	0.0313	0.0207	0.0137	0.0091	0.0061
50	0.0339	0.0213	0.0134	0.0085	0.0054	0.0035

Present Value of Ordinary Annuity of $1 per Period: $P_{\overline{n}|i} = \dfrac{1 - \dfrac{1}{(1+i)^n}}{i}$

$n \backslash i$	3%	4%	5%	5.5%	6%	6.5%
1	0.9709	0.9615	0.9524	0.9479	0.9434	0.9390
2	1.9135	1.8861	1.8594	1.8463	1.8334	1.8206
3	1.9135	1.8861	1.8594	1.8463	1.8334	1.8206
4	3.7171	3.6299	3.5460	3.5052	3.4651	3.4258
5	4.5797	4.4518	4.3295	4.2703	4.2124	4.1557
6	5.4172	5.2421	5.0757	4.9955	4.9173	4.8410
7	6.2303	6.0021	5.7864	5.6830	5.5824	5.4845
8	7.0197	6.7327	6.4632	6.3346	6.2098	6.0888
9	7.7861	7.4353	7.1078	6.9522	6.8017	6.6561
10	8.5302	8.1109	7.7217	7.5376	7.3601	7.1888
11	9.2526	8.7605	8.3064	8.0925	7.8869	7.6890
12	9.9540	9.3851	8.8633	8.6185	8.3838	8.1587
13	10.6350	9.9856	9.3936	9.1171	8.8527	8.5997
14	11.2961	10.5631	9.8986	9.5896	9.2950	9.0138
15	11.9379	11.1184	10.3797	10.0376	9.7122	9.4027
16	12.5611	11.6523	10.8378	10.4622	10.1059	9.7678
17	13.1661	12.1657	11.2741	10.8646	10.4773	10.1106
18	13.7535	12.6593	11.6896	11.2461	10.8276	10.4325
19	14.3238	13.1339	12.0853	11.6077	11.1581	10.7347
20	14.8775	13.5903	12.4622	11.9504	11.4699	11.0185
21	15.4150	14.0292	12.8212	12.2752	11.7641	11.2850
22	15.9369	14.4511	13.1630	12.5832	12.0416	11.5352
23	16.4436	14.8568	13.4886	12.8750	12.3034	11.7701
24	16.9355	15.2470	13.7986	13.1517	12.5504	11.9907
25	17.4131	15.6221	14.0939	13.4139	12.7834	12.1979
26	17.8768	15.9828	14.3752	13.6625	13.0032	12.3924
27	18.3270	16.3296	14.6430	13.8981	13.2105	12.5750
28	18.7641	16.6631	14.8981	14.1214	13.4062	12.7465
29	19.1885	16.9837	15.1411	14.3331	13.5907	12.9075
30	19.6004	17.2920	15.3725	14.5337	13.7648	13.0587
31	20.0004	17.5885	15.5928	14.7239	13.9291	13.2006
32	20.3888	17.8736	15.8027	14.9042	14.0840	13.3339
33	20.7658	18.1476	16.0025	15.0751	14.2302	13.4591
34	21.1318	18.4112	16.1929	15.2370	14.3681	13.5766
35	21.4872	18.6646	16.3742	15.3906	14.4982	13.6870
40	23.1148	19.7928	17.1591	16.0461	15.0463	14.1455
45	24.5187	20.7200	17.7741	16.5477	15.4558	14.4802
50	25.7298	21.4822	18.2559	16.9315	15.7619	14.7245

Present Value of Ordinary Annuity of \$1 per Period: $P_{\overline{n}|i} = \dfrac{1 - \dfrac{1}{(1+i)^n}}{i}$

$n \diagdown i$	7%	8%	9%	10%	11%	12%
1	0.9346	0.9259	0.9174	0.9091	0.9009	0.8929
2	1.8080	1.7833	1.7591	1.7355	1.7125	1.6901
3	2.6243	2.5771	2.5313	2.4869	2.4437	2.4018
4	3.3872	3.3121	3.2397	3.1699	3.1024	3.0373
5	4.1002	3.9927	3.8897	3.7908	3.6959	3.6048
6	4.7665	4.6229	4.4859	4.3553	4.2305	4.1114
7	5.3893	5.2064	5.0330	4.8684	4.7122	4.5638
8	5.9713	5.7466	5.5348	5.3349	5.1461	4.9676
9	6.5152	6.2469	5.9952	5.7590	5.5370	5.3282
10	7.0236	6.7101	6.4177	6.1446	5.8892	5.6502
11	7.4987	7.1390	6.8052	6.4951	6.2065	5.9377
12	7.9427	7.5361	7.1607	6.8137	6.4924	6.1944
13	8.3577	7.9038	7.4869	7.1034	6.7499	6.4235
14	8.7455	8.2442	7.7862	7.3667	6.9819	6.6282
15	9.1079	8.5595	8.0607	7.6061	7.1909	6.8109
16	9.4466	8.8514	8.3126	7.8237	7.3792	6.9740
17	9.7632	9.1216	8.5436	8.0216	7.5488	7.1196
18	10.0591	9.3719	8.7556	8.2014	7.7016	7.2497
19	10.3356	9.6036	8.9501	8.3649	7.8393	7.3658
20	10.5940	9.8181	9.1285	8.5136	7.9633	7.4694
21	10.8355	10.0168	9.2922	8.6487	8.0751	7.5620
22	11.0612	10.2007	9.4424	8.7715	8.1757	7.6446
23	11.2722	10.3711	9.5802	8.8832	8.2664	7.7184
24	11.4693	10.5288	9.7066	8.9847	8.3481	7.7843
25	11.6536	10.6748	9.8226	9.0770	8.4217	7.8431
26	11.8258	10.8100	9.9290	9.1609	8.4881	7.8957
27	11.9867	10.9352	10.0266	9.2372	8.5478	7.9426
28	12.1371	11.0511	10.1161	9.3066	8.6016	7.9844
29	12.2777	11.1584	10.1983	9.3696	8.6501	8.0218
30	12.4090	11.2578	10.2737	9.4269	8.6938	8.0552
31	12.5318	11.3498	10.3428	9.4790	8.7331	8.0850
32	12.6466	11.4350	10.4062	9.5264	8.7686	8.1116
33	12.7538	11.5139	10.4644	9.5694	8.8005	8.1354
34	12.8540	11.5869	10.5178	9.6086	8.8293	8.1566
35	12.9477	11.6546	10.5668	9.6442	8.8552	8.1755
40	13.3317	11.9246	10.7574	9.7791	8.9511	8.2438
45	13.6055	12.1084	10.8812	9.8628	9.0079	8.2825
50	13.8007	12.2335	10.9617	9.9148	9.0417	8.3045

SEARS CANADA INC.

SEARS*

Annual Report

Growing **Relationships**

FORWARD THINKING
New insights into how Sears gains strength by better understanding customers

TRANSFORMING SEARS INSIDE OUT
An inside look at Sears $300 million nationwide revitalization program

CLOSER TO HOME
Sears Whole Home Furniture Stores and dealer stores key to Sears innovative off-mall growth strategy

1997

Financial Highlights

For the 53 weeks ended January 3, 1998 and the 52 weeks ended December 28, 1996	1997	1996
RESULTS FOR THE YEAR (in millions)		
Total revenues	$ **4,584**	$ 3,956
Interest expense	**86**	96
Earnings from operations		
before unusual items and income taxes	**215**	70
Unusual items expense	**-**	45
Income tax expense	**99**	16
Net earnings	**116**	9
YEAR END POSITION (in millions)		
Working capital	$ **971**	$ 741
Total assets	**3,007**	2,734
Shareholders' equity	**1,042**	949
PER SHARE OF CAPITAL STOCK (in dollars)		
Net earnings	$ **1.10**	$ 0.09
Dividends declared	**0.24**	0.24
Shareholders' equity	**9.84**	8.98

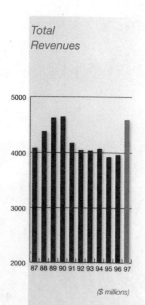

Total Revenues

($ millions)

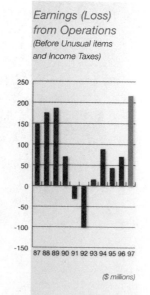

Earnings (Loss) from Operations
(Before Unusual items and Income Taxes)

($ millions)

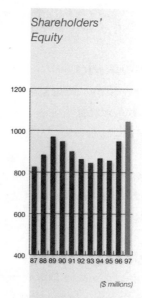

Shareholders' Equity

($ millions)

To our Shareholders

1997 was an outstanding year for our Company. Revenues increased 15.9% to $4.6 billion, contributing to the best performance in our 45 year history. Most importantly, earnings more than tripled and at $116.5 million also represent a new high for our Company.

These results are extremely gratifying for all of us as our customers responded to our efforts to improve their shopping experience in the numerous sales and merchandise distribution channels that make us uniquely Sears. A key measure of our success is our strong sales gain in stores open for at least a year. Sales increased 14.7% during 1997, more than double the 6.4% posted by the industry.

The dedication of our 39,000 associates from coast to coast is at the core of our success and their satisfaction with Sears as a Great Place to Work continues to improve. We are committed to creating a winning team that treats every person with dignity and challenges them to place customer satisfaction as their top priority in everything they do.

LEVERAGING OUR STRENGTHS FOR GROWTH

Delivering a superior return to our shareholders is also squarely embedded in our goals, benefiting investors and associates alike. We are especially pleased that Sears shares posted a total return of 98% in 1997.

Last year I had indicated in my message to shareholders that the growth of our business was a key focus for us over both the short and longer term. Buoyed by a much improved economic environment in Canada, our strategies to grow our Company and create value by leveraging the strengths that make us uniquely Sears are clearly working.

Without exception, all of our sales channels posted strong growth, well in excess of the market.

We are focused on the continuous improvement of our business strengths which include our reputation for trust, integrity and value, as well as our excellent store locations, our growing stable of private and national brands and our portfolio of high quality Sears Card charge account receivables.

"Our continuing challenge is to use all our resources to better serve our target customer and build a

Our continuing challenge is to use these unique resources to better serve our target customer and build a lifelong relationship with her and her family.

Our full-line store repositioning strategy, launched in the all-important Greater Toronto Area (GTA) market earlier this year, is an important example of our commitment to make the Sears proposition more attractive to her on every dimension.

These repositioned stores have performed exceptionally well both during and after their transformation, and we believe we have a compelling format with which to move forward. As a result, in 1998 we will reposition a further 14 stores in major markets across Canada including Vancouver, Edmonton, Toronto and Montreal.

Our catalogue business had an exceptional year and was solidly profitable on a stand-alone basis. Our Christmas Wish Book, the biggest ever in our history, was a huge success reflecting our commitment to expand our merchandise assortments, value and service delivery to millions of customers in some of Canada's remotest communities.

OFF-MALL STRATEGY EXTENDS OUR PRESENCE

Our dealer store format now includes 79 locations, an addition of 19 stores over last year. These stores take the best of Sears, our strength in merchandise categories like appliances and lawn and garden equipment, and combine them with our world class brands such as Craftsman and Kenmore. Our strategy here is to continue to grow our market leading share of these businesses by extending our presence further into the market by making store access easier for our customers.

In 1997 we continued the development of our successful Sears Whole Home Furniture Stores. We added 4 stores over the past year, concentrating on the Greater Toronto Area market.

In two of these locations we added our Sears Brand Central major appliance assortment and expanded the stores by 25%. Coupled with Canada's broadest furniture assortment under one roof, this represents a substantial growth opportunity for us. In the coming year our plans are to accelerate the growth of this format by tripling the number of locations. In 1998 we will open Sears Whole Home Furniture Stores featuring Sears Brand Central in British Columbia, Alberta, Ontario and Quebec.

Home services will also play an important role in the future growth of Sears. In this highly fragmented business where reputation is paramount, we are ideally positioned to serve our customer base via Sears 2,800 repair technicians and a network of home improvement and home maintenance specialists, together making more than a million home visits annually.

SEARS

lifelong relationship with her and her family."

GIVING CREDIT WHERE IT IS DUE

The Sears Card is one of the most important ways we strengthen our relationship with our 8 million customer households.

Our Credit business continues to perform very well and providing credit is critical to the ability of moderate-income families to finance the purchases they require. Our portfolio of charge account receivables is of very high quality and we enjoy one of the lowest write-off rates in the industry.

While 1997 represents a year of substantial progress for our Company on all fronts, we are nevertheless well aware that we have much work ahead of us. The consumer recovery is still somewhat fragile and our year-over-year comparisons will now become more difficult.

We are extremely appreciative and proud of the support we have received from our associate team and from our supplier partners who share our commitment and vision for sustained growth in revenues and earnings.

The confidence within our organization continues to build and when combined with dedication and effort, success is usually the result. On behalf of all of our management and associates we thank our shareholders for their support of our business and rededicate ourselves to providing you with the return on your investment that you expect and deserve.

I would like to express my gratitude to Harold Corrigan for his contribution to Sears Canada during his 18 years on the Board of Directors and to extend my warmest wishes for his good health and happiness in his retirement. On a sadder note, Sears Canada would like to reflect on the passing of Michel F. Bélanger, a distinguished Director of our Company for almost 20 years.

In addition to Mr. Bélanger's significant contribution to the growth and success of Sears Canada, he also played an important role in the business community and political life of Quebec and Canada. He held various positions in the Provincial Civil Service and was one of the principal architects of the nationalization of Quebec's hydro-electric resources and the establishment of Hydro-Quebec. A former Chair of the National Bank of Canada, he became well known in the early 1990s when the late Premier Robert Bourassa recruited him to serve as Co-Chair of the Bélanger-Campeau Commission on Quebec's constitutional future. His last prominent role was as Co-Chair of the NO Committee in the 1995 Quebec Referendum Campaign. His sound advice and counsel were of constant help and guidance to the management of our Company. We will all miss him greatly.

P.S. Walters

Paul S. Walters,
Chairman & CEO

SEARS✦CANADA

How did Sears achieve growth this year at a rate above market growth, and significantly improve shareholder return? The bottom line: in 1997, Sears became more relevant to its customers.

"To move our business into the future, our first step was to better understand who our customers were," says Paul Walters, Chairman and Chief Executive Officer. "She is a woman, 25 to 54, the CEO and CFO of the family. She is the leader who makes 80% of the family's buying decisions even in categories like automotive, electronics and appliances. Another key customer segment is the 18-25 year olds, who are making major changes in their lives, moving into new homes and entering into new relationships. In many ways, Sears is the store for every generation."

REINVENTING THE SHOPPING EXPERIENCE

Concurrently, Sears adapted a number of the successful strategies of its U.S. parent and began the process of branding Sears as the place to go for consistent quality in goods. "After all, a powerful brand is the first step to building a closer relationship with our customers," explains Rick Sorby, Executive Vice-President, Marketing. "It is what makes people come into our stores, and what makes them come back, time after time."

To achieve our **best performance ever**, Sears *became* more **relevant** to **customers**

Sears made a major investment in the revitalization of 9 stores in the Greater Toronto Area market resulting in a 31% sales increase in the fourth quarter of 1997 compared to the same period last year. Based on the success of this program, the Company started rolling out a number of these innovative changes to many of its stores across Canada. Major national and Toronto-focused marketing programs, created to bring to life the new Sears brand and to highlight 'The Many Sides of Sears', supported these efforts.

Growth in 1997 was also a result of Sears firmly repositioning itself as a fashion apparel retailer, as it dramatically expanded its exclusive private label program and added 50% more national brands to its apparel assortments.

The Company continued its initiative to retain the loyalty of Sears traditional market. This was accomplished by increasing its established dominance in such areas as major appliances and furniture with its Sears Brand Central concept, Sears Whole Home Furniture Stores and dealer stores. Sears also enhanced its catalogue offerings and began looking at the vast new opportunities that exist with electronic commerce. ✦

Sears
MD&A and
Financial
Highlights

"1997's record profit performance is a tribute to the entire Sears organization and their efforts over the last several years. During this period we repositioned the Company and each business strategically, operationally and financially. We invested in our core businesses and in new formats. We also invested in redesigning business processes and in technology designed to make Sears Canada more efficient, more responsive and more flexible. It is those strategic initiatives executed by all Sears associates that drove our improved performance in 1997."

"Although we are pleased with 1997's performance, we recognize that shareholder value is built on consistent and profitable growth. We accept this challenge and believe Sears Canada is well positioned to achieve this goal."

James R. Clifford,
President and Chief Operating Officer

Financial
Information
1997

Eleven Year Summary [1]

Fiscal Year	1997	1996	1995	1994	1993	1992	1991	1990	1989	1988	1987
Results for the Year (in millions)											
Total revenues	$ 4,584	$ 3,956	$ 3,918	$ 4,066	$ 4,032	$ 4,042	$ 4,169	$ 4,642	$ 4,621	$ 4,377	$ 4,079
Depreciation	78	78	74	67	69	70	56	55	48	47	45
Earnings (loss) from operations before unusual items and income taxes	215	70	43	88	15	(101)	(31)	70	186	175	148
Unusual items gain (loss)[2]	0	(45)	(21)	(5)	(5)	(46)	(8)	(31)	0	0	27
Earnings (loss) from operations before income taxes	215	25	22	83	10	(147)	(39)	39	186	175	175
Income taxes (recovery)	99	16	10	38	6	(56)	(10)	19	83	82	73
Net earnings (loss)	116	9	12	45	4	(91)	(29)	21	106	96	107
Dividends declared	25	23	23	23	23	21	20	20	21	21	21
Capital expenditures	160	63	76	60	37	55	235	204	116	118	63
Year End Position (in millions)											
Accounts receivable	$ 1,225	$ 1,033	$ 926	$ 1,324	$ 1,101	$ 909	$ 1,090	$ 1,877	$ 1,784	$ 1,496	$ 1,272
Inventories	640	491	507	559	563	628	693	665	807	747	740
Net capital assets	825	744	763	800	813	941	997	803	665	572	504
Total assets	3,007	2,734	2,554	2,949	2,746	2,796	3,069	3,581	3,512	3,103	2,793
Working capital	971	741	661	1,016	888	885	1,112	1,486	1,451	1,177	1,172
Long-term obligations	836	634	662	1,032	947	1,063	1,245	1,362	1,185	964	944
Shareholders' equity	1,042	949	856	867	845	863	900	948	970	883	825
Per Share of Capital Stock (in dollars)											
Net earnings (loss)	$ 1.10	$ 0.09	$ 0.13	$ 0.47	$ 0.05	$ (1.04)	$ (0.34)	$ 0.25	$ 1.23	$ 1.11	$ 1.22
Dividends declared	0.24	0.24	0.24	0.24	0.24	0.24	0.24	0.24	0.24	0.24	0.24
Shareholders' equity	9.84	8.98	9.02	9.13	8.90	9.10	10.67	11.25	11.26	10.27	9.43
Financial Ratios											
Return on average shareholders' equity (%)	11.7	1.0	1.4	5.2	0.5	(10.3)	(3.1)	2.2	11.4	11.2	13.7
Current ratio	1.9	1.7	1.7	2.0	2.0	2.1	2.4	2.3	2.1	2.0	2.2
Return on total revenues (%)	2.5	0.2	0.3	1.1	0.1	(2.2)	(0.7)	0.5	2.3	2.2	2.6
Debt/Equity ratio	45/55	46/54	48/52	59/41	58/42	59/41	61/39	67/33	66/34	65/35	63/37
Pre-tax margin (%)	4.7	0.6	0.6	2.0	0.3	(3.6)	(0.9)	0.8	4.0	4.0	4.3
Number of Selling Units											
Retail stores	110	110	110	110	110	109	106	97	92	84	80
Furniture stores	8	4	1	0	0	0	0	0	0	0	0
Outlet stores	8	9	10	11	12	13	15	18	17	16	15
Dealer stores	79	60	19	4	0	0	0	0	0	0	0
Catalogue selling locations	1,752	1,746	1,623	1,542	1,483	1,579	1,701	1,701	1,708	1,726	1,719

1 Certain amounts have been restated to reflect accounting changes related to the consolidation of the Company's proportionate share of the assets, liabilities and expenses of real estate joint ventures as recommended by the Canadian Institute of Chartered Accountants. The change in policy, effective in 1995, has been applied retroactively.

2 Extraordinary items have been restated in 1987 to reflect the reclassification of items from extraordinary items to unusual items. All amounts are restated in pre-tax dollars and the income tax amounts have been adjusted accordingly.

Management's Discussion & Analysis

Sears is Canada's largest single retailer of general merchandise, with department and specialty stores as well as catalogue selling units located across Canada. The Company emphasizes quality, value, and service in appealing to a broad cross-section of Canadian consumers.

The Company's vision is to be Canada's most successful retailer by providing customers with total shopping satisfaction, associates with opportunities for career advancement and personal growth, and shareholders with superior returns on their investment.

OVERVIEW OF CONSOLIDATED RESULTS

For purposes of this discussion, "Sears" or "the Company" refers to Sears Canada Inc. and its subsidiaries together with the Company's proportionate share of the assets, liabilities, revenues and expenses of real estate joint ventures.

The 1997 fiscal year refers to the 53 week period ended January 3, 1998 and comparatively, the 1996 fiscal year refers to the 52 week period ended December 28, 1996.

The following table summarizes the Company's operating results for 1997 and 1996.

(in millions, except per share amounts)	1997	1996
Total revenues	$ 4,583.5	$ 3,955.9
Earnings from operations before interest, unusual items and income taxes	301.3	166.3
Interest expense	86.1	96.3
Earnings from operations before unusual items and income taxes	215.2	70.0
Unusual items expense[1]	-	45.0
Income taxes	98.7	16.2
Net earnings	$ 116.5	$ 8.8
Earnings per share	$ 1.10	$ 0.09

1 Refer to Financial Statement Note 10.

Total revenues increased in 1997 by $627.6 million or 15.9% over 1996 due primarily to an increase in merchandise revenues of 16.8%, with strong growth in both retail and catalogue operations. Fiscal 1997 contained 53 weeks. On a comparable 52 week basis, total revenues increased by 14.4%.

In 1997, Sears achieved significant growth in revenues, building on the initiatives implemented in recent years. The Company's strategy for growth is directed at meeting the needs of its target customer, and involves increased investment in inventories, fixed assets, and marketing. In 1997, the Company completed substantial renovations to nine stores in the Greater Toronto Area, opened four new **Sears Whole Home Furniture Stores**, and nineteen dealer stores.

The Company's earnings from operations before unusual items and income taxes were $215.2 million in 1997, just over three times 1996 earnings of $70.0 million. Operational expenses, and investments in inventory and capital assets were all effectively managed, resulting in a substantial increase in net earnings. Interest expense declined by $10.2 million primarily due to a reduction in the average amount of debt outstanding during the year. (Refer to the section entitled "Analysis of Funding Costs" on page 30).

Number of Associates

	1997	1996
Full-time associates	9,221	9,033
Part-time associates	29,324	26,263
Total associates	38,545	35,296

The total number of associates increased by 9.2% in 1997, reflecting the Company's emphasis on customer service.

SEGMENTED BUSINESS ANALYSIS

The Company's operations can be grouped into three major businesses: merchandising, credit, and real estate joint ventures.

Management's Discussion & Analysis continued

MERCHANDISING OPERATIONS

The merchandising business segment includes Sears full-line department store and catalogue operations, in addition to Sears Whole Home Furniture Stores, dealer stores and outlet stores.

(in millions)	1997	1996
Revenues	$ 4,210.6	$ 3,605.7
Earnings from operations before interest, unusual items and income taxes	$ 141.7	$ 27.0
Capital employed	$ 553.6	$ 585.8

Merchandising Operating Analysis

Merchandising revenues were $4.2 billion in 1997, an increase of 16.8% over 1996. All regions experienced increases in revenues in 1997. The Ontario region recorded the largest increase at 20.5%.

Merchandising Revenues by Region

(in millions)	1997	% of Total	% of Total Households[2]
Atlantic	$ 402.6	9.6	7.8
Quebec	876.9	20.8	26.1
Ontario	1,667.7	39.6	36.3
Prairies	754.2	17.9	16.4
BC/Yukon/NWT	509.2	12.1	13.4
Total	$ 4,210.6	100.0	100.0

2 Total Households is based on Statistics Canada, 1996 Census.

Number of Selling Units

As at January 3, 1998

	Atlantic	Que.	Ont.	Prairies	BC Yukon NWT	Total
Retail	11	25	43	19	12	110
Furniture	0	0	8	0	0	8
Outlet	1	0	5	1	1	8
Dealer	16	8	21	12	22	79
Catalogue	327	417	472	386	150	1,752

Retail Stores – 110 department stores ranging in size from 24,500 square feet to 162,000 square feet.

Furniture Stores – stores ranging in size from 35,000 square feet to 48,000 square feet featuring an expanded selection of furniture, decorator rugs and, in two stores, major appliances.

Outlet Stores – selling returned and surplus merchandise in stores ranging in size from 25,000 square feet to 104,000 square feet.

Dealer Stores – independent locally operated stores serving smaller population centres, selling home appliances and electronics, as well as lawn, garden and snow removal merchandise.

Catalogue Selling Locations – include 1,551 independent catalogue agent locations, plus catalogue pick-up locations within Sears retail stores, outlet stores and dealer stores.

During 1997, the Company opened four new Sears Whole Home Furniture Stores and 19 dealer stores.

Merchandising Gross Floor Area

(square feet – in millions)	1997	1996
Retail	13.6	13.6
Furniture	0.3	0.1
Outlet	0.6	0.7
Total	14.5	14.4
Merchandise service centres:		
Active	6.8	6.8
Subleased or dormant	1.9	2.8
Total merchandise service centres	8.7	9.6

Merchandise service centres include two catalogue order fulfillment facilities and five service centres supporting national merchandising operations.

Recent Merchandising Initiatives

- In 1997, Sears completed major renovations to nine full-line department stores in the Greater Toronto Area (GTA). Approximately $60 million was invested in major upgrades to store presentation such as fixtures and lighting. The renovated stores allow Sears to offer a broader and deeper assortment of merchandise presented in an up-to-date store environment. These stores feature an expanded assortment of fashion apparel, cosmetics, accessories and "soft" home fashions. During these renovations, Sears was able to reclaim more than 160,000 square feet of selling space by eliminating surplus stockroom and office space. The renovation of nine GTA full-line department stores completes the first phase of a three year, $300 million capital investment program to reposition Sears retail stores nationally.

- Expansion of the Sears Whole Home Furniture Store concept, launched in 1995, continued with openings in Burlington, Woodbridge, Barrie and Newmarket, Ontario in 1997. Both the Woodbridge and Barrie locations carry **Sears Brand Central** selection of major appliances in addition to the broad selection of furniture, decorator rugs and accent decor items available at all Sears Whole Home Furniture Stores. This combination of furniture and appliances offers one of Canada's widest assortments of home merchandise under one roof. The Company plans to open fourteen additional Sears Whole Home Furniture Stores in 1998. Many of these stores will also feature Sears Brand Central appliances.

- The Company continued to enhance its assortment of national brands in 1997. Sears has combined these brands with strong private label offerings in order to provide customers with a broad range of fashionable merchandise. National brands introduced this year include **First 1 Issue, Jones Studio, Calvin Klein, Point Zero, Daniel David, Private Member** and **Calvin Klein Khakis** in apparel; **Fieldcrest Royal Velvet** and **Joseph Abboud** in bed and bath; and **Pfaltzgraff** in housewares.

- In 1997, Sears invested $40.4 million to install improved fixturing in stores across the country. Fashion tables for the presentation of folded goods were installed in all apparel departments. **Levi's** shops, a unique branded shopping environment, were rolled-out to 80 retail stores in 1997 to provide a consistent and attractive presentation in men's, women's and children's apparel departments. As well, fixtures which allow for the display of approximately 50% more merchandise were installed in hardware and seasonal merchandise departments.

- Sears introduced Shop By Phone across Canada in 1997. This innovative program allows customers to purchase selected items featured in retail flyers and bearing the Shop by Phone symbol, either at a local Sears retail store, or by calling 1-888-607-3277. This initiative is designed to enhance customer convenience and service.

Management's Discussion & Analysis continued

• The dealer store program, introduced in 1994, expanded to a total of 79 stores, with 19 locations being added in 1997. The Company plans to open an additional 20 dealer stores in 1998. Dealer stores are operated under independent local ownership. These stores offer a selection of **Kenmore** and other name brand appliances, electronics, and lawn and garden furniture and equipment. Dealer stores are designed to provide the small market customer with a broad shopping selection, together with personal local service.

• 1997 marked the launch of the biggest Christmas **Wish Book** in Sears 44 year catalogue history. This year's Wish Book was larger than last year's book with 38% more pages. It featured expanded toy, fashion apparel and home electronics sections, as well as an increased national brand selection. The 1997 Sears Wish Book was distributed to almost five million Canadian households.

• Several initiatives were introduced during the year designed to improve synergies between the catalogue and retail sales channels. As part of the GTA store renovations, the presentation of catalogue shopping areas located in several Sears retail stores was updated. An inviting atmosphere was created through the use of modern fixturing, seasonal posters, and a central area in which to browse through catalogues. These catalogue shopping areas were also equipped with fitting rooms, enabling customers to try on merchandise they have ordered. In addition, the Company continued to install catalogue outposts in various areas of the store. These outposts permit customers to order merchandise via the catalogue if their particular selection is unavailable in the retail store, thereby enabling the customer to access the catalogue's expanded selection of styles and specialty sizes.

CREDIT OPERATIONS

Sears credit operations finance and manage customer charge account receivables generated from the sale of goods and services charged on the Sears Card.

(in millions)	1997	1996
Total service charge revenues	$ **364.8**	$ 361.6
Less: SCRT share of revenues[3]	**(54.2)**	(69.2)
Net service charge revenues	**310.6**	292.4
Earnings before interest, unusual items and income taxes	$ **127.5**	$ 109.1
Capital employed	$ **1,090.8**	$ 943.6

3 Refer to the section entitled "Analysis of Funding Costs" on page 30.

Credit operations contributed $127.5 million to the Company's 1997 consolidated earnings before interest, unusual items and income taxes, compared to $109.1 million in fiscal 1996. The increase of $18.4 million in earnings reflects the increase in the Company's net revenues.

Total service charge revenues earned on customer charge account receivables increased slightly in 1997. Through its securitization program, the Company securitizes customer charge account receivables in order to obtain a more favourable cost of funding. The cost of this funding is deducted from the total service charge revenues earned on the portfolio. After adjusting for amounts securitized, net service charge revenues increased by $18.2 million or 6.2%. (Refer to the section entitled "Securitization of Charge Account Receivables" on page 29.)

Charge Account Receivables Analysis

(in millions – except average account balances)	1997	1996
Active customer accounts	**3.8**	3.8
Average outstanding balance of receivables per customer account at year end	$ **439**	$ 424
Charge account receivables written-off during the year (net of recoveries)	$ **46.4**	$ 49.9

Net write-offs as a percentage of the monthly average amounts outstanding were 3.2% in 1997 compared to 3.4% in 1996 and 2.7% in 1995. This write-off rate continues to be at the low end of industry norms.

Since October 1993, Sears has been accepting third party credit cards in addition to the Sears Card. In 1997, Sears began accepting debit cards in major centres. The chart below details the trend in method of payment.

	1997	1996	1995
Sears Card	**64**	66	65
Third Party Credit Cards	**13**	11	10
Cash	**23**	23	25
Total	**100 %**	100 %	100 %

The percentage of sales charged by customers to their Sears Card decreased to 64% of total sales from 66% in 1996. The percentage charged to third party cards increased to 13% from 11% last year. The share of cash sales remained constant at 23%.

Recent Credit Initiatives

The following initiatives have been directed at increasing usage of the Sears Card.

- A new auto club developed exclusively for Sears Card holders was launched in September 1997. **Sears AutoAssist** provides access to roadside assistance 24 hours a day, 365 days a year, anywhere in Canada or the U.S.A. Roadside services include; emergency towing, battery boosts, flat tire service, lock-out service, emergency gasoline delivery, and up to $500 for accommodations, meals and transportation for road accidents away from home.

- In 1997, Sears enhanced the **Sears PhonePlan** program. Effective December 1, 1997 the discount offered to Sears PhonePlan members on all "time and day" billing rates for long distance calls increased from 25% to 33 1/3%. In 1997 Sears PhonePlan also introduced the **Sears Card Calling Card**. This card allows members to conveniently place long distance calls when they are away from home. All long distance calls made by members also earn Sears Club points. As at January 3, 1998, the Sears PhonePlan program had 485,640 members.

REAL ESTATE JOINT VENTURE OPERATIONS

As at January 3, 1998, the Company held joint venture interests in 19 shopping centres, 17 of which contain a Sears store. The Company has 15% to 50% interests in these joint ventures. Accordingly, the Company carries its proportionate share of the assets, liabilities, revenues and expenses of these joint ventures on its books.

(in millions)	1997	1996
Revenues[4]	$ **62.3**	$ 57.8
Earnings from operations before interest, unusual items and income taxes	$ **32.1**	$ 30.2
Capital employed	$ **245.7**	$ 238.8

4 Excluded from revenues is the Company's proportionate share of rental revenues earned from retail stores of Sears Canada Inc. of $3.7 million ($3.6 million – 1996).

The market value of Sears interest in these properties is estimated to be approximately $400 million ($365 million – 1996). It is the Company's policy to have one-third of the properties independently appraised each year, while the appraisals of the remaining two-thirds are reviewed and updated by management. The Sears portion of the debt of these properties is $229.8 million ($223.2 million – 1996).

Management's Discussion & Analysis continued

OVERVIEW OF THE CONSOLIDATED STATEMENTS OF FINANCIAL POSITION

Assets

(in millions)	1997	1996
Cash	$ 68.3	$ 201.2
Accounts receivable	1,224.6	1,033.0
Inventories	640.3	491.1
Net capital assets	825.1	744.4
Other assets	249.0	264.3
Total assets	$ 3,007.3	$ 2,734.0

Total assets increased by $273.3 million or 10.0% in 1997.

In 1997, cash decreased $132.9 million. The 1996 cash balance of $201.2 million included proceeds from the issue of 10.3 million common shares in December 1996.

Accounts receivable increased by $191.6 million or 18.5% in 1997.

Accounts Receivable

(in millions)	1997	1996
Charge account receivables	$ 1,655.7	$ 1,568.5
Less amount securitized[5]	(965.6)	(961.2)
Net charge account receivables	690.1	607.3
Deferred receivables	497.4	456.1
Less amount securitized[5]	(24.4)	(97.6)
Net deferred receivables	473.0	358.5
Other receivables	61.5	67.2
Total accounts receivable	$ 1,224.6	$ 1,033.0

5 Refer to the section entitled "Securitization of Charge Account Receivables" on page 29.

Deferred receivables represent credit sales not yet billed to customers' accounts. These credit sales are billed to the customers' accounts at the end of an interest-free deferral period.

Inventories increased by $149.2 million in support of the Company's revenue growth initiatives.

Net capital assets increased by $80.7 million. Capital expenditures totaled $160.4 million in 1997, of which approximately $114 million was spent on retail store renovations and the opening of four new Sears Whole Home Furniture Stores. Depreciation expense for the year was $78.1 million.

Liabilities

(in millions)	1997	1996
Accounts payable and accrued liabilities	$ 878.6	$ 797.8
Long-term obligations due within one year	11.6	183.2
Long-term obligations	836.1	634.2
Other liabilities	238.6	170.1
Total liabilities	$ 1,964.9	$ 1,785.3

Total liabilities increased by $179.6 million or 10.1% in 1997.

Long-term obligations increased by $201.9 million due to the issuance of $125.0 million of 6.55% unsecured debentures and the refinancing of certain joint venture debts. Including amounts due within one year, long-term obligations increased by $30.3 million. (Refer to the section entitled "Analysis of Funding Costs" on page 30.)

Liquidity

As at January 3, 1998, the ratio of current assets to current liabilities increased to 1.9:1 from 1.7:1 in 1996. Working capital was $971.1 million as at January 3, 1998 compared to $741.0 million as at December 28, 1996. The increase in working capital is primarily attributable to growth in accounts receivable and merchandise inventories.

FINANCING ACTIVITIES

The Company has the flexibility to raise funds through bank borrowings, by issuing equity and corporate debt securities, and through the securitization of charge account receivables.

In 1997, the Company carried out the following significant financing activities:

- On February 26, 1997, the outstanding 9.25% unsecured debentures of Sears Canada Inc. in the amount of $100.0 million matured and were repaid.
- On November 5, 1997, Sears Canada Inc. issued $125.0 million of 6.55% unsecured debentures due November 5, 2007.
- During 1997, long-term financing for new capital projects of real estate joint ventures was obtained in the amount of $9.9 million. In addition, $81.8 million of joint venture debt matured in 1997, of which $78.5 million was refinanced.

Securitization of Charge Account Receivables

Sears Acceptance Company Inc. ("Acceptance"), a wholly owned subsidiary of Sears, purchases all Sears Card charge account receivables (including deferred receivables) generated by merchandise and service sales. Through the Company's securitization program, Acceptance sells undivided co-ownership interests in the charge account receivables (excluding deferred receivables) to Sears Canada Receivables Trust (Trust 1) and Sears Canada Receivables Trust – 1992 (Trust 2). In addition, Acceptance sells undivided co-ownership interests in its portfolio of charge account receivables (including deferred receivables) to Sears Canada Receivables Trust – 1996 (Trust 3). Trust 1, Trust 2 and Trust 3 are collectively referred to as SCRT.

As the equity units of Trust 1, Trust 2 and Trust 3 are held by independent parties, the assets and liabilities of SCRT are not reflected in the Company's consolidated financial statements. The cost to the Company of the securitization program is reflected as a reduction in the Company's share of Sears Card service charge revenues.

SCRT is an important financing vehicle which is able to obtain favourable interest rates because of its structure and the high quality of the portfolio of charge account receivables backing its debt. Securitization provides the Company with a diversified source of funds for the operation of its business.

Trust 1 – Trust 1, which was established in 1991, issues short-term commercial paper to finance the purchase of undivided co-ownership interests in charge account receivables (excluding deferred receivables).

The commercial paper of Trust 1 is rated A-1+ by CBRS Inc. (CBRS) and R-1(High) by Dominion Bond Rating Service Limited (DBRS), the highest ratings assigned by these rating agencies for commercial paper.

In order to reduce its exposure to fluctuations in short-term interest rates on Trust 1 borrowings, the Company has entered into floating-to-fixed interest rate swaps in the notional amount of $200 million with remaining terms to maturity of up to 5 years. The average amount securitized under Trust 1 in 1997 was $415.6 million, at an average rate of 4.0% ($509.0 million in 1996 at an average rate of 5.7%).

Trust 2 – Trust 2, which was established in 1993, issues long-term senior and subordinated debentures to finance the purchase of undivided co-ownership interests in charge account receivables (excluding deferred receivables).

The senior debentures of Trust 2 are rated A++ by CBRS and AAA by DBRS, the highest ratings assigned by these agencies for long-term debt. The subordinated debentures of Trust 2 are rated A by CBRS and A (High) by DBRS.

Trust 3 – Trust 3, which was established on October 22, 1996, finances the purchase of undivided co-ownership interests in Acceptance's portfolio of charge account receivables (including deferred receivables) through drawdowns under revolving senior and subordinated note facilities.

Management's Discussion & Analysis *continued*

The senior notes of Trust 3 are rated A++ by CBRS and AAA by DBRS, the highest ratings assigned by these agencies for long-term debt. The subordinated notes of Trust 3 are rated A+ by CBRS and A by DBRS.

Summary of Debt Ratings

	CBRS	DBRS
Sears Canada Inc.		
Unsecured debentures	B++ (High)	BBB
SCRT		
Commercial paper (Trust 1)	A-1+	R-1 (High)
Senior debentures (Trust 2)	A++	AAA
Subordinated debentures (Trust 2)	A	A (High)
Senior notes (Trust 3)	A++	AAA
Subordinated notes (Trust 3)	A+	A

Summary of SCRT Obligations

	1997	1996
Commercial paper	$ 374.8	$ 311.5
Senior debt:		
5.65%, due January 14, 1997[6]	-	27.9
6.50%, due December 16, 1998	150.0	150.0
8.95%, due June 1, 2004	175.0	175.0
Floating rate, due April 1, 2001	150.0	150.0
Floating rate, due June 30, 2006	43.1	139.4
	518.1	642.3
Subordinated debt:		
7.67% to 9.18%, due 1998 to 2004	7.2	7.2
Floating rate, due 1997 to 2004	13.7	18.1
Floating rate, due June 30, 2006	0.4	1.4
	21.3	26.7
Accrued liabilities	3.5	6.0
Trust units (floating rate, due 1998 to 2006)	72.3	72.3
Total SCRT obligations	$ 990.0	$ 1,058.8

6 Face value of $100.0 million debenture shown net of permitted investments as at December 28, 1996 of $72.1 million.

Analysis of Funding Costs

The following table summarizes the Company's total funding costs including the cost of the securitization program:

(in millions)	1997	1996
Interest Costs		
Total debt at end of year	$ 847.7	$ 819.5
Average debt for year	758.4	836.6
Interest on long-term debt	$ 74.5	$ 82.8
Other interest (net)[7]	11.6	13.5
Interest expense	$ 86.1	$ 96.3
Average rate of debt[8]	11.2 %	11.5 %
Securitization Costs[9]		
Amount securitized at end of year	$ 990.0	$ 1,058.8
Average amount securitized for year	1,019.6	1,103.9
Cost of funding	54.2	69.2
Average rate of securitized funding[8]	5.2 %	6.3 %
Total Funding		
Total funding at end of year	$ 1,837.7	$ 1,878.3
Total average funding for year	1,778.0	1,940.5
Total funding costs for year	140.3	165.5
Average rate of total funding[8]	7.8 %	8.5 %

7 Other interest includes $13.2 million in 1997 ($12.8 million – 1996) for payment of the interest rate differential on floating-to-fixed interest rate swaps.

8 1997 calculation based on 365 day year rather than fiscal period of 53 weeks.

9 Securitization costs for 1996 comparative figures reflect the cost of Trust 1 and Trust 2 for the fiscal year and the cost of Trust 3 for the period from November 1, 1996 to December 28, 1996.

Total funding costs for 1997 decreased by $25.2 million due primarily to lower average funding levels and lower average interest rates applicable to floating rate funding outstanding in SCRT.

Capital Structure

The chart below highlights the improving trend in the debt to equity ratio, due primarily to the contribution of net earnings and a 1996 common share issue.

(in millions)	1997	% of Total	1996	% of Total
Current debt:				
Bank advances and				
short-term notes	$ 0.0	0.0	$ 2.1	0.1
Long-term debt due				
within one year	11.6	0.6	183.2	10.4
	11.6	0.6	185.3	10.5
Long-term debt	836.1	44.2	634.2	35.8
Total debt	847.7	44.8	819.5	46.3
Shareholders'				
equity	1,042.4	55.2	948.7	53.7
Total capital	$1,890.1	100.0	$1,768.2	100.0

CAPITAL EXPENDITURES

The Company expects to commit approximately $214 million for capital expenditures in 1998, compared to capital expenditures of $160.4 million in 1997. Planned expenditures for 1998 include $110.5 million for retail store enhancements and new Sears Whole Home Furniture Stores. The balance of the capital expenditures will be spent primarily on information technology, logistics and real estate operations.

ANALYSIS OF TOTAL CORPORATE TAXES

Total corporate taxes increased by $77.7 million in 1997. Income taxes increased $82.5 million, commensurate with an increase in earnings from operations before income taxes. (Refer to Financial Statement Note 11.)

(in millions)	1997	1996
Provincial capital tax	$ 6.7	$ 6.9
Property tax	45.7	54.4
Payroll taxes[10]	68.6	64.5
Total taxes expensed in cost of		
merchandise sold, operating,		
administrative and selling expense	121.0	125.8
Corporate income tax	93.9	11.2
Large corporations tax	4.8	5.0
Income taxes	98.7	16.2
Total corporate taxes	$ 219.7	$ 142.0

10 Represents contributions to the Canada and Quebec Pension Plans, Employment Insurance, health care levies and WCB premiums.

RISKS AND UNCERTAINTIES

The key elements of the Company's strategy for minimizing risk are as follows: .

Interest Rates

Trust 1 has financed purchases of undivided co-ownership interests in the portfolio of charge account receivables with the issuance of $374.8 million of commercial paper as at January 3, 1998 ($311.5 million – 1996). To reduce the risk associated with fluctuating interest rates, floating-to-fixed interest rate swap transactions in the notional amount of $200 million ($250 million – 1996) have been utilized. This brings the Company's fixed-to-floating funding ratio, including securitized funding to 66/34, which is within its target ratios.

Management's Discussion & Analysis *continued*

Foreign Exchange

The Company's foreign exchange risk is limited to currency fluctuations between the Canadian and U.S. dollar. The Company's total forecasted requirement for foreign funds in 1998 is approximately U.S. $300 million. From time to time, the Company uses forward contracts to fix the exchange rate on a portion of its expected requirement for U.S. dollars. As at January 3, 1998, there were no foreign exchange contracts outstanding.

Concentration of Credit Risk

The Company's exposure to credit risk relates mainly to customer account receivables. Sears Card customers are a large and diverse group. The average balance per customer at year end was $439.

Leases

Twenty-two of Sears 110 retail stores are Company-owned and two of the eight Sears Whole Home Furniture Stores are Company-owned, with the balance held under long-term leases which include favourable renewal options. As a result, the Company's retail store rental expense is expected to remain stable.

Merchandise Sources

A major aim of the merchandise procurement process is to ensure that Sears, together with its merchandise sources, fulfills its promises and obligations to its customers. Sears will continue to work with its merchandise sources to ensure that they share this commitment.

Sears shops the world market to provide its customers with the best value for their dollar. As a result, Sears is confident in its ability to continue providing consumers with high quality merchandise at competitive prices.

Year 2000

The Year 2000 poses a significant global challenge. Date dependent systems and processes that use two digits to represent the year must be adapted in order to avoid risk of error with the turn of the century.

Sears has been preparing to meet the Year 2000 challenge for the past three years, as the Company is a significant user of current technologies. The Company has established a cross-functional team to oversee and manage the Sears Year 2000 project. The first phase of the project, which included identifying and evaluating the Company's systems and applications for Year 2000 capability, determining necessary modifications and replacements and communicating with third parties, including merchandise and non-merchandise suppliers to discuss and assess their Year 2000 readiness, was completed early in 1997.

Remedial action and testing are underway. The project is continuing to progress in accordance with the project schedule. The Company has established December 31, 1998 as the date that its critical systems will be converted, tested and Year 2000 ready. To date, approximately $7 million has been spent on personnel and contractor costs. Costs are expensed as incurred. The total estimated cost for the project is approximately $28 million for internal and external resources.

Competitive and Economic Environment

Sears believes that the general economic environment will remain positive, providing additional opportunities for growth in 1998. Although the retail market remains highly competitive, Sears is well positioned to take advantage of emerging trends in retailing, including those in the areas of specialty stores and services.

Sears is optimistic that consumer confidence will remain high in 1998, despite continuing high levels of household debt. Strong growth is forecast for the Canadian economy again this year, as labour markets are expected to further improve and inflation is forecast to remain low.

Outlook

Sears continues to position itself to capture a larger share of consumer spending through its aggressive programs of store renovations and enhanced merchandise assortment and presentation. The Company also continues to evaluate new and innovative methods of retailing. By meeting customers' needs in terms of merchandise selection, pricing, and the total shopping experience, Sears anticipates growth in revenues and profits into the future.

SEARS ✦ CANADA

Quarterly Results *Unaudited*

	First Quarter 1997	First Quarter 1996	Second Quarter 1997	Second Quarter 1996	Third Quarter 1997	Third Quarter 1996	Fourth Quarter 1997	Fourth Quarter 1996
Total revenues	$ 875.1	$ 821.7	$ 1,054.3	$ 899.2	$ 1,065.5	$ 928.5	$ 1,588.6	$ 1,306.5
Earnings (loss) from operations before unusual items and income taxes	(2.6)	(36.1)	42.3	(12.2)	37.1	1.3	138.4	117.0
Net earnings (loss)	$ (2.8)	$ (21.8)	$ 22.8	$ (31.9)	$ 19.4	$ (0.5)	$ 77.1	$ 63.0
Earnings (loss) per share	$ (0.03)	$ (0.23)	$ 0.22	$ (0.34)	$ 0.18	$ 0.00	$ 0.73	$ 0.66

Common Share Market Information*

	First Quarter 1997	First Quarter 1996	Second Quarter 1997	Second Quarter 1996	Third Quarter 1997	Third Quarter 1996	Fourth Quarter 1997	Fourth Quarter 1996
High	$ 13.95	$ 6 5/8	$ 20.00	$ 8.15	$ 25.20	$ 8.15	$ 25.75	$ 12.00
Low	$ 10.00	$ 5 4/8	$ 12.50	$ 6 3/8	$ 18.25	$ 7.40	$ 19.00	$ 7.75
Close	$ 13.35	$ 6 6/8	$ 18.40	$ 8.05	$ 25.00	$ 7.75	$ 19.80	$ 10.10
Avg. daily trading volume	229,870	88,198	295,137	84,790	127,992	62,142	189,641	202,507

* The Toronto Stock Exchange

Statement of Management Responsibility

Management is responsible for the accuracy, integrity and objectivity of the financial information contained in this Annual Report. The consolidated financial statements have been prepared in accordance with generally accepted accounting principles in Canada and include certain amounts that are based on estimates and judgements. Financial information used elsewhere in the Annual Report is consistent with that in the financial statements.

Management has developed, maintains and supports an extensive program of internal audits that provides reasonable assurance that financial records are reliable and that assets are safeguarded.

The Board of Directors, through the activities of its Audit and Corporate Governance Committee, ensures that management fulfills its responsibilities for financial reporting and internal control. The Audit and Corporate Governance Committee, the majority of whom are outside directors, meets periodically with the financial officers of the Company, the internal auditors and external auditors to discuss audit activities, internal accounting controls and financial reporting matters. The Board of Directors, on the recommendation of the Audit and Corporate Governance Committee, has approved all of the information contained in the Annual Report.

The Company's external auditors, Deloitte & Touche, have conducted audits of the financial records of the Company in accordance with generally accepted auditing standards. Their report is as follows.

President and
Chief Operating Officer

Senior Vice-President and
Chief Financial Officer

Auditors' Report to the Shareholders of Sears Canada Inc.

We have audited the consolidated statements of financial position of Sears Canada Inc. as at January 3, 1998 and December 28, 1996 and the consolidated statements of earnings, retained earnings and changes in financial position for the 53 weeks and 52 weeks then ended. These financial statements are the responsibility of the Company's management. Our responsibility is to express an opinion on these financial statements based on our audits.

We conducted our audits in accordance with generally accepted auditing standards. Those standards require that we plan and perform an audit to obtain reasonable assurance whether the financial statements are free of material misstatement. An audit includes examining, on a test basis, evidence supporting the amounts and disclosures in the financial statements. An audit also includes assessing the accounting principles used and significant estimates made by management, as well as evaluating the overall financial statement presentation.

In our opinion, these consolidated financial statements present fairly, in all material respects, the financial position of the Company as at January 3, 1998 and December 28, 1996 and the results of its operations and the changes in its financial position for the 53 weeks and 52 weeks then ended in accordance with generally accepted accounting principles.

Deloitte & Touche
Chartered Accountants

Toronto, Ontario
February 9, 1998

Consolidated Statements of Financial Position

SEARS CANADA

As at January 3, 1998 and December 28, 1996 (in millions)	1997	1996
Assets		
Current Assets		
Cash and short-term investments	$ 68.3	$ 201.2
Charge account receivables (Note 2)	690.1	607.3
Other receivables (Note 3)	534.5	425.7
Inventories	640.3	491.1
Prepaid expenses and other assets	48.9	46.5
Short-term deferred income taxes	41.9	40.0
	2,024.0	1,811.8
Investments and Other Assets (Note 4)	22.8	29.6
Net Capital Assets (Note 5)	825.1	744.4
Deferred Charges (Note 6)	135.4	148.2
	$ 3,007.3	$ 2,734.0
Liabilities		
Current Liabilities		
Bank advances and short-term notes	$ 0.0	$ 2.1
Accounts payable	560.2	472.9
Accrued liabilities	318.4	324.9
Income and other taxes payable	162.7	87.7
Principal payments on long-term obligations due within one year (Note 8)	11.6	183.2
	1,052.9	1,070.8
Long-term Obligations (Note 8)	836.1	634.2
Long-term Deferred Income Taxes	75.9	80.3
	1,964.9	1,785.3
Shareholders' Equity		
Capital Stock (Note 9)	450.9	448.3
Retained Earnings	591.5	500.4
	1,042.4	948.7
	$ 3,007.3	$ 2,734.0

Approved by the Board:

P.S. Walters
Director

J.M. Tory
Director

Consolidated Statements of Earnings

(in millions, except per share amounts)	For the 53 weeks ended January 3, 1998	For the 52 weeks ended December 28, 1996
Total revenues	$ 4,583.5	$ 3,955.9
Deduct:		
Cost of merchandise sold, operating, administrative and selling expenses	4,204.1	3,712.1
Depreciation	78.1	77.5
Interest	86.1	96.3
	4,368.3	3,885.9
Earnings from operations before unusual items and income taxes	215.2	70.0
Unusual items (Note 10)	0.0	(45.0)
Earnings from operations before income taxes	215.2	25.0
Income taxes (Note 11)		
Current	105.0	9.4
Deferred	(6.3)	6.8
	98.7	16.2
Net earnings	$ 116.5	$ 8.8
Earnings per share	$ 1.10	$ 0.09

Consolidated Statements of Retained Earnings

(in millions, except per share amounts)	For the 53 weeks ended January 3, 1998	For the 52 weeks ended December 28, 1996
Opening balance	$ 500.4	$ 514.4
Net earnings	116.5	8.8
	616.9	523.2
Dividends declared	25.4	22.8
Closing balance	$ 591.5	$ 500.4

Consolidated Statements of Changes in Financial Position

SEARS ✦ CANADA

(in millions)	For the 53 weeks ended January 3, 1998	For the 52 weeks ended December 28, 1996
Cash Generated From (Used For) Operations		
Net earnings	$ 116.5	$ 8.8
Non-cash items included in net earnings, principally depreciation	88.9	86.2
Funds from operations	205.4	95.0
Changes in working capital (Note 12)	(106.5)	183.2
	98.9	278.2
Cash Generated From (Used For) Investment Activities		
Purchases of capital assets	(160.4)	(63.2)
Proceeds from sale of capital assets	1.1	8.9
Charge account receivables	(82.8)	(189.3)
Deferred charges	(1.9)	(2.4)
Investments and other assets	6.8	(14.4)
	(237.2)	(260.4)
Cash Generated From (Used For) Financing Activities		
Issue of long-term obligations	134.9	100.0
Repayment of long-term obligations	(104.6)	(71.3)
Net proceeds from issue of capital stock	2.6	106.3
	32.9	135.0
Cash (Used For) Dividends	(25.4)	(22.8)
Increase (decrease) in cash net of bank advances and short-term notes at end of year	(130.8)	130.0
Cash, net of bank advances and short-term notes at end of year	$ 68.3	$ 199.1

Notes to Consolidated Financial Statements

1 SUMMARY OF ACCOUNTING POLICIES

Principles of Consolidation

The consolidated financial statements include the accounts of Sears Canada Inc. and its subsidiaries together with its proportionate share of the assets, liabilities, revenues and expenses of real estate joint ventures ("the Company").

Fiscal Year

The fiscal year of the Company consists of a 52 or 53 week period ending on the Saturday closest to December 31. The 1997 fiscal year for the consolidated statements presented is the 53 weeks ending January 3, 1998 and the comparable period is the 52 weeks ending December 28, 1996.

Inventories

Inventories are valued at the lower of cost or net realizable value. Cost is determined for retail store inventories by the retail inventory method and for catalogue order and miscellaneous inventories by the average cost method, based on individual items.

Prepaid Advertising Expense

Catalogue production costs are deferred and amortized over the life of each catalogue on the basis of the estimated sales from that catalogue.

Deferred Receivables

Deferred receivables are charge account receivables that have not yet been billed to the customers' accounts. Service charges are not accrued on these accounts over the deferral period which generally ranges from six to thirteen months.

Capital Assets

Capital assets are stated at cost. Depreciation and amortization provisions are generally computed by the straight-line method based on estimated useful lives of 2 to 10 years for equipment and fixtures, and of 10 to 40 years for buildings and improvements.

The Company's proportionate share of buildings held in joint ventures is generally depreciated by the sinking fund method over 20 to 40 years.

The Company capitalizes interest charges for major construction projects and depreciates these charges over the life of the related assets.

Deferred Charges

The cumulative excess of contributions to the Company's pension plan over the amounts expensed is included in deferred charges.

Debt issuance costs are deferred and amortized by the straight-line method to the due dates of the respective debt issues. Securitization set up costs are amortized on a straight-line basis over a maximum of five years.

Consulting fees for major projects are amortized by the straight-line method over the period of future benefit ranging from three to five years.

Certain other costs are deferred and amortized by the straight-line method over the remaining life of the related asset.

Deferred Income Taxes

The Company follows the comprehensive method for accounting for deferred taxes. Deferred income taxes arise from timing differences between tax and financial reporting. Short-term deferred income taxes relate principally to the reporting of such items as reserves for returns and allowances, and insurance provisions. Long-term deferred income taxes relate principally to the reporting of such items as depreciation and pension expense.

Foreign Currency Translation

Obligations payable in U.S. dollars are translated at the exchange rate in effect at the balance sheet date or at the rates fixed by forward exchange contracts.

Transactions in foreign currencies are translated into Canadian dollars at the rate in effect on the date of the transaction.

Pensions

The Company maintains a defined benefit, final average pension plan which covers substantially all of its regular full-time associates as well as some of its part-time associates. The plan provides pensions based on length of service and final average earnings.

Current service costs under the Company's pension plan are charged to operations as they accrue. The excess of the market value of pension fund assets over the actuarial present value of the accrued pension obligations as at January 1, 1986 and any surpluses or deficits arising since that date are amortized over the expected average remaining service life of the associate group covered by the plan. Actuarial valuations are calculated using the projected benefit method pro-rated on services, based on management's best estimate of the effect of future events (Refer to Note 7).

The Company provides life insurance, medical and dental benefits to eligible retired associates. These benefits are accrued in the year that an associate retires. The accumulated obligation as at January 1, 1989, for previously retired associates, is being amortized over 10 years beginning January 1, 1989.

Earnings per Share
Earnings per share is calculated based on the weighted average number of shares outstanding during the fiscal year.

2. CHARGE ACCOUNT RECEIVABLES

Details of charge account receivables are as follows:

(in millions)	1997	1996
Charge account receivables	$ 1,655.7	$ 1,568.5
Less: amounts securitized	(965.6)	(961.2)
Net charge account receivables	$ 690.1	$ 607.3

3. OTHER RECEIVABLES

Other receivables consist of the following:

(in millions)	1997	1996
Deferred receivables	$ 497.4	$ 456.1
Less: amounts securitized	(24.4)	(97.6)
Net deferred receivables	473.0	358.5
Miscellaneous receivables	61.5	67.2
Total	$ 534.5	$ 425.7

4. INVESTMENTS AND OTHER ASSETS

(in millions)	1997	1996
Unsecured debentures	$ 20.1	$ 20.1
Subordinated loans	2.2	9.0
Other	0.5	0.5
Total	$ 22.8	$ 29.6

Unsecured debentures in the amount of $14.1 million and $6.0 million are due in 2010 and 2011 respectively. Subordinated loans are due in 2006. All bear interest at floating rates.

5. NET CAPITAL ASSETS

Capital assets are summarized as follows:

(in millions)	1997	1996
Land	$ 68.1	$ 65.8
Buildings and improvements	561.3	524.5
– held by joint ventures	266.6	256.2
Equipment and fixtures	694.7	598.2
Gross capital assets	$ 1,590.7	$ 1,444.7
Accumulated depreciation		
Buildings and improvements	276.6	261.8
– held by joint ventures	41.5	36.3
Equipment and fixtures	447.5	402.2
Total accumulated depreciation	765.6	700.3
Net capital assets	$ 825.1	$ 744.4

The carrying values of land and buildings are evaluated by management on an ongoing basis as to their net recoverable amounts. This is a function of their average remaining useful lives, market valuations, cash flows and capitalization rate models. Situations giving rise to a shortfall in the net recoverable amounts are assessed as either temporary or permanent declines in the carrying values; permanent declines are adjusted. Management does not foresee adjustments in the near term.

Notes to Consolidated Financial Statements continued

6. DEFERRED CHARGES

(in millions)	1997	1996
Excess of pension contributions over amounts expensed, including contributions for post retirement benefits of $3.1 million ($4.8 million – 1996)	$ 107.5	$ 117.0
Deferred consulting fees	0.7	4.4
Tenant allowances for proportionate interests in joint ventures	9.4	8.5
Debt issuance and securitization set up costs	6.2	6.6
Other deferred charges	11.6	11.7
Total deferred charges	$ 135.4	$ 148.2

7. PENSION PLAN

Selected financial information relating to the Company's pension plan is summarized as follows:

(in millions)	1997	1996
Pension plan assets at market value	$ 1,137.8	$ 1,015.0
Present value of accrued pension obligations	$ 697.1	$ 701.0

8. LONG-TERM OBLIGATIONS

(in millions)	1997	1996
Unsecured Debentures:		
9.25% due February 26, 1997	$ -	$ 100.0
11.00% due May 18, 1999	150.0	150.0
11.70% due July 10, 2000	100.0	100.0
8.25% due December 11, 2000	125.0	125.0
7.80% due March 1, 2001	100.0	100.0
6.55% due November 5, 2007	125.0	-
Proportionate share of long-term debt of joint ventures with a weighted average interest rate of 9.0% due 1998 to 2013	229.8	223.2
Capital lease obligations: interest rates from 8.0 % to 17.0%	17.9	19.2
	847.7	817.4
Less principal payments due within one year included in current liabilities	11.6	183.2
Total long-term obligations	$ 836.1	$ 634.2

The Company's proportionate share of the long-term debt of joint ventures is secured by the shopping malls owned by the joint ventures and, in some cases, guaranteed by the Company. The Company's total principal payments due within one year include $10.5 million ($81.8 million – 1996) of the proportionate share of the current debt obligations of joint ventures.

SEARS✦CANADA

Principal Payments

For fiscal years subsequent to the fiscal year ended January 3, 1998, principal payments required on the Company's total long-term obligations are as follows:

(in millions)	
1998	$ 11.6
1999	158.7
2000	253.7
2001	134.3
2002	33.4
Subsequent years	256.0
Total debt outstanding	$ 847.7

Significant Financing Transactions

On January 5, 1996, Sears Canada Inc. issued $100.0 million of 7.8% unsecured debentures due March 1, 2001.

On April 1, 1996, the outstanding 15.125% Series V secured debentures of Sears Acceptance Company Inc. ("Acceptance"), a wholly owned subsidiary of Sears Canada Inc., in the amount of $66.4 million matured.

On October 22, 1996, Sears Canada Receivables Trust – 1996 (Trust 3) was created. This new financing vehicle allows the Company to securitize charge account receivables, including deferred receivables.

On February 26, 1997, the outstanding 9.25% unsecured debentures of Sears Canada Inc. in the amount of $100.0 million matured.

On November 5, 1997, Sears Canada Inc. issued $125.0 million of 6.55% unsecured debentures, due November 5, 2007.

During 1997, long-term financing for new capital projects of real estate joint ventures was obtained in the amount of $9.9 million. In addition, $81.8 million of joint venture debt matured in 1997, of which $78.5 million was refinanced.

9. CAPITAL STOCK

An unlimited number of common shares are authorized. Changes in the number of outstanding common shares and their stated values since December 31, 1995 are as follows:

	1997		1996	
	Number of shares	Stated value (millions)	Number of shares	Stated value (millions)
Beginning Balance	105,610,910	$ 448.3	94,946,372	$ 342.0
Issued pursuant to stock options	348,594	2.6	340,728	2.4
Issuance of shares	-	-	10,323,810	103.9
Ending Balance	105,959,504	$ 450.9	105,610,910	$ 448.3

As at January 3, 1998, details of stock option transactions under stock option plans are as follows.

Options granted and accepted	Option price	Expiry date	Options exercised	Options outstanding
213,125	$ 9.07	Mar. 1997	183,185	-
175,975	$ 5.69	Feb. 1998	148,498	27,477
142,150	$ 7.53	Feb. 1999	97,100	45,050
195,200	$ 7.49	Feb. 2000	135,642	59,558
232,301	$ 5.58	Feb. 2001	174,479	57,822
275,375	$ 5.58	Feb. 2006	30,243	245,132
60,000	$ 9.72	Nov. 2006	-	60,000
286,750	$ 10.65	Jan. 2007	-	286,750
30,000	$ 10.82	Feb. 2007	-	30,000

Options to purchase up to 322,000 common shares have been authorized to be granted under stock option plans in 1998.

The Company is authorized to issue an unlimited number of non-voting, redeemable and retractable Class 1 Preferred Shares in one or more series. As at January 3, 1998, the only shares outstanding were the common shares of the Company.

Notes to Consolidated Financial Statements *continued*

10. UNUSUAL ITEMS

(in millions)		1997		1996
Costs related to the restructuring of business units and processes, including severance	$	-	$	(42.2)
Loss incurred on closure of buildings as a result of operational efficiencies		-		(6.2)
Gain on sale of two service centres		-		3.4
Unusual items	$	-	$	(45.0)

11. INCOME TAXES

The average combined federal and provincial statutory income tax rate, excluding Large Corporations Tax, applicable to the Company was 43.5% for 1997 and 43.2% for 1996.

A reconciliation of income taxes at the average statutory tax rate to actual income taxes is as follows:

(in millions)		1997		1996
Earnings from operations before income taxes	$	215.2	$	25.0
Income taxes at average statutory tax rate		93.6		10.8
Increase (decrease) in income taxes resulting from:				
Non-taxable portion of capital gains		(0.1)		(0.1)
Non-deductible items		0.4		0.5
Large Corporations Tax		4.8		5.0
Income taxes	$	98.7	$	16.2
Effective tax rate		45.9%		64.8%

12. CHANGES IN WORKING CAPITAL

The cash generated from (used for) working capital is made up of changes in the following accounts:

(in millions)		1997		1996
Other receivables	$	(108.8)	$	81.9
Short-term deferred income taxes		(1.9)		6.7
Inventories		(149.2)		16.0
Prepaid expenses and other assets		(2.4)		8.6
Accounts payable		87.3		22.9
Accrued liabilities		(6.5)		24.0
Income and other taxes payable		75.0		23.1
Cash generated from (used for) working capital	$	(106.5)	$	183.2

13. COMMITMENTS

Minimum capital and operating lease payments, exclusive of property taxes, insurance and other expenses payable directly by the Company having an initial term of more than one year as at January 3, 1998 are as follows:

(in millions)		Capital leases		Operating leases
1998		2.9		66.1
1999		2.7		66.8
2000		2.7		63.9
2001		2.7		62.6
2002		2.7		59.8
Subsequent years		16.9		421.6
Minimum lease payments	$	30.6	$	740.8
Less imputed interest		12.7		
Total capital lease obligations	$	17.9		

Total rentals charged to earnings under all operating leases for the year ended January 3, 1998 amounted to $79.4 million ($75.0 million – 1996).

SEARS✦CANADA

14. SEGMENTED INFORMATION

Segmented Statements of Earnings for the 53 weeks ended January 3, 1998 and the 52 weeks ended December 28, 1996

(in millions)			1997				1996	
			Real Estate Joint				Real Estate Joint	
	Mdse.	Credit	Ventures[2]	Total	Mdse.	Credit	Ventures	Total
Total revenues[1]	$ 4,210.6	$ 310.6	$ 62.3	$ 4,583.5	$ 3,605.7	$ 292.4	$ 57.8	$ 3,955.9
Segment operating profit	141.7	127.5	32.1	301.3	27.0	109.1	30.2	166.3
Interest expense				86.1				96.3
Unusual items				-				45.0
Income taxes				98.7				16.2
Net earnings				$ 116.5				$ 8.8

Segmented Statements of Financial Position as at January 3, 1998 and December 28, 1996

(in millions)			1997				1996	
			Real Estate Joint				Real Estate Joint	
	Mdse.	Credit	Ventures[2]	Total	Mdse.	Credit	Ventures	Total
Assets								
Cash	$ 64.9	$ -	$ 3.4	$ 68.3	$ 199.4	$ -	$ 1.8	$ 201.2
Total receivables	90.9	1,130.3	3.4	1,224.6	83.0	946.5	3.5	1,033.0
Inventories	640.3	-	-	640.3	491.1	-	-	491.1
Net capital assets	568.4	-	256.7	825.1	495.3	-	249.1	744.4
Other	230.5	14.0	4.5	249.0	235.1	22.3	6.9	264.3
Total assets	$ 1,595.0	$ 1,144.3	$ 268.0	$ 3,007.3	$ 1,503.9	$ 968.8	$ 261.3	$ 2,734.0
Liabilities								
Accounts payable	$ 555.2	$ -	$ 5.0	$ 560.2	$ 464.1	$ 1.7	$ 7.1	$ 472.9
Accrued liabilities	294.5	21.8	2.1	318.4	302.2	22.2	0.5	324.9
Other	191.7	31.7	15.2	238.6	151.8	1.3	14.9	168.0
Total liabilities excluding debt	$ 1,041.4	$ 53.5	$ 22.3	$ 1,117.2	$ 918.1	$ 25.2	$ 22.5	$ 965.8
Capital employed	$ 553.6	$ 1,090.8	$ 245.7	$ 1,890.1	$ 585.8	$ 943.6	$ 238.8	$ 1,768.2
Capital expenditures	$ 147.3	$ -	$ 13.1	$ 160.4	$ 62.2	$ -	$ 1.0	$ 63.2
Depreciation and amortization	$ 72.6	$ -	$ 5.5	$ 78.1	$ 71.6	$ -	$ 5.9	$ 77.5

1 The real estate joint venture revenues are net of $3.7 million ($3.6 million – 1996) representing the elimination of rental revenues earned from retail stores. Rental expense of the real estate joint venture segment has been decreased by the same amount having no effect on segment operating profit.

2 The real estate joint ventures had cash generated from operations of $8.7 million ($7.2 million – 1996), cash used for investment activities of $13.9 million ($4.4 million – 1996), and cash used for financing activities of $6.8 million ($3.6 million – 1996).

Notes to Consolidated Financial Statements *continued*

15. RELATED PARTY TRANSACTIONS

Sears, Roebuck and Co. is the beneficial holder of the majority of the outstanding common shares of Sears Canada Inc.

During the year, Sears, Roebuck and Co. charged the Company $5.5 million ($2.6 million – 1996) in the ordinary course of business for shared merchandise purchasing services. These amounts are included in the cost of merchandise sold, operating, administrative and selling expenses.

Sears, Roebuck and Co. charged the Company $18.4 million ($19.2 million – 1996) and the Company charged Sears, Roebuck and Co. $4.6 million ($4.8 million – 1996) for other reimbursements. These reimbursements were primarily in respect of customer cross-border purchases made on the Sears Card, and the Sears, Roebuck and Co. charge card, as well as software and support services.

There were no significant commitments, receivables or payables between the companies at the end of 1997 or 1996.

16. FINANCIAL INSTRUMENTS

In the ordinary course of business, the Company enters into financial agreements with banks and other financial institutions to reduce underlying risks associated with interest rates and foreign currency. The Company does not hold or issue derivative financial instruments for trading or speculative purposes and controls are in place to prevent and detect these activities. The financial instruments do not require the payment of premiums or cash margins prior to settlement. These financial instruments can be summarized as follows:

Foreign Exchange Risk

From time to time the Company enters into foreign exchange contracts to reduce the foreign exchange risk with respect to U.S. dollar denominated goods purchased for resale. There were no such contracts outstanding at the end of 1997 or 1996.

Securitization of Charge Account Receivables

Securitization is an important financial vehicle which provides the Company with access to funds at a low cost. Acceptance sells undivided co-ownership interests in its portfolio of charge account receivables and deferred receivables to independent trusts, collectively referred to as SCRT. Acceptance retains the income generated by the undivided co-ownership interests sold to SCRT in excess of SCRT's stipulated share of service charge revenues (Refer to Notes 2 and 3).

Interest Rate Risk

To manage the Company's exposure to interest rate risks, the Company has entered into interest rate swap contracts with Schedule "A" Banks. Neither the notional principal amounts nor the current replacement value of these financial instruments are carried on the consolidated balance sheet.

As at January 3, 1998, the Company had two interest rate swap contracts in place to reduce the risk associated with variable interest rates associated with the commercial paper issued by Trust 1. For the year ended January 3, 1998, a net interest differential of $13.2 million ($12.8 million – 1996) was paid on the floating-to-fixed interest rate swap contracts and was recorded as an increase of interest expense of the Company.

Credit Risk

The Company's exposure to concentration of credit risk is limited. Accounts receivable are primarily from Sears Card customers, a large and diverse group.

Interest Rate Sensitivity Position

Interest rate risk reflects the sensitivity of the Company's financial condition to movements in interest rates.

The table below identifies the Company's financial assets and liabilities which are sensitive to interest rate movements and those which are non-interest rate sensitive. Financial assets and liabilities which do not bear interest or bear interest at fixed rates are classified as non-interest rate sensitive.

(in millions)	1997		1996	
	Interest Sensitive	Non-Interest Sensitive	Interest Sensitive	Non-Interest Sensitive
Cash net of bank advances and short-term notes	$ 68.3	$ -	$ 199.1	$ -
Investments and other assets	$ 22.8	$ -	$ 29.6	$ -
Total receivables	$ -	$1,224.6	$ -	$1,033.0
Long-term obligations (including current portion)[3]	$ (33.7)	$ (814.0)	$(179.9)	$ (637.5)
Net balance sheet interest rate sensitivity position	$ 57.4	$ 410.6	$ 48.8	$ 395.5

3 Interest sensitive portion includes long-term prime-rate based debt and current portion of long-term debt due to be renegotiated.

In addition to the net balance sheet interest rate sensitivity position, the Company is also affected by interest rate sensitive debt outstanding in SCRT. Any change in short-term interest rates will impact floating rate debt and debt with maturities of less than one year held by SCRT, which totaled $811.1 million at January 3, 1998 ($726.6 million at December 28, 1996). An increase in the cost of this off-balance sheet debt will result in a decrease in the Company's share of service charge revenues. This interest rate exposure is offset by interest rate swap contracts held by the Company in the notional amount of $200 million ($250 million – 1996).

Fair Value of Financial Instruments

The estimated fair values of financial instruments as at January 3, 1998 and December 28, 1996 are based on relevant market prices and information available at that time. As a significant number of the Company's assets and liabilities, including inventory and capital assets, do not meet the definition of financial instruments, the fair value estimates below do not reflect the fair value of the Company as a whole.

Carrying value approximates fair value for financial instruments which are short-term in nature. These include cash and short-term investments, charge account receivables, other receivables, prepaid expenses and other assets, bank advances and short-term notes, accounts payable, income and other taxes payable, and principal payments on long-term obligations due within one year. For financial instruments which are long-term in nature, fair value estimates are as follows:

(in millions)	1997		1996	
	Carrying or Notional Amount	Fair Value	Carrying or Notional Amount	Fair Value
Financial Assets and Liabilities				
Investments and other assets	$ 22.8	$ 22.8	$ 29.6	$ 29.6
Long-term obligations	$ (836.1)	$(895.7)	$(634.2)	$ (713.9)
Off-Balance Sheet Interest Rate Swaps				
9.32%, expiring April 1997	$ -	$ -	$ 50.0	$ (1.5)
9.40%, expiring April 1999	$ 100.0	$ (6.4)	$ 100.0	$ (12.1)
9.54%, expiring April 2002	$ 100.0	$ (16.5)	$ 100.0	$ (19.1)
	$ 200.0	$ (22.9)	$ 250.0	$ (32.7)

The fair value of investments and other assets and long-term obligations was estimated based on quoted market prices, when available, or discounted cash flows using discount rates based on market interest rates and the Company's credit rating. As long-term debt coupon rates are higher than current market interest rates, the fair value of the Company's long-term debt exceeds its carrying value.

The fair value of the interest rate swap contracts was estimated by referring to the appropriate yield curves with matching terms of maturity. A negative fair value reflects the estimated amount that the Company would pay to terminate the contracts at the reporting date.

Corporate Governance

In December, 1994, the Report of The Toronto Stock Exchange Committee on Corporate Governance in Canada recommended 14 guidelines for improved corporate governance which were adopted by the Montreal Exchange and The Toronto Stock Exchange.

The Corporation has considered the TSE Report and these guidelines in developing and formalizing its corporate governance practices. A Statement of Corporate Governance Practices has been prepared in accordance with the requirements of the Exchanges and is contained in the Management Proxy Circular of the Corporation.

The Board of Directors is responsible to oversee the business and affairs of the Corporation and to act with a view to the best interests of the Corporation, providing guidance and direction to the management of the Corporation in order to attain corporate objectives and maximize shareholder value.

The Board of Directors and the Audit and Corporate Governance, Compensation, and Nominating Committees of the Board are each responsible for certain corporate governance functions in accordance with their respective mandates. The Audit and Corporate Governance Committee is responsible for monitoring and guiding the corporate governance approach and practices of the Corporation.

Directors and Officers (as at January 3, 1998)

SEARS ◆ CANADA

Board of Directors

Jalynn H. Bennett ◆
President, Jalynn H. Bennett and Associates Ltd.

James R. Clifford ●
President and Chief Operating Officer, Sears Canada Inc.

Gary L. Crittenden ◆
Executive Vice President and Chief Financial Officer,
Sears, Roebuck and Co.

William A. Dimma ◆●
Corporate Director

Jeanne E. Lougheed ■
Corporate Director

Arthur C. Martinez ■
Chairman of the Board, President and Chief Executive Officer,
Sears, Roebuck and Co.

James W. Moir, Jr. ●
President and Chief Executive Officer,
Maritime Medical Care Inc.

Alfred Powis ◆■●
Corporate Director

Anthony J. Rucci ■
Executive Vice President, Administration,
Sears, Roebuck and Co.

James M. Tory ◆■
Partner, Tory Tory DesLauriers & Binnington,
Barristers & Solicitors

Paul S. Walters ■●
Chairman of the Board and Chief Executive Officer,
Sears Canada Inc.

Committees

■ Compensation ◆ Audit and Corporate Governance ● Nominating
J.R. Clifford and P.S. Walters are ex officio members of the Nominating Committee.

Honorary Directors

James W. Button
Former Senior Executive Vice President
of Merchandising, Sears, Roebuck and Co.

C. Richard Sharpe
Former Chairman of the Board and Chief Executive Officer,
Sears Canada Inc.

Officers

Paul S. Walters
Chairman of the Board and Chief Executive Officer

James R. Clifford
President and Chief Operating Officer

Patricia E. Beaudoin
Senior Vice-President, Human Resources

H. Ray Bird
Senior Vice-President, Credit

John T. Butcher
Senior Vice-President and Chief Financial Officer

Brent V. Hollister
Executive Vice-President, Sales and Service

Richard W. Sorby
Executive Vice-President, Marketing

William R. Turner
Executive Vice-President, Merchandising and Logistics

Rudolph R. Vezér
Senior Vice-President, Secretary and General Counsel

Corporate Information

Head Office
Sears Canada Inc.
222 Jarvis Street
Toronto, Ontario
Canada M5B 2B8

Transfer Agent and Registrar
CIBC Mellon Trust Company
Toronto, Ontario
Montreal, Quebec

Answerline: (416) 643-5500 or 1-800-387-0825

Internet Address: www.cibcmellon.ca (website) or
inquiries@cibcmellon.ca (e-mail)

Listings
The Montreal Exchange
The Toronto Stock Exchange

Trading Symbol
SCC

Annual and Special Meeting
The Annual and Special Meeting of Shareholders of
Sears Canada Inc. will be held on Monday, April 20, 1998 at
10:00 a.m. in the Burton-Wood Auditorium
Main Floor
222 Jarvis Street
Toronto, Ontario, Canada

Édition française du Rapport annuel
On peut se procurer l'édition française de ce
rapport en écrivant au:

S/703, Relations publiques
Sears Canada Inc.
222 Jarvis Street
Toronto, Ontario
Canada M5B 2B8

Pour de plus amples renseignements au sujet de la
Société, veuillez écrire au Service des relations
publiques, ou composer le (416) 941-4425

For More Information
Additional copies of the Annual Report can be obtained through the
Public Affairs Department at the Head Office of Sears Canada Inc.

For more information about the Company, write to
Public Affairs, or call (416) 941-4425

Internet Address: www.sears.ca (website) or enquiries:
home@sears.ca

Produced by Sears Canada Inc.
Public Affairs

Design by Compendium Design International Inc.

Photography of Chairman of the Board by Christopher Campbell,
Publication: Canadian Retailer.

Printed in Canada by Kempenfelt Graphics Group Inc.

Front cover: Fashions by Jones Studio
Back cover: Fashions by Nygard Collection

Certain brands mentioned in this report are the trademarks of Sears
Canada Inc., Sears, Roebuck and Co., or used under license. Others are
the property of their owner.

Appendix D: The Basics

1. Accounting Equation:

Assets = Liabilities + Owner's Equity

2. T Account:

Account Title	
Left Side debit	Right Side credit

3 Rules of Debit and Credit:

Balance Sheet Accounts

ASSETS		LIABILITIES	
Asset Accounts		Liability Accounts	
Debit for increases	Credit for decreases	Debit for decreases	Credit for increases

OWNER'S EQUITY

Owner's Equity Accounts	
Debit for decreases	Credit for increases

Income Statement Accounts

Debit for decreases in owner's equity Expense Accounts		Credit for increases in owner's equity Revenue Accounts	
Debit for increases	Credit for decreases	Debit for decreases	Credit for increases

▨ Normal Balance

4. To Analyze a Transaction:

1. Determine whether an asset, a liability, owner's equity, revenue, or expense account is affected by the transaction.
2. For each account affected by the transaction, determine whether the account increases or decreases.
3. Determine whether each increase or decrease should be recorded as a debit or a credit.

5. Financial Statements:

INCOME STATEMENT
A summary of the revenue and the expenses of a business entity for a specific period of time, such as a month or a year.

STATEMENT OF OWNER'S EQUITY
A summary of the changes in the owner's equity of a business entity that have occurred during a specific period of time, such as a month or a year.

BALANCE SHEET
A list of the assets, liabilities, and owner's equity of a business entity as of a specific date, usually at the close of the last day of a month or a year.

STATEMENT OF CASH FLOWS
A summary of the cash receipts and cash payments of a business entity for a specific period of time, such as a month or a year.

6. Accounting Cycle:

1. Analyze and record transactions in journal.
2. Post transactions to ledger.
3. Prepare trial balance, assemble adjustment data, and complete work sheet.
4. Prepare financial statements.
5. Journalize and post adjusting entries.
6. Journalize and post closing entries.
7. Prepare post-closing trial balance.

7. Types of Adjusting Entries:

1. Deferred expense (prepaid expense)
2. Deferred revenue (unearned revenue)
3. Accrued expense (accrued liability)
4. Accrued revenue (accrued asset)
5. Amortization expense

Each entry will always affect both a balance sheet and an income statement account.

8. Closing Entries:

1. Transfer revenue account balances to Income Summary.
2. Transfer expense account balances to Income Summary.
3. Transfer Income Summary balance to Capital.
4. Transfer withdrawals account balance to Capital.

9. Special Journals:

Rendering of services
on account ⟶ recorded in ⟶ Revenue (sales) journal
Receipt of cash from
any source ⟶ recorded in ⟶ Cash receipts journal
Purchase of items
on account ⟶ recorded in ⟶ Purchases journal
Payments of cash for
any purpose ⟶ recorded in ⟶ Cash disbursements journal

10. Shipping Terms:

	FOB Shipping Point	FOB Destination
Ownership (title) passes to buyer when inventory is...........	delivered to freight carrier	delivered to buyer
Transportation costs are paid by	buyer	seller

11. Format for Bank Reconciliation:

Cash balance according to bank statement .... $xxx
Add: Additions by depositor not on bank
         statement .... $xx
         Bank errors xx   xx
                                        $xxx

Deduct: Deductions by depositor not on bank
         statement .... $xx
         Bank errors xx   xx
Adjusted balance .... $xxx

Cash balance according to depositor's records .... $xxx
Add: Additions by bank not recorded by depositor.. $xx
       Depositor errors xx   xx
                                        $xxx

Deduct: Deductions by bank not recorded
        by depositor .... $xx
        Depositor errors xx   xx
Adjusted balance .... $xxx

12. Inventory Costing Methods:

1. First-in, First-out (FIFO)
2. Last-in, First-out (LIFO)
3. Average Cost

13. Interest Payment Computations:

Interest Payment =
Face Amount (or Principal) × Stated Rate × Time

14. Effective Interest Method:

Interest Expense =
Carrying Value (present value) × Effective Rate × Time

15. Methods of Determining Annual Amortization:

STRAIGHT-LINE: $\dfrac{\text{Cost} - \text{Estimated Residual Value}}{\text{Estimated Life}}$

DECLINING-BALANCE: Rate* × Book Value at Beginning of
Period

*Double-declining rate is twice the straight-line
rate (1 ÷ Estimated Life).

16. Cash Provided by Operations on Statement of Cash Flows (indirect method):

Net income, per income statement .... $xx
Add: Amortization of capital assets .... $xx
        Decreases in current assets (receivables,
         inventories, prepaid expenses) xx
        Increases in current liabilities (accounts
         and notes payable, accrued liabilities) .. xx
        Losses on disposal of assets and retirement
         of debt xx   xx

Deduct: Increases in current assets (receivables,
         inventories, prepaid expenses) .... $xx
        Decreases in current liabilities
         (accounts and notes payable,
         accrued liabilities) xx
        Gains on disposal of assets and
         retirement of debt xx   xx
Net cash flow from operating activities .... $xx

Appendix E: Abbreviations and Acronyms Commonly Used in Business and Accounting

ASB	Accounting Standards Board
CA	Chartered Accountant
CAAA	Canadian Academic Accounting Association
CBCA	Canada Business Corporations Act
CCA	Capital cost allowance
CEO	Chief Executive Officer
CGAAC	Certified General Accountants Association of Canada
CGA	Certified General Accountant
CIA	Certified Internal Auditor
CICA	Canadian Institute of Chartered Accountants
CMA	Certified Management Accountant
CPP	Canada Pension Plan
Cr.	Credit
Dr.	Debit
EFT	Electronic funds transfer
EHT	Employment Health Tax
EI	Employment Insurance
EPS	Earnings per share
FASB	Financial Accounting Standards Board
FIFO	First-in, first-out
FOB	Free on board
GAAP	Generally accepted accounting principles
GST	Goods and Services Tax
HST	Harmonized Sales Tax
IASC	International Accounting Standards Committee
IIA	Institute of Internal Auditors
LIFO	Last-in, first-out
LCM	Lower of cost and market
n/30	Net 30
n/eom	Net, end-of-month
NBV	Net book value
NSF	Not sufficient funds
P/E Ratio	Price-earnings ratio
POS	Point of sale
PST	Provincial Sales Tax
ROI	Return on investment
SMAC	Society of Management Accountants of Canada
UCC	Undepreciated capital cost
WC	Workers' Compensation

Appendix F: Classification of Accounts

Account Title	Account Classification	Normal Balance	Financial Statement
Accounts Payable	Current liability	Credit	Balance sheet
Accounts Receivable	Current asset	Debit	Balance sheet
Accumulated Amortization	Capital asset	Credit	Balance sheet
Accumulated Depletion	Capital asset	Credit	Balance sheet
Advertising Expense	Operating expense	Debit	Income statement
Allowance for Doubtful Accounts	Current asset	Credit	Balance sheet
Amortization Expense	Operating expense	Debit	Income statement
Appropriation for _____	Shareholders' equity	Credit	Retained earnings statement/ Balance sheet
Bonds Payable	Long-term liability	Credit	Balance sheet
Building	Capital asset	Debit	Balance sheet
Canada Pension Plan Payable	Current liability	Credit	Balance sheet
_____ Capital	Owners' equity	Credit	Statement of owner's equity/ Balance sheet
Capital Stock	Shareholders' equity	Credit	Balance sheet
Cash	Current asset	Debit	Balance sheet
Common Shares	Shareholders' equity	Credit	Balance sheet
Cost of Goods Sold	Cost of goods sold	Debit	Income statement
Depletion Expense	Operating expense	Debit	Income statement
Discount on Bonds Payable	Long-term liability	Debit	Balance sheet
Dividend Income	Other income	Credit	Income statement
Dividends	Shareholders' equity	Debit	Retained earnings statement
Dividends Payable	Current liability	Credit	Balance sheet
Donated Capital	Shareholders' equity	Credit	Balance sheet
Employees Income Tax Payable	Current liability	Credit	Balance sheet
Employment Health Tax Payable	Current liability	Credit	Balance sheet
Employment Insurance Payable	Current liability	Credit	Balance sheet
Equipment	Capital asset	Debit	Balance sheet
Future tax asset	Current asset/Long-term asset	Debit	Balance sheet
Future tax liability	Current liability/Long-term liability	Credit	Balance sheet
Gain on Disposal of Capital Assets	Other income	Credit	Income statement
Gain on Sale of Investments	Other income	Credit	Income statement
Goodwill	Intangible capital asset	Debit	Balance sheet
GST Payable	Current liability	Credit	Balance sheet
HST Payable	Current liability	Credit	Balance sheet
Income Tax Expense	Income tax	Debit	Income statement
Income Tax Payable	Current liability	Credit	Balance sheet
Insurance Expense	Operating expense	Debit	Income statement
Interest Expense	Other expense	Debit	Income statement
Interest Income	Other income	Credit	Income statement
Interest Payable	Current liability	Credit	Balance sheet
Interest Receivable	Current asset	Debit	Balance sheet
Inventory	Current asset	Debit	Balance sheet
Investment in Bonds	Long-term asset	Debit	Balance sheet
Investment in Shares	Long-term asset	Debit	Balance sheet
Land	Capital asset	Debit	Balance sheet
Lease Liability	Current liability/Long-term liability	Credit	Balance sheet
Leased Asset	Capital asset	Debit	Balance sheet
Loss on Disposal of Capital Assets	Other expense	Debit	Income statement
Loss on Sale of Investments	Other expense	Debit	Income statement
Marketable Securities	Current asset	Debit	Balance sheet
Notes Payable	Current liability/Long-term liability	Credit	Balance sheet
Notes Receivable	Current asset/Long-term asset	Debit	Balance sheet

Account Title	Account Classification	Normal Balance	Financial Statement
Organization Costs	Intangible capital asset	Debit	Balance sheet
Patents	Intangible capital asset	Debit	Balance sheet
Payroll Tax Expense	Operating expense	Debit	Income statement
Pension Expense	Operating expense	Debit	Income statement
Pension Liability	Long-term liability	Credit	Balance sheet
Petty Cash	Current asset	Debit	Balance sheet
Preferred Shares	Shareholders' equity	Credit	Balance sheet
Premium on Bonds Payable	Long-term liability	Credit	Balance sheet
Prepaid Insurance	Current asset	Debit	Balance sheet
Prepaid Rent	Current asset	Debit	Balance sheet
Prepaid Pension Cost	Long-term (other) asset	Debit	Balance sheet
PST Payable	Current liability	Credit	Balance sheet
Purchases	Cost of goods sold	Debit	Income statement
Purchases Discounts	Cost of goods sold	Credit	Income statement
Purchases Returns and Allowances	Cost of goods sold	Credit	Income statement
Rent Expense	Operating expense	Debit	Income statement
Rent Income	Other income	Credit	Income statement
Retained Earnings	Shareholders' equity	Credit	Balance sheet/Retained earnings statement
Salaries Expense	Operating expense	Debit	Income statement
Salaries Payable	Current liability	Credit	Balance sheet
Sales	Revenue from sales	Credit	Income statement
Sales Discounts	Revenue from sales	Debit	Income statement
Sales Returns and Allowances	Revenue from sales	Debit	Income statement
Sales Tax Payable	Current liability	Credit	Balance sheet
Sinking Fund Cash	Long-term asset	Debit	Balance sheet
Sinking Fund Investments	Long-term asset	Debit	Balance sheet
Stock Dividends	Shareholders' equity	Debit	Retained earnings statement
Stock Dividends Distributable	Shareholders' equity	Credit	Balance sheet
Supplies	Current asset	Debit	Balance sheet
Supplies Expense	Operating expense	Debit	Income statement
Transportation In	Cost of goods sold	Debit	Income statement
Transportation Out	Operating expense	Debit	Income statement
Uncollectible Accounts Expense	Operating expense	Debit	Income statement
Unearned Rent	Current liability	Credit	Balance sheet
Utilities Expense	Operating expense	Debit	Income statement
Utilities Payable	Current liability	Credit	Balance sheet
Vacation Pay Expense	Operating expense	Debit	Income statement
Vacation Pay Payable	Current liability/Long-term liability	Credit	Balance sheet
Workers' Compensation Payable	Current liability	Credit	Balance sheet

Appendix G: A Classified Balance Sheet

Assets

Current		
Cash	$ 8,200	
Temporary investments	1,000	
Accounts receivable	25,250	
Inventory	43,100	
Prepaid expenses	1,100	
Total current assets		$78,650
Long-term Investments		
Capital Assets		
Land	50,000	
Building	110,000	
Equipment	80,000	
	240,000	
Less: Accumulated amortization	47,000	
	193,000	
Intangible assets (net)	2,200	
Total capital assets		195,200
Total Assets		$273,850

Liabilities and Owner's Equity

Current Liabilities		
Bank loan	$ 10,000	
Accounts payable	28,000	
Wages payable	3,100	
Sales taxes payable	2,150	
Current portion of long-term debt	5,000	
Total current liabilities		$ 48,250
Long-term Liabilities		
Mortgage payable (net of current portion)		120,000
Total liabilities		168,250
Owner's Equity		
A. Androkov, Capital		105,600
Total Liabilities and Owner's Equity		$273,850

Glossary

Accelerated amortization method. An amortization method that provides for a high amortization expense in the first year of use of an asset and a gradually declining expense thereafter. (400)

Account. The form used to record additions and deductions for each individual asset, liability, owner's equity, revenue, and expense. (44)

Account form of balance sheet. A form of balance sheet with assets on the left side and liabilities and owner's equity on the right side. (21)

Account payable. A liability created by a purchase made on credit. (15)

Account receivable. A claim against a customer for services rendered or goods sold on credit. (16)

Accounting. The process of identifying, measuring, and communicating economic information to permit informed judgments and decisions by users of the information. (3)

Accounting cycle. The sequence of basic accounting procedures during a fiscal period. (149)

Accounting equation. The expression of the relationship between assets, liabilities, and owner's equity; it is most commonly stated as Assets = Liabilities + Owner's Equity. (11)

Accounting period concept. In order to provide timely information relevant to users, accountants divide the economic activities of the entity into artificial time periods. (94)

Accounting system. The methods and procedures used by a business to record and report financial data for use by management and external users. (179)

Accounts payable subsidiary ledger. The subsidiary ledger containing the individual accounts with suppliers (creditors). (189)

Accounts receivable subsidiary ledger. The subsidiary ledger containing the individual accounts with customers (debtors). (189)

Accrual basis. Recognizes revenues in the period earned and expenses in the period incurred in the process of generating revenues. (94)

Accruals. Expenses incurred or revenues earned that have not yet been recorded. (98)

Accrued expenses. Expenses incurred, but not yet recorded. Sometimes called accrued liabilities. (98)

Accrued revenues. Revenues earned, but not yet recorded. Sometimes called accrued assets. (98)

Accumulated amortization. Contra asset account used to accumulate the amortization recorded to date on capital assets. (108)

Adjusting entries. Entries required at the end of an accounting period to bring the ledger up to date and ensure that revenues and expenses are recorded in the correct period. (97)

Adjusting process. The process of updating the accounts at the end of the period. (97)

Administrative expenses. Expenses incurred in the administration or general operations of a business. (243)

Aging the receivables. The process of analyzing the accounts receivable and classifying them according to various age groupings, with the due date being the base point for determining age. (324)

Allowance method. A method of accounting for uncollectible receivables, whereby we make advance provision for the estimated uncollectibles. (320)

Amortization. Systematic allocation of the cost of a capital asset over its useful life in order to match the cost of the asset with the periods in which it provides service to the business. (107, 395)

Assets. Economic resources owned or controlled by an entity. (11)

Average cost method. A method of inventory costing that is based on the assumption that costs should be charged against revenue in accordance with the weighted average unit costs of the items sold. (362)

Balance of the account. The amount of difference between the debits and the credits that have been entered into an account. (46)

Balance sheet. A financial statement listing the assets, liabilities, and owner's equity of a business entity as of a specific date. (19)

Bank reconciliation. The analysis that details the items responsible for the difference between the cash balance reported in the bank statement and the balance of the cash account in the ledger. (293)

Betterment. An expenditure that increases operating efficiency, productive capacity, and/or useful life of a capital asset. (404)

Book of Original Entry. The journal in which we first record a business transaction. (47)

Business transaction. The occurrence of an economic event or a condition that must be recorded in the accounting records. (11)

Canada Pension Plan (CPP). Federal program for providing retirement, disability, and similar benefits. Requires employers to withhold employee's contribution from employee's pay and to remit this to the government along with a matching contribution from employer. (442)

Canadian Institute of Chartered Accountants (CICA). The professional self-regulating accounting body whose *CICA Handbook Recommendations* have legal status as authoritative pronouncements regarding generally accepted accounting principles in Canada. (6)

Capital asset. Long-lived asset owned by a business that provides benefits over more than one period and is used in business operations. (107, 392)

Capital cost allowance (CCA). Deduction allowed for amortization expense of physical capital assets in computing taxable income. Rates and method of computing CCA are specified by the Income Tax Act. (401)

Capital expenditures. Costs that add to the usefulness of capital assets for more than one accounting period and increase the operating efficiency, productive capacity, and/or useful life of the asset. (403)

Capital leases. Leases that transfer substantially all of the benefits and risks of ownership of the leased property from the lessor to the lessee. (409)

Cash. Cash on hand and demand deposits, coins, currency (paper money), cheques, traveller's cheques, money orders, and money on deposit that is available for unrestricted withdrawal from banks or other financial institutions. (283)

Cash basis. Recognizes revenue when cash is received and expenses when cash is paid. (94)

Cash disbursements journal. The journal in which all cash and cheque payments are recorded. (196)

Cash equivalents. Short-term, highly liquid non-equity investments that are readily convertible to cash and subject to an insignificant risk of changes in value. (296)

Cash receipts file. An electronic listing of customer cash receipts information. (201)

Cash receipts journal. The journal in which all cash receipts are recorded. (192)

Chart of accounts. The system of accounts that makes up the ledger for a business. (44)

Closing entries. Entries necessary to eliminate the balances of temporary accounts in preparation for the following accounting period. (141)

Comparability principle. Financial reports should be presented in a way that enables users to identify similarities in and differences between the information provided by different financial statements. (368)

Compensated absences. Periods when employers are obligated to pay employees for time off work due to statutory holidays, vacations, and illness. Accrued during periods when worker renders service to employer. (444)

Conservatism. The concept that requires accountants, when uncertainty exists, to select the alternative that ensures that assets and revenues are not overstated, and that liabilities and losses are not understated. (332)

Consistency principle. A firm is normally expected to employ the same accounting policies from year to year. (369)

Contingency. Existing situation involving uncertainty as to possible gain or loss, the outcome of which will ultimately be resolved when future events occur. (447)

Contingent liability. A liability arising from an existing situation involving uncertainty as to possible loss arising from a past event whose outcome will not be resolved until the future; potential obligations that will materialize only if certain events occur in the future. (336, 447)

Contra account. Account that is offset against (deducted from) another account in the financial statements. (108)

Contractual commitment. Contract that may obligate firm to undertake substantial future liabilities. (448)

Control account. The account in the general ledger that summarizes the balances of the accounts in a subsidiary ledger. (189)

Corporation. A separate legal entity that is organized in accordance with provincial or federal statutes and in which ownership is divided into shares of stock. (9)

Cost-benefit principle. Financial statements should only disclose information whose benefit to users is greater than the costs of presenting it. (137)

Credit. (1) The right side of an account; (2) the amount entered on the right side of an account; (3) to enter an amount on the right side of an account. (46)

Credit memorandum. The form issued by a seller to inform a buyer that a credit has been posted to the buyer's account receivable. (228)

Current assets. Cash or other assets that are expected to be converted to cash or sold or used up usually within a year or less, through the normal operations of a business. (198)

Current liabilities. Liabilities that will be due within a short time (usually one year or less) and that are expected to be paid out of current assets. Debts that a business expects to pay out of current assets or through the creation of another current liability. Includes amounts payable within one year or the operating cycle of the firm, whichever is longer. (139, 434)

Debit. (1) The left side of an account; (2) the amount entered on the left side of an account; (3) to enter an amount on the left side of an account. (46)

Debit memorandum. The form issued by a buyer to inform a seller that a debit has been posted to the seller's account payable. (234)

Debt security. A security that represents an obligation between a creditor and the business issuing the obligation. (330)

Declining-balance amortization method. A method of amortization that provides declining periodic amortization expense over the estimated life of an asset. (399)

Deferral. Delay in recognizing a cash payment as an expense or a cash receipt as a revenue. (97)

Deferred expense. Cash expenditure recorded as an asset, which will be recognized as an expense in the future as it is used up over time or through the normal business operations. Sometimes called prepaid expense. (97)

Deferred revenue. Cash receipt recorded as a liability, which will be recognized as revenue in the future when it is earned. Sometimes called unearned revenue. (97)

Depletion. The cost of natural resources removed from the earth. (410)

Direct write-off method. A method of accounting for uncollectible receivables, which recognizes an expense only when specific accounts are judged to be uncollectible. (320)

Discount. The interest deducted from the maturity value of a note receivable. (335)

Discount on note payable. Difference between the maturity value of the note and the fair value of the consideration received for the note when issued. Represents the "real" interest being charged on a non-interest-bearing note. (435)

Double-declining-balance amortization method. Declining-balance amortization method using twice the straight-line rate. (399)

Double-entry accounting. A system for recording transactions, based on recording increases and decreases in accounts so that debits always equal credits. (50)

Electronic funds transfer (EFT). A payment system that uses computerized information rather than paper (money, cheques, etc.) to effect a cash transaction. (297)

Employment Health Tax (EHT). Payroll tax levied on employers by some provinces to help pay for health care system. (444)

Employment Insurance (EI). Federal program for providing benefits to unemployed workers. Requires employers to withhold employee's contribution from employee's pay and to remit this to the government along with employer's contribution, calculated at 1.4 times employees' contributions. (442)

Entity concept. The concept that accounting applies to individual economic units and that each unit is separate from the persons who supply its assets. (13)

Equity security. A security that represents ownership in a business, such as shares in a corporation. (330)

Estimated liability. Obligation that definitely exists, but that is uncertain as to its amount and due date. (445)

Expense. The amount of assets or services used in the process of earning revenue. (16)

Financial Accounting Standards Board (FASB). An authoritative body for the development of accounting principles in the United States. (9)

First-in, first-out (FIFO) method. A method of inventory costing based on the assumption that the costs of goods sold should be charged against revenue in the order in which the costs were incurred. (361)

Fiscal year. The annual accounting period adopted by a business. (148)

FOB destination. Terms of agreement between buyer and seller whereby ownership passes when merchandise is received by the buyer, and the seller pays the transportation costs. (230)

FOB shipping point. Terms of agreement between buyer and seller whereby ownership passes when merchandise is delivered to the freight carrier, and the buyer pays the transportation costs. (230)

Full disclosure principle. Financial reports should provide any information that is important enough to influence the decisions of an informed user. (137)

General journal. The two-column form used for entries that do not "fit" in any of the special journals. (190)

General ledger. The primary ledger, when used in conjunction with subsidiary ledgers, that contains all of the balance sheet and income statement accounts. (189)

Generally accepted accounting principles (GAAP). Generally accepted guidelines for the preparation of financial statements. (4)

Going concern concept. The principle that assumes the entity will not go out of business in the foreseeable future. (13)

Goods and Services Tax (GST). Federal tax levied on most transactions involving delivery of products or services to customers. Businesses are required to act as agents to collect these taxes and remit them to the government, but may claim a refund for GST paid on their own purchases and capital assets. (439)

Goodwill. An intangible asset of a business due to such favourable factors as location, product superiority, reputation, and managerial skill. May only be recorded when a business is purchased. (412)

Gross pay. The total earnings of an employee for a payroll period. (441)

Gross profit. The excess of net sales over the cost of merchandise sold. (224)

Gross profit method. A means of estimating inventory based on the relationship of gross profit to sales. (372)

Historical cost principle. The principle that assets should be recorded at the actual cost incurred to acquire them. (13)

Income from operations. The excess of gross profit over total operating expenses. (243)

Income statement. A summary of the revenues and expenses of a business entity for a specific period of time. (19)

Income summary. The account used in the closing process for transferring the revenue and expense account balances to the owner's capital account at the end of the period. (140)

Intangible assets. Long-lived assets that are useful in the operations of a business, are not held for sale, and are without physical qualities. (411)

Internal control. The policies and procedures established and maintained by management to assist in achieving its objective of ensuring, as far as practical, the orderly and efficient conduct of the entity's business. (182)

Internal control framework. Consists of five major elements: (1) the control environment, (2) risk assessment, (3) control procedures, (4) monitoring, and (5) information and communication. (183)

Inventory (merchandise inventory). Merchandise on hand and available for sale to customers. (224)

Inventory shrinkage. Loss of inventory due to shoplifting, employee theft, or errors in recording or counting inventory. (244)

Invoice. The bill provided by the seller (who refers to it as a sales invoice) to a buyer (who refers to it as a purchase invoice) for items purchased. (226)

Invoice file. An electronic listing of customer billing information in a computer. (200)

Journal. The initial record in which we record the effects of a transaction on accounts. (47)

Journalizing. The process of recording a transaction in a journal. (47)

Last-in, first-out (LIFO) method. A method of inventory costing based on the assumption that the most recent costs incurred should be charged against revenue. (362)

Ledger. The group of accounts used by a business. (44)

Liabilities. Obligations due by an entity. (11)

Liability. An obligation that (1) will require a future outflow of economic benefits, (2) the entity has little or no discretion to avoid, and (3) is due to a transaction or event that has already occurred. (434)

Long-term assets. Assets that will not be sold or used up within one year. (139)

Long-term liabilities. Liabilities that are not due for a long time (usually more than one year). (139)

Lower of cost and market method. A method of valuing temporary investments or inventory at the lower of their cost or current market value. (332, 369)

Marketable securities. Investments in securities that can be readily sold when cash is needed. (330)

Matching. The concept that expenses incurred in generating revenue should be matched against the revenue in determining the net income or net loss for the period. (19)

Matching principle. Accountants should record expenses in the same period as the revenue that they helped to generate. (95)

Materiality concept. Financial reports need only disclose information that is significant enough to affect a user's decision. (65)

Maturity value. The amount due (face value plus interest) at the maturity or due date of a note or bond. (328)

Monetary unit assumption. The principle that states that accounting transactions should be measured and recorded in terms of money (dollars). (14)

Multiple-step income statement. An income statement with several sections, subsections, and subtotals. (241)

Natural business year. A year that ends when a business's activities have reached the lowest point in its annual operating cycle. (148)

Natural resources. Wasting assets such as timber, oil, gas, and mineral deposits, which are physically consumed as they are removed from the ground. (410)

Net book value of a capital asset. The difference between the cost of a capital asset and the accumulated amortization that has been recognized to date on the asset. (108, 399)

Net income. The final figure in the income statement when revenues exceed expenses. (19)

Net loss. The final figure in the income statement when expenses exceed revenues. (19)

Net pay. Gross pay less payroll deductions; the amount the employer is obligated to pay the employee. (441)

Net realizable value. A market value determined as the estimated selling price less any direct cost of disposal. (369)

Nominal accounts. Revenue or expense accounts that are periodically closed to the income summary account; temporary owner's equity accounts. (140)

Note payable. A written promise to pay a stated amount at a specific date. May have an interest rate stated on the note or be non-interest bearing. (435)

Note receivable. A written promise to pay, representing an amount to be received by a business. (318)

Operating leases. Leases that do not meet the criteria for capital leases and are accounted for as rent expenses by the lessee. (409)

Other expense. An expense that cannot be traced directly to operations. (243)

Other income. Revenue from sources other than the primary operating activity of a business. (243)

Owner's equity. The rights of the owner to the residual assets in a business left over after creditors have been paid. (11)

Partnership. An unincorporated business wherein two or more persons carry on a business together for profit. (9)

Payroll. The total amount paid to employees for a certain period. (440)

Periodic inventory system. A system of inventory accounting in which only the revenue from sales is recorded each time a sale is made. Purchases are recorded in the purchases account. The cost of goods on hand at the end of a period is determined by a detailed listing (physical inventory) of the merchandise on hand. (231)

Perpetual inventory system. A system of inventory accounting in which both the revenue from sales and the cost of merchandise sold are recorded each time a sale is made, so that the records continually disclose the amount of the inventory on hand. Purchases are recorded in the inventory account. (231)

Petty cash fund. A special cash fund used to pay relatively small amounts. (288)

Physical capital assets. Long-lived tangible assets used in the operations of a business and not held for resale. (392)

Physical inventory. The detailed counting and listing of inventory on hand. (231, 357)

Post-closing trial balance. A trial balance prepared after all of the temporary accounts have been closed. (147)

Posting. The process of transferring debits and credits from a journal to the accounts. (53)

Prepaid expenses. Purchased commodities or services that have not been used up at the end of an accounting period. (15)

Private accounting. The profession whose members are accountants employed by a business firm or not-for-profit organization. (5)

Proceeds (of a note). The net amount available from discounting a note. (335)

Promissory note. A written promise to pay a sum of money on demand or at a definite time. (318)

Provincial Sales Tax (PST). Tax imposed by most provinces on sales to final consumers of products. Businesses are required to act as agents to collect these taxes and remit them to the government. (439)

Public accounting. The profession whose members render accounting services on a fee basis. (5)

Purchases account. Temporary account in which we record purchases of inventory during the period under a periodic inventory system. (235)

Purchases discounts. An available discount taken by a buyer for early payment of an invoice; a contra account to Purchases. (233)

Purchases journal. The journal in which all items purchased on account are recorded. (194)

Purchases returns and allowances. Reductions in purchases, resulting from merchandise being returned to the seller or from the seller's reduction in the original purchase price; a contra account to Purchases. (233)

Real accounts. Balance sheet accounts. (140)

Refundable deposits. Security or container deposits that the business intends to return to customers in the future. (438)

Relevancy concept. Accounting information is relevant if it is timely and can influence the decisions of those who use it. (12)

Reliability concept. Accounting information is reliable (objective) if it represents what it is supposed to represent, is free from bias, and is verifiable. (12)

Replacement cost. The current cost to replace inventory at the inventory date. (369)

Report form of balance sheet. A form of balance sheet with the liabilities and owner's equity sections below the assets section. (21, 246)

Residual value. The estimated recoverable cost of a capital asset as of the time of its removal from service. (396)

Retail inventory method. A means of estimating inventory based on the relationship of the cost and the retail price of goods. (371)

Revenue. The gross increase in owner's equity as a result of business and professional activities that earn income. (16)

Revenue expenditures. Expenditures that do not increase the productive capacity of useful life of a capital asset. (403)

Revenue journal. The journal in which all sales of goods or services on account are recorded. (191)

Revenue recognition principle. Recognizes revenue in the period in which it is earned. Requires that both performance and measurability criteria can be met before revenue is recorded. (95)

Sales discounts. An available discount granted by a seller for early payment of an invoice; a contra account to Sales. (227)

Sales returns and allowances. Reductions in sales, resulting from merchandise being returned by customers or from the seller's reduction in the original sales price; a contra account to Sales. (228)

Selling expenses. Expenses incurred directly in the sale of merchandise. (243)

Single-step income statement. An income statement in which the total of all expenses is deducted in one step from the total of all revenues. (243)

Slide. The erroneous movement of all digits in a number, one or more spaces to the right or the left, such as writing $542 as $5,420. (66)

Sole proprietorship. An unincorporated business owned by one individual. (9)

Special journals. Journals designed to be used for recording a single type of transaction. (190)

Statement of cash flows. A summary of the major cash receipts and cash payments for a period. (19)

Statement of owner's equity. A summary of the changes in the owner's equity of a business that have occurred during a specific period of time. (19)

Straight-line amortization method. A method that provides for equal periodic amortization expense over the estimated life of an asset. (398)

Subsidiary ledger. A ledger containing individual accounts with a common characteristic. (189)

T account. A form of account resembling the letter T. (46)

Temporary accounts. Revenue or expense accounts that are periodically closed to the income summary account; nominal accounts. (140)

Temporary investments. Investments in securities that can be readily sold when cash is needed. (330)

Trade accounts payable. Amounts owed for goods or services purchased on credit. (435)

Trade discounts. Special discounts from published list prices offered by sellers to certain classes of buyers. (229)

Trade-in allowance. The amount a seller grants a buyer for a capital asset that is traded in for another asset. (407)

Transportation-in. Temporary account in which we record freight costs on inventory purchases under a periodic system. (236)

Transportation-out. Selling expense incurred when seller pays freight on a sale. (230)

Transposition. The erroneous arrangement of digits in a number, such as writing $542 as $524. (66)

Trial balance. A summary listing of the titles and balances of the accounts in the ledger. (64)

Units-of-production amortization method. A method that provides for amortization expense based on the productive output of the asset during a period proportionate to the total expected productive capacity of the asset over its lifetime. (398)

Voucher. A document that serves as evidence of authority to pay cash. (287)

Voucher system. Records, methods, and procedures used in verifying and recording liabilities and paying and recording cash payments. (287)

Warranty. A seller's promise to provide parts and/or labour to fix a product that proves to be defective during some specified period of time. (445)

Withdrawals. The amount of drawings made by the owner of a sole proprietorship. (44)

Work sheet. A working paper used to summarize adjusting entries and assist in preparation of financial statements. (109)

Workers' Compensation (WC). Provincial program to provide assistance to employees injured on the job. Employers pay premiums based on payroll at rates set according to industry risk for worker injuries. (444)

Index

INDEX OF REAL COMPANIES

Photo Credits

Check Figures for Selected Problems

Problem	Check Figure
1–2A	1. Net income, $36,655
1–3A	1. Net income, $4,350
1–4A	2. Capital, $10,750
1–5A	2. Total assets, $47,550
1–6A	3. Total liabilities and owner's equity, $150,950
1–2B	3. Total assets, $26,400
1–3B	2. Ed Seaquest Capital, $13,770
1–4B	1. Net income, $3,075
1–5B	3c. Net income, $1,775
1–6B	3. Total assets, $290,515
2–1A	2. Cash, $11,310
2–2A	3. Total debit balances, $35,550
2–3A	2. Cash, $1,865
2–4A	4. Total debit balances, $237,865
2–5A	5. Total debit balances, $78,190
2–1B	3. Total debit balances, $46,100
2–2B	2. Cash, $17,050
2–3B	3. Cash, $5,607
2–4B	3. Cash, $5,910
2–5B	1. Cash, $5,825
3–5A	3. Total adjusted debit balances, $482,270
3–6A	2. Correct owner's equity, $166,650
3–5B	3. Total credit adjustments, $16,025
3–6B	2. Corrected net income, $66,350
CP3–3	Accrual net income, $109,065
4–1A	1. Total debit adjustments, $12,580
4–2A	2. Net income, $32,295
4–3A	3. Net income, $44,870
4–4A	4. Total debits, adjusted trial balance, $158,430
4–1B	2. Sylvia Akai, capital August 31, 1999, $59,290
4–2B	2. Net income, $21,780
4–3B	1. Total debits, adjusted trial balance, $468,420

Problem	Check Figure
4–4B	2. Total debit adjustments, $17,590
CP4–1	3. Total assets, $81,000
CP4–3	2. J. Service, capital at year end, $31,810
Cont. Prob.	4. Net income, $1,522
Comp. Prob.	3. Total adjusted debit balance, $27,300
5–1A	3a. Total, $15,045
5–2A	3. Total cash receipts, $76,910
5–3A	5a. Total, $44,910
5–4A	3. Total credits to accounts payable, $46,990
5–5A	4. Ending cash balance, $5,960
5–1B	2. Total debits to accounts receivable, $15,045
5–2B	5. Ending balance in accounts receivable, $11,060
5–3B	5. Total accounts payable, $49,300
5–4B	2. Total credits to cash, $48,040
5–5B	4. Ending balance in cash, $7,740
6–7A	1. Total assets, $970,000
6–8A	1. Net income, $90,000
6–9A	2. Net income, $176,855
6–6B	3. Total assets, $360,200
6–7B	3. J. Lucas, capital, June 30, 1999, $301,500
6–8B	4. Total assets, $507,375
6–9B	4. Total assets, $489,365
CP6–1	Net income, $41,000
CP6–2	Net income, $38,000
Comp. Prob.	3. Net income, $69,500
7–4A	1. Adjusted bank balance, $17,764.30
7–5A	1. Adjusted bank balance, $20,879.87
7–6A	1. Adjusted bank balance, $9,650.02
7–4B	1. Adjusted bank balance, $20,645.00
7–5B	1. Preliminary book balance, $14,531.33
7–6B	1. Preliminary book balance, $7,885.59
CP7–1	1. Adjusted bank balance, $10,019.60

Problem	Check Figure
8–2A	Allowance, end of year 3, $7,500
8–3A	Net accounts receivable, $76,450
8–7A	2. Unrealized loss, $2,625
8–2B	Allowance, end of year 2, $4,650
8–3B	Uncollectible account expense, $6,490
8–7B	2. Interest receivable, $250
CP8–1	Uncollectible account expense, $1,352
CP8–3	Cash proceeds on discounted note, $5,073.25
CP8–4	Uncollectible account expense, $2,131
9–1A	2. Cost of goods sold, $1,436,750
9–2A	2. Total sales, $1,656,500
9–3A	1. Unit cost, August 10, $6.19
9–4A	Fifo inventory, $8,681
9–5A	1. Estimated inventory, $157,500
9–1B	3. Gross profit, $5,705
9–2B	2. Total sales, $21,445
9–3B	1. Unit cost, May 4, $226.58
9–4B	2. Lifo inventory, $10,793
9–5B	2a. Estimated inventory, $372,550
CP9–2	b. Cost of goods sold, $14,200
10–1A	1. Total building, $964,050
10–2A	Year 2000 declining balance, $20,000

Problem	Check Figure
10–3A	Year 1999 declining balance, $40,500
10–4A	1b. Book value end of year 3, $37,800
10–7A	1a. Amortization, $70,000
10–1B	Land improvements total, $37,500
10–2B	Year 1998, units of production, $42,000
10–3B	Year 2000, Straight-line, $12,000
10–4B	4. Loss on disposal, $10,000
10–6B	April 2, 2000, loss on disposal, $3,042
10–7B	1c. Amortization, $1,667
CP10–3	c. Loss on disposal, $15,006
11–2A	B. Total current liabilities, $28,604
11–3A	Total payroll expenses, $8,904
11–4A	A. Warranty liability December 31, 2001, $105,000
11–6A	Total current liabilities, $145,900
11–7A	2d. Total payroll taxes, $15,621.92
11–2B	a. May 31 debit prepaid property taxes, $15,088
11–3B	Net pay December 14, $36,157
11–4B	b. Promotions liability, end of 1999, $150,000
11–6B	Total current liabilities, $110,333
11–7B	Total gross pay, $4,872.00
CP11–2	b. Total current liabilities, $44,180
Comp. Prob.	5. Total assets, $1,042,230